LLOYD GEORGE

LLOYD GEORGE

WAR LEADER,
1916–1918

JOHN GRIGG

faber and faber

This edition first published in 2011
by Faber and Faber Ltd
Bloomsbury House, 74–77 Great Russell Street
London WC1B 3DA

Printed by CPI Antony Rowe, Eastbourne

A CIP record for this book is available from the British Library

ISBN 978-0-571-27749-0

Contents

List of Illustrations

(Photographic acknowledgements appear in parentheses)

1 Lloyd George with Lord Reading at Chequers (Photo: Camera Press)
2 Robert Georges Nivelle, 1916 (Photo: Hulton Archive)
3 Aristide Briand (Photo: Hulton Archive)
4 Luigi Cadorna, June 1916 (Photo: Hulton Archive)
5 Georges Clemenceau, c. 1917 (Photo: Hulton Archive)
6 Sir Eric Geddes, September 1916 (Photo: Hulton Archive)
7 Lord Beaverbrook, 1918 (Photo: House of Lords Record Office)
8 US Admiral Sims, J. L. Garvin and Lord Northcliffe, October 1918 (Photo: Hulton Archive)
9 David Lloyd George at the 14th Army Corps headquarters at Mesulte, with Sir Douglas Haig, General Joffre and Albert Thomas, 12 September 1916 (Photo: Hulton Archive)
10 Winston Churchill speaking at a munitions factory, 1916 (Photo: *Illustrated London News*)
11 Lloyd George, Lord Milner and Philip Kerr, 1917 (Photo: House of Lords Record Office)
12 Sir George Riddell, Lloyd George, Charles Masterman and Gwilym Lloyd George playing golf at Walton Heath (Photo: Walton Heath Golf Club Archives)
13 Lloyd George and Arthur Balfour, 26 July 1917 (Photo: Courtesy Trustees of the Imperial War Museum [Q57038])
14 General Sir William Robertson and Major-General Sir Frederick Maurice at the Paris Allied conference (Photo: Courtesy Trustees of the Imperial War Museum [Q58590])
15 Sir Maurice Hankey, J. T. Davies and Frances Stevenson during Lloyd George's visit to Rapallo, from Stephen Roskill, *Hankey: Man of Secrets*
16 Lloyd George, 1917 (Photo: Owen Lloyd George)

Abbreviations Used in Footnotes

ABL	Andrew Bonar Law
AJB	Arthur James Balfour
Crawford diary	*The Crawford Papers*, ed. John Vincent (1984)
DLG	David Lloyd George
FSD	Frances Stevenson, *Lloyd George: A Diary*, ed. A. J. P. Taylor (1971)
IWC	Imperial War Cabinet
MLG	Margaret Lloyd George
RWD	*Lord Riddell's War Diary: 1914–1918* (1933)
Scott diary	*The Political Diaries of C. P. Scott, 1911–1928*, ed. Trevor Wilson (1970)
Wilson diary	Charles Edward Callwell, *Field-Marshal Sir Henry Wilson: His Life and Diaries* (2 vols., 1927)
WM	*The War Memoirs of David Lloyd George* (6 vols., 1938; paginated continuously)
WPC	War Policy Committee

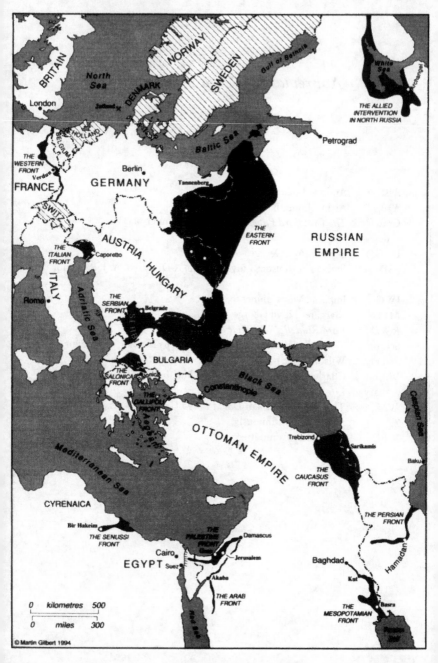

Map 1. The war fronts

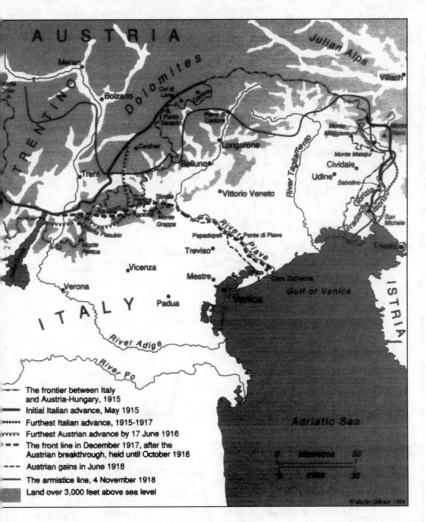

AUSTRIA

Julian Alps

Merani

Dolomites

Bolzano

Col di Lana

Cortina

Trentino

Punto Sarauto

Piave di Cadore

Monte Maggiore

Trent

Cardinal

Monte Mataiur

Longarone

Udine

Cividale

Sabatino

Asiago

Vittorio Veneto

River Tagliamento

Gorizia

Monte Grappa

Monte Pasubio

Monte Piatica

Papadopoli

Ponte di Piave

Gradisca

Isonzo

San Michele

Treviso

River Piave

Trieste

Vicenza

Mestre

Clara Duchessa

Verona

Venice

Gulf of Venice

ISTRIA

Padua

ITALY

River Adige

River Po

Adriatic Sea

-·-·- The frontier between Italy
and Austria-Hungary, 1915

▬▬▬ Initial Italian advance, May 1915

••••• Furthest Italian advance, 1915-1917

ʌʌʌʌ Furthest Austrian advance by 17 June 1916

▬ ▬ The front line in December 1917, after the
Austrian breakthrough, held until October 1918

- - - Austrian gains in June 1918

▬▬▬ The armistice line, 4 November 1918

███ Land over 3,000 feet above sea level

0   kilometres   50

0   miles   30

© Martin Gilbert 1994

Map 2. The Italian front

Map 3. The Western front, 1918

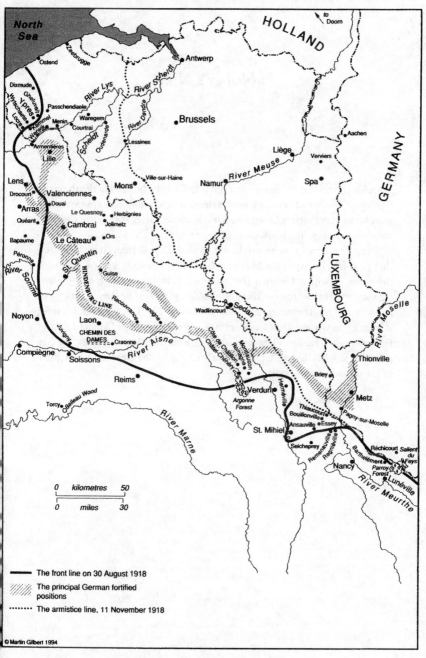

Map 4. *The Western front, the last three months*

Publisher's Note

John Grigg worked on this book until a few weeks before his death on 31 December 2001, and very nearly completed it. The publishers are extremely grateful to Mrs Patricia Grigg and Mr Alexander Grigg for their indispensable help in seeing the book through the press.

When he realized that he would not finish the book, John Grigg indicated that he would be happy for Margaret MacMillan to write a postscript from the point at which his own text stopped, half-way through the present Chapter 33. He had reviewed her book *Peacemakers: The Paris Conference of 1919 and Its Attempt to End War* warmly in *The Times* on publication; it went on to win the Duff Cooper Prize and the BBC Four Samuel Johnson Prize for Non-Fiction. The publishers are most grateful to her for her contribution. Margaret MacMillan is also, happily, the great-granddaughter of the subject of this book.

Acknowledgements

John was very grateful to Ian Gilmour who read the typescript and made useful comments and criticism. Richard Ollard and Stuart Proffitt also greatly helped him with their detailed notes. (He did not live to see the proofs so cannot be held responsible for any errors that may have crept in.) He would have wished to thank Earl Lloyd George of Dwyfor who was, as ever, very helpful and also found the negatives of two photographs (one of his grandfather and the other of his grandmother with three of their children) which were taken by his mother in 1917 and which are reproduced in the book. He was also indebted to Mrs Jennifer Longford for material about her mother, Frances Stevenson (later Countess Lloyd George of Dwyfor), and to her daughter, Ruth Longford; Inez Lynn, Librarian of the London Library, her predecessor, Alan Bell, and indeed the whole staff of the Library; the Bodleian Library; the House of Lords Record Office; the National Library of Wales, and the Public Record Office. He also consulted the Hankey Papers at the Churchill College Archive Centre, the Astor Papers at Reading University Library and the Lothian Papers at the Scottish Record Office; he would have wished me to thank the keepers of each of them, as he would have wished me to thank Her Majesty the Queen for gracious permission to quote the memorandum of the conversation between Curzon and Stamfordham quoted on p. 41.

At a crucial moment, the Rhodes Trust gave extremely generous support to John and he was very grateful to them, and to William Waldegrave too. I would also like to thank Robin Prior for his help and advice and Elizabeth Greenhalgh for her meticulous checking of the footnotes. Among others who have helped me in various ways and to whom I am very grateful are Catherine Haddon, Caragh Hanning, Denis Moloney and above all Alexander Grigg who has been enormously helpful throughout. Sir Martin Gilbert, CBE, very generously allowed us to reproduce some of the maps from his *First World War*. I also owe particular thanks to Stuart Proffitt for all his support and advice.   Patricia Grigg

Acknowledgements

I

Extreme Danger

The task facing Britain's new Prime Minister at the end of 1916 was truly enormous, and the dangers besetting the country at the time were as dire as they would be in May 1940, if not more so. It is commonly believed that Lloyd George's predicament may have been bad, but that Winston Churchill's in 1940 was far worse. A glance at the facts should help to correct this mistaken view. Both men had to deal with situations of extreme peril, but there are good reasons for regarding Lloyd George's as the more perilous of the two, in reality if not in appearance.

In December 1916 things *seemed* less desperate than they would do after Dunkirk. Far from being in retreat from the Continent, the British were firmly established there with an army of nearly 1.5 million men. Beside them on the Western front was a French army of even greater numerical strength, which had withstood the German attempt to destroy it at Verdun. In the southern Alps and on the Isonzo the Italians were engaging part of the forces of Austria-Hungary. In eastern Europe Russia still had masses of men in the field, so obliging the Central Powers to continue to wage war on two main fronts. Superficially, the position on land was a far cry from the catastrophe of 1940.

Yet on closer inspection the contrast does not necessarily favour the time when Lloyd George took over. At that moment the war was not, as would be the case in 1940, in its early stages; it had been going on for over two years, and in varying degrees all the combatants were affected by war-weariness. Least affected, as yet, were the Germans, because they had palpable gains to set against their heavy losses in battle and the domestic sufferings caused by blockade. On both fronts they held the strategic advantage; while their own country remained intact, they were occupying large areas of foreign territory, east and west. The Austro-Hungarians had their misgivings, but they were effectively tied to Germany. Besides, they had the satisfaction that Serbia was overrun, and that Roumania's intervention in 1916 had been swiftly counteracted, with German help.

Beyond question, war-weariness was more pronounced on the Entente side. In Russia, extreme demoralization in the army, spreading to the civilian population, would soon lead to the downfall of the Tsarist regime and the progressive collapse of Russia as a fighting ally. Before long, also, there would be a crisis of morale in France – less comprehensive than in Russia, but still very serious – which would be reflected in army mutinies and a marked weakening of the French war effort, until Clemenceau came to power in November 1917. For much of the year the burden of fighting the Germans on land would fall largely on the British army, and this would subject British morale, particularly at home, to an unprecedented test.

Britain was not used to fighting wars on foreign soil at a heavy cost in life to its own citizens. Traditionally, its land campaigns had involved a limited number of British volunteers, supplemented (on the Continent) by foreign allies and mercenaries. At Waterloo, for instance, the army under Welling-ton's command – to say nothing of Blücher's Prussians – had consisted of more foreign troops than British. The scale of military casualties to which Britain had been accustomed was, therefore, very low by Continental stan-dards. In each of Britain's two most substantial wars before the First World War, the Crimean and the South African, about 25,000 British lives had been lost, mostly from disease. These totals were not much larger than the number of British soldiers killed on one day in 1916, the first day of the battle of the Somme. During the Crimean War John Bright had disturbed his compatriots with the words: 'The angel of death has been abroad throughout the land; you may almost hear the beating of his wings.' By the end of 1916 the beating of those wings had become a familiar sound in every part of Britain. Though the country's human toll was still scarcely comparable with that of Russia or France, in relation to previous British experience it was enormous and uniquely traumatic. Moreover, since the voluntary principle of recruitment that had applied in the early phase of the war had given way to compulsion, a growing proportion of the soldiers who were now dying were conscripts.

Despite the circumstances there was, as yet, no appreciable sign of defeat-ism either in the army or among the people at large. Morale was holding up remarkably well, but Lloyd George knew that it could not be taken for granted. War-weariness was evident and could easily turn to demoralization if losses continued to mount without any prospect of victory. The spirit of the nation was not what it had been in 1914, or would be again in 1940. After Dunkirk, the British people may have been alarmed and apprehensive, but they were not war-weary. After a period of 'phoney war' the real thing was beginning. Along with the sense of acute danger there was exhilaration in the air, and even a perverse feeling that the country might be better off on its own, without allies. British insularity was at a premium. Churchill exploited this mood to glorious effect, but it was not available to Lloyd George when he became leader. Both the situation and the national mood were more complex.

The country was, indeed, faced with a mortal threat, but one of which few members of the public were properly aware. This supreme menace came from the sea, the element on which Britain had to prevail in order to survive. Throughout the First World War Germany was an altogether more formidable naval power than it would be in the Second. The German High Seas Fleet which had been built as a deliberate challenge to the Royal Navy remained in existence, as a brooding presence, from start to finish. The only major engagement between the two fleets, at Jutland in mid-1916, was inconclusive. Before returning to base the German ships did more damage than they sustained, and there was every reason to fear that they might one day attempt another such sortie. There had been no Trafalgar, and the big enemy ships might at any time emerge for another trial of strength, in which Britain's fate could be decided, adversely, in a few hours. By contrast, in the Second World War Hitler's surface fleet was never remotely a match for the Royal Navy, and less so than ever by the summer of 1940, after its losses in the Norwegian campaign.

In 1916–17 it was not, however, Germany's surface fleet – dangerous though it was – which posed the deadliest threat. More terrible by far was the submarine menace to the sea-lanes on which Britain depended for survival. Germany was now operating with U-boats of longer range and a heavier armament of torpedoes, which it was planning to use indiscriminately against all ships bringing supplies to Britain. Instead of seeking first to knock France out of the war, the strategic priority to date, at more or less exactly the time Lloyd George became Prime Minister Germany was switching to the elimination of Britain as its first objective. The plan was not only to sink double the tonnage of British merchant shipping within a few months, but also to deter all neutrals from carrying goods to British ports. This was an entirely new departure in warfare, and an unprecedented threat to Britain's island existence. Already, in November 1916, Board of Trade experts were predicting a complete breakdown in shipping well before the middle of the following year. How much more dire would their prophecies have been had they then known of the impending escalation in the German submarine campaign.

When this began to take effect the Admiralty had no answer to it, and in the spring of 1917 the Germans came near to achieving their aim. Probably at no other time in either war was the country closer to defeat. The extent of the peril was brutally apparent to Lloyd George and his colleagues in government, but hardly suspected by the general population. Before he became Prime Minister figures of shipping losses were not published, because it was felt that they would be bad for morale. Though he soon arranged for the figures to be published, people nevertheless had to be persuaded to accept and implement measures appropriate to a state of siege without at first – or perhaps ever – fully understanding how beleaguered the country was. In 1940 its isolation was obvious. Of course, there was also a grave threat from German U-boats in the Second World War, but it was not then an utterly new threat, to which an effective response had to be improvised from scratch. The experience of the First World War was available to British leaders in the next struggle, and the U-boats were, indeed, defeated again by much the same methods at sea as those evolved under Lloyd George, with the added resource of reconnaissance and attack from the air.

Air power was clearly of much greater significance in the Second World War, but was not – like the U-boats in the First – an absolute novelty. Northcliffe's famous remark that Britain (actually he said England) was 'no longer an island' was made in 1906, after Alberto Sandos-Dumont had flown 722 feet in an aeroplane. By 1914 aviation technology had advanced to the point that the aeroplane was, from the first, a factor in the war; then the war itself acted as a mighty spur to invention and production. At the end of 1916 Britain had nearly 600 military aircraft on the Western front, supporting the army as its 'eye in the sky'. But there were already those who saw the potential of aircraft in war as far transcending the functions of intelligence-gathering and help for the artillery. Air power was being conceived as an offensive, even war-winning, arm in its own right. Before the end of the war the Royal Flying Corps had been transformed into the Royal Air Force, a separate service, and Hugh Trenchard, so-called 'Father of the RAF', was propounding his wildly exaggerated notion of what could be achieved by air-bombing alone. (His disciples in the Second World War, and during the rest of the century, were to cause much futile havoc through their misguided adherence to his doctrine.)

Britain was by no means immune to air raids during the First World War. German bombs were dropped as far west as Birmingham and Shrewsbury, as far north as Yorkshire and even the Scottish Highlands; but most of them naturally fell in the south-east of the country. For two years or so the attacks were delivered mainly by Zeppelin airships, but by the time Lloyd George became Prime Minister the Zeppelins had been so hard hit by gunfire and interceptor planes that their role was being taken over by bomber aircraft, including the Gotha and a few Giants, the largest aeroplanes used against Britain in either war. Damage and casualties were, of course, far less severe than in the later Blitz, but still not negligible; about 1,000 British civilians died in air raids during the First World War, compared with roughly 60,000 in the Second. Above all, the mere fact of being subject to such attacks, and the precautions, such as black-out, that had to be taken against them, made the British people most unpleasantly aware of their new vulnerability.

Despite the development of air power, however, the English Channel remained a tough obstacle for any would-be invader. Even in 1940 the value of Britain's 'moat defensive', though seriously diminished, was still very considerable. Four years later the Allies, with total command of sea and air, and overwhelming superiority in most forms of equipment, had some difficulty in carrying out a successful cross-Channel invasion.

When Churchill became war leader in 1940 he offered only 'blood, toil, tears and sweat'. They were noble words, evoking a noble response. But he was speaking at a time when little had, as yet, been demanded of the British people in warlike effort or sacrifice. Lloyd George, on the other hand, assumed the premiership when there had already been any amount of toil and sweat, and an all-too-copious effusion of blood and tears. He had to tell the people that the ordeal would continue, and he could predict no early end to it. In a much-quoted interview with an American reporter in August 1915 he had said that there was 'neither clock nor calendar' in the British war effort; only the result would count. But he was under no illusion that British soldiers and their families would be content to suffer indefinitely on the scale of the past two years. Stoical and dedicated though they had shown themselves to be, there must be a limit to their endurance. He was expected, he knew, to prosecute the war more energetically and effectively; it was for that reason that he was Prime Minister. But he was also determined that the war should be fought, if possible, in a manner more economical of British life.

Since the first winter of the war he had been looking for a way to escape from the deadlock on the Western front. Like Churchill and a few others, he wanted to find an alternative strategy for defeating the Central Powers. In early 1915 he had argued that the numerical superiority of the Entente could best be used to mount an Allied onslaught on Austria-Hungary through the Balkans. His proposal, as it evolved, was that there should be a massive attack on the Habsburg Empire's most vulnerable frontier, in which the Serbs and Russians would be joined not only by new Balkan allies, but by more than half a million troops transferred from the West, to operate from the Dalmatian coast or Salonica. On a visit to Paris at the beginning of February he had secured the backing of some leading French politicians and soldiers for his project, though not that of the Frenchman whose word was virtually law, General Joffre. At home, his plea for a diplomatic offensive in the Balkans, to bring at least Roumania and Greece into the war on the Entente side, had prompted a suggestion by the Foreign Secretary, Edward Grey, that such a mission, if conducted by Lloyd George himself, might have a chance of success. But Grey was dissembling; in fact he was dead against the idea and nothing came of it.

As well as his grand scheme for the Balkans, Lloyd George had advocated a secondary eastern move – against the Ottoman Empire, which had been an ally of the Central Powers since late 1914. Turkey's presence in the enemy ranks in 1914–18 is a factor that needs to be emphasized, when we compare the two world wars. Though to some extent offset by the different allegiance of Italy (an Entente partner from May 1915), on balance the Turkish factor is the more important. The Ottoman Empire counted for more as an enemy than did Italy as an ally – or than Italy counted as an enemy in 1940–43. In the Second World War the Ottoman Empire no longer existed. Large parts of it were under British control, including Iraq (Mesopotamia) with its oilfields. Turkey itself was neutral.

In 1915 Lloyd George had advocated an expedition to the Levant, to cut off the Turkish forces deployed against Egypt. But in the event neither this nor his Balkan project carried the day. Instead, an attempt was made to force the Straits leading to the Sea of Marmara by a naval action which, it was hoped, would result in the fall of Constantinople and the opening of warm-water access to Russia. This plan appealed to 'Easterners' and 'Westerners' alike – to the former because it was a potentially decisive stroke in the East, to the latter because it seemed to involve no significant deflection of forces from the Western front. But, through a combination of bad luck and bad management, it proved disastrous. The naval action on its own did not succeed, and then a growing number of Allied troops were landed on the Gallipoli peninsula in a vain attempt to secure the heights dominating the Narrows. The Gallipoli campaign thus became a lesser, but still substantial, version of the deadlock on the Western front. At the end of 1915 the decision was taken to abandon the campaign, and by early January 1916 all the troops had been withdrawn.

Meanwhile, an Anglo-French force of two divisions had, at last, been landed at Salonica, but not as part of the comprehensive Balkan strategy earlier advocated by Lloyd George. This had been overtaken by events. In October 1915 the Austrians, with German help, and also with the assistance of Bulgaria which had decided it had more to gain from siding with the

Central Powers, had knocked Serbia out of the war (though many Serbs continued to fight outside their country). In the summer of 1916 Roumania belatedly opted for the Entente, only to be crushed by the Austro-Germans, with neither the Russians (by then) nor the Allied force at Salonica able to affect the issue. The Salonica bridgehead remained, indeed, little more than an internment camp for Allied troops until September 1918, by which time the war in the West was nearly over.

Lloyd George's Balkan dream at the beginning of 1915 was not pure fantasy. Certainly he underrated some of the difficulties, military, logistical and political. Yet it is conceivable that, if he had been sent at that time to undertake a concerted negotiation with the Balkan states, he might have persuaded Serbia and Greece to make the necessary concessions to Bulgaria (which had lost territory to its neighbours in 1913), and so have constructed a solid alliance against the Austro-Germans and the Turks. By the time he was Prime Minister such a prospect had utterly vanished, the Balkan scene having been transformed to the Allies' disadvantage. Serbia and Roumania were defeated, Bulgaria was an enemy, and Russia was nearly a spent force. Greece was still neutral, though with Allied troops on its soil at Salonica.

The bad turn of events in the Balkans cannot, therefore, be blamed on Lloyd George, though he had to live with the consequences. Nor can he be blamed for the Gallipoli catastrophe. He supported the navy's attempt to force the Straits on its own, but warned against the danger of committing troops on the peninsula. The Army should not, he argued, be 'expected to pull the chestnuts out of the fire for the Navy'. He did not share the contempt of some of his colleagues for the fighting qualities of the Turks. Having observed their dogged performance in the recent Balkan wars, he was convinced that they would fight hard at Gallipoli in defence of their home-land; and so it proved. Lloyd George as Prime Minister had to face an Ottoman Empire that seemed quite a menacing enemy, having inflicted a heavy defeat on the British and French at Gallipoli, and another – in April 1916 – on the British alone in Mesopotamia.

Politically, Lloyd George's position was far less secure than Churchill's would be in the Second World War. Though both men headed coalition governments, Churchill's was a 'grand' coalition embracing all major parties in the state. Moreover, his own (Conservative) party was the largest com-ponent, and, when Neville Chamberlain died at the end of 1940, he took the precaution of becoming leader of it. His Parliamentary base was thus exceptionally strong. Lloyd George's was, from the first, very much less so. His coalition included neither the Irish National Party (with eighty-odd seats in the House of Commons) nor about half of his own Liberal Party.

The Asquithians, like Asquith himself, refused to serve under him. A party that was not his, the Conservatives, provided the bulk of his support. For political ascendancy he had to depend, therefore, very largely on his own adroitness and personal prestige. Though opposition to him in Parliament remained for some time patriotically quiescent, he had to face one Parliamentary challenge, at a critical moment in May 1918, of a kind that Churchill never had to face. Lloyd George's government could never have survived the humiliations and strategic disasters of 1941 and 1942.

Two other political factors should be noted when Lloyd George's situation in 1916 is compared with Churchill's in 1940. They can be summarized in two words: Ireland and America. The country over which Churchill came to preside was united in a sense that Lloyd George's ostensibly undivided country was not. Ireland had been the scene, in 1916, of a rebellion for which, at the time, there was little popular support, but whose suppression had been so mishandled that it had generated an extreme nationalist myth of disastrous potency. After the failure of Lloyd George's attempt to negotiate a settlement (or rather, his and Asquith's failure to push through the settlement that he negotiated) in the immediate aftermath of the Easter Rising, Gaelic Ireland became for the rest of the war more of a headache than the neutral Irish Free State ever was in Churchill's time. And the growing disaffection of the Gaelic Irish, reflected in the decline of the Irish National Party and the rise of Sinn Fein, was damaging to Britain in other parts of the world where Irish influence was strong, such as Australia and, above all, America.

The policy of the United States as a neutral was, in any case, very much less helpful to Britain under President Woodrow Wilson than it would be under President Franklin D. Roosevelt. Wilson's outlook was truly neutral. He viewed the struggle in Europe with lordly impartiality, from a supposed moral eminence, and his aim was to broker a compromise peace between the combatants. Until German actions eventually forced him into 'co-belligerency', he did not feel that the United States was seriously threatened and took hardly any steps to prepare his country for war. Roosevelt, by contrast, never doubted that an expansionist Germany was a potentially mortal threat to the United States and did all that he could, within the restraints imposed by the Congress and public opinion, both to build up American armed strength and to enable Britain to survive. Though his country remained formally neutral until the end of 1941, Roosevelt himself was not neutral and used all his political ingenuity to bend the rules in Britain's favour. He did this, not because he was any more pro-British than Wilson, but because he had a more enlightened and realistic grasp of American interests.

Finally, the greatest difference between the two world wars (already mentioned in relation to the U-boat threat) is so obvious that it tends, paradoxically, to be overlooked or taken entirely for granted. The First World War, precisely because it was the first, was a new experience for all concerned in it. Ordinary people had never before witnessed or felt the effects of warfare on such a colossal scale; leaders, both civilian and military, had never before had to adapt themselves to the problems that such warfare created. The leaders, in particular, were like explorers in a strange land full of unimaginable dangers. They made, as was only natural, many grievous mistakes and some were slower than others to adapt themselves to wholly unfamiliar challenges. But it is only fair to remember that they were pioneers making painful, hazardous progress in the unknown. They may not be so worthy of sympathy as the men who fought and died, but they are surely entitled to rather more understanding than they have received from posterity.

Lloyd George himself, writing about the experience some years later, asks us to try to enter into his feelings:

What must be the sensation of a man who took a leading part in the direction of this tremendous war and undertakes to recall these events with their horrors, their perils and their amazing escapes. It is like that of a traveller who revisits dangerous rapids through which once upon a time he helped to pilot a boat without map, without knowledge, and without experience to guide him or any of the crew as to the course of the river, its depths and its shallows, its sharp and unexpected bends, the strength and whirl of its current, or the location of the hidden rocks in its channel.[1]

The civilian leaders suffered from an additional disadvantage, compared with their successors in the next war. Nearly all of them were totally lacking in first-hand experience of life in the armed forces. Churchill was the one outstanding exception; in 1914 no other member of the Cabinet (apart from Kitchener, who was brought in as a warlord to boost public confidence) had ever heard a shot fired in anger. Consequently there was a psychological gulf between the civilian and service chiefs, which the latter were able to exploit. In the Second World War many of the country's civilian leaders had seen active service in the previous war, and so could deal with the top brass on level terms. Some, indeed, had served with such distinction that, had they chosen to remain in uniform, they might themselves have been occupying top military positions when the next war came.

1. *WM*, p. 1120.

Lloyd George's uneasy relationship with the service chiefs had been apparent during the first two years of the First World War. As Chancellor of the Exchequer, and then as Minister of Munitions, he dealt with them intermittently and at a remove. Even so there were frequent clashes. As Secretary of State for War, from July to December 1916, he was directly involved with the military professionals, especially the Chief of the Imperial General Staff (CIGS), Sir William Robertson, but this period of close involvement did not produce harmony or understanding. As Prime Minister during the last twenty-three months of the war he was in almost day-to-day contact with all the service chiefs, naval and military. The resulting friction (or worse) had some beneficial effects, but also many tragic consequences.

2

War Cabinet

*Lloyd George and Law – The indispensable Hankey – First
Commons speech as premier – French plan and Rome
conference*

The first month of Lloyd George's premiership established his style of
government, for good or ill. Its most notable features were vitality, urgency,
improvisation, ideas ranging from the inspired to the foolhardy, ruthlessness, resourcefulness, and an astonishing disregard for convention. All of
these characteristics were soon apparent.

On the face of it, nothing could have been less conventional than the new
War Cabinet, which seemed more akin to the Committee of Public Safety
established during the French Revolution than to the traditional British
Cabinet maintained, even during the war, by Asquith. The War Cabinet was
particularly unorthodox in being so small. Of the five original members two
were Tory peers, the famous and controversial former proconsuls Milner
and Curzon. They, together with the leader of the Conservative Party, Bonar
Law, gave majority representation in the War Cabinet to the party which
was providing most of the Parliamentary support for Lloyd George's
coalition. The only non-Tory members were the Labour leader, Arthur
Henderson, and Lloyd George himself.

In principle the War Cabinet was meant to consist of ministers without
departmental responsibilities, free to devote their minds to the war as a
whole, and to preside over powerful Cabinet committees. Accordingly,
Milner and Henderson were ministers without portfolio. Curzon, as Lord
President of the Council and Leader of the House of Lords, had little to
distract him from War Cabinet work. Lloyd George was careful to shuffle
off the serious burden of leadership of the House of Commons, so that he
could exercise national leadership more in the manner of an American
president than a British prime minister. Law alone had major tasks outside
the War Cabinet; he was both Leader of the House of Commons and, as
Chancellor of the Exchequer, head of one of the great departments of state.

A simple but telling measure of Lloyd George's detachment from Parliament, and of Law's resulting workload, is to be found in the general index
of Hansard for the period February 1917 to February 1918. In this Lloyd

George occupies only four columns, Law thirty-seven. It was lucky for the Prime Minister that his deputy was so patient, loyal and diligent. Law had been a widower since 1909, and work was his refuge from solitude; also from the anxiety of having his two elder sons at the front, followed by the grief of losing both of them in 1917. Despite the heavy demands of his work at the Treasury and in the War Cabinet, he would sit late in the House of Commons listening to humdrum debates, though implored by subordinates to go home. His command of the House of Commons has been compared with Walpole's, though he differed from Walpole in at least one respect: he was a byword for integrity and indifference to material reward. As Chancellor he was highly competent, with a freakish memory for figures which enabled him to deliver a Budget speech from notes written on two small sheets of paper. Altogether he was the government's indispensable anchor-man.

His qualities perfectly complemented Lloyd George's, and for the rest of the war and some time afterwards the two men worked as close partners, without a hint of rivalry. Though there had been a transient period of coolness on Law's side after the formation of Asquith's coalition, when he felt, with reason, that Lloyd George had blocked his claim to the Exchequer, on the whole their personal relations had been particularly good for many years, notwithstanding the intensity of party warfare before the war. The Scots-Irish Presbyterian and the Welsh Baptist, neither university-educated, had come to the centre of British power from the outside, owing nothing to social or academic privilege. Yet both were well read and shared a vivid sense of history. These were strong bonds.

In temperament they were poles apart, but this was a great asset to the state. Law recognized Lloyd George's creative genius, while Lloyd George was equally respectful of Law's critical judgement. From early 1917, every morning, after breakfast, he would walk along the connecting passage from Number 10 to Number 11 Downing Street to spend an hour or so with Law discussing the business of the day and any ideas that might be germinating in his mind. In his war memoirs he describes Law's way of reacting to such ideas, and how it helped the process of decision-making:

Bonar's first impulse, when a project or a prospect was placed before him, was to dwell on its difficulties and dangers. I found that idiosyncrasy useful and even exhilarating. . . . He had an incomparable gift of practical criticism. When he had finished marshalling his objections I knew there was nothing more to be said against my plans. Sometimes I felt the force of his adverse criticisms was so great as to be insuperable, and I abandoned the project altogether; at other times I found it necessary to alter or modify the idea in order to meet some obstacle which I had not foreseen but which he had pointed out. But if I came to the conclusion that his objections were not sufficient to deter the Government from initiating and carrying out the particular scheme, I went away strengthened in my resolve. . . . He usually acquiesced, as he knew that I never failed to listen to his views and to give full weight to them.[1]

Of course Lloyd George could not have ignored Law's opinion even if he had thought it unworthy of respect, because he was dependent on the party that Law led. But in fact he respected Law's opinion for its own sake. He was also genuinely fond of him, and the sentiment was mutual. As Robert Blake says, their collaboration showed 'a harmony seldom found in high politics' and 'was never marred by a single quarrel'.[2] Though mistakes and disasters nevertheless occurred, their partnership served to limit the number, and so contributed largely to the government's relative success.

Before Lloyd George, only prime ministers who were peers had not also been leaders of the House of Commons. (Most recently, during the second and third premierships of Lord Salisbury, the House had been led by his nephew, Arthur Balfour.) When Law took Lloyd George's place after the fall of the coalition in 1922, the traditional practice was restored and stayed in force until the Second World War. Churchill then separated the functions again, and they have remained separate ever since. But modern prime ministers have been less remote from Parliament than Lloyd George became. Even as war leader from 1940 Churchill often showed his face there and regularly answered questions, warned by the example of Lloyd George's self-inflicted isolation. For a remarkably long time, however, this isolation was not unduly damaging to him. His prestige in the country and in the world, reinforced by occasional speeches in Parliament, was enough to maintain his dominance.

A historic innovation associated with the War Cabinet was its secretariat, and another key figure in the new regime – next to Law, perhaps the most influential – was the War Cabinet's secretary, Sir Maurice Hankey. Lloyd George was supremely good at creating machinery of government, and providing the energy and inspiration to keep it going; but he was not at all good at running it in a methodical way. Smooth, efficient administration was never his forte; indeed his working habits were disorderly, verging on the chaotic. Fortunately, Hankey had all the higher bureaucratic qualities

1. WM, pp. 1026–7.
2. Robert Blake, *The Unknown Prime Minister: The Life and Times of Andrew Bonar Law, 1858–1923* (1955), p. 342.

that he lacked; it was for this reason that Lloyd George appointed him. His extraordinary efficiency, already demonstrated as secretary of, in turn, the Committee of Imperial Defence, the War Council, the Dardanelles Committee and the War Committee, found its ultimate fulfilment when Lloyd George attached him to the Cabinet itself, which had previously worked without a secretariat, even in wartime.

The War Cabinet's procedure was largely evolved by Hankey. It was his idea that the Cabinet should meet at least once every weekday, and if necessary more often. Between its first meeting on 9 December 1916 (a Saturday) and the end of 1917 it held 308 meetings. Hankey made all government departments aware of its overriding authority, stipulating that they should keep it supplied, through him, with all relevant information, while he in return would convey to them information that he and the Cabinet received from various sources. Heads of department, or experts deputed by them, were to attend when items of concern to them were on the agenda, and it was their duty to bring such items forward. The agenda consequently tended to be long, with the result that business often had to be postponed. Arrears would then be made up, at intervals, in marathon sessions of the Cabinet, or by referring some matters to subordinate committees. The Cabinet's decisions were meant to be implemented as soon as its minutes had been initialled by the Prime Minister. When, as was often the case, he could not be bothered to initial them, Hankey would issue them on his own authority. Either way, the fact that he was known to have the Prime Minister's confidence enabled him to spur departments to action. Though far from achieving perfect efficiency, the new system was certainly a great improvement on the old.

Hankey was a master of detail who could also take a broad view of affairs. He had never confined himself to the role of a super-secretary, but from early in the war had made a point of expressing views on grand strategy, which carried weight with his political masters. His mind was in many ways unconventional; for instance, he deserves, with Churchill, the chief credit for promoting the idea of the tank. As a Royal Marines officer he had no exclusive service prejudice. Asquith had thought as highly of him as Lloyd George did, though without giving him quite so important a role. Before the first meeting of the new Cabinet Lloyd George asked him for a memorandum on the state of the war and priorities for the future. In the course of one day (8 December) Hankey produced a thirty-page document, with a covering letter summarizing its contents.

His top priority was the maintenance of sea power and victory over the U-boats, though he did not yet mention convoys. He asserted the primacy of the Western front (a concept to which he had been reluctantly converted the previous year) and envisaged the necessity for a major Allied offensive there in 1917, if only to forestall another Verdun. He saw little chance, as yet, of smashing the German army. At Salonica the Allies should, he thought, adopt a defensive stance, but he favoured sending guns to Italy to support offensive operations on that front, and also suggested reinforcing Egypt in preparation for a northward move from there. Production of all kinds should be stimulated at home, to reduce the need for imports, and compulsion should be used to the utmost that Labour would tolerate. Towards Ireland he recommended 'an entirely conciliatory policy'.[3]

The War Cabinet itself was small, but its meetings were not held in seclusion. From the first they were occasions involving, as well as the principals, other ministers summoned *ad hoc*, officials, service chiefs and civilian experts. For the Cabinet's first meeting on 9 December all its five members were present, and Hankey was in attendance with one of his assistants, Colonel Dally Jones. Also present for the whole meeting were the First Lord of the Admiralty, Sir Edward Carson, the permanent under-secretary at the Foreign Office, Lord Hardinge of Penshurst, and the two Chiefs of Staff, Sir John Jellicoe and Sir William Robertson. There were eleven items on the agenda, of which the first two concerned the Cabinet secretariat. It was decided that Hankey and his enlarged staff should move temporarily into Montagu House (in Whitehall), while two houses on either side of their existing premises in Whitehall Gardens were absorbed and adapted to provide more space. Several items related to the situation in Greece, where a civil war was going on between the King, Constantine I, and his pro-Allied Prime Minister, Venizelos, whom the King had dismissed and who was running a rival government at Salonica. The Foreign Office was authorized to send a telegram demanding that royalist troops be withdrawn from Thessaly, under the threat of war. At the time, however, Allied policy towards Greece, and about operations on the Salonica front, was bedevilled by Anglo-French disagreements. The French wanted to send four more divisions (two French, two British) to Salonica, but Robertson was opposed to this, regarding it as an unwarrantable diversion of strength, and also because he had no confidence in the Allied commander there, the French General Maurice Sarrail. The Cabinet could only instruct him, lamely, to communicate his views to Joffre.

Two items concerned the crisis in financial relations with the United States, and for these the Governor of the Bank of England, Lord Cunliffe,

3. Stephen Roskill, *Hankey: Man of Secrets* (3 vols., 1970–74), vol. i, pp. 335–7.

and the joint permanent secretaries to the Treasury, Sir John Bradbury and Sir Robert Chalmers, were present. The Cabinet decided that there should be an early conference of the European allies, and that meanwhile orders in the United States should be curtailed, though without any public announcement. Under another item Lloyd George informed the Cabinet of his appointment of Sir Joseph Maclay as Shipping Controller, and Hankey was asked to request 'every possible facility and assistance' for him from the Admiralty and the Board of Trade.

Finally, under item 11 – for which the Secretary of State for India, Austen Chamberlain, attended – the Cabinet considered the expediency of sending a force to Rabegh, on the Arabian coast of the Red Sea, to give support to the Arab revolt against the Turks. This had begun in June 1916, under the leadership of the Sherif of Mecca, Hussein, and had achieved initial success as the rebels, with help from the Royal Navy, overran some of the main Red Sea ports, including Rabegh. But by October the Turks were fighting back strongly and threatening the rebels' gains, with reinforcements sent along the railway line to Medina.

The Cabinet decided to order the General Officer Commanding (GOC) Egypt (Sir Archibald Murray) to prepare a brigade for possible dispatch to Rabegh, and the Foreign Office to ask if the French would be willing to send a similar force. Robertson argued – and made sure that his opinion was recorded in the minutes – that one brigade would be insufficient, and anyway could not be spared from 'more important theatres'; while Curzon and Chamberlain insisted that the Allies could not allow the Sherif to be overwhelmed. (The view of T. E. Lawrence, already working with Hussein's sons, Abdullah and Feisal, happened to coincide with Robertson's, because he did not regard the intervention of large regular forces as appropriate to the local situation. But his name did not come up at the Cabinet meeting; he had yet to make his mark at that level.)

The agenda on 9 December covered a number of issues that were to bulk large in the months ahead. The meeting also demonstrated how the War Cabinet would function; not as five men sitting in isolation, but as a larger group of people among whom the five alone had the power to decide. The presence of the Chiefs of Staff when operations were being discussed, usually in the early part of each meeting, was to become a matter of course – though there was soon to be one important occasion when Robertson was deliberately not summoned. Others, like the financial experts or departmental ministers at the first meeting, would be called in for particular items in which they had an interest. Not all of the questions raised were resolved with clinical decisiveness; and so it would continue. Despite the smaller executive body and the secretarial infrastructure, both undoubted aids to the processes of decision and action, there would still be a fair amount of shilly-shallying, postponement and fudge. All the same, the routine of Cabinets every weekday – announced in a communiqué to the press after the first meeting – ensured a more urgent and sustained attention to the manifold problems of the war.

Members of the War Cabinet sat at the centre of the Cabinet table, on both sides, while ministers and experts summoned to attend sat towards the ends of the table. The secretary, normally Hankey himself, sat on the Prime Minister's right, with an assistant to his right. The procedure for taking and circulating the minutes is best described in Hankey's own words:

I had to insist on permission to bring assistant secretaries, except when matters of special secrecy were under consideration, as it would have been impossible for me to undertake the actual drafting of the whole of the . . . Minutes. As it was, I had to take single-handed all the more secret meetings both of the War Cabinet, of the Prime Minister's own conferences, and of international meetings. In order to expedite the business – for in war-time Minutes may make the difference between success and failure – the assistant secretary would be changed several times during the meeting. As each assistant secretary left the room . . . I would hand him a rough pencil draft of the conclusions reached while he was present. Returning to the office he would at once dictate a draft of the conclusions, and his successor would follow the same procedure. The moment the meeting was over . . . I would return to the office and rough drafts would be brought for my approval. When approved, they were roneo-ed on a wax sheet and circulated as a draft to the War Cabinet, the Minutes on each item being sent in addition to those who had been present only for that item. A copy was also sent for printing under conditions of great secrecy. The drafts had to be returned within twenty-four hours together with any corrections or suggestions. These were then incorporated in the print, after which final copies were struck off and sent to all concerned. Only the King, the War Cabinet and a small selection of Ministers, Chiefs of Staff, and high officials received the full Minutes, extracts being sent as necessary to others.[4]

At the outset this procedure required some explanation to Buckingham Palace, since under the old system the Prime Minister used to write to the King in his own hand after Cabinet meetings, and these letters provided, in fact, the only written record of conclusions reached. Lloyd George, who hated writing letters, could never have been induced to conform to this practice.

4. Maurice Hankey, *The Supreme Command, 1914–1918* (2 vols., 1961), vol. ii, pp. 585–6.

He gave Hankey an argument to put to the King's private secretary, Lord Stamfordham: that the War Cabinet had taken over the business of the old War Committee and that Asquith had sent no written report of this to the King, since proper minutes of it were kept. Stamfordham affected to assume that Lloyd George would nevertheless report to the King in person on traditional Cabinet business, as distinct from the type of business taken over from the War Committee. But this assumption (or pious hope) was vain. The King had to be content with printed minutes of the new unified body.[5]

During the next ten days Lloyd George was absent from seven meetings of the War Cabinet. At one of these Curzon presided; at all the others, Law. The reason for Lloyd George's absence was that he had a severe cold, followed by throat trouble of a kind that intermittently afflicted him in times of stress. Never one to make light of physical ailments, he was also prone to occasional bouts of illness whose root cause may well have been nervous. He had a prolonged bout of throat trouble during and after the second general election of 1910, at the end of what had certainly been a testing year for him; and he was similarly afflicted in 1914, when the preparation of his Budget was proving very difficult, and he was also involved in the Ulster crisis. In December 1916 the effects of a cold may well have been aggravated by the strain of getting his government formed, and of taking stock of the many daunting challenges of his new job. He was still complaining of his throat when he addressed the House of Commons for the first time as Prime Minister on 19 December, and even said at one point that he had almost not been able to make the speech at all. Nevertheless he spoke for nearly two hours.

He dealt, first, with the peace offensive that had been launched during the past week by the German government. This took the form of a note presented by the German Chancellor, Bethmann Hollweg, to the American Ambassador in Berlin, for onward transmission to the Allied governments; followed by a speech the same day (12 December) in the Reichstag. The note proclaimed German willingness to negotiate, but without stating terms. The offer was disingenuous, because so long as the balance of military and, still more, of territorial advantage lay with Germany, no terms that Germany would have agreed to could possibly have been acceptable to the Allies. The true purpose of the 'peace' move was to wrongfoot the Allies, particularly

5. Hankey to Stamfordham, 10 December 1916; Stamfordham to Hankey, same date. Hankey shared Lloyd George's dislike for 'time-honoured customs that waste time' (Roskill, *Hankey*, vol. i, pp. 340–41).

in regard to American opinion, and so prepare the ground, diplomatically, for the declaration of unrestricted submarine warfare on which the German high command was intent.

When Lloyd George spoke, the French and the Russians had already rejected the German offer, and he gave them the British government's firm backing. 'They have the unquestionable right to give the first answer . . . The enemy is still on their soil; their sacrifices have been greater.' With an eye to President Wilson and the American people, he quoted tellingly some words of Abraham Lincoln (always a hero of his): 'We accepted this war for an object, and a worthy object, and the war will end when that object is attained. Under God, I hope it will never end until that time.' It was difficult enough for the British, 'with the protection of the broad seas', to understand what the war had meant to the French and the Russians, so how much more so for 'those who were fortunate enough to live thousands of miles away'. He repeated the Allies' unalterable demand for 'complete restitution, full reparation, effectual guarantees'.

In the next part of his speech he emphasized the size of the task ahead. 'If there be any who have given their confidence to the new Administration in expectation of a speedy victory they will be doomed to disappointment.' His picture of the military situation would not be 'gloomy', but it had to be 'stern'. He explained the need for a small War Cabinet, while assuring members that Parliament would retain control. He spoke of the new ministries he was setting up, dwelling at some length on the vital importance of shipping, and of making best use of the country's labour resources. For the duration of the war shipping would be 'nationalized in the real sense of the term', and power would be taken to move workers from inessential to essential tasks. He also had much to say about the food problem. The harvest had been bad, and rough weather was impeding the sowing of winter wheat. Consumption had to be cut by voluntary self-sacrifice. He called for a 'national Lent'; but there was no word, yet, of rationing. At the same time home production of food had to be boosted; 'every available square yard' must be made to produce.

Praising the great contribution that the Dominions were making to the war effort, he announced that an imperial conference would soon be held, at which the 'whole position' would be placed before them and their advice sought. Though he spoke at length about the achievements and growing professionalism of the new army, he forgot to pay a similar tribute to the navy and had to be prompted to do so by an Admiral of the Fleet (Sir Hedworth Meux). In response to the Admiral's interruption he poured unction on the troubled waters: 'I do not think that anything I can say would be in the least adequate to recognise the enormous and incalculable services that the great Navy of Britain has rendered, not merely to the Empire, but to the whole Allied cause.'

There was more unction as he ended with 'one personal note'. It was 'one of the deepest regrets of his life' that he had had to part from his predecessor, Asquith, under whom he had been proud to serve. He 'never had a kinder or more indulgent chief', and if there were any faults of temper they had been entirely on his side. 'For eight years we differed as men of such different temperaments must necessarily differ, but we never had a personal quarrel.' (It was true that they had worked together closely and, except when mischief was made between them by others, had got on remarkably well.) His decision, at length, to resign from Asquith's government had been taken 'with deep genuine grief', but there were moments when 'personal and party considerations must sink into absolute insignificance'.

Asquith, who spoke next, began with gracious congratulations, the hope that Lloyd George would 'sustain a full measure of physical strength and energy', and an assurance of 'whole-hearted sympathy'. And the outgoing Prime Minister would not be outdone in non-partisanship. 'That is a claim which others may make also.' If he spoke from the Opposition front bench, it was not because he claimed 'in any sense to be the leader of what is called an opposition'. He believed that there was no such thing, though in the last few weeks he had received 'most gratifying testimony' of the confidence of his 'old political associates'. Party had ceased to exist until the end of the war, though 'in good time' it would revive.

On the German peace offer Asquith was no less firm than Lloyd George. It was 'wrapped up in the familiar dialect of Prussian arrogance', and 'born of military and economic necessity'. The only peace worth having was one that promised to be durable and achieved the purposes for which Britain had entered the war. There was nothing to be said for 'a patched-up and precarious compromise'.

If there had been no other speech Lloyd George could have felt that his first encounter with Parliament as Prime Minister had passed off reasonably well. But unfortunately Asquith was followed by John Redmond, leader of the Irish National Party, who was indignant that in the 'general programme of energy, promptness, quick decisions' the Irish question alone, apparently, was to be 'allowed to drift'. Lloyd George in his speech had suggested no palliatives, still less a cure. Between 500 and 600 prisoners from the 1916 Easter Rising were still being held, without trial, in English prisons. If Lloyd George really wanted, as he said, to improve the atmosphere in Ireland, at the very least those prisoners should be released at once. But more drastic action was needed to settle the larger Irish question, and Redmond urged Lloyd George to take a bold initiative, at a time when he could count on the maximum support at home and abroad.

Redmond was a man on Lloyd George's conscience. After the Easter Rising he had negotiated a settlement between the leading Nationalists and Unionists, but had failed to push it through against the opposition of lesser figures. Asquith and Lloyd George were both to blame for this failure, but special blame attaches to Lloyd George for having gone back on a promise to Redmond that he would resign rather than allow the deal to be shipwrecked. It would have been bad for the country if Lloyd George had left the government at the time, but the promise should not have been given unless he was sure that he would, if necessary, be prepared to honour it. The collapse of the deal undermined the position of Redmond and his party in Ireland, already weakened by acceptance of the postponement of Home Rule until after the war, and so contributed to the eventual triumph of Sinn Fein.

Lloyd George interrupted Redmond's speech in a rather tetchy and defensive tone, pleading that he had had no time, as yet, to discuss Irish matters in depth since becoming Prime Minister, and that he had been further handicapped by illness. But he did not emerge very creditably from the exchange.

The Cabinet did not meet on Christmas Eve or Christmas Day, but a meeting was held during the morning of Boxing Day, in preparation for a conference with French ministers who came over from Paris and stayed three days. The visiting party consisted of the veteran Finance Minister, Alexandre Ribot, and the Armaments Minister, Albert Thomas, together with a brilliant Quai d'Orsay official and future Foreign Minister, Philippe Berthelot.

The Prime Minister, Aristide Briand, did not attend, nor did the new War Minister, General Lyautey, who had been appointed when Briand reconstructed his government immediately after Lloyd George formed his. To some extent Briand copied Lloyd George, in reducing the number of ministers in his Cabinet; but he did so by the opposite method, cutting out senior ministers of state and so having a Cabinet that contained only departmental ministers. Another change had occurred, however, which was far more important than any political reshuffle, and incidentally the cause of Briand's absence from the London talks. This was the removal of General Joffre from the post of Commander-in-Chief, which was tantamount to a change of regime in France.

The victory of the Marne had given Joffre a prestige that no French politician could match, and so long as his faithful spokesman Alexandre Millerand was War Minister his word on all matters of war policy was as good as law. Even when General Galliéni, who had a rival claim to credit for the Marne victory, replaced Millerand in October 1915, Joffre's position was at first little affected, because Galliéni was a sick man and anyway quite unsuited to a political role. But during 1916 Joffre's authority was progressively undermined as French opinion, both civilian and among the military rank-and-file, became disenchanted with the strategy of attrition, which seemed to leave the enemy in undisturbed possession of nearly all of the French territory he had occupied, despite the huge losses incurred in the Somme offensive. As for Verdun, Joffre was blamed for its initial vulnerability, while others received the glory for its heroic and successful defence. Meanwhile the politicians, reflecting the public mood, began to assert a measure of control through parliamentary commissions, and General Roques, who took over from Galliéni in March 1916, administered a further blow to Joffre when he backed Sarrail, the commander at Salonica, in a dispute with the Commander-in-Chief.

Joffre's eventual fall occurred in two stages. First, Briand persuaded him, in the early part of December, to agree to the appointment of a new operational chief of the French armies, while retaining his existing title and nominal supremacy. But General Lyautey, simultaneously appointed War Minister, was not consulted about the arrangement and, on his arrival in Paris from Morocco (where he was already a much-admired proconsul), refused to go along with it. Joffre then had no choice but to resign, and he did so on 26 December, accepting as a consolation prize the rank of marshal of France which, because of its Napoleonic overtones, had not been conferred on any soldier since the foundation of the Third Republic. (The last holder, Marshal Canrobert, who died in 1895, had received it under the Second Empire.) The man appointed to the chief operational command, with Joffre's approval, then inherited the supreme position in name as well as in fact, though without the lustre of national saviour that had made Joffre, for a time, so uniquely dominant in the French state.[6]

6. According to one who later achieved even greater dominance, there was no legitimate authority in France between the fall of Joffre and the advent of Clemenceau in November 1917. Near the end of his life, after he had stood down as president, Charles de Gaulle told one of his intimates: 'It was not the government of the Third Republic that won the Great War. The French people led, successively, by Joffre, Clemenceau and Foch had the legitimacy.' He added that he himself had embodied this mysterious essence since 1940, and would continue to embody it until his death (François Flohic, *Souvenirs d'Outre-Gaulle* (1979), p. 195). This bizarre view of history – particularly bizarre in the suggestion that Foch was, in some sense, Clemenceau's successor – illustrates the problem of legitimacy that has dogged the French state ever since the Revolution. Of course de Gaulle regarded the Fifth Republic that he had founded as, by extension, legitimate.

The new Commander-in-Chief was General Robert Nivelle, whose relatively brief tenure of the post was to have fateful consequences. Though only four years younger than Joffre, he had been a mere colonel at the outbreak of war, when Joffre was already an army group commander. But since then his rise had been extremely rapid – too rapid for his own good. A cavalryman turned gunner, he had shown initiative and dash in the early battles of the war, and by the end of 1915 was a corps commander. In this capacity he so distinguished himself at Verdun that in August 1916 he was given command of the Second Army, the army of Verdun, when Pétain was promoted commander of the central group of armies. In October and November his troops recaptured the symbolic forts of Douaumont and Vaux, so completing the triumphant saga of Verdun.

At the moment when Joffre's ascendancy was coming to an end, Nivelle stood out as his apparently providential successor. He was a new man, associated with victory but as yet unburdened with any responsibility for costly large-scale battles. He also had a way with politicians, which was a crucial asset at the time. Pétain conspicuously lacked it, so he was passed over. Foch, whose offensive spirit Nivelle fully shared, but who bore considerable public odium for losses on the Somme and earlier, was sidelined to prepare for a possible German attack through Switzerland. Joffre himself proposed Nivelle for the operational high command when Briand suggested the division of functions – imagining that a man so quickly promoted would defer to his own experience and seniority. This was a naïve idea and was anyway never put to the test, because by the end of the year Joffre had been forced out, as we have seen, and Nivelle remained as military overlord without even a nominal superior. Briand judged that his appointment would be politically popular, and so at first it was. Nivelle moved the general headquarters from Chantilly to Beauvais, and was soon, far more significantly, preparing to change the strategy for 1917.

The visit of French ministers to London during the Christmas holidays gave Lloyd George a better excuse than usual for not going to Criccieth. It was always a time of year he particularly disliked being there. If he had to stay in Wales at all, he preferred to do so in the summer. From early in his career he had tried, whenever possible, to spend Christmas in a warmer climate abroad, the Mediterranean having a special attraction for him. But he would write to his relatives at Criccieth saying how much he was missing the spiritual warmth of home. It was so at the end of 1916. He wrote to his brother William:

I am so disappointed not be able to join you all Xmas day. It would have been such happiness to spend my holidays in the midst of the family. But I am not the only one deprived of the joy by this sad War. I could not dream of leaving things until the Asquith muddle has been straightened out. That will take some time.

Love and happiness to you all.

In a postscript he added:

Do you know I can get to Paris in less time than I can get to Cric. It shows how far you are.[7]

He spent Christmas at Walton Heath with Frances Stevenson.

His meetings with the French on Boxing Day and the two following days were important but inconclusive. Much time was devoted to Salonica, but the visitors also revealed that General Nivelle was planning a new offensive on the Western front and gave some indication of its proposed character.

How would this differ from what had gone before? Joffre's plan for the coming year had envisaged a continuation of pressure all round – on the Eastern front, in the Balkans, and above all in the West. The Western offensive was to be, in effect, a renewal of the battle of the Somme at the earliest opportunity. Judging correctly that the Germans had been very hard hit by the operations of 1916, Joffre was determined that they should be allowed no respite. From the beginning of February the British were to move against the German salient between Arras and the Somme, while the French were to tackle the larger one between the Somme and the Aisne. If these attacks went well, a French reserve group would strike northwards from the Rheims area a fortnight later, with a view at least to capturing large numbers of Germans trapped in the salients, and possibly bringing about a total collapse of the German front.

It is one of the many cruel ironies of the First World War that this strategy might conceivably have worked. The enemy would have been hit while he was still punch-drunk from the previous year's fighting, and while much of his line was still dangerously exposed. From the French point of view, the plan had the merit of avoiding any frontal assaults on positions naturally favouring defence, such as the escarpment of the Chemin-des-Dames, which was to be turned rather than attacked head-on. Joffre had at last learnt some important tactical lessons from the bloody experiences of 1914–16. But this was not how it appeared to the politicians who brought him down. To them

7. DLG to William George, 23 December 1916.

he was the same man promising to pursue the same discredited type of warfare, with as little chance as ever of achieving a decisive result.

Nivelle, by contrast, was a new man, offering what seemed to be a new and more promising formula for success. He believed that he could win the war outright, and swiftly, by applying on a larger scale the formula that had worked so well for his recapture of the Verdun forts.

Under a creeping artillery barrage his main thrust would be against the Chemin-des-Dames, which he intended to capture within forty-eight hours. Through the hole thus opened he would then pour reserves in overwhelming force to roll up the entire enemy line. Operations further north were to be more or less as projected in Joffre's plan, though with the sole purpose of deceiving the enemy and deflecting his strength from the vital sector. But one notable difference was that Nivelle wanted the British to take over part of the French line, so as to release French units for what he meant to be an essentially French victory.

The change of command and plan necessarily involved delay, which was itself to prove calamitous. In retrospect there can be little doubt that any chance of decisive success in France in 1917 depended upon the resumption of attacks as early in the year as Joffre desired. His removal, and the timing of it, had dire consequences.

At the London meetings after Christmas the French, having outlined Nivelle's plan, sought full co-operation from the British in carrying it out. The War Cabinet expressed general sympathy, but reserved its position on the length of French line to be taken over and insisted that there must be time to 'go into the matter' with Haig.[8] At this stage the plan did not at all appeal to Lloyd George. He was still opposed to any further massive onslaughts in the West and was hoping, if possible, to find a way round. Regarding the Habsburg Empire as the enemy's most vulnerable flank, he wanted to concentrate upon attacking it, not least as a means of helping Russia and forcing the Germans to divert strength from the Western front. Since a major move against Austria-Hungary from the Balkans was not, in the circumstances, practicable – despite the current interest of the French in the Salonica bridgehead – his thoughts turned to the idea of an offensive on the Italian front, for which powerful artillery support would be provided by Britain and France.

He did not mention this project to the French during the London talks. Instead, he proposed that an Allied conference should very soon be held at some Mediterranean venue, at which Salonica (definitely) and the general course of operations in 1917 would be discussed. The second, broader topic

8. War Cab., 28 December 1916 (morning meeting).

would (he privately hoped) give him the opportunity to raise his Italian scheme with the advantage of enthusiastic Italian backing. After their return to Paris the French agreed to the suggested conference, though with considerable reluctance, and it was eventually settled that it should be held in Rome in early January.[9] Those attending would be the leaders of the Western Allies, together with Russian representatives at the official level.

Lloyd George went to the conference with a free hand from the War Cabinet to clinch any arrangement that might be negotiated. He took with him Milner, whom he had already asked to go to Russia early in the New Year as the chief British representative on an Allied mission to that country. He was also accompanied by Robertson and Hankey, and a number of other professionals. But the Foreign Secretary, Arthur Balfour, was not in the party.

Before Lloyd George's premiership the form of political activity that has come to be known as summitry – international meetings involving heads of government – was almost unknown. Disraeli attended the Congress of Berlin in 1878, with his Foreign Secretary, Lord Salisbury. But Salisbury himself, during three terms as Prime Minister, never attended any conference abroad.[10] The same was true of Balfour and Campbell-Bannerman during their relatively brief premierships, and of Asquith before 1914. As leader of the country in wartime, Asquith travelled to Calais in November 1915, to Paris and Rome in March–April 1916, and in November of the same year to Paris again for an Allied conference. But Lloyd George's addiction to summitry was apparent throughout his premiership in war and peace. He was to become the most compulsive exponent of the practice before the air age.

Opinions will always differ as to the value of summit conferences. Cynics tend to dismiss them as little more than an opportunity for leaders to indulge their vanity, while briefly escaping from the less glamorous demands of domestic politics. Others maintain that there are some questions that only leaders can decide, and that their decisions are likely to be prompter and better if they meet face to face and get to know each other. On one point, however, there is general agreement: to have any serious value a summit conference must be carefully prepared. Before the principals meet much work needs to be done through the normal processes of diplomacy and this

9. The precise venue was not settled until the last moment. At first Brindisi was mentioned, for the convenience of General Sarrail who would be coming from Salonica. On the eve of Lloyd George's departure the choice still lay between Naples and Rome (War Cab., 1 January 1917).
10. In March 1897 – on his way to the French Riviera for health reasons – he had talks in Paris with the French Foreign Minister. But these did not amount to a proper summit conference.

rule applies in war as well as in peace, save only in sudden grave emergencies.

It is hard to agree with Dr Thomas Jones that Lloyd George prepared for the Rome conference in early January 1917 'with his usual thoroughness'.[11] Neither the French nor the Italians had any prior warning of his chief motive for proposing it. Though he talked to Briand and Lyautey in Paris on his way to Rome, and travelled with them on the same train, he seems to have made no attempt, before the conference, to convert them to the idea of an Italian offensive. As for the Italian government, the first of its members to be apprised of his thinking on the subject was the Socialist leader, Leonido Bissolati, who was known to favour a forward strategy on the Italian front. Lloyd George talked to him at the British embassy on the evening of his arrival in Rome, but the Italian Prime Minister, Paolo Boselli, received no direct advance notice of the plan. A last-minute attempt was made to nobble the Italian Commander-in-Chief, General Luigi Cadorna. Lloyd George sent Hankey to talk to the General while he talked to Bissolati, but Robertson moved more swiftly, reaching Cadorna first and clearly planting in his mind thoughts adverse to Lloyd George's project. Hankey found him 'not nearly as enthusiastic [about it] as he should have been' and concluded that 'he had been got at by Robertson'.[12] He would, in fact, have been likely to oppose the plan anyway.

Lloyd George and Hankey had indeed prepared a long memorandum on options facing the Allies in 1917, including a strong statement of the case for offensive action on the Isonzo front, with the support of British and French heavy artillery. This (it was argued) would not only ensure the safety of Italy, pre-empting a possible offensive by the Central Powers; it would also give Italy the chance to inflict a decisive defeat and then 'to press forward to Trieste and to get astride the Istrian Peninsula'. It might also enable the Allies to attack the naval base at Pola, threatening the Austrian fleet with destruction and hampering enemy submarine activity in the Mediterranean.

Contrary to what Lloyd George states in his memoirs, copies of his memorandum were not 'distributed amongst the civilian, military and naval members of the various delegations before the Conference met', giving them the chance to study it with due care. Far from being made available to other participants beforehand, it was circulated only during the afternoon of the first day of the conference, 5 January. If Lloyd George believed he could best advance his main proposal by such shock tactics, he could hardly have made a worse miscalculation. To gain support for it he needed, above all,

---

11. Thomas Jones, *Lloyd George* (1951), p. 108.   12. Hankey diary, 5 January 1917.

to persuade the French to think again about the Nivelle offensive on which they had set their hearts. Such persuasion would have been hard enough to achieve even if he had devoted himself to the task from the moment he heard about Nivelle's plan, and their espousal of it, at the London talks. To delay the presentation of his own plan until after the Rome conference had begun was to ensure that it would be rejected, as in effect it was. (It was referred to the Chiefs of Staff for further consideration, which was tantamount to killing it.)

With a view, no doubt, to humouring the French, he did not present his plan as an alternative to theirs, but suggested that the Italian offensive might be launched earlier 'to take advantage of a period when the weather on the Western Front [was] unfavourable for the development of a great offensive' there. It would, however, be 'absolutely necessary' for the heavy guns lent by the British and French in support of the Italian attack to be withdrawn in good time 'to enable the British and French Armies to pursue their offensive on the Western Front'. In saying this, Lloyd George was not only concealing, or attempting to conceal, his true motive for proposing an Italian offensive; he was also fatally weakening any attraction his plan might have had for the Italian high command. Cadorna naturally questioned the value of guns lent for such a limited period, and Lloyd George then said, off the top of his head, that although he could not answer for the French the guns lent by Britain might, if necessary, be kept for longer. Thus he flatly contradicted the statement in his memorandum that British guns, no less than French, would 'absolutely' have to be returned in time for the Western front offensive. His argument had no consistency or logical coherence.[13]

The French were determined that nothing should detract from the Nivelle offensive, and after the London talks Lloyd George had little excuse for failing to understand how committed they were to it. Did he really fail to understand? The fact that he felt obliged to write his memorandum on the assumption, so damaging to his Italian proposal, that the Western offensive would go ahead, suggests that he understood the French commitment all too well. In retrospect, he affected surprise and disappointment at the line taken in Rome by Briand, and by his old comrade Albert Thomas (his opposite number when he was Minister of Munitions). He complains in his memoirs that Briand and Thomas turned out to be just two more French

13. '. . . the conditions as to the return of the guns by May might apply to the French guns, but I myself had not, up to the present, excluded the possibility of allowing British guns to remain for a longer time on the Italian front' (WM, p. 1440). In his chapter on the January 1917 Rome conference (WM, pp. 1413–51), Lloyd George quotes his memorandum almost in full, as well as key exchanges arising from it.

politicians enslaved to the Joffre strategy of massive assaults in the West, though he had believed them to be as eager as he was to escape from it. He ignores the crucial point that they regarded Nivelle's strategy as radically different from Joffre's; they were looking to Nivelle to deliver a quick victory at relatively low cost. The French had outlined Nivelle's plan to Lloyd George and his colleagues in London (though Briand himself was not there) whereas he had kept them in the dark about his Italian scheme. In fairness one must say that they had more reason to complain of his behaviour in Rome, than he of theirs.

Despite the collapse of the project which he had secretly intended to be the Allied leaders' principal business there, in other respects the conference was not entirely useless. Most of its time was devoted, as the French wished, to the military future at Salonica and the political problem of relations with Greece. The Allied army at Salonica had a total strength of 300,000, in which the British component was 90,000. Briand pleaded eloquently for two further British divisions to be sent, but Lloyd George refused, giving – significantly – shortage of shipping as his reason. (He did his best to impress upon the conference the gravity of the threat to Britain's shipping resources, upon which France and Italy were heavily dependent for the transport of essential supplies. It was agreed that an Allied naval and shipping conference should be held in the near future.)

On the political side, there were grounds for uneasiness about Greece, in whose territory Salonica was situated, since it had been annexed at the end of the Balkan War of 1912–13. Greece was formally neutral, but its King, Constantine I, had dismissed his pro-Allied Prime Minister, Venizelos, and his intentions were understandably suspect. The French commander at Salonica, General Sarrail, came to Rome seeking authority to overthrow the Greek King. Sarrail was a strong republican (unusually for a French general); his military judgement was therefore tinged with ideology. Lloyd George held no brief for Constantine and took quite a liking to Sarrail, but he was sure that it would be wrong to move directly against the King and his army – which would mean shedding Greek blood and so risking a conflict with the Greek people, as well as exposing the Allied army at Salonica to war on two fronts. He would not assent to such action at the time, but suggested combining the pressure of blockade with insistence that the Greek army be moved, within a stated period, to the Peloponnese. The Italians supported him on this issue, while the Russian representative sided with the French. In the end Lloyd George's policy was adopted.

By 10 January he was back in London, after an unpleasant Channel crossing in a destroyer, and that morning he reported to the War Cabinet.

Though he made the most of what had been achieved in Rome, he knew that the cause for which, above all, he had promoted the conference had failed. The implications of his failure were to be far-reaching.

3

Conference at Calais

*Lloyd George and Robertson – Nivelle in London – Last
meeting with Uncle Lloyd – Calais on his heart*

During his first month or so as Prime Minister Lloyd George had shown all
the vigour and freshness of mind that were expected of him. He had formed
a government that not only looked different, but in many ways was different.
He had delivered a speech in Parliament in which his attitude to the war
and his sense of priorities were clearly signalled. He had emphasized the
vital importance of two related problems, shipping and food. He had ruled
out any compromise peace that would, in reality, be no more than an armed
truce heavily favouring the enemy. Vividly aware that the British war effort
was an effort involving the whole Empire, and most conspicuously the
self-governing Dominions, he had declared his intention of bringing the
Dominion leaders into the process of central decision-making at an early
date. He had remained at work in London through the Christmas holidays,
and his Italian trip, whatever its true value, had served to enhance in the
public mind an impression of feverish activity. People everywhere could feel
that a change of direction and momentum had indeed occurred in Britain.

   Yet in one respect, as he knew too well, things had not changed at all. The
military establishment had lost none of its power. In securing full Conservative participation in his government Lloyd George had more or less guaranteed Haig's position as Commander-in-Chief, while Sir William Robertson
retained, as CIGS, the unique prerogatives that had been given him in January
1916, when he was brought in as an answer to the Kitchener problem.[1] These

---

1. Kitchener, appointed War Secretary at the outbreak of war in response to public and press
demand, had become a liability by 1916. He had made two great contributions – predicting a
long war and raising a mass army to fight it – but he was a chaotic administrator and never
conformed to the minimum requirements of Cabinet government. Since his popular standing
made it impossible to oust him, he was eventually bypassed by the device of appointing
Robertson as CIGS with special powers conferred on him by Order in Council – an arrangement
with which, surprisingly, Kitchener was quite content. A few months later he went down with
the *Hampshire*, but his disappearance did not cause Robertson's powers to be removed. The
CIGS kept his anomalous and unduly exalted status under Kitchener's successor as War
Secretary, Lloyd George. And he kept it still when Lloyd George became Prime Minister.

entitled him to deal direct with the Cabinet, and to be the sole channel through which military command was exercised.

In an ideal world Lloyd George and Robertson would have formed an ideal partnership, like Lloyd George and Bonar Law. Of all senior army officers of the period none should have appealed more to Lloyd George, in at least one way, than Robertson; and in the same way no politician should have appealed more to Robertson than Lloyd George. Both were self-made men, who had reached the top in their different spheres through their own talents and force of character. At a time when the political world was still dominated by men of hereditary position and wealth, and when membership of the officer corps of the British army was still largely determined by social privilege, Lloyd George and Robertson had risen to the top from obscure origins. Lloyd George was, indeed, born into a localized cultural élite (that of Welsh Nonconformity), which helped him to win a seat in Parliament at an early age; but thereafter he had to compete with men whose material advantages he did not remotely share. Robertson was born into no kind of élite. His father was a village tailor and postmaster in Lincolnshire, and after leaving school at thirteen he went into domestic service as a footman. In his autobiography he tells us nothing about his life before, at eighteen, he joined the army as a ranker. But the book's dedication points to an otherwise unsung heroine: 'To the memory of my mother to whose affectionate and inspiring teachings in early life is attributable such merit, if any, as may attach to my career.'[2]

In 1888, after eleven years in the ranks, Robertson was commissioned and posted to a regiment in India, where an officer without private resources could have some hope of being able to live on his meagre pay. Even so, Robertson had to supplement it by learning Indian languages, for which financial reward was offered. After a time his marriage to the daughter of an Indian Army general made it easier for him to mix with his 'social superiors'.[3] By 1905 – when Lloyd George became a Cabinet minister – he was a full Colonel, having distinguished himself as a staff officer in the South African War, and having afterwards been appointed to a key post in War Office intelligence. From the outbreak of war until his appointment as CIGS he was first Quartermaster General, then Chief of Staff, to the British army in France. He had hardly any experience as a fighting soldier, and none at all of command in the field.

2. William Robertson, *From Private to Field-Marshal* (1921).
3. *The Military Correspondence of Field-Marshal Sir William Robertson*, ed. David R. Woodward (1989), p. 3.

As a staff officer he was, however, supremely competent, and he was just the man to advise on the feasibility of bright ideas that might spring from a mind more imaginative than his own. He was also well qualified to administer the great army that had been built up since 1914. As a foil to Lloyd George's mercurial genius he could have acted, on the military side, much as Bonar Law acted on the civilian. In practical hard-headedness and negative wisdom he was analogous to Law. Unfortunately there was a crucial difference. As fellow-politicians Lloyd George and Law belonged, as it were, to the same trade union. Robertson belonged to the military trade union, which regarded all politicians with suspicion and felt that they had no right to intrude into its mysteries. Moreover, Robertson's loyalty to the military caste was intensified by a factor peculiar to himself. Having broken down so many internal barriers to reach the summit of his profession, he was all the more adamant in his determination to defend it against what he saw as ignorant and improper interference by outsiders.

In the Great War there was (as has already been noted) a psychological gulf between civilian and service leaders that did not exist, to anything like the same degree, in the next war. Between Lloyd George and Robertson the gulf was made even wider by personal incompatibility. Lloyd George and Law could hardly have been less alike in temperament, yet they were not at all incompatible. On the contrary, their solidarity as politicians and coalition partners was reinforced by a personal friendship that began long before the war and survived the extreme rancour of pre-war party politics, in which, of course, they were on opposite sides. No such friendship, transcending disagreements and quarrels, ever developed between Lloyd George and Robertson. Far from being friends, they never really got on at all.

One reason, no doubt, was that Robertson was at heart a very conventional man. He was also a bit of a prig, who brought to his dealings with Lloyd George strong moral disapproval of his character as a public man. As well as condemning his methods, Robertson was very apt to impugn his motives. In the *Dictionary of National Biography* entry on Robertson, Lloyd George is said to have been 'essentially an opportunist', whereas Robertson was 'a firm believer in principles'. Since the entry was written by Robertson's faithful acolyte, Sir Frederick Maurice, we may be sure that it reflected his own view, both of himself and of the Prime Minister.[4] At any rate the contrast is absurd. Lloyd George may have been opportunistic in his methods, but his aims were strikingly constant throughout his career. They were patriotic and, to a large degree, idealistic, though combined with strong personal

4. *DNB* (Supplement 1931–1940) (Robertson died in 1933).

ambition. Much the same was true of Robertson, and it was also true that Robertson could resort, in promoting his aims, to the very methods that he condemned in Lloyd George, such as intrigue and use of the press.

With all his faults, Lloyd George was less of a humbug than most successful public figures. He was humorous and unpompous, and although a high moral tone occasionally crept into his speeches (in particular when he was addressing Welsh audiences) it did not come naturally to him. He liked to do business informally, face to face, whereas Robertson much preferred exchanges on paper. Lloyd George's style was cheerfully uninhibited, Robertson's stiff and unyielding. Even Louis Spears, who admired Robertson, is compelled to say that 'a little mansuetude and affability would have helped him mightily'.[5]

Another flaw in Robertson, admitted by Spears, was his blind loyalty to Haig. 'For the sake of standing by Haig he probably put aside and overrode many ideas of his own.'[6] The pros and cons of Haig will be considered later; here it is enough to say that, while he was War Secretary in 1916, Lloyd George came to regard the cons as substantially outweighing the pros. He looked to Robertson, as CIGS, to help him in the search for a possible replacement for Haig. But Robertson refused to co-operate. As Robertson records:

More than once during 1917, when affairs on the Western Front were being discussed, [Lloyd George] said to me that his chief complaint was that I would persist in always supporting what Haig did, and there is no doubt in my mind that a recommendation from me ... to appoint a new Commander-in-Chief would have met with his instant approval. Without such a recommendation, which could if necessary be publicly quoted in support of the appointment, [he] was not prepared to act and therefore no change was made.[7]

Whatever his private opinion of Haig, Robertson was on principle ('firm believer in principles' that he was) loyal to the Commander-in-Chief rather than to the Secretary of State who became Prime Minister. In defending Haig he felt that he was defending the army against a meddlesome civilian, who had no qualifications to form a judgement on strategy or military leadership. Perhaps also, despite his own origins – or because of them – there lingered in him a residue of deference towards the traditional officer class that Haig epitomized.

5. E. L. Spears, *Prelude to Victory* (1939), p. 34.   6. Ibid., p. 35.
7. William Robertson, *Soldiers and Statesmen, 1914–1918* (2 vols., 1926), vol. ii, pp. 213–14.

Lloyd George, faced with a CIGS who would not help him in his search for an alternative to Haig, should have done more on his own initiative to make direct contact with the army while he was at the War Office. But he largely wasted the opportunity. He was ill at ease with soldiers, not only because he had never been one himself (apart from brief service in the Volunteer Force during his youth in Wales), but still more because he had reason to feel that he would have been unable to endure what the soldiers in the trenches were enduring. Though he showed, as a rule, exceptional moral courage, his physical courage was seriously deficient. He was always squeamish about illness and death, and he had a special fear of high explosives. He did not therefore pay many visits to the army in the field, and – unlike Clemenceau, when he became Prime Minister of France – seldom visited the front. Had Lloyd George got to know the army better, he would certainly have overcome some of the prejudice against him as a politician, and might have discovered for himself a potential alternative to Haig.

The deadlock between Lloyd George and Robertson, neither trusting the other and each working to frustrate the other's intentions, constituted a grave weakness at the heart of government. Lloyd George did not feel free to get rid of the over-mighty CIGS at the outset of his premiership, and was further obliged to appoint, as War Secretary, the 17th Earl of Derby, who was as much the mouthpiece of the generals as Millerand had been of Joffre. In attempting to circumvent the War Office, and to conduct war policy with Hankey as, in effect, his only Chief of Staff, Lloyd George went to Rome without the full professional back-up he needed. He did not consult Robertson about his Italian scheme, because he knew that the CIGS would be against it *a priori*. Yet some hints of it must have reached Robertson because, as we have seen, he acted swiftly to prejudice General Cadorna against it (not that Cadorna would have been likely to agree to it, in any case). Knowing that he lacked Lloyd George's confidence, Robertson should have offered his resignation. Instead, he chose to stay where he could best obstruct the threat that Lloyd George posed, in his view, to the army's and the country's interest.

Lloyd George's failure to promote a campaign on the Italian front left him under the urgent necessity to reach a decision on the Nivelle plan, to which the French had shown that they were inflexibly committed. As he travelled back from Rome he could reflect that this would at least have the merit of cramping Haig's style. The French intended their army to have the lion's share of the fighting, because they were counting on Nivelle to strike a war-winning blow. Lloyd George was still sceptical of any attempt to win the war by a massive attack on the Western front; but if there had to be such an attack he would prefer it to be undertaken mainly by the French, since he was determined to avoid British casualties in 1917 on anything like the scale of 1916. Besides, he tended to have more confidence in French generals than their British counterparts, having formed the view – for which there was some justification – that French troops had been more effectively and economically led in the Somme fighting.[8] To that extent he was predisposed in favour of Nivelle.

It is, however, a myth that he experienced a sudden, dramatic conversion to Nivelle's plan, and to the man himself, when they met at a station during Lloyd George's return journey from Rome. According to Robertson, the talk on that occasion was 'desultory'.[9] But it was agreed with the French ministers that Nivelle should come to London the following week to expound his strategy to the War Cabinet, with Haig also present. The two commanders-in-chief had already been discussing its implications both in correspondence and face to face. Nivelle from the first took account of Haig's intention to clear the Belgian coast by the end of the summer, but argued that a German withdrawal there would follow automatically from the success of his own plan. Haig agreed to play his part in this, but only on the strict understanding that, if its objectives were not achieved within the time stated, he would be free to launch his own attack in Flanders, with the necessary degree of French co-operation.[10]

Nivelle attended two meetings of the War Cabinet, on 15 and 16 January. He was accompanied by the French Ambassador, Paul Cambon, and several staff officers. Every member of the War Cabinet was present, as were Balfour, Robertson and Haig. Before the first meeting, which was held during the afternoon of the 15th, the two British soldiers had an unpleasant encounter

8. On the whole the French had more to show in the way of captured territory and a lower level of casualties. Trevor Wilson attributes their relative success to three factors, all of which must have had something to do with the quality of command: surprise, a much heavier weight of artillery bombardment, and superiority in infantry tactics (*The Myriad Faces of War: Britain and the Great War, 1914–1918* (1986), p. 325).
9. The story that Lloyd George was instantly converted on his way back from Rome was given wide currency by John Buchan (*A History of the Great War* (4 vols., 1921–2), vol. iii, p. 436). Lloyd George dismisses it in his memoirs with the comment: 'When a brilliant novelist assumes the unaccustomed role of a historian it is inevitable that he should now and again forget that he is no longer writing fiction.' It is hard to be sure where the meeting actually took place, because accounts differ. Robertson tells us that Nivelle met the British and French delegates 'at a railway station near Paris' (*Soldiers and Statesmen*, vol. ii, p. 196).
10. The two commanders first met on 20 December 1916 and subsequently corresponded about Nivelle's plan.

with Lloyd George. The Prime Minister was still, clearly, not at all en-amoured of the prospect of any large-scale attack on the Western front, having deduced from the experience of previous campaigns that conditions there would always favour the defending army. Yet he showed that, if there had to be an attack, he would much prefer the French to take the leading role in planning and execution. According to Haig's contemporary record, Lloyd George said that to win the war it was necessary to 'attack a soft front, and we could not find that on the Western Front'. Nevertheless, he regarded the French army as 'better all round', and 'able to gain success at less cost of life'. The country would not stand for any more squandering of British lives, as on the Somme.[11]

In his appearance before the War Cabinet Nivelle presented his case with such force and charm that the politicians were won over. He converted not only Lloyd George but all of his colleagues. Hankey also was persuaded, noting in his diary that Nivelle 'made a very favourable impression on the War Cabinet *and on me*'.[12] The General had the unusual advantage of being a fluent English speaker, since his mother was English. (One must emphasize that the language barrier was a far bigger problem in the First World War than in the Second, when the two principal Western Allies spoke the same language.) In addition, his looks and manner inspired instant confidence:

He was good-looking, smart, plausible and cool. Typically French in appearance, he showed no [visual] sign of his mother's English blood. He was a man of medium height . . . with regular well-drawn features, thoughtful brown eyes, a slightly greying well-brushed moustache, dark hair showing white at the temples, and a *mouche* or tuft of hair, also turned grey, under the lower lip. He gave an impression of vigour, strength and energy.[13]

Robertson and Haig did not share the politicians' – and Hankey's – buoyant confidence in Nivelle or his plan. Yet they deferred to the emphatic collective judgement of the War Cabinet and signed an agreement with the French General. As a warning against any inclination to drag their feet,

11. Haig diary, 15 January 1917.
12. Hankey diary, same date (my italics). With the passage of time Hankey seems to have forgotten about his own enthusiasm for Nivelle after hearing him at the War Cabinet meetings, because Hankey's account of the war mentions only the General's success in persuading Lloyd George and the War Cabinet (*The Supreme Command, 1914–1918* (2 vols., 1961), vol. ii, pp. 613–14).   13. Spears, *Prelude to Victory*, p. 31.

the War Cabinet formally instructed them to honour the agreement 'both in the letter and in the spirit'.[14]

Lloyd George came back from Rome with presents for Frances Stevenson ('an exquisite little marble model of the child taking a thorn out of his foot [and] a beautiful necklace of corals').[15] But he spent the following weekend at Walton Heath with his wife, Margaret. It would not, he explained to Frances, have been fair to send for her, his mistress, during the weekend, because Margaret knew all about their relationship and was 'very tolerant'.[16] In fact, she was deeply resentful, but in certain indestructible ways she and Lloyd George remained close, and he managed somehow to maintain the balance of his quasi-bigamous life.

At the end of January it was reported that the Lloyd Georges had taken possession of 10 Downing Street. The Asquiths having moved out on 16 December, why were the new tenants so slow to occupy the house? Lloyd George was too busy to attend to the matter on his own, and Margaret was at Criccieth over Christmas and the New Year. Besides, it is easy to understand why they were in no hurry to move. They already had a base in Downing Street, since Lloyd George had stayed on at Number 11 when he left the Treasury in May 1915. As the undisputed second man in the government, he did not relinquish the Chancellor's official residence while serving as, in turn, Minister of Munitions and War Secretary. For a month or so before the change of government he had, in fact, been living in a flat provided for him by his friend David Davies, having closed down Number 11 for economy reasons. But he moved back after becoming Prime Minister, and since there was a connecting door was able to use Number 10 for business purposes, in particular Cabinet meetings, before making it his personal home. He was, in any case, largely indifferent to the trappings of office. When the family eventually moved, they 'walked in from next door, by the garden gate'.[17] Bonar Law was then able to establish himself at Number 11, so becoming Lloyd George's closest neighbour as well as his closest colleague.

At the beginning of February Lloyd George visited his homeland for the first time as head of the government, travelling by train to Bangor, and on

14. War Cab., 17 January 1917 (incidentally, Lloyd George's fifty-fourth birthday). Woodward describes this instruction as an 'unusual step' (David R. Woodward, *Lloyd George and the Generals* (1983), p. 143).
15. FSD, 10 January 1917. The marble figure was obviously a copy of the famous Roman statuette in the Campidoglio museum.   16. FSD, 15 January 1917.
17. Olwen Carey Evans, *Lloyd George Was My Father: The Autobiography of Lady Olwen Carey Evans* (1985), p. 87.

by car to Criccieth, on Friday the 2nd. At Criccieth he saw his ailing uncle, Richard Lloyd, who had given him so much encouragement throughout his life. He may have guessed that they would never meet again.

On the Saturday evening he spoke at the Pavilion, Caernarvon, scene of many earlier oratorical triumphs. On the platform he was supported by his wife and daughter Olwen, many Welsh MPs, an array of local mayors, the Anglican bishops of St Asaph, Bangor and St David's, and the Roman Catholic archbishop of Cardiff. He hardly needed to emphasize (though he did) the non-party character of the occasion, and it was most piquantly illustrated at the end when Sir Hugh Ellis Nanney, the Tory squire whom he had defeated in his first Parliamentary election, seconded the vote of thanks to him.

The speech was made against the background of Germany's recent proclamation of unrestricted submarine warfare, and Lloyd George laid heavy stress on the maritime threat:

I want the nation to realise what this most recent move of Germany really portends . . . it is an advance along the road to complete barbarism. [The Germans know they cannot win on land, but] if they destroy our transports at sea our armies will languish for lack of support and sustenance and our people will die of hunger. . . . I have never been a believer in concealing the realities of the situation from my fellow-countrymen. You cannot get the best out of them until they face the facts.

One of the facts was that, apart from the men in the trenches, Britain had so far not suffered on anything like the scale of other belligerents. The civilian population must therefore brace itself for greater sacrifices.

He ended on a high note, with typical imagery:

There are rare epochs in the history of the world when in a few raging years the character, the destiny, of the whole race is determined for unknown ages. This is one. The winter wheat is being sown. It is better, it is surer, it is more bountiful in its harvest than when it is sown in the soft spring time. There are many storms to pass through, there are many frosts to endure, before the land brings forth its green promise. But let us not be weary in well-doing, for in due season we shall reap if we faint not.

Before sitting down he repeated his peroration in Welsh.[18]

18. Report in *The Times*, 5 February 1917. In December 1910, at the height of the controversy over the Lords' rejection of his 1909 Budget, he had spoken in the same place of the violence of nature, though with a different twist – saying that the great storm they were passing through would tear up 'many a rotten tree', and that the best time to collect firewood was after such a storm.

The speech was, of course, widely reported, but shortly beforehand news had broken of an alleged plot to assassinate him. Four people, members of the same family – two living in Derby, two in Southampton – had been charged and remanded in custody. At the time Lloyd George appears to have been unperturbed by the news itself, but concerned that it might distract attention from his speech, remarking to an old friend that people seemed to be 'very much more interested in preparations for my death than in my speech, which was what I wanted them to read'.[19]

After the London conference at which Nivelle had taken the War Cabinet by storm, and Haig had been instructed to co-operate with him to the full in the implementation of his plan, relations between the two commanders did not develop well. Haig was irritated by Nivelle's increasingly high-handed attitude, while Nivelle tended to regard even the genuine practical difficulties raised by Haig as mere obstructionism. At the same time Haig damaged himself at home by giving a tactless interview to French journalists, in which his worst mistake was to suggest that the British army was suffering from a shortage of guns. This could only be taken as a reflection on the Munitions Ministry that Lloyd George had created, and so inevitably aggravated the Prime Minister's ill-will towards him. Haig complained that the journalists had, in general, misrepresented him, but on the subject of guns there can be little doubt that his words were roughly as reported, because even Derby, his slavish mouthpiece, was forced to make a defensive and rather absurd explanation of them to Lloyd George. The statement that the army was short of big guns was, Derby wrote, 'only an expression of opinion that has found vent in many other ways, viz., that nobody can have too many big guns. The ideal of enough big guns can probably never be reached.' He admitted that the interview was an 'indiscretion', though not one for which the country would expect Haig to be driven to resign.[20]

An Anglo-French conference involving political and military leaders was arranged for the end of the month at Calais, and Lloyd George approached it with a determination to subordinate Haig to Nivelle. On 15 February – significantly, the day that reports of Haig's interview appeared in the press – he made a proposal to this effect to Commandant Berthier de Sauvigny, the assistant French military attaché in London, whom he met, apparently by chance, in Hankey's office. De Sauvigny naturally passed the Prime

19. Herbert Lewis diary, entry for 6 February 1917 (National Library of Wales). Lewis was one of Lloyd George's oldest political friends, but he remained in the junior ministerial post at the Board of Education to which he had been appointed in 1915, with the satisfaction, now, of serving under H. A. L. Fisher. Reports of the alleged plot appeared in the newspapers on 1 February 1917.   20. Derby to DLG, 19 February 1917 (Lloyd George Papers).

Minister's thoughts on to Nivelle. Lloyd George's policy had the support of his War Cabinet colleagues, who at the time shared his enthusiasm for Nivelle and his doubts about Haig (though he probably mentioned to none of them his conversation with de Sauvigny). At a meeting of the War Cabinet on the 24th, which Robertson was told he need not attend, the Prime Minister was authorized to seek at Calais 'such measures as might appear best calculated . . . to ensure unity of command both in the preparatory stages of and during the operations'. Later, explaining the War Cabinet's view to the King's private secretary, Stamfordham, Curzon gave the following arguments in favour of Nivelle:

1. The French had practically twice the number of troops in the field that we had.
2. We were fighting on French soil to drive the enemy off French soil.
3. Independent opinion shows that without question French Generals and Staffs are immeasurably superior to British Generals and Staffs, not from the point of view of fighting but from that of generalship . . .
4. The War Cabinet did not consider Haig a clever man. Nivelle made a much greater impression on the members of the War Cabinet – of the two in existing circumstances Nivelle was the right man to have supreme command.[21]

The King, however, like Robertson (and Derby), was kept in the dark about the War Cabinet's policy during the days preceding the Calais conference.

Lloyd George would have been wise to go to Calais accompanied by at least one Conservative colleague, preferably Bonar Law, and to make sure that his tactics there were fully understood and agreed in advance. As it was, he went on his own, politically speaking, and compounded the ill effects of a dubious policy by the inept methods he used to promote it. There was no secret about the purposes of the conference. The idea that it was called only to settle the problems of transport behind the lines is false; it was also the clear intention that general operational matters should be reviewed. But the proposal to put Haig under Nivelle was kept a secret, so far as the British military were concerned, until the conference assembled during the afternoon of the 26th at the Hotel of the Gare Maritime.

There was first a brief discussion of railway matters (which were then referred to a sub-committee), but in the early evening Haig and Nivelle spoke about the forthcoming offensive. The two prime ministers, who had talked privately before the opening session, were hoping that Nivelle would

21. Memorandum of a conversation between Curzon and Stamfordham, 4 March 1917 (Royal Archives).

broach the issue of overall command, arguing the case for its exercise by himself. But to their annoyance he failed to do so, even when prompted with leading questions from Lloyd George. The confidence and mastery that he had shown in London seemed to have deserted him.

When the conference adjourned for dinner, Lloyd George asked the French for a statement in writing of what they – and he – wanted. A typed document was then produced (earlier drafted at Nivelle's headquarters) in which it was proposed that Haig's army should be put under Nivelle's command in all essential respects. Haig was to be left responsible for little more than administration and discipline. Hankey claims to have been dumbfounded when he saw the document ('It fairly took my breath away'), and Robertson's reaction was almost apoplectic. He immediately contacted Haig, and they went together to see Lloyd George, who had dined alone in his room.

A furious row ensued, during which Lloyd George was 'extremely brutal to Haig'. When the Field-Marshal said the 'Tommies' would not stand being under a Frenchman, the Prime Minister replied that he knew the British private soldier and there were people he criticized 'a good deal more strongly' than General Nivelle. Without any lowering of the temperature the combatants separated for the night, but Hankey, who felt that his position was acutely invidious, did not go to bed before drafting a formula which, he hoped, might serve to resolve the dispute.[22]

To a very limited degree his hope was fulfilled, though in reality the outcome was profoundly unsatisfactory all round. Next day – after Lloyd George had slept badly, and Robertson not at all – an agreement of sorts was reached, and it was based on Hankey's formula. This followed the precedents of Gallipoli and Salonica, where the commander of the larger element in an Allied force (British in the first case, French in the second) was accorded the leading role, though the other commander had a right of appeal to his own government if he felt unhappy about any decision affecting his troops. The precedents were scarcely relevant to a theatre as vast as the Western front, or to a situation in which the supposed subordinate was higher in rank and more experienced at the top level of command than his nominal superior. Under the Calais agreement Haig not only had the right of appeal to London; he also retained control of operations in his own sector. Faces were saved, but the prize of an effective joint command eluded Lloyd George, Briand and others who sought it.

Lloyd George's pursuit of this prize (since 1915) was laudable, but his

22. Hankey diary, entry for 26 February 1917.

attempt to grasp it by giving overall command to Nivelle was doubly flawed. Granted the scale of operations, not to mention the political sensitivities involved, it was a practical absurdity for the commander of one of the component national forces also to be the supreme Allied commander. When, the following year, an Allied supremo in the West was eventually appointed, he was, indeed, a Frenchman, but not Commander-in-Chief of the French armies, responsible to the French government; he was formally an Allied officer responsible to an Allied war council. The Nivelle set-up in 1917 was, therefore, institutionally misconceived.

Still more was it a mistake in personal terms. Nivelle was simply not equal to the task assigned to him. His poor performance at Calais should have made all who witnessed it aware that he was out of his depth. It was not the performance of a man with clear vision or the moral authority to impose his will on others. During the weeks that had elapsed since his appearance before the War Cabinet, the difficulties of his position had started to overwhelm him, and his limitations were becoming increasingly apparent to those not blinded by wishful thinking.

Despite the evidence of Calais, Lloyd George remained in the latter category. He had been slow to come round to the idea of Nivelle's offensive, but had been forced to accept it as, he thought, the only way – the Italian option having failed – of avoiding a costly Haig offensive in Flanders. At first reluctant to acquiesce in the plan, he had then been converted, like his War Cabinet colleagues, by the plan's author. Now he was determined to see the project through. It was one of his outstanding qualities that, once committed to a course of action, he threw himself into it with the utmost energy and enthusiasm. This quality could, however, become a defect and a liability, if the course of action was ill-judged and the individual upon whom it depended unworthy of his ardent support. It was so with Nivelle and his plan.

On his return to London Lloyd George admitted to Frances Stevenson that Nivelle had 'floundered about most hopelessly', but made the excuse for him that he was 'in a very awkward position as the new proposals concerned himself '. He expressed no doubt at all about putting Nivelle in overall command, claiming to have forced Haig and Robertson to accept this proposal, and suggesting that at one point it looked very much as though either he (Lloyd George) or Haig would have to resign. He seems to have given her no indication that the proposal had been considerably modified, on lines worked out by Hankey in the small hours, before Haig and Robertson would accept it.[23]

23. FSD, entry for 28 February 1917.

At Calais Lloyd George reached the nadir of his relations with the British high command. He had repeated, in an aggravated form, the mistake he made the previous September, when he discussed with Foch the relative British and French performances in the battle of the Somme, by implication criticizing Haig's generalship. Foch at once reported what had been said to Haig, who then briefed the Conservative press against Lloyd George. The coup attempted at Calais was a far worse blunder. Based on unsound reasoning in any case, it was maladroit in execution, and all the more so for being attempted by Lloyd George on his own. Though he could argue that the War Cabinet had given him a more-or-less free hand, in fact he badly needed the presence and support of a leading Tory colleague at the conference. Without it, he alone was bound to be vulnerable if the outcome proved disastrous. For the time being he was dependent on Nivelle. If Nivelle failed, he would be at a fatal disadvantage in his dealings with Haig. Queen Mary I is well known for the statement that when she died 'Calais' would be written on her heart. In retrospect, Lloyd George could have echoed the sentiment.

4

Crisis at Sea and Revolution in Russia

Crisis at sea – Russian Revolution – Imperial War Cabinet

However unsatisfactory Lloyd George's efforts on the military side during his first months as Prime Minister, it was not there that the war was in imminent danger of being lost. In 1917 the Germans were seeking victory, not on the Western front in France and Flanders, but on the western approaches to Britain. In all of his utterances Lloyd George rightly dwelt upon the supreme importance of the maritime threat, and in tackling it he had a freer hand, and made fewer mistakes, than in his dealings with the military. The men he appointed, and the measures that he and they together took, can fairly be said to have saved the country. But it was a close-run thing.

His key decision was to set up a Ministry of Shipping to control Britain's merchant marine, hitherto controlled (to the extent that it was controlled at all) by the Admiralty and the Board of Trade. To run the new department he chose the Glaswegian shipowner Sir Joseph Maclay, whose name was suggested to him by Bonar Law. The appointment was providential. Maclay was to prove one of the great successes of Lloyd George's government, in a sphere where failure would have been catastrophic. His ministry strikingly exemplified Lloyd George's flair for improvisation and disregard for convention. Though Maclay's personal politics were Liberal, he was allowed to be almost uniquely apolitical while serving as a member of the government. No seat was found for him in the House of Commons, and he accepted a peerage only after he had left office, his vital work done. He insisted on being unpaid for his services.

Another mark of the new department's originality was the physical environment created for it. A makeshift wooden building was constructed on the bed of the lake in St James's Park, which was drained for the purpose, becoming what Lloyd George called a 'desiccated duckpond'. Maclay's Ministry was thus situated within a few minutes' walk of the Admiralty, from which, however, its distance in character could hardly have been greater.

Maclay himself has been well depicted by Arthur Salter, one of his principal aides at the Ministry:

A spare form, above medium height; a head of light red hair; blue eyes with a glint of steel; a straight slit of a mouth; a slightly jutting chin – constituted an unmistakable Scottish figure which would have been a good subject for Raeburn, and at once suggested self-discipline, a strong will, and an inner life. A certain hesitancy in speech and a natural courtesy sometimes veiled, but did not long disguise, a confident judgement of men and things which did not easily yield to either pressure or persuasion.

His 'inner life' was essentially religious. He was a devout and austere Presbyterian, whose only publication (in 1918) was not an account of his remarkable achievements as self-made businessman and major contributor to national survival, but a book of prayers for family worship.[1]

Salter came to the Shipping Ministry soon after its creation. He was one of an exceptionally talented group of young officials who served under Maclay, some of them destined for very high positions later. At their head was John Anderson, already regarded as the most promising civil servant of his generation, who would go on to be (among other things) permanent under-secretary at the Home Office, Governor of Bengal, and Chancellor of the Exchequer in Churchill's wartime coalition, before completing his career as the panjandrum Lord Waverley. He was only thirty-four when he was appointed official head of the new Ministry. Though Scottish to the core like his ministerial chief, he was a product of Edinburgh, whose citizens do not always harmonize perfectly with Glaswegians. Nevertheless, he and Maclay established an excellent working relationship, and the whole official team was notable for its freedom from personal friction and its high collective morale.[2]

Less easily assimilated was Lloyd George's choice as junior minister and spokesman in the House of Commons, Sir Leo Chiozza Money, who started life in Genoa as Leo Chiozza. His father was Anglo-Italian, his mother

1. Salter, entry on Maclay in *DNB* (Supplement 1951–1960). Maclay survived another world war, dying in 1951 at the age of ninety-three. So strict was his sabbatarianism that he would not even read newspapers on Sunday (private information from one of his sons, Lord Muirshiel).
2. Among other future stars recruited for the new ministry were Cyril Hurcomb, Graeme Thomson and Henry Bunbury. Salter returned to the task of Allied shipping control during the Second World War, playing a dominant role as head of the British shipping mission in Washington. By then he was an MP (for Oxford University), and had held ministerial office under Chamberlain, as he did later under Churchill.

46

English, and he assumed the additional name of Money (for eponymous reasons) soon after he came of age. He was educated privately, and began his career as a journalist. Moving into politics, he became a Liberal MP in 1906, and Lloyd George's PPS at the Ministry of Munitions in 1915–16. Lloyd George valued his ability to come up with new ideas, and was amused rather than irritated by his self-advertising tendency. His *Who's Who* entry, prepared by himself, was full of items such as 'member of the Restriction of Enemy's Supplies Committee . . . in which he suggested the Rationing Blockade Policy which was adopted by the Government'. In the Lloyd George coalition he was, at first, junior minister for pensions as well as shipping, and although he held the former post for only a fortnight this was long enough for him to claim that he 'drafted the new Pensions Scheme of 1917'.

Such a character was hardly made to appeal to Maclay, and for some months the Minister (or Controller, as he was more often called) tried hard to get rid of the bumptious colleague who had been foisted on him. In a typical letter to the Prime Minister he wrote:

After our conversation about Sir Leo G. Chiozza Money I had serious talk with him . . . and determined to make an effort to work with him. After further experience I am forced to the conclusion that we cannot go on – as not only with myself but with all those here associated I am convinced there will be constant friction difficulty and worry doing away with all pleasure in work. . . . He is clever – very clever – but impossible. He seems to live in an atmosphere of suspicion and distrust of everyone – satisfied only with himself and his own views.[3]

But Lloyd George had confidence in his appointment, feeling no doubt that Maclay and Chiozza Money had complementary qualities. His judgement was vindicated, and by slow degrees the two men came to appreciate each other.

When the Ministry came into being less than half of the country's merchant shipping was under public control. Requisitioning of ships for war purposes was carried out by the transport department of the Admiralty (in which Salter served), but most of the available tonnage was still unrequisitioned. An immediate decision was taken to transfer that department to the new Ministry, and soon nearly 90 per cent of Britain's mercantile marine was subject to public control, while remaining privately owned. Lloyd George had given a pledge to the House of Commons that shipping would

3. Maclay to DLG, 24 January 1917.

be 'nationalised in the real sense of the term', but the term was open to more than one definition, and he made it clear that he did not have the socialist definition in mind when he said that the nation's shipping would be put on the same footing as its railways (still in private hands) for the duration of the war.[4] As a shipowner Maclay was naturally opposed to public ownership, and argued convincingly against it. He also persuaded the War Cabinet that the taxation of owners' profits should not be so severe as to reduce their efficiency. While accepting the case for taxing excess profits, he maintained that it was 'a mistake not to leave an incentive to men to exert themselves to the utmost'.[5] But above all he was determined to make the fullest and most economical use of the ships he controlled, and to use his influence with colleagues in other ministries to find answers to the U-boat threat.

In the short run the most telling measures taken were the concentration of shipping on the North Atlantic route and the drastic restriction of imports. The first was a direct consequence of the Shipping Ministry's assumption of control over the greater part of Britain's merchant fleet. Hitherto, many ships had been bringing freights from the ends of the earth, involving a waste of time and precious cargo space that was quite unacceptable as the U-boats took an ever-increasing toll. The Ministry quickly decided that nearly all of the country's essential imports could be brought from the North American continent, and the resulting economy in the use of ships, combined with stricter criteria for essential imports, helped to avert total disaster in the early part of 1917.[6]

For a time Maclay was also made responsible for merchant shipbuilding, in which he took strong initiatives, approving designs for four standard types of ship and placing orders for well over a million tons. But he was handicapped at home by shortages of labour and steel, and when America entered the war in April ships under construction for him in American yards were appropriated by the United States government. Consequently the bare statistics of his shipbuilding effort do him less than justice; but he made a valuable start.[7]

In May 1917 Lloyd George put one of his favourite technocrats, Sir Eric Geddes, in charge of all shipbuilding, naval and mercantile. This

4. House of Commons, 19 December 1916 (see p. 19 above).
5. Maclay to DLG, 2 February 1917.
6. David French, *The Strategy of the Lloyd George Coalition, 1916–1918* (1995), p. 77, and *WM*, pp. 1234–5. Chiozza Money deserves substantial, though not exclusive, credit for the scheme to concentrate shipping in the North Atlantic.
7. Britain launched 495,000 tons of new shipping during the first half of 1917, but 820,000 tons were sunk during the first quarter alone.

arrangement was bound to produce occasional friction, because Geddes worked from the Admiralty (where he was soon to succeed Carson as First Lord). But on the whole the two men made the new system work, and Maclay continued to play an influential part on the side of shipbuilding that concerned him. His achievement during the five months when it was his direct responsibility is acknowledged in Lloyd George's memoirs: '[He] greatly speeded up the completion of vessels already under construction, and devised a programme that would eventually yield upwards of 3,000,000 tons of merchant shipping a year.'[8]

Maclay drew on the services of other shipping magnates, such as Sir Thomas Royden and Sir Percy Bates (both of Cunard). Like Maclay himself they worked unpaid for his ministry, just as many leading industrialists had responded to Lloyd George's call to work for the Ministry of Munitions. Each of these improvised organizations, taking over functions formerly controlled by a service department, had the supreme advantage of being infused with a civilian ethos, encouraging discussion and the propagation of new ideas. In the Admiralty junior officers tended to accept what the top brass said, whatever their private reservations.[9] Through contact with the Shipping Ministry such officers had a chance to make their views known, and this process had a crucial bearing on the all-important issue of convoys.

As Lloyd George later pointed out, there was nothing new in the idea of merchantmen being escorted by ships of the Royal Navy; after Trafalgar, 'the main function of our ships-of-war was to convoy our merchant vessels through seas infested with French privateers'.[10] Faced, however, with the unprecedented factor of submarine warfare, most senior naval officers took the view that convoy was no answer to the menace. When Lloyd George and Bonar Law raised the subject at a War Committee meeting in November 1916, before the change of government, they were told by the admirals in attendance – one of whom was Sir John Jellicoe – that ships in convoy presented too large a target for U-boats, and that in any case the masters of

8. *WM*, p. 1223. Geddes was a fellow Scot but, like Anderson, from Edinburgh.
9. 'I recall the deep impression made on me by a conference at which I was once present at the Admiralty. The presiding Admiral expressed opinions on methods of naval protection which were in complete opposition to those I knew to be held strongly, and indeed passionately, by the junior naval officers to whom he was speaking. . . . To my shocked surprise all they said was, "Yes, sir". I reflected on what this meant. There is great disadvantage in applying the kind of discipline appropriate to the field of battle to the council chamber.' (Arthur Salter, *Memoirs of a Public Servant* (1961), p. 89). Salter is referring to his time in the transport department of the Admiralty before it was taken over by the Ministry of Shipping, where those working in it came to enjoy 'the greater freedom of civilian traditions'. 10. *WM*, p. 1138.

merchant ships lacked the skill to maintain an orderly formation (in the technical lingo, to 'keep station').[11]

When Maclay became Shipping Controller he gave short shrift to the second argument, which he knew from personal experience to be false; and he was always strongly in favour of convoys. But Admiralty resistance to the change remained obdurate, and Lloyd George's efforts to promote it were less consistently pressing than he (and others on his behalf[12]) later claimed. Until the indiscriminate U-boat campaign began in early February, he seems to have hoped that the steps he had already taken would be enough to counter the maritime threat. He had established the Shipping Ministry; he had met most of Maclay's initial demands; and he had put men who might be expected to co-operate with Maclay in charge of other civilian departments most relevant to national survival – the Board of Trade, Munitions, Agriculture and Food.[13]

There was also a new regime at the relevant service department, the Admiralty. But the First Lord, Carson, proved a weak administrator, and became as much a mouthpiece for the top sailors as Derby at the war office was for the top military. There was also a new First Sea Lord, who had been appointed just before Lloyd George took over, and he was Jellicoe – the very Jellicoe whose sceptical attitude to convoys was already apparent. He brought with him as anti-submarine chief an officer who shared his scepticism, Admiral Alexander Duff. In January it was still the collective opinion of the Board of Admiralty that convoys would make merchant ships more, rather than less, vulnerable to U-boats, quite apart from other objections.[14]

Fortunately, a junior officer engaged in anti-submarine work, Commander R. G. H. Henderson, took a quite different view, and even more fortunately he was brought into close contact with officials at the Ministry of Shipping, particularly Salter and Norman Leslie, a shipbroker seconded

11. *WM*, pp. 1139–40.

12. Notably Winston Churchill in *The World Crisis* and Lord Beaverbrook in *Men and Power, 1917–1918*.

13. Sir Albert Stanley, a transport expert of proven ability, was President of the Board of Trade in the new government. He worked well with Maclay. Christopher Addison was Minister of Munitions, having previously served as junior minister under Lloyd George and Edwin Montagu. He was equally helpful. R. E. Prothero at Agriculture and Lord Rhondda at Food (from mid-1917) were also co-operative colleagues.

14. 'The system of several ships sailing together in a convoy is not recommended in any area where submarine attack is a possibility. It is evident that the larger the number of ships forming the convoy, the greater is the chance of a submarine being enabled to attack successfully . . .' (Admiralty pamphlet, January 1917).

to the Ministry. Together they were able to develop an overwhelming case for convoys. One argument used, in good faith, by the opponents of convoy was that, even if it could be justified on other grounds, the number of merchant ships needing to be escorted was far too large for the resources of the Royal Navy. Henderson and his civilian colleagues were able to demonstrate that this argument was based upon a gross fallacy. The figure quoted of 2,500 ships completing voyages every week was shown to consist mainly of coastwise vessels, whereas the number of ocean-going ships arriving weekly was between 120 and 140, which was certainly quite manageable for purposes of escort.

Within days of the German escalation of U-boat warfare at the beginning of February, Hankey wrote a memorandum for Lloyd George arguing the case for 'scientifically organised convoys'. There had been no reference to the subject in the memorandum on war policy that he prepared the weekend after Lloyd George took office, and it is virtually certain that his conversion was brought about by Henderson and the Shipping Ministry officials with whom he (Henderson) was in close touch.[15] Lloyd George, already sympathetic to the idea, was in turn convinced by Hankey, and immediately summoned Carson, Jellicoe and Duff to discuss it with him at breakfast on 13 February. At this meeting the Admiralty group maintained its opposition in principle, but at least agreed to conduct experiments. Hankey, who attended the breakfast, felt that the 'discussion did good'.[16]

Yet two and a half months were still to pass before the Admiralty chiefs were induced to change their minds, and then only tentatively. Why so long a delay? The statistics of sinkings gave a clear enough message. With the onset of unrestricted U-boat action the monthly rate of British tonnage lost

15. Though there is no contemporary evidence that Hankey's proposal was inspired by Henderson and his colleagues, Stephen Roskill gives strong reasons for believing that it must have been. The most telling piece of evidence *ex post facto* is a letter from Churchill to Hankey in 1937, recalling 'how you [Hankey] played an essential part in saving the country over the convoy system, and *how when young officers came to you and told you the truth against service rules, you saw that the seed did not fall on stony ground*'. Roskill suggests that Hankey could not record Henderson's approach at the time, because to have put anything on paper might have imperilled the young officer's professional future (Stephen Roskill, *Hankey: Man of Secrets* (3 vols., 1970–74), vol. i, pp. 357–8).

Henderson died a full admiral – but prematurely – on the eve of the Second World War, in which he might well have achieved the fame that his talents and character merited. In the 1930s he had given further proof of his far-sightedness in the work he did to promote the Fleet Air Arm and the construction of aircraft carriers (*DNB* article by Sir Vincent Baddeley). Lloyd George acknowledges Henderson's vital role over convoys (*WM*, pp. 1155–7).

16. Hankey diary, 13 February 1917.

more than doubled, from just over 150,000 tons in January to well over 300,000 tons in February, while Allied and neutral losses increased in proportion. Week by week the rate of destruction became more alarming. In the first nine days of April the figure far exceeded the total for January. In April about 850,000 tons of British, Allied and neutral shipping went down (525,000 tons of British alone). How could Lloyd George have been so slow to enforce a measure of whose necessity he seemed to be convinced in mid-February?

In his memoirs he makes much of the time needed for the experiments to be conducted, and of the fact that one of them (between Britain and Norway) was not a success – because, he says, it was badly organized by the Admiralty. He also blames Jellicoe for obtaining statements from some merchant captains to the effect that they would, indeed, have difficulty keeping station in convoy. According to Lloyd George, the captains were quite unrepresentative, and their views were solicited behind Maclay's back. These arguments, or excuses, are not without substance. But they are not the whole story.

The truth is that Lloyd George was less urgent and single-minded about convoy, even after Hankey's conversion, than he may have come to believe by the time he wrote his memoirs, or than posterity has been taught to accept.[17] He was also understandably reluctant to have a direct showdown with the Admiralty. Carson was still a redoubtable politician, whatever his limitations as a minister. Together with Law and Lloyd George himself he had been a member of the triumvirate that engineered the change of government, and his appeal to the Tory rank-and-file could not be ignored. He stood unquestioningly behind the admirals, and might resign if Lloyd George attempted to overrule them. Moreover a prime minister whose relations with the top soldiers were already so bad had good reason to hesitate before taking on the top sailors as well. Lack of absolute certainty on the issue, and a sense of political vulnerability, are enough to explain Lloyd George's cautious approach.

During April circumstances moved in favour of convoy. The figures of shipping losses, growing at such a monstrous rate, served to concentrate minds. The United States entered the war, and American naval resources became available for escort duty; while the US Admiral William S. Sims made his pro-convoy views known. In the higher ranks of the Royal Navy,

17. Frances Stevenson's diary contains no record of any outburst by him on the subject, or for that matter any reference to it. On the other hand Hankey's diary contains clear evidence that the Prime Minister's sense of urgency about it was, to say the least, intermittent.

too, Lloyd George found a powerful advocate of convoy in Admiral Sir David Beatty, who had succeeded Jellicoe in command of the Grand Fleet. On 15 April the Prime Minister visited him at Invergordon, and Beatty afterwards wrote to his wife: 'There is no doubt he is a wonderful man with a mass of energy ... Our conversation was interesting and varied and, I hope, will have far-reaching results.'[18] On 25 April the War Cabinet authorized Lloyd George to take a hard look at the anti-submarine campaign, in order to make sure that it was being properly co-ordinated. He then announced that he would pay a personal visit to the Admiralty on the 30th. By the time he arrived, the Admiralty had decided to run an experimental convoy from Gibraltar, and Admiral Duff had submitted a minute to Jellicoe recommending the general adoption of convoy.

We shall probably never know quite how far this was an instance of cause and effect, but we may be sure that the imminence of Lloyd George's visit at the very least accelerated a process that was already in motion. Besides, the process itself owed much to him indirectly, since without the Ministry of Shipping – his creation – fresh thinking about convoy would not have been encouraged, and Admiralty resistance to it might not have been overcome in time. The idea that he went to the Admiralty, sat in the First Lord's chair, and imposed the convoy system upon a still implacably hostile board is in the strict sense mythical; and it is also a myth that his visit was the culmination of a sustained and unrelenting struggle on his part. But myth is often an exaggeration or oversimplification of the truth, and it was something of both in this case.

The Gibraltar experiment was successful, but even so it was not until mid-August that the convoy system was accepted and in general use. By then the rate of sinking by U-boats was already in decline compared with the April peak, though the figure for July had shown a blip in the downward trend. In October the loss of British merchant ships fell to about 270,000 tons, and in December it was only a little over 170,000 tons. Convoy was by no means the only factor in the defeat of the U-boats; it was one of many, though rightly regarded as the most important. In sum, the credit for a victory analogous to that of the Battle of Britain a generation later has to

18. *The Beatty Papers*, ed. B. McL. Ranft (2 vols., 1989), vol. i, p. 415. Professor Ranft stresses the importance of Beatty's backing for the convoy system, while suggesting that it may have been rather more recent than he liked to make out. '[He] *claimed to have been* an early advocate of convoy. The fact that he made his views known in influential places, and a particularly timely meeting with the Prime Minister, must have added substantially to the arguments which led to the Admiralty's change of heart in April 1917' (vol. i, p. 379; my italics).

be widely shared, but on the whole Lloyd George seems to deserve the largest share.

While the war at sea was reaching its climax in the West, in the East an event was occurring whose significance for the land war – and for world politics during the rest of the century – was incalculable. On 16 March British newspapers reported revolution in Russia; three days later it was confirmed that Tsar Nicholas II had abdicated and that the rule of the Romanovs was at an end.[19]

The causes of Russia's revolution were profound and various, but only a brief summary of them is appropriate in a life of Lloyd George. One major factor was the process of industrialization, which the war accelerated. Between 1914 and 1916 the industrial proletariat rose by at least a million, and in January 1917 state factories alone were employing 400,000 workers, one-third of them in the then capital, Petrograd. Though the vast majority of Russia's 175 million inhabitants were still peasants living on the land (emancipated since 1861), the shift in population from country to town, combined with the army's demands, had drastically and adversely affected the rural economy. One leading scholar even suggests that 'the countryside lost more men of working age to industry than to the army'.[20]

Another cause of unrest was inflation far worse than that experienced by any other belligerent. By January 1917 prices had increased fourfold since the beginning of the war. Government attempts to control prices led to widespread black marketeering and frequent shortage of necessities in the shops. Even food, which should have been plentiful, often ran short in the cities, partly on account of defects in Russian farming, aggravated by war conditions, but mainly because of the gross inefficiency of the country's transport system.[21] Shortage of bread in Petrograd helped to precipitate the revolution.

There was deep disaffection among Russia's fighting men and their families. Millions had died from enemy action or disease, with nothing to show for the sacrifice but a lamentable record of military failure, or at best advances followed by retreats. Despite many heroic episodes, the Russian

19. Since Russians were using the Old Style (Julian) calendar, which was thirteen days behind the New Style (Gregorian) calendar used in the West, the revolution began in Russia at the end of February and is known there as the February revolution, to distinguish it from the October revolution which brought the Bolsheviks to power later in the year. The Tsar abdicated on 2 March (15 March in the West). In early 1918 the Bolshevik government changed to the New Style calendar.   20. Norman Stone, *The Eastern Front, 1914–1917* (1975), p. 285.
21. By contrast, its munitions industry responded to the demands of war 'with remarkable success' (John Keegan, *The First World War* (1998), p. 153).

army suffered on the whole from low morale. For every hundred Russians who fell in battle during the First World War, three hundred surrendered (compared with only twenty-six Germans, twenty-four French and twenty British).[22] Desire to get out of the army, and reluctance to be drafted into it, contributed strongly to the revolutionary mood.

Above all, the regime was vulnerable because it had failed to evolve politically. While in many ways Russia had been undergoing dynamic change, at the summit the autocracy of the Tsar remained intact. Nicholas II embodied the authority of the state, and was also supreme commander of the army (since September 1915, when he replaced his uncle, the relatively competent Grand Duke Nicholas). Such a concentration of power was anyway undesirable and out-of-date, but what made it catastrophic was that the Tsar was not an intelligent man and a hopelessly weak ruler. He had a mystical belief in his right and duty to rule, but none of the qualities needed to give effect to it. Far from being able to dominate a situation which would have tested the most formidable of his ancestors, he was himself largely dominated by his wife, Alexandra Fedorovna (a German princess by origin, though in her way loyal to Russia), and she in turn was for several years dominated by the 'mad monk' Grigori Rasputin, who thus became – until his murder at the end of 1916 – the most powerful man in the country. Rasputin owed his ascendancy over the Imperial couple to his supposed ability to cure the haemophilia of their only son, the Tsarevich Alexis. This poor child's illness both symbolized and compounded the weakness of the dynasty during its last, doomed phase.

If the Tsar had been prepared to take even a modest step towards constitutionalism, it is just possible that disaster might have been averted; but he would not budge. When Milner lunched with him and the Tsarina in early February it was made clear that discussion of internal politics would not be tolerated. Milner was leading the British part of a fifty-strong mission from the Western Allies, which stayed in the country for over a month.[23] Its purpose was to co-ordinate strategy and supply, but in the circumstances it was wasting its time. On his return Milner reported to the War Cabinet that there was

22. Richard Pipes, *The Russian Revolution 1899–1919* (1990), p. 419.
23. Other leading members of the British party were General Sir Henry Wilson, Lord Revelstoke (finance expert) and Walter Layton (economist and munitions expert). David Davies MP also joined the mission at the last moment. Landowner and philanthropist, and a former PPS to Lloyd George, he was at the time serving in the political secretariat in the so-called 'Garden Suburb' (see p. 231 below). The French delegation was led by an ex-premier and future president, Gaston Doumergue, and its chief military member was General de Castelnau. The Italians also sent a delegation.

plenty of discontent in Russia, but that administrative chaos was a more imminent threat than revolution. A fortnight later revolution occurred.

In his memoirs Lloyd George makes fun of Milner's failure to perceive what was happening, but it is notoriously difficult to predict the exact moment when a potential revolution will become actual.[24] The February revolution took nearly everyone by surprise. Like many others Lloyd George was aware of the revolutionary potential, having remarked in January: 'The position is similar to that in France before the French Revolution. You have a kindly, patriotic well-meaning monarch, dominated by a masterful wife with ... narrow reactionary ideals.'[25] But even he, with political antennae incomparably more sensitive than Milner's, might not have been able to make an accurate assessment had he visited the country in February. Most Russians, even those with a vested interest in revolution (such as Lenin), were taken by surprise. So were the Germans. Admiral Tirpitz later confessed: 'Had we been able to foresee ... the Russian Revolution, we should perhaps not have needed to regard the submarine of 1917 as the last resource.'[26]

In early February (Russian dating) there was a shortage of bread in Petrograd, aggravated by weather so severe that it brought transport to a standstill, preventing the delivery of flour and fuel to the bakeries. A spell of milder weather began on 23 February, which favoured open-air demonstrations. Workers started to go on strike and parade in the streets. Within two days the strike was general and – more ominously – troops of the city's large garrison were showing reluctance to act against the crowds. By 27 February the garrison as a whole was in a state of mutiny. From then onwards the city swiftly passed into the hands of the people. Prisons were opened and police stations set on fire. The arsenal was seized and weapons from it distributed. Looting and violence followed; about 1,500 were killed and 6,000 wounded in Petrograd during the 'February days'.

When the Tsar realized how grave the situation was, he tried to return from his headquarters to the summer palace at Tsarskoe Selo, but his train was

---

24. Milner (Lloyd George writes) 'was by training and temperament a bureaucrat. He knew nothing of the populace that trod the streets outside the bureau. He did not despise them. He just left them out of his calculations' (*WM*, p. 1587). Davies, who submitted his own report on the mission, was more prescient, in Lloyd George's view, though his forecast was neither definite nor strictly accurate: 'What *may* happen is a *palace* revolution, ending in the removal of the Emperor and Empress' (my italics). There is evidence, however, that most members of the mission thought, unlike Milner, that revolution would occur before the end of the war (George Clerk's report, quoted in *WM*, pp. 1589–91; Davies's report was delivered only a few days before the Tsar abdicated).   25. *RWD*, 14 January 1917.
26. Alfred von Tirpitz, *My Memoirs* (2 vols., 1970), vol. ii, p. 442.

halted at Pskov, about a hundred miles south of the capital. There he heard that popular feeling in Petrograd was overwhelmingly against the monarchy. He also heard that the acting Commander-in-Chief, General Alexeyev, regarded any attempt at counter-revolution as futile. Finally he heard from the court physician that his son's illness was incurable. He therefore decided to abdicate in favour of his brother, the Archduke Michael, and on 2 March, in a mood of quiet and almost relieved fatalism, he signed his throne away. (The form that his abdication took was legally invalid, since he had no right to alter the law of succession. But at such a time legal niceties were of no importance, and in any case the Grand Duke almost immediately waived the dubious right conferred on him, so ending the 300-year rule of the Romanov dynasty.)

There was now a formal power vacuum, to match the anarchy which was beginning to spread from the capital to all parts of the empire. In the Tauride Palace in Petrograd the Duma remained in session, despite the Tsar's recent attempt to prorogue it. This body was based on an extremely restricted franchise, but could nevertheless claim to be the nearest approach to a parliament representing the Russian people. With the collapse of the autocracy its chance seemed to have come. Unfortunately, events in the capital had brought into being another body, occupying another part of the same building, and purporting to represent the workers and soldiers whose joint action was making the revolution. The Petrograd Soviet was, in fact, by no means perfectly representative of those it was supposed to represent; most of its moving spirits were not proletarians, uniformed or civilian, but bourgeois intellectuals. All the same, the Soviet was the assembly created by the revolution, and it became the model for similar revolutionary assemblies throughout the country. Two parliamentary institutions therefore coexisted in the capital; indeed, within the same building. Which was to inherit the authority of the tsardom?

Before long it was apparent that the answer would be neither. But in the short term a clumsy form of diarchy was established. The Soviet had the power, but did not wish its members to govern. So the Duma was invited to form a provisional government, pending the introduction of a new political system to be devised by a constituent assembly. The Soviet thus acquired 'power without responsibility', while the provisional government had 'responsibility without power'.[27] Such an arrangement could hardly be expected to last.

27. Orlando Figes, *A People's Tragedy: The Russian Revolution 1891–1924* (1996), p. 334. Trotsky, a major participant in the events he later described, is interesting about the Soviet's shyness of power: 'the democracy did not trust its own support, feared [the] masses, did not believe in their . . . confidence in itself, and worst of all dreaded what they called "anarchy" . . . In other words, the democracy felt that it was not called to be the leader of the people at the

The first head of the provisional government was Prince Georgi Lvov. He was a widely respected figure, with a good record of local administration and paternalistic reform. Though he belonged to the Constitutional Democratic (Cadet) Party, he was not really much of a party man and so was acceptable to other groups. The founder and leader of the Cadets, Pavel Milyukov – scholarly and impressive, but more controversial – became Foreign Minister. One member of the Soviet took office in the government, despite the former's self-denying ordinance. This was the nominally socialist Alexander Kerensky, whose fervid eloquence enabled him to win the Soviet's subsequent assent to the step he had taken.

When news of the revolution reached London in mid-March (in the western calendar) Lloyd George at first reacted to it as Fox did to the French Revolution, writing to his brother: 'Russia is triumphant. Worth the whole war and its terrible sacrifices.'[28] Soon afterwards he was reported as saying 'he was confident that the Russian people would find that liberty [was] compatible with order, even in revolutionary times'.[29]

On 23 March prominence was given to a message from him to Prince Lvov, which read:

It is with sentiments of the most profound satisfaction that the people of Great Britain and the British Dominions across the seas have learned that their great ally Russia now stands with the nations which base their institutions upon responsible government. Much as we appreciate the loyal and steadfast cooperation which we have received from the late [sic] Emperor and the armies of Russia during the past two and a half years, yet I believe that the revolution whereby the Russian people have based their destinies on the foundation of freedom is the greatest service which they have yet made to the cause for which the Allied peoples have been fighting since August 1914.

It reveals the fundamental truth that this war is at bottom a struggle for popular government as well as for liberty. It shows that, through the war, the principle of liberty, which is the only sure safeguard of peace in the world, has already won one resounding victory. It is the sure promise that the Prussian military autocracy which

moment of its revolutionary uprising, but the left wing of a bourgeois order, its feeler stretched out towards the masses. It called itself ... "socialistic", in order to disguise not only from the masses, but from itself too, its actual role' (Leon Trotsky, *The History of the Russian Revolution*, trans. Max Eastman (1977), p. 189).

28. DLG to William George, 16 March 1917 (National Library of Wales). The same day Herbert Lewis wrote in his diary: 'Great news from Russia. A revolution – successful so far.'
29. *The Times*, 20 March 1917.

began the war, and which is still the only barrier to peace, will itself, before long, be overthrown.

Freedom is the condition of peace, and I do not doubt that as a result of the establishment of a stable constitutional government within their borders the Russian people will be strengthened in their resolve to prosecute this war until the last stronghold of tyranny on the Continent of Europe is destroyed and the free peoples of all lands can unite to secure for themselves and their children the blessings of fraternity and peace.[30]

In reality, the new regime in Russia was anything but 'stable'. The Duma–Soviet diarchy was inherently weak and unworkable. One instance alone is enough to show how hopeless the arrangement was. At the very first meeting of the provisional government a delegation from the Soviet demanded approval of an order which, in effect, released troops from the authority of their officers. Neither the government nor the Duma ever approved the order, but word of it spread to the army and in many units discipline was undermined. Despite the provisional government's intention to continue the war, the revolution immediately reduced Russia's value as a combatant, and the course of events during the rest of the year would result in the country's elimination from the war.

Yet it was only natural for the Western Allies to react hopefully to the news from Petrograd. Russian absolutism had been an embarrassment to them, and the prospect of a fully democratic alliance had to be welcomed in public, whatever misgivings might be felt by some in private. Lloyd George, even at the outset, was not wholly euphoric. Several days before sending his high-flown message to Lvov, he expressed doubts and fears to Riddell: 'L.G. says he fears that Russia is not sufficiently advanced for a republic. The position is an anxious one; the elements involved are so various and antagonistic.'[31]

Anxiety was justified. There was no proper government in Russia, and the power vacuum remained. But someone all too capable of filling it was waiting in the wings. Vladimir Ilyich Ulyanov, known to history as Lenin,

---

30. *The Times*, 23 March 1917. It had been announced that Lloyd George would make a statement in Parliament, asking for a fraternal message to be sent to the Duma. But instead he sent his telegram to Lvov, while the Commons statement was made – typically – by Law.

The tone of Lloyd George's message, and in particular his use of the word 'revolution' in a favourable sense, evoked a mild protest from the King, who felt that the word 'had a disagreeable sound coming from a monarchical government'. But Lloyd George replied that the British monarchy was founded upon a revolution (Kenneth Rose, *King George V* (1983), p. 210).

31. *RWD*, 17 March 1917.

had been living in Switzerland since 1906. Most of his adult life had been spent as an exile, in Siberia or abroad. He knew little of Russia, but he knew what he wanted. He was single-minded in pursuing power for himself as the agent of Marxist revolution. He had no time for liberalism or democracy. He was determined to end Russia's participation in the war, at any price. On 3 April 1917 he returned to the city which, for most of the rest of the century, would bear his name. His return had been facilitated by the Germans, and with good reason. Injecting him into the turmoil of Petrograd was, from their point of view, a strategic master-stroke. Before the end of the year he was in power, and Russia was at their mercy. An abject peace with Germany, followed by civil war in Russia, were needed to secure his power, but in the end he succeeded in imposing a tyranny more efficient and comprehensive than that of the Tsars.

Meanwhile the outgoing Tsar and his family were kept, until August, under house arrest at Tsarskoe Selo. On 19 March Milyukov sent a request through the British Ambassador that the family be given asylum in England. Lloyd George and Law considered the request within a few days and felt that it could not be turned down, provided the Russian government would ensure that the Romanovs came with funds adequate to maintain themselves in reasonable dignity. But Stamfordham on behalf of the King made difficulties from the first, and was soon putting the government under relentless pressure to deny asylum to the Imperial family. The King was afraid that his own dynasty might be threatened by association with the Tsar, and still more with the Tsarina, to whom Labour opinion in Britain was strongly opposed. Both were cousins of the King and the personal tie between him and Nicholas had been close; but for that very reason he shrank from helping them in the existing climate.

There were problems, too, on the Russian side. Milyukov's sympathy for the Romanovs, and desire to put them out of harm's way, were not shared by most of his colleagues, to say nothing of militants in the Soviet who wanted the Tsar to be imprisoned and tried. When Milyukov received the British government's qualified assent to his proposal, he did not immediately respond, perhaps because he doubted his ability to act on it. There was the further complication that the Tsar's daughters were unfit to travel because they had measles. The brief period of opportunity was therefore lost. In April the British government shifted its ground in deference to the King's wishes, and in May Milyukov resigned. Little hope then remained of getting the Imperial family out of the country. In August they were moved to Tobolsk, beyond the Urals, and in the spring of 1918 – after the Bolshevik revolution – they were brought to Ekaterinburg where, in July, they were murdered.

Lloyd George had not been enthusiastic about having them in England. He would have preferred them to go to some neutral country, such as Denmark or Switzerland. But rather than abandon them to an uncertain fate he would have been willing to admit them. The same was not true of George V, whose attitude in the matter was uncharacteristically craven and cold-blooded. In his memoirs Lloyd George blames the Russians for their 'divided counsels', but makes no reference to George V's part in the affair – thus going some way towards atoning for his often cavalier treatment of the King while he was Prime Minister.[32]

Lloyd George's message to Lvov was sent on behalf of 'the British Dominions across the seas' as well as Great Britain, and this was no idle flourish. Four days earlier an Imperial War Cabinet had begun its first series of meetings in London.

The creation of such a body was foreshadowed in Lloyd George's first speech to Parliament as Prime Minister, and it gave effect to a concept of empire that he had held from the beginning of his career. Though his opposition to the Boer War had misled many into regarding him as a Little Englander, in fact he had always been, and was to remain, a liberal imperialist. His journey across Canada in 1899 had greatly impressed him, and he proclaimed his imperial vision in a speech delivered before the end of the Boer War. A great empire, he said, must be 'fearlessly just', and must be free from 'racial arrogance'. It could be held together only on the basis of national freedom. 'We ought to give freedom everywhere – freedom in Canada, freedom in the Antipodes, in Africa, in Ireland, in Wales, and in India. We will never govern India as it ought to be governed until we have given it freedom.'[33] There was a paradox in Lloyd George's vision, and in the long run the paradox could not be resolved. But he meant what he said,

32. *WM*, p. 1645. The King's adamant opposition to refuge in Britain for the Russian Imperial family can be inferred from a careful reading of Harold Nicolson's official life (*King George the Fifth: His Life and Reign* (1952)). But the story is told in greater detail, and without a trace of courtly reticence or evasion, in Kenneth Rose's unofficial life (*King George V*, pp. 210–18). Rose comments that 'the British Government would willingly have offered [the Tsar and his family] asylum but for the fears expressed by Buckingham Palace; and . . . at that most critical moment in their fortunes they were deserted not by a radical Prime Minister seeking to appease his supporters, but by their ever affectionate Cousin Georgie'.

33. Speech at Birkenhead, 21 November 1901. He was a liberal imperialist, but not (one should stress) a Liberal Imperialist. The capital letters denote a more restricted meaning not at all applicable to Lloyd George, since the term thus used relates to those Liberals – such as Rosebery, Asquith and Grey – who supported the Unionist government's Boer War policy.

and the liberal imperial experiment that he promoted was, while it lasted, of vital importance to the world.

By the time he became Prime Minister the validity of his concept of empire already seemed to be proving itself. The white Dominions, including the recently formed Union of South Africa – run by the supposedly defeated Boers – were freely engaged in the war at Britain's side, and were making a contribution out of all proportion to their numbers. By the end of the war they had raised, from a total white population of 15.5 million, a total of 1.3 million troops, of whom nearly a million served overseas with exceptional credit. In addition, the Indian Empire's volunteer army was expanded from 160,000 to a million, more than half of whom served overseas, also most creditably. The Indian war effort was strongly supported by representative Indians, not least by M. K. Gandhi, who was confident that his country's loyalty to the common cause would be rewarded by Dominion status at the end of the war.

As early as 1897 the Canadian leader, Sir Wilfrid Laurier, had offered a challenge to the mother-country: 'if you want our aid, call us to your councils.'[34] To a limited degree the challenge was taken up during the years before the war. Imperial conferences were held in London in 1902, 1907 and 1911. But these were occasions for talk rather than action. After the outbreak of war there was no gathering of Dominion prime ministers until Lloyd George became Prime Minister, though one of them, the Australian W. M. (Billy) Hughes, was invited by Asquith to attend meetings of the Cabinet and War Committee while on a visit to Britain in the spring of 1916. (During this visit his admiration of his fellow North Welshman, then Minister of Munitions, was confirmed, though later relations between them were not destined to be always smooth.)

Lloyd George's idea of imperial consultation was far more ambitious than anything that had gone before. Invitations were sent to the Prime Ministers of Canada, Australia, New Zealand, South Africa and Newfoundland (then separate from Canada). Moreover, it was decided that India, though not a self-governing Dominion, should – in view of its outstanding contribution to the war – for the first time be represented at an imperial conference. The Indian delegation was to consist of the Secretary of State for India (Austen Chamberlain) and three assessors, one British and two Indian. The latter were not representative in the sense of being elected, but could certainly not be dismissed as men of straw. The Maharaja of Bikaner was a majestic figure representing the princely states, and Sir S. P. Sinha was an eminent Bengali lawyer who had been the first Indian to serve as a member of the

34. Britain was not strictly Laurier's mother-country, since he was a French-Canadian.

Viceroy's council, and who until very recently had been president of the Indian National Congress.

At the end of January Lloyd George gave an interview to the influential Australian journalist Keith Murdoch, in which he discussed the forthcoming council and its significance. 'The great reformer', Murdoch reported, 'allowed his imagination to kindle.' Lloyd George explained to Murdoch the sort of imperialist he was and was not. 'The people of the Dominions know that I am not a Jingo ... Yet I regard this council as marking a new epoch in the history of the empire.' He asserted India's claim to be represented, and emphasized the unifying effect of the common struggle. 'Of this I am certain, the peoples of the empire will have found a unity in the war such as never existed before it – a unity not only in history, but of purpose. What practical change in imperial organisation that will mean I will not venture to predict.' Asked if he was sanguine about the empire's future, he replied: 'If we see the war through I certainly am.'[35]

The practicalities developed strikingly before the first series of meetings in March–May 1917. Two different forms of meeting were to occur on alternate days. There was to be a conference, at which matters of long-term interest, though not of pressing urgency, were to be discussed. And there was also to be an Imperial War Cabinet, in which the Dominion leaders would sit as equals with members of the British War Cabinet, dealing with the problems of war direction as they arose from day to day. Membership of both bodies would be the same, so far as the Dominions were concerned, but at meetings of the conference the Colonial Secretary (Walter Long) would preside, whereas at meetings of the Imperial War Cabinet Lloyd George would take the chair.

At the 1917 meetings Australia was not politically represented, since Hughes had been in London the year before and was now faced with serious difficulties at home. New Zealand, having a coalition government, sent two representatives – W. F. Massey and Sir Joseph Ward – and Canada therefore insisted on having two as well – the Prime Minister, Sir Robert Borden, and a colleague. Borden (like Lloyd George, a lawyer) had defeated Laurier in 1911. Always describing himself as a Liberal Conservative, he dominated Canadian politics until 1920.

South Africa sent only one representative in 1917, but he was talented enough to count as two. The Afrikaner General J. C. Smuts was one of the very few people to play a key role in both world wars. Soldier, scholar,

---

35. *The Times*, 26 January 1917. Murdoch had made his name with a sensational report on the Gallipoli campaign.

lawyer, philosopher and notably sharp politician, he acquired a reputation for judgement and wisdom which came to be rather exaggerated. But his versatility and industry are beyond question. After the Imperial War Cabinet sessions in 1917 Lloyd George asked him to stay on as a member of the British War Cabinet, and he did so until January 1919, often giving his attention to British domestic issues as well as the broader issues of war policy and strategy.[36] There was powerful symbolism in the fact that in the War Cabinet he was a colleague of Milner, who had been the Boers' principal antagonist twenty years earlier.

The Imperial War Cabinet was not formally a responsible executive, though it acted as such. It was to meet again during two extremely important periods in 1918, but the groundwork was laid in the first series, and it was obviously of enormous value that most of the leaders of the self-governing empire, together with representatives of India, were in joint session during a period which included the climax of the war at sea, the Russian Revolution and America's decision to enter the war.

---

36. Like Maclay's, his position was constitutionally anomalous, since he was not a member of the British Parliament while holding high office in a British government. The Prime Minister of South Africa, General Louis Botha, was unable to attend the first series of meetings, but made his presence felt later.

5

America Comes In

Family matters – America comes in – A letter from
Mr Guggenheim

The day Lloyd George returned from the ill-fated Calais conference (28 February), his uncle and guardian died at Criccieth. The two had seen each other for the last time when Lloyd George was in North Wales at the beginning of the month. In his eighty-third year, and mortally ill with bowel cancer, Uncle Lloyd had lived long enough to see his cherished nephew at the summit of national and imperial power. Now he was ready to go, cared for to the end by his younger nephew, William – in whose house he lived and whose wife, Anita, was a trained nurse – while Lloyd George fussed about him from afar.

On 11 February he officiated and preached for the last time at the Berea chapel in Criccieth, after nearly sixty years as an unpaid minister in the Baptist sect, the Disciples of Christ. He clearly knew that the sermon would be his last, because he chose as his text the fourth verse of the 23rd Psalm, 'Yea, though I walk through the valley of the shadow of death, I will fear no evil.' The congregation was deeply affected. After the service he took to his bed at William's house, Garthcelyn, and never got up again. Indeed, the words of his sermon were almost his last words.[1]

As he lay dying, the press began to take notice. On 17 February his name appeared as a distinguished invalid on the Court page of *The Times*: 'Mr. Richard Lloyd, the Prime Minister's uncle, is seriously ill, and Mrs. Lloyd George left London yesterday for Wales.' Further bulletins recorded his weakening state until, on 1 March, it was announced that he had died, with Margaret present. Two days later Lloyd George attended the funeral, travelling overnight from London.

At Uncle Lloyd's request the funeral was simple – a ceremony at the house, to which only members of the family, officers of the chapel and a few old friends were invited, followed by burial beside his sister (Lloyd George's mother) in the Criccieth cemetery. Nevertheless the importance of

---

1. William George, *My Brother and I* (1958), p. 38.

the chief mourner was reflected in the proceedings. As well as a Welsh oration (by a nephew of Lloyd's former co-pastor) there was a tribute in English by the chairman of the Disciples of Christ for Great Britain, and a telegram was read from the Italian Prime Minister.

The occasion was moreover covered by the national press. One 'special correspondent' described the scene after the cortège left Garthcelyn:

It was a grey day, and drops of rain fell every now and then. The mist played about Snowdon and, a mile out at sea, obscured the grey waters . . .

The village people, quietly reverent, had gathered . . . The Prime Minister walked behind the hearse, and with him were his [elder] son, Major [Richard] Lloyd George, and his brother [William]. The whole attendance at the cemetery was not above a hundred people. . . . It was the very keynote of democracy. Here was the most highly placed man in the world's greatest Empire burying his foster-father and uncle, the village cobbler.

The mourning party, not 30 people, stood alongside the grave, the Prime Minister at the front. He stood with his head bared, and the expression on his face was the index of his feelings. The wind ruffled his grey hair, and the few drops of rain fell unheeded. . . .

[After the service] the Prime Minister walked to the edge of the grave and looked down at the plain oak coffin. He walked from the cemetery bare-headed, and so down the hill.[2]

The funeral ceremonies were in the morning, and after them Lloyd George spent an hour or two at his own house, Brynawelon, before driving with Margaret, Dick, Olwen and his private secretary, J. T. Davies, to Llandudno, where they caught the afternoon train to London.

The Italian premier was not the only statesman to take note of the occasion. There were also messages in the press from Asquith, the French Prime Minister, Briand, the President of the French Chamber of Deputies and the Prime Minister of Serbia. Newspaper tributes were written by T. P. O'Connor and Marie Corelli, which Lloyd George sent to his brother describing them as (respectively) 'beautiful' and 'exquisite', and adding a rhapsodic comment of his own:

The old boy has already passed into the history of the world, for his part of it is a world story and will interest readers in Korea just as much as readers in Carmarthen. The romance of his share in life will always fascinate and inspire; in fact the interest

2. *The Times*, 5 March 1917.

in what he did will long survive any interest there may be in what I have or ever can achieve.[3]

He may have believed this nonsense as he wrote it, but obviously Richard Lloyd is remembered only because he is part of the romance, indeed the mythology, of Lloyd George's life, which the letter illustrates in an extreme form. Certainly Lloyd George owed a lot to the 'old boy' who perceived and nurtured his genius as a child. But of course the genius was his own, as were (very largely) the ideas that he formed and the way he conducted himself as a grown man. Uncle Lloyd gave him boundless encouragement and, even in his early years, the minimum of criticism. As his career blossomed and his fame grew, his uncle's indulgence turned almost to idolatry. When he became Prime Minister Uncle Lloyd regarded him as larger than the office.[4]

The notion that Uncle Lloyd remained a constant 'mentor' to him (as O'Connor wrote, and many still believe) is sheer fantasy. He went his own way. If his uncle had ever failed to back him he would have been sorry, but it would have made no difference. In fact, Uncle Lloyd always ultimately supported anything he thought or did, and was rewarded with genuine gratitude and an affectionate pretence of subordination. The myth to which this pretence contributed was useful to Lloyd George, because it reassured Welsh Nonconformists and appealed to sentimentalists everywhere. It must also have pleased his vanity to imagine that the story of his relationship with his uncle was a talking-point in places as remote as Korea.

The relationship inspired mixed feelings in William George, who was to some extent a victim of it. 'He [David] was the apple of Uncle Lloyd's eye, the King of the castle and, like the other King, could do no wrong. . . . Whether this unrestrained admiration was wholly good for the lad upon whom it was lavished, and indeed for the man who evolved out of him, is a matter upon which opinions may differ.'[5] William had reason to feel some resentment, having been treated as an ordinary child while David was worshipped and pampered. Though he was not a high-flyer, his natural abilities were far from ordinary, and his conscientious work as a solicitor helped to sustain his brother's early career. This was seemingly taken for

3. DLG to William George, 6 March 1917. T. P. O'Connor was a well-known journalist and politician, the only Irish Nationalist representing an English constituency (the Scotland division of Liverpool). Marie Corelli was the pen-name of Mary Mackay, an extravagantly romantic novelist whose work was very popular at the time but has not endured. She had a cottage in Criccieth. (Her piece appeared in the *Pall Mall Gazette*, O'Connor's in *Lloyd's Weekly News*.)
4. FSD, 24 February 1917.   5. George, *My Brother and I*, p. 33.

granted, as was the care that he and his wife devoted to Uncle Lloyd from day to day. When David added the name Lloyd to his patronymic, partly no doubt as a gesture to Uncle Lloyd, the latter would not allow William to do the same. (It is true that Lloyd was David's second baptismal name, whereas William was just William; but it was nevertheless gratuitously wounding to prevent him from sharing the new composite surname that David came to assume.)

Richard Lloyd was certainly a remarkable man. His Christianity was sincere, and not at all bigoted. He was tolerant of those who were unable to match his certainty of faith or his puritanical standards of behaviour – which was just as well for one cast as cheer-leader to Lloyd George. There was in his character a good deal, perhaps, of the frustrated politician, which found an outlet in helping his elder nephew to achieve in the world what he could never have achieved himself. History should salute him, though not quite as a saint and still less as a Svengali.

Frances Stevenson was aware that her role in Lloyd George's life was, in a sense, similar to his, and Lloyd George reminded her of it as soon as he heard that his uncle had died. 'He will miss the old man very much, and he says . . . that I shall have to fill the old man's place. God knows I shall try.'[6] More than ever she had to be a source of predictable adulation and moral support.

Very soon after the family's oldest member had died, the youngest had a brush with death. Like the poor Russian princesses – and at about the same time – Megan (now nearly fifteen) went down with measles, and there were fears that the disease might go to her head. Lloyd George, always afraid of illness, and with the ever-painful memory of his daughter Mair's death ten years earlier, was sure from what he heard that Megan would contract meningitis. Fortunately this did not occur, but the attack of measles was severe and one night a doctor was with her from 9.30 p.m. to 4.30 a.m.[7] Then the crisis passed. To help him through a difficult time Lloyd George took to drinking every morning 'a wonderful concoction of egg, port wine, honey and cream', which seemed to 'buck him up a lot'.[8]

By 7 April Megan was well enough to act as a maid of honour when her brother Richard was married. His bride was Roberta McAlpine, youngest daughter of Robert McAlpine, head of the already successful building firm. The marriage was a whirlwind affair. Richard was at an officers' convalescent home in Bath (recuperating from trench fever) when Roberta accompanied

6. FSD, 1 March 1917.   7. DLG to William George, 16 March 1917.
8. FSD, 10 March 1917.

her father on a visit to the city, for the traditional purpose of taking the waters. She and Richard met, and within weeks they were married in Bath Abbey.

The Lloyd Georges were privately unenthusiastic about this turn of events, but put the best face on it they could. The McAlpine connection was not ideal for Lloyd George's image, particularly in Wales, and in any case they liked the Welsh girl, Dilys Roberts, whom Richard had seemed likely to marry. Unfortunately she broke off the engagement (before he met Roberta), and it may have occurred to them that he was now marrying on the rebound.

Richard's best man was a brother officer, in the absence of Gwilym who could not get leave from the front. The bride wore a dress 'of white charmeuse with an Empire tunic of silver lace and semi-court train attached by crystal and diamanté ornaments'. She wore a string of pearls, a present from her father, and carried a bouquet of lily-of-the-valley. Care was taken, however, that press reports of the occasion should not give an impression of undue lavishness. 'Only immediate relatives and old friends' were invited to the service, and at the wedding breakfast afterwards at the Empire Hotel 'no alcohol was served'. A large crowd gathered outside the hotel and there were calls for a speech from Lloyd George, but he did not oblige. The people had to be content with sprigs of white heather and pieces of wedding cake distributed by the bride.[9]

After the wedding Lloyd George visited the Pump Room, where he signed the visitors' book. He and Margaret then went for a drive in the Mendips before spending a second night in Bath. The following morning (Easter Sunday) they motored back to London.

Richard and Roberta spent their honeymoon in Cornwall. In due course they had two children, Valerie (later Lady Valerie Daniel) and Owen (3rd Earl Lloyd George of Dwyfor). The marriage did not ultimately last, but proved the medium through which a noble dynasty was established – an outcome few would have predicted in April 1917, granted Lloyd George's colourful denunciations of the hereditary peerage.

Before going to Bath on the eve of his son's wedding Lloyd George had received, and reacted to, news of the highest importance. America had at last entered the war.

Since the failure of his peace initiative at the end of 1916, events had been edging President Woodrow Wilson away from the proud neutrality which he had maintained for so long. But still he was slow to move and appeared to remain a neutral at heart, to the despair of three of his closest advisers –

9. *The Times*, 9 April 1917.

Colonel Edward M. House, Secretary of State Robert Lansing and the American Ambassador in London, Walter Hines Page. Perhaps he reflected American opinion more accurately than they did; certainly he was in a position where it was more necessary to take account of it. But he was also convinced of his own wisdom and rectitude, and infused with a sense of destiny as the agent of what he saw as America's mission to the world. The first intellectual to hold the American Presidency since Thomas Jefferson, he was a Calvinistic egotist in the Scots-Irish tradition. At one level he was a philosopher and dreamer, at another a ruthless exponent of American national interests, at another still the most hard-bitten of party politicians. Though he doubtless believed that his motives were simple and noble, they were in fact complicated and not wholly admirable. Over the next two and a half years his personality was to arouse irrational hopes throughout the world, but would also doom those very hopes to cruel disappointment.

On 22 January President Wilson delivered an address to the United States Senate, which was both a personal and an American manifesto. He called for the war to end in a 'peace without victory', which would be followed by the creation of a league of nations to prevent future wars. In this the United States would play its part. The old order would be replaced by a new order, the old diplomacy by a new diplomacy based on 'the equality of nations'. There had to be 'not a balance of power, but a community of power; not organised rivalries, but an organised common peace'. These, he proclaimed, were 'American principles, American policies', which were also those of 'forward-looking men and women everywhere'. The Republican Senator Henry Cabot Lodge (a name to remember) soon raised doubts about the practicality of Wilson's lofty vision, and questioned its detailed implications. But the *New York Times* described the address as 'The President's greatest utterance', and representatives of the American Union Against Militarism said that it was 'destined to an immortality as glorious as that of the Gettysburg Address'.[10]

Meanwhile, the Germans were intent upon real victory, with a view to imposing a peace to suit themselves. They had no interest in Wilson's 'peace without victory'. Within days of his address they launched their indiscriminate U-boat campaign, which was in effect a declaration of maritime war on all neutrals trading with the Western Allies, particularly Britain. But Wilson did not treat this as a *casus belli*. He merely broke off diplomatic relations with Germany, while expressing the hope that American ships

---

10. Thomas J. Knock, *To End All Wars: Woodrow Wilson and the Quest for a New World Order* (1992), pp. 111–14 and 124.

would not be sunk (a hope which, if heeded, would have negated the whole purpose of German strategy). In fact, only three American ships were sunk during the couple of months while Wilson continued to dither, but a more serious blow to the policy of neutrality was the disclosure, at the beginning of March, of a plot by the German Foreign Minister, Arthur Zimmermann, to inveigle Mexico into war with the United States, on the promise of regaining the 'lost provinces' of Arizona, New Mexico and Texas. This flagrant challenge to the Monroe Doctrine and America's territorial integrity provoked public outrage and created a climate on the whole favourable to war with Germany.[11] On 2 April Wilson asked Congress to recognize that a state of war existed, in an address containing the famous words 'The world must be made safe for democracy'. By 6 April, after four days' debate, the declaration of war had received Congressional approval.[12]

Wilson had been forced to change his position by American public opinion, itself transformed by German actions and the evidence of German intentions. He was also influenced by the desire to play a suitably commanding role in the negotiations that would follow Germany's defeat – an event that he expected the mere fact of American participation to hasten. Since he had been balked in his ambition to promote, as a non-combatant, a peace without victory for others, he could at least hope that, as a combatant, he would be able to secure the kind of peace he wanted, after American intervention had brought about a fairly early victory. During his long period of indecision Lloyd George, sensing his susceptibility in this respect, appealed to him through Ambassador Page: 'The President's presence at the peace conference is necessary for the proper organisation of the world ... Convey to him this deep conviction of mine. He must help make peace if the peace made at the conference is to be worth keeping. American participation would enable him to be there and the mere effect of his participation would shorten the war, and might even end it very quickly.'[13] Such words may have contributed to Wilson's inner debate, if only by strengthening a line of thought that was already present in his mind.

11. The so-called 'Zimmermann telegram' was intercepted by British intelligence in mid-January, but for a time kept secret for fear of compromising British code-breaking. A month later it was communicated to the American government, and Wilson then immediately released it to Congress and the press. Its authenticity was never doubted in Washington; more surprisingly, it was never denied by Zimmermann.
12. The crucial vote for war in the Senate (on 4 April) was 82:6. In the House of Representatives the vote (two days later) was 363:50. A fortnight earlier Wilson had canvassed the views of his Cabinet, and had found that its members were unanimously for war.
13. Page to Lansing, 11 February 1917.

On the first day of April Lloyd George was aware that Wilson might be on the point of reaching a decision, though also uneasy about the form it might take. 'I wonder if America will come in this week? It would be the best piece of luck we have had for some time. But I fear Wilson will only half come in.'[14] Both the hunch and the fear were justified. Within the week America was indeed in, but only half in. War was declared on Germany, but not – until the end of the year – on Austria-Hungary, and never on the Ottoman Empire or Bulgaria. Moreover, America condescended to become only an associate, not an ally, of the European democracies that had been fighting for so long, and at such heavy cost, against what was now a common enemy. The distinction was irritating and insulting, if largely meaningless.

All the same, American involvement in the war, however belated and limited, was immensely significant and had to be welcomed. The Imperial War Cabinet took stock of the new situation at its eighth meeting on 6 April, and afterwards Lloyd George made a statement on behalf of his colleagues and himself – but in words unmistakably his own – to a group of leading American journalists summoned to Downing Street. (Parliament had risen for the Easter recess, so he was free to waive the normal procedure of a Commons statement.) He said:

America has at one bound become a world power in a sense she never was before. She waited until she found a cause worthy of her traditions. The American people held back until they were fully convinced the fight was not a sordid scrimmage for power and possessions, but an unselfish struggle to overthrow a sinister conspiracy against human liberty and human right. Once that conviction was reached, the great Republic of the West has leaped into the arena, and she stands now side by side with the European democracies who, bruised and bleeding after three years of grim conflict, are still fighting the most savage foe that ever menaced the freedom of the world.

The glowing phrases of the President's noble deliverance illumine the horizon and make clearer than ever the goal we are striving to reach. . . . [the phrase about making the world safe for democracy was one of three here quoted].

The Imperial War Cabinet, representative of all the peoples and nations of the British Empire, wish me, on their behalf, to recognise the chivalry and courage which call the people of the United States to dedicate the whole of their resources to the service of the greatest cause that ever engaged human endeavour.

The words were well chosen, hailing the new partner and endorsing the Americans' view of themselves, yet with more than a hint of irony.

14. RWD, 1 April 1917.

72

Apart from the obvious psychological value of the United States' entry into the war, what were its practical effects? On the military side nothing much could be hoped for in 1917, since the country was in a state of extreme military unpreparedness. In size the United States army ranked seventeenth in the world; in equipment it was obsolete and ill-supplied. 'Its field artillery had enough rounds to sustain a bombardment on the western front for no more than a few minutes. With no poison gas, flame throwers, tanks, mortars, hand and rifle grenades, heavy field howitzers, or modern aircraft, the United States army remained a nineteenth-century force and a very small one at that.'[15] The former President Theodore Roosevelt was eager to raise a force of volunteers, like the Rough Riders with whom he had won fame and glory in the Spanish-American War, to expedite American action on the Western front. But any idea of Roosevelt's was likely to be viewed with disfavour by Wilson, and this one certainly was. Wilson was still hoping to avoid large-scale military involvement in Europe, and was anyway determined that, if it had to happen, it should happen in a way that would preserve his own control and reflect America's complete independence. He therefore decided to expand the United States army by means of conscription, operated selectively to safeguard the needs of industry. This was found to be a slow process, and the result was that the United States was not a serious military factor until 1918, though a token unit was sent over to parade in Paris on the Fourth of July.

In the short term the benefits of American co-belligerency were chiefly felt in the maritime and financial spheres. Though America's ocean-going merchant fleet was very small (most of its tonnage being used in coastal traffic or on the Great Lakes), it received an immediate boost from about half a million tons of German shipping seized in American ports when war was declared. Another boost came from the requisitioning (as already mentioned) of ships under construction for Maclay in American yards. Obviously this was of no net advantage to Britain, but Britain did gain substantially from the diversion of American destroyers to anti-submarine warfare. A flotilla of six was sent at once to assist in escort work in the European war zone, and major reinforcements soon followed, authorized by the young assistant Secretary of the Navy, Franklin D. Roosevelt.

The Canadian-born Admiral William S. Sims was appointed the United States navy's representative in London and he fortunately did not at all share the view of America's top sailor, Admiral Benson, that he would 'as

15. David R. Woodward, *Trial by Friendship: Anglo-American Relations, 1917–1918* (1993), p. 20.

soon fight the British as the Germans'.[16] Sims proved thoroughly helpful and co-operative, not least (as we have seen) in adding his voice to the pro-convoy lobby.

On the financial side, America's entry steadied relations after what had been a rather bumpy period. Towards the end of 1916 British credit in the United States was damaged by a statement from the Federal Reserve Board, warning American banks and private investors against subscribing to Allied loans. The temporary crisis so precipitated was partly due to incompetence by J. P. Morgan & Co., the 'bankers' banker' and sole purchasing agent for the Entente powers in America; but above all it was due to President Wilson, who 'directly influenced the Board's warning'.[17] Wilson was using financial pressure in support of his peace initiative, and an additional motive was annoyance with Morgans for backing his Republican opponent in the Presidential election. Alarm in London was increased by the Treasury's leading expert in foreign matters, John Maynard Keynes, who was given to unnecessary pessimism and anyway shared Wilson's desire to promote a compromise peace. Before the change of government he had drafted for the then Chancellor, Reginald McKenna, the words: 'If things go on [as] at present, I venture to say with certainty that by next June or earlier the President of the American Republic will be in a position, if he wishes, to dictate his own terms to us.'[18] And Keynes continued in the same vein when Law succeeded McKenna, finding the new Chancellor amenable to his influence.

Lloyd George, on the other hand, was temperamentally immune to panic about the financial means for conducting the war. In this respect his cavalier attitude to money served him well. He knew that there was much sympathy for the Allied cause in the United States, as well as hostility in certain quarters. He also knew that American farmers and industrialists had a strong interest in the maintenance of British credit. Any attempt to starve Britain of funds would penalize the customers of American banks no less than the banks themselves. Even before the escalation of the U-boat war a new loan was issued with the Federal Reserve Board's blessing, and when the United States entered the war it was clearly out of the question for its European associates to be denied the means to carry on fighting. Despite continuing argument and friction over terms, from then onwards American money was ultimately available.

16. Woodward, *Trial by Friendship*, p. 65.
17. Kathleen Burk, *Britain, America and the Sinews of War, 1914–1918* (1985), p. 87.
18. Robert Skidelsky, *John Maynard Keynes: A Biography* (3 vols., 1983–2000), vol. i, p. 334.

Too dramatic a view has often been taken of the Anglo-American financial crisis that coincided with the start of Lloyd George's premiership. To regard it as marking the establishment of American economic hegemony is premature. Keynes is chiefly responsible for its being so regarded, but he had his own subjective motives for putting forward the gloomy prognoses which were repeatedly disproved. When, at the end of 1940, Lord Lothian said to American reporters 'Well, boys, Britain's broke,' he was scarcely exaggerating. But in 1917 Britain was far from broke. While there were substantial transfers of gold, and sales of British holdings in the United States, Britain remained a formidable economic power as well as a political superpower. Its Latin American portfolio was untouched, and at the end of the war the country was still a net creditor. Nevertheless it is, of course, undeniable that American economic power grew, absolutely and relatively, during the war, and with it America's political power in the world.

As soon as the news came through that Wilson was asking Congress for a declaration of war, the Cabinet decided that a mission should be sent to the United States to co-ordinate all aspects of Anglo-American activity, including finance. The twenty-five-strong party was to consist of soldiers, sailors, financiers, economists, diplomats, and experts on food, transport, munitions and trade. Balfour himself offered to lead the mission, provided Wilson was agreeable. The President showed some reluctance, fearing that his compatriots might suspect 'an attempt in some degree to take charge of us as an assistant to Great Britain'.[19] But after a few days he gave his consent and the mission sailed from Greenock on 13 April.

The previous day Lloyd George addressed the American Luncheon Club at the Savoy Hotel in London. Knowing that many American journalists would be in the audience, and that the occasion would enable him to speak, through them, to the American people, he prepared his speech carefully after 'an impromptu dinner' the evening before in Frances Stevenson's room at 10 Downing Street.[20] The advent of America as a belligerent, he said, gave 'the final stamp and seal to the character of the conflict as a struggle against military autocracy throughout the world'. He conceded that in Europe 'most of the great wars of the past were waged for dynastic aggrandisement and for conquest', but the fact that the United States had made up its mind 'finally' showed that this was 'a great fight for human liberty'.

He made good rhetorical use of the Germans' new line in France (to be explained in the next chapter), which was already known as the Hindenburg line. He described it as 'the most characteristic of all Prussian institutions

19. Woodrow Wilson to Col. E. M. House, 6 April 1917.   20. FSD, 11 April 1917.

75

... a line drawn in the territory of other people, with the warning that the inhabitants of those territories shall not cross it at the peril of their lives'. Similarly, 'a Hindenburg line [had been] drawn along the shores of America and Americans were told that they must not cross it'. But America had said: 'The place for that line is not the Atlantic, but on the Rhine, and we mean to help you to roll it up'.

He referred to the Russians, who had fought for freedom and had now made their own country free. But his strongest emphasis was on the maritime war. 'The road to victory, the guarantee of victory, the absolute assurance of victory, is to be found in one word – ships.' He urged the Americans to learn from Britain's mistakes. 'We are a slow people in these islands. Yes, but sure! We have made blunders; we generally do; we have tried every blunder. It is worth America's while to study our blunders so as to begin just where we are now – not where we were three years ago.' (In saying this he neatly combined self-deprecation as a Briton with a reminder to the Americans of their long sojourn on the sidelines.)

The speech ended in a vein of high optimism. The peace that would follow the war would be 'a real peace'. Just as troops attacked with the dawn, so the war itself would bring a new dawn to humanity. When he arrived for the lunch, and at the end of his speech, Lloyd George was given a standing ovation.[21]

That evening there was another Anglo-American occasion at the Savoy, a Pilgrims' dinner at which Lord Bryce presided and Ambassador Page was the principal speaker. Many leading figures from Britain and the overseas Empire attended, but Lloyd George was not among them. After lunch he drove to Windsor to discuss an important and secret matter with the King. Frances Stevenson accompanied him, and while he was in the Castle she went off to have tea on her own in the town. Then they drove together to Walton Heath, where Lloyd George was 'in excellent spirits & very pleased with his speech'.[22] How successful was it? Did the warm reception from those who heard it represent their true feelings? One of them, Admiral Sims, told Riddell a month later that his compatriots present had not understood it 'at the time'.[23] Yet a distinguished American journalist who was there, Isaac F. Marcosson, described it as a 'great speech'.[24] What mattered most, perhaps, was that it was widely reported in the American press. Lloyd George's name was more familiar to American newspaper readers than that of any other Allied politician, and his words never failed to command attention.

21. *The Times*, 13 April 1917.   22. FSD, 12 April 1917.   23. *RWD*, 15 May 1917.
24. Isaac F. Marcosson, *Adventures in Interviewing* (1920), p. 98.

Balfour was far less well known in America, though unlike Lloyd George he had visited the country – more than forty years earlier, while he was on a world tour. Now he was returning as Foreign Secretary and a former Prime Minister. For all his Old World sophistication, he was an admirer of the New World and ready to be impressed by it again, as he had been in his youth by San Francisco, Salt Lake City, the Yosemite Valley and Niagara. After landing at Halifax, Nova Scotia, he and his party travelled by train to Washington, arriving there on 22 April. House also travelled on the train from New York to Baltimore, briefing Balfour helpfully in preparation for his meetings with Wilson.

The mission – which stayed in America until the end of May – was on the whole a success, though some of its expert groups did better than others. Balfour was 'nearly an unalloyed success',[25] and nowhere more so than at the White House. Wilson's initially grudging attitude to the visit gave way to cordiality and trust. The eminence of the emissary was flattering to him, and he enjoyed the company of one who, like himself, was an intellectual in politics.[26] Balfour, far from trying to lead him by the nose, showed genuine respect for the man, and still more for his office, writing later that the President was 'at that moment by far the most important man in the world'.[27] At one of their business meetings – after a family dinner at the White House – Balfour took the risk of informing Wilson about the secret treaties that existed between the Allied powers, telling him secretly 'as man to man'. Wilson did not betray his confidence – to the extent of subsequently making out he knew nothing about the treaties before he went to the peace conference.[28]

When, during the visit, Balfour addressed Congress, Wilson came to listen to him; and before he left the President 'broke all precedents by visiting him in person to say goodbye'.[29] The understanding he established with Wilson enabled him to overcome some difficulties that arose in the specialist work of his mission, notably in the negotiations between Treasury experts (one of whom was the Governor of the Bank of England, Lord Cunliffe) and the

25. Burk, *Britain, America and the Sinews of War*, p. 99.

26. Wilson had been a professor at Princeton, and then President of the University, before turning to politics as Governor of New Jersey.

27. A. J. Balfour, *Chapters of Autobiography* (1930), p. 239.

28. This rather annoyed Balfour, though he was prepared to put it down to forgetfulness. 'You see when Wilson had made up his mind about coming into the war, it was the *present* and the future that interested him, not the past. I felt the same – those Treaties had no importance by that time' (AJB talking to his niece and biographer, Mrs Dugdale, in 1928; Blanche E. C. Dugdale, *Arthur James Balfour* (2 vols., 1936), vol. ii, p. 201).   29. Ibid., p. 200.

United States Treasury. But in general he left the specialists to get on with their jobs, while seeking himself 'to impress the American public with his statesmanship and amiability'.[30] This he did by giving press interviews and by personal contact with politicians and other leading figures.

The invitation to address Congress showed how well he had succeeded, even with people who had no reason to be prejudiced in his favour. In particular, all but the most implacable Irish-Americans found that the man nicknamed 'Bloody Balfour' for his toughness as Chief Secretary for Ireland early in his career was not the monster they had expected. It was a nice twist that he was the first British Parliamentarian to address Congress since Charles Stewart Parnell (in 1880).

A French mission was visiting America at the same time, led by the former Prime Minister Viviani, and including Marshal Joffre; but Balfour stole the show. Of course, he had the advantage of language, but that alone could not account for his success. He performed a difficult task with quiet mastery and showed that he was the right person for the job.[31] Lloyd George himself would have made a bigger splash, with his charisma and demotic appeal, and having a style more akin to that of American politicians. But for that very reason Wilson would have balked at having him (as he did when the question arose later in the year). The Balfour mission was a most effective instance of Lloyd Georgian summitry, though without Lloyd George in the starring role.

Apart from affairs of state, another Anglo-American matter impinged upon Lloyd George during the early months of 1917. And his handling of it was curious, to say the least.

On 27 March a letter was sent to him from New York by the American copper magnate and art collector, Solomon R. Guggenheim. It read:

My dear Mr. George,

I write to ask if you will be so kind as to donate to whatever relief work you consider most worthy and in the greatest need, the enclosed draft for Twenty thousand pounds, of the American Exchange National Bank, of our City, on the Capital & Counties Bank Limited, London.

My only excuse for taking advantage of my acquaintance with you, formed on two different occasions at dinner in England, by asking for even a moment of your

---

30. Burk, *Britain, America and the Sinews of War*, p. 104.
31. His visit included a token appearance in the South, at Richmond, Virginia. This was appropriate, since Wilson was the first Southern-born President since the Civil War.

precious but apparently inexhaustible time, is my ardent desire to help Britain's sufferers, my ignorance at this distance, and your knowledge of the best way to do so.

Since the outbreak of the war in Europe, I have followed as closely as I have been able the varying fortunes of Great Britain, whose cause has ever had my heartfelt sympathy, and now for the indomitable way in which she is gradually surmounting her colossal difficulties she commands my deepest admiration; and by this means I wish, even in a slight degree, to give expression to my feelings.

I am,

Yours sincerely

S. R. Guggenheim

Lloyd George and Guggenheim must have met as fellow guests of another copper millionaire, Sir Charles Henry, and his wife Julia, who entertained lavishly at their grand London house, 5 Carlton Gardens, and at their two houses in the country (including one within easy reach of London, at Henley-on-Thames). Henry, Australian-born but educated in England and Germany, had been a Liberal MP since 1906. His wife, formerly Julia Lewisohn of New York, was a darkly glamorous and rather intense woman, with whom Lloyd George had an affair – never serious on his side – before Frances Stevenson came into his life. When it ended, relations between him and the Henrys naturally cooled, though not to the point of total estrangement. It suited Henry to keep in touch with such a powerful political friend, whom he anyway admired; and Julia, despite her hurt feelings, continued to ply Lloyd George with fruit from her greenhouses (always welcome) and with invitations (which he only occasionally accepted).[32]

Apart from personal contact through the Henrys, Lloyd George had in a sense encountered Guggenheim at long range, since at the beginning of the war there was considerable tension between Britain and the American copper industry, in which the family firm of Guggenheim was one of the biggest concerns. The trouble was that American copper was being supplied in large quantities to Germany as well as to the Entente powers – the supplies to Germany being often delivered in the first instance to neutral countries and thence passed on. The British were determined to stop this practice and after a time succeeded in doing so. By March 1915 the American

---

32. For further information on Lloyd George's relations with the Henrys see my *Lloyd George: The People's Champion* (1978), pp. 127–9, and *Lloyd George: From Peace to War* (1985), pp. 85–8 and 404–6.

industry was selling 95 per cent of its exportable copper to Britain, and had acquiesced in the blockade of Germany. But Lloyd George suggests in his *War Memoirs* that Guggenheims, for their part, did not agree to this arrangement out of sympathy for Britain. 'One of the last to come in', he writes, 'was the great Guggenheim group. Its hand was forced by an announcement made, in reply to a question in Parliament, that the firms whose consignments were safeguarded by agreements with us were welcome to announce the fact, so that orders might be placed with them. Thereupon Guggenheim cabled their representative in London to sign an agreement with the Admiralty.'[33]

Such was the background to Solomon R. Guggenheim's letter of 27 March 1917. Ostensibly, any ill-will there may once have been at the commercial and political level had been replaced, in Guggenheim's mind, with a cordial attitude towards Britain and in particular its new leader. We have no record of the 'different occasions' on which they had met in England, so cannot know if they had met at all since the war began. But we can safely assume that the original link was through the Henrys. (Subsequent statements indicate that this must have been so.)

It is possible that Guggenheim was trying to resurrect a slight pre-war acquaintance for purposes that were self-serving as well as philanthropic. But it is equally possible that he meant exactly what he said, and that his donation was prompted by wholehearted sympathy for Britain and its cause, whatever may have been his attitude in the past. Either way, there can be no justification for Lloyd George's behaviour about the letter and its contents. In 1917 £20,000 would have been worth more than £500,000 in today's money. So handsome a gift, from so important an American, ought to have been announced immediately, and the money either transferred at once to named war charities or placed in the hands of trustees. But nothing of the sort happened.

It was over a month before the letter was acknowledged, and even then Guggenheim was not told how his money would be used. In a brief cable to him Lloyd George merely said:

Pray accept my most cordial thanks for the generous gift you have forwarded for war relief in England and for your expression of sympathy and goodwill. We are most grateful for this token of the spirit in which your great country has entered the

33. WM, pp. 664–5. This is the only reference to Guggenheim in the memoirs. There is no mention at all of S. R. Guggenheim's letter and donation (hardly surprising in view of the sequel).

war. Letter will follow to let you know the use to which your contribution has been put as soon as an appropriate decision has been arrived at.[34]

The promised letter did not follow. Guggenheim waited for it until nearly the end of the year, when he wrote again:

Dear Mr George,

Your cablegram of May 1st acknowledging receipt of the donation which accompanied my letter of the 27th of March came to hand. Please do not think me unduly anxious, but as your letter stated you would let me know later the use to which the donation had been put, and not having heard, it has occurred to me that possibly, in these days of enemy under-sea activity, your letter may have been lost.

I receive from time to time requests from my friends in England for subscriptions to various war charities, and if I knew the institutions among which you have distributed my donation, it would be of great help to me in giving further to others.

Sincerely yours,

S. R. Guggenheim.[35]

This letter was not answered until April of the following year, and then not by Lloyd George himself but by his private secretary, J. T. Davies. And the reply was thoroughly unsatisfactory. Further developments in this murky story will be described in due course. This was an instance in which Lloyd George's cavalier attitude to money did not serve him well.

34. 1 May 1917.   35. 30 November 1917.

6

Nivelle's Nemesis

*Doubts about Nivelle – Vimy, Arras, Compiègne – Saint-Jean
de Maurienne – Nivelle's nemesis*

Before the eventual launch of Nivelle's offensive in April, the whole com-
plexion of the war had been changed by revolution in Russia and America's
decision to enter the war. In theory, either of these enormous developments
might have prompted reconsideration of Allied strategy in the West; together
they might have dictated a wholly different approach. But in the real world
it could not be so. Western leaders must be forgiven for not perceiving at
once that the Revolution would put an end to Russia's effective participation
in the war. As for American entry, it occurred too late to have a serious
influence on the plans for 1917, since it more or less coincided with the first
shots in the Allied campaign.

There was, however, one development which both could and should have
caused the Nivelle plan to be modified, if not abandoned. Even while the
Anglo-French leaders were holding their ill-fated conference at Calais, news
came through that the Germans were retreating from the large salient which
they had defended the previous year at such heavy cost in the battle of the
Somme. Before long they had succeeded in pulling back, in good order, to
a line of defences between Arras and Soissons, which had been under
preparation for several months – the so-called Hindenburg line referred to
by Lloyd George in his speech to the American Luncheon Club. The move
was calculated, and performed with systematic ruthlessness. The territory
from which the Germans withdrew was left in a state of utter devastation,
with booby-traps cunningly laid to take a toll of Allied personnel. (One
exploded in the Town Hall of Bapaume a week after the British occupied
the place, killing a number of Australian soldiers and two French deputies.)

Nevertheless the spectacle of the Germans in retreat, for whatever reason,
was at first encouraging – particularly, of course, to the French, who were
regaining a small part of their homeland. Since 1914 Georges Clemenceau
had been insistently reminding his compatriots 'The Germans are at Noyon'
(a town about sixty miles from Paris). Now the Germans were no longer at
Noyon, but the fillip to morale was short-lived. The elimination of the bulge

deprived Nivelle's plan of its original rationale and necessitated awkward adjustments, even though the plan itself was not scrapped. Worse, the Germans' withdrawal so reduced their length of front that a dozen divisions were made available to help counter the coming Allied offensive.

Haig was quick to perceive that the move had dangerous implications, but he either misread the danger or chose to misrepresent it, arguing that the German divisions freed by the shorter line might be used on his front between Lille and the sea, so threatening the Channel ports. He failed to understand that the German strategy for 1917 was to avoid large-scale operations on land, while the U-boats would supposedly be winning the war. Lloyd George was infuriated by Haig's reaction, seeing it as a manœuvre to win support for his cherished Flanders plan. The Prime Minister may have been right about Haig's motives, but Calais had left him with diminished moral authority in his dealings with the Field-Marshal, while it had left Nivelle under the impression that he could treat Haig as a subordinate, with the British government's assured backing.

About a week after Calais Nivelle sent Haig two directives whose tone might have seemed haughty if addressed to one of his own French corps commanders; and a telegram from Briand to the British government accused Haig of a deliberate intent to sabotage Nivelle's plan.[1] The effect of these communications was to unite Lloyd George's colleagues behind Haig and against Nivelle. Lloyd George then had to switch from seriously considering how he could get rid of Haig to giving him strong backing at another Anglo-French conference, hastily assembled in London on 12–13 March.[2] The result of the conference was an improvement in Haig's position compared with the Calais compromise, which itself had marked a success for him and Robertson. Another result was that his relations with Nivelle took a turn for the better.

The same could not be said of Nivelle's relations with his fellow-countrymen, among whom his stock was falling by the day. Some military colleagues who had never believed in his plan – notably Pétain – were now being joined by others. The inflexibility of his reaction to the first evidence of German withdrawal in the bulge – his failure to move in hot pursuit – undermined confidence in his judgement and flair. The commander of the northern army group, General Franchet d'Esperey, was beside himself with frustration at not being allowed to carry out an *attaque brusquée*. Replying after some delay to his urgent requests, Nivelle still would not assent,

1. E. L. Spears, *Prelude to Victory* (1939), pp. 170–79.
2. David R. Woodward, *Lloyd George and the Generals* (1983), pp. 151–2.

maintaining that the enemy was unlikely to abandon without a fight any-where so close to Paris as Noyon. A vital opportunity was thus lost. D'Esperey's loss of faith in Nivelle is of special significance, because his attitude was not warped by jealousy or rancour; on the contrary he was personally attached to the Commander-in-Chief.

Political opinion reflected the changing mood of the army. By the time of the London meeting in March few leading politicians apart from Briand were still supporting Nivelle; and Briand did not attend the conference. After reluctantly agreeing to it, he deputed leadership of the French party to his Finance Minister, the veteran Alexandre Ribot, who was accompanied by the War Minister, Lyautey, the Navy Minister (an Admiral), Albert Thomas and Nivelle. Lyautey was loyal to the beleaguered General, but also sympathized with Haig. Lloyd George had no such sympathy, but was unable to fight for Nivelle, because the attitude of his colleagues compelled him to support Haig. At the end of the conference Hankey noted that the French ministers seemed quite pleased with its results.[3]

Within a week Briand resigned and Ribot took his place as Prime Minister and Foreign Minister. The change of government was precipitated by a row in the French Parliament which Lyautey, no politician, handled badly; so Lyautey left with Briand, to be succeeded as War Minister by Paul Painlevé, whose views on war policy were closely akin to Pétain's. The isolation of Nivelle was thus almost complete. The French premier who had been his principal champion had gone, while the new War Minister did not believe in his plan. Painlevé wanted to stop the offensive, but could find no way of removing Nivelle or imposing an alternative strategy. Like Lloyd George with Haig, he did his best to undermine the Commander-in-Chief, but felt incapable of sacking him. Such was the position as the time came for the first stage of the plan to unfold.

The first stage was entrusted to the British, who were to attack north and east of Arras. Their role, as Nivelle conceived it, was to keep German forces away from those sectors of the front, on either side of Rheims, where the French army was to deliver its war-winning blow. It was the French who were expected to make the decisive breakthrough.

As things turned out, the best chance of performing such a feat fell to the British. After a preliminary bombardment, which began on 4 April, Haig's troops went into action on the 9th and achieved, at the outset, remarkable success, despite bitterly cold and wet weather. The Canadian corps captured

3. Hankey diary, 18 March 1917. Hankey's observation may not have been quite accurate, because Thomas was among Nivelle's dwindling band of supporters.

Vimy ridge, an objective of prime tactical importance, while to the east of Arras the attackers penetrated to a depth of three and a half miles or more, on a front of seven to nine miles. Had preparations been adequate, and conditions less adverse, this was the moment when a great victory might have been won. Ludendorff later recorded that the situation at the end of 9 April was, from the German point of view, 'extremely critical, and might have had far-reaching and serious consequences if the [British] had pushed further forward'.[4] For various reasons, however, they failed to exploit the initial gains, and before long were bogged down in a manner all too familiar on the Western front, with heavy losses on both sides but the balance of loss substantially favouring the defence. When the operations known as the battle of Arras at length petered out in mid-June, German casualties were over 100,000 but British casualties were about 150,000.

In relation to Nivelle's plan Haig did what was chiefly expected of him. Though the British did not reach Cambrai, as Nivelle had hoped, they certainly kept plenty of Germans busy during the crucial period. And the capture of Vimy ridge was a bonus, since it was not part of the original plan, but insisted on by Haig as a means of securing his left flank.

While the British guns were already firing in preparation for the Arras attacks, a strange meeting of French political and military leaders took place, on 6 April, at Compiègne. It was held under the chairmanship of the President of the Republic, Raymond Poincaré, in the drawing-room coach of his presidential train. The conference was his idea, since he was aware of the conflicting views between politicians and generals, and among the generals themselves, and felt that they ought to be resolved before the great French offensive was launched. His own opinion was that Nivelle should receive unqualified backing at such a time, but he acted as an impartial chairman.

Painlevé spoke first (with Ribot's consent), on behalf of the government. While not questioning the Commander-in-Chief's right to conduct operations without intrusion from ministers, he pointed to the new situation created by the German withdrawals, events in Russia, and – now – American entry into the war; and he emphasized the need to conserve French manpower. There should be no repetition of the grim pattern of losses disproportionate to results.

Nivelle, who spoke next, restated the case for his offensive, and renewed the pledge that it would be called off if there was no breakthrough within forty-eight hours. Then his leading subordinates were invited to speak.

4. Erich Ludendorff, *My War Memories, 1914–1918* (2 vols., 1919), vol. ii, p. 421.

Franchet d'Esperey was honest about the difficulties, but concluded that the French part of the joint Allied operation could not be abandoned when the British part had already begun. The two generals known to be most hostile to the plan were Micheler (commander of the reserve group of armies) and Pétain (commander of the central group). Painlevé may have been counting on them to achieve what he could not achieve himself.

If so, he was disappointed; both failed, though in quite different ways. Micheler made a poor showing, creating an impression of shiftiness and equivocation. Pétain was clear enough, but his quiet and deadly critique stung Nivelle into a *coup de théâtre*. Without the confidence of the government or his subordinates, he said, the only course open to him was to resign. Poincaré and the ministers then hastened to reassure him, with the result that he and his plan survived and many thousands of *poilus* were doomed to die.

The conference at Compiègne was a purely French affair. No British ministers or soldiers were invited to attend, though it vitally concerned the future course of what was supposed to be a joint Allied offensive. Haig was asked to the lunch afterwards, but the invitation must have been issued in the confident (and correct) expectation that he would be unwilling to leave his headquarters when an attack was imminent, to travel a long distance for what might be little more than a social occasion. The Compiègne meeting exhibits with brutal clarity the basic flaw in the arrangement promoted at Calais: Nivelle was not a truly Allied leader responsible to Allied politicians, but the French Commander-in-Chief responsible to the French Cabinet. If he had insisted on resigning, or if his offer to resign had been accepted, the British would have been left committed to a major attack while the French part of the offensive was called off. At the conference only d'Esperey seems to have regarded this as a relevant consideration.[5]

Three days later Painlevé was in London for talks with the British government, in particular Lloyd George, who had been receiving confused and worrying accounts from France. Obviously it would have been more appropriate for Painlevé to visit London before the Compiègne meeting; indeed, he should have explained his own and his colleagues' doubts about the

---

5. Spears, *Prelude to Victory*, pp. 356–83. Among participants in the conference, Poincaré and Painlevé left accounts of it, which at some points conflict but which nevertheless provide the best first-hand evidence of what happened. Spears has their accounts to go on, but is able to supplement them, and where necessary suggest corrections to them, in the light of what was said to him by participants emerging from the meeting. Another French-speaking British officer hovering around the conference, without having the right to attend it, was General Henry Wilson, head of the British mission at Nivelle's headquarters.

Nivelle plan before its implementation began with the British bombardment. Lloyd George had reason to feel much aggrieved, and a lesser man might have made a bad situation worse by wrangling about the past. Instead, the Prime Minister looked only to the future, with an air of buoyant optimism that proved infectious.

Painlevé belatedly told Lloyd George of his anxiety about Nivelle, but Lloyd George was able to counter his fears with an argument more powerful than mere words. As they talked on 9 April reports were coming through of the success of British attacks that day, and Painlevé could reflect that if so much was being achieved by action that was only meant to be subsidiary and diversionary, the main part of the offensive – the French part – was bound to succeed. Sadly, this turned out to be a false deduction, but to the mathematician that Painlevé was it must have seemed logical.

Lloyd George took the Frenchman into his confidence about the war at sea, alarming him with the figures of shipping lost to the U-boats, but at the same time convincing him that Britain would overcome the threat. Afterwards Painlevé told Spears that he 'had carried away two main impressions' from his talk with Lloyd George (which lasted until 8 p.m.). He had 'grasped as he had never done before the overwhelming might of British sea power', and he had been much comforted by the assurances given him of 'Great Britain's unshakable resolution'. This was 'exactly the moral tonic he needed', and he told Spears 'how much it had meant to him at that particular time'.[6]

The following morning Painlevé had a meeting with the whole War Cabinet, which reinforced the good effect produced by the Prime Minister, and in the afternoon he conferred with Derby and Robertson at the War Office. That evening (10th) Derby gave a banquet in his honour at Derby House.

Encouraging as the visit was to Painlevé, it was markedly less so to Lloyd George. Though relieved that the French part of the Allied offensive would be going ahead, he was beginning to wonder if it would succeed, or if, after all, he had backed a loser in Nivelle. In her diary entry on the visit Frances Stevenson reflects his mood: 'It appears that the new Fr[ench] Gov[ernment] have their doubts about Nivelle . . . I do hope he will not fail, for D. has backed him up against Haig, & it will rather let D. down if he proves to be a failure.'[7] The uneasiness that the visitor had caused was evidently concealed from him. Painlevé left London, on the 11th, in much better heart than when he arrived.

*

6. Ibid., pp. 439–40.   7. FSD, 10 April 1917.

Lloyd George accompanied him to Folkestone, not as a final gesture of goodwill – which would have been far beyond the demands of protocol or Allied camaraderie – but for a quite different reason. Before Painlevé sailed away (for a meeting with the King of the Belgians at Dunkirk, on his way back to Paris), a ship bearing the French Prime Minister docked at Folkestone. Ribot had come to discuss with Lloyd George a secret matter of which Painlevé as yet knew nothing. The two prime ministers talked during the afternoon for three hours before returning to their respective capitals, and the fact that Ribot (like Nivelle) was fluent in English enabled their discussion to be a confidential tête-à-tête.

The subject that the French premier came to broach with Lloyd George was a peace overture from the new Austrian Emperor, Karl, who had succeeded his aged great-uncle Franz Josef the previous November. Karl was eager to get out of the war, if he could do so on terms favourable to his empire and dynasty. In his innocence, he felt that there might be scope for doing a deal with the French, while ignoring the Italians and largely disregarding the British. His wife, Zita (the stronger character of the two), was Franco-Italian, a princess of Bourbon-Parma, and her brother, Sixte, was well placed to act as an intermediary, since he was serving as a Belgian army officer, having been debarred from the French army by his royal status.

In early March Prince Sixte approached President Poincaré on behalf of his brother-in-law, suggesting terms attractive to the French but without any reference to Italian claims, and with a crudely mischief-making innuendo that the French were seen as mere pawns of the British. For two or three weeks Poincaré and Briand (still Prime Minister) said nothing about Sixte's approach, mainly because it took a form that would be bound to antagonize France's principal ally. But after much toing and froing a letter was written by Karl to Sixte, which both committed him personally (rather than merely by proxy) and was fit for British as well as French eyes. In this letter the Emperor confirmed that he favoured the return of Alsace-Lorraine to France, and would use his influence to bring it about; that he wished to see the complete restoration of Belgium, including colonies, without prejudice to her claim to be compensated for losses; and the re-establishment of a sovereign Serbia, with access to the sea through Albania, subject only to the condition that secret societies threatening the Habsburg Empire must be ruthlessly suppressed. There was no mention of Italy.

Poincaré would have liked Sixte to go to England to expound Karl's proposals to the King and Lloyd George; but Ribot, who had just succeeded Briand, preferred to handle the matter himself. Hence his day trip to Folkestone. At the meeting there, he showed Lloyd George the Emperor's letter, and Lloyd George made a copy of it in his own hand. He responded to the overture with interest, even excitement, having long believed that the Habsburg Empire was the vulnerable part of the enemy structure, whose elimination from the war would knock away the props on which German power rested. Two years previously he had dreamt of mobilizing a Balkan coalition against Austria-Hungary, and at that time the project was certainly worth considering, Serbia being still unconquered and Russia a major force. Even then, however, Lloyd George was apt to underrate the difficulties, political and logistical, that his scheme entailed, while exaggerating the Habsburg Empire's value as a prop to Germany. By 1917 the situation in the Balkans had been transformed to the Allies' disadvantage. Their attempt to force the Straits and occupy Constantinople had been a ghastly failure; Bulgaria had soon afterwards taken sides with the enemy; Serbia had been overrun (though a Serb army was still fighting outside the national territory); Roumania had entered the war on the Allied side, only to be defeated; the Salonica bridgehead remained, but seemingly as little more than a giant internment camp for Allied forces; and, above all, the revolution in Russia had drastically reduced the effectiveness of the Allies' Eastern front.

As for Austria-Hungary, its position was weak enough in 1914, and with every year of the war became weaker. By 1917 it was 'no longer a fully sovereign power, given its dependence on German financial, material and military aid'.[8] Since Bismarck had brutally asserted German supremacy in 1866, the Habsburg Empire had been of dwindling importance. At the turn of the century it was 'slipping out of the ranks of the Great Powers'.[9] In 1914 it allowed itself, fatally, to be pushed into war by Germany, to serve the ends of German aggrandizement. The all-embracing conflict, which many still believe to have been 'caused' by the Archduke's assassination at Sarajevo, was in reality determined by the warlords in Berlin. Austria's quarrel with Serbia would never have led to general war had the Germans not been ready for one and looking for a *casus belli*. In the resulting struggle the Habsburg Empire was heavily engaged on the Eastern front and suffered enormous casualties – 1,200,000 before the end of 1914, and another 800,000 in the first quarter of 1915 – but all to no avail. Only German support saved the Austrians from collapse after the Masurian battle in early 1915, which left them 'at their last gasp'.[10] When Italian intervention forced them to fight on another front, German stiffening was needed from the first;

8. Holger H. Herwig, *The First World War: Germany and Austria-Hungary 1914–1917* (1997), p. 317.   9. A. J. P. Taylor, *The Struggle for Mastery in Europe* (1954), p. xxviii.
10. John Keegan, *The First World War* (1998), p. 187.

and in 1916 they depended on German help for conquering Serbia, for holding Brusilov's Russian offensive, and for dealing with Roumania. Far from acting as a prop to Germany, the Habsburg Empire had to be propped up by Germany, and was therefore incapable of acting independently, whether for peace or war.

Lloyd George nevertheless felt that the overture from Karl was well worth pursuing, and turned his mind to it eagerly. The evening he returned from Folkestone he had to prepare his speech for the American Luncheon Club, but the following day, after delivering it, he drove down to Windsor to discuss Karl's letter with the King. Six days later he was travelling to an Alpine destination at which he and Ribot were to meet the Italian Prime Minister (still Boselli) and Foreign Minister (still Baron Sonnino). He had persuaded Ribot that something had to be said to the Italians; but, since both Sixte and Poincaré felt it would be dangerous to show them, or even to mention, the Emperor's letter, the meeting was arranged ostensibly to confer about other matters, but with the intention of raising possible peace terms for Austria as a hypothetical question, without any suggestion that there had been an actual overture.

Lloyd George crossed the Channel – a rough crossing – on 18 April, arriving in Paris at 6 p.m. He then had an interview with Painlevé, and a highly secret meeting with Sixte, before joining Ribot on a night train to Saint-Jean de Maurienne, a small town near the French end of the Mont Cenis tunnel, where the Italians arrived for the conference the following morning. At his meeting with Sixte, Lloyd George made a last attempt to persuade the Prince to allow him to come clean with the Italians about the overture, but without success. He claims, however, to have stressed the necessity for Italian agreement to any peace terms that might be negotiated.[11] Before catching the train he told Hankey about the Sixte affair, because he felt that in case of an accident to himself another British person ought to share the secret.[12] (He clearly discounted the risk that both of them might be killed if the train crashed, which was anyway a much rarer occurrence then than now.)

At Saint-Jean de Maurienne, still under snow, the Allied leaders talked through the day (19 April) in a railway carriage. When the subject of peace terms with Austria was brought up in a roundabout way, Sonnino expressed

11. WM, pp. 2003–4.

12. Hankey diary, 18 April 1917. On the French side the Ambassador in London, Paul Cambon, and his brother, Jules, were privy to the secret. Spears, too, claims to have known 'all about' the overture and resultant discussions, though he does not say how he came by the information (Spears, *Prelude to Victory*, p. 450).

strong opposition to any idea of a separate peace. Italy had gone to war to achieve certain objectives – the Trentino, Trieste and the Dalmatian coast, as well as territory in Asia Minor and some addition to her colonial empire.[13] These aims would be realized only if and when the Central Powers were comprehensively defeated. Any hint of willingness to settle for less would be a betrayal of Italy's dead, and might lead to revolution in the country. Lloyd George seems to have been quite rough with him, arguing that the Italians expected vast rewards though they were doing nothing more than defend their own country.[14] According to Frances Stevenson, reporting what he told her on his return, he even issued a threat that the British and French could make peace with Austria '*tomorrow*' (her italics).[15] But Sonnino would not budge, and his words carried weight because it was he, above all, who had brought Italy into the war. At that time the Austrians had been forced by the Germans to offer the Trentino as the price for Italian neutrality (further evidence of their subjection to Germany). But Sonnino had persuaded his colleagues to reject the offer and to enter the war on the Entente side, with far more ambitious aims. Obviously he could not contemplate peace on terms remotely resembling those that had been available before hundreds of thousands of Italians had been killed or wounded in battle.[16]

The conference at Saint-Jean de Maurienne ended with acceptance of a formula that suited Sonnino. The Allied leaders 'reached an agreement that it would not be opportune to enter on a conversation which, in present circumstances, would be particularly dangerous and would risk weakening the close unity that exists between the Allies and is more than ever necessary'.[17] This

---

13. In the secret treaty of London (April 1915), under which Italy entered the war, the Italians 'were so eager to define their Adriatic terms precisely that they accepted vague, and ultimately unprofitable, phrases in regard to colonies and the Near East' (Taylor, *Struggle for Mastery*, pp. 546–7).   14. Hankey diary, 19 April 1917.

15. FSD, 23 April 1917. Lloyd George is silent about this threat in his memoirs.

16. By early 1917 the Italians had already suffered well over a million casualties, including nearly 400,000 killed. Their losses were not much less heavy than those of Great Britain (as distinct from the British Empire as a whole), and for the time that they had been in the war probably heavier.

17. WM, p. 2006. Absent from the Saint-Jean de Maurienne formula was any agreement to give Italy part of south-eastern Anatolia, including Smyrna, if and when the Ottoman Empire was dismembered. An offer to this effect seems to have been made by Lloyd George to Sonnino during the conference, in the hope that it would make him more inclined to contemplate a separate peace with Austria. Sonnino accepted the offer, but without the hoped-for response. In any case Ribot seems not to have been a party to the offer, though he may not expressly have dissociated himself from it. The so-called 'agreement of Saint-Jean de Maurienne' is, therefore, mythical so far as Smyrna is concerned. Several months later (in August) an agreement on the

formula was put forward by Ribot. Though secret talks about peace with Austria continued for another two months or so, and Sixte was in England for a time in late May and early June, for all practical purposes the project was killed at Saint-Jean de Maurienne. The French soon lost interest in it, for two good reasons. From their point of view, the most attractive feature of it was the proposed return of Alsace-Lorraine, but the Austrians were in no position to give effect to this. It was not they who were occupying Alsace-Lorraine, but the Germans, who had no intention whatever of returning the annexed provinces. All that Karl could offer was his influence with the rulers of Germany, which was, in fact, zero. The French could also see that a settlement with Austria that would satisfy Italy would be a serious threat to France, since it would deprive most Italians of their primary motive for staying in the war. Sonnino might want his compatriots to keep fighting for more far-flung spoils, but most of them would be content with the territories that they hoped to gain at Austria's expense. Italy had gone to war, in the first instance, with the Habsburg Empire alone; it was not until August 1916 that she declared war on Germany. Austria was Italy's chief enemy, and if Austria were prepared to make peace on terms acceptable to the majority of Italians the latter's warlike zeal would soon evaporate.

In fact, the Austrians were not prepared to concede even minimal Italian demands. Behind Sonnino's back, General Cadorna and some Italian politicians, uneasy about the state of army morale, were approaching the enemy with an offer of peace in return for nothing more than the Trentino. One has to say 'the enemy' rather than 'the Austrians' because the emissary went first to the German minister in Berne, which shows that those who sent him had no illusions about Austrian independence. In any case the Austrians replied, presumably with German approval, that the Trentino would be conceded only in return for substantial compensation, in the form of territory in Greece or in Italy's African colonies. This was too little even for Italian peacemongers, and Sonnino's strong policy was not undermined. Italy stayed in the war, nervously and without enthusiasm, but still in the hope of doing well out of a general Allied victory.

Lloyd George had a wildly exaggerated idea of what could be achieved by a separate peace with Austria in 1917. In his memoirs he suggests that such a peace would have made up 'tenfold' for the defection of Italy. Millions of Austrian troops would have been withdrawn from the war; Turkey and

---

partition of Anatolia *was* reached between Britain, France and Italy, but subject to Russian assent – which, after the Bolshevik Revolution, provided a plausible excuse for treating it as invalid at the Peace Conference.

Bulgaria would have been 'cut off from Germany and forced to make terms'; Austrian submarines would have ceased to operate in the Mediterranean; Allied armies in Salonica, Egypt, Palestine and Mesopotamia could have been 'reduced to garrisons'; the 'corn of Russia and the Danube' could have been brought to France, while 'food, petroleum and other supplies' of the Habsburg Empire and Roumania would have been 'withheld from Germany'; and Prussian militarism, 'deserted by all its allies, and opposed by the most powerful nations in the world', would have been 'forced into a position of foredoomed defeat'.[18] This euphoric projection of events ignored the reality of German power. Even if it had been possible for Austria to escape from its condition of thraldom, the Germans would not have allowed it to happen. They would have moved at once into the vacuum, at the very least to prevent any breach between themselves and their allies to the east. It was quite unrealistic to imagine that they would allow themselves to be cut off from Bulgaria or the Ottoman Empire. The Saint-Jean de Maurienne meeting and other clandestine activity resulting from the Austrian overture was all, essentially, a waste of time.

When Lloyd George boarded the night train from Paris on 18 April he had just received the most profoundly disheartening news. At his meeting with Painlevé, the French War Minister told him that Nivelle's offensive had, in its own terms, failed. The attacks had begun on the 16th, and after forty-eight hours of desperate fighting, involving very heavy casualties, there had been no breakthrough.

We have seen how protracted and controversial was the process leading to the offensive. The change in the high command, whereby Nivelle replaced Joffre, itself caused delay, compared with the strategy agreed on by the Allies at the end of the previous year. Further delay was caused by arguments with Haig over transport behind the front and the lengthening of the British line. Then there was the Calais imbroglio and all the trouble it created. Meanwhile the Germans decided to withdraw to the Hindenburg line, and were allowed to carry out the manœuvre unmolested. Nivelle's critics in the higher ranks of the army were becoming ever more numerous and more vocal, as were his political critics. Within weeks of his offensive the Prime Minister who had appointed and backed him resigned, and he had to deal instead with a Prime Minister, and more especially a War Minister, who had no faith in his plan. When the Allied operation had already begun the French part of it came near to being aborted at the Compiègne meeting.

18. *WM*, p. 2028.

There was always too much talk about Nivelle's intentions. As Churchill neatly puts it, the General's 'preparations for surprise continued to rivet the attention of the enemy'.[19] From the first he and his staff spoke with culpable freedom about the operation they were planning, whose main features thus became a *secret de Polichinelle*. The Germans had long warning of the sector in which it would take place, and so were given plenty of time to prepare for it. To compound this general lack of security (so different from the hush-hush atmosphere surrounding the Austrian peace overture), an order was captured by the Germans in mid-February showing that the French would attack on the Aisne in April, and only twelve days before the attack a French NCO was taken prisoner with a document indicating precise corps objectives.

The long-awaited French onslaught on the 16th had to be carried out in the same atrocious weather that the British had experienced when the Arras battle was launched. But it was not sleet and snow that made the attackers' task hopeless, but rather the depth of the German defences. Too great a distance had to be covered, against an enemy who was well prepared and insufficiently hurt by the preliminary bombardment. Even so, gains were made that would have seemed remarkable and gratifying if expectations had been less high. On the first day the ridge of the Chemin-des-Dames was reached at several points and on the right of the Aisne front there was also a substantial advance. But on the Chemin-des-Dames it proved impossible to penetrate the defences of the reverse slope, while the other advance was soon checked. Before long some of the ground gained at heavy cost was having to be surrendered. The same pattern was repeated in the attacks to the east of Rheims, which began on the 17th: a pattern of initial progress that could not be sustained. Altogether, the great victory that had been promised failed to materialize. The battle seemed to be just another typical Western front operation, with gains pathetically modest in relation to the human toll. By early May 270,000 French soldiers had been killed, as the price of a few miles gained. Enemy losses were heavy too, but less so; and above all the German defences, though dented, were not broken.

The continuance of the fighting into May shows that the idea of a forty-eight-hour offensive, which would be stopped if a breakthrough were not achieved within that time, was abandoned. The idea was never practical; operations on such a scale cannot be ended so abruptly without the risk of worse disaster. Nivelle did not make good on his pledge to resign at once if his plan failed, but his authority and credibility were destroyed and it was

19. *The World Crisis*, p. 719 (single-volume edition, 1931).

only a matter of time before he was removed. On 29 April Painlevé appointed Pétain as his Chief of Staff at the War Ministry. On 15 May Nivelle was sacked, and Pétain then took his place as Commander-in-Chief, with Foch (who had been in limbo since the battle of the Somme) as his Chief of Staff.

The supreme casualty of the Nivelle offensive was French army morale. In early May the first case of mutiny occurred, when a division was ordered into the line and the other ranks refused, at first, to march. In that case the officers managed to restore discipline, but soon there were comparable incidents of varying magnitude in no fewer than sixteen army corps. Since 1914 French soldiers had been carrying the heaviest burden in the West, and had suffered more than other combatants there, Allied or enemy. Though France was a slightly less populous country than Great Britain, the French had lost in battle nearly twice as many men as the British. They had also lost more, in proportion to their numbers, than the Germans. The *poilus* had other grievances as well. Their food and drink in the line was 'monotonous, at best', and accommodation when they were resting behind the lines was 'often wretched'. Leave was always irregular and, because of delays to the offensive, had been stopped since February.[20] The attitude of most of those who mutinied was that they were as willing as ever to go into the trenches to defend the country, but not to have their lives sacrificed in apparently futile attacks.

This was an attitude with which the new Commander-in-Chief had much sympathy. Pétain's temperament was defensive and pessimistic. From the obscurity of a colonel about to go into retirement in 1914, he had risen to fame and glory as commander of the Second Army defending Verdun. His observation of the war told him that the defence, on one side or the other, had so far had the upper hand, and he felt that the French army had taken more than its fair share of punishment in attempts to defeat the Germans by offensive action. He was therefore convinced that French strategy in 1917 should be to stand firm and wait for the Americans. It was on this principle that he had opposed the Nivelle plan, and the same principle guided him when he was given the task of repairing the effects of Nivelle's failure. He handled the mutinies with a judicious blend of firmness and compassion. Only a hundred and fifty death sentences were passed, of which about fifty were carried out. Meanwhile every effort was made to improve the conditions in which ordinary soldiers had to serve, and to organize leave and rest periods more efficiently and equitably. In addition, Pétain made it his business to visit units throughout the army, including those in which

20. Denis Brogan, *The Development of Modern France* (1940), p. 497.

there had been trouble, and to speak directly to the troops. He exercised a 'magic of natural authority allied to true affection', and so established a reputation unlike that of any other warlord – which was to be tragically abused in the greater crisis of 1940.[21]

Mercifully, no word of the French army mutinies reached the Germans until July, by which time the situation was completely under control. The British high command had some inkling of what was happening in May, but preferred to keep the politicians in ignorance. Lloyd George knew nothing about the mutinies until some time later. Nevertheless he was well aware of the need to boost French morale – an awareness he had shown when Painlevé visited London before the attack, and which he had reason to feel more acutely after its failure. On his way back from Saint-Jean de Maurienne he obtained an assurance from the French that they would continue their attacks to enable Haig's army to make the most of its success in the Arras sector. This was, of course, an inversion of the original plan, under which the French were to have achieved a decisive victory while the British provided a subsidiary covering operation. Lloyd George was now asking the French at least to keep up enough pressure on their front to help the British to exploit their success. In fact, Haig's advance was held up; his chance of a breakthrough had been missed. But even if Lloyd George had fully understood the state of affairs on the Arras front, he would have regarded a continuation of Haig's attacks there as a welcome means of deflecting his thoughts from the dreaded Flanders project.

Lloyd George was back in Paris again on 4 May, for the purpose (as Hankey records) of trying 'to ginger up the French' at a time when 'they were very down on their luck about their heavy losses and depleted reserves'. On arrival he immediately sent 'scouts' out to discover all the political gossip.[22] One of these was Lord Esher who, after lunching with him at the Crillon, wrote to his hero Haig: 'He has entirely changed his point of view as to the respective merits of the chiefs of the Allied army, their staffs, and powers of offence. For the moment I do not think *you* could do wrong.'[23] Esher felt that Lloyd George's 'instability of vision' was a danger when combined with 'his tremendous vitality and indestructible spirit'. But Esher also found him 'amazingly alert', and capable of 'laughing at jokes made at

---

21. Jacques Chastenet, *Histoire de la Troisième République* (7 vols., 1952–63), vol. iv, p. 291.

As a small example of Pétain's prestige in France after the Great War, the present author can remember going to a play in Paris during the 1930s and an announcement being made, before the curtain rose, that Pétain's *wife* – 'Madame la Maréchale Pétain' – was in the theatre. The whole audience rose and turned towards the little figure in the stalls, cheering fervently. 22. Hankey diary, 4 May 1917. 23. Esher to Haig, 4 May 1917.

his expense'.[24] Before returning to London Lloyd George visited Haig at his headquarters at Arras and the Field-Marshal noted that he was 'particularly pleased with his visit to Paris', feeling that he had encouraged the French and 'got them to do what he wanted'. Haig also noted, with exclamation marks, that Lloyd George had 'heartily congratulated' him on the success of his operations.[25] (Lloyd George spent the night with 'the thunder of the guns' in his ears, and experienced 'a near miss from a bomb').[26]

In fact, the Prime Minister's view had not changed, except in recognizing that he had made a disastrous mistake about Nivelle. Before attending the Allied conference in Paris the War Cabinet had instructed him to 'press the French to continue the offensive'. Though 'his heart was not in this assignment', he 'had no choice but to support his generals', because 'he could not afford another Calais'. He also realized that, 'at this critical moment in the war, it might be dangerous to support any slackening of the Allied effort because an almost irresistible momentum for a compromise peace . . . might be the result'.[27] A further consideration, as suggested, was that Arras was at least preferable to Flanders. But any victory he may have scored in Paris was short-lived. Though Nivelle attended the conference, still as Commander-in-Chief, his days were numbered, as were the days of the offensive that he had planned and launched. Pétain was in the ascendant, and his alternative strategy would soon prevail.

Three days before Nivelle's formal removal, Frances Stevenson wrote in her diary:

Nivelle has fallen into disgrace, & let D. down badly after the way D. had backed him up at the beginning of the year. Sir Douglas Haig has come out on top in this fight between the two Chiefs, & I fear D. will have to be very careful in future as to his backings of the French against the English. However D. appears to take it as the fortunes of war, and has accepted his defeat cheerfully, though he was very sick as it gradually became apparent that the French were failing hopelessly in the offensive.[28]

It was surely unfair to put so much blame on a man who was over-promoted, not least by Lloyd George. Some pity should be spared for Nivelle. He ought never to have been appointed Commander-in-Chief, and still less Allied supremo while retaining the French command. If Joffre's original plan had

24. James Lees-Milne, *The Enigmatic Edwardian: The Life of Reginald 2nd Viscount Esher* (1986), p. 301.   25. Haig diary, 6 May 1917.
26. Stephen Roskill, *Hankey: Man of Secrets* (3 vols., 1970–74), vol. i, p. 387. On his way to Arras Lloyd George and his party visited the cathedrals at Beauvais and Amiens.
27. Woodward, *Lloyd George and the Generals*, p. 163.   28. FSD, 12 May 1917.

gone ahead, very early in the year, with Nivelle as field commander under his control, it is just possible that a great victory might have been won. The Germans were still suffering from their recent hammering in the Somme battle – which, though they had held most of their ground, was immensely costly to them – and they were still vulnerable in their salient. In that case, Nivelle might have added to his Verdun reputation and ended the war as one of France's most acclaimed leaders.

Instead he was appointed to take Joffre's place, and the very timing of his appointment prejudiced his chances of success, since it caused delay when speed was of the essence. Besides, he could never inherit Joffre's unique prestige, deriving from the Marne victory, nor was he as well equipped as Joffre, in temperament or judgement, for the highest position of responsibility. At such an altitude he felt insecure, and his sense of insecurity brought out, and aggravated, his defects. He became arrogant and high-handed, and so antagonized not only Haig but many of his own compatriots, civil and military. (Indeed, he was eventually in the strange position of being supported by Haig while his fellow countrymen were turning against him.) He lacked the flexibility of mind to adapt himself either to the German withdrawal or to the change of government in France. He linked his fate to outright victory within a short and specified period of time, and stuck to this commitment regardless of altered circumstances.

After his dismissal he was given a command in North Africa, and during the remainder of the war he had to watch from afar the triumph and apotheosis of other generals, some responsible for more costly offensives than his. For him, there was no marshal's baton; no streets, squares or avenues bear his name. Briefly, he was the most conspicuous military figure in the Western world, but when he died – in 1924 – even France hardly noticed. Lloyd George, after initial reluctance, had endorsed both the man himself and his plan to an excessive degree and in an inappropriate manner. It was poetic justice that he was in part a victim of Nivelle's nemesis, though many innocent, unknown warriors paid a far higher price.

7

Electoral Reform and Industrial Unrest

Curious pact – Guildhall speech – Electoral reform –
May strikes

The entry in Frances Stevenson's diary for 23 April 1917 contains one of its strangest passages:

We went down to Walton H[eath] on Saturday afternoon [21 April] & had a perfect weekend. I do not think we have ever loved each other so much. D. says that ours is a love that comes to very few people and I wonder more & more at the beauty and happiness of it. It is a thing that nothing but death can harm, and even death has no terrors for me now, for D. asked me yesterday if I would come with him when he went. He begged me not to stay behind, but for both of us to go together, and I promised him to do so, unless I have any children of his to claim me. So, I am not now afraid of the misery if D. is taken away, for then I shall go too & his end will be my end, and until then everything is happiness, if our love stays. I hope by any chance I shall not go first, for I know his misery would be great, and he could not leave his work, which is a great one. I am so happy now that we have decided this, for sometimes my heart would stop beating with terror at the thought of life without D.

The circumstances of this one-sided *Liebestod* pact should be noted. Lloyd George had just returned from his excursion to Paris and Saint-Jean de Maurienne, on which he had heard of the failure of the Nivelle offensive. His own hopes for the year's Western front strategy were severely damaged, probably ruined. The war at sea was in its most critical phase. The chance of a peace with Austria-Hungary seemed elusive. Beyond question the pressure on him was very great, and due allowance should be made for his tortured state of mind.

All the same, it is hard to understand how he can have made such a request of a woman young enough to be his daughter, for whom he believed himself to have a deep love. He had insisted from the first that their relationship had to be on his terms, and had demonstrated that this could involve a brutal disregard for her interests and feelings. So long as Margaret lived, Frances could not become his wife, since divorce would put an end to his career, given the public mores of the time. (In fact, he had no desire to be divorced from Margaret anyway, though he pretended otherwise to Frances.) Evidence suggests that she aborted a child at the beginning of 1915, and long afterwards she told her daughter Jennifer that she had had two abortions during her early years as Lloyd George's mistress. In 1915–16 he tried to arrange for her to be married to a complaisant husband, which would have made her status less equivocal and his own relations with her in some ways easier. Much as she hated the idea, she agreed for a time to contemplate formal marriage to the man of his choice (Captain Hugh Owen), who was prepared to act as her slave as well as his. But by 1917 the project had lapsed.[1]

Now he was asking her to take her own life in the event of his death – to throw herself, as it were, upon his funeral pyre. In the nature of things he was likely to die long before she did (she was born the year he married), and it was quite possible that he might die soon, because war travel was dangerous, as Kitchener's fate had shown. Indeed, on his recent return journey from Paris Lloyd George had been lucky to avoid a clash with enemy destroyers in the Channel.[2] The pledge that she gave might have to be acted upon at any time. It was bad enough to have asked her to forgo the experience of marriage and motherhood, but to ask her now to promise to make the supreme sacrifice – while, as could be expected, in the fullness of health and strength – was obviously far worse. There was, moreover, no reciprocal pledge on his part. If she were to die, it was understood that he would not leave the world with her, because 'he could not leave his work'.

Even allowing for his fraught mental state, one can only be appalled that it ever occurred to him to make such a proposition. He had been spoilt since his childhood, and retained much of the character of a spoilt child. He had the driving egotism so often seen in major creative artists, and his temperament was always that of a demanding taskmaster. At the same time he differed from many great men in being genuinely interested in ordinary people, and in being sensitive to the feelings of others. He was on the whole good-natured and affectionate; though capable of cruelty, he was certainly

---

1. For a detailed account of her probable abortion in 1915, and of the proposed mock-marriage to Owen, see my *Lloyd George: From Peace to War* (1985), pp. 221–6 and 395–400.

2. 'he ought, upon an ordinary calculation, to have returned by the midnight tide on Friday night, & there were 5 destroyers waiting to catch him in the Straits. The boat that he should have crossed on, & one other, attacked them, & accounted for three. But fortunately D. elected to cross by day on Saturday, & so avoided them' (FSD, 23 April 1917).

not a cold man. How can he have brought himself to make such a barbaric demand, particularly of a person so close to him, who was also so young?

Jealousy may have been the key factor. In the biblical sense he was a jealous god; intensely possessive, and unwilling to let go of anyone or anything that belonged to him. In that sense he had been jealous even of the weak and inoffensive Hugh Owen, while promoting him as a husband for Frances and a respectable cover for his own affair with her. At one stage he was 'making himself miserable about the idea of [her] belonging to someone else even in name'; several times he 'cried & sobbed as a child when speaking of it'.[3] If such could be his attitude to an arrangement designed by himself for his own convenience, in which he would have been not only alive but effectively in control, we can well imagine how abhorrent it must have been to him to think of Frances being possessed, and not only in name, by another man after his death. He may also have been jealous in the sense of wondering if he could continue to hold her, or if one day she would succumb to the charms of a younger man. Though she gave him little enough cause to doubt her absolute devotion to him, he may all the same have felt that he could not take her entirely for granted.

There was, in fact, an admirer on the horizon, who had far more to offer than poor Owen, and who, though older than Frances, was fifteen years younger than Lloyd George. Colonel Albert Stern was lively, intelligent and rich. He came from a Jewish family, comfortably established, and was educated at Eton and Christ Church. Before the war he was a banker, but in the war he showed outstanding ability on the technical side, playing an important part in the evolution of tanks. He worked under Lloyd George at the Ministry of Munitions, and by 1917 was head of its mechanical warfare department. (He was knighted in 1918.)

The references to him in Frances's diary are intriguing. He clearly knows all about the relationship between her and Lloyd George, and quite often entertains them together, though with others present. We can sense that she is attracted to him, and he to her. In November 1916 he asks her and J. T. Davies to a dinner and concert party, and she sees a side of him that excites her – the ' "Bertie Stern" of the Smart Set'. She likes the 'glitter & light', while professing to be glad that she does not 'go *home* to it'. Stern is 'one of the least frivolous' members of the set, 'though he seems to have a considerable reputation!'[4] The weekend before that of the suicide pledge she stays, with a woman friend, at Stern's house on the south coast – 'right

3. FSD, 5 October 1915 – a passage that does not appear in the printed version.
4. FSD, 15 November 1916.

on top of the Downs, with a beautiful garden, & inside every comfort one can desire'. Lloyd George is visiting the Grand Fleet, and Stern is away in France. But a rumour has reached her: 'Mamma told me that she had heard that I should marry Colonel Stern. Was nevermore surprised in my life.'[5]

Lloyd George's antennae must have alerted him to the situation developing between her and Stern, and if she told him about her visit to his house only the week before – as she probably did – his jealousy may well have been sharpened, even though Stern was not there. There was never any danger that Stern would make a move while Lloyd George was alive and in power; Lloyd George must have known that. But what if he were to die? And what, meanwhile, were her feelings for Stern? These questions may have been in his mind when he asked her to promise to go with him. He may have been testing her, as Jehovah tested Abraham. She proved her fidelity to the extent of giving the pledge, but he was less merciful than Jehovah in not immediately releasing her from it once her fidelity was proved.

Stern was still around two years later, and there is clear evidence that by then the pledge was for practical purposes forgotten. There is no further reference to it in her diary, and she does not mention it in her autobiography.[6] It was never, in any case, quite unconditional, but was to apply only if there were no 'children of his' to claim her attention. In 1929 she gave birth to Jennifer, whom Lloyd George accepted privately as his child. Thereafter the pledge, even if remembered, could be treated as null and void. When Lloyd George died in 1945 Frances did not take her life (as some members of his family might have wished) but lived on for a period longer than the difference in their ages, dying in 1972.

Soon after the weekend of the pact, on 27 April, Lloyd George went to Guildhall to receive the freedom of the City of London, one of the ultimate marks of worldly acceptance in Britain. He used the occasion to make a wide-ranging speech, to which many responded at the time with enthusiasm, but which also provoked some strong criticism – Asquith, for one, describing it as 'singularly impudent & mendacious'.[7] In retrospect it cannot, certainly, be regarded as one of his best, though it had its good points.

He began by observing that he was not the first Welshman to receive the honour, since Dr Richard Price had received it for protesting against the

5. FSD, 14 April 1917.
6. Frances Lloyd George, *The Years that Are Past* (1967). There is also no mention of it in her granddaughter's life of her (Ruth Longford, *Frances, Countess Lloyd George: More than a Mistress* (1996)).   7. Asquith to Sylvia Henley, 1 May 1917.

oppression of the American colonies.[8] In the month of America's entry into the war this was an apt historical allusion. But his method of dealing with recent operations on the Western front was altogether less apt. Of course, he could not be expected to say that the Nivelle offensive had failed; in that respect, he had to be mendacious, or anyway misleading. But he should have said something about the French, instead of more or less ignoring them; and in his remarks about the British attack he should not have singled out General French, who had nothing to do with it, for laudatory mention.

We can guess at his reason for doing so. He must have wanted to praise the troops and, implicitly, his own achievements at the Ministry of Munitions, while giving no praise at all to Haig or any of the senior commanders under him. To loud cheers, he said:

The way in which the British infantry stood the guns of Napoleon for one day is one of the epics of military history. Their descendants stood greater guns, for days and nights and weeks and months, and never flinched.

The nation's gratitude should go 'for ever' to the troops, and it should also go to

that brave little man who led them through all those trying months under very great difficulties, and was never beaten, and never lost heart – Lord French. [*No cheers are recorded at this point.*]

Now the army had the guns and ammunition that it needed, and so was able to win battles. He could see a new pattern emerging, in which victory was assured and would be gained 'at less cost'.

This statement must have haunted him later in the year. As for his failure to give any credit to Haig – which must have puzzled many present, and angered some – he had to make amends for it when he visited France in early May. Hence his fulsome references to Haig in his conversation with Esher, and his ingratiating demeanour at Haig's headquarters.

On the war at sea and measures to defeat the U-boat blockade he had a better story to tell and told it quite straightforwardly, though with necessary reticence. (He did not, for instance, mention the subject of the convoys, since he was speaking three days before his visit to the Admiralty, and anyway the subject was not one to advertise.) He went too far in saying that

8. Price is perhaps better known for his warm welcome to the French Revolution, which infuriated Edmund Burke and prompted him to write his *Reflections*.

the Germans had been driven to 'black piracy on the high seas' because they knew they were beaten on land. The truth was that they had decided there was a better chance of winning the war quickly by indiscriminate submarine warfare than by massive land attacks, in which the advantage seemed always to lie with the defence. This was not the same as knowing that they were beaten on land. Moreover, their view on mass attacks was shared by Lloyd George, though he could hardly state it, since it obviously cut both ways. It would also be seen to conflict with what he had said about the new pattern of Allied land warfare leading (as he claimed) to inevitable victory at lower cost. By contrast with his silence on Haig, he paid a generous compliment to Maclay.

There was a strong passage in the speech on 'that great commonwealth of nations which is known as the British Empire'. The meetings with Dominion leaders then in progress did not involve merely carrying resolutions, but gave them 'a real share in our councils, and in our decisions'. They had been 'a great source of strength and wisdom'. Orthodox Free Traders present must have winced when he announced that the principle of Imperial Preference had just been agreed.[9]

He spoke with special emphasis about Ireland and India. Ireland, he said, must be converted 'from a suspicious, surly, dangerous neighbour to a cheerful, loyal comrade' (this remark was cheered). He warned that failure to achieve a settlement in Ireland would have dangerous repercussions in America, Australia and elsewhere, as he knew from facts being borne in on him 'every hour'. Of the Indians he said that 'these loyal myriads should feel, not as if they were a subject race in the Empire, but as partner nations'. (Speaking in the presence of the Maharaja of Bikaner he could refer to Indians as a race but not as a single nation, since he had to take account of the princely states – that, presumably, explains his wording.) Both questions, Ireland and India, required 'bold statesmanship'.

The most striking feature of the speech was Lloyd George's suggestion that British politics would never be the same again – that the non-party spirit prevalent in the war might carry over into the peace:

We are a thousand years older and wiser. The experience of generations has been crowded into just a few winters, and we should indeed be unworthy of the great destiny to which Providence has called this generation of men if we threw all that away for the sake of any formulas that were framed before the Flood.

9. It was agreed, as a 'principle' rather than as a 'system', at the meeting of the Imperial War Cabinet on 26 April 1917. Lloyd George had stipulated that 'it should be made clear that we were not actually committed to taxes on food' (Amery diary, 26 April 1917).

Though in his short speech at the Mansion House lunch which followed the ceremony in Guildhall he seemed to admit that party politics were necessary to 'any system of democracy', the clear purport of his earlier remarks was that a different system might and should emerge after the war.[10]

In one vital respect he had already missed a supreme opportunity to change the political system, and the consequences were to prove disastrous for him later. At the end of January he had received the report of the conference on electoral reform, set up before he became Prime Minister under the chairmanship of the Speaker of the House of Commons, James Lowther. The conference embraced Parliamentarians of every shade of opinion, from right to left, and the radical tenor of its recommendations was, therefore, all the more astonishing.[11] Lowther, himself a moderate Conservative, was a superb chairman, but even he could not have secured the result he did at any other time. For a brief moment it could almost be said that none was for a party, all for the state; and the conference reflected the national mood. As one historian writes:

In the third bitter winter of trench warfare this group of thirty-two middle-aged and elderly politicians found in the conference one of the few ways open to them of making a personal contribution to the cause of national unity; at the least they were sparing the Lloyd George government a disruptive distraction from the war, and at best they might conjure all-party unity out of a dismal and perennial controversy.[12]

The most important recommendations concerned reform of the franchise and the system of voting. The conference decided unanimously in favour of extending the vote to virtually all adult males (compared with the existing barely 60 per cent), and by a majority for granting 'some measure of woman suffrage' (the suggested qualifying age for women to be thirty or thirty-five). But the most remarkable proposals of all envisaged a drastic departure from the first-past-the-post system of election. In single-member constituencies, where more than two candidates were standing, election should, it was proposed, be by the alternative vote system (AV); and in multi-member urban

10. *The Times*, 28 April 1917. Perhaps he was got at by some anxious colleagues on his way to the lunch.
11. Its membership ranged from arch-Conservatives such as Henry Page Croft to the left-wing Liberal Ellis Davies and the Labour Stephen Walsh. Prominent figures on it included T. P. O'Connor and Sir John Simon; and, among peers, Lord Bryce and Lord (Herbert) Gladstone. Lord Salisbury was an original member, but withdrew in December 1916. The conference had twenty-six sittings, and reported the day after its last sitting, on 27 January 1917.
12. Martin Pugh, *Electoral Reform in War and Peace, 1916–18* (1978), pp. 75–6.

constituencies – which were to be enlarged to conurbation size for the purpose – election should be by the single-transferable-vote proportional method (STV). The first of these proposals was, like that of women's suffrage, supported by a majority of the conference; the second was unanimous.

It was widely felt that all the report's recommendations should be treated as an indivisible package; what would nowadays be called a historic compromise. This was very much the view of the Colonial Secretary, Walter Long, squirearchical Tory and former candidate for the party leadership, who advised his colleagues to 'take advantage of an opportunity which may never recur and decide to legislate on the lines of the report'.[13] Though a fair number of Tory MPs did not agree with him, among those who did were three who really mattered, Law, Balfour and Austen Chamberlain. Their combined authority was likely to prevail with most Conservatives.

The initiative, however, lay with Lloyd George, who was not only head of the government but also the politician who seemed to represent, in a unique degree, the patriotic and progressive spirit of the hour. If he had acted at once, as Long advised, proposing to the Cabinet that a government bill should be introduced without delay to give effect to all the recommendations, the whole package would probably have gone through with relative ease. But he hesitated, partly because he knew that a Parliamentary reform bill would deny him the chance of holding a snap election on the old register – an option that he was reluctant to lose.[14] For two months, therefore, the report was in the public domain (because it was decided to publish it at once), but without any pledge of action by the government or even a Parliamentary debate.

Eventually, at the end of March, a debate was held on a resolution, moved by Asquith, calling on the government to implement the report. Lloyd George, making one of his infrequent Commons appearances, intervened in the debate – saying that he had little time for preparing speeches, so he hoped the House would allow him to 'indulge in a little plain talk'. He argued broadly in favour of Asquith's resolution, but went out of his way to discredit proportional representation (PR):

I do not put the proposals about proportional representation in quite the same category as the others. I express no personal opinion upon it . . . I never made up my

13. Memorandum for the Cabinet, 2 February 1917.
14. Talking to C. P. Scott the day after receiving the report, he said that the government would introduce a bill but that if it were carried 'he would be morally estopped from dissolving till it came into operation, which would take some time'. Clearly he was in two minds, at any rate about the need for urgency (Scott diary, 28 January 1917).

mind, and I really have no time to make up my mind upon it. Unless I am really forced to do so, I do not propose even to study it during the War. It is an entirely novel suggestion; it is not an essential part of the scheme. I think that the feeling of the members of Mr. Speaker's conference . . . is that they would not imperil the rest of their plan by pressing this. . . . The common sense they have shown generally in their conclusions proves to me that they are sensible enough not to press this at the expense of the whole of their scheme, and I earnestly trust that it will not be regarded as an integral part of the proposals, because if it is it will undoubtedly make it much more difficult for the government to find the necessary time to carry this into effect.

Thus he dismissed one of the conference's unanimous recommendations, and in so doing showed that the package was not to be treated as an integral whole. He did not distinguish between STV and AV, and said nothing about the proposed application of the latter (a majority recommendation) to single-member seats. Yet to another majority recommendation – that the vote should be extended to women – he gave the strongest support consistent with leaving it to a free vote of the House. To deny women a voice in the future would be 'an outrage . . . ungrateful, unjust, inequitable', and he had 'not the faintest doubt' what the decision of the House would be.[15]

The line taken by Lloyd George effectively destroyed the best chance of changing the voting system in his own lifetime or for many years to come. If he had backed the proposals of the Speaker's conference, using the argument that its recommendations should be implemented in full, the Commons would almost certainly have voted for them, as in due course women's franchise was accepted, however reluctantly in the case of some MPs. Despite his withering comments, PR was in fact very nearly carried when the matter was first voted on in the Commons on 12 June. The majority against it was only seven (150 to 143) and it is hard to believe that the sort of endorsement that he gave to women's suffrage – a cause to which he had always been committed – would not have been more than enough to turn the scale in favour of changing the voting system.

His attitude also delayed the passage of the reform bill, because the issue that he shelved was thereafter contested over many months between the two Houses of Parliament. PR appealed to many Conservatives as a means of guarding against the left-wing extremism which, they feared, might well result from the adoption of universal manhood suffrage. STV for the big cities was therefore taken up by the House of Lords, only to be rejected on four subsequent occasions by the House of Commons (by majorities always

15. Hansard, fifth ser., vol. cii: Lloyd George's speech, cols. 486–96.

substantially larger than in the first vote). At the same time, people on the left tended to feel that the alternative vote would work to their advantage in the Tory-dominated country seats; so attempts were made in the Commons to insert AV into the bill.

Eventually, in February 1918, the bill passed into law without any serious provision for changing the voting system – with consequences that Lloyd George was to rue very bitterly in the 1920s. His Representation of the People Act was a great measure, making Britain more nearly a true democracy, with votes for all adult men and, at last, many women (for whom the qualifying age was fixed at thirty). But it had one palpable defect, for which he was chiefly to blame.

Like other British politicians, Lloyd George had had ample opportunity to familiarize himself with the arguments for changing the voting system, but had not bothered to do so, relying instead upon sheer prejudice. It was not true that he had 'no opinion' on the subject. He had an all-too-robust opinion, rooted in ignorance, which he expressed to C. P. Scott. PR was, he said, 'a device for defeating democracy' (whose principle was that 'the majority should rule') and 'for bringing faddists of all kinds into Parliament'.[16] But it should have been obvious to him that the first-past-the-post system did not ensure a clear-cut Parliamentary majority for a single party. From 1910 onwards the Liberal government was dependent upon the support of Labour and, more especially, of the Irish party, since it had no majority at all over the Tories in Parliament, and in the country had polled fewer votes than they had in both 1910 elections. The supposed virtues of the traditional voting system were not much in evidence during the period immediately preceding the First World War.[17]

PR was far from being 'an entirely novel suggestion', as he described it in his speech. It had received the blessing of John Stuart Mill before Lloyd George was born.[18] As for AV, a Royal Commission had reported almost unanimously in its favour in 1910, though the evidence contained in the report seemed to point more logically to PR. Either way, the Commission gave further publicity and credibility to the case for changing the voting system.[19]

Politicians are naturally tempted to assume that any system through

16. Scott diary, 3 April 1917.
17. Ireland was grossly over-represented in Parliament, since the number of its MPs still reflected the population before the period of famine and mass emigration in the first half of the nineteenth century. Incidentally, the Speaker's conference made no recommendations about Ireland.   18. In *Thoughts on Parliamentary Reform* (1859).
19. Royal Commission on Systems of Election – chairman, Lord Richard Cavendish – appointed by Asquith in 1908.

which they have made their way into Parliament must be essentially sound. Lloyd George was not immune to this temptation, which must have been all the stronger in his case, since the system had brought him to the summit of political life. A truly democratic voting system should be based on two principles: one person one vote, and one vote one value. Lloyd George paid too little heed to the second principle – until it was too late.[20]

Throughout the war the attitude of industrial workers was a prime preoccupation of government, and of Lloyd George above all. In his own words: 'the contentment and cooperation of the wage-earners was our vital concern, and industrial unrest spelt a graver menace to our endurance and ultimate victory than even the military strength of Germany.' The immediate pre-war period had been marked by growing trade union strength and militancy. There were massive strikes in 1910–12, and there would (he believed) have been 'industrial unrest without precedent' in the autumn of 1914, had the war not supervened. When it began, the trade union leaders called off their programme of strikes and proclaimed industrial peace for the duration. 'But if the threat of unrest based on peace-time issues was thus dissolved . . . there were new troubles and problems of infinite complexity created . . . by the conditions under which industry had to be carried on in a world war.'[21]

One of the troubles soon apparent was price inflation, with which wages did not begin to keep pace. During the first six months of the war prices rose by more than 20 per cent, while wages hardly moved. The ill-feeling that this naturally caused was aggravated by the manifest profiteering of some industrialists. Another problem that came to the fore as war industry expanded was the need to modify trade union restrictive practices. In March 1915 Lloyd George was asked to negotiate a deal with the leaders of labour, and his talks with them resulted in the so-called Treasury Agreement, under which the unions accepted compulsory arbitration as an alternative to strikes, and the suspension of traditional workshop regulations for the rest of the war, so as to permit male and female 'dilution' of the labour force. In return, a rather vague assurance was given on the control of profits, and the unions had the satisfaction of being treated by the government as an estate of the realm, separate from the employers. A National Labour Advisory Committee was set up, with Arthur Henderson as chairman; and soon afterward Henderson joined the first wartime coalition, formed by Asquith.

20. His own constituency of Caernarfon Boroughs had one of the smallest electorates in the country, and so conspicuously violated the principle of one vote one value, making it a rather unsuitable political base for a champion of democracy. 21. WM, pp. 1925–7.

By 1917 new difficulties, even dangers, had arisen. The introduction of conscription for the armed forces made it necessary to find a way of exempting essential workers. In the early months of the war many skilled men were lost to industry as they volunteered for the army; now there was a danger that such men would be lost through conscription. A trade card scheme, devised in haste towards the end of 1916, gave the leaders of certain unions the right to determine which workers should be exempted. This proved to be an unsatisfactory arrangement, not least because it was much resented by those union leaders not chosen to operate it. Christopher Addison, Lloyd George's Minister of Munitions, therefore sought to replace it with a wider schedule of exemption, drawn up in consultation with the Admiralty, the War Office and the National Labour Advisory Committee. The War Cabinet endorsed the new schedule, but the idea of scrapping the trade card scheme did not at all appeal to those who were operating it, notably the powerful Amalgamated Society of Engineers (ASE).

The government also ran into trouble with its proposal to extend dilution to private industry. Under the Treasury Agreement dilution applied only to controlled establishments, and the ASE leaders had accepted it in that sphere because they thought they had 'guarantees that it would not be extended to private and commercial work (the work the bulk of engineers would return to after the extraordinary war work in munitions had ended)'.[22] Their fear was that 'dilutees' would be enabled to capture the peacetime jobs of skilled engineers. Nevertheless, Addison went ahead with legislation to extend dilution.

The trouble caused by specific government policies was compounded by the persistence of working-class grievances, ranging from the high cost of living and inadequate housing to dilution of another kind, that of beer. There was tension not only between Labour and the government, but also within the labour movement itself, as local, unofficial leaders began to challenge the authority of the official leadership. Labour politicians were in the coalition, and responsible trade union leaders seemed to many of their followers to be closer to the government than to the rank-and-file. And then came the Russian Revolution, which 'lit up the skies with a lurid flash of hope for all who were dissatisfied with the existing order of society . . . [and] encouraged all the habitual malcontents in the ranks of labour to foment discord'.[23] As May Day approached, even the level-headed Henderson felt that 'the situation was one which would need careful handling'.[24]

Industrial conflict was in the air, but the timing and scale of it could not

22. Chris Wrigley, *David Lloyd George and the British Labour Movement: Peace and War* (1976), p. 185.   23. *WM*, p. 1933.   24. Wrigley, *David Lloyd George*, p.189.

be foreseen. In the event it took everyone by surprise, even the shop stewards' rank-and-file movement which was the principal destabilizing force. In mid-March the directors of a Rochdale firm, Tweedales and Smalleys, had put some of its women employees on to a form of skilled work for which the principle of dilution had not been agreed with the unions. Ignoring a warning from the Ministry of Munitions, the firm then sacked some men who refused to instruct the women in the work. As a result 400 men walked out in protest. After an interval a mass meeting of 2,000 trade unionists at Rochdale called for the prosecution of the firm within three days. The action it had taken was, certainly, in breach of the Munitions of War Act, and a prompt move against the firm might have averted the trouble that ensued. But the Ministry hesitated, hoping that the directors would undergo a change of heart. This was a fatal miscalculation. As Lloyd George describes the directors, they were 'all of that stubborn autocratic type that was in its way at least as dangerous to industrial peace as the worst communist agitator'.[25] They did not respond to appeals to their good nature and common sense. Meanwhile sympathetic strike action was spreading. By 5 May 60,000 men were out in Lancashire, and soon workers in Liverpool, Sheffield, Coventry and London followed their example (though important areas, including the Clyde, did not). At their peak the May engineering strikes involved 200,000 men, and they cost the country 1,500,000 working days.

Lloyd George was always wary of trade unions, seeing them as a potential threat to the authority of the state. But he recognized that most of their members were thoroughly patriotic and largely immune to subversive influences, as were most of their official leaders. Two of his ministerial colleagues concerned with handling the strikes, Henderson and the Minister of Labour, John Hodge, were themselves leading trade unionists. In any case, neither his mixed feelings about trade unions as institutions – nor, for that matter his high regard for go-ahead businessmen – prevented him from sympathizing with the poor. He knew that many working-class grievances were genuine, and that they provided a far stronger motive for trouble in industry than left-wing ideology, even after the Russian Revolution. He therefore approached the crisis created by the May strikes with a judicious blend of firmness and flexibility.[26]

On the government side, Addison led the detailed negotiations, and his

25. *WM*, p. 1940.
26. Charles Dickens – one of his literary heroes – had a similar attitude to organized labour. In *Hard Times* Dickens shows infinite compassion for the poor, but suspicion verging on hostility towards trade unions.

opposite number was R. Brownlie, president of the ASE. Lloyd George kept in touch and authorized key decisions. Brownlie, like Henderson and Hodge, felt that the strikes were directed as much against the official union leadership as against the government. He wanted the trouble-makers to be defeated, but also to win some concessions. On 17 May Lloyd George presided over a meeting at which it was decided to prosecute up to ten unofficial strike leaders. (Next day seven were arrested and placed in Brixton gaol.) Meanwhile a conference representing a hundred strike committees was in session at Walworth, and an attempt was made to obtain direct access to Addison and his colleagues. But he, with War Cabinet backing, refused to receive an unofficial deputation behind the backs of the official union leaders. The latter agreed to a tripartite meeting, which took place at the Ministry of Munitions on 19 May (a Saturday). At this the strikers' representatives stated their case in the presence of the union leaders, and then left all further negotiation to the ASE executive. Addison hinted at the meeting that the arrested men would be released if and when there was a return to work. Later the same day agreement was reached and Lloyd George sanctioned the withdrawal of charges against the men, on the understanding that they would honour the agreement. The trade card scheme was dropped, the government's new schedule accepted, and the shop stewards' power at least checked. The government seemed to have scored a considerable triumph.

Unfortunately it was accompanied by an early manifestation of what we now call spin-doctoring. The agreement was signed by Addison and Brownlie, who were indeed the prime negotiators, and at 4 p.m. it was approved by Lloyd George at 10 Downing Street. The document was then left by Addison in the Cabinet Room, with the assurance that it would be published without delay. So it was, but in a doctored form. In the version given to the press the signatures of Addison and Brownlie were cut out, and the opening sentences were changed in such a way as to imply that the agreement had been reached at 10 Downing Street under Lloyd George's chairmanship. For two days there had been newspaper comment adverse to Addison's Ministry and its handling of the dispute. Now the doctored version of the agreement suggested that Lloyd George had had to step in to clear up the Ministry's mess.

Addison was furious, and others who had been party to the talks shared his indignation. 'God knows' (he wrote in his diary) 'that I of all men have never been backward in getting L.G. all the credit I could and that he deserves, and I hate the idea of trying to advertise myself, but this business discredits the whole Ministry as well as myself.' According to him, he managed to reclaim the original document, which showed alterations 'in the handwriting of one of the men at No. 10 . . . well known to all of us'. When he confronted Lloyd George with it, the Prime Minister 'professed to be as angry as [he] was', and said that if the facts were as stated his press man, William Sutherland, 'would have to go'.[27] Addison also demanded a statement in Parliament to repair the damage, and Lloyd George made one on 21 May, emphasizing that the settlement had been reached on his Right Honourable friend's initiative, and subsequently brought to him for confirmation. He asked the House to join him in congratulating Addison on the skill with which he had conducted the negotiations.[28]

Addison was important to Lloyd George, and not only because he was the most highly placed fellow-Liberal in the government. He had been a faithful acolyte ever since they had worked together during the passage of the 1911 National Insurance Act. A physician and former professor of anatomy, as well as a Liberal MP, he had then helped to bridge the gap between Lloyd George and the British Medical Association. In 1915, when Lloyd George was setting up the Ministry of Munitions, he chose Addison as his junior minister, and at the end of the following year Addison canvassed support for him among Liberal MPs during the crisis from which he emerged as Prime Minister. The contretemps over the press release did not cause any lasting estrangement (that was to come later). For a time their relations remained as close as ever.

Was Lloyd George responsible for the press rubbishing of Addison and his Ministry, and for the doctored press release? On the latter question one biography of Addison asserts that what was done 'surely cannot have been the initiative of Sutherland alone'.[29] This may be unfair to Lloyd George, but only to a limited extent. It is quite possible that Sutherland acted without reference to his master in changing the opening sentences of the agreement, and removing the signatures, before issuing the document to the press. But if he did so, it must have been because he knew the sort of thing that was expected of him. If we give Lloyd George the benefit of doubt on the narrow issue, we have to fault him on a wider one. He must have observed the bad press that Addison was getting during the last phase of the negotiations, but obviously did nothing to counteract it. Sutherland was Lloyd George's

27. Diary entry on 25 May 1917, describing events of the previous few days. This was published in Addison's *Four and a Half Years* (2 vols., 1934, vol. ii, pp. 384–5) but with a dash in place of Sutherland's name, presumably for fear of libel (Sutherland died in 1949).

28. The statement was made in reply to an arranged private notice question.

29. Kenneth and Jane Morgan, *Portrait of a Progressive: The Political Career of Christopher, Viscount Addison* (1980), p. 65.

employee, and Lloyd George must have been well aware of his methods of news management. Besides, whatever may have been said to Addison during the row about the press release, Sutherland kept his job. He remained as press secretary until 1918, and thereafter continued to serve Lloyd George – in positions of growing consequence – until the end of his premiership.[30]

Of course, the Ministry of Munitions deserved criticism for its failure to act more swiftly against Tweedales and Smalleys, so giving shop stewards in other parts of the country time to exploit a small dispute and work it up into a major crisis. Addison cannot escape some responsibility for that failure. It is also true that the policy which led to the settlement was essentially Lloyd George's, and it is worth noting, as a detail, that the 4 p.m. meeting at 10 Downing Street on 19 May was arranged before the final, decisive encounter between Addison's team and the ASE executive. Knowledge that it was to occur may have helped to concentrate minds, much as Lloyd George's impending visit to the Admiralty almost certainly did in the matter of the convoys. Nevertheless, Addison was justified in feeling rather hard done by when he read the newspapers on Sunday, 20 May, and Lloyd George's role in the affair was far from blameless.

Yet he read the lessons of the strikes correctly, and showed no complacency when the strikers returned to work. His immediate concern was to tackle the social grievances which, he knew, had contributed greatly to the industrial unrest. Unless they were tackled, he was sure that there would soon be even worse trouble. Eight regional commissions were appointed to investigate and report within a month. Each commission had an independent chairman, and included a representative of labour as well as an employer. Evidence was taken from unofficial as well as official sources. Even before the commissions reported, Lloyd George anticipated the main thrust of their reports by announcing a policy of subsidies to hold down the price of food. At the same time he redoubled efforts to increase domestic food production (as will be described later). In response to the commissions' reports, which were in by mid-July, action was also taken to deal more generously with pension claims resulting from the war. Whereas such claims had been rejected at the rate of over two thousand a month before April 1917, by October rejections had been cut to an average of under a hundred a month.[31] Bad housing was another matter raised, but with so much competition for resources, particularly manpower, only the worst cases of overcrowding

30. He entered Parliament at the 1918 election and was for two years Lloyd George's PPS, before becoming a whip and, in April 1922, Chancellor of the Duchy of Lancaster and a Privy Counsellor. Like Addison, he had worked with Lloyd George on social reform before the war.
31. Wrigley, *David Lloyd George*, p. 200.

(and by no means all of them) could be attended to during the war. One should add that the government's proposal to extend dilution to private industry was quietly dropped.

Sceptical as he was of any serious revolutionary threat in Britain, Lloyd George did not overreact when he heard that there was to be a convention at Leeds in early June, whose purpose was 'to hail the Russian Revolution and to organise the British Democracy to follow Russia'. A letter – signed by Ramsay MacDonald, among others – was sent to trade unions, trades councils, local Labour parties and other such bodies, inviting them to be represented at the convention. Lloyd George was urged by some to ban it, but he decided against doing so and the War Cabinet supported him, only soldiers in uniform being prohibited from attending. His relaxed attitude proved wise. The convention 'seemed imposing' and carried resolutions 'by sweeping majorities', but its true significance was negligible. The views expressed at it did not reflect the mass opinion of British labour. The so-called delegates at Leeds were not really delegates at all, but 'individual enthusiasts who came without authority or instructions'. Most of the leaders were the sort of people 'who think something is actually done when you assert vociferously that it must be done'.[32] (For all his eloquence, Lloyd George himself did not make this mistake. He treated words as accessory to action, never as a substitute for it.)

Though not a portent of revolution, the industrial unrest of 1917 was nevertheless the worst of the war. Lloyd George deserves credit for his handling of it, and in retrospect he paid a generous tribute to the King for his contribution. In May, when the strikes were spreading, the King 'arranged to spend a week touring the areas where the trouble was most acute', and he made a further extended tour in June. His visits were never 'marred by any kind of unpleasantness'; on the contrary, 'the loyalty of the people was heartened to new vigour' by his presence.[33] The value attached to the visits at the time may be judged from the fact that the arrest of strike leaders was postponed to allow his tour of northern industrial towns to go ahead.

32. WM, p. 1948.
33. WM, pp. 1961–3. Another example of Lloyd George making amends?

8

Farming and Food

Irish sop – Northcliffe in America – Farming and food

After Lloyd George's first Commons speech as Prime Minister a discordant note was struck, as we have seen, when the leader of the Irish National Party, John Redmond, complained that the speech offered no policy for progress in Ireland, and that several hundred Irish prisoners from the 1916 Easter Rising were still being held without trial in English gaols. Lloyd George replied at the time with some impatience and irritation. But soon afterwards, as a goodwill gesture for Christmas, he released all prisoners who had not been tried and sentenced by court martial, 560 in all. One of them was the founder of Sinn Fein, Arthur Griffith, whose aim was to establish an Irish monarchy co-equal with Great Britain but under the same sovereign, on the Habsburg model. Another was a still virtually unknown young man, Michael Collins. His aim was to win independence for Ireland as a republic, and to do so by the use of covert terrorist violence rather than by the sort of open rebellion, provenly futile, in which he had taken part the previous year.

After the Easter Rising Lloyd George had been asked by Asquith to negotiate an Irish settlement, and had produced a deal which might have worked if the speed of its negotiation had been matched by prompt implementation. The deal involved acceptance of Home Rule by the Ulster Unionists, on the understanding that six of the nine Ulster counties would be excluded for the indefinite future, if not for ever, while Redmond managed (with difficulty) to sell the deal to his supporters on the understanding that exclusion could be for a limited period. Lloyd George's deliberate ambiguity on this point was justified, since the only realistic chance of a settlement lay in bringing a Home Rule regime into being for most of Ireland, in the hope that the Ulster Unionists would gradually be won over to the idea of joining it of their own free will. But it was essential to move very fast, before opposition to the deal had time to mobilize. Sadly, Lloyd George and Asquith did not expedite amending legislation (to the Home Rule Act which was in cold storage for the duration of the war), and the delay proved fatal.

Opposition to the deal was bound to come from Nationalists, when they discovered the exclusion of the six counties might not be temporary. But if a Parliament and government had swiftly been set up in Dublin, and if Redmond had thus acquired the additional persuasive resource of patronage, it is just possible that this opposition might have been contained, granted the will to contain it. For quite different reasons, the deal was opposed by Southern Unionists and their natural allies in the British Tory Party, who did not want Home Rule at all, but disliked it even more in the form that Lloyd George's deal would have brought about. Southern Unionists felt that they were being abandoned by both the British government and their fellow Unionists in Ulster. They had many sympathizers at Westminster but, with Bonar Law, Balfour and F. E. Smith supporting the deal, the hostility of lesser Tory leaders and even a majority of Tory backbenchers might not have wrecked it if it had been promoted with due urgency by the government.[1]

Lloyd George had a bad conscience about his failure of judgement and will in the spring of 1916. He knew that he had let Redmond down by promising to make the deal a resigning issue and then not honouring the pledge. The following year Ireland was a much tougher proposition for him, even though he was Prime Minister. Redmond would no longer look at the terms that he and his party had agreed to in 1916, and was under growing pressure from Sinn Fein and the more militant elements in his own ranks. As for the Ulster Unionists, they would make no further concessions, and their political strength was reinforced by the Conservatives' predominance within the Lloyd George coalition, in particular by Law's indispensability to the Prime Minister.

At the beginning of March there was an adjournment debate on Ireland, in which Lloyd George intervened. His speech was remarkable for a passage that showed his understanding of the basic problem in Ireland, to which, in one or other of its aspects, most of his contemporaries were blind. The Tory policy of trying to kill Home Rule with kindness had manifestly failed:

After all this great record of beneficent legislation, in spite of the fact that Ireland is more materially prosperous than she has ever been, there remains one invincible fact

1. One of the lesser leaders, Walter Long, more or less admitted to Riddell that a bill would have gone through if it had been introduced 'without delay' (*RWD*, 21 July 1916). The terms of the deal were in many ways highly favourable to the Nationalists, and could not have been secured without reassurance to the Ulster Unionists, who had shown before the war that it was politically impossible to coerce them. (See my *Lloyd George: From Peace to War* (1985), pp. 349–55.)

today, that she is no more reconciled to British rule than she was in the days of Cromwell. . . . It is something which has to do with the pride and self-respect of the people. I entreat the House of Commons and the British people to get that well into their mind. It is a fact which must be grasped . . . by any Government which means to attempt a settlement of this question.

But something else also needed to be grasped.

The other fact is that in the north-eastern portion of Ireland you have a population as hostile to Irish rule as the rest of Ireland is to British rule, yea, and as ready to rebel against [Irish rule] as the rest of Ireland is against British rule. . . . As alien in blood, in religious faith, in traditions, in outlook – as alien from the rest of Ireland in this respect as the inhabitants of Fife or Aberdeen.

Asquith spoke after Lloyd George, and then Redmond got up. He had listened to Lloyd George, he said, 'with the deepest pain'. His message was simple: the Home Rule Act must be put into operation at once. After speaking, he led his party out of the House. Soon it would be passing out of history.[2]

Redmond did not understand the genuineness of Scots-Irish resistance to Home Rule. Like most Irish Nationalists, north and south, he regarded it as a spurious device for prolonging British rule in Ireland, rather than as an autonomous force – an illusion that was to persist among the Gaelic-Irish until late in the century. At the same time most Unionists, north and south, failed to understand that the yearning of the Gaelic-Irish for self-government and recognition of their national identity was, as Lloyd George said, 'invincible'. It could not be conjured away by any palliative measures. Yet there was a crucial difference between Southern Unionists and Ulster Unionists. The former were prepared, in the last resort, to accept devolved government for a united Ireland, provided it remained part of the United Kingdom; the latter would accept devolution to Dublin only if they were free to opt out of it.

As the ostensible leader of Ulster Unionism, Carson was in an ambiguous position. He was not an Ulsterman, but a Dubliner; he represented Dublin University (Trinity College); and his prime concern was to preserve the unity of the British Isles and the British Empire. He had become Protestant Ulster's

---

2. Hansard, fifth ser., vol. xci, 7 March 1917; Lloyd George's speech, cols. 454–66; Redmond's, cols. 473–81. The debate was opened by T. P. O'Connor, and he was followed by Redmond's brother William, a serving officer soon to die in action on the Western front.

champion because he regarded Gladstonian Home Rule as a mortal threat both to British and imperial unity, not because he ever contemplated the division of Ireland. In April he told C. P. Scott that he would 'do all he could to bring about a compromise, [though] there were very strict limits to his powers and the moment he went beyond them his people in Ulster would throw him over and choose another leader'.[3] (He had already proposed to them that, if their right to opt out were accepted, they in turn should agree to a national consultative assembly for the whole of Ireland, to consist of Parliamentarians from both parts, and to hold yearly meetings alternating between Dublin and Belfast.[4])

Lloyd George was acutely conscious of the need for some new Irish initiative, above all to mollify Dominion and American opinion, the latter more important than ever now that the United States was in the war. Appealing to Carson to agree to county option, he showed a rare contrition about his own failure the previous year, to judge from his version of the conversation recorded by Frances Stevenson:

At every stage . . . the Irish question is a stumbling-block in the conduct of the war. It ought to have been settled last year. I feel that I was a coward not to insist upon a settlement then. It has done much harm in Australia. Hughes begged me last year to settle it for the sake of Australia, but I failed to do so. Twice since then he has sent me messages saying that it is essential that the matter should be settled. I have refrained from pressing the question, knowing your [Carson's] difficulties. But I feel that it can remain in abeyance no longer. Now that America has come in I get the same representations from that side . . . If we do not settle it now, this government will not be able to continue.[5]

A few days later at Guildhall he was openly proclaiming the need for a settlement, saying that Ireland had to be converted from surly suspicion to loyal comradeship.[6]

3. Scott diary, 19–21 April 1917.
4. Ian Colvin, *Carson, the Statesman*, repr. in Edward Marjoribanks and Colvin, *The Life of Lord Carson* (3 vols., 1932–6), vol. iii, pp. 242–6. The idea of an 'Irish dimension', later so abhorrent to Ulster Unionists, was the brainchild of their own charismatic leader – a nice irony.
5. FSD, 25 April 1917. In 1916 W. M. Hughes, Australian Prime Minister, had narrowly lost a plebiscite on the issue of conscription, much of the opposition coming from Irish Australians. As a result, he split his own Labour Party and formed a coalition with the Liberals, under the label Nationalist. It was these domestic preoccupations that caused him to miss the Imperial War Cabinet sessions in 1917. In another plebiscite conscription was again defeated, but Hughes remained as Prime Minister. 6. See p. 104 above.

There was, however, no basis for a deal on the lines he was canvassing. County option was unacceptable to the Ulster Unionists, because it would have meant the loss of Fermanagh and Tyrone, in which there were National-ist majorities. The most that the Ulstermen would agree to was a 'clean cut' of six counties, including those two. On the Nationalist side the demand was now for the Act and nothing but the Act. The Irish Party was no longer prepared to consider an Ulster opt-out in any form or for any period. Redmond told C. P. Scott that the 'true policy' for Ireland was Dominion status, 'or something like it', with a subordinate assembly for the whole of Ulster. He was 'emphatic in his rejection' of Carson's idea of a consultative assembly, or council, for Ireland, since it presupposed a departure from the principle of Home Rule for the whole island.[7]

In the middle of May the impasse was broken by a device which arose, as things so often do in politics (and in life generally), in a casual and serendipit-ous way. Lloyd George was about to write a letter to the Irish parties, offering Home Rule at once with exclusion for six Ulster counties – subject to reconsideration by Parliament after five years – and with Carson's proposed council for Ireland. When the letter was already drafted, but not yet sent, there was a dinner at the House of Lords in honour of Smuts, at which the gist of the letter was conveyed to Redmond by Lord Crewe. (Crewe had heard about it from Asquith, with whom Lloyd George had recently been discussing the Irish question.) Redmond replied that the offer was quite unacceptable, but then on an impulse asked Crewe if he thought 'it would be right to copy what had been done in the Dominions and leave the constitutional question to a convention entirely Irish'. Crewe was so inter-ested that he went to 10 Downing Street later the same evening and put the suggestion to Lloyd George. Next day Lloyd George put it to the War Cabinet, and a decision was taken to include it in the letter as an alternative to the original offer. The letter, as amended, was then immediately sent.[8]

The original proposal foreshadowed the future course of events, but in the short term the convention idea prevailed, because it gave a breathing-space to all concerned. An Irish Convention was duly set up, and held meetings in the Regent House at Trinity College, Dublin, from 25 July 1917 to 5 April 1918. Over a hundred representatives of various Irish bodies took part, and Sir Horace Plunkett was chosen to preside. Plunkett had symbolic merits. He was a figure from the Anglo-Irish Ascendancy who had been converted to Home Rule. He had a good record as an agricultural reformer.

7. Scott diary, 10–11 May 1917.
8. R. B. McDowell, *The Irish Convention, 1917–18* (1970), pp. 76–7.

He had strong links with America. As a character he was well-meaning and idealistic. Unfortunately he was a hopeless chairman – loquacious but inaudible, and indiscreet.[9] In any case, he had a no-hope job.

From the first the Convention was doomed to be no more than a talking-shop. It was absolutely boycotted by Sinn Fein, which was enough to make its proceedings nugatory. The Ulster Unionists were represented, but on the understanding that they would agree to nothing that involved Home Rule for the whole island. This set them on a collision course with Redmond's party, and with the Southern Unionists as well. Lloyd George would have preferred a settlement on the lines of his first option, but found the Convention (in Nicholas Mansergh's words) 'a qualified disappointment rather than a failure'.[10]

For him it provided a useful and tolerably effective way of demonstrating to America and the Dominions that an attempt had been made to resolve the Irish question, while yet carrying an inbuilt assurance that nothing would come of it, and that failure would be attributed to the inability of Irishmen to agree among themselves. In other words, it was to Lloyd George much as the Cripps mission to India would be to Churchill twenty-five years later. Lloyd George undertook to give effect to any 'substantial agreement' that might emerge from the Convention. But it must soon have been obvious to him that no such agreement was conceivable.

The growing support for militant nationalism and republicanism was already apparent in by-election victories for Sinn Fein. Only a week before Lloyd George sent his letter a Sinn Fein candidate won a spectacular victory over the Redmondite candidate in South Longford. The winner was an IRB (Irish Republican Brotherhood) man, who was helped in his campaign by prisoners from the Rising, recently released. Worse was to follow. In June Redmond's brother William was killed in Flanders, and his death caused a vacancy in the East Clare constituency. Sinn Fein chose as its candidate for the by-election one of the leaders of the Rising, who was lucky to have escaped execution after it, and who had just been released in a final batch of 118 prisoners as a gesture by Lloyd George 'to create a favourable climate for the Convention'. Éamon de Valera did not stand for what was known as constitutional Sinn Fein (the Griffith variety). He stood for an Irish republic totally independent of Britain, and had proved his willingness to

9. Ibid., pp. 97–8. Plunkett was selected by a committee of ten, which first chose a candidate proposed by the Southern Unionists, but switched to Plunkett on the insistence of the Independent Nationalists.

10. Nicholas Mansergh, *The Unresolved Question: The Anglo-Irish Settlement and its Undoing 1912–72* (1991), p. 106.

use force in pursuit of his dream. His Redmondite opponent was a popular local man. Nevertheless, de Valera won in a landslide.

The East Clare result was the *coup de grâce* to Redmond, who died within a year, and it was also the surest signal that his party was losing the battle with Sinn Fein for the soul of Irish nationalism. Occurring a fortnight before the Convention held its first meeting, and greeted with 'rejoicings throughout the rest of Ireland', it demonstrated the Convention's irrelevance to Irish, as distinct from British, politics.[11] Moreover, in launching de Valera on his political career it cast a long shadow over the British Isles for the rest of the century.

In the negotiations leading to the Convention, the Chief Secretary for Ireland, H. E. Duke, was marginalized, as his predecessor, Augustine Birrell, had been during the pre-war Anglo-Irish talks. Duke was a Unionist, appointed by Asquith and kept on by Lloyd George, who described him as a 'steady, careful man' but had little direct contact with him.[12] His share in the birth of the Convention was significant only for his speech at the opening session, when he took the chair before Plunkett was chosen to preside. In his peroration Duke showed that, however careful he might be in other ways, he could be less than careful in his choice of a word. His speech ended: 'Gentlemen, one thing I have learned in the course of my experiences, *never despair of the republic.*' According to one witness, a 'faint titter went through the room', and the Southern Unionists 'looked aghast'.[13]

While Balfour was returning from the United States in early June 1917, a very different, but in his way equally high-powered, emissary was crossing the Atlantic in the opposite direction. Lloyd George had decided to send Lord Northcliffe to co-ordinate the various British and Allied missions in America. Balfour was opposed to the appointment and so, at first, was President Wilson. But having persuaded the press lord to do the job Lloyd George sent him swiftly on his way, so presenting both the Foreign Office and the White House with a *fait accompli.*

The Prime Minister's motives were mixed. Though he genuinely believed that Northcliffe's extraordinary talents could be used to great public advantage in America, he was also keen to divert the press lord's energies, at least temporarily. Since the outbreak of war Northcliffe had used the power of his newspapers to goad and berate the nation's leaders with increasing force.

11. Robert Kee, *The Green Flag* (1976), pp. 600–603.   12. *RWD*, 8 October 1916.
13. Quoted in McDowell, *Irish Convention*, p. 104. Duke, a lawyer, had no personal or ethnic links with Ireland. He was an Englishman, from Devon.

Standing outside constitutional politics, yet feeling himself to be a vital part of the political process, he acted as a one-man leader of the opposition who was nevertheless irked by being confined to the role of a critic. His one attempt to be elected to the House of Commons having failed, he was resentful of elected politicians, even of the one – Lloyd George – whom he regarded as the best fitted to lead the country to victory.[14] They, in turn, naturally viewed him with a mixture of resentment and fear. In an age when scientific opinion polling was unknown, Northcliffe could claim to be more in touch with the general public, including even soldiers at the front, than any regular politician, since he had unrivalled sources of information, at home and abroad. He also had ideas, which could be brilliantly right or disastrously wrong. Either way, he had the means to give them the maximum impact, possessing in *The Times* the acknowledged organ of the British élite, and in the *Daily Mail*, his own creation, the supreme British popular newspaper.

To Lloyd George in 1917, Northcliffe was a menace chiefly because he had become a blind supporter of Haig (despite his attacks two years earlier on another military idol, Kitchener). By sending him to America, in public harness, the Prime Minister managed to secure a few months of 'partial respite' from the Northcliffe press. *The Times*, which was in any case semi-independent editorially even under Northcliffe, was all the more so in his absence, and it was a further convenience that the editor, Geoffrey Dawson, was a friend and disciple of Milner. But even the *Daily Mail*'s attacks 'lacked vigour' while Northcliffe was away.[15] It was not so much his physical absence that counted; as a rule he was very good at exercising remote control when he was out of the country, as he often was. The difference in this case was that he was absorbed in other work. For the first time he had been entrusted with major responsibility on behalf of the country, and as the patriot he undoubtedly was he gave of his best.

Nevertheless it was a gamble to send him, and few prime ministers would have dared to make an appointment so fraught with risk, whatever the fringe benefits. Lloyd George rightly judged that Northcliffe would do

14. In 1895, when he was thirty, he had stood for Parliament as Unionist candidate for Portsmouth. Though he put a lot of money and effort into the contest, he was not elected, and he never tried again. In 1905 he received his peerage, on Balfour's recommendation, but hardly ever attended, or spoke in, the House of Lords. By nature he was the opposite of a Parliamentarian.

15. J. Lee Thompson, *Politicians, the Press, & Propaganda: Lord Northcliffe & the Great War 1914–1919* (1999), p. 170. Northcliffe's American mission is fully described in chapter 8 of this valuable work.

the job well. As an outstanding self-made entrepreneur he was in tune with the American ethos, and he was already a familiar figure in the United States, having paid twenty visits to the country before 1917. Balfour had appealed above all to the politicians and the Washington establishment, but Northcliffe was capable of making a more direct appeal to the American people. He was a living contradiction of the stuffy image of Britain, even in the matter of dress. He usually wore a blue serge suit, soft white collar, red checked tie and soft grey hat. His manner was informal, his methods unorthodox. As a journalist of genius he had many friends and admirers in the American press, and his sayings and doings were always good copy. It was helpful, too, that his family origins were Irish, and that his views on Ireland were well informed and progressive.

Northcliffe arrived in New York on 11 June, and spent a few days there before moving on to Washington, meeting journalists and giving lunch parties in his hotel suite. By the time he reached Washington he was already big news, and press comment on him was, on the whole, glowingly favourable. In the capital he lost no time in making contact with senior officials, most of whom were eager to meet him; and within a week he had his first meeting with the President, which was a success on both sides.

There was, however, one person in Washington who did not at all welcome his presence, and that person was a compatriot. The British Ambassador, Sir Cecil Spring-Rice, felt upstaged by a visiting celebrity who had no formal diplomatic status, but who reported direct to the Prime Minister. Partly to avoid friction with Spring-Rice, Northcliffe decided to set up his headquarters in New York; but his main reason for doing so was that he regarded New York as the centre of American life, financially, industrially and culturally. Though he often had occasion to be in Washington again during his time in America, and a branch of his mission, with some of the key personnel, was maintained there, his principal office was in New York.

Under its aegis he brought together the various departmental missions in America, which had previously been working more or less independently: those representing the Admiralty and War Office, the Ministries of Munitions, Shipping, Transport and Food, the Board of Trade, and numerous other *ad hoc* bodies. Before long he was presiding over an organization employing 10,000 people and spending $10 million a day. To help him in this giant task, he drew on his own staff in London. Andrew Caird, editor of the *Daily Mail*, was brought over to be general administrator of the combined British war mission, and *The Times*'s Washington correspondent, Arthur Willert, was attached to the Washington office.

Finding that the work of his mission was hampered by slow and incoherent means of communicating with London, he arranged for a central office to be created there to handle all cables to and from the United States; and he prevailed upon all the relevant departments to co-operate with the office by expediting their procedures. At the same time he made sure that all cables from him to the War Cabinet, or addressed to him in New York, were to have priority.

At first he himself conducted negotiations with the US Treasury, and he got on well with the Secretary of the Treasury, William Gibbs McAdoo, who admired his 'great energy and purpose'. But the task was too large and important to be combined with running the whole mission, and in any case the niceties of finance – as distinct from the process of making money – were not Northcliffe's forte. He realized, therefore, that the financial end of his mission needed to be the full-time responsibility of a major figure with the relevant expertise. After discussion with Colonel House he decided that Lord Reading would be the man for the job, and began to press for his appointment.

Lord Reading's career is one of the most bizarre in British history. Few have possessed to such a degree the capacity to rise, and keep on rising, whatever the circumstances. Born Rufus Isaacs, one of the numerous children of a prosperous Jewish fruit-merchant in the City of London, he had a patchy education and desultory employment before being called to the Bar at the age of twenty-seven. From then onwards his advance in life was relentless. As a flourishing silk he became a Liberal MP (for Reading) in 1904, and in the Liberal government that came to power the following year he was soon appointed a law officer. His central role in the Marconi scandal while he was Attorney-General did not prevent his being made Lord Chief Justice in 1913, and he held the post until 1921, though for most of the time he was engaged in other public work, unconnected with the law.

He was a born go-between and fixer, quick to master a technical brief and adept at handling human beings. In 1914 Lloyd George had enlisted his help in dealing with the financial crisis caused by the outbreak of war, and he quickly established an easy working relationship with City potentates (who were prepared to forget Marconi and the fact that, long before, during his brief experience as a stockjobber, he had been 'hammered' on the Stock Exchange). An office in Whitehall was put at his disposal and he continued to do important war work on behalf of the government, particularly the Treasury. At a time of intense Germanophobia, it was not held against him that his wife was of German-Jewish extraction.

In September 1915 he had led the British team in a joint Allied financial mission to the United States. While negotiating a loan he made valuable

American contacts, from the President downwards, and won the special friendship of Colonel House. After the change of government in 1916 he was as close as ever to Lloyd George, while remaining on good terms with Asquith. In May of the following year he was Lloyd George's intermediary in an attempt to persuade Asquith to join the government; but even he could not remove the former premier's adamant objection to serving under his successor.[16] In September Reading returned to America, as Northcliffe wished, with a wider remit than two years before, taking charge of all the government's financial business in the United States, and in Canada as well. Northcliffe gave him full backing until his own departure in November. But there were predictable difficulties with Spring-Rice, whose position became increasingly anomalous. The eventual solution was for Reading to replace Spring-Rice, and this occurred at the beginning of 1918.[17]

Meanwhile Northcliffe rounded off his mission with a major effort of political salesmanship. An information office had been opened in New York during Balfour's visit. It was run by Geoffrey Butler (a distinguished academic on temporary secondment) and supervised by the Foreign Office's information department under John Buchan. Inevitably Butler's activities were limited and cautious, since the Foreign Office was fearful of giving offence to the American government. But Lloyd George believed in appealing robustly to the American people, and Northcliffe had the same attitude. He would have liked the Prime Minister or Smuts to come over, but since they could not be spared he did the job himself.

Northcliffe's aim was to tell the Americans what Britain was doing in the war, how great were the dangers still to be surmounted, and how much depended upon the speed and effectiveness of American support. He wrote articles for American newspapers and magazines, some of which were

16. The overture was made during a weekend spent by Reading at Asquith's country house at Sutton Courtenay, near Oxford. According to Asquith's contemporary record, Reading said that he and many others regarded his (Asquith's) participation in the government as essential and hinted that Lloyd George would offer him any post he chose, apart from the premiership. Asquith's reply was unequivocal. In no circumstances would be serve in any government led by Lloyd George, or indeed in any of which he was not himself the head.

17. Reading became, as well as Ambassador, head of the British War Mission, leaderless since Northcliffe's departure. (And, amazingly, he continued to draw his emoluments as Lord Chief Justice.)

Spring-Rice died suddenly, while staying in Ottawa on his way home. Shortly before he died he wrote the poem 'I vow to thee, my country', for which he is chiefly remembered. He composed it for a farewell letter to the former American Secretary of State, William Jennings Bryan.

suppressed by nervous editors. But one that did appear (in the October issue of *Current Opinion*) contained the striking and salutary comment:

The motive which brought the United States in was not sympathy for any other nation, was not desire for gain, was not an abstract fondness for democratic as opposed to autocratic government; it was self-interest, self-preservation, self-respect. The American people are not fighting to make the world safe for democracy, but to make the world safe for themselves.

House felt that there might be 'serious trouble should the President chance to see' this article.[18] Surely he must have seen it, or at least heard about it, and it says much for Northcliffe's standing in America that he got away with such a challenging statement. His outspokenness about all politicians, domestic or foreign, was accepted as a precious virtue.

As well as writing for the press, he went about the country addressing large audiences. Though he was far from being a natural orator, with a weak voice and reliant upon notes, he improved with practice and gained confidence as he went on. At a rally in July he spoke to 14,000 people in New York's Madison Square Garden, and was enthusiastically received despite being inaudible to part of the crowd. Another speaker at the rally said: 'I wish to God we had in this country a Lord Northcliffe. We need one perhaps even more than Great Britain did.'[19] At a meeting in Atlantic City, from which 4,000 had to be turned away, he spoke in Lloyd Georgian terms of the war's unprecedented character: 'this is a war of engineers and chemists as well as soldiers . . . It is essentially a businessman's war . . . that requires the brains of men of business.'[20]

His boldest foray was into the Middle West, where there were large German-American communities and 'America First' sentiment was at its strongest. In Cleveland he rallied support for a Liberty Loan and called for more ships to be built. In Chicago his message was the same, and he seems to have got it across, since at the end of his visit to the city the *Chicago Herald* commented: 'We can accept his statements . . . as facts, and his conclusions as sound.'[21] His impact was similar in Kansas City, St Louis and other places on his tour. A week after completing it he sailed for home.

18. Quoted in Thompson, *Politicians, the Press & Propaganda*, p. 161.
19. Reported in *Public Ledger*, Philadelphia, 20 September 1917.
20. Thompson, *Politicians, the Press & Propaganda*, p. 163. In February 1915 Lloyd George had proclaimed, in a speech at Bangor, 'This is an engineers' war'; and as Minister of Munitions he had drawn heavily on the services of businessmen, as he continued to do as Prime Minister.
21. Ibid., p. 166.

Tributes were paid to his all-round achievement by numerous American leaders, and by the Prime Minister of Canada. Lloyd George sent him this message:

I wish . . . to thank you for the invaluable work you have done in the United States as head of the British War Mission . . . the War Cabinet desire to express to you their complete satisfaction. They would also like to congratulate you on the great energy and effect with which you have striven to explain what Great Britain has been doing and the needs of the Allies to the American public, and the success of your efforts to combat attempts of the enemy to sow dissension between the people of the U.S. and Great Britain.[22]

Northcliffe regarded his American mission as 'the most important task in his life'.[23] It was certainly his most important official service to his country. After his return he was to be given further public employment by Lloyd George, but his work in America in 1917 was the high point in his intermittent and always somewhat unnatural career as an insider. It was also the high point in his relations with Lloyd George. There was stormy weather ahead.

In most respects, Lloyd George's assumption of supreme power represented a change of gear rather than a change of direction. The differences that resulted were highly significant, and some were vital, but what happened was seldom entirely new. Rather, it was a development of procedures and policies that had been initiated – many of them by Lloyd George himself – while Asquith was Prime Minister. This was notably true in the sphere of food supply and distribution, in which Lloyd George's government made dramatic advances on work already begun, or at least contemplated.

Of all belligerents Britain seemed the most vulnerable to defeat by starvation. At the outbreak of war the country was importing 60 per cent of its total food supply, 80 per cent of its staple food grain, wheat, and 100 per cent of its sugar (considered more essential then than now). Until the end of 1916 'business as usual' remained the governing principle in keeping the nation fed, though in practice the state was increasingly forced to intervene, overtly or surreptitiously. An immediate step was taken to ensure the supply of sugar, through the appointment of a Royal Commission with monopoly purchasing power; and two years later, in October 1916, an analogous body was established for imported wheat. Meanwhile other state agencies were

22. 1 November 1917.
23. Arthur Willert, *Washington and Other Memories* (1972), p. 101.

in varying degrees involved in the process of food supply, though without co-ordination or exclusive responsibility. A Cabinet committee on food supplies was created by Asquith in August 1914, and continued to meet for the rest of his premiership; but since it had to refer all its decisions to the main Cabinet, and had no independent power of enforcement, its 'ability to direct and control was limited'.[24]

The formation of the first coalition seemed, at first, to presage a more drastic interventionism. Lord Selborne, the Tory-appointed President of the Board of Agriculture, aimed at nothing less than making the country self-sufficient in food. At a time when the U-boats were causing their first serious scare, he set up a committee under Milner, whom he greatly admired, to advise on methods to boost the production of home-grown food. The Milner committee did its work quickly, recommending a four-year minimum price for wheat in return for an expansion of arable farming by one-fifth compared with pre-war. There should also be higher wages for farm workers, and county councils should appoint committees of experts to promote every form of agricultural production in their areas. Only the last of these recommendations was Selborne allowed to implement; the rest of the Milner programme was shelved in 1915, since to the Asquith Cabinet as a whole it seemed too far-reaching, while for a time the U-boat threat to supplies became less acute. But in the critical circumstances in which Lloyd George formed his government it was essentially the programme of his chosen President of the Board of Agriculture, R. E. Prothero.

Prothero was an excellent choice. A Tory of the best sort, he was no narrow partisan and was quite prepared to be radical when necessary. Though he was closely associated with the landed interest, and had strongly opposed Lloyd George's policies, including his Land Campaign, before 1914, when faced with the emergency of war he soon decided that the man he had fought against was the most effective minister to deal with its problems and wrote to tell him so, graciously apologizing for any undue acerbity shown towards him earlier.[25] Prothero was in his mid-sixties, and had been in Parliament only since 1914, as one of the two MPs for Oxford University. He was in no sense a professional politician, but rather a versatile scholar with a special interest in agriculture, on which he had written a classic work.[26] For some years a fellow of All Souls, Oxford, and thereafter for a time editor of the *Quarterly*, in 1898 he accepted an invitation from

24. L. Margaret Barnett, *British Food Policy in the First World War* (1985), p. 22.
25. Prothero to DLG, 27 November 1915 (Lloyd George Papers).
26. *The Pioneers and Progress of English Farming* (1888), revised and reprinted as *English Farming, Past and Present* (1912).

the Duke of Bedford to be agent-in-chief of his estates, in town and country – a post he was still holding in 1916, when the Duke granted him leave of absence to join the new government.[27]

He took office knowing that the Prime Minister would back a vigorous effort to boost food production at home, and in his memoirs he acknowledges the constancy of Lloyd George's support. 'At once sympathetic and stimulating, his determination and courageous optimism were a perpetual inspiration . . . from the first my relations with him were of the friendliest character.'[28] (A running gag between them concerned Lloyd George's ill-informed reference, in a pre-war speech, to the consumption of mangel-wurzels by pheasants.) As well as the Prime Minister, Prothero had another powerful War Cabinet ally in Milner. He and Milner had been friends from undergraduate days, and he had served on Milner's 1915 food committee, to whose recommendations he was now in a position to give substantial effect. He lost no time in making sure that he had the means to carry out his ambitious programme. DORA (the Defence of the Realm Act) was extended to permit the commandeering of any land, machinery or farm stock needed to raise agricultural production. In appealing to the farming community to give its full co-operation and not to resist the revolutionary changes he was proposing, he took the positive line that by doing so they would bring the long agricultural depression to an end and get 'back to the Seventies and better'.[29]

In January 1917 he wrote to Lloyd George to explain the measures he was taking. The war agricultural committees set up by Selborne, though a valuable innovation, were too large to be efficient. Prothero arranged that real work should be done by sixty-one small executive sub-committees, to which most of the new compulsory powers would be delegated. Each should send a weekly report of its activities to the Board of Agriculture, which would also be represented by commissioners in twenty-one districts, close enough to the county executives to keep an eye on them. Since the War Office was demanding 30,000 men for front-line service, Prothero was obtaining 16,000 substitutes from the home army, and hoped to obtain more for the spring sowing (which would, in fact, be long delayed by exceptionally bad weather). He was also seeking to make up the country's serious deficiencies in machinery, seeds, feedstuff and fertilizers.[30]

---

27. Bedford was an enlightened landowner, maintaining a family tradition of helping tenants and employees through the lean times of agricultural depression.

28. Lord Ernle (as Prothero became in 1919), *Whippingham to Westminster: The Reminiscences of Lord Ernle (Rowland Prothero)* (1938), p. 285.

29. Prothero, Circular Letter, 28 December 1916.   30. Prothero to DLG, 11 January 1917.

Prothero had a clear mind and knew what needed to be done. But he did not pretend to be a dynamic administrator, preferring wherever possible to delegate. Thus he showed his awareness of the top priority of his job in deciding to make the food production department a separate branch of his Ministry; and he was delighted when Lloyd George proposed that one of his men of 'push and go', Arthur Lee, should be its Director-General. Lee had been left out when the new government was formed, to his understandable surprise and distress. Though a Conservative MP, he was one of Lloyd George's most fervent acolytes, and had served with marked success as an under-secretary at the Ministry of Munitions. But Lloyd George felt unable, at first, to give Lee a place in his own government, because there was a strong prejudice against him among his fellow-Conservatives at all levels, which a new Prime Minister dependent upon the Conservative Party could not afford to ignore.

Lee's trouble was not that he was ambitious (which he was), but that in a party where it was considered ungentlemanly to *seem* ambitious he made no effort to conceal the fact. His all-too-obvious desire to get on was held against him, and his wealth, derived from marriage to an American heiress, attracted both envy and snobbish scorn. In addition, he was combative and devoid of humour. There were some who appreciated his more than compensating merits, but they did not include Bonar Law (perhaps surprisingly, in view of Law's attachment to the thrusting parvenu Beaverbrook). As a result no post was offered to Lee in December, and he heard nothing from Lloyd George for over two months. Even a piteous letter offering to make his Parliamentary seat and his London house available to the Prime Minister went unanswered.[31]

Then, in early February, he was suddenly invited to breakfast at 10 Downing Street and questioned by Lloyd George about agriculture with all the regard due to 'an equal and valued colleague'. A week later he was asked to be head of the food production department and accepted the job, having satisfied himself that he would be implementing a policy that he believed in, and that he would be subordinate only to Prothero.[32] The Minister, for his part, warmly welcomed the appointment. He was a Tory who felt no hostility to Lee and could see that his qualities would complement his own. Far from seeking to restrict the scope of his work, he asked that it should

31. Lee to DLG, 11 December 1916. His seat, he said, might be needed 'for any one of your new colleagues', and his house (in Great College Street, Westminster) had 'certain unique features as regards privacy'.

32. Ruth Lee's diary entries for 7, 8 and 14 February 1917, quoted in *A Good Innings: The Private Papers of Viscount Lee of Fareham*, ed. Alan Clark (1974), p. 165.

be as wide-ranging as possible.[33] The two men worked well together until the following year, when friction developed, leading to Lee's resignation. In retrospect Prothero recorded his own and the country's debt to Lee: 'His organising gift amounted to genius. In his hands the Department became a living force.'[34]

When offering him the job, Lloyd George made the equivalent of an apology for his neglect of Lee since becoming Prime Minister. He 'said quite frankly that he just *couldn't* see him; he was so *ashamed*; that he had said to "Maggie" (his wife) again and again: "I just *can't* see him!" L.G. added: "You see we weren't colleagues only; we had been such *pals*".'[35] This was typical Lloyd George treatment – both the neglect and the disarming explanation. Clearly he was protesting too much, but the kindness and candour were by no means entirely bogus. He could be very ruthless with old colleagues under the stress of political expediency. With him, politics always came first. But he was genuinely good-natured as well as driven, and his simple, unpompous way of explaining himself to Lee was a sign of grace as well as guile.

Equally typical of Lloyd George was the unconventional character of Lee's appointment. Though in effect Prothero's deputy, he held no ministerial rank as Director-General of the food production department. The junior minister at the Board of Agriculture was, from February, the Duke of Marlborough. Both the Prime Minister and Prothero must have relished the irony of a ministerial team formally responsible for the land in a Lloyd George government, consisting of a Duke and a Duke's agent.

Incidentally, in April the Lees became absolute owners of the Chequers estate, of which they had been life-tenants since 1909. This was to make possible the great public benefaction for which Lee's career is chiefly remembered and which will be discussed in a later chapter. Meanwhile, his work at agriculture, though less spectacular, was in fact an even larger boon, since it helped the country to survive.

The results achieved by the Prothero–Lee regime were very significant in 1917 and even more so in 1918. Britain did not, indeed, become self-sufficient in food or anything like it; that was an unattainable goal. But the forty-year agricultural depression, which the war had hitherto tended to deepen (despite a bumper harvest in 1915), was checked and put into reverse. The wheat for 1917 had already been sown in the autumn, so that

33. Prothero to DLG, 16 February 1917.
34. Ernle, *Whippingham to Westminster*, p. 310.
35. Ruth Lee's diary, 14 February (*A Good Innings*, p. 165).

production of it in the first year showed only a modest increase. But total food production was 6 per cent higher in 1917 than the previous year, and the output of oats and potatoes was, respectively, 15 and 50 per cent higher. In 1918 there were further large increases. Some loss of output in meat and dairy products has to be set against the cereal and potato gains, since the conversion of 2 million acres of grassland to arable had inevitable implications for stock farming. Yet overall the effect of the government's food production programme was to make the country substantially less dependent on imported food.

The feat was achieved by a judicious blend of direction and persuasion. The DORA regulations (supplemented in April by a corn production bill, which was not strictly necessary and proved, in the long run, more trouble than it was worth) provided the compulsory element, while persuasion took the form of propaganda from on high, technical help and advice for farmers, and the crucial device of guaranteed prices. The local executive committees were of immense value for both purposes, and they brought elasticity into the system, enabling it to adapt itself to local conditions. Labour was always a problem, but to some extent the War Office was induced to make up for its depredations by supplying home-based troops for *ad hoc* work on the land, while the women's branch of the Board of Agriculture succeeded in recruiting 260,000 village women for farm work, and also formed a Women's Land Army, eventually 12,000-strong, whose members could be sent wherever they were needed. (Apart from its practical utility, the WLA was symbolically important and had an immeasurable effect on national morale, rather like the Home Guard in the Second World War.) Another source of manpower was German prisoners-of-war; by the autumn of 1918, 30,000 of them were working on British farms.

The alternative to manpower was mechanization, and Lee took a bold initiative, with Lloyd George's backing, in placing an order for 10,000 Ford tractors. Having read in a magazine that Henry Ford had been experimenting with a small tractor-plough for his own private farm, Lee sent him the order by cable and Ford promptly built a new factory at Detroit to carry it out. (Later he told Lee that he had framed the order and that it always hung behind his desk.)[36] Unfortunately, delivery of the tractors was slow, and when they came they proved not well suited to 'the sloping fields and differing soil conditions of the United Kingdom'.[37] Advances in mechanization were not, therefore, a decisive factor in food production during the last phase of the war. But improved supply of fertilizers undoubtedly was. For

36. Lee, *A Good Innings*, pp. 166–7.　　37. Barnett, *British Food Policy*, p. 199.

instance, 'the tripling of agricultural usage of sulphate of ammonia' after 1916 'contributed strongly' to the big harvest of 1918. (Sulphate of ammonia was developed as a substitute for the potash formerly imported from Germany.)[38] Altogether, the fertilizer programme was one of the triumphs of Lee's department.

The Board of Agriculture was a newish ministry; it had been in existence since 1889 and its concerns were the farming community and the production of food in the United Kingdom. Alongside it Lloyd George created an entirely new Ministry to handle the other main aspect of food supply, distribution. The Ministry of Food was concerned with the consumers rather than the producers, though its precise status and functions were, at the outset, rather loosely defined. Unfortunately, its first chief did not come to it with clear ideas of his own as to what it should be and how it should work. Lloyd George's selection of Hudson Kearley, Lord Devonport, for the post of Minister, or 'Food Controller', seemed sensible and promising. Devonport had made his fortune in the grocery business, as founder of a pioneering chain of high-street stores. As a Liberal MP, he had served in the Campbell-Bannerman government as junior minister to Lloyd George at the Board of Trade, and in that capacity had shown political competence. Among other things, he had helped Lloyd George to establish the Port of London Authority, of which he then became chairman (leaving the House of Commons and soon afterwards taking a peerage). As head of the PLA he was generally thought to have done quite well in a new situation, though he had incurred labour hostility by refusing the dockers' demand for a minimum wage. His appointment as Food Controller was welcomed in the press.

The qualities needed for top ministerial office are, however, of a rare and special kind, and all the more so when a new Ministry has to be set up from scratch. Despite his varied experience, Devonport was found not to possess these qualities. As an entrepreneur he had worked outside the worlds of politics and officialdom; at the Board of Trade he had been only a junior minister; at the PLA he had duties and powers defined by statute. Now, as Food Controller, he had to write his own job specification and impose it. In the absence of clear guidance from the War Cabinet, he needed to take the matter into his own hands. Prothero came in with a policy of his own, and on the understanding that the War Cabinet would back it. Maclay did not hesitate to lay down the lines on which he intended his new Ministry to operate. He acted as Lloyd George himself did when asked to create a Ministry of Munitions. Devonport, by contrast, expected the structure of

---

38. Barnett, *British Food Policy*, pp. 201–2.

his department and the policy it was to carry out to be dictated by the War Cabinet. Left to his own initiative, he floundered.

Another bad defect was that he was incapable of making proper use of civil servants or outside experts. Rather like Kitchener, he tried to do everything himself. Even his junior minister, Charles Bathurst, was not given the information he needed to answer questions in the House of Commons. William Beveridge, who was transferred to the new Ministry with the Board of Trade's food department (of which he was head), found his talents spurned by Devonport. Understandably, he later wrote a scathing account of the Controller's proneness to attend personally to the most trifling matters, such as 'the construction of buns'. On one occasion a selection of sugared cakes was brought to his office for evaluation, and afterwards 'furnished a sumptuous tea for the typists of the sugar department'. In Beveridge's view, such activities suggested to the public either that the food problem was 'not serious', or that Devonport was 'missing its seriousness'.[39]

Devonport's short stint as Food Controller was not wholly barren of achievement. He won an important battle with the Treasury over the release of funds for the purchase of American wheat. Law, like McKenna before him, was worried about the trade deficit with North America, but when Devonport made a strong representation to him, on behalf of the wheat commission, he agreed to lift the Treasury restrictions. Devonport also pursued the process, begun just before the change of government, of lengthening the extraction rate of wheat and diluting wheat flour with flour from other grains, to make a 'war loaf'. At first he acted by administrative order, but in April he took over the country's larger flour mills, as a big step towards establishing a government monopoly in the manufacture of flour (which soon followed, under his successor).

Yet his moves towards increased control were contrary to his free market-eering instincts. He preferred exhortation and symbolic gestures, such as 'meatless days', to an outright system of control. This made him unpopular, particularly on account of the steep rise in food prices that was occurring. At the start of 1917 the retail cost of food was already 87 per cent above the pre-war level; five months later the figure had risen to 102 per cent. Rising food prices were among the principal grievances highlighted by the wave of strikes in May. By now Lloyd George felt that Devonport had

39. William H. Beveridge, *British Food Control* (1928), pp. 35–6. Beveridge joined the public service in 1908, at the Board of Trade under Churchill. In 1915–16 he worked at the Ministry of Munitions under Lloyd George, before returning to the Board of Trade. Originally he was an Oxford academic, and then a Toynbee Hall social idealist. He is, of course, best known for his report on social insurance in 1942.

become a liability, and the Controller's illness in May, followed by his resignation at the end of the month, were convenient to the Prime Minister, though he feigned deep regret at losing a valued colleague.[40]

He had some difficulty in finding a replacement. Robert Smillie, the miners' leader, was the first to be offered the job, but refused it. Next, Lloyd George tried to persuade Addison to take it on, but he preferred to stay at Munitions and (so soon after the Sutherland incident) his wishes had to be respected. Finally Lord Rhondda, President of the Local Government Board, accepted the post 'with unconcealed reluctance'.[41] As will be seen, he proved a remarkable success in it, though it cost him his life.

40. Devonport, promoted Viscount, returned to the PLA, whose chairmanship (like the office of Lord Chief Justice in Reading's case) he had not been obliged to relinquish. His illness was short-lived, and he remained chairman of the PLA until 1925. He died in 1934.
41. Beveridge, *British Food Control*, p. 50.

9

Honours

*Honours lists – New awards – A wedding from Downing
Street – Allenby in Egypt*

Many who have only a slight awareness (if any) of Lloyd George's true importance in history think of him above all as a man of unbridled sexual appetite,
or as one who corrupted the honours system. The first view of him is much
exaggerated, and anyway of doubtful relevance to his value as a political
leader. The second rests upon the assumption that, before Lloyd George,
honours were awarded solely with regard to personal merit and the public
interest. It also ignores the positive and constructive impact that he had upon
the honours system, which should be set against his undeniable abuse of it.

   The method of distributing honours in Britain has always been inherently
corrupt, for the obvious reason that it has been controlled by the rulers of
the state, to whose power it has served as a useful adjunct. When kings and
queens ruled, they conferred peerages upon favourites, or upon those whose
position in the country made it expedient to honour them. The Order of the
Garter was similarly used, and James I invented the lesser hereditary rank
of baronet simply as a means of raising funds. After the Glorious Revolution
the honours patronage of the Crown largely passed, first to a Parliamentary
oligarchy, then to government based on a wider, but still limited, franchise,
and finally to today's big government based on universal suffrage. But
the honours system has remained, through all the constitutional changes,
manifestly susceptible to the influences of money and power.

   Merit has, of course, made considerable headway. In the eighteenth
century the Order of the Bath was instituted, mainly for the recognition of
martial services. Victorious commanders, too, were likely to be made baronets or peers, and this practice continued. In the early nineteenth century
another order was created, that of St Michael and St George, whose chief
purpose was to lend dignity to the country's growing army of diplomats
and proconsuls.[1] The same century also witnessed some recognition of

---

1. Separate orders were created for the Indian Empire, but these died with it, though a few
members of them still survive.

technological innovators (such as Brunel and Paxton), and there were peerages for a poet (Tennyson), a painter (Leighton) and a surgeon (Lister).[2] But the bulk of honours, and the highest, went to politicians and the representatives of new money, the entrepreneurs and captains of industry, who needed social status and knew how to obtain it.

In 1902 the Order of Merit was established, in the personal gift of the Sovereign. Confined to twenty-four members (plus a few eminent foreigners) it has, on the whole, proved worthy of its name.[3] This inaugurated an age in which, at all levels, the truly deserving were to have a better chance of recognition. Yet the broadening of the system to include many categories of meritorious service – a process which, as we shall see, Lloyd George greatly assisted – has not removed its underlying tendency to serve the self-interest of the party, or parties, in power. In the twentieth century financiers and industrialists were joined by press magnates and media personalities as outstanding beneficiaries of the system. From absolute monarchs to democratic leaders the element of corruption has remained, though some have been more adept than others at disguising it.

When Lloyd George became Prime Minister he had more pressing matters to attend to than the honours system, and the list for New Year 1917 did not, in fact, appear until mid-February. But meanwhile he recommended one man for a peerage: W. M. Aitken, already (since the previous year) a baronet. The King objected strongly, but was overridden.[4] Aitken, who thus became Lord Beaverbrook, was Law's nominee – and it should be made clear that most of the political honours conferred during Lloyd George's premiership went to Conservatives. Since their party was dominant in his coalition, it naturally felt entitled to the lion's share of the traditional spoils.

The immediate reason for ennobling Aitken was that his Parliamentary seat was needed for a new minister.[5] He was also Law's closest friend, and had been privy to the negotiations leading to the change of government, though his role in them was rather less important than his own account of

2. Macaulay might be added as a historian, but since he was also a politician, who sat in Cabinets, his position is somewhat equivocal.

3. A few years earlier the personal honours patronage of the Sovereign had been substantially revived, when the Victorian Order was created. And after the Second World War the right to confer the ancient Orders of the Garter and Thistle was restored to the Sovereign (by a Labour prime minister, Clement Attlee).

4. In law, the Sovereign is the fountain of honour, but in practice most honours are conferred on the Prime Minister's advice. The Sovereign can express an opinion, but can withhold formal assent only at the risk of a constitutional crisis.

5. Sir Albert Stanley, President of the Board of Trade.

them might suggest.[6] Since he had just gained control of the *Daily Express*, he became the latest 'press baron', following Burnham (of the *Daily Telegraph*) and Northcliffe, both elevated by Balfour in 1903, and Northcliffe's brother Rothermere, who received his peerage from Asquith in 1914.

When Lloyd George's first list eventually appeared, on 13 February, it contained few surprises, and was similar in character to Asquith's last Birthday honours the previous June. This had named five new peers, twelve baronets (headed by Aitken) and thirty-one knights. Lloyd George's total was slightly smaller: one peer, seven baronets and twenty-eight knights. The peer was Sir Hugh Graham (who took the title Atholstan). Like Aitken he was a Canadian and a press magnate – founder and proprietor of the *Star* group in Montreal – but one who had stayed in Canada. His prominence in the list aroused some interest, and seemed to be in keeping with Lloyd George's desire to make suitable gestures to the Dominions. There was also recognition for men who had served him and the country well at the Ministry of Munitions; among others, his director of area organization there, James Stevenson, was awarded a baronetcy, and W. A. Tritton, to whom the development of tanks was (according to the citation) 'largely due', a knighthood.[7] Among other knights were the naval historian Julian Corbett and the medievalist Paul Vinogradoff.

The 1917 Birthday honours list, published on 4 June, was rather larger, including five peers, twenty-five baronets and forty-six knights. There was nothing abnormal about the list, apart perhaps from the award of knighthoods to three Canadians. It was on the whole just the usual concoction of political nominees, men from outside politics contributing to the war effort, and a few others of miscellaneous merit. Yet it was precisely because it represented no significant departure from the norm that it was attacked by *The Times* in a powerful leader, under the heading 'Party Honours and Party Funds':

we may be allowed to wonder ... whether our political system really requires a wholesale periodical output of peerages, baronetcies and knighthoods *in return for some heavy disbursement* or for purely party services. MR. LLOYD GEORGE, after some hesitation, seems to have swallowed the system whole. For sheer bulk *his recommendations will challenge comparison with those of any of his predecessors,*

6. Lord Beaverbrook, *Politicians and the War, 1914–1916* (1928), chapter XVI.
7. Tritton had none of the boastfulness that we have observed in Sir Leo Chiozza Money. His *Who's Who* entry after the war was conspicuously brief (five lines) and claimed much less than the citation for his knighthood: 'sometime at Ministry of Munitions; took a share in development of Tanks'.

none of whom can afford to cast a stone at him ... [Despite good names] the old atmosphere of party bargaining hangs heavy over the List. *One would say, at a casual glance, that it was compounded in the main from an ancient file of pledges in the Unionist Central Office*, reinforced by certain special obligations contracted under the present regime.

This was 'a public outrage', while 'thousands were making the supreme sacrifice unrecognized'. Party funds should be audited and reasons given for party-political honours. There would be 'a great future' for the statesman who had 'the courage to get rid once and for all of *a cynical traffic* and incidentally to restore the value of decoration for real service to the State'.[8]

It is clear that *The Times* was attacking Lloyd George, not for making the honours system corrupt, but for missing a historic opportunity to purge it of corruption. This should be noted by anyone who thinks that the sale of honours was started by Lloyd George. In fact, it neither started with him nor ended with him. The same critique of the system could have been written at any time before or after his premiership. Attempts to make the system respectable have hitherto (up to the end of the twentieth century) been largely cosmetic. The system remains essentially flawed, because it has never ceased to be under the ruling establishment's control.

The leader-writer (probably the editor, Geoffrey Dawson) was mistaken in suggesting that Lloyd George considered abandoning the traditional system. There is no evidence that he hesitated for this reason. Delay in producing his first list was due to overwhelming pressure of work, rather than to any need to give himself time to reflect on the way honours should be conferred. He was genuinely radical, but never systematically so. On some issues he could be thoroughly conservative and he was always pragmatic rather than philosophic in his approach. Good men of action are seldom philosopher-kings, and he was not one of the rare exceptions.

After his fall from power, when the honours scandal was being laid exclusively at his door by people who had participated in it under his regime, and who were carrying it on (if more discreetly), Lloyd George put a case for what *The Times* called 'a cynical traffic'. Talking to Stanley Baldwin's henchman, J. C. C. Davidson, he said:

You and I know perfectly well it is a far cleaner method of filling the Party chest than the methods used in the United States or the Socialist Party. . . . In America the

8. *The Times*, 4 June 1917, my italics. It was a peculiarity of *Times* style that the names of individuals mentioned in leading articles were printed in capital letters (until July 1968).

steel trusts support one political party, and the cotton people support another. This placed political parties under the domination of great financial interests and trusts . . . Here a man gives £40,000 to the Party and gets a baronetcy. If he comes to the Leader of the Party and says I subscribe largely to the Party funds, you must do this or that, we can tell him to go to the devil. The attachment of the brewers to the Conservative Party is the closest approach to political corruption in this country. The worst of it is you cannot defend it in public, but it keeps politics far cleaner than any other method of raising funds.[9]

The argument had a great deal of force, and was refreshingly free from hypocrisy and cant. But of course it was not true that selling honours was the cleanest possible method of financing parties. It might be – indeed was – less damaging to the public interest than a method which resulted in the control of parties by large corporations or trade unions. But it was surely casuistical to suggest that no cleaner method could be found. If Lloyd George had had the time and inclination, he could have devised a method which would have removed all taint from the honours system while guaranteeing the independence of parties. But he was short of time, and anyway had no more inclination than his predecessors and successors to forgo a singularly convenient aid to political management.

Even so, he was less conservative about honours than about the voting system. Though he did not change the basic *modus operandi*, he used it with imagination and much altruism, as well as with guile. In the matter of hereditary honours (the most coveted), he showed a complete disregard for the assumption, still at the time widely held, that they needed to be 'supported' by social and economic status of a particular kind. Right through the nineteenth century and into the twentieth it was expected of a peer or baronet that he should have a place in the country, if not inherited then acquired. Land was seen as an almost indispensable concomitant of rank. There were some signs before Lloyd George that this idea was beginning to be called in question; after him it was generally felt to be obsolete. He

---

9. *Memoirs of a Conservative: J. C. C. Davidson's Memoirs and Papers, 1910–37*, ed. Robert Rhodes James (1969), p. 279. Baldwin liked to give the impression that he had restored probity and decency to public life after the Lloyd George regime, but the same source betrays the truth: 'lunched with Sir William Berry. He is very anti-Lloyd George . . . At the end he asked me whether . . . it would be possible for him to be considered for a peerage. I told him that it was more than possible and that I was quite certain the Prime Minister [Baldwin] would be favourably disposed. For many reasons I felt it would be better if it were after the election' (ibid., pp. 296–7). Berry, who had recently taken possession of the *Daily Telegraph*, duly became Lord Camrose just after the next election.

extended the ambit of hereditary honours, and in particular made the peerage more representative than it had ever been (though it was still, of course, by no means representative of society as a whole).

Yet it was not in relation to hereditary honours or other established forms of public recognition that Lloyd George's influence on the system was most marked. By far the most important change associated with his regime was the introduction of new honours, whose effect was wide-ranging and, on the whole, salutary. They did not spring suddenly from his mind when he became Prime Minister, nor can he be regarded as the inventor of them at all. For some time there had been talk, in royal circles and elsewhere, of new awards to meet the demands and deserts of the nation at war. But it was no coincidence that the matter came to a head when Lloyd George assumed the premiership, and in the awards themselves, as they emerged, his views and outlook were unmistakably reflected.

The first intimation was a news item early in the New Year: 'We understand that an official announcement may shortly be expected of the creation by the King of a new Imperial Order . . . with a view to rewarding suitably those who have rendered signal services, both in military and civil capacities . . . all subjects of the Crown, both at home and overseas, will be eligible.'[10] The reference to 'all subjects of the Crown' may have been a hint that the male monopoly of honours, hitherto almost absolute,[11] was about to be broken. But whether or not it was so intended, the point was not clarified until six months later, when details of the new awards were given.

Soon after the routine Birthday honours list the creation of two new orders was announced. They were to be named the Order of the British Empire and the Order of the Companions of Honour. Both were to be open to women as well as men. The former was to consist of five classes, in which the top two would carry knighthoods for men as in the Orders of the Bath and St Michael and St George (as well as the Indian and the Victorian Orders), while female members in the same classes would be entitled to the style 'Dame'. The Companions of Honour, who were to be 'closely restricted

10. *The Times*, 4 January 1917.

11. The Order of the Garter was open to royal ladies, and peerages had occasionally been given to women in their own right; for instance, to the philanthropist Angela Burdett-Coutts and to Disraeli's wife, Mary Anne (who anticipated him in taking the title Beaconsfield). The Order of Merit did not exclude women, though it was only with difficulty Edward VII had been persuaded to appoint Florence Nightingale to it in her extreme old age.

in numbers', would put the letters CH after their names, but the order would carry 'no title or precedence'.[12]

It was not until the end of August that the first lists appeared and even then it was stated that there would have to be a further delay before publication of lists for the Dominions and India, and for 'the Civil, Military and Naval Services'. The first list of appointments to the Order of the British Empire was, in any case, long enough – 268 names of people selected mainly for voluntary war work on the home front. To emphasize the sexual equality that the order was asserting, the first name was that of the Queen, who headed the list of GBEs (Grand Masters). Of the five original DBEs, three were peeresses (Lady Dufferin, Lady Byron and Lady Londonderry). The other two were Mrs Alfred Lyttelton, widow of a Tory Cabinet minister, and Mrs Charles Lees, Mayor of Oldham. The preponderance of blue blood in this quintet cannot be denied, but all, in their different ways, were worthy of the honour.[13]

The original CBEs (Commanders) included Gertrude Bell, scholar and Arabist, Margaret McMillan, pioneer of nursery schools and physical education, and Havelock Wilson, founder of the Seamen's and Firemen's Union. More trade unionists appeared among the OBEs (Officers) and MBEs (Members), as did other figures of evidently solid worth. In the list as a whole the party-political flavour was slight, granted the numbers involved.

Originally part of the order, but later separated from it, was the British Empire Medal (BEM). The first list appeared on the same day (25 August), and the first recipient, alphabetically, was Jenny Algar, who was awarded the medal 'for presence of mind and good example on the occasion of an explosion at a shell-filling factory'. The citations were various, but the common theme was courage or devotion beyond the line of duty, shown by ordinary people doing ordinary jobs.

Taking the Order of the British Empire and the BEM together, one is struck by the novelty of what was occurring. Hitherto the honours system had touched only a tiny section of the population – the political class, the rich and powerful outside politics, the higher ranks of the armed forces and the civil service, and a very few others. The great mass of the people did not,

12. *The Times*, 22 June 1917.
13. Lady Dufferin had been her husband's consort in a remarkable variety of posts, as Ambassador to Russia, Turkey, Italy and France, as Governor-General of Canada, and as Viceroy of India. Lady Byron, an ardent campaigner for women's suffrage (though not a suffragette), was donor and administrator of the first Rest Home for Tired Nurses. Lady Londonderry was founder of the Women's Legion. Mrs Lyttelton (a 'Soul') was a general do-gooder, whose citation singled out her work for war refugees. Mrs Lees was an outstanding regional figure, concerned with nursing and music as well as local government.

apparently, qualify for honours in the estimation of those who controlled the system. Soldiers and sailors received campaign medals, and other awards culminating in the Victoria Cross, but there was no comparable recognition for civilian services, which could be no less arduous and were often dangerous, particularly in wartime. As for titles and membership of the orders of chivalry, these were confined to a minuscule privileged élite.

All this changed in 1917. The Order of the British Empire was, as we should now say, a people's order; and where its five classes did not reach, the BEM did. For the first time there was potential public recognition for all citizens. The comprehensive character of the order ensured its rapid expansion. Its membership soared, and within four years had reached a figure of over 25,000. The publishers of *Burke's Peerage* then produced a similar bible for the Order of the British Empire, describing it as 'British Democracy's Own Order of Chivalry'.[14]

By contrast, the other order created at the same time, the Companions of Honour, was élitist in character, though non-titular and for both sexes. The first list of seventeen names was headed by that of 'Lieut.-Gen. Right Hon. J. C. Smuts', a natural choice for Lloyd George. An outstanding woman in the list was Violet Markham, then at a quite early stage in her long and beneficent career. Though a Liberal, and sister of Lloyd George's old friend (and enlightened coal-owner) Arthur Markham, she could not be thought to owe her selection merely to partisan or personal favour. Before 1914 she had done important slum relief work in her native Derbyshire, and since the outbreak of war had worked with Robert Morant on national relief before being appointed to a high post in the new Ministry of National Service. Among the original Companions of Honour there were also two trade union leaders, and one of Lloyd George's star recruits to the Ministry of Munitions, Lord Chetwynd.

The CH was less restricted than the OM, but still restricted enough to give it scarcity value and prestige. (Its membership came to be limited to sixty-five.) Over the years it has maintained a tolerably high standard; one recipient[15] called it 'the poor man's OM'. Since recommendations for it lie with the Prime Minister, it has been used rather too often for the reward or consolation of politicians, some distinctly mediocre. One who could certainly not be so described, however, was Winston Churchill. He was recommended for it by Lloyd George in 1922, and it was the only such honour that he held until 1946, when he received the OM. Apart from politicians, its recipients have tended to be people of distinction in a wide variety of fields.

14. *Burke's Handbook to the Order of the British Empire* (1921), introduction.
15. Maurice Bowra.

The net effect of the new honours introduced in 1917 was advantageous to the state. But there was undeniably a debit side. The vast extension of patronage in the hands of government, especially the Prime Minister's, was a potential menace. Multiplying the number of honours a thousandfold and more, without depoliticizing the method of appointment, could in theory have led to wholesale corruption. But in fact it neither did so under Lloyd George nor has done so since. The grey expanses of the Order of the British Empire have doubtless concealed, over the years, a fair amount of skulduggery. But routine party-political abuse of it though ever-present, has never been quite flagrant enough, or on a large enough scale, to bring the order into serious discredit.

Towards the end of Lloyd George's premiership the honours system became an issue on which an increasingly mutinous Conservative Party chose to denounce him, though with very questionable moral credentials for doing so. Meanwhile, as a warning against facile or oversimplified judgements, we should note the strange but instructive case of Horace Farquhar, who appeared as a viscount in the 1917 Birthday honours list.

Farquhar had an extraordinary talent for flourishing under different regimes. Though a Tory, he also did well out of Liberal Prime Ministers. Originally a friend of Edward VII, he became very close to George V and a senior member of his Household. He bought a barony from Lord Salisbury's government in 1898 – paying, as he put it, more than the 'accepted tariff'. Campbell-Bannerman recommended him for a privy counsellorship, and Asquith for the office of Lord Steward (then political) during the period of the first wartime coalition. In 1917 he was treasurer of the Conservative Party, and it was through him that negotiations with would-be honorands were conducted on the Tory side. Under Lloyd George he became a viscount and later an earl, as well as GCB (Grand Cross of the Order of the Bath), without, of course, a word of protest from his Tory colleagues or from his friend the King.

After the fall of Lloyd George's government, it was found that at least half of the money he had raised from Tory sources had been paid into the Coalition Liberal fund (of which Lloyd George retained control) and that much of the Tory share of the spoils had disappeared. When, soon afterwards, he died, his estate had to be sold to pay off enormous personal debts. Throughout his career there were people who knew that he was (to put it mildly) a financial adventurer, but refrained from exposing him because his connections were so exalted.[16]

16. Kenneth Rose, *King George V* (1983), pp. 274–80.

At one o'clock on 19 June Lloyd George took out his watch and told his War Cabinet colleagues that he would have to bring their meeting (a vital one, as we shall see) to an end, because he had an important engagement that afternoon. He had, in fact, to attend the marriage of his daughter Olwen to Captain Thomas Carey Evans, and to give her away. The bridegroom's family, from Blaenau Ffestiniog, was well known to the Lloyd Georges, and they had none of the reservations about the marriage that they had felt about Dick's. Fortunately for all concerned, their optimism was justified.

Olwen, born in 1892, was the Lloyd Georges' third child and elder surviving daughter. She had been to school at Roedean, and then sent for cultural improvement to Dresden and Paris before the war. Her French became good enough to enable her to interpret for her father when French politicians were visiting. In 1915 she went to France as member of the Voluntary Aid Detachment and stayed for about a year, before returning to help with her mother's war work. She was therefore at home when Tom Carey Evans, on leave from Mesopotamia in 1916, came to lunch at 11 Downing Street.

He was eight years older than Olwen, and in 1907 was already a practising surgeon in North Wales, having been educated at Brighton College, and having done university courses at Cardiff and Glasgow as well as in Brussels. In 1910 he joined the Indian Medical Service as an army officer attached to an Indian regiment, and in this capacity served throughout the Gallipoli campaign, being awarded the MC and three mentions in despatches. He and Olwen got on well at their first meeting, and before his leave ended he proposed to her. She did not accept at once, but in January 1917 cabled him in Mesopotamia: 'Happy birthday. Yes. Love Olwen.'[17]

Lloyd George nevertheless asked her if she was quite sure she loved him. Would she be 'frightfully upset if he didn't come home'? Her answer was entirely positive, but the question might have proved all too apposite, because Tom was lucky to get home for the wedding. His ship was torpedoed, and for a time – during which Lloyd George kept the news from Olwen – his fate was uncertain. But eventually a telegram to the Admiralty gave the news that he was safe, and he himself arrived with four days to spare.

The wedding was simple, involving only the couple's families and a few friends. After lunch at 10 Downing Street, Lloyd George drove with Olwen, in his Rolls Royce, to the Welsh Baptist chapel in Castle Street, where he

---

17. His birthday, 17 January, was the same as Lloyd George's.

was a frequent attender.[18] The service was conducted mainly in Welsh, though there was an address by Dr John Clifford, veteran Nonconformist gladiator, and Annie Rees sang 'The King of Love' by Ivor Novello. The bridesmaids were Megan and two young cousins of Tom on his mother's side, Elaine and Gwendoline Armstrong-Jones.[19] Olwen wore a white satin dress with a chiffon train, lined in shell pink. As she and Tom left the chapel a group of wounded soldiers from Millbank Hospital formed a guard of honour, and some girl munition workers presented her with a bouquet of carnations.

Back at Number 10, the reception was even more austere than Dick's had been at the Empire Hotel in Bath. There, at least there had been a real wedding cake, but Olwen had only an imitation one made of cardboard, in deference to the government's cult of voluntary frugality. Like Dick and his wife, the Carey Evanses went to Cornwall for their honeymoon, but a delay in Tom's recall to Mesopotamia gave them a few extra days, which they spent in Wales. They were at Criccieth when he received his summons.[20]

Their marriage was a success, and ended only with his somewhat premature death in 1947. Olwen lived on into extreme, but robust, old age, and from 1967 until her death in 1990 was the last surviving child of the Lloyd Georges. Her own family consisted of four children (two girls and two boys), the first Margaret – born in 1918. Her attitude towards her father was more relaxed than that of Dick or Megan, who were both, in their different ways, obsessional about him. The nearest to her, in this respect, was Gwilym, but he differed from her in being also relatively relaxed about Frances Stevenson, which she most certainly was not. To her, as to Megan and her other brother, Frances never ceased to be an object of resentment and hatred. This was a little surprising, because unlike them Olwen was capable of seeing some faults in her mother, and of admitting that she might not always have been an absolutely dedicated wife to the politician that, when she married him, she knew Lloyd George intended to be.[21]

Olwen's independent spirit was matched and sustained by her husband's. Carey Evans had his own distinguished career, which only at one point

18. Since Lloyd George was a Baptist, his wife a Methodist, their children alternated between the two denominations – Richard the eldest, a Baptist, Mair a Methodist, Olwen a Baptist and so on. In practice it made little difference, the family not being given to sectarian purism.
19. Aunts of the future Lord Snowdon.
20. There was hardly any press coverage of the wedding, perhaps at Lloyd George's request. The account of it given here is based largely on Olwen's own memoir (*Lloyd George was my Father: The Autobiography of Lady Olwen Carey Evans* (1985), pp. 84–5 and 91–6), and on Harry Harrison's *Lloyd George Family History* (privately circulated).
21. This matter is discussed in detail in my *Lloyd George: The Young Lloyd George* (1973), particularly pp. 77–81.

could be said to have owed anything to his father-in-law. His appointment as medical adviser to Lord Reading, when he was Viceroy of India, must surely have been influenced, at least indirectly, by Lloyd George. (Other things being equal, people tend to give jobs to the close relations of old friends.) But this appointment, though it brought him a knighthood, Carey Evans regarded as a mixed blessing, since it probably denied him the chance to become head of the Indian Medical Service. In any case, while he respected Lloyd George – and the respect was mutual – he was never over-awed by him, but on the contrary often stood up to him, sometimes quite aggressively.

Olwen's wedding brought Lloyd George a friendly and philosophical letter from a Tory colleague with whom, in the past, he had often crossed swords. Lord Robert Cecil (Minister of Blockade) wrote:

Just a line to offer you my heartiest . . . congratulations on the marriage of your daughter. I did not feel that my very slight acquaintance with Mrs Evans justified me in sending her personally my good wishes but perhaps if you have the opportunity you will convey them to her. These things are like flowers in the waste of war. It is after all only a stupendous interlude in human history & the happiness of young people reminds us that in a few years all the carnage & cruelty – yes & all the heroism as well – will be memories of the past.[22]

Cecil had been one of Lloyd George's severest critics over the Marconi affair. During debates on the Welsh Church bill in 1912 he had attacked him for seeking to plunder Church property, while Lloyd George had replied that the hands of families such as Cecil's were 'dripping with the fat of sacrilege'. Cecil was later to resign from Lloyd George's post-war government on the same issue, after many other disagreements. His letter shows how strong, meanwhile, was the spirit of political ecumenism in 1917, and how transformed Lloyd George was in the eyes of former opponents.

During the past six months things had been looking up in the theatre to which Carey Evans returned after his marriage and honeymoon. In February the Indo-British army in Mesopotamia, commanded by General Sir Frederick Maude, recaptured Kut-al-Amara on the Tigris – lost in humiliating circumstances the previous year – and in March went on to capture Baghdad. A further advance up the river enabled the food-control points to be secured, so consolidating the army's gains. These successes were achieved by heavy superiority over the Turks in numbers and equipment, combined with

22. Robert Cecil to DLG, 20 June 1917.

careful planning. Their chief value was for British morale at home, at a time when cheering news was in particularly short supply. Even Robertson, in principle no friend to 'sideshows', wrote in anticipation of Maude's campaign: 'Moral effect counts for more than usual at this stage of the war.' He was enthusiastic about Maude's progress, and determined at least to enable him to hold on to what he had won, against an enemy potentially strengthened by the disappearance of a Russian threat on the Caucasus front.[23]

Victory in the Middle East was not, indeed, merely a question of morale, important though that was. The war against the Ottoman Empire was a sideshow only when compared with the war against Germany. In other respects it was a major struggle, in which substantial interests were at stake. Politicians and generals could agree that to lose the war in the Middle East would be a catastrophe, and that defeat of the Turks and the break-up of their empire were thoroughly desirable ends. The problem was to agree on the allocation of forces needed to accomplish them. Lloyd George intended that Mesopotamia, with its oil resources, should be a British sphere of interest after the war, a policy to which the Asquith government had been committed. He also regarded Palestine as an objective of special significance, both because of its appeal to the popular imagination (including his own) and because it could serve as a protective buffer to the British position in Egypt. After Maude's success in Mesopotamia he looked for a comparable advance from Egypt into Palestine.

The commander of the British Egyptian army was Sir Archibald Murray. He was a capable but unlucky general. For a very short time in the autumn of 1915 he had been CIGS, but at the end of the year he had to make way for Robertson and was sent to Egypt. Accepting his diminished role with a good grace, he made an excellent start in it throughout 1916. After defeating a Turkish force within a few miles of the Suez Canal he pushed forward to the Palestine border, laying a railway line and a water main to sustain the position thus gained. But when ordered to invade Palestine the following March he could not get beyond Gaza. Indeed, after capturing the town at the first attempt he soon had to withdraw from it, and at the second found the Turks well prepared and was repulsed. His force was in any case inadequate for a full-blooded campaign in Palestine, as he tried to explain. Despite his earlier achievements the setbacks at Gaza unfairly tarnished his record. He was now associated with failure and had to go.[24]

23. Maude did not live to be showered with honours at the end of the war, as other victorious commanders were, since he succumbed to cholera in November 1917. But his gains were held.
24. On his return to England he was appointed to the Aldershot command, but retired from the army in 1922. He lived on until 1945.

For a successor Lloyd George turned at first to Smuts, to whom he offered the prospect of undertaking 'the last and greatest Crusade'.[25] Smuts toyed with the idea for a month before deciding against it. (During the same period he was offered, and refused, the chairmanship of the Irish Convention.) When Smuts ruled himself out another name emerged, that of Sir Edmund Allenby. Allenby was commander of the Third Army in France, and as such had conducted the recent battle of Arras. Relations between him and Haig, never good, had been exacerbated by disagreements over the battle.[26] Robertson, however, thought highly of Allenby and proposed that he should take Murray's place, judging that more than one purpose would thus be served; Allenby would be removed from Haig's sphere, while the army in Egypt would acquire a dynamic new leader, yet one who would conform to his (Robertson's) view of strategic priorities. Lloyd George was amenable to the suggestion, having himself formed a good opinion of Allenby, which Allenby warmly reciprocated. In Robertson's presence Lloyd George gave him the objective of capturing Jerusalem 'as a Christmas present for the British nation', and promised him the necessary reinforcements.[27] He arrived in Egypt and took up his command at the end of June.

His impact upon a bruised and demoralized army anticipated Bernard Montgomery's in the same theatre a quarter of a century later. Allenby moved his headquarters forward from Cairo to the Palestine front, and within weeks of his arrival had visited most of the units under his command, leaving a sense of vitality and confidence wherever he went. In the words of the Australian Official History, 'he went through the hot, dusty camps of his army like a strong, fresh, reviving wind'.[28] The relative independence of his new role, and the change of scene from the Western front, seemed also to have a liberating effect upon himself. He had earned the nickname 'the Bull' for his brusque manner and proneness to violent outbursts of temper,

25. Smuts to his mother, 27 April 1917 (letter translated from the original Afrikaans in *Selections from the Smuts Papers*, ed. W. K. Hancock and Jean van der Poel (7 vols., 1966–73), vol. iii).

26. Though both were cavalrymen, they had incompatible temperaments. This was already evident when they were contemporaries at the staff college at Camberley. Allenby was far more popular and defeated Haig for the coveted post of master of the drag-hounds (Lawrence James, *Imperial Warrior: The Life and Times of Field-Marshal Viscount Allenby, 1861–1936* (1993), p. 23).

27. Archibald Wavell, *Allenby: A Study in Greatness* (1940), p. 186. (Wavell, then a colonel, was appointed to Allenby's staff in July, as Robertson's representative. He soon became a devoted admirer of Allenby.)

28. The army in Egypt included, at the time, one Australian and one Anzac mounted division.

which could often conceal his fundamental warm-heartedness. The former characteristics remained, but with less frustration and more scope for action his good qualities flowered. Before long he was to prove one of the most effective commanders of the war. (It should be added that a marked point of difference between him and Montgomery was that he was generous in acknowledging what he and his army owed to the work of his predecessor, whereas Montgomery's attitude to Auchinleck was brutally mean.)

Before launching the dramatic operations that will be described in Chapter 19, Allenby needed to be sure that he had overwhelming superiority in numbers and equipment. He had been promised reinforcements, but they could not be spared from the Western front. One new division was therefore formed from troops in India, and another source of manpower was the Salonica front, from which two divisions were in due course transferred, together with substantial artillery. The reduction of the British force at Salonica could hardly have been contemplated without French agreement, however grudging. But this Lloyd George was able to obtain as part of a bargain in which, during May, he changed his policy towards Greece.

At the Rome conference in January he had resisted General Sarrail's demand for the removal of King Constantine; but by May he had changed his mind, partly because circumstances had changed. Venizelos's provisional Greek government at Salonica, and the military supporting him, had gained in strength. It seemed less likely than in January that an Allied *coup* in Athens, deposing the King and restoring Venizelos to power there, would provoke a civil war. On the contrary, Lloyd George now felt that the risk of allowing Constantine to remain, as an unfriendly neutral to the rear of the Allied position, was more than that of taking action which stood a fair chance of bringing Greece as a whole into the war as an ally.

There was no early prospect of moving forward from Salonica. Sarrail's offensive against the Bulgarians in April had been a failure (though it had enabled the Serbians to regain a small piece of their national territory, at Monastir). With the Russians an increasingly doubtful factor, the most that could be expected of the Salonica front for the time being was that it would hold. Since the war seemed to have demonstrated that fewer troops were needed for defence than for attack, there was reason to believe that two British divisions could be withdrawn without endangering the Allied line. But the line would obviously be more secure if Greece were under a single government and part of the Alliance.

Lloyd George therefore agreed to the enforced deposition of Constantine and gave the French a free hand to carry it out.[29] In return, they accepted that the British force at Salonica would be reduced. The gamble underlying this bargain paid off. After a show of strength by the French, Constantine abdicated, *de facto* if not *de jure*, and retired to Switzerland, accompanied by the Crown Prince George, while Venizelos reasserted his power in Athens, acknowledging Constantine's second son, Alexander, as King. There was no civil war, though the schism in Greek political life between Constantinists and Venizelists was not healed. Opponents of Venizelos were purged from the army, the police and the public services, and a number of dissident politicians were, like Constantine, exiled. But Venizelos was a genuine national leader. He brought his country into the war on the Allied side. This had been his consistent policy. He was never anybody's puppet. Though he prudently refrained from holding an immediate election to validate his return to power, he had a respectable claim to democratic legitimacy in 1917. Two years earlier Constantine had forced him to resign as Prime Minister, though he had a Parliamentary majority and an electoral mandate recently renewed. The issue on which the breach had occurred was Venizelos's belief that the Allies would win and that Greece should make common cause with them.[30]

Lloyd George and Venizelos had first met in December 1912, when the latter came to London and was asked to breakfast at 11 Downing Street. They were already in touch through the Greek Consul-General in London, John Stavridi, whom Lloyd George had first got to know as a fellow-lawyer. The personal and political rapport between the two leaders was instant. Both were adventurous politicians with large ideas; both had moved, geographically, from the periphery to the centre – Lloyd George from Wales, Venizelos from Crete. After their first encounters Venizelos praised Lloyd George's 'splendid capacities and clear insight', while Lloyd George

29. Hankey thought that the French had deceived Lloyd George and committed a 'horrid breach of faith' (Hankey diary, 17 June 1917). But he was clearly mistaken. Lloyd George either helped Painlevé to arrange the *coup* or, at the very least, knew what the French were planning and showed that he approved of it (*RWD*, 10 and 16 June 1917; FSD, 28 and 29 May 1917).

30. He and Constantine had not always been at cross-purposes. During the Balkan wars of 1912–13 they worked together, Venizelos leading the country, Constantine commanding the army. (He became King in 1913, when his father was assassinated at Salonica – which Greece had acquired in the second war.) On the question of Greek participation in the First World War Constantine became the rallying-point for those who thought that it was in the country's interest to remain neutral. His own attitude must also have been influenced by the fact that the Kaiser was his brother-in-law.

described Venizelos as 'a big man, a very big man'.[31] Their mutual admiration and shared aspirations were to have disastrous consequences a few years later, for themselves and for their countries. In particular, the link with Venizelos was to contribute, in no small measure, to Lloyd George's downfall. But few could have foreseen this in 1917, and meanwhile the war had to be won.

One victim of the fighting at Gaza was Bonar Law's second son, Charlie, a lieutenant in the King's Own Scottish Borderers. Though he was reported missing in mid-April, for weeks there was hope that he might have been taken prisoner, which seemed to be confirmed when a list of British prisoners including his name was received from the Vatican. But soon the cruel truth emerged that there had been a deciphering error omitting the word 'not'. Charlie was not a prisoner; he was dead.

Though Lloyd George lived next door to Law and saw him almost every day, he felt moved to write:

My dear Bonar,

My heart bleeds for your sorrow, for I know from experience the anguish you must be passing through.

The fact that you are one of a vast multitude who are treading the dark valley of grief will not I know bring consolation, for each man carries his own burden on that tear-sodden road; but the knowledge that your gallant boy gave his life for a great cause must sustain you in your trial.

May I again drawing on experience urge you to remember that time and work acting in concert are the only healers. I threw myself into hard work without waiting a day, and it saved me.

However, I know how little words of the sincerest sympathy avail. All the same believe me, my dear Bonar, I feel in my heart for you.

Ever sincerely
D.Ll.G.[32]

Lloyd George was recalling the supreme bereavement in his own life, the death in 1907 of his eldest daughter, Mair. His well-meant advice was redundant, because Law had taken refuge in non-stop work when devastated by his wife's death in 1909, and did so again when faced with the loss of

31. Conversations recorded in Sir John Stavridi's diary 1912–15 (quoted in Michael Llewellyn Smith, *Ionian Vision: Greece in Asia Minor, 1919–1922* (1973), p. 18).
32. DLG to ABL, 6 June 1917.

Charlie. The same remedy had to serve him yet again a few months later, when his eldest son, Jim, was killed in action.

Lloyd George clearly knew that his words could do little to console a man who was prone, at the best of times, to pessimism and melancholy. But he also knew that Law had a toughness of spirit that few could match. However miserable, he did not give in.

10

Haig Gets His Way

Lloyd George and Haig – Plan for Third Ypres – Discussed at
War Policy Committee – Haig gets his way

In Paris at the beginning of May Lloyd George was at pains to make amends
to Haig for the damage inflicted at Calais, and for his failure to mention the
Field-Marshal in his recent Guildhall speech. We have seen how warmly he
spoke of Haig to Esher, and at the Allied conference he seems to have openly
pledged all-out support for him, disclaiming any pretension to be a strategist
and saying that he left that side of things to his military advisers. He gave
Haig 'full power to attack where and when [he] thought best', adding that
he wished the French government would treat its own commanders in the
same way.[1]

We should note the exact timing and context of these injudicious remarks.
Nivelle's offensive had failed, while Haig's subsidiary operations had apparently succeeded. The capture of Vimy ridge was a palpable triumph, and it
could still be hoped that the advance beyond Arras would continue. In any
case, it was necessary to persist with the Arras battle to take the heat off the
French and to encourage them to keep fighting. According to Hankey, the
main purpose of the conference was 'to ginger up the French to renew their
efforts on the western front, and to give the enemy no respite'.[2] Lloyd
George had no idea of the extent of demoralization in the French army. He
may not yet have entirely despaired of Nivelle, who was still Commander-in-
Chief (though Pétain had been appointed Chief of Staff to the War Minister).
He knew that Nivelle had suffered from confused political attitudes to his
offensive, which may account for the hint that the French government
should back its military commander.

Even the weather may have affected Lloyd George's state of mind. Warm
sunshine had come to Paris after a period of cold and rain, and Lloyd George
always responded to the sun. Above all, he was a natural optimist, quick to
look on the bright side – on this occasion, too quick.

1. Haig diary, 3 May 1917. There is no reason to doubt the essential accuracy of this record.
2. Hankey diary, 4 May 1917.

Haig too was a natural optimist. In this he and Lloyd George were akin, and another bond was that both tended to think on a large scale. The differences between them, though indeed profound, were often exaggerated and misunderstood, not least by themselves. It has been written of Haig that he 'greatly disliked men, clever or foolish, whom he did not consider straight', and that 'there was something in Lloyd George, a love of intrigue, a lack of fixed principle, a curious inconsistency, which at once puzzled [him] and aroused his suspicion'.[3] But Haig himself was no stranger to intrigue, having used it to secure the removal of his predecessor, French. (He wrote to Kitchener to complain of French's dispositions at the battle of Loos, and took advantage of his special standing with the King to make the latter aware of French's limitations.)[4] In his own eyes he was a straightforward officer and gentleman, as well as a professional soldier of unerring strategic grasp. Lloyd George he liked to regard as an ill-bred specimen of a profession for which he affected a supreme contempt, that of the politician.

Lloyd George in his memoirs made many telling criticisms of Haig, but could not bring himself to do justice to a man who got the better of him as well as (eventually) the Germans. While conceding that he had 'the courage and stubbornness of his race', he dismissed Haig's intelligence as 'of secondary quality'. In his view, Haig lacked the 'imagination to plan a great campaign', and had 'none of that personal magnetism which has enabled great leaders of men to inspire multitudes'.[5] The implication was that while he (Lloyd George) had genius and intuition, Haig was a highly competent plodder fit only for subordinate command, who won in 1918 only because he was under Foch. That was what Lloyd George chose to believe, and wanted the world to believe.

The truth was more complicated, on both sides. Both men were born to lead, and to exercise personal ascendancy. Haig may not have had the magnetism to 'inspire multitudes', but magnetism he certainly had. Nearly all who came into contact with him, including people as different as Esher and Northcliffe, were apt to fall under his spell and to recognize his authority. And the multitudes, though perhaps not inspired by him – without, for the most part, ever seeing or hearing him – were nevertheless affected by his prestige. He had none of Lloyd George's eloquence or adroitness in off-the-cuff argument. But he wrote clearly, in a tidy, well-formed hand. He was inarticulate (relatively)

3. *The Private Papers of Douglas Haig, 1914–1919*, ed. Robert Blake (1952), Introduction, p. 42.
4. Haig was a personal friend of George V. His wife had been a maid of honour to Queen Alexandra, and their marriage took place at Buckingham Palace.
5. *WM*, pp. 2266–7 and 3378–9.

only in the spoken word; on paper he was fluent and often cogent. His power came, above all, from his unwavering self-belief, to which his military competence was accessory. He had a Calvinistic faith in Divine Providence which merged with his self-belief, giving him a conviction that the war would be won and that he would win it, whatever the cost.

If Lloyd George was an amateur strategist (as of course he was, despite his statement to the contrary in Paris), Haig was an amateur politician, showing considerable finesse in arts that he ostensibly despised. He made good use of the press, and he chose a Conservative MP, Philip Sassoon, to serve as his Parliamentary private secretary and to keep him in touch with the London political world. Lloyd George paid him an unintended compliment by later picking Sassoon to be his own PPS. Similarly, Haig appointed one of Lloyd George's principal 'men of push and go', Eric Geddes, to run and reorganize the transport behind his lines.[6] Geddes remained devoted to Lloyd George, but his experience of working under Haig left him with a good deal of respect for the Field-Marshal as well.

Lloyd George's responsibilities as national leader were, of course, much wider than Haig's as Commander-in-Chief. He also had an overall strategic judgement that was often, though by no means always, superior to Haig's. Inevitably, Haig's thoughts were concentrated on the Western front, which was, indeed, where the principal enemy had to be defeated. His plans for that front did not suffer from being insufficiently imaginative. On the contrary, his imagination tended to override his practical sense, well versed though he was in the business of his profession. His worst fault was a defect of his most important quality. The stubbornness that Lloyd George noted in him (as a Celtic characteristic) could take the form of moral courage and a steady nerve in critical times, but could also show itself as inflexibility and refusal to accept the logic of inconvenient facts. Lloyd George had plenty of stubbornness of the good kind, (though it occasionally failed him), but he was always capable of modifying, or completely abandoning, a course of action when he could see that it was getting nowhere. It was this adaptability that Haig and others were too ready to stigmatize as lack of principle.

In the summer of 1917 Lloyd George and Haig were at loggerheads over a strategic decision of immense consequence. Haig's plan was full of flaws, and Lloyd George's argument against it exceptionally strong. Yet it was Haig who got his way – an outcome heavily influenced, if not predetermined, by earlier events.

*

6. Lloyd George suggested the appointment, but Haig had the acumen to act on the suggestion.

Before he went to Paris at the beginning of May, Lloyd George had received a long memorandum on war policy from General Smuts who, at his request, had visited Haig's headquarters to make an assessment. Lloyd George set great store by Smuts's opinion not only because of his outstanding intellect and his status as a former enemy reconciled to the British Empire, but also because he wore uniform and could be regarded as a military, as well as a political, leader.

Unfortunately, his military credentials were irrelevant to the scale and complexity of warfare on the Western front. His reputation as a soldier rested on a daring commando raid into Cape Colony during the South African War, and on three operations in Africa during the current war: the suppression (under Botha) of a local rebellion by hardline Boers, and the conquest (again under Botha) of German South-West Africa, followed by independent command in East Africa, where he had driven Colonel Lettow-Vorbeck's force out of Kenya. But these were the merest sideshows, involving small numbers of men, unsophisticated equipment, and terrain wholly dissimilar from that of the Western front. For the purpose of appraising the situation there Smuts was scarcely less amateur than his civilian colleagues.

Nevertheless Lloyd George seems to have hoped that he would advise against the sort of offensive in Flanders on which Haig's heart was set. In fact, Smuts proved to be yet another person susceptible to Haig's personality. After mentioning that Palestine offered 'very interesting military and even political possibilities', he argued most strongly that a defensive policy on the Western front would be disastrous. The key passage was this:

Our forces should be concentrated towards the north, and part should go to the rear as a strategic reserve, while the rest should endeavour to recover the northern coast of Belgium and drive the enemy from Zeebrugge and Ostend. This task will be most formidable, especially if both the Russian and French lines remain passive, and every pressure should be exerted to induce them to be as aggressive as possible, even if they cannot actually assume the offensive. But, however difficult the task, something will have to be done to continue our offensive, and I see more advantages in an offensive intended to recover the Belgian coast and deprive the enemy of two advanced submarine bases, than in the present offensive, which in proportion as it succeeds in driving the enemy out of France will make the French less eager to continue the struggle . . .[7]

7. Smuts memorandum, 29 April 1917. Despite his interest in a Palestine campaign, he considered that, if necessary, troops from Salonica should go to Haig's command rather than to Egypt.

Smuts thus gave blanket endorsement to Haig's plan. He did not even make his support for it conditional upon simultaneous action by the French and Russians. In his view, it had to go ahead regardless, or the Germans would win the war before the Americans could become a significant factor.

The same view was taken by Hankey, another adviser on whom Lloyd George could normally rely:

We must do the enemy all the damage we can. This can best be done by fighting a great battle with the object of recovering the Flanders coast, which would be the most effective way of reducing our shipping losses. We must not anticipate quick results. But even a battle of the Somme type . . . might produce great results. If the enemy retires he gives us what we want. If he stands, he exposes himself to colossal losses from our heavy artillery. Either way we stand to gain.[8]

This was the remorseless strategy of attrition, to which Lloyd George remained utterly opposed. Another 'battle of the Somme type' was what he had been seeking, above all, to avoid.

Among senior military figures Lloyd George's best potential ally was, of all people, Robertson. The CIGS did not believe that a major offensive in Flanders could succeed if the French did nothing. He said as much in his formal comment on Smuts's memorandum.[9] Shortly beforehand he had written a remarkable letter to Haig which might almost have been written by Lloyd George:

To my mind no war has ever differed so much from previous wars as does the present one, and it is futile, to put it mildly, hanging on to old theories when facts have shown them to be wrong. At one time audacity and determination to push on regardless of loss were the predominating factors, but that was before the days of machine guns and other modern armament. Of course there must still be audacity and determination to push on otherwise nothing would be done, but there is no doubt that in these days these qualities must be governed . . . by the effects of modern fire and modern entrenchments. Your recent splendid operations are a proof of this . . . for it seems to me that your success was mainly due to the most detailed and careful preparation, to thorough knowledge of the ground by battalions and batteries and the higher units, and to well observed artillery fire. It seems to me that these factors will continue to the end of the war to be vitally essential, and if they are not so regarded success will be rather in the nature of a fluke, *and will probably entail*

8. Hankey memorandum, 18 April 1917.
9. He doubted that such an attack without French support, and against German opposition of undiminished strength, would be 'feasible'.

heavier losses than will justify the few hundred yards of trench or additional village gained. I cannot help thinking that Nivelle has attached too much importance to what is called 'breaking the enemy's front'. The best plan seems to me to be . . . that of defeating the enemy's army, and that means inflicting heavier losses upon him than one suffers oneself. If this old principle is kept in view . . . the front will look after itself, and the casualty bill will be less.[10]

Though in this letter Robertson tactfully used Nivelle's plan to illustrate his argument, he was clearly seeking to moderate Haig's ambitions and to dissuade him from embarking on another Somme-style offensive. Yet, as will be seen, he was never prepared to impose his judgement upon Haig, or to advise the War Cabinet to overrule him. In the last analysis he acted as Haig's champion against the civilians, rather than as chief military adviser to a democratic government.

The line Lloyd George took in Paris in early May could easily be misunderstood, but certainly did not represent any conversion on his part to the idea of a massive British operation in Flanders. It was dictated by the desire to atone for Calais, by the hope that continuing success on the Arras front might provide an alternative to Haig's Flanders project, and by the need to rally French spirits after the Nivelle débâcle. A month later the situation had changed in such a way as to revive his worst fears. The Arras operation had stalled, Nivelle was sacked, and it was clear that for the rest of 1917 French activity would be largely defensive. It was also increasingly doubtful that anything significant could be expected of the Russians. Meanwhile Haig's Flanders plans were going forward.

His choice of operational commander for the main offensive reflected his grandiose intentions. Generals with intimate knowledge of the Ypres salient, whose approach would have been more cautious, were passed over in favour of Sir Hubert Gough, whose temperament was better suited to what Haig had in mind. Gough was brave but intellectually limited; also impulsive and irascible. His leading role in the Curragh 'mutiny' in March 1914 might well have ended his career, but he had emerged from it unscathed. Nevertheless he had done nothing since to indicate that he was remotely qualified for the task now assigned to him by Haig. Indeed, it has been suggested that his lack of qualifications was, paradoxically, a qualification, since it made him 'peculiarly dependent on the commander-in-chief '.[11]

10. Robertson to Haig, 20 April 1917; my italics.
11. Robin Prior and Trevor Wilson, *Passchendaele: The Untold Story* (1996), p. 51.

Since he came from another part of the front and needed time to familiarize himself with the terrain, the original plan for the campaign had to be modified in a drastic and disastrous way. The opening move in the offensive, the capture of Messines ridge to the south of the ruined city of Ypres, was to have preceded the main attack by only a matter of days. Instead, the Messines battle took place in early June and Gough's attack was delayed until the end of July.

Messines itself was a big success. The assault on the ridge resulted in its swift capture by Sir Herbert Plumer's Second Army. Plumer had been planning the operation for months. At 3.10 a.m. on 7 June nineteen enormous mines, long planted under the ridge, were detonated, blowing away the German advance positions. The noise was audible even in London, and in Lille people felt they were experiencing an earthquake. After the mines, an overwhelming weight of artillery provided a barrage ahead of the infantry, and well before the end of the day the ridge was secured. Haig visited Plumer at his headquarters to congratulate him, and that evening wrote in his diary: 'the operations today are probably the most successful I have yet undertaken. Our losses are reported to be very small. *Under* 11,000 for the nine Divisions which attacked.'[12]

Four days later a new committee of the War Cabinet held its first meeting. Known as the War Policy Committee its function was to review the major strategic issues facing the country and the Alliance. In reality, it was the War Cabinet itself under another name, since membership of the two bodies was almost identical. Henderson did not attend, because he was out of the country on a mission to Russia. Smuts attended from the first, though he did not formally become a member of the War Cabinet until 22 June. But essentially the two bodies were the same. The regular attenders of the committee were Lloyd George, Law, Curzon, Milner and Smuts, with Hankey taking the minutes and various experts called in to advise.[13] It was set up, at Milner's suggestion, because ordinary meetings of the War Cabinet were becoming clogged with miscellaneous business.

The first meeting opened with a report by Spears on the state of affairs in France. He was accompanied to 10 Downing Street by Robertson, and what he said was clearly influenced by Robertson's fear that the politicians, especially Lloyd George, would try to avoid action on the Western front. Spears referred to the French mutinies (about which ministers were still less

12. Haig diary, 7 June 1917. It was typical of Haig to describe nearly 11,000 as a very small number of casualties. Another man might have written 'relatively' rather than 'very'. The eventual figure of British casualties at Messines was 25,000, a large figure but perhaps just acceptable in relation to the advantage gained.

13. It is often stated that Balfour attended, but in fact he did not. (He was not strictly a member of the War Cabinet, though always free to attend its meetings.)

well informed than the military, though shortly beforehand General Wilson had reported on them to the War Cabinet). According to Spears, they were due to the failure of the Nivelle offensive combined with the news from Russia. He believed that there was a danger revolutionary ideas might spread among the French population. For the moment the situation was 'extraordinarily improved' by the British success at Messines, and there was no doubt that we were at present 'the mainstay of the French nation'. But it was vital that the Ribot government should not be upset, because there was no credible alternative to it. Poincaré had 'lost influence', Briand was 'to some extent discredited', and Clemenceau was 'too old'. The only alternative would be a government led by Joseph Caillaux, whose 'advent to power would mean peace'.

Robertson spoke next, confirming that the French army was for the time being incapable of large-scale action. Yet the 'Allied armies could not sit still and do nothing', and this was true, above all, of the British army, in which there was a prevalent opinion that 'they could beat the Germans by themselves'. It was necessary to maintain 'an offensive spirit', and operations such as Messines were 'very suitable for this purpose'. He did not, however, believe that 'great attacks against a distant objective were at present practicable'. Haig would be coming over in a few days, and meanwhile he thought that 'it would be desirable to modify [Haig's] orders to a certain extent, owing to the changed situation'.

Instead of jumping at the hint that the CIGS might be willing to see Haig confined by the politicians to limited offensive action, Lloyd George unfortunately returned to his old obsession with the Italian front. He read a message from the British Ambassador in Rome, Sir Rennell Rodd, suggesting that Cadorna regarded his front as the enemy's most vulnerable point in the West, but needed more guns to exploit its potential. Robertson, instantly on guard, said that he doubted Cadorna could break through to Trieste, even with more guns. He also argued (correctly, as it turned out) that if the Austrians were ever in trouble 'the Germans might turn upon the Italians'.

Lloyd George concluded that the committee 'must think out the whole position'. He 'could see no serious indication of cracking in Germany'. The Germans on the Western front seemed 'stronger than ever in men, guns and leadership'. Yet he felt that only 'bold, determined action' could save the Allied cause.[14]

14. WPC, 11 June 1917. The meeting was held at 5 p.m. According to Spears, Lloyd George asked him if he would give his word of honour that the French army would recover, and he replied that he could not give his word of honour but would stake his life. Hankey, he said, could record in the minutes that Lloyd George could shoot him if he was proved wrong (Max Egremont, *Under Two Flags: The Life of Major-General Sir Edward Spears* (1997),

Unlike Lloyd George, Haig did think that the Germans were cracking, and was encouraged to do so by his chief intelligence officer, Brigadier John Charteris. In an appreciation dated the day after the first meeting of the War Policy Committee, Haig said that popular discontent in Germany had 'already assumed formidable proportions' and that the German army was showing 'unmistakable signs of deterioration in many ways'. He estimated that Germany was 'within 4 to 6 months of a date at which she will be unable to maintain the strength of her units in the field'. It was, therefore, his 'considered opinion' that with adequate and concentrated resources his army could be relied on 'to effect great results', which would make final victory more assured and might even bring it about in 1917. In an appendix he gave figures supporting his view of enemy weakness.[15]

Robertson did not share his optimism, but nevertheless said that he agreed with Haig's views and would give them his full backing. At the same time he was so sceptical of the figures in Haig's appendix that he proposed its deletion before the paper was circulated to ministers, and Haig assented. Robertson's concern to coach Haig before the forthcoming encounter in London is most revealing:

to forewarn you of what is in the air so that you may be ready for them next week, the L.G. idea is to settle the war from Italy, and today the railway people have been asked for figures regarding the rapid transfer of 12 Divisions and 300 heavy guns to Italy! They will never go while I am C.I.G.S., but all that will come later. What I do wish to impress on you is this: Don't argue that you can finish the war this year, or that the German is already beaten. Argue that your plan is the best plan – as it is – that no other would even be *safe* let alone decisive, and then leave them to reject your advice and mine. They dare not do that . . .

P.S. We have got to remember, as we do, that the Government carry the chief responsibility, and that in a war of this kind many things besides the actual Army must be considered. Having remembered this, however, we are entitled to see that unsound military plans are not adopted – or all other plans may come to nought.[16]

Robertson was prepared to tell Haig what Lloyd George had in mind as an alternative to the Flanders operation, while withholding from the Cabinet evidence of the false assumptions on which Haig's plans were based. He

---

p. 58). Whether or not this exchange occurred in the melodramatic form recalled by Spears, no note of it was kept by Hankey. (Incidentally, Spears's name appears in the minutes as Spiers, its original spelling which he changed to Spears in September of the following year.)

15. Haig, 'Present Situation and Future Plans', 12 June 1917.

16. Robertson to Haig, 13 June 1917.

was acting more honestly and zealously as adviser to Haig than to the ministers who were carrying 'the chief responsibility'. It seems not to have occurred to him that his own chief responsibility was to the government which represented the British people.

After preparing another paper arguing the case for his offensive, Haig appeared before the War Policy Committee on 19 June. This happened to be his birthday. It was also (as will be recalled) Olwen's wedding day. The meeting was held at 11 a.m. at the Privy Council office. The next two hours, before Lloyd George had to go off to the pre-nuptial lunch, witnessed one of the most important discussions of the war.

Most of the record of it that follows is taken from Hankey's sober minutes. But there is an unforgettable description of Haig's performance at it in Lloyd George's *War Memoirs*:

When Sir Douglas Haig explained his projects to the civilians, he spread on a table or desk a large map and made a dramatic use of both his hands to demonstrate how he proposed to sweep up the enemy – first the right hand brushing along the surface irresistibly, and then came the left, his outer finger ultimately touching the German frontier with the nail across . . .

The War Policy Committee were then taken up into an aerial tower built during the past six months or more by the industry and imagination of G.H.Q. to view this thrilling prospect. It is not surprising that some of us were so captivated by the splendour of the landscape . . . that their critical faculties were overwhelmed. Mr Bonar Law, Lord Milner and I remained sceptical.[17]

According to the minutes, Lloyd George complimented Haig on the 'very powerful' statement of his case. Haig then said that the German guns were short of ammunition and not as good as formerly, which Robertson endorsed. Lloyd George described this 'a very satisfactory piece of information', but pointed out that the Allies had no superiority in heavy guns, and a superiority in men of only 15 per cent or (without the Belgians and Portuguese[18]) 10 per cent. What rate of loss did Haig contemplate? In the Somme battle it had averaged 100,000 a month. Haig replied that he had

17. *WM*, pp. 2157–8. Haig was dead when Lloyd George's memoirs appeared, but other witnesses of the occasion, including Hankey, were alive and did not dispute the accuracy of this recollection. Presumably Haig's general survey was given at the beginning of the meeting.
18. Portugal had entered the war on the Allied side in March 1916. It had an army corps on the Western front. The Belgian army held the extreme left of the Allied line from 1914 through to the end of the war.

originally estimated similar losses for the new campaign, but the small rate of loss at Messines encouraged him to hope for better.

When Curzon asked if he could promise a successful outcome, he replied that 'no soldier could say that any operation of war was a certainty', but his campaign would be 'the beginning of a very great strategical operation'. Milner expressed doubt that the operation could be carried through, and Lloyd George echoed the doubt. Haig had 'a splendid conception', but was it 'practicable at the present time'? Law asked if there would be any support from the French, should the Germans concentrate all their resources against the British army. Haig referred the question to Lloyd George, who said that according to his information the French could not be counted on.

When Haig mentioned Vimy in support of his case, Lloyd George suggested that what was achieved there was due, above all, to surprise; but Haig thought it more attributable to German delay in starting counter-battery work. Lloyd George said that he was sure the Germans would defend the positions Haig was proposing to attack 'desperately'. Haig could only reply that the Germans had failed to hold Messines, though he also exploited the civilians' sensitivity about Nivelle by adding that Pétain's operations in support would be 'very different from those designed by General Nivelle, in which he had never had much confidence'.

His army, he told Curzon, 'would be by no means exhausted by the operation'. In any case, if we did not attack in the current year the enemy would attack us, and we should be likely to 'lose the same number of men and guns without any advantage'. When Lloyd George disputed this statement, Haig again cited Vimy, and Lloyd George reminded him that at the time of Vimy the Germans were 'awaiting a tremendous attack by general Nivelle'. Milner then deviated momentarily from his sceptical attitude by saying that it would be worth 500,000 men to 'get the enemy away from the Belgian coast'. Smuts intervened strongly in support of Haig.

At the end of the meeting Lloyd George summed up. While assuring Haig that the Committee was 'most anxious to support him' in view of his 'brilliant successes', the Prime Minister asked the generals to consider all the difficulties. He personally wanted to reserve our strength until the following year, to 'hold our hand until the French army had been resuscitated by the intervention of America'.[19] The discussion was then adjourned and Lloyd George went off to get Olwen married.[20]

19. WPC, 19 June 1917.
20. Hankey accompanied him to the chapel, where Lloyd George was discussing the issues raised at the meeting up to the moment when he had to lead Olwen to the altar (Hankey diary, 30 June 1917).

After the wedding celebrations Lloyd George wrote a long memorandum disputing Haig's arguments, which he hoped the generals would consider carefully before discussion resumed next day. He stressed the Allies' slender margin of numerical and material superiority, the impossibility of relying upon the French (for whose plight he showed sympathetic understanding), and the likelihood that Haig's offensive would, therefore, turn into another indecisive bloodbath. 'Brilliant preliminary successes followed by weeks of desperate and sanguinary struggles, leading to nothing except perhaps the driving of the enemy back a few barren miles – beyond that nothing to show except a ghastly casualty list.' In a final section headed 'Alternatives' he dwelt mainly upon the chance of defeating Austria with the help of British guns. He did not mention the transfer of troops, and showed that he was hoping for victory at the expense of Italian lives. 'What does it matter whether we fight Germans in the north of France or in Italy? The only difference would be that if we fought them in France we should be doing it at the expense of our own troops, whereas in Italy we can use the enormous reserves of the Italians.'[21]

The following day the Committee met again at the same place, at noon. Robertson, replying to Lloyd George's overnight memorandum, argued against the Italian option. He did not think that Austria would make a separate peace, and feared that if the Italians made a serious advance the Germans would step in with devastating effect. He believed that Haig's plan should go forward, but that heavy casualties should not be incurred 'without a corresponding return'.

Haig then made a statement which has a hollow resonance in history. He was 'fully in agreement with the committee that we ought not to push in attacks that had not a reasonable chance of success, and that we ought to proceed step by step. He himself had no intention of entering into a tremendous offensive involving heavy losses. His plan was aggressive without committing us too far.'

The Commander-in-Chief was followed by the First Sea Lord, Jellicoe, who said that unless the Germans were removed from the Belgian ports before winter it was improbable we could go on with the war. Haig privately deplored Jellicoe's pessimistic outlook, but did not challenge it on this occasion, since what the First Sea Lord said reinforced the case for his offensive.[22]

The third meeting involving Haig was held next day, again at the Privy Council office, at 11.30 a.m. Robertson was also there. Lloyd George said that he had 'devoted many hours of anxious consideration' to Haig's plan,

21. Memorandum dated 19 June 1917, quoted in *WM*, pp. 2163–75.
22. WPC, 20 June 1917.

which Robertson supported, and had discussed it 'very fully with his colleagues'. Speaking for himself and 'no doubt' also for them,

he considered it would be too great a responsibility for [the Committee] to take the
strategy of the war out of the hands of their military advisers. [But this] made it all the
more important that the military advisers . . . should carefully weigh his misgivings in
regard to the advice they had tendered. If after hearing his views, and after taking
time to consider them, they still adhered to their previous opinion, then the responsibility for their advice must rest with them.

He felt that Robertson had changed his ground, having earlier maintained
that large-scale aggressive operations were dependent upon strong French
co-operation. Now he seemed to be supporting an attempt 'to fight right
through to a depth of 20 miles, while the French contented themselves with
relatively minor operations further to the south'. He listed conditions which,
in his view, were necessary if such an offensive were to have any chance of
success. There must be an overwhelming weight of men and guns. The
enemy must be attacked so strongly elsewhere that his reserves would be
drawn off. And his morale (a word at the time always spelt *moral*) must be
so broken that he would no longer be able to put up a fight. None of these
conditions at present obtained.

He reminded the generals that 'during nearly three years of war he had
never known an offensive to be undertaken without sure predictions of
success', and gave reasons for regarding the examples of Arras (Vimy) and
Messines as misleading. In both cases surprise had been a vital factor, and
in the second there had also been the pending French offensive further south.
(Haig here intervened to say that the Germans had known of the mines at
Messines, and that some of his divisional commanders had said they would
prefer to attack without them – a dubious statement.)

Turning to his alternatives, Lloyd George suggested either Pétain-style
tactics, 'a punch here and there, and a process of wearing down the enemy',
or concentration militarily and politically against Austria. Having mentioned the former option he said no more about it, but went on at length
about the latter. At the end he repeated his self-denying ordinance. Even if
his colleagues were to agree to imposing the Committee's views upon the
military, he personally would not do it.[23]

In effect, Haig got his way, and certainly acted on the assumption that he
had. After hearing that the politicians would not overrule their military

23. WPC, 21 June 1917.

advisers, he felt free to go ahead with his preparations and, when he saw fit, to start the battle. He was quite unmoved by what Lloyd George or any of his colleagues had said at the meetings. It seems not to have bothered him at all that at least three members of the War Cabinet, including the Prime Minister, were opposed to his plan.

While he prepared to launch the offensive in Flanders, the civilians, and Lloyd George in particular, continued to agonize. The War Policy Committee held its last meeting (the sixteenth) on 18 July, before briefly reconvening in late September. But meanwhile the War Cabinet resumed its overall responsibility, and was slow to give formal, explicit endorsement to Haig's campaign. It did so, eventually, on 25 July, six days before the infantry went into action and five days *after* the preliminary bombardment had begun.

Robertson in his heart shared the politicians' misgivings, but Haig could count on him not to break ranks. On 18 July he wrote to the Commander-in-Chief:

Up to the present no official approval of your plans has been given. I understand however that the War Cabinet are now in favour of your plans ... Apparently the Prime Minister is the only one who is sticking out ... and who continues to favour the Italian venture ... I had a long talk with one of the Cabinet ... yesterday and impressed upon him that I thought they need have no fear as it is well understood that the extent of the advance must, roughly speaking, be limited by the assistance of the guns until such times as a real breakthrough occurs. He replied that so long as this step by step system of advance was adhered to he would back your plan for all it was worth.

Three days later Robertson wrote again:

The Prime Minister is still very averse from your offensive and talks as though he is hoping to switch off to Italy within a day or two after you begin. I told him that unless there were very great miscalculations on your part, and unless the first stage proved to be a more or less disastrous failure – which I certainly did not expect it would be – I did not think it would be possible to pronounce a verdict on the success of your operations *for several weeks*. He seemed to have in mind what the French said last spring when Nivelle told them that he would be able to say in one or two days whether his operation had been successful or not.

He is also very keen on capturing Jerusalem and this of course I also had to fight ...[24]

24. Robertson to Haig, 21 July 1917; my italics.

Haig had no intention of being tied to a precise time-table like Nivelle. Though three weeks to prove himself was far less exacting than the forty-eight hours that Nivelle had recklessly proposed as the test for his offensive, Haig did not wish to be committed at all but to have complete freedom. Sensing a little weakness in Robertson, he told the CIGS to 'be firmer and play the man'.[25] The formula at length agreed to by the War Cabinet contained no specific reference to time, but did contain an undertaking that Haig's views would be sought before 'any decision as to cessation of operations'.[26] Since he also had Lloyd George's repeated guarantee that the War Cabinet would never go against the considered opinion of its military advisers, and since he knew that Robertson would never side with the politicians against him, this amounted to *carte blanche* and he should have been well satisfied. Yet he complained of the absence of wholehearted support for his offensive, by contrast with that given to 'the Frenchman' earlier in the year.[27]

Could Lloyd George have prevented the launching of Third Ypres, a battle better known by the name that marked its final phase, Passchendaele? Use of this familiar name tends to confuse two questions that should be considered separately: should the battle, or campaign, ever have occurred, and (granted that it did occur) should it have been allowed to drag on for so long? The second question will be discussed in a later chapter; here we are concerned with the first.

When Haig agreed to co-operate with Nivelle there had been an understanding that, if Nivelle's offensive failed, Haig's long-cherished Flanders project would go ahead, with French support. Flanders was obviously a sector of prime importance to the British. It was the closest part of the front to Britain, posing the greatest potential threat and offering the greatest opportunity. If the Germans were to capture the French Channel ports they would cut the communications between France and Britain (as they did in 1940), with catastrophic results for both countries. On the other hand, if they could be comprehensively defeated in Flanders – with the possible help

25. Haig diary, 22 July 1917. Robertson was on a visit to Haig's headquarters.
26. Telegram from Robertson to Haig, reporting decision of War Cabinet, 25 July 1917. Robertson's view of that body's members was given soon afterwards in a letter to Haig: '[Lloyd George] is a real bad 'un. The other members . . . seem afraid of him. Milner is a tired, dyspeptic old man. Curzon a gas-bag. Bonar Law equals Bonar Law [whatever that might mean]. Smuts has good instinct but lacks knowledge. On the whole he is best, but they help one very little' (Robertson to Haig, 9 August 1917). Haig did not share Robertson's low opinion of Milner, whom he regarded as 'the strongest member of the War Cabinet as well as . . . the best informed' (Haig to Lady Haig, 7 May 1917). But Milner's doubts about Haig's plan still counted for nothing with the Field-Marshal.   27. Haig to Derby, 29 July 1917.

of amphibious action – they might then have to abandon the Belgian ports, from which one-third of their U-boat flotillas operated, and even evacuate the whole of Belgium. One way or the other, it was a sector where the war could, in theory, be won.

In 1914 the Germans had failed to capture the French Channel ports, when they were stopped by the small British army and its allies at Ypres. In 1915 they had been held there again, primarily by the British, in the second battle to which the city gave its name. Ypres had thus become a symbol of resistance almost as potent as Verdun became in 1916. It remained such a symbol in 1917, though the city had been reduced almost to rubble. It was also a liability, since the Ypres salient was a death-trap for British troops even in 'quiet' times. To withdraw from it, as the Germans had withdrawn from their salient on the Somme, was morally unthinkable. The alternative was to advance.

Yet advance did not necessarily have to take the form of a major offensive. Limited action, such as the recent capture of the Messines ridge, could have been taken to straighten the line and remove the Germans from other commanding ground in the area. But Haig's project was far more ambitious. His aims were, first, to reach the general line Courtrai–Roulers–Thorout as soon as possible, forcing the Germans to leave Ostend, and then to press on north-eastwards and eastwards, clearing the whole Belgian coast and eventually driving the enemy out of Belgium. It was this grand scenario that he expounded to the War Policy Committee on 19 June, using a map and illustrating his points with eloquent gestures, as described by Lloyd George.

Through his own fault, and for reasons already explained, the Prime Minister was at a disadvantage in dealing with Haig. But others were at a disadvantage too. Lloyd George's War Cabinet colleagues (apart from Smuts, who was not then involved) were equally embarrassed by having been swept off their feet by Nivelle when he addressed them at the end of January, and by having issued a peremptory order to Haig to co-operate with him in his plan of campaign. Haig now benefited not only from Nivelle's failure, but from his own successes at Vimy and Messines, which to some extent eclipsed the painful memory of the Somme. Robertson, too, was at a disadvantage, as a promoted ranker and perennial staff officer dealing with a gentleman field commander.[28] In every respect, and with all concerned, Haig had the psychological edge.

It is hard, therefore, to see how the politicians could have vetoed the launch

28. Moreover he was only a general, whereas Haig was already a field-marshal (Robertson did not become a field-marshal until 1920). His exceptional powers as CIGS were held at the expense of the politicians.

of his campaign, even if they had been united in believing that it should not be launched. But in fact they were not united on the issue. As we have seen, Milner and Bonar Law shared Lloyd George's scepticism, while Smuts and (more equivocally) Curzon favoured the campaign. The War Policy Committee was misled by Haig about enemy strength, because he was misled himself and anyway wanted to believe that the Germans were cracking. Evidence that the sort of French supporting action originally expected would not be forthcoming, and that the Russians were ceasing to count as effective allies, was not enough to deter Haig or to undermine his ascendancy in the debate.

He prevailed by force of character and the inherent strength of his position, rather than by the persuasiveness of his arguments. He repeatedly invoked Vimy and Messines in support of his case, though those instances could more aptly be used against it, because they were restricted, well-prepared and clearly defined operations, not all-out offensives with distant and chimerical goals. Lloyd George rightly questioned their relevance, and Haig replied with statements of dubious honesty. He was also highly disingenuous in asserting that he had 'no intention of entering into a tremendous offensive involving heavy losses'.

It has been suggested, by no less an authority than Trevor Wilson, that Lloyd George's response to Haig's plan was less hostile at the time than he remembered, or was prepared to admit, later. His description of Haig and the map of Flanders is quoted with this comment:

By the time he came to write about it his response was one of rage. Nearer the event, Haig's exposition may have aroused in him – however unwillingly – some responsive chord. Indeed, it is quite probable that it got home to him much more nearly than to the more stolid Robertson. After all, when on other occasions Lloyd George had expounded his own strategic views, his hands must have moved with similar fluency over maps of the Balkans and southern Austria, sweeping across mountain peaks and rivers as if they presented little obstacle.[29]

Certainly Lloyd George could be cavalier, when it suited him, about physical and logistical difficulties. But on his reaction to Haig's Flanders plan Wilson, most unusually, seems guilty of unfairness. We need not rely at all on what Lloyd George wrote in the 1930s. The contemporary record shows beyond the possibility of doubt that he was in no sense carried away by Haig's enthusiastic presentation. The minutes of the War Policy Committee bear

29. Trevor Wilson, *The Myriad Faces of War: Britain and the Great War, 1914–1918* (1986), p. 464.

out his subsequent account, as does the memorandum that he wrote after Haig had spoken on 19 June.

This is not to say that his words and actions bearing upon the launch of Third Ypres were above reproach. Having already erred in giving too much encouragement to Haig in early May, overcompensating for Calais, he made further mistakes in his conduct of the discussion on which so much, and so many lives, depended. For one thing it is hard to understand why he allowed Jellicoe's pessimism to be vented, without expert challenge, at the meeting on 20 June. He himself contested the First Sea Lord's dismal view, and said that it would be necessary to hear him and Maclay together to arrive at a balanced judgement. But why had he not called Maclay to take part in the discussion? Why did he not call the two men together to any meeting of the Committee?[30]

Above all, why did he press only the Italian alternative to Haig's Flanders plan? His idea of what could be accomplished on the Italian front was another grandiose concept, though one involving the loss of Italian rather than British lives. Unfortunately it was a flawed concept, as the generals could easily demonstrate. The Italians wanted more than guns; they wanted men as well, and in any case did not at all relish the thought that theirs would be the only active front. Robertson was right to treat as illusory the prospect of an Italian breakthrough to Trieste, or a separate peace with Austria. The Germans would never allow this to happen. And Haig was right to point out that, when it came to sending troops to the Italian front, the Germans had the advantage of interior lines.

It is a great pity that Lloyd George allowed an alternative that he mentioned at the meeting on 21 June to go by default. He said then (though he had not said it in his memorandum two days earlier) that instead of another big offensive reminiscent of the Somme Haig might engage in more limited operations, 'a punch here and a punch there', as a better and less costly means of 'wearing down the enemy'. There was no need to identify such actions with Pétain, as he did rather tactlessly. Among Haig's army commanders Plumer had shown himself to be a most effective exponent of them, and in 1915 Sir Henry Rawlinson had invented for them the name 'bite and hold'.[31]

30. Maclay attended a meeting of the Committee with Carson (on 18 June) but never with Jellicoe.
31. After the battle of Neuve Chapelle he wrote: 'What we want to do now is what I call "bite and hold". Bite off a piece of the enemy's line . . . and hold it against counter-attack' (Rawlinson to Colonel Clive Wigram, 25 March 1915, quoted in Robin Prior and Trevor Wilson, *Command on the Western Front: The Military Career of Sir Henry Rawlinson, 1914–18* (1992), p. 78). Rawlinson was commander of the Fourth Army in the Somme battle, his cautious plans for which were altered by Haig. Naturally he was marginalized in the 1917 Flanders campaign.

Lloyd George failed to put any weight behind this alternative, perhaps because it seemed to him too humdrum. It was indeed unlikely to bring the war to an end, and would not have been cost-free, as Vimy and Messines testified. We can only speculate as to his reasons for raising the option so casually, and passing over it so quickly. Had he developed a strenuous argument in favour of it, both in his memorandum and at the Committee, his record of sound judgement in the debate before Third Ypres would be more impressive than it is. Even so it is undeniably impressive on the critical side.

There remains the question, were he and his colleagues wrong to defer, in the end, to the soldiers' advice? They decided, however slowly and reluctantly (on the majority's part), to let Haig's campaign go ahead, having subjected the case for it to lengthy discussion. Lloyd George said that he would not 'impose his strategical views' even if his colleagues wished him to do so. But he knew very well that they had no such wish, and would probably turn against him if he attempted to dictate to the generals in the circumstances of the moment. Haig was riding high and Robertson was acting as his accomplice in fixing the politicians, while privately doubting the soundness of his plan. Besides, Haig made a show of heeding the sceptics' concerns when he said that his offensive would not be 'tremendous', and that he would 'proceed step by step'. With such reassurance, how could the War Cabinet have prevented him from taking the first step, large though it was and ghastly though its consequences were to be?

The politicians did not abdicate their constitutional responsibility. Lloyd George said that the generals must accept responsibility for their *advice*, which was tantamount to admitting that responsibility for the *decision* rested with the War Cabinet. If it was the wrong decision, it was almost certainly inevitable.

II

New Appointments

Change at the Admiralty – Montagu's appointment – Addison
moved – Churchill brought back

During the period before the start of Third Ypres Lloyd George made important changes to his government. In late June, as already mentioned, Devonport resigned as Food Controller, and was succeeded by Rhondda. Rhondda's replacement at the local government board was a Conservative, Hayes Fisher, who proved a bad choice. (He was sacked the following year.)

At about the same time Smuts's membership of the War Cabinet was formalized. Despite its unorthodoxy this was a relatively easy appointment for Lloyd George to make, because Smuts had already ingratiated himself with the British political establishment, regardless of party or faction. But in one household his decision to join Lloyd George's government was *mal vu*. When it was still only a rumour Margot Asquith did her best to dissuade him:

Our Dear General Smuts,

In the Westminster Gazette tonight it says on the first page that you have 'special qualifications' for membership of the War Cabinet. I hope you will not let this statement remain uncontradicted. All the Lloyd Georgites – anti-Asquithites – and Tories are *overjoyed* and say to me 'There, you see how wrong you were! He *has joined Lloyd George* after all.' You might write a short note to *The Times* [to explain that] you are only doing what you and all the Imperial Conference Premiers do – go to the War Cabinet when you are asked to, but that you have not joined it. This would delight my husband as he is being deserted by another of his ministers . . . I do think he has every reason to believe you will *never* desert him.

You have a fine loyal nature and everything Henry could do for your people he has done. He is the most loyal man in the world as you all know. One or two of our friends were very sad today and said 'To think of a fine man like Smuts joining the War Cabinet sitting with a man like Lloyd George and men as foolish as Milner and above all Curzon.' Dear friend do make your position *clear*. It is so humiliating to have men say that everyone does what the Press tells them to do and are afraid of the Press. Forgive your unhappy

Margot Asquith

She added her own draft of a letter he might write to *The Times*.[1]

Smuts did not, of course, comply with her request, and his appointment to the War Cabinet was announced three days later. But he kept in touch with the Asquiths, as will be seen. His was not exactly a 'fine loyal nature'. Even in the world of politics, where absolute loyalty is in short supply, he was one of the sharpest of operators. In any case, why should he have felt any partiality for Asquith, who had strongly supported the Tory government's Boer War policy when Lloyd George was opposing it?

The other addition to the War Cabinet during this period involved the Prime Minister in serious difficulty. The man in question was Carson, and the difficulty consisted in removing him from the Admiralty. Carson's deficiencies as First Lord have already been noted. He was to the admirals what Derby was to the generals, an uncritical spokesman and champion; and this was all the more unfortunate since the principal admiral with whom he had to deal, the First Sea Lord (Jellicoe), was still pessimistic about defeating the U-boats. Lloyd George wanted to be rid of Jellicoe and thus (he hoped) change the prevailing ethos at the Admiralty, still unsatisfactory despite the reluctant acceptance of convoys. But so long as Carson was there Jellicoe was guaranteed immunity. It was clear that as a first step Carson would have to go.

But who was to succeed him? Sir Eric Geddes, already at the Admiralty as controller, was an obvious candidate. Lloyd George had brought him into public service at the Ministry of Munitions, and had later recommended him to Haig as Director-General of transport in France.[2] He must have been in the Prime Minister's mind for the job of First Lord, but before any offer was made to him two surprising alternatives were considered.

The first arose at a working breakfast at 10 Downing Street on 26 June. Those present were Geddes, Haig and Milner. Haig's involvement is a striking example of his political ruthlessness and flair. He had already talked

---

1. Margot Asquith to Smuts, 19 June 1917.
2. He assumed (1916–17) the further role of Inspector-General of transport on all fronts. Haig thought so highly of his work that he wished to keep him theoretically liable to recall to the staff of the British Expeditionary Force (BEF) when he was moved to the Admiralty. So Geddes retained the rank of Major-General while assuming that of Vice-Admiral – an unprecedented double. (In the next war Lord Louis Mountbatten held similar rank in all three services as head of Combined Operations.)

to Geddes and heard of his deep dissatisfaction with the current regime at the Admiralty. He had also discussed the matter with Curzon and Asquith, as well as with the Prime Minister. At the War Policy Committee on the 20th he had heard Jellicoe speak in pessimistic terms of the war at sea, and seems not to have uttered a word of dissent, presumably because Jellicoe's line was convenient to the case for his own Flanders offensive. But in fact he did not at all share the Admiral's outlook. Whatever his faults, he was no pessimist. Now that he had got his own way about Flanders (as in effect he had, and knew he had) he was free to intrigue against Jellicoe and Carson, and quite ready to earn Lloyd George's gratitude by helping him in a different sphere.

He may also – conceivably – have had a further motive, as his tantalizing account of the breakfast meeting suggests:

I breakfasted with the Prime Minister at 9.15 am . . . Geddes gave his views very definitely, much as he told me last Sunday [two days before] . . . L.G. seemed much impressed. . . . He decided something must be done at once. . . . the proposal to put Robertson in Carson's place was considered, replacing Jellicoe and one or two other 'numbskulls' now on the Board. I left about 10.30. L.G. said he was firmly decided to take immediate action to improve matters, but was uncertain as to what was the best decision to take at present.

The diary entry ends:

I saw Sir William Robertson at the War Office. He said he would not become First Lord as that would mean becoming a politician![3]

What are we to make of this curious episode, of which Haig is the only participant to have left a record?[4] There is no way of knowing how Robertson's name came up, or how seriously it was taken. Who made the 'proposal'? Haig's account leaves that question and others unanswered, but we are free to infer that he may have been asked to sound the CIGS out, without conveying a definite offer. If so, did he mention the idea to Robertson

3. Haig diary, 26 June 1917. Milner joined the party while it was going on, brought by Haig's car from his home in Great College Street, Westminster.

On Monday the 25th Haig had a talk with Balfour (at Philip Sassoon's house) and probably the Admiralty was one of the matters discussed, though Haig does not explicitly say so – as he does in recording his meetings with Curzon, Asquith and Lloyd George.

4. Robertson nowhere refers to the possibility that he might have become First Lord, and the same is true of Lloyd George and Milner.

in the hope that he would be interested, or confident that he would reply as he did? May the idea of Robertson's translation to the Admiralty perhaps have appealed to him, as it must have done to Lloyd George, though for opposite reasons? Lloyd George would certainly have liked Robertson to be elsewhere, because from his point of view the CIGS was too supportive of Haig. But from Haig's point of view there may have been some attraction in the thought of Robertson's removal, because he knew, as Lloyd George did not, that the CIGS had grave doubts about the character of his Flanders offensive. And he may have been prepared to gamble that he could convert any successor to enthusiastic support of his plan. The mystery has to remain unsolved for want of evidence. In any case, Robertson would not look at the proposal.

Two days later Lloyd George discussed the Admiralty with Hankey, who made a suggestion that the Prime Minister can hardly have expected:

He rather inclined to Geddes, but was undecided. . . . Perhaps unwisely I asked him if he had ever thought of me in this connection. He simply fastened on to it, and would, I believe, there and then have forced me to accept the post of First Lord, but for my many protests of unfitness in many respects. I pointed out that, while I believed that I could improve matters as regards anti-submarine warfare and produce better results, I should be quite hopeless as regards parliamentary matters, deputations, etc.

He also said that he would be taking an enormous personal risk, exchanging a post which suited him and in which he was happy for 'a rather rocky Ministry' and the odium of sacking 'some of the most distinguished admirals'. But Lloyd George 'was absolutely bitten with the idea, and would talk of nothing else'.[5]

That Hankey should have made such a suggestion is only less astonishing than Lloyd George's apparent eagerness to act on it. Certainly Hankey had taken a close interest in the war at sea, on which national survival depended, and his advice and influence on the subject had been of measureless value. But he was quite right in thinking that he lacked essential qualifications for an exposed political post.[6] His ambition ran away with him in making the suggestion, but at least he immediately saw and stated the arguments against it. Lloyd George's excitedly positive response is harder to understand. For

5. Hankey diary, 30 June 1917 (written up two days after the event).
6. Long afterwards he served as a member of Neville Chamberlain's War Cabinet 1939–40, and was kept on by Churchill in sinecure posts outside the War Cabinet until 1942. But his presence in both governments was largely symbolic; he was not cut out to be a minister.

the technocratic side of the Admiralty job there was little to choose between Hankey and Geddes, whereas in the post of War Cabinet secretary Hankey was all but irreplaceable.

The discussion occurred while the two men were being driven from Walton Heath to Downing Street. That evening Lloyd George had Milner to dinner and tried the idea out on him. Milner argued against it for all the right reasons. Besides, he had already proposed his own solution to the problem. After the breakfast meeting with Haig he had written to Lloyd George suggesting that Carson be brought into the War Cabinet and that Geddes be appointed First Lord.[7] When forming the government Lloyd George had, in fact, intended that Carson's place should be in the War Cabinet, and that Milner should go to the Admiralty; but he had been persuaded by the King to reverse the roles. Now Milner was doing such good work in the War Cabinet that Lloyd George could not bring himself to revert to both parts of his original plan. But after his brief flirtation with the idea of appointing Hankey he fell in with Milner's proposal and on 6 July offered Geddes the post of First Lord, which was accepted.

There could be no announcement, however, until Carson agreed to be elevated to the War Cabinet, and this proved to be a trickier business. When Lloyd George wrote to him about it he replied:

My dear Prime Minister,

Have read yr letter by special messenger. Of course I am ready to fall in with yr views that a change shd be made at the Admiralty if you consider it in the public interest. It is vital that you should have confidence in the administration of so important a department. As regards my entering the Cabinet I am very grateful for all you say but I shd prefer not to have to give an answer today. I am suffering from a bad attack of neuralgia but hope to be all right by Monday.

Yrs ever sincerely
Edward Carson[8]

This letter set off alarm bells in Lloyd George's mind. It seemed to contain at least a hint that Carson might resign if he were forced to leave the Admiralty. Lloyd George feared him as a potential focus of discontent on the back benches, and so did Law. The result was swift back-tracking:

7. Milner to DLG, 26 June 1917.
8. Carson to DLG, 7 July 1917. Apparently Lloyd George had floated the War Cabinet idea in conversation with Carson a day or two earlier, but the letter putting it in writing reached Carson after 11 p.m. on Friday 6th, at a bungalow lent to him at Birchington on the Isle of Thanet. He had to get out of bed to receive the special messenger.

My dear Carson,

I am afraid from your letter that you have misunderstood mine. We sincerely want you in the War Cabinet, but if you cannot see your way to join the Cabinet & prefer to remain at the Admiralty then the suggestion falls to the ground. We must have your help in this terrible war. I have all along – & so has Bonar – wanted you here. But it is for you to decide.

The changes I wanted at the Admiralty could be effected under your leadership . . . [In fact, this was just what Lloyd George did not think.]

I am so sorry that you are suffering from neuralgia. It is a plague . . .

Ever sincerely

D. Lloyd George[9]

Lloyd George may have tended to underrate his own political strength at this time. Because he was so conscious of his dependence upon the Conservative Party, and of Carson's importance within it, he may have shown undue timidity on receiving from him what appeared to be a veiled threat of resignation. The Tory Party had no figure who could match Lloyd George's credentials for leadership of the nation at war, and the fact that Carson and Law were, to some extent, rival Tory leaders was a further advantage to him. Yet his mastery of the scene was not unquestioned. An assessment by F. S. Oliver sent to Carson at about this time is worth quoting:

Lloyd George's position with the country is still very strong: perhaps stronger than ever. He is the only dramatic figure. He is regarded as the personification of energy and the 'will to victory'. But his position with the departments and in political circles is not so strong, and he appears to me to be losing ground rather rapidly. If this is correct then it will be only a question of time before the same sort of impression begins to affect the country.

He is not accused of being unable to take a decision, but he is accused of taking decisions without due forethought; of deciding wrongly, and having accordingly to go back upon them when he ought to stick to them.[10]

9. DLG to Carson, 7 July 1917. Neuralgia, whatever its cause and however it might be defined, was an ailment that often plagued Lloyd George himself. Moreover, both men were given to hypochondria.

10. Appreciation of the political situation by F. S. Oliver, sent privately to Carson, 13 July 1917. Oliver was rare, if not unique, in being a man of letters who was also successful in business (managing the firm Debenham & Freebody). His book on the war, *Ordeal by Battle* (1915), had a wide readership. Close to Milner and Carson, he was generally influential in Conservative circles. His attitude to Lloyd George, formerly hostile, was changed by the latter's performance in the war, particularly at the Ministry of Munitions.

Lloyd George's reluctance to risk a breach with Carson has to be considered in relation to a greater risk that he was intent on taking (to be described later in this chapter). More than a week went by after his emollient letter to the First Lord before he decided to force the issue, and it seems that another intervention by Milner helped him to make up his mind:

Forgive my worrying. I am very anxious about the Admiralty . . . the longer we wait, the more likely it is that something will get out . . .

It would be best to make all Ministerial changes at once, but if this is not practicable, cannot the Carson–Geddes business in any case be settled right away? It is very urgent.[11]

The day after Lloyd George received this letter from Milner, Carson's appointment to the War Cabinet and Geddes's as First Lord were announced, along with other major changes. However bruised his feelings, Carson stayed on board.

There was no certainty about Geddes's appointment until a late stage, despite the Prime Minister's offer and his acceptance. Lloyd George more or less offered the post of First Lord to another man three days before the reshuffle.[12] When Geddes was eventually installed in the job he 'took a long time to settle down', and it was also quite a long time before the ostensible purpose of the change was fulfilled, since Jellicoe remained as First Sea Lord until the end of the year. Nevertheless 'things at the admiralty tended to improve'.[13]

Another appointment announced the same day (18 July) was that of a new Secretary of State for India. The post became vacant on 12 July, when Austen Chamberlain resigned after publication of the Mesopotamian Report and on the first day of a debate on it in the House of Commons. The report was the work of a commission set up by Asquith at the end of May 1916, to investigate the disastrous Mesopotamian operations which culminated

11. Milner to DLG, 16 July 1917. He had earlier written to Carson urging him to agree to Lloyd George's proposal, which was also his own. By means of this letter (7 July 1917) Milner 'made patent his support of Lloyd George', and showed that if Carson tried to oppose his wishes 'he would have to reckon with Milner's disapproval and hostility' (A. M. Gollin, *Proconsul in Politics: A Study of Lord Milner in Opposition and in Power* (1964), p. 439).

12. See p. 186 below.

13. Maurice Hankey, *The Supreme Command, 1914–1918* (2 vols., 1961), vol. ii, p. 655. Unlike Maclay, Geddes did not stay outside Parliament when he became a minister. A seat was found for him and he was returned as Unionist MP for Cambridge at a by-election later in the year. He held the seat until 1922.

in the surrender of a large British and Indian force at Kut-al-Amara in April. At the same time another commission was given the task of investigating the Dardanelles fiasco. The appointment of these commissions was a serious mistake by Asquith, since it was a sign of weakness and involved immense time-wasting by busy people. (Hankey had to spend 174 hours preparing the government's case for the Dardanelles commission.) The effect of the commissions was also to start time bombs ticking, whose explosion could only do considerable damage. Though the investigations concerned events in the past, under a different government, the reports were not good for public morale at the time of their publication, and were also embarrassing to some people still in office.

The Mesopotamian Report was scathing about mismanagement by the government of India, for which Chamberlain's direct responsibility as Secretary of State was minimal. But as head of the India Office he regarded himself as morally responsible and therefore honour bound to resign. (Such punctilio is very rarely shown in politics, and if carried to its logical conclusion would make the tenure of high political office impossible.) The Viceroy at the time, Lord Hardinge of Penshurst, was more directly responsible and did, in fact, offer to resign the post of permanent under-secretary at the Foreign Office, to which he had been appointed (or rather reappointed) on his return from India. But Balfour would not hear of it and he stayed on.[14] Chamberlain was determined to go and could not be dissuaded. Lloyd George was sorry to lose him, at the very least because he represented a family tradition and regional fiefdom that carried a lot of weight in politics. But he also knew that Chamberlain was less likely than Carson to be a source of danger on the back-benches. He had not resigned on any issue of contention with his colleagues, and anyway was by nature an insider, not given to rebellion.

To succeed him, Chamberlain urged Lloyd George to appoint the under-secretary at the India Office, Lord Islington, a moderate reformer who knew the background and would work well with others.[15] Islington had paid two visits to India as chairman of a Royal Commission on Indian

---

14. Hardinge's career took off when he accompanied Edward VII to Paris for the Entente Cordiale visit in 1904. Two years later he became official head of the Foreign Office, and in 1910 Viceroy of India. He survived an assassination attempt in 1912, when a bomb filled with gramophone needles was thrown into the howdah of his elephant from an upper window in Delhi, as he was entering the city in procession. Many of the needles remained in his body for the rest of his life. Nevertheless he returned to his former post at the Foreign Office in 1916 and held it for the rest of the war and through the peace conference. He was ambassador in Paris 1920–22.   15. Austen Chamberlain to DLG, 13 July 1917.

public services, before becoming Chamberlain's junior minister. Earlier, as Sir John Dickson-Poynder MP, he had been slightly troublesome as leader of a Liberal group opposed to the land clauses of Lloyd George's 1909 budget. But Lloyd George did not hold this against him, and was, indeed, quite well disposed towards him. If there had been no candidate with more compelling claims Islington might well have been appointed. But there *was* such a candidate in Edwin Montagu, whose knowledge of India was – for a politician – exceptional, and who had already held high office. A further point in his favour was that he was a prominent Liberal with close Asquithian links but also a strong attachment to Lloyd George.

As an acolyte of Asquith, treated almost as a member of his family, Montagu had risen rapidly in politics. In 1915 he was brought into the Cabinet at the early age of thirty-six, and during the second half of 1916 followed Lloyd George as Minister of Munitions. His relationship with Asquith was shaken, but not broken, by his sudden and surprising marriage to Venetia Stanley, whom Asquith loved. But his growing admiration for Lloyd George, under whom he had served for a time at the Treasury, was perhaps harder for his old patron to bear. During the crisis that led to the change of government he genuinely sought a compromise that would have kept the two men working together. He tried in vain to persuade Asquith to join the Lloyd George government, but having failed was ready, indeed eager, to join it himself.

Unfortunately he was viewed with hostility by most Conservatives, and with some suspicion by Lloyd George, who felt that his loyalty might be divided. At the outset he was offered no more than the post of Financial Secretary to the Treasury, after all the top posts in the new government had been filled. Moreover the offer was made not by Lloyd George in person, but by Bonar Law, who visited him at home where he was ill in bed. Immediately afterwards he wrote Lloyd George a long letter, from which extracts must be quoted for the light they throw on his character:

My dear Prime Minister,

Greeting and the best of good wishes on writing to you by this title for the first time! . . . I have been very much perplexed to know what I should do if you offered me a place in your new Government; but that offer never came. I never regarded it as a lack of confidence on your part . . . it is impossible to think that I should ever be in opposition to you and I do not think it is likely to occur. . . . It was . . . quite unthinkable to me that I had suddenly lost your confidence when you were forming your Government, and although I received no invitation from you I sat and waited knowing that in good time you would give me . . . your explanation, and that this explanation would be satisfactory . . .

Looking back over the ten days, I remember in my pride that two dazzling offices had been mentioned by you as offices that I was fitted to fill, the Chancellorship of the Exchequer and the First Lord of the Admiralty. . . . [These offices] you were forced to fill by appointing two men whose claims I do not for one moment question . . .

I have no doubt you felt what I have often told you about my personal relations with Asquith, and it may well have been that you felt that I might have to refuse, although I hope you could have counted on me not to publish or swank about my refusal.

But now . . . I have received, naturally, the condemnation of those who thought I ought to have been with you. I have also received the equally unwelcome plaudits of those who thought that I could, and did not, join with you.

I feel that if I now accept an office of a subordinate nature, it will at once be said that I have taken the only office I was offered . . . I should be so discredited by the fact that I was not offered anything better (for which please understand that I do not blame you for one moment) . . . that I should be a weakness and not a support to your Government.

Yours always

Edwin S. Montagu[16]

Lloyd George respected Montagu's talents, but was often irritated by him and never felt quite at ease with him. In this the Prime Minister was not alone. Montagu had an unsure touch with colleagues and in Parliament. In an age when anti-Semitism was normal (though in varying degrees), he conformed all too well to the Jewish stereotype that existed in most gentile minds.[17] By turns self-assertive and self-abasing, he inspired feelings of aversion and distrust that were compounded by ethnic prejudice. His greatest strength was a fertile imagination, his worst weakness a febrile temperament.

Whatever Lloyd George may have said to him in the past – in casual conversation – about his fitness for certain posts, it was quite out of the question for him to be made Chancellor of the Exchequer or First Lord when the new coalition was formed, or later. All the same, Lloyd George wanted to employ his talents and retain his allegiance. After his refusal of

16. Montagu to DLG, 13 December 1916.
17. He was the second son of the banker Samuel Montagu, 1st Lord Swaythling, whose orthodox Judaism Edwin did not at all share. But to safeguard his financial inheritance he had to feign orthodoxy, and Venetia had to convert to Judaism.

another post, that of Director of National Service, a place was found for
him as vice-chairman of a committee to concoct plans for reconstruction
after the war. Though outside the government, this seemed to give him scope
for creative work, and since the committee's chairman was to be Lloyd
George himself he had reason to hope that he would be in constant touch
with the Prime Minister.

He was soon disillusioned. After addressing the first meeting of the
committee Lloyd George never again attended, as he had little interest in
discussing post-war problems while the war was still far from won. Montagu
made the mistake of bombarding him with letters, some of intolerable
length. (Like Curzon, he never learnt that this was a profitless way of
communicating with Lloyd George.) He also pleaded, usually in vain, for
the sort of intimate colloquy with the Prime Minister that he craved. On
one occasion he resorted to free verse:

Dear Prime Minister,

> As the desert sand for rain,
> As the Londoner for sun,
> As the poor for potatoes,
> As the landlord for rent,
> As Drosera rotunderfolio for a fly,
> As Herbert Samuel for Palestine,
> As a woman in Waterloo Road for a soldier,
> I long for a talk with you.
> Will you breakfast or dine tomorrow?

But Lloyd George did not have time for him, and began to feel that he
would be less of a nuisance if his desire for ministerial status were suitably
gratified.

His first job in government had been as under-secretary for India from
1910 to 1914. During this term of office he paid a long visit to India and
acquired a considerable knowledge of its affairs. The India Office seemed,
therefore, an appropriate place for him even before it unexpectedly became
vacant. But his own preference was to become Minister for Reconstruction,
or to return to the Ministry of Munitions. These options were talked about
and Montagu mentioned them to the Asquiths. (Hence Margot Asquith's
reference, in her letter to Smuts, to the impending desertion of her husband
by 'another of his Ministers'.) Then matters were brought to a head by the
Mesopotamian debate and Chamberlain's resignation. Montagu spoke in

the debate in terms calculated to make him more acceptable to Conservatives. He argued for a large measure of devolved power to the provinces of British India which, together with the princely states, should be federated within a single union. But he ruled out the 'one great Home Rule country' to which Indian nationalists aspired. At the centre British paramountcy should remain for the indefinite future.[18]

His speech was not intended as a bid for Chamberlain's job, which he coveted less than Munitions or Reconstruction. India fascinated him, but the post of Secretary of State had so many built-in constraints that he did not really fancy it. Nevertheless his speech had the effect of making Lloyd George decide that he could most conveniently be accommodated as Chamberlain's successor. It was a last-minute decision, when the other options had been closed. On 17 July, just before Lloyd George went to Buckingham Palace with his list of government changes, he saw Montagu and offered him the India office, which was accepted *faute de mieux*. At the same time Lloyd George asked him to write a letter outlining his policy for India, with a view to reassuring Conservatives, in particular Balfour and Curzon, that the British Raj would be safe in his hands. In the letter he repeated his assertion that Home Rule for India was 'not possible'.

Lloyd George had consulted Balfour about the appointment the day before, pointing out that Montagu's speech in the Mesopotamian debate had been 'cautiously worded'. Balfour's reply was rather equivocal, but disclaimed any wish to block the appointment:

Montagu is very able; he knows a great deal about India; he would be very popular with the Indians. I'm certain he would be disliked by the Anglo-Indians; partly because he is too much (in their opinion) of a 'reformer', partly because he is a Jew. I should certainly not raise any objection to his appointment and I should be interested to see how the experiment succeeded.[19]

A Liberal colleague, the Education Minister H. A. L. Fisher, was altogether more positive, volunteering the opinion that Montagu would be 'an excellent Secretary of State'. He was 'already very popular with Indians', had shown 'a real imaginative insight into Indian problems', and was 'a man of ideas ... with a great deal of the *future* in his mind'. When he was in India he was 'well liked by the Anglo-Indian community', who 'might be a little

18. Hansard, fifth ser., vol. xcv, 12 July 1917: Montagu's speech (cols. 2199–2210) immediately preceded Chamberlain's, in which the latter announced that he had resigned.
19. DLG to AJB, 16 July 1917; AJB to DLG, same date.

apprehensive of his visionary spirit' but realized that he had 'ballast and weight' and would be 'duly sensible of their point of view'.[20] No more promising appointment was ever made to the India office. If in the end the promise was blighted the fault was only partly Montagu's. The Reconstruction Ministry option was closed to him, by 17 July, because Lloyd George had decided that the post should go to Addison. The Munitions Ministry, to be vacated by Addison, was also bespoken.

Lloyd George had been discussing Reconstruction with Addison for some time. After the ending of the May strikes and the row over Sutherland's press release, the Prime Minister went out of his way to consult Addison about policies and personalities (just as Montagu vainly wished to be consulted). But it was not only to mollify Addison that this was done. Lloyd George had abundant proof of Addison's loyalty, and the two men saw eye to eye on most issues. In early June Addison volunteered to leave the Ministry of Munitions in a few weeks' time, when the recent adverse publicity would, he hoped, have been effaced by his introduction of the Ministry's estimates and vindication of his record.[21] The new role for him might then be membership of the War Cabinet with wide scope for inter-departmental planning and co-ordination, particularly on the domestic side. Milner, who felt overburdened with such work, was privy to the suggestion and strongly supported it.

Unfortunately, the War Cabinet idea was killed by premature press speculation, in which Addison suspected Montagu of having a hand. But Lloyd George was still keen to take Addison up on his offer and to move him to another post that would be congenial to him. On 12 July he lunched privately at 10 Downing Street. Lloyd George told him that Chamberlain would be resigning and that Montagu might succeed him. He also said that Carson would be leaving the Admiralty and asked Addison if he would like to be First Lord (Geddes's acceptance of the post again disregarded). Addison replied that he 'had better stick to the less spectacular job of dealing with Reconstruction and Future Policy questions'. Lloyd George said that he had 'long been anxious' such questions should be 'dealt with', and felt Addison was the man for getting together 'a Reconstruction party'. Addison agreed to do the job provided he had 'sufficient powers'.[22]

20. Fisher to DLG, 17 July 1917. Fisher had served on the Islington commission.
21. Kenneth and Jane Morgan, *Portrait of a Progressive: The Political Career of Christopher, Viscount Addison* (1980), p. 67.
22. Addison diary, 13 July and 22 July 1917. The reference to a reconstruction *party* suggests that Lloyd George was hoping to give substance to his dream of a post-war realignment of British politics.

Four days later, after a War Cabinet meeting which Addison attended, Lloyd George 'took him aside' with Law and told him that the changes had to be made 'immediately'. Addison was annoyed at being asked 'to take up Reconstruction straight-away', before the necessary powers had been worked out and agreed; but he did not demur. In the late afternoon he had a further meeting with Lloyd George, at which both men 'got pretty angry'; but the row, understandable on both sides, did not last long, and agreement was reached on the powers Addison would have as Reconstruction Minister. He went away to prepare a draft of them and returned with it in the evening, when Lloyd George 'initialled all the powers', and the two 'finished up by having a chop together'.[23] Lloyd George thus ended the day of the reshuffle in good Liberal company.

In his own interest, Addison might have done better to accept the Admiralty, where he would have had a more focused job and the backing of a long-established department. But he was a social reformer at heart. Having done his bit for the war effort at the Ministry of Munitions throughout the two years of its existence, as deputy and then chief, he was tempted by the prospect of working on plans to improve and regenerate the country after the war. Hitherto such matters had been worked on only by a committee, the first set up by Asquith, the second by Lloyd George. Asquith's reconstruction committee, with himself as chairman, consisted of Cabinet Ministers, one of whom was Montagu. Though it lasted only from early 1916 until Asquith's fall, it did valuable groundwork. Lloyd George's committee had a wider membership, representative of many different points of view. It carried out research and produced policy papers. But Montagu felt that the subject was so important and so varied that a Minister was needed to give coherence to the work, and to have enough power to tackle departments and ensure action. When the post was offered to Addison, he did his best to gain the necessary authority as a condition of acceptance. According to the document prepared by him, and initialled by Lloyd George, he would have the right to appoint committees, to call for information from all relevant quarters, and to make recommendations to the War Cabinet. His achievements and frustrations as Minister of Reconstruction will be described in Chapter 31.

When Addison offered to leave the Ministry of Munitions in early June, he did so with a view to facilitating the return to government of the most talented and controversial of all the Liberal exiles from power, Winston

23. Addison diary, 17 July 1917.

Churchill. When the government was formed Lloyd George had been obliged to leave him out, because Tory hostility to him was so intense. Several leading Tories refused to join the government unless Lloyd George gave them a guarantee that Churchill would not be in it. For his part, Churchill deeply resented his exclusion and unfairly blamed Lloyd George, telling C. P. Scott in March that he would have 'gone a long way with George if George had wanted him'. He regarded Lloyd George's excuse that the Tories would not have him as bogus. 'He did not behave well to me.'[24] (In 1940, when Churchill formed his own coalition, he did not immediately offer Lloyd George a place in it. Even though his political position was far stronger than Lloyd George's in December 1916, he felt that he could not invite Lloyd George without the agreement of his predecessor, Neville Chamberlain. When this was obtained and an offer was made, Lloyd George declined it, partly because he was so annoyed that Chamberlain had been given an arbitral role in the matter.)

Lloyd George, in fact, genuinely regretted having to exclude Churchill at the outset, and was always keen to find some way of harnessing his prodigious ability. It was one of Lloyd George's special merits that he liked to surround himself with colleagues and advisers of superior talent. He had no fear of the first-rate, and did not allow any differences of temperament or opinion to inhibit his choice. Churchill's was a unique case, since in him Lloyd George recognized the only contemporary of voltage equivalent to his own, and the recognition was mutual. Though there was always, and inevitably, an element of rivalry between them, and although they could often quarrel and make sharp remarks about each other on the spur of the moment, there was nevertheless a profound affinity which survived until Lloyd George's death in 1945 – when Churchill delivered a tribute to him the warmth of which was in notable contrast with the relative formality of his tribute, soon afterwards, to Franklin D. Roosevelt.

In retrospect Churchill acknowledged that Lloyd George could not have brought him in earlier than he did, and that he took an enormous risk in bringing him in at all. On the former point he writes in *The World Crisis*:

The new Prime Minister wished to include me in his Government; but this idea was received with extreme disfavour by important personages whose influence ... was decisive. ... He therefore sent me a message a few days later, through a common friend, Lord Riddell, that he was determined to achieve his purpose, but that the

24. Scott diary, 15–16 March 1917.

adverse forces were too strong for the moment. . . . I replied through the same channel with a verbal declaration of political independence.

Nevertheless my relations with the new Prime Minister, especially after a speech which I made in the Secret Session of May 10, were such that although holding no office I became to a large extent his colleague. He repeatedly discussed with me every aspect of the war and many of his secret hopes and fears.[25]

In the 10 May secret session Churchill made the sort of speech that Lloyd George would have made, had he been in the same position. Exercising the 'freedom of action' of a politician unshackled by collective responsibility, he argued that it would be wrong 'to squander the remaining armies of France and Britain before the American power [began] to be felt on the battlefields'. Replying, Lloyd George could not commit himself against a renewed offensive, though of course he entirely agreed with Churchill's argument.[26] Afterwards he and Churchill met behind the Speaker's chair and Lloyd George said that he wanted Churchill at his side. This cannot have been news to Churchill and represented no sudden shift in Lloyd George's attitude to him. For some time the two men had been meeting and Lloyd George had been taking Churchill into his confidence about the war. In March Churchill had written to his friend Archibald Sinclair: 'I see a good deal of L.G. and hear how things are going.'[27] When the Prime Minister visited Beatty in mid-April (to discuss the convoys), he picked Churchill up afterwards at Inverness and the two spent the night at Aviemore.[28] They were already quasi-colleagues long before their casual exchange on 10 May.[29]

25. *The World Crisis*, chapter XLIV (p. 688 of the single-volume edition, 1931). His mind was not then distorted by rancour, as it had been when he spoke to C. P. Scott. Riddell's contemporary record confirms his later and juster version: 'Called upon Winston and gave him my message. . . . Winston said, "I don't reproach him. His conscience will tell him what he should do. Give him that message and tell him that I cannot allow what you have said to fetter my freedom of action. I will take any position which will enable me to serve my country. My only purpose is to help to defeat the Hun, and I will subordinate my own feelings so that I may be able to render some assistance" ' (*RWD*, 11 December 1916). The day before, Lloyd George had told Riddell: 'I am sorry for some of my friends. They would not have Winston at any price' (*RWD*, 10 December 1916).

26. Randolph Churchill and Martin Gilbert, *Winston Spencer Churchill*, vol. iv (1975), pp. 16–17 (vol. iv is by Gilbert only).   27. WSC to Sinclair, 22 March 1917.

28. Beatty to his wife, 15 April 1917.

29. Some historians have exaggerated the significance of what then happened. For instance, A. J. P. Taylor writes: '[Lloyd George] made an effective speech, but it was Churchill who dominated the House. Lloyd George did not waste a moment. He caught Churchill behind the Speaker's chair . . .' (*Politics in Wartime and other Essays* (1964), p. 41). This dramatic wording suggests that Lloyd George was suddenly pursuing Churchill, having previously ignored him.

Of course Churchill's interventions during the first half of the year were calculated to make his friends, and even more his enemies, aware of the danger of leaving him out in the cold. In attacking the government he was often, though not always, saying what Lloyd George would have liked to say.[30] He was certainly a more effective critic than Asquith and his followers who constituted the official opposition (in so far as such a thing existed). After his partial vindication by the Dardanelles commission, which reported in March, and after his successful speech in the Commons debate on the report, it became easier to consider his re-employment, though the political obstacles remained daunting.

Lloyd George's first thought was to give him a job which – on the analogy of Lee's at the Board of Agriculture – would be powerful and worthwhile, but outside the government. Within days of the Dardanelles debate he suggested to Addison that Churchill might be associated with tanks and mechanical warfare at the Ministry of Munitions, but Addison was against the idea, rightly perceiving that only a manifestly major post would do for him. Anything less 'would be bound to lead to trouble'.[31] Nevertheless Lloyd George did not abandon the idea for over a month.

Churchill was, indeed, interested only in a ministerial post at Cabinet level, and one directly bearing upon the war (despite his statement to Riddell that he would 'take any position'). And Lloyd George more than ever wanted him in the government, not least for the stimulus of his company:

He says he wants someone who will cheer him up and help & encourage him & who will not be continually coming to him with a long face and telling him that everything is going wrong. At present, he says, he has to carry the whole of his colleagues on his back. . . . D. feels that he must have someone a little more cheerful to help him to cope with all these mournful faces – Bonar Law not the least of them. I think D. is thinking of getting Winston in in some capacity. He has an intense admiration for his cleverness, & at any rate he is energetic and forceful.[32]

But how was Churchill to be brought into the government, on terms suitable and satisfactory to him, without provoking a Conservative revolt of fatal proportions?

Churchill himself only says that their relations were 'especially' close after 10 May, not that their renewed partnership began then. The contemporary evidence shows that their exchange that day was part of a continuum, not a new departure.
30. He specifically, though not too harshly, attacked Lloyd George in a Commons adjournment debate on the ill-judged suppression of a series of articles in H. W. Massingham's *Nation* (17 April 1917).   31. Addison diary, 23 March 1917.   32. FSD, 19 May 1917.

At the end of May he visited France, with Lloyd George's blessing, and met most of the top people, French and British. On 2 June he had lunch with Haig, who had just received an unflattering assessment of him from Esher:

He handles great subjects in rhythmical language, and becomes quickly enslaved by his own phrases.

He deceives himself into the belief that he takes broad views, when his mind is fixed upon one comparatively small aspect of the question.

At this moment he is captured by the picture of what 1918 may bring forth in the shape of accumulated reserves of men and material poured out from England in one great and final effort; while at the same time a million Americans sweep over Holland on to the German flank.

He fails to grasp the meaning to France, to England, to Europe, of a postponement of effort.... It seems not unlikely that L. George will put Winston into the Government.... His [Churchill's] temperament is of wax and quicksilver, and this strange toy amuses and fascinates L. George, who likes and fears him ...

To me he appears not as a statesman ... I hope therefore that he may remain outside the Government.[33]

Churchill was obviously on his best behaviour with Haig, who found him 'most humble', though 'aiming at reaching a decision in August 1918'.[34]

Lloyd George did not fear Churchill, but he did fear the potential results of bringing him back. He therefore moved warily. When the two were not meeting face to face, they had a useful go-between in Frederick (Freddy) Guest, Lloyd George's chief whip and Churchill's cousin. The first Cabinet office that Lloyd George had in mind for Churchill was that of President of the Air Board, one of his inventions and currently held by Lord Cowdray. But when rumours appeared in the press the reaction from Conservative sources was so menacing that Lloyd George felt he had to back down and pause. Milner and Curzon were both opposed to the appointment, and Sir George Younger, the Conservative chairman, wrote that it 'would strain to breaking point the Unionist Party's loyalty to [Lloyd George]'. Cowdray, though a Liberal, wrote that Churchill in office would be a 'grave danger'.[35]

Balked in his first attempt Lloyd George proposed, as an alternative, the job, or non-job, of Chancellor of the Duchy of Lancaster. But Churchill could hardly be expected to accept again the post to which he had been

33. Esher to Haig, 30 May 1917.   34. Haig diary, 2 June 1917.
35. Churchill and Gilbert, *Churchill*, vol. iv, pp. 23–6. Guest became chief whip in May, when Neil Primrose left to rejoin his regiment (having failed to receive the political promotion he expected). He was killed before the end of the year.

relegated when forced out of the Admiralty in 1915. Guest, who conveyed the offer and received Churchill's refusal, told Lloyd George that Churchill would accept 'any war department' with adequate powers. Since there could be no question of the War Office or the Admiralty, the Ministry of Munitions emerged as the only answer to a tough problem. On 16 July Lloyd George went through the motions of asking Churchill which job he would like, but both knew that Munitions was the only realistic option. Churchill 'chose' it, and Lloyd George then made the appointment without consulting any of his Conservative colleagues.

When it was announced they accepted the *fait accompli* – but only just. For a time it seemed that the shock might destroy the coalition. The back-bench Tory 1900 Club passed a unanimous motion of protest, and Law had to face his outraged colleagues. When Beaverbrook was given (by Lloyd George) the task of breaking the news to him – the day after the appointment and the day before the public announcement – Law's comment was: 'Lloyd George's throne will shake.'[36] If Law had resigned it is hard to see how the government could have survived. But he did nothing to topple the shaking throne. He did not feel that he or anyone else would be a better prime minister than Lloyd George.

It was probably good judgement on the Prime Minister's part not to consult even his faithful comrade and principal Tory colleague. Though Law was at first angered, and perhaps hurt, it was fairer to him as well as more politic to leave him in ignorance until the deed was done. That way he was innocent of complicity. Had he been consulted, he would have been forced either to do all in his power to frustrate Lloyd George's intention, at whatever cost to the government and the country, or to share in the odium occasioned by a step of which he profoundly disapproved. Yet in acting as he did Lloyd George subjected his crucial partnership with Law to its most severe test.

Churchill himself was taken aback by the storm that his appointment caused. A few days later Hankey found him in 'a chastened mood', admitting that 'he had no idea of the depth of public opinion against his return to public life'.[37] If he had ever doubted the difficulty and risk that Lloyd George would incur in engineering his return, he could have no doubts after the event. Even H. A. L. Fisher thought that Lloyd George had committed 'a pretty big error of judgment'.[38] (Esher, ironically, wrote Churchill a fawning letter, referring to his 'fiery energy and keen outlook'.[39])

36. Lord Beaverbrook, *Men and Power, 1917–1918* (1956), p. 137.
37. Hankey diary, 22 July 1917.   38. Fisher to his wife, 20 July 1917.
39. Esher to WSC, 24 July 1917.

Asquith wrote to his confidante, Venetia Montagu's sister Sylvia:

The Tory tornado against Winston is blowing today with full & increasing fury. The wretched Whips . . . are having the worst time of their life. It is astonishing to me to see how widespread & deep-seated is the hostility to him. Ll.G. appears to have nominated him without consulting any of his Tory so-called colleagues. . . . In all this hurly-burly E.S.M[ontagu]'s appointment escapes almost without notice.

He added an interesting titbit:

General Smuts, who was here to lunch today, gave me a very frank view of the situation. He thinks the present lot helpless and doomed, but is against forcing matters to a head. This is quite private.[40]

So much for 'Slim Jannie's' team spirit.

40. Asquith to Sylvia Henley, 19 July 1917.

I 2

Arthur Henderson and Neville Chamberlain

Glasgow speech – Loss of Henderson – Manpower and
Neville Chamberlain

Glasgow was a city whose robust character Lloyd George knew from experience. When the controversy over dilution of labour was at its height he went there to promote the policy and faced, on Christmas Day 1915, one of the rowdiest meetings of his career, held in St Andrew's Hall.[1] He was then Minister of Munitions. Eighteen months later, as Prime Minister, he returned to the same hall to receive the freedom of the city and to make one of the more important of his wartime speeches, to an audience which showed no inclination to deny him a hearing.

He travelled overnight from London, accompanied by his wife and William Sutherland, and his arrival at Glasgow Central Station was well choreographed. A contingent of flag-waving women munition workers, wearing overalls and trousers, formed a guard of honour as he walked down the platform, serving to advertise the triumph of dilution. He then visited the station canteen for soldiers and sailors, where he was warmly received, before driving off to the City Chambers through cheering crowds.

After breakfast and a little time to collect his thoughts, he emerged shortly before noon to drive from City Chambers to St Andrew's Hall. All along the route buildings were decked with flags and bunting, as for a royal procession. Outside the hall there was, indeed, a crowd of militant workers protesting against his being awarded the city's freedom, but their behaviour was innocuous apart from some singing of 'The Red Flag'. No attempt was made to break into the hall, and a 'large posse of police' had no need to interfere. Inside the hall decorum reigned, giving way only to bursts of friendly laughter or cheers.

He began his acceptance speech by recalling with suitable awe the names

1. Members of the Clyde Workers' Committee, present in strength in the hall, almost denied him a hearing. Though they constituted, in fact, only a minority of those present, they were numerous and vocal enough to cow the majority into silence. The demonstration did not reflect the true state of working-class opinion on the Clyde, where dilution was in due course grudgingly accepted. (See my *Lloyd George: From Peace to War* (1985), pp. 297–301.)

of former honorands, concentrating upon the statesmen, to whom he referred in studiedly non-partisan terms, as befitted a coalition leader. Lord John Russell and Palmerston were mentioned, as was the 'dazzling career' of Disraeli, the 'towering figure' of Gladstone, and the 'great peace minister' Salisbury.[2] The list concluded with 'that fine old Glasgow man' who was Lloyd George's 'first chief ', Sir Henry Campbell-Bannerman.

After reaffirming Germany's and (to a lesser extent) Austria's responsibility for the war, which Britain had done everything possible to avoid, he spoke of the war's progress. 'I am steeped every day – morning, noon and night – in the perplexities and difficulties and the anxieties of this grim business, but all the same I feel confident.' Events in Russia had modified the military situation 'temporarily to our disadvantage, but permanently for the better'. Before very long Russia would once again be a major force in the war, and when it was over we should be spared the embarrassment of having 'the most reactionary autocracy in the world' as an ally at the peace conference.

He attacked those who hailed the Russian Revolution while deploring Britain's participation in the war (primarily the anti-war wing of the labour movement). Without the assistance of our 'great army' and 'enormous equipment', the 'great old democracy of France' would have been destroyed. And how could the new Russian democracy then have survived? 'Not long, and you would have had one great outstanding autocracy in Europe governing from the East to the West, and only these little islands standing between the world and disaster.'

This (he knew) was the truly compelling argument for British intervention in 1914, though it was the violation of Belgian neutrality and the spectacle of Belgium's resistance that had moved public opinion. In mid-June the moral and emotional appeal of Russia was comparable, since its new regime could still be seen as a budding democracy. As a means of countering anti-war sentiment in the 'Red' city of Glasgow Lloyd George's approach was artful.

He gave a confident prognosis of the war against the U-boats. Even in May and June, when shipping losses were very heavy, they were 'hundreds of thousands of tons beneath the Admiralty forecast' (a dig at Jellicoe). Measures to defeat the U-boat campaign were beginning to take effect, and if all played their part 'the German submarine [would] be almost as great a failure as the German Zeppelin'. On the home front, people must adapt their eating habits:

2. He cited Salisbury's pacific handling of the Venezuelan dispute and the Fashoda incident, but said nothing of the fact that he had led the country into the Boer War. Nor did he mention that his own first article, written in his teens, had been an attack on Salisbury's foreign policy.

LLOYD GEORGE

You might be driven to eat less wheat and more barley and oats, the food of the men and women who made Scotland; yes and made my little country too . . . I am running the war on the stock of energy which I accumulated on that fare when I was young, and I am not going to weep over the hardships of a country which is driven back to oats and barley. [A voice – 'Gi' us a haggis.'] We were never able to aspire to those luxuries in Wales. [Laughter.] We never got further than a bannock. [Laughter.][3]

Shipbuilding was vital, he stressed. 'We have heard of the battle of the Marne. This is the battle of the Clyde.' When he spoke of the land war he naturally highlighted Vimy and Messines; and he paid a tribute to the valour of the French army 'against the dense hordes of the German troops' (since he could hardly celebrate the results of the Nivelle offensive). Again, as at Guildhall, he avoided any mention of Haig, but at least he did not invidiously praise Haig's predecessor, as he had on that occasion. Indeed he mentioned no military commander by name, but gave a qualified salute to generals, among other more or less worthy groups, in a passage that led to an unexpected climax:

Our army is great, and the army is now the people . . . everybody is doing his best within human limitation – generals, officers, soldiers, admirals, sailors, officials, employers, workmen, yea, ministers of the Crown – forgive me saying it – we are doing our best in our way . . . and will you allow me to say that there is one man who is working as hard as the hardest-worked man in this country, and that is the Sovereign of this realm.

At these words the whole audience rose spontaneously and sang the National Anthem. Lloyd George had achieved a remarkable *coup de théâtre*. Within days of his losing battle with Haig over the Flanders plan he was less disposed than ever to glorify the Commander-in-Chief. But in eulogizing the King, the symbolic head of the armed forces, he was, as it were, trumping Haig's ace and disarming those who might have resented his silence about Haig. At the same time he was exalting the democratic concept of equality of service – under the Crown. It was a most ingenious passage.

He turned, next, to the terms on which the war could be ended, conscious of the false hopes aroused by rumours of peace overtures:

In my judgment this war will come to an end when the Allied powers have reached the aims which they set out to attain . . . I hear there are people going about saying

3. A bannock = 'a large cake, usually of barley or pease-meal, round or oval in form, and flattish' (*OED*).

that Germany is prepared to give you peace now, an honourable peace, and a satisfactory peace. Well, let us examine that . . . Germany will give us peace now – at a price . . . but do you know what it would be?

Lloyd George replied to the question. It would be like the Romans buying off the Goths. There was no intention on the Germans' part of restoring Belgium to freedom. The country would remain under German economic hegemony, and Germany would continue to control the Belgian ports. 'That is not independence – that is vassalage.' Edward I had had similar ideas for Scotland, but the Scots gave their answer at Bannockburn.

Then Lloyd George spoke of the idea spreading from Russia that there should be a peace without annexations or indemnities: 'But what does indemnity mean? A man breaks into your house, turns you out for three years, murders some of the inmates . . . and turns round and says, when the law is beginning to go against him, "Take your house". [Laughter.] I am willing to give you the *status quo*.' Even a pacifist, Lloyd George suggested, would seek compensation if such things were done in his house.

A peace without annexations? Here the speaker was on more difficult ground, but he picked his way adroitly. Britain, he could fairly claim, had no territorial ambition in Europe. But what about the Middle East and the German colonies? He took the instance of Mesopotamia:

Mesopotamia is not Turkish, never has been Turkish. The Turk is as much an alien in Mesopotamia as the German, and everyone knows how he ruled it. This was the Garden of Eden. What a land it is now! What will happen to Mesopotamia must be left to the peace congress, but . . . it will never be returned to the blasting tyranny of the Turk.

Colonies, too, must be left to the peace congress, and he mentioned the word 'trusteeship', suggesting that German colonies should be entrusted to 'gentler hands than those who [had] had the governing of them up to the present time'. His audience was free to speculate whose gentle hands he had in mind.

The best guarantee of peace would, he said, be 'the democratisation of the German government':

One of the outstanding features of the war has been the reluctance with which democratic countries entered it . . . it is right that we should say we could enter into negotiations with a free government in Germany . . . with less suspicion, with more confidence [than one governed] by the aggressive and arrogant spirit of Prussian militarism. . . . Democratic France was a more sure guarantee for the peace of Germany than the fortress of Metz or the walled ramparts of Strassburg.

He ended on a quasi-religious note, asking the audience not to forget 'the great succession of hallowed causes', which were 'the Stations of the Cross on the road to the emancipation of mankind'. He urged them to endure as their ancestors had done. Every birth was an agony, and a new world was being born out of the agony of the old.

From St Andrew's Hall he returned to City Chambers for lunch in the banqueting hall, where he made a short speech in response to the Lord Provost's proposal of his health. When he came to Glasgow, he said, he hardly felt that he had changed his atmosphere, because in the government he was surrounded by Glasgow men, such as Law, Henderson and Maclay.

Later he went to Bute Hall at the University to receive an honorary doctorate of laws. Throughout the ceremony the crowd, mainly of students, 'kept up a good-natured fusillade of interruptions'. When Lloyd George began his third speech of the day, expressing thanks for the award, a voice from the back of the hall shouted 'Speak up, Davie' – to which he replied: 'This is my first lesson as a student, and I am glad that it is a lesson in elocution' (he had never attended a university). The doctorate was the third distinction of its kind conferred on him, and he 'found himself getting more and more learned without making the slightest effort to acquire any further knowledge'.

After the university he visited an air services exhibition in the McLellan Galleries, where he made 'a rapid inspection of the various exhibits', and then was entertained to dinner at the Western Club. He left the city, finally, not for London, but for Dundee, where the following day he was to be similarly honoured – and also effusively praised by the local Liberal MP, Winston Churchill.[4]

At Glasgow on 29 June Lloyd George put down a few highly significant markers for the future. He asserted the principle of German responsibility for the war – and Austria's too, though he played this down a little,

---

4. Report of visit and speeches, *The Times*, 30 June 1917. Lloyd George's stamina must certainly have seemed a good advertisement for his early diet of oats and barley. His main speech at St Andrew's Hall – delivered, of course, without artificial amplification – lasted an hour and 26 minutes, in a day that included two further speeches and other wearisome activities.

Churchill had represented Dundee since 1908. After his appointment as Minister of Munitions a fortnight or so later he had to re-contest the seat (according to the rule then still in force) and was returned with a majority of over 5,000. His opponent was Labour, as was the other MP for the two-member seat.

presumably as an incentive to the Austrians to make a separate peace (a continuing pipe-dream). He also asserted the right to proper compensation of those who had suffered immensely from the effect of enemy occupation, clearly meaning above all Belgium and France, since it was into their 'houses', literally and metaphorically, that the Germans had broken. At the same time he hinted at the desirability of a European peace without annexations.

While saying that Britain had no territorial ambitions on the Continent, he mentioned in a derogatory way German seizure of French territory after the 1870 war, intending surely to suggest that such annexations by other Allies, at Germany's expense, should be avoided for the sake of a lasting peace. (He did not refer to France's demand for the restoration of Alsace-Lorraine, which he delayed endorsing until October.) He allowed for *de facto* annexations outside Europe, as a result of the dismemberment – on which he insisted – of the Ottoman Empire, and of the probable destruction of the German colonial empire. But he invoked the concept of trusteeship, which could appeal to radical critics of imperialism, while leaving all practical dispositions to the peace conference.

His statement that it would be easier for the Allies to make peace with a democratic Germany was almost a truism, but nevertheless contained potential for misunderstanding. In the absence of an explicit statement to the contrary, the Germans might be tempted to believe that by merely changing their regime they could escape responsibility for compensating the countries that they had invaded and ravaged. In this and other respects the speech anticipated problems that were to beset the peacemakers in 1919.

For two months in the spring of 1917 Albert Thomas, the French Armaments Minister, was in Russia on a special mission to the provisional government, replacing the French Ambassador, Maurice Paléologue. It had been felt that, as a socialist and politician, he would be more effective than a traditional diplomat in establishing close relations with the new regime and maintaining the Russians' fighting spirit. Impressed by this initiative Lloyd George and the War Cabinet decided that a British Labour leader should be sent to Petrograd as a substitute for Sir George Buchanan, who had been Ambassador there since 1910. The man chosen for the task was Labour's representative in the War Cabinet, Arthur Henderson, who accordingly spent six weeks in Russia from the beginning of June until early July. His mission made no perceptible impact on the course of events in Russia, but was of boundless significance for himself, Lloyd George and the future of British politics.

From the outset the business was clumsily handled. Buchanan was told by the Foreign Office that Henderson would be coming, and the reasons for his mission were disingenuously explained. The Ambassador was asked to stay at his post for a few weeks after Henderson's arrival to brief him thoroughly and to enable him to find his feet on unfamiliar ground. Then Buchanan was to return home for consultations. But he was assured that there was no question of his being permanently recalled, like Paléologue. His absence was to be no more than a temporary interlude. In fact it was Lloyd George's intention that Henderson should take over as Ambassador. The idea of sending him was proposed and decided on behind his back. Of course, he could have refused, but as a member of the War Cabinet he should have been present when the idea was discussed, and thus have been fully party to the decision. He left at short notice, accompanied by G. M. Young, historian and Fellow of All Souls, who had been recruited to the War Cabinet secretariat the previous December. In Petrograd, Henderson soon made friends with Buchanan and came to the conclusion that it would be quite wrong to replace him, telling Lloyd George in a letter that Prince Lvov thought 'very highly' of the Ambassador and said that he 'gave great help to him [Lvov] and his friends during the last phase of the old regime'.[5] Buchanan appreciated Henderson's confidence in him, and in his memoirs praised the visitor's 'most gentlemanly and straightforward manner'.[6]

What sort of man was Henderson, and how had he reached such an eminent position in the state? Lloyd George listed him among Glaswegian colleagues, and he was indeed Glasgow-born. But at the age of nine, when his father died, his mother took him to Newcastle-upon-Tyne, and thereafter his life was spent in England. Leaving school at twelve he joined Robert Stephenson's works and was soon making his way in the Ironfounders' Union. He continued to educate himself, mainly by reading newspapers. Before he was thirty he was elected to Newcastle City Council, and in 1903, his fortieth year, he entered Parliament at a by-election as member for Barnard Castle, on the Independent Labour Party ticket. In 1906 he moved to London.

In that year the Labour Party as such came into being as a loose federation of bodies within the labour movement,[7] comprising ideological socialists, moderate social reformers and trade unionists (categories which could, of

5. Henderson to DLG, 6 June 1917.
6. George Buchanan, *My Mission to Russia and Other Diplomatic Memories* (2 vols., 1923), vol. ii, p. 146.
7. It already existed, from 1900, as the Labour Representation Committee, and the party's centenary was therefore celebrated in February 2000. But the name Labour Party dates from 1906. In the general election of that year twenty-nine Labour MPs were returned.

course, to some extent overlap). In 1911 he became secretary of the party, a post which he held until 1934. At the outbreak of war in 1914 the leader of the Parliamentary party, Ramsay MacDonald, declined to vote for war credits and, being in a minority, resigned. Henderson took his place and was followed by the bulk of trade unionists and party members in giving support to the war. When Asquith formed the first wartime coalition in May 1915, Henderson took office in it;[8] the following year, as we have seen, he joined Lloyd George's War Cabinet.

The Labour Party did not, however, formally split on the issue of the war. The pro-war majority and the anti-war minority continued to coexist and the division of opinion between the leaders of the two factions was less fundamental than it seemed. Though some opponents of the war (and most members of the ILP) were against war on principle, MacDonald was not a pacifist. His attitude to the war was idiosyncratic to the point of absurdity. Britain should not have entered the war, he maintained, but having entered she must win it. Those who could enlist should do so and those who worked in war industry should do so wholeheartedly. Yet he would not give unqualified endorsement to the war effort, and some of his statements could easily be used in enemy propaganda.

Henderson, too, was critical of pre-war foreign policy, but the invasion of Belgium converted him to the need for Britain to intervene and from then onwards he never wavered in his commitment to the war or shrank from any of the practical implications. His stand was unequivocal, and in taking it he had the overwhelming backing of the labour movement as a whole, though on particular issues, such as dilution, he had to face some hostility and resistance. The pain of the war touched him personally when his eldest son was killed on the Somme. In everything that he did he was sustained by a strong Methodist faith which he had acquired in his teens. From the start of his career he was a lay preacher as well as a political activist.

He and MacDonald are a fascinating pair, contrasted but complementary – rather in the manner of Law and Lloyd George, though without the bond of affection. They could work together for the sake of the party, but were never soul-mates. Both were Scots, but of a very different kind, MacDonald with Highland imagination and flair, Henderson excelling as a down-to-earth organizer. Their partnership, never quite severed by disagreement over the war, was soon to be restored in some measure by events.

Before Henderson went to Russia an international socialist conference was already being mooted. It was to be held in Stockholm, under the

8. First nominally, as Minister of Education, then as Paymaster-General.

presidency of a Swedish socialist, and delegates from all belligerent countries were to be free to attend. Though the French socialists and the executive of the British Labour Party voted against taking part, Lloyd George at first saw some potential advantage in the gathering, and he telegraphed Albert Thomas in Petrograd to ask his opinion:

I understand that German Socialists of both sections are to be there and also Russian Socialists. I am afraid that unless Allied cause is represented also bad impression may be produced on Russian Socialists. . . . It would no doubt be proper to see that none of the delegations were anti-patriotic or in favour of peace at any price or any separate peace by Russia, but subject to that it would probably be necessary to allow French and English Socialists to be represented by those whom they might select.[9]

Thomas replied that he would be prepared, at a price, to accept attendance by the Russians without conditions. If his own government agreed, he would personally attend the conference 'at any cost'.[10]

Soon after this exchange MacDonald made an attempt to visit Russia, travelling via Stockholm. The government decided to allow him to go, on the understanding that he would merely convey fraternal greetings to Russian socialists, while doing his utmost to dissuade them from any idea of a separate peace. Such a peace (he said) he regarded 'with absolute horror, as it would mean the destruction of everything he cared for in Europe'.[11] He dined with Lloyd George at Walton Heath on 8 June, and was taken back to London in the Prime Minister's car. The following day he left for Aberdeen to embark on his journey, but it did not take place because members of the Seamen's Union refused to transport him. The prospect of his joining Henderson in Petrograd, though on a separate, unofficial mission, was thus aborted. Henderson had agreed to the government's decision to allow him to travel, but at this stage was thoroughly sceptical about the proposed Stockholm conference, plans for which remained on hold.

Events in Russia during Henderson's time there, and immediately following his return, transformed the situation in that country. When he arrived Lvov was still Prime Minister, but Milyukov had been replaced as Foreign Minister by a member of the Soviet, and Kerensky had become Minister of War. Thus began Kerensky's brief period of ascendancy. His gifts as an orator, unsupported by the qualities needed in a man of action, created a popular illusion, which he shared, that he could both win the war and save

9. DLG to Albert Thomas, 22 May 1917.   10. Albert Thomas to DLG.
11. Robert Cecil to DLG, 29 May 1917.

the country from revolutionary chaos. He saw himself as another Napoleon, and put a bust of his hero on his desk at the War Ministry. He toured the front and delivered passionate speeches to the troops. Their applause misled him into believing that they were eager to fight. Brusilov, whom he appointed Commander-in-Chief in place of Alexeyev, soon came to the conclusion that their morale was not equal to another offensive. But Kerensky blindly insisted, and in mid-June the Russian army was thrown into battle, mainly on the southern front, towards Lemberg, but with subsidiary attacks in the centre and north. After two days of apparent success, the Germans counterattacked with divisions brought from the West and Kerensky's offensive swiftly collapsed. By early August the Russians had been driven out of Galicia and Bukovina. If it had suited the Germans to invade Russia itself they could have done so at that time. But they preferred to allow the internal situation to develop to their advantage, while they contented themselves with the capture of Riga (in September).

Meanwhile Kerensky survived the calamitous failure of his offensive. After an attempted Bolshevik coup in Petrograd (regarded as premature by Lenin) had been scotched by the local military, acting independently, Lvov gave up the premiership and retired to a monastery. Kerensky succeeded him on 7 July, though it was to the city's garrison rather than to the War Minister that the regime owed its temporary reprieve. The Bolsheviks were still unpopular, because they were thought (correctly) to be in German pay. The army was prepared to reimpose order in the capital but the people, including most of the army's rank and file, above all wanted peace. Since the Bolsheviks alone stood for peace at any price, it was only a matter of time before power fell into their hands.

In July Kerensky was 'the only major politician who had a base of popular support yet who was broadly acceptable to the military leaders and the bourgeoisie'. But he had no grip on affairs, while his megalomania increased. 'His offices were transferred to the Winter Palace [and he] slept in the Tsar's enormous bed . . . he also kept on the old palace servants, and changed the guards outside his suite several times a day. As he came and left, the flag on the palace roof was raised and lowered, just as it had been for the tsars.'[12] The only difference was that it was a red flag. A new autocracy was, indeed, in the offing, but Kerensky was scarcely better fitted than Nicholas II to play the part of an autocrat in desperate times.

Henderson was in Russia when Kerensky's doomed offensive was

12. Orlando Figes, *A People's Tragedy: The Russian Revolution 1891–1924* (1996), pp. 437–8.

launched, and throughout his time in the country he witnessed the turmoil of its politics. His last impression of Petrograd was of the uprising in the streets which the military had to quell. He had a slow journey home, involving a delay in Norway and was not back in England until the last week of July. How deeply was he affected by his Russian experience? To what extent did it determine what he did on his return?

Certainly his mind changed about the Stockholm conference, while Lloyd George's was changing the other way. But the fact that Henderson's changed as it did while he was in Russia does not necessarily mean that the events he witnessed there caused the change. According to G. M. Young, his head was 'turned a bit by . . . hearing 180 millions of Russians chanting ["peace without annexations or indemnities"]'. As a result he 'had it in his mind to "rat" and head a great British labour-socialist peace movement', but was 'drawn in the opposite direction by the sweets and emoluments of office'. Young claimed to be 'working on him to lead the socialists without leaving office, and without . . . abandoning our war aims'. Such was Young's report to Hankey immediately after he and Henderson returned together from Russia, and Hankey at once communicated all that he had said to Lloyd George.[13]

In his memoirs Lloyd George gives a similar account of Henderson's state of mind on his return:

Fresh from the glow of that atmosphere of emotionalism and exaltation which great Revolutions excite, Mr. Henderson was out of tune with the stern . . . self-control which was dominant here. When he came back from Russia the fine steel of his character was magnetised by his experiences. He was in an abnormal frame of mind. He had more than a touch of the revolutionary malaria.[14]

Lloyd George's appraisal was much influenced by G. M. Young's reports at the time. But was Young right?

Obviously the contemporary evidence of a highly intelligent man, who accompanied Henderson to Russia and returned with him, deserves serious attention. Nevertheless it is hard to accept the view that Henderson was carried away by what he saw and heard in Russia. He was surely not the man to be magnetized or infected (whichever metaphor is preferred) by revolutionary manifestations. Throughout his career he had been dead

---

13. Hankey diary, 25 July 1917. Hankey gives the Russian words for 'peace without annexations or indemnities' incorrectly, presumably as they had been give to him by Young. The author of the slogan was Lenin.   14. *WM*, p. 1900.

against political extremism and mob rule, and the spectacle of both in Russia is far more likely to have alarmed him than to have inspired him. Indeed, we know from other contemporary evidence that it was so. The *Times* correspondent wrote that he 'was completely overwhelmed and upset by his surroundings',[15] and he himself wrote at the time:

The new Provisional Government has had imposed upon it a task of serious magnitude, for it would have been bad enough to have had the war or the revolution, but both is almost beyond human capacity and more especially when the people are suffering from *the form of intoxication* that has followed upon their newly won freedom. Unfortunately both in civil life and in the armies a great percentage have no desire whatever to get on with the war. They try to excuse themselves by stating that they are prepared for a defensive war but nothing more. I think the indications go to prove that they have been permeated by pacifist theories.[16]

In Henderson's vocabulary 'intoxication' was a pejorative word. He was a lifelong abstainer and his devotion to the cause of temperance 'drew to him much hostility during his political career'.[17] In the metaphorical sense, too, he was clearly appalled by the political intemperance from which, as he saw it, the Russians were 'suffering'. His opposition to syndicalism had always been particularly strong, and is reflected in another of his letters from Russia:

Unfortunately there are no steadying influences akin to our trade unions and the demands that are put forward to the employers are so outrageous that it is obvious they are not prompted by a desire for economic improvement so much as with a view to obtaining complete control of the industry.[18]

These words and the others quoted, written when he had been in the country for several weeks, are not those of a man touched by 'revolutionary malaria'. Nor are they those of a man who had it in mind to lead, as G. M. Young suggested, 'a great British labour-socialist peace movement'. They showed beyond doubt that he was deeply troubled by the drift to pacifism and uncontrolled radicalism that he saw in Russia.

So how did G. M. Young come to misunderstand his attitude so seriously? Intellectuals can be very obtuse, and one can only assume that Young put a

15. Letter from 'Our Petrograd Correspondent' (Robert Wilton) to *The Times*, 31 December 1917. Some months had elapsed since Henderson's visit, but it was still a fairly recent memory.
16. Henderson to T. W. Dawson, 19 June 1917; my italics.
17. Chris Wrigley, *Arthur Henderson* (1990), p. 3.
18. Henderson to J. G. Dale, 19 June 1917.

false construction on Henderson's support for Kerensky, and on his switch from opposing the Stockholm conference to strong advocacy of it. When Henderson left Petrograd Kerensky seemed the only leader capable of holding the line against both the Germans and the Bolsheviks. Lenin was against the conference, because he regarded it as the means whereby Russian social democracy might survive and Russia be kept in the war. For precisely the same reason Henderson came round to the idea. He was convinced that 'there was no possibility for any Russian government of keeping the Russian people in the war unless they could be made to believe in the aims for which it was being pursued'. A 'fully representative' conference might achieve this. 'As he worked things out on the slow journey home . . . it seemed to him that his first duty was to swing the British Labour Party into action, in support.'[19] His companion on the journey may have got the impression that he was backing Kerensky as a radical firebrand, and looking to Stockholm as an occasion for promoting a 'peace movement', rather than for defining peace aims as the only means (he believed) of maintaining the Russians' fighting spirit. In some way or other Young certainly reached the wrong conclusion.

But this is not to say that the alternative and generally accepted view of what happened to him in Russia is the whole truth. On the basis of nothing more than hunch and common sense it is surely fair to speculate that while he was there, and on his way to and fro, he may have changed his mind about his place in British politics. The whole journey gave him plenty of time to think, and his thoughts may often have turned to the domestic scene, since there was not much that he could do about the alien events he was witnessing. Though he was a true patriot, he was also a shrewd and ambitious politician. The war had divided both his own party and – more recently – the Liberals, while the Conservatives were united and increasingly strong. But the division within Labour had never been formalized and was limited to a single issue; he himself remained secretary of an ostensibly united party. The Liberal rift, on the other hand, showed every sign of widening. The issue separating the Asquithians from the Coalition Liberals was essentially personal. It derived from Asquith's refusal to serve under Lloyd George, and from the belief held by him and his supporters that an act of usurpation had occurred the previous December. Such personal rifts are often more damaging and lasting than disagreements on substantial issues of policy. The two Liberal factions were at one on the origins of the war and the need to fight through to genuine victory; but they were already

19. Mary Agnes Hamilton, *Arthur Henderson: A Biography* (1938), pp. 133–4.

206

behaving as distinct parties, with their own whips. Labour was still divided on the war, but showed every sign of becoming a coherent force in the post-war period.

From afar, and with time on his hands, Henderson may have been able to see more clearly the configuration of British politics, and how things might develop, than would have been possible at close range, amid the press of daily business. He may have felt intuitively that it was time for him to devote more of his energy to party organization, so that Labour would have the means to exploit its opportunity; and he may also have felt that, if he had to choose between his duty to Labour and continued membership of a Tory-dominated government, the latter would have to be sacrificed. This interpretation cannot be documented, let alone proved, but his conduct after his return from Russia tends to support it.

He arrived back in England on 24 July. The following day, before talking to Lloyd George or any of his War Cabinet colleagues, he attended a meeting of the Labour Party executive, at which he advised that a special conference of the party should be summoned to consider the question of sending a delegation to Stockholm. He would state at it his own view that delegates should be sent, and meanwhile would go to Paris to confer with the French socialists. Significantly, he would be accompanied by MacDonald (as well as another Labour MP, George Wardle,[20] and two delegates from the Petrograd Soviet).

Before leaving he attended a meeting of the War Cabinet over which Law presided, Lloyd George being already in Paris for an Allied conference. Henderson's colleagues – all Conservatives – then heard about his intended trip and expressed their strong disapproval. He telegraphed Lloyd George in Paris to inform him of the trip, but the Prime Minister could reasonably complain that he had never been consulted about Henderson's course of action. Apparently the two men did not meet while they were in Paris.

If Henderson had spoken to Lloyd George before taking his initiative about Stockholm, he would have found that circumstances had changed the Prime Minister's thinking on the subject. Much had, indeed, happened since he told Albert Thomas in late May that he broadly favoured the Stockholm idea. There had been mutinies in the French army and the War Cabinet had heard of a potentially revolutionary situation in France. The French government was opposed to French socialists participating in any conference involving delegates from enemy countries, at which peace terms would be discussed. The American and Italian governments were equally opposed to

20. Wardle, a railwayman, was acting chairman of the Labour Party.

the idea, agreeing that the conference might suggest the Allies' will to win was flagging. Lloyd George's War Cabinet colleagues were emphatically of the same view, which he had come round to himself.

The position in Russia was hopelessly confused, as was Kerensky's attitude to Stockholm. Lloyd George had spoken in bullish terms of Russian democracy at Glasgow at the end of June, but he had done so as a preliminary to contesting the Russian radicals' demand for a peace without indemnities. Even then – indeed from the beginning – he had his private doubts about the viability of democracy in Russia. While Henderson was on his slow journey home Kerensky's offensive had been seen to fail, and it was evident that the morale of the Russian army was far worse than that of the French. Henderson still had faith in Kerensky and was sure that British representation at Stockholm would help him. Whether or not Kerensky favoured Stockholm became a matter of dispute between Henderson and Lloyd George, but the argument was academic. In reality Kerensky's power was waning and Russia's value as a belligerent was effectively at an end.

Back in London, Lloyd George and Henderson met at 10 Downing Street early on 1 August, their first encounter since Henderson's return from Russia. The Stockholm issue was discussed, but without any meeting of minds. Henderson's course was set, and he was unlikely to be deflected from it by anything that Lloyd George could say. He had never been susceptible, as so many were, to the Prime Minister's charm. Having a rather limited sense of humour, he found Lloyd George's light-hearted banter objectionable. On one occasion, when the two of them were together supporting the electoral reform bill, Lloyd George had said: 'You do the heavy truculent working man and then I will do my bit.' Obviously he was talking in fun, but Henderson was not amused.[21] Of the two coalition chiefs under whom he served Henderson preferred Asquith (whose flippancy was confined to talk and correspondence with intimates). Lloyd George for his part respected Henderson and did not want to lose him, but now felt that he had to choose between service to the Labour Party and his duty as a senior minister of the Crown.

Later the same day (at 4 p.m.) Henderson arrived for a meeting of the War Cabinet, but was told to wait in the secretary's room while his position was discussed. After an hour he was admitted, and Lloyd George explained that he had been kept outside to spare his feelings. Whatever the merits of this explanation, the so-called 'doormat' incident was a serious tactical error by Lloyd George, since it gave Henderson a plausible grievance. It was bad

21. Wrigley, *Arthur Henderson*, p. 114.

enough that his mission to Russia had been decided behind his back; this was far worse. Nevertheless he did not at once submit his resignation, though he had offered to do so at the meeting before he went to Paris. And Lloyd George did not ask him to resign, presumably still hoping to be able to talk him round.

On 10 August the special Labour conference, whose convening Henderson had requested, took place at the Central Hall, Westminster. MacDonald called for a clear statement of peace terms at Stockholm so that 'our German friends' could be asked how far they agreed and how far they disagreed. But Henderson's was the decisive speech. He advised the conference to reverse previous Labour Party policy on Stockholm, and was thus asking it to vote against the policy of the government of which he was still a member, though he neglected to make this particular point clear. When the vote was taken it showed a three-to-one majority in favour of Stockholm.

Lloyd George was now quite sure that Henderson had to give up his party office if he was to remain a member of the War Cabinet, and lost no time in telling him so. Henderson, therefore, wrote the following day:

Dear Prime Minister,

At our interview last night I gathered you had reached the conclusion that my retention of the post of Secretary of the Labour Party was no longer compatible with my membership of the War Cabinet. Recent experiences have impressed me with the embarrassing complications arising from this duality of office. In the circumstance, therefore, I deem it advisable to ask you to release me from further membership of your Government.

I continue to share your desire that the war should be carried to a successful conclusion, and trust that in a non-Government capacity I may be able to render some little assistance to this end.

> I remain,
> Yours sincerely,
> Arthur Henderson

Lloyd George replied at some length in an argumentative letter to 'My dear Henderson', which began by noting 'with satisfaction the assurance of [his] unabated desire to assist in the prosecution of the War to a successful conclusion', and expressed great regret that he could 'no longer be directly and officially associated' in the enterprise.[22]

Two days later Henderson made a personal statement to the House of

22. Henderson to DLG and DLG to Henderson, 11 August 1917.

Commons, which lasted over an hour. Reading it now, one has the feeling that he was protesting too much, and indulging in an excess of self-righteousness, though he scored some palpable hits, not least on the 'door-mat' incident. He suggested that it was without precedent for a Cabinet minister to be kept in another room while his 'conduct was being investigated by his colleagues'. Lloyd George spoke much more briefly, perhaps because he had already said so much in his reply to Henderson's resignation letter. But he maintained that he and his colleagues had been led to suppose that Henderson would not, after all, be asking the Labour conference to endorse Stockholm. Asquith also spoke.[23] The arguments are now of little interest. What mattered was that Lloyd George had lost a colleague of exceptional importance, and that his loss was to be Labour's great gain.

For a time it seemed that Henderson's gamble might have failed. His place as Labour's representative in the War Cabinet was taken by the Minister of Pensions, G. N. Barnes, another respected figure in the trade union movement;[24] and no Labour minister resigned with him. Indeed Wardle, who had accompanied him to Paris, actually joined the government (as junior minister at the Board of Trade). Asquith made no attempt to exploit the situation; his few remarks were, on balance, helpful to the Prime Minister. As for Stockholm, it was soon evident that the recent Labour vote did not represent the opinion of most trade union leaders, who continued to support the government. When it was decided that passports should not be issued for delegates to Stockholm, the decision was accepted without fuss, and in September the TUC resolved that 'a conference at Stockholm at the present moment could not be successful'. The project petered out, while events in Russia followed a course more consistent with Lloyd George's judgement than with Henderson's.

Yet in a longer perspective Henderson's resignation was a disaster for Lloyd George. After his 'release' from ministerial office Henderson was free to devote himself to party organization, and no one could have done the job more effectively. He saw that 'Labour needed machinery to match its increased political and economic strength',[25] and set about providing it. The results were first apparent in the general election of 1918, and a few years later enabled the party to win power. Henderson's departure can be seen in retrospect to signal the end of Lib–Lab partnership and the emergence of

23. Hansard, fifth ser., vol. xcvii, cols. 909–34.
24. Barnes had been acting as substitute Labour member of the War Cabinet during Henderson's absence in Russia.   25. Wrigley, *Arthur Henderson*, p. 120.

Labour as an autonomous force. It also made Lloyd George more dependent than ever upon the Conservatives.

Among the innumerable problems that faced British leaders in the First World War, none was more vexatious than that of manpower. In the rush of voluntary recruitment in the early months of the war thousands of skilled workers joined Kitchener's army, and so were lost to industry, at a time when the creation of a military machine unprecedented in British history demanded a parallel growth in war production. In 1915 Lloyd George's Ministry of Munitions started a reverse trend. With the backing of legislation he mobilized British industry to produce guns and material on a vast scale, but in the process he caused a shortage of the manpower needed to make good the army's heavy losses. In consequence, the voluntary principle was reluctantly abandoned and in May 1916 conscription was introduced for Great Britain (though not yet for Ireland).

Towards the end of Asquith's time a manpower distribution board was set up, under Austen Chamberlain, to administer the new system, but it had no executive powers and so could do little to reconcile the competing claims on the country's human resources. The armed forces now had the power to compel, but the needs of war industry were as great as ever; indeed, they were to become greater with Lloyd George's expansion of home agriculture.

The first Minister of Labour was John Hodge who, like Henderson, was a product of the Glasgow area and a trade union leader, and who, also like Henderson, had moved south during his career – first to Manchester and then to London. He had been in Parliament since 1906. Lloyd George no doubt chose him because he was a thoroughly representative Labour figure, known for his moderation. His new department was to be responsible for the employment exchanges but little else.

The Directorate, or Ministry, of National Service was intended by Lloyd George to have a more potent role, but much would depend upon the choice of a man to run it. Lloyd George first offered the post to Edwin Montagu (as we have seen) but Montagu refused it, ostensibly because he felt that the task of building up a new ministry was beyond him. Lloyd George then turned to Austen Chamberlain's half-brother, Neville, who was just starting his second term as Lord Mayor of Birmingham. His name was proposed by Austen, not directly to Lloyd George but to Curzon, who brought it forward at a meeting of the War Cabinet on 19 December 1916, with Milner's support. The same afternoon Lloyd George saw Neville Chamberlain in his room at the House of Commons and offered him the job, asking for an immediate reply. With whatever misgivings Chamberlain accepted, and news of the appointment was at once given to the press.

The new Director-General was previously unknown to Lloyd George, but by no means unknown to the public. Birmingham was a great city, whose politics had a national dimension, and Chamberlain had made a success of his first term as Lord Mayor. People had heard of him. But apart from his family connections he had no experience of Westminster or Whitehall. Unlike his half-brother he had pursued a career in business, which began with seven lonely and frustrating years trying to grow sisal in the Bahamas. On his return to Birmingham he had prospered in the management of metallurgical firms, while throwing himself into the city's municipal affairs, as his father had done. But Joseph Chamberlain had entered Parliament at the age of forty. Neville, eight years older at the time of his appointment, had never stood for Parliament, and was not asked to do so by Lloyd George. (He did not, in fact, become an MP until he was fifty, remarkably late for a future prime minister.)

He would attribute his failure in the National Service job partly to having not served a Parliamentary apprenticeship. But this is hardly a convincing explanation. Maclay showed that a man unversed in politics of any kind, and unwilling to enter Parliament, could establish a new war department and run it with the utmost efficiency. Chamberlain made the mistake of waiting to be told what to do, rather than deciding what needed to be done and then demanding the means to do it. A friendly biographer, who could write with special insight, has stressed this point:

By Christmas Day, instead of bemoaning his lack of clear instructions, [Chamberlain] should have been banging his fist on the table at 10 Downing Street. And he should have taken his resignation with him. A Minister, particularly the head of a new department, is never so strong again as in his first few weeks of office. His resignation, which in a few short months may have become just a 'little local difficulty', is not to be thought of when he has just been selected for a new post.[26]

Lloyd George gave hostages to fortune when speaking of Chamberlain's job in the House of Commons immediately after appointing him. He implied that the government might extend compulsion to the civil sphere, and that Chamberlain would swiftly produce a new system of enrolment for

26. Iain Macleod, *Neville Chamberlain* (1961), p. 61. This book, published when the author was Colonial Secretary, was ghost-written (by Peter Goldman). But the passage quoted has an authentic ring.

industrial purposes. His speech 'aroused expectations ... which neither Chamberlain nor any other man could fulfil'.[27] But it was up to Chamberlain to decide upon a realistic programme and then to make sure that he had the War Cabinet's full backing. Unfortunately, in making his début in national politics, he showed a dearth of self-confidence. Twenty years later, as Prime Minister, he showed an excess of it – with far more dire consequences.[28]

Failure to write his own job specification and to insist upon a course of policy devised by himself was not his only mistake at the National Service Ministry. He also spurned good advice from Lloyd George about the sort of people he needed to assist him, and chose instead to surround himself with officials who had served him in Birmingham. These men were out of their depth and merely compounded his own lack of metropolitan experience. When, reluctantly, he accepted one man recommended by Lloyd George – James Stevenson from the Ministry of Munitions – as his deputy for civil recruiting, the arrangement did not work and was short-lived.

In general Lloyd George showed little consideration for him, not even bothering to make him a Privy Counsellor, though he was the head of a government department. This was only a detail, but symbolic of his low standing. The weakness of his position was soon apparent. The armed forces continued to control their own recruitment, and he also encountered stiff resistance from civilian departments, in particular Munitions and Labour. When, for instance, he proposed that all men up to the age of twenty-one should be taken out of industry and put into the army, Addison had no difficulty in shooting the proposal down. 'I pointed out that we already had an arrangement exempting skilled men and his proposal would involve taking away 70,000 skilled men who had been through apprenticeships.'[29]

As the months went by he came to see that his position was hopeless. His speeches were quite effective in persuading men to come forward, but he had no power to determine where they should serve. In June he nearly resigned when he read in the press that he had a new Parliamentary secretary, about whose appointment he had not been informed, let alone consulted, by the Prime Minister. Lloyd George explained that the discourtesy was inadvertent, and Chamberlain stayed on, though not for much longer. On 8 August he found another cause to resign, and this time his resignation was accepted. Lloyd George, while maintaining that his complaints were

27. David Dilks, *Neville Chamberlain*, vol. i: *Pioneering and Reform, 1869–1929* (1984), p. 202.
28. It is fair to say that between the two 'extreme' periods he was an outstanding Minister of Health (1924–9) and a competent Chancellor of the Exchequer (1931–7).
29. Addison diary, 19 January 1917.

unjustified, thanked him for the 'high-minded patriotism' with which he
had undertaken 'one of the most complicated and difficult tasks', and for
his 'unwearying devotion and assiduity'.[30] Of more value to Chamberlain
were the friendly messages he received from many quarters, including his
staff at St Ermin's Hotel, Westminster, where the Ministry was housed.

He never forgave Lloyd George. In the 1930s no member of the national
government was more implacably opposed to any suggestion that Lloyd
George might be brought into it, and Lloyd George returned the hostility
with interest, writing in his memoirs:

We needed a man of exceptional gifts . . . Mr. Neville Chamberlain is a man of rigid
competency. Such men have their uses in conventional times . . . and are indispensable
for filling subordinate posts at all times. But they are lost in an emergency or in
creative tasks at any time.[31]

And in May 1940 he had the last word in the vendetta, when his devastating
intervention in the Norway debate helped to end Chamberlain's premiership.

Lloyd George's replacement for Chamberlain at National Service was
Auckland Geddes, brother of Eric, who had been director of recruiting at
the War Office since early 1916, having previously been Adjutant-General
in France. On appointment he was made a Privy Counsellor and given rather
more power than Chamberlain had ever had. He also received more support
from the War Cabinet. Under him the problems of manpower were more or
less contained for the rest of the war, though they were never solved.

We can now see that Lloyd George should have established a single
Ministry of Labour and National Service when he became Prime Minister,
as was done (with poetic justice by Chamberlain) at the beginning of the
Second World War. But the unified ministry did not achieve its full effect
until Ernest Bevin was put in charge of it by Churchill. Was anyone in Bevin's
class available to Lloyd George? The nearest equivalent was Henderson, who
had similar prestige as a trade unionist, and who possessed a similar talent
for mass organization – though this was not recognized by Asquith or Lloyd
George. While he was a minister in both coalitions he was taken seriously

30. DLG to Neville Chamberlain, 9 August 1917.
31. *WM*, p. 1368. It is often said that Lloyd George took against Chamberlain at once,
regarding the shape of his head as phrenologically suspect. (Lloyd George had a quirky interest
in phrenology.) There is no contemporary evidence for this, but certainly by the end of January
he was telling C. P. Scott that he was 'rather disappointed with Neville Chamberlain' (Scott
diary, 28 January 1917).

as a Labour stalwart and intermediary in labour disputes but not as a potential man of action. Lloyd George discovered too late, and at his own expense, that he was 'the greatest political organiser of his day'. If Henderson had been given control of Labour and National Service, with the necessary panoply of power, he might have done as well as Bevin. And with such a challenging executive task he might have been less easily tempted to resign.

13

Lloyd George's Boswell

Lloyd George's Boswell – Opening phase in Flanders – Retreat to Criccieth

There is a long gap in Frances Stevenson's diary between the spring and autumn of 1917. She stops in the middle of a sentence on 29 May and does not resume until 5 November. There had been similar, though shorter, mid-year gaps in 1915 and 1916, and for 1918 there was to be no diary at all, or none that has been preserved. In the absence of a contemporary record by her, George Riddell's diary becomes more important than ever. He was, in any case, the nearest equivalent to a Boswell in Lloyd George's life, because he was a close observer and admirer who had an independent position, and because he records conversational exchanges in the Boswellian manner. Moreover, his diary covers the whole period of Lloyd George's greatest power, from 1908 to 1922.

Riddell was a curious man, in both senses. As well as being widely and systematically inquisitive, he was a man of considerable mystery. In particular, he was at pains to conceal his own origins and early life. He managed to keep essential facts about himself hidden while he was alive and for some time after his death. This was particularly true of his matrimonial past. His *Who's Who* entry mentioned only one marriage, to Annie Allardice, and his obituary in *The Times* followed suit.[1] In the *Dictionary of National Biography* supplement published in 1949, the entry on him by the journalist Hamilton Fyfe mentions an earlier marriage, to Grace Williams, though without any indication how or why he became free to marry for a second time.[2] Only in 1956 was it revealed in print, by Lord Beaverbrook, that Riddell was divorced, and that he was the first divorced man to become a peer.[3] The truth had long been known in establishment circles, and on this account Lloyd George had some difficulty with the King over Riddell's peerage in 1920 – though there seems to have been no trouble when

1. *The Times*, 6 December 1934.   2. *DNB* (Supplement 1931–1940).
3. Lord Beaverbrook, *Men and Power, 1917–1918* (1956), p. 246 (and biographical sketch, pp. xxii–xxiii).

he received a knighthood (on Asquith's recommendation) in 1910 and a baronetcy (on Lloyd George's) in 1918.[4]

There was similar obfuscation about his birth, family background and education. *Who's Who* gave only the year of his birth (1865), but did not say where he was born or give any details of his parentage. The *Times* obituary stated that he was born in Scotland, that his father was a civil servant, and that he was educated in London. Hamilton Fyfe corrected his birthplace to Brixton, described his father as a photographer, and confirmed that he was educated in London, though 'privately'.

He was indeed born in South London, but preferred it to be thought that his birthplace was Duns in Berwickshire, whence his paternal grandfather had migrated early in the century. His father – who died before he was two – had drifted from job to job and could therefore be identified with a variety of occupations. Riddell may have felt that the civil service was more respectable than photography, and so have put it around that his father was a civil servant. For the same reason he may have told Hamilton Fyfe (for whose *DNB* entry 'private information' was cited as a source) that his education was private, though in fact he was sent to a Church of England school in his neighbourhood – where he had no difficulty with his lessons and showed early signs of a phenomenal memory.

Riddell's widowed mother was a woman of strong character and Calvinist principles. She was largely responsible for the upbringing of her only child, and she instilled into him a work ethic which dominated his life. Though she had little money herself, some of her relations were quite well off, and when Riddell was seventeen one of his uncles placed him in a firm of solicitors. Six years later he qualified with first-class honours and won the Law Society's prize. Through his marriage to Grace Williams (from a London Welsh family) he acquired enough money to set up a partnership with two other young men. He then devoted himself single-mindedly to achieving professional and financial success.

His firm's clients came to include the Cardiff *Western Mail*, whose proprietor was Lascelles Carr. Soon afterwards Carr bought the *News of the World*, making Riddell its legal adviser and, in 1903, its chairman. Thus he entered the world of newspaper management and ownership, in which he prospered immensely. While maintaining the *News of the World*'s distinctive formula of petty prurience, he moved the paper slightly up-market in other

4. Kenneth Rose, *King George V* (1983), pp. 249–50. We must assume that gossip about Riddell's past had been slow to reach the King, since he would surely have applied the same moral test to a new knight or baronet as to a new peer.

respects. Within ten years its circulation doubled to 100,000, and within the next ten passed the million mark. By the time of his death it was well on the way to becoming the largest-selling newspaper in the world. He also gained effective control of the Newnes empire, adding *Country Life* and *John o' London's Weekly* to its list of titles.

During the period of his escape from the genteel poverty of his childhood to the wealth that his efforts brought him in middle life he had no time for distractions of any kind. His wife, Grace, hardly saw him at all and (according to him) took to drink. In 1900 they were divorced, with Riddell as the 'guilty party'. He then immediately married a cousin of his in her mid-thirties, Annie Allardice, who was content to live with him on his own terms. They were cousins – his own second name was Allardice – but otherwise had little in common. Yet she furnished with some taste the house that he acquired in Westminster, 20 Queen Anne's Gate, and ran it for him with quiet efficiency.

It is understandable that he wished to suppress all knowledge of his first marriage and divorce. In the late nineteenth century the marriage bond was sacrosanct and anyone judged responsible for breaking it was beyond the pale. Indeed, such a predicament was likely to destroy any public career until the Second World War. The wonder is not that Riddell was so secretive about his matrimonial record, but rather that the secret was kept for so long. The probable explanation is that, as a newspaper proprietor himself, he benefited from the 'dog don't eat dog' tradition, reinforced in his case by the fact that he was, on the whole, liked and respected by his fellow proprietors.

However unattractive Riddell may have seemed as he went about accumulating his wealth, he was generous and enlightened in the use that he made of it. Since both his marriages were childless, there were few family obligations to compete with his philanthropy. When he died most of his estate of £2.3 million (more than £75 million in today's money) was left to newspaper and other charities, and he had already given away large sums during his lifetime. Medicine was one of his special interests, and he gave £100,000 each to the Royal Free Hospital and the Eastman Dental Clinic. Another recipient of his largess was the London Library, since he was a bibliophile and wished to be remembered as an author. He wrote articles on a variety of subjects, some later collected in hard covers, and above all he wrote his diary, extracts from which were published in three volumes before he died. His coat of arms as a peer showed a printing press of Caxton's day with two printers as supporters, and his crest was a carrier pigeon with an open scroll in its beak.

Politics fascinated him, but unlike Northcliffe and some others he had no urge to wield power, preferring the role of confidant and discreet go-between. At the Paris peace conference and several other post-war gatherings he acted as liaison between the British delegation and the press, in which essentially diplomatic work he excelled, since both the politicians and the journalists trusted him.

Lloyd George was the politician to whom he was closest, from 1908 until the last phase of the former's premiership. Thereafter they were partly estranged, though there was never a complete breach. When Riddell died he left Lloyd George £1,000, and he also left £500 each to Frances Stevenson and A. J. Sylvester. He encouraged Sylvester to keep a diary, in which the latter records Riddell's account of how he and Lloyd George first met.

It was at the house of Mr and Mrs Timothy Davies in Fulham, to which he had come at Lloyd George's request to give advice on a libel case. There he found Lloyd George 'lying on a settee, his brow being mopped by . . . Mrs Timothy Davies'.[5] This meeting must have been in the summer of 1908, several months before Riddell's diary begins. The libel about which he was being consulted must have been an item that appeared in the *Bystander* in July of that year, suggesting that a man of Lloyd George's 'temperament' found it difficult to resist the flattery of 'the fair sex'. No female name was mentioned, but Lloyd George secured a complete retraction, together with damages of £300 which he gave to the Caernarfon Cottage Hospital.

The irony of the situation would not have been lost upon Riddell, whose alertness to human feelings and foibles was akin to Lloyd George's own. He must have sensed at once that 'Mrs Tim' was rather more to the Chancellor than merely the hospitable wife of a Parliamentary colleague, and that Davies himself was a complaisant husband.[6] To be summoned to discuss, in such company, the supposedly defamatory character of an innuendo that Lloyd George was susceptible to female charm cannot have failed to amuse Riddell; but no doubt his professional skill contributed to the satisfactory outcome.

When Frances Stevenson became, in effect, a secret second wife to Lloyd George, Riddell was quick to perceive the relationship. She writes of him in her memoirs:

I found him at first rather forbidding, with his piercing blue eyes, gaunt figure, and his habit of cross-examining everyone with whom he came into contact. He had an

5. A. J. Sylvester, *Life with Lloyd George*, ed. Colin Cross (1975); diary entry for 6 October 1933 (p. 101).
6. For the origins of this triangle see my *Lloyd George: The Young Lloyd George* (1973), pp. 239-45.

insatiable curiosity, and he simply had, if possible, to get at one's private life, more, I think, because he liked to be able to form a complete picture of the person in question than from any morbid motive.[7]

Riddell's motive, in this instance, was certainly to protect Lloyd George. In 1916, when he moved to the War Office and Frances's place in his secretariat attracted unwelcome publicity – her photograph appearing in the papers – Riddell gave her a veiled warning that care was more than ever necessary, since the Minister's enemies would 'stoop to the trick that was played on Parnell' to bring him down.[8]

Riddell looked after Lloyd George's comforts as well as his reputation, building for him the house at Walton Heath where, during the war, he spent many weekends and weekday nights. The house was built beside the golf course. Both men loved the game, and Riddell did much to extend its appeal to the middle class. Among Walton Heath's many advantages was its convenience as a retreat for Lloyd George and Frances, where they could be under the same roof but away from the pressure of Downing Street and central London. Riddell also took larger country houses, where he could entertain the Prime Minister and enable him to talk at leisure to people he needed to see, including foreign statesmen. Annie Riddell is occasionally mentioned as being present at one of these house parties, but as a rule Riddell acted as host and impresario on his own. For August 1917 he rented Great Walstead, at Lindfield in Sussex, where Lloyd George spent a substantial part of the month.[9]

At Great Walstead Riddell recorded his own assessment of the Prime Minister's qualities and defects:

His energy, capacity for work, and power of recuperation are remarkable. He has an extraordinary memory, imagination, and the art of getting at the root of a matter . . . He is not afraid of responsibility, and has no respect for tradition or convention. He is always ready to examine, scrap or revise established theories and practices. These qualities give him unlimited confidence in himself . . . he is one of the craftiest of men, and his extraordinary charm of manner not only wins him friends, but does much to soften the asperities of his opponents and enemies. He is full of humour and a born actor . . . He has an instinctive power of divining the thoughts and intentions of people with whom he is conversing. His chief defects are: (1) Lack of appreciation

7. Frances Lloyd George, *The Years that Are Past* (1967), p. 58.   8. FSD, 28 July 1916.
9. Some writers tend to confuse Great Walstead with Danny Park, which Riddell took for a longer period the following year, and where much important business was done in the closing months of the war.

of existing institutions, organisations and stolid, dull people ... their ways are not his ways and their methods are not his methods. (2) Fondness for a grandiose scheme in preference to an attempt to improve existing machinery. (3) Disregard of difficulties in carrying out big projects ... he is not a man of detail.[10]

These comments are broadly fair so far as they go, but two points on the credit side need to be qualified. Not everyone was susceptible to Lloyd George's charm; Robertson and Henderson were important exceptions, and there were others. Moreover, the Prime Minister's self-confidence, though certainly great, was not 'unlimited'. In particular, it tended to fail him – after Calais – in his dealings with Haig.

The month of August witnessed the first phase of Haig's long-delayed campaign in Flanders. The delay in launching it was, of course, only partly his fault. He cannot be blamed for the priority given to Nivelle's offensive; but when, as a result of its failure, the initiative passed to him, he wasted precious time by appointing to the key operational command, that of the Fifth Army, a man who was unfamiliar with the terrain. Seven weeks elapsed between Plumer's victory at Messines and Gough's attack on 31 July. This would have been bad enough if Gough had been the right man for the job; but, in fact, as already explained, he was not.

The Germans made good use of the time Haig allowed them to prepare against the coming attack. They deepened their defences and massed artillery behind the Passchendaele ridge and the Gheluvelt plateau. Gough's intelligence grossly underrated the strength of the German batteries facing him. As for his own artillery, it was adequate for destroying the German forward positions, and for providing a creeping barrage for the first assault troops; but his field guns did not have the range to cover the depth of advance envisaged in his plan, while his heavy guns were bound to be largely preoccupied with counter-battery work.

Gough hoped to achieve a north-easterly advance of up to 5,000 yards on a ten-mile front, in four swift stages. This was a far more ambitious plan than Rawlinson or Plumer had put forward, and it was in expectation of such a plan that Haig had appointed Gough. But even Gough had some doubts about the time it would take him to achieve a decisive breakthrough, and Haig, as the date approached, became concerned about the danger of enfilade from the right. Nevertheless the attack went ahead more or less as planned.

10. *RWD*, 13 August 1917.

The first day was certainly a big improvement on the dreadful opening of the battle of the Somme the previous July, when for the capture of three and a half square miles the British had sustained 57,000 casualties, compared with the Germans' one to two thousand. On 31 July 1917 the human cost was roughly equal, at about 27,000 casualties on either side, while Haig's forces captured eighteen square miles.

But success was by no means uniform along the whole of the front. The corps on the left of the Fifth Army, and the French First Army operating on its left, made gains of up to 3,000 yards which were consolidated by the end of the day, at the cost of relatively light casualties. In the centre similar advances were made, though at greater cost and without securing all the ground gained. Before nightfall British troops in this sector were forced to make significant withdrawals, and an important contributory factor was enfilade fire from German batteries behind the Gheluvelt plateau – the very danger that Haig had belatedly perceived. On the right the attack on the Gheluvelt plateau itself was the least successful part of the day's work, leaving the Germans largely in control of a key position.

Bad strategy was compounded by bad luck. The original aims of Haig's offensive, extravagant enough in the best of circumstances, were utterly stultified by the weather. During the afternoon of 31 July rain began to fall, and it continued unremittingly for the next four days. There was further heavy rain, at intervals, for the rest of the month, and the intervals were never long enough to allow the ground to dry. The battlefield became waterlogged, all the more so because the preliminary bombardment had wrecked the drainage system. Both sides suffered from the weather, but the attacking forces were the more heavily penalized. While the Germans could sit tight in their concrete pillboxes (a novel device), Haig's troops had to advance against them through an expanse of mud and water, and without accurate artillery support – since the Allied gunners largely depended upon observation from the air (the Germans being more favourably placed on the ground) and low cloud made this impossible.

It was certainly unfortunate for Haig – but far more unfortunate, of course, for the troops – that August 1917 turned out to be such a wet month in Flanders. Two out of five Augusts during the war (1914 and 1918) were fine and dry there. But rain was a known hazard, and in any case a good commander should be capable of adapting to vagaries of weather, as to other unforeseen developments. Haig did not adapt well to the situation created by the rain. Though his intellect told him it would be futile to persist in attacking without the necessary artillery cover, he was slow to impose this logic upon Gough, partly because it conflicted with his own instincts.

The result was that, while complaining of Gough, he acquiesced in further large-scale attacks, and in one moment of euphoria even said that, if the offensive were maintained, the war might be won in December.[11]

At the end of August, however, when the toll of casualties had risen to 70,000 with hardly anything to show for it, he decided to reduce Gough's role and to settle, in effect, for a different sort of campaign, in which Plumer would be the chief executant and capture of the Gheluvelt plateau the prime immediate objective. Meanwhile any idea of an amphibious operation to link up with the Ypres offensive was quietly postponed. (It was later quietly abandoned.) Henceforth the unspoken purpose of the campaign was to wear the enemy down by the old attritional method, and to prevent the deflection of substantial force to other theatres. According to Haig's postwar line, taken up by his apologists, his overriding motive was to keep the Germans so busy that they would be unable to exploit the weakness of the French. But there is little contemporary evidence to sustain this rationalization, and we should note that in August the First French Army under his command performed exceptionally well.[12]

When the offensive began, not only members of the War Cabinet were kept in the dark about its progress, or the lack of it. Even Robertson had to plead for information, writing to Haig's Chief of Staff, Sir Lancelot Kiggell:

I am sure your Chief is very busy. I do not wish to be given any secrets you do not care to entrust to me, then I cannot give them to the Cabinet or to anyone else, but I would like to have a few lines occasionally giving your opinion as to how matters are progressing – of course with the knowledge of the Commander-in-Chief. *Not unnaturally the Cabinet ask me my opinion every morning and it is rather difficult for me to say much as I have nothing to rely upon but the Communiqué and the slight additions you occasionally send to me* . . . our Ministers have a good deal of anxiety to

11. Haig diary, 19 August 1917.
12. In his biography of Haig, Duff Cooper quotes a letter the Field-Marshal wrote on 5 March 1927 to General Charteris, his former Chief of Intelligence, referring to Churchill's *World Crisis*: 'it is impossible for Winston to know how the possibility of the French Army breaking up in 1917 compelled me to go on attacking . . . You [Charteris] even did not know the facts, as Pétain told them to me in confidence.' Cooper goes on to remark that, although Pétain intensified trench warfare in the Verdun area from 20 August onward, it was not until 23 October that he 'dared to use his troops for an offensive, and then only on a comparatively minor scale' (Duff Cooper, *Haig* (2 vols., 1935–6), vol. ii, p. 134). In fact, the crisis in the French army following the Nivelle débâcle was well under control by August, and Pétain's avoidance of another major offensive in 1917 was a deliberate strategy, to preserve French strength until the Americans came. Any danger that his army might break up had passed.

carry and it is all for the good of the war that I should be able to give them a good account of what is taking place . . . they asked me for my opinion this morning as to how matters were going and my answer was 'very well'. So far as I know they are . . . Apparently there has been some very hard fighting . . . but I imagine that your task will be easier now that you have got the Pilckem Ridge [on the left of the front, where the attack had been most successful on the first day] . . . The rain is a great nuisance . . . *All I want is some interesting information that I can properly give to these people*, to which I think you will agree they are entitled. Good luck to you all.[13]

It is clear from this characteristic letter that there was quite a lot that Robertson did not consider 'these people' – the responsible government of the country – were entitled to know. But he wanted to have a few harmless scraps to throw to them. He acknowledged their right to be concerned, but not to have any effective say in military affairs. The letter also shows that Robertson felt distinctly aggrieved by the inadequate flow of information to himself. He had made Haig, if not the War Cabinet, aware that he had serious doubts about the range and sweep of the Flanders plan, and Haig therefore had serious doubts about him. But the Field-Marshal had no reason to fear that the CIGS would ever violate his code of professional and caste loyalty.

General Kiggell had been Haig's Chief of Staff since December 1915. Coming to the post from the War Office he 'had no experience of large-scale modern war in the field', and his thinking was 'orthodox and doctrinaire'.[14] Throughout his time with Haig he acted as 'servant rather than adviser'.[15] Even John Terraine admits that he 'never was, nor aspired to be, more than a mouthpiece for Haig',[16] which is almost tantamount to saying that Haig should have picked somebody capable of forming independent views and giving him the benefit of them. When Robertson arranged for Lloyd George to meet Kiggell, on his way back from the Rome conference in January, the encounter was not a success, Kiggell reporting afterwards to his master that the Prime Minister 'poured out a lot of heretical, amateur strategy of the most dangerous and misleading kind'.[17] Lloyd George's memoirs do not refer to the occasion, but describe Kiggell as having, in general, 'the air of a silent craftsman, whose plans, designed . . . in the seclusion of his workshop,

13. Robertson to Kiggell, marked secret, 2 August 1917; my italics.
14. Correlli Barnett, entry on Kiggell in *DNB* (Supplement 1951–1960).
15. David R. Woodward, *Lloyd George and the Generals* (1983), p. 75.
16. John Terraine, *Douglas Haig: The Educated Soldier* (2000), p. 176. The author adds that Kiggell was 'always a shadowy figure in the background, signing orders, circulating papers, minding the machine'.   17. Cooper, *Haig*, vol. ii, p. 23.

were turning out well and proceeding inexorably without a hitch to the destined end'.[18]

Despite the War Cabinet's grudging and qualified assent to Haig's offensive, Lloyd George continued to hope, up to the last minute, that some means would be found of averting it. At an Allied conference in Paris after the bombardment had begun he talked of potentially decisive action against Austria and Turkey. But the French were unresponsive. He tried again at the next meeting of Allied leaders in early August, when the first results, or non-results, of Haig's offensive were becoming obvious and when Cadorna announced that he was bringing forward his attack on the Austrians from September to mid-August. Lloyd George argued strongly for action in support of the Italians, but the French still did not respond. Robertson told Kiggell that the Prime Minister was 'twice as bad as on the occasion you had a discussion with him in the train', adding, most unsuitably, that he was 'an under-bred swine'.[19]

At the same time Hankey was coming round to Lloyd George's view: 'I agree with him that rain has spoiled Haig's Flanders plan & that we ought to do something else.'[20] This was the Cabinet secretary's comment after the London meeting, and three days later he wrote: 'the days are slipping by, it is time to reconsider whether Haig's offensive should be permitted to continue in the bad weather conditions, and whether the alternative for a great offensive on the Italian front should not be adopted. In a few days Cadorna starts and it will be too late.'[21] Haig, however, replying to Robertson's report of the 'doings' in London, reasserted his belief that he would be victorious in Flanders, basing his opinion on 'actual facts viz: the poor state of German troops, high standard of efficiency of our own, power of our artillery to dominate enemy's guns, etc. etc.' An occasional glance at his intelligence summaries would, he said, 'convince even the most sceptical'.[22] (Haig himself, unfortunately, was one of the least.)

Cadorna opened his offensive on 19 August – the eleventh battle to be fought on the Isonzo front. At first it went well. After a week Lloyd George received, at Great Walstead, a telegram from the British Ambassador in Rome, Sir Rennell Rodd, suggesting that the battle might result in 'a complete smashing of the Austrian army'.[23] This was just what the Prime Minister wanted to hear, and Hankey was summoned from a brief holiday with his family to discuss the new situation and how to exploit it. He found Lloyd

18. WM, pp. 2224–5.   19. Robertson to Kiggell, 9 August 1917.
20. Hankey diary, 8 August 1917.   21. Ibid., 11 August 1917.
22. Haig to Robertson, 13 August 1917.   23. Cipher telegram from Rodd, 26 August 1917.

George 'in a ferment of excitement', in which he admits to having shared. While they were talking in the garden, 'Ll.G. climbed high up a plum tree, and out on to a very rotten branch after plums'.[24] (Always a fruit-lover, he had raided orchards around Llanystumdwy as a child.) Albert Thomas joined the party in the evening, when Lloyd George pressed the case for sending guns from the Western front to help the Italians. Late at night he wrote letters in the same sense to Robertson and Bonar Law. His aim was to enable the Italians 'to convert the Austrian retreat into a rout'.[25]

All this occurred on a Sunday, and Lloyd George stayed on at Great Walstead until the following Wednesday, while the War Cabinet held meetings in his absence. On Tuesday evening Milner came down from London for dinner and showed himself 'in substantial agreement with Ll.G. on the Italian question'.[26] The following day Robertson arrived mid-morning with his acolyte, General Frederick Maurice, director of military operations since 1915 (when Robertson became CIGS). It was agreed that a telegram should be sent offering help for Cadorna if he could guarantee that it would produce 'a really great victory'. In Hankey's view Robertson agreed only because he was sure that no such assurance would be given. Maurice told Hankey that Haig still believed the Flanders coast could be cleared, but Hankey was unable to share his optimism, having been very differently briefed by a former member of his staff who was now a corps chief of staff in Haig's army.[27]

Riddell did his best to make Robertson's visit go smoothly, ordering for lunch an apple suet pudding which he happened (typically) to know was one of the General's favourite dishes. Robertson had two helpings of it, but more than an apple pudding was needed to create harmony between him and Lloyd George. In the afternoon the party dispersed, Lloyd George returning briefly to Downing Street before going out to Walton Heath.[28]

He stayed there for most of the next week and was absent again from the War Cabinet when, on 3 September, word was received from Maurice in Paris to the effect that the French wanted to send a hundred guns to Italy,

24. Hankey diary, 26 August 1917.
25. DLG to Robertson, same date. Also staying were Lord Burnham (proprietor of the *Daily Telegraph*), Lord Reading (about to leave for America), Philip Kerr and the interpreter Paul Mantoux.
26. Hankey diary, 28 August 1917. The telephone lines had been brought down by windy weather, with the result that Hankey had to walk two or three times with Riddell to the post office at Lindfield.   27. Ibid., 29 August 1917.
28. Hankey diary, same date. Robertson asked Riddell to congratulate his cook (*RWD*, 29 August 1917).

to be taken from the First French Army under Haig's command. This request was no doubt prompted by Thomas, who had been swayed by Lloyd George's arguments at Great Walstead; but it was also supported by Foch whose attitude to peripheral activities had been changing. Foch and Haig came to London, and Lloyd George came up from Walton Heath to preside over discussion of the French proposal. The result was essentially a victory for Haig. Lloyd George found that his colleagues, including even Milner who had so recently favoured his Italian idea, were unwilling to agree to anything that would detract from Haig's chances in Flanders. Lloyd George appealed to Haig to make some concession, and in the end he agreed to release fifty guns from the First French Army, if the remaining fifty could be taken from French units in other sectors. But this practical gesture to the Italians was too little and too late. Cadorna's offensive was already in trouble and by 12 September was completely stalled. Austria had not been defeated, but had been hurt enough to make the Germans feel that their ally needed to be actively supported – with consequences that would soon be apparent.

In Hankey's view at the time, Lloyd George's policy of guns for Italy might, if adopted earlier, have 'led to big results'. He also thought that the issue gave the Prime Minister a good opportunity to impose his will on Haig and Robertson, but that 'when he came to the point, he funked it', telling Hankey it was 'not the moment for a row with the soldiers'. In a longer perspective Hankey may have modified the latter judgement,[29] and certainly it is not endorsed by the American historian who has written the fairest study of Lloyd George and the generals. David Woodward considers it 'fortunate' for Lloyd George that he recoiled from a showdown at that moment and on that issue. If he had laid himself open to the charge of undermining Haig's campaign for the benefit of Cadorna's, when Cadorna was anyway about to revert to the defensive, he 'could well have destroyed his premiership'.[30]

Cheerfulness and high spirits were among Lloyd George's most valuable qualities. They seldom failed him, and never (until old age) for long. But on the rare occasions when, like Othello, he found himself 'perplexed in the extreme', his fraught state of mind tended to be accompanied by physical symptoms. It was so, for instance, at the end of 1910, when his attempt to

29. Hankey diary, 4 September 1917. It is surely significant that Hankey omits the reference to funking when he quotes this diary entry in *The Supreme Command* (2 vols., 1961), vol. ii, p. 696.
30. Woodward, *Lloyd George and the Generals*, pp. 198–9.

promote a coalition to tackle outstanding national problems had ended in frustration. He developed, then, a curious throat complaint, never specific- ally diagnosed, which was cured by a combination of fringe medicine (in the form of a 'voice restorer' called Miss Hicks) and working holidays away from London.

A similar crisis occurred in September 1917. Though the symptoms were different, it is hard to doubt that they were at least partly the product of acute mental stress. Lloyd George had declined Haig's invitation to witness the opening of Third Ypres, and never showed any desire to observe the battle at first hand. He could too well imagine what was happening, and the thought of it tormented him. He had tried to prevent the further massive loss of young British lives – in an offensive whose aims he regarded as extravagant and unrealistic even without the rain – but had felt unable to force the generals to conform to his strategic judgement. After more than a month of the campaign he felt that his judgement was vindicated, but could still see no way of stopping the carnage.

For much of August, as we have seen, he had been out of London, at Great Walstead or Walton Heath. After the Allied meetings in early September he took the increasingly unusual step of turning to Criccieth as a holiday retreat. Though always close to his Welsh roots psychologically, he was rarely attracted by the physical environment of Wales, and since the start of the war his visits to Criccieth had been briefer and less frequent than ever. Now, however, he felt the need to go there, and his state of health probably made his stay longer than intended.

With Margaret and Megan he left London on 5 September, travelling first to Cheshire, where he stayed with Lord Leverhulme while carrying out engagements in Birkenhead. Hankey was 'very glad to see him go', having recently found him 'restless and neurotic, unstable and rather infirm in purpose, neuralgic and irritable, exacting and difficult to please'.[31] The Welsh National Eisteddfod was meeting at Birkenhead, and Lloyd George appeared at it twice. On 6 September he spoke on one of his favourite themes, that 'an intense love for Wales [was] compatible with the most fervent British patriotism'. He related it to the current struggle:

Humanity at the end of this war will know that it largely owes its freedom to the fact that the British Empire has proved to be a reality and not a sham. But if this is the day of great empires, it is also pre-eminently the day of little nations. . . . Great empires are necessary for protection, for security, for strength; the smaller nations

31. Hankey diary, 5 September 1917.

for concentrated and intensive effort . . . Go to the Far West, and there you will find giants of the forest which have defied the storms of centuries . . . You are overawed by the majesty of their strength . . . However, it is the little trees which bear fruit . . .[32]

The following evening he spoke again at the Eisteddfod, in Welsh and on the subject of Welsh music.

Meanwhile, during the morning of 7 September, he received the freedom of Birkenhead at the Town Hall and spoke on the progress of the war. The local alderman who introduced him gave him the chance to begin with a light-hearted reassertion of his Welsh patriotism:

Alderman Solly, in a very happy speech, made one statement which, as a Welshman, did not cheer me very much, when he referred to the fact that the first visitor to this town hall was, I think, Edward the First – not a very popular personality. He was the man who suppressed the Eisteddfod, but I am comforted by the fact that Birkenhead has put that right.

We can visualize his expression as he produced the name 'Edward the First', and the effect of what must have been a pregnant pause before he added the words 'not a very popular personality'.

On the war, he gave an honest but upbeat assessment of the fight against the U-boats, praising Birkenhead's contribution to war production, in particular shipbuilding. He also spoke at some length about Russia, admitting that the news from there was 'disappointing' but hoping, all the same, that Kerensky's government would keep Russia in the alliance and improve its military performance.

Then, after referring to the 'triumphs won by the Italian armies', he had just this to say about the campaign in Flanders:

On the Western Front the Germans are meeting soldiers, British and French, who not merely stand up to them but seek them out in their concrete dug-outs. They have beaten them in a dozen pitched battles and scores of thousands of men from picked legions of Germany have been led into captivity by the foe whom a short time ago they affected to despise.[33]

He could hardly have said less without imperilling national morale, but clearly could not bring himself to say more.

From Cheshire the Lloyd George family trio motored on to Criccieth,

32. *The Times*, 7 September 1917.   33. Ibid., 8 September 1917.

accompanied by Riddell and Philip Kerr. They had a picnic lunch on the way, and as they neared their destination Lloyd George began to recite Welsh poetry, 'all the time holding his wife's hand as if they were a newly married couple'.[34] On Saturday, 8 September he fell ill, and by the following evening had a high temperature, the highest he had had for years (as he told Frances Stevenson in a letter three days later). He believed he was 'in for a serious illness', but was saved by his 'old trick of perspiration'. After sweating 'gallons' during the night, on Monday morning he was 'normal but feeble', and got up to attend a ceremony at the village institute in Llanystumdwy (built from libel damages paid to him by the *People* in 1909). He unveiled there two portraits – one of the local squire, Sir Hugh Ellis-Nanney, whom he had defeated in two Parliamentary elections, the other of his old schoolmaster, David Evans. To both men he paid graceful compliments, though only Ellis-Nanney was present to hear them, Evans having recently died.

Not surprisingly, Lloyd George was still far from well, but his indisposition (officially described as a cold) gave him an excuse to prolong his stay at Criccieth. At the same time he missed Frances:

I must stay down as long as I can be spared. Otherwise P[ussy – his nickname for her] will soon have to find another Tom Cat . . . Now I have a proposal to make. Couldn't you & Muriel [her sister] come down here and stay at the Marine Hotel. We might snatch one or two walks along the riverside – you Muriel & self. You could come Saturday . . . I could then meet you on the cliff under Muriau beyond Marine Terrace at 10.30 Sunday morning. Just think of it sweet . . . I am simply mad to see you.[35]

Evidently she came, because when he returned to London she was a member of the party. It may have been no coincidence that Margaret left for London a few days earlier.[36]

Meanwhile Lloyd George had also summoned Hankey to Criccieth, again interrupting his leave. When he arrived he found the Prime Minister 'still

34. *RWD*, 9 September 1917.
35. DLG to FLS, 13 September 1917. In *My Darling Pussy: The Letters of Lloyd George and Frances Stevenson, 1913–41*, ed. A. J. P. Taylor (1975), 'Muriau' is incorrectly transcribed 'Murian' (p. 21). Lloyd George seems to have told C. P. Scott that his illness was ptomaine poisoning, but there is no other evidence of this (Scott diary, 28 September 1917).
36. Hankey diary, 21 and 23 September 1917. Margaret is said to have returned to London with Megan on Wednesday the 19th.

looking out of sorts and only convalescent'.[37] But *The Times* reported that he was 'much better than when he arrived at Criccieth', and that he had 'transacted business with his secretaries'.[38]

The private secretary who was with Lloyd George for the whole of the visit was Philip Kerr, already one of the most influential figures in his entourage. Now in his middle thirties, Kerr was a foundation member of the so-called 'Garden Suburb', the secretariat established by Lloyd George at the start of his premiership and occupying huts in the garden of 10 Downing Street. Appointed on the recommendation of Milner, whom he had served in South Africa and never ceased to revere, Kerr became Lloyd George's principal adviser on imperial and foreign affairs. He was a man of fascinating contradictions. In some senses nobody could have been more of an élitist. He was an aristocrat *pur sang*, on his father's side heir presumptive to the marquessate of Lothian and great estates north and south of the Border (which he inherited in 1930), on his mother's side a grandson of the 14th Duke of Norfolk. He had a first-class degree from Oxford, and as a prominent member of the Round Table group, dedicated to the furtherance of Milnerian ideals, belonged to a self-conscious élite. Yet there was also an egalitarian streak in his nature, which made the social atmosphere of the United States and the self-governing Dominions highly congenial to him. His sympathies extended far beyond the class into which he was born, and he got on easily with people of all backgrounds. Such a man was naturally attractive to, and attracted by, Lloyd George. Before entering Lloyd George's service he was, if anything, a Conservative; thereafter he was a Liberal for the rest of his life.

In one respect, however, his cast of mind was very unlike Lloyd George's. He was far more religious and needed absolute belief in a way Lloyd George did not. Both had intensely religious upbringings; in Kerr's case as a Roman Catholic. (He was sent to the Oratory School in Birmingham, founded by Newman.) But when, as a young man, he developed doubts – mainly, it would seem, under the influence of Bernard Shaw and H. G. Wells – he did not move to a moderate and vaguely theistic position, but soon espoused another absolutist faith, that of Christian Science. To this he was converted by the wife of his close friend Waldorf Astor, herself a recent convert.

Nancy Astor became, also, the love of his life, though the precise nature of their relationship is open to some doubt. The accepted wisdom is that they were lovers only in the platonic sense, because (it is said) he was a natural celibate and she tended to recoil from sex. It may well have been so,

37. Ibid., 14 September 1917.   38. 17 September 1917.

though in such a matter it is perhaps best for outsiders not to be too sure in their opinions, one way or the other. What is certain is that she and Kerr were very close, and that after her own conversion to Christian Science (in 1914) it took her only a few weeks to convert Kerr, whereas her husband's conversion took ten years.[39]

His only letter to her from Criccieth during the September visit tells us more about his religious enthusiasm than anything else:

from holiday making we have settled down to hard work with occasional intervals of golf. The weather has been foul. But bad weather is never very bad when there are hills & the sea. There is always something to look at, as is not the case in flat country.

I don't get a great deal of time for [Christian] Science, but enough. And every moment is a chance of demonstrating the truth of it. Life can never be dull again . . .

Everything is heating up for a difficult & trying time ahead of us . . . Do you notice that the [Christian Science] Monitor keeps on saying that the war will be over before the spring if everybody does their bit. So let's do our bit. Envy hatred malice & fear have no power & the man of God's creating does not & cannot reflect them. Peace is the reality of things . . .[40]

This letter conveys nothing of Kerr's humour, or of his practical and worldly side, without which he would have been of no use to Lloyd George. Religion was vital to Kerr, but public affairs also enthralled him, and he was at his best when harnessed to political work at the highest level. In the last year or so of his life his talents were fully revealed when he was serving as Ambassador to the United States at a time of supreme crisis. To Winston Churchill he then seemed 'a changed man . . . earnest, deeply stirred . . . primed with every aspect and detail of the American attitude'. Churchill also records his earlier impression of Kerr: 'Airy, viewy, aloof, dignified, censorious, yet in a light and gay manner, he had always been good company.'[41] In 1940 he was, in fact, changed only in the sense that he was, once

39. Both men were ultimately more serious in their commitment to it than she was. Kerr died from uraemia which might have been successfully treated if he had consented to receive medical aid. Astor suffered acutely at the end of his life because he would not accept any medical treatment for his cardiac asthma. But when Nancy Astor was ill, in her last years, she agreed to see a doctor.

40. Kerr to Nancy Astor, 20 September 1917. The letter begins 'Dear Nancy' and ends 'Yours, Philip Kerr'.

41. Winston S. Churchill, *The Second World War* (6 vols., 1948–54), vol. ii, p. 490. When Kerr, by then Marquess of Lothian, died in December 1940 the Americans gave him a state funeral and his remains were buried at first in Arlington National Cemetery. Later they were brought home and buried amid the ruins of Jedburgh Abbey.

again, engaged in work that really mattered, and work at the top, as in 1917. But Churchill's remark about his manner was entirely apt. Whatever his views, they were always, in conversation, lightly and humorously expressed.

On 17 September the party at Criccieth was joined by Milner – Kerr's original political master and still his political guru. Milner stayed for four days, and during the visit wrote to his close friend and future wife, Violet Cecil:

Here I am marooned, with an exceedingly entertaining, rather mad, host, who will neither come to the point nor let me get away to do some work. I don't know yet when I shall get out of it, as though you are fond of saying that I always get my way, I really find it very difficult to have my way with L.G., he is so extraordinarily elusive.

If I could do what I wanted, I should leave this place by the next train . . .

Country here really beautiful, weather perfectly beastly. There is no hope for the harvest – I mean for such of it – the greater part I fear in these regions – as has not been collected. And by the same token I should think the offensive in Flanders must by now be literally a 'wash-out'. That may be a blessing in disguise – but I fear the consequences here 1) upon the country, wh. I think will be fearfully discouraged 2) upon the relations between the Govt. & the soldiers. Big breakers ahead, though some new development in the huge World – Chaos may, at any moment, create a diversion!!

Well, you will see from this that I am not having a restful time, or much peace of mind, except that modicum wh. always remains to a man who is doing his best & has no axe of his own to grind . . .[42]

Bonar Law, as usual holding the fort in London, wrote to Lloyd George the day after Milner travelled to Criccieth:

Sutherland tells me that you wish me to send you a line and I am sorry that I have not written you before . . .

As regards the military situation, nothing has happened in your absence and I know that Milner, whom I saw just before he left to go to you, is aware of everything that has come to my knowledge. The only thing at all new is that, in speaking to Robertson yesterday, I said to him that I had lost absolutely all hope of anything coming of Haig's offensive and, though he did not say so in so many words, I understood that he took the same view. I do not know when the next attack is

42. Milner to Violet Cecil, 20 September 1917.

supposed to take place but I believe it may happen at any time. *It is evident, therefore that the time must soon come when we will have to decide whether or not this offensive is to be allowed to go on . . .*

I have no doubt that you have been thinking of nothing except the war during your absence and will come back full of ideas and they will be needed.[43]

There are heavy pencil markings by Lloyd George beside the second paragraph of this letter. He was clearly impressed by Law's absolute pessimism concerning the Flanders offensive, and by his belief that it was shared by Robertson. This belief was correct up to a point, as a letter from the CIGS to Haig written a few days previously shows:

Of course the difficulty is the ground in Flanders. It will never be good for tanks I am afraid . . . It seems to me that the tactical situation has become rather difficult. A year ago we thought that victory lay in having a large amount of heavy artillery. We have got a large amount now, but the enemy's machine-guns are still a difficulty, not yet surmounted. Our hope is, I gather, that the artillery will knock out the hostile machine-guns, but unfortunately this entails the entire destruction of the surface of the ground and renders it almost impassable, especially in Flanders. We would therefore seem to be confronted with the problem that unless we use a great deal of artillery fire we cannot get on, and if we do use it the ground is destroyed. Of course this is a very crude way of stating the case . . .[44]

The logic of these words was, surely, that the Flanders campaign should be discontinued. But Robertson could never bring himself to say so in plain terms to Haig, and of course would never have backed the War Cabinet against him, even if its members had been united.

Haig had good reason to know that they were not united from the mouth of the War Cabinet's most recent member, Carson, who spent two nights at his headquarters in mid-September. The Field-Marshal found him 'so straightforward and single-minded', noting in his diary:

He is convinced that the military experts must be given full power, not only to advise, but to carry out their plans. He is all opposed to the meddling now practised by the Prime Minister and others . . . He considers that Lloyd George has considerable value as P.M. on account of his driving powers, but he recognises his danger.

43. ABL to DLG, 18 September 1917; my italics.
44. Robertson to Haig, 15 September 1917.

Before leaving, Carson assured his host that 'the War Cabinet would not be allowed to interfere' with him or his arrangements. For good measure he urged Haig 'to talk freely' to Asquith, who was to be his next visitor, since in his (Carson's) view the former premier still had 'very great power'.[45] Such talk came oddly from a man who had taken a leading part in bringing Asquith down, and who was now supposedly a loyal colleague of his successor. There was some idea that Carson might go to Criccieth on his return, but in the event he did not, which was probably just as well.

Lloyd George's working holiday in Wales seems to have been of limited therapeutic value. Two days before it ended Hankey observed that his neuralgia was 'not much better'.[46] To what extent did he benefit from the opportunity to think about the war at a greater physical distance, in surroundings familiar to him from his childhood? Perhaps a little, though it is hard to be sure. His discussions with Hankey and Milner showed agreement on two propositions: that there was 'little hope of achieving definite success on the Western front', and that Britain's 'proper course in the war' was now 'to concentrate on Turkey'.[47] But there was no agreement that the Flanders campaign should be stopped, or that the generals should be overridden. Hankey hoped, unrealistically, that Robertson could be talked round, and when Milner left he told Riddell, who accompanied him to Llandudno junction, that he was opposed to any quarrel with the soldiers, 'which would dishearten our people and hearten the enemy'.[48] Apart from the switch from Austria to Turkey as the prime target for alternative, peripheral strategy, little emerged from the Criccieth retreat.

When Lloyd George returned, it was not to take the decision over Flanders for which Law seemed to be hoping, but mainly to deal with an urgent matter raised by the Foreign Office. But for this he might have stayed in Wales until the end of the month. In fact, he left Criccieth on the morning of Sunday, 23 September and drove to Shrewsbury with Riddell, Kerr and Frances, 'by a glorious route over high mountains & through Bala'. From Shrewsbury the party travelled on by train to London. When Lloyd George reached Downing Street he lost no time in having a 'long yarn' with Law about 'the war and the German peace proposal'.[49] This development must now be described.

---

45. Haig diary, 14, 15, 16 September 1917. Asquith told him that the government was 'very shaky', and said that he was 'all in favour' of Haig's offensive.

46. Hankey diary, 21 September 1917.   47. Ibid., 17 September 1917.

48. *RWD*, 22 September 1917.   49. Hankey diary, 23 September 1917.

14

War from the Air

*Kühlmann's tempting approach – A libel action – Air raids –
Air policy*

Lloyd George received at Criccieth a memorandum from the Foreign Secretary, Balfour, carrying news of a German peace overture and his own preliminary thoughts about it. The German Foreign Minister, Baron Richard von Kühlmann, had indicated through Spanish diplomatic channels that he would like to enter into conversations with the British government. Balfour speculated that he might have made this overture 'probably with a view of arriving at some basis of discussion as regards the terms of peace', but also 'possibly with the amiable purpose of sowing dissensions among the Entente Powers'. The Foreign Secretary therefore considered that, while the overture could not be ignored, the British government should make no response without fully informing its allies, and he explained his thinking:

I have little doubt that Kühlmann would greatly prefer that the conversations . . . should be kept secret, and he would desire this whatever be his motives in initiating this new policy. If his object is to make mischief between the Allied Powers his best course is evidently to carry on negotiations secretly until they have reached a stage which lends itself to misrepresentation, and then to betray them. If, on the other hand, as I am inclined to believe, he is genuinely anxious to find a basis for settlement, this end might well seem to him easier of attainment if he begins . . . with a dialogue rather than a general debate.

Whatever his motive, Balfour feared the potential consequences. If, for example, France or Italy were now offered all that ultimate victory would be likely to give them, 'it might be exceedingly difficult . . . to induce them to go on fighting for interests that were not their own'. (Britain and America were different, since their people were not 'moved in the main by national considerations' – a curious view.) The best chance of 'parrying this danger' lay in full disclosure of Kühlmann's approach to the ambassadors of France, Italy, America, Russia and Japan, but not of the minor allies (since to inform them would be tantamount to 'a proclamation at Charing Cross'). Balfour doubted that the Germans would consent to negotiate even with the great powers of the Entente, and was 'by no means sure that a refusal on their part to proceed further in the matter . . . would not, *at the moment*, be the best thing that could happen'.[1] He clearly regarded any move to negotiate as premature, and was hoping that the procedure he advocated would have the effect of scuppering it.

Balfour's memorandum and the relevant telegrams reached Criccieth on Saturday 22nd, as did a letter from Law suggesting that the French at least should be consulted before any response was made to the German overture. Law also regretfully urged Lloyd George to curtail his holiday, 'which no one ever needed more', and to be back in London by Monday to preside over discussion of the matter by the War Cabinet. Hence Lloyd George's return journey on Sunday.[2]

He did not at first share Balfour's view. His immediate reaction to the overture was excited and hopeful, as it had been to the Emperor Karl's in the spring. This overture, moreover, seemed to have greater possibilities, since it came from Germany, which was the supreme enemy. The Prime Minister had lost none of his determination to achieve Britain's essential war aims in the West. On land, he would never have settled for anything less than the full restoration of Belgium and those parts of France occupied since 1914, with proper compensation. Yet he was increasingly sceptical of the soldiers' claims that they could inflict a comprehensive defeat on the German army, and his scepticism was sharpened by a growing belief that Russia's contribution to the war was effectively over. At the same time he also believed that Germany was suffering from general war-weariness on the home front, in particular from the food shortages and malnutrition caused by the Allied blockade, and that she might therefore be willing to sacrifice her gains in the West in return for an implied free hand in the East. In other words, he was prepared at least to contemplate abandoning a Russian ally which – despite his upbeat remarks at Birkenhead – he now regarded as hardly worth the name for practical purposes, if in so doing he could end the carnage in the West on terms satisfactory to the Western Allies.

When the War Cabinet met on Monday morning it was known that an approach had also been made to the French government, through a high official of the German occupation regime in Belgium and the former French premier, Briand. (The intermediary between them was a lady friend of Briand, of Franco-German parentage.) It was obvious, therefore, that a

1. Memorandum by AJB, 20 September 1917.   2. ABL to DLG, 21 September 1917.

meeting between British and French leaders had to be arranged as a matter of urgency, and the War Cabinet decided, contrary to Balfour's advice, that the other major Allies should meanwhile be kept in the dark. To this extent Lloyd George got his way. He knew that any hint of what was afoot, particularly to the Russians, would destroy all hope of a fruitful outcome. Yet his own hope that there might be such an outcome was not, on the whole, shared by his colleagues, and it was significant that Milner and Law were foremost among the doubters.[3]

No time was lost. Lloyd George left London on Monday night, with Hankey as his sole companion, and crossed the Channel in a destroyer early the following morning, to confer with his French opposite number at Boulogne. The opposite number now was Painlevé, who had succeeded Ribot less than a fortnight before, while remaining War Minister.[4] Ribot was still Foreign Minister, but did not accompany Painlevé to the meeting.

The two premiers conferred in a railway carriage, for a time on their own, and then with a few advisers, notably Robertson and Foch. Lloyd George found Painlevé 'entirely preoccupied about his political difficulties',[5] to which the German approach was a serious addition, as it was doubtless intended to be. Though it lacked the diplomatic formality of the overture to Britain, it was potentially more alluring, and therefore more dangerous. The proposal was that a meeting should take place in Switzerland, at which Briand would discuss peace terms with a leading German personage – who might even be the Chancellor, Georg Michaelis[6] – and then report back to the French government. The terms vaguely floated were the restoration of Belgium and Serbia, and all occupied French territory including most of Alsace-Lorraine, together with unspecified territorial concessions to Italy, and colonial concessions, also unspecified, to Britain. Briand was far from sure what precisely the Germans would agree to, but was nevertheless eager to go ahead with the proposed Swiss rendezvous.

Painlevé (and the absent Ribot) were dead against it. To them it seemed all too likely to prove a trap. Quite apart from the rather dubious

3. War Cab., 24 September 1917.
4. The Ribot government fell after the resignation of two important ministers: the Minister of the Navy, Admiral Lacaze, who resented the degree of scrutiny to which his department was subjected, and the Minister of the Interior, Louis Malvy, who was thought – not without reason – to be a defeatist. Malvy had been mercilessly attacked in Parliament by Clemenceau, whose hour was approaching.   5. Hankey diary, 25 September 1917.
6. Michaelis had succeeded Bethmann Hollweg in July. He was an unknown figure, formerly under-secretary in the Prussian Ministry of Finance, and appointed chiefly because the military regarded him as dependable.

character of the German approach, and the implied requirement to desert their Eastern allies, they felt that any negotiations at a time when the French army and French public opinion had still not fully recovered from the Nivelle trauma could lead to irretrievable disaster. If it got out that peace talks were taking place, and that the Germans might withdraw from Belgium and, more especially, Alsace-Lorraine, it would scarcely be possible, in their view, to restore the fighting spirit of the French people, should the talks break down on other issues vital to French security and a stable European order.

Lloyd George had hitherto been the strongest British exponent of the view that negotiations should not be entered into with Germany until that country's military power was broken. A year previously he had given a resounding interview to the American Roy Howard of United Press, in which he had said:

The fight must be to a finish – to a knock-out . . . The inhumanity and the pitilessness of the fighting that must come before a lasting peace is possible is not comparable with the cruelty that would be involved in stopping the war while there remains the possibility of civilisation again being menaced from the same quarter.[7]

In the altered circumstances of September 1917 he clearly had a serious wobble, caused above all by his impotent distress at what he regarded as the futile loss of British lives in Flanders. The Russians were collapsing, the Americans hardly in sight and the French still not pulling their weight. (He heard at Boulogne that another French offensive in support of Haig had been postponed.) He may have agreed with Painlevé that Briand's proposed trip to Switzerland should not go ahead; in any case the decision to veto it was the French government's affair. But he continued to feel that a positive, if suitably guarded, response should be made to the more formal overture to Britain.

Playing for time, he sought the opinion of Robertson, Foch and Haig on 'the effect of [Russia's] defection, if it occurred before America was ready to take her place'. Robertson alone gave the answer he wanted, that in such an event 'the chances of our achieving a military victory were gone'. Foch 'did not accept Robertson's estimate' and Haig – predictably – agreed with Foch.[8] Lloyd George met the Field-Marshal at his headquarters after leaving Boulogne. Though Haig was preoccupied with Plumer's attack on the Menin

---

7. Interview published 28 September 1916 (for details see my *Lloyd George: From Peace to War 1912–1916* (1985), pp. 423–34).   8. *WM*, pp. 2101–2.

Road, then in full swing, he gave his opinion tersely and emphatically. We 'could not desert Russia'. The right course for us 'was to go on hammering now, and to make the French fight without delay'. The Germans 'were now very worn out and had some very poor material in the fighting line'.[9] To impress the last point upon Lloyd George he was shown a cage of German prisoners, captured in the current operation, who were 'a weedy lot . . . deplorably inferior to the manly samples [he] had seen in earlier stages of the War'. Later he was allegedly told on 'unimpeachable' authority that an order had been sent down to remove able-bodied men from the cage before his inspection, though he claimed (perhaps tongue-in-cheek) to have been sure that Haig 'had no part' in this deliberate act of deception.[10]

In any case Lloyd George's mind was not changed by his visit to Haig. He remained open to a German offer, without prejudice. But his colleagues were less than ever disposed to support him on the issue. Balfour was the most adamant and had probably helped to instigate a speech by Asquith while Lloyd George was away, in which the former premier made evacuation of all Russian territory a necessary condition of peace.[11] In the War Cabinet there was almost unanimous opposition to any thought of a compromise peace at Russia's expense. It was therefore decided that the representatives of America, Russia, Italy and Japan should be informed of the German overture, and that a reply should be sent to Germany expressing willingness to receive any communication relating to peace 'and to discuss it with [Britain's] allies'. The Germans did not respond to this message, but the day after it was sent Kühlmann made a speech in which he declared that Germany would 'never' surrender Alsace-Lorraine. The inference must be that the approach to France had been no more than a mischief-making exercise.

Was the approach to Britain equally so? In his speech ruling out any question of returning France's lost provinces Kühlmann said nothing about Belgium, which he knew to be a matter of paramount concern to Britain. The Germans had of course noted that Britain had never endorsed France's claim to Alsace-Lorraine, and therefore had some reason to believe that a separate peace with Britain was on the cards, or at any rate a separate negotiation which might lead to pressure on France to abandon her irredentist claim. Kühlmann was sincere in the sense that he genuinely wanted

9. Hankey's note of meeting, 26 September 1917. Haig later confirmed his views in writing, stating that 'an unsatisfactory peace' would lead to 'the almost certain renewal of the war . . . at a time of Germany's choosing'.   10. *WM*, p. 2225.
11. The suggestion that Asquith should speak as he did, and the reason for doing so, came from Sir Eric Drummond of the Foreign Office, formerly Asquith's private secretary and now Balfour's (David R. Woodward, *Lloyd George and the Generals* (1983), p. 203).

peace in the West, and particularly with Britain. He did not share the anglophobia that was prevalent in German ruling circles, having served in London as counsellor for some years before the war, achieving personal and diplomatic success. He was prepared to go further than any other German statesman to satisfy Britain about Belgium, but still nothing like far enough. For one thing he would not commit himself to making any concessions at all about Belgium in advance of a British commitment to negotiate. His intention was to use Belgium as 'a bargaining counter', and any prior statement of willingness to restore the Belgian state would have spoilt 'his diplomatic game'.[12]

His reading of British policy was that it was powerfully motivated by the desire to end the war before the Americans had time to establish ascendancy within the alliance. When he sent his message to the British government via Spain he believed that he was responding to an overture rather than initiating one. This misunderstanding was caused by Britain's reaction, the previous month, to a plea from the Vatican to all belligerents to end the war by negotiation. Benedict XV had called for withdrawal from all occupied territory, including colonies, and all claims to indemnity. His public appeal was followed by secret talks conducted by Eugenio Pacelli, the future Pope Pius XII, then nuncio in Bavaria.[13] When the British government replied to the Vatican that negotiation would be useless in the absence of a general statement of war aims by the Central Powers and a specific declaration from Germany that the independence of Belgium would be restored and the damage done to her made good, Pacelli passed the reply on to Michaelis with the gloss that Germany's security needs should be stated. The German government took this to mean that 'Britain might be putting out serious peace feelers', but could not 'feel certain that, if the desired declaration were given, Britain would open (separate) peace negotiations on a basis acceptable to Germany in other respects'.[14] Hence the Kühlmann overture, or counter-overture.

12. Fritz Fischer, *Germany's Aims in the First World War* (1967), p. 420.

13. Benedict XV's initiative won him no plaudits on either side. The Germans did not take kindly to the proposal that they should abandon their hard-won conquests, East and West, and that even the Alsace-Lorraine question might be settled on a basis of compromise. Austria-Hungary equally resented the attempt (by an Italian) to promote territorial concessions to Italy. On the other hand, the Entente Powers were angered by the call for a peace without indemnities, when most of the damage had been suffered by them and inflicted by Germany. In France Benedict was spoken of as 'the *Boche* pope' – though ironically an outstanding achievement of his reign, after the war, was reconciliation between the Vatican and the French republic, culminating in his canonization of Joan of Arc in 1920.

14. Fischer, *Germany's Aims*, p. 419.

If Britain had become involved in a separate negotiation at the time, there was, in fact, no prospect of any deal that could remotely have justified the breach in Allied solidarity. There was no question of a return to the *status quo ante* on land. Kühlmann could not have delivered, even on Belgium, terms that Britain could have agreed to without gross danger and dishonour. Policy in Germany was not in the hands of civilian ministers like Michaelis and Kühlmann; they were subservient to the high command, whose minimal requirements for Belgium were quite incompatible with Britain's. There was, indeed, a difference between the military and naval warlords. The latter wished to retain the coast of Flanders and a wide corridor through the country to enable the German position there to be supplied. Hindenburg and Ludendorff were prepared to withdraw from the coast, though not from the whole of Belgium's national territory, part of which, including Liège, was to be retained as a protective *glacis* for the German Empire. Moreover Belgium was not to be restored as a truly independent country; despite an outward show of sovereignty, it was to be closely tied to Germany, economically and politically. And far from any compensation being paid to the Belgians for the damage done to their country, they were to be expected to pay, themselves, for the phoney freedom they would be receiving.

The German warlords were still confident that Britain would be defeated by the U-boats; they were unmoved, as yet, by the evidence that their campaign at sea was failing. In their eyes, Britain was the principal Western enemy. Even the limited concessions they were prepared to envisage for Belgium would have been made only in return for prior British withdrawal from the Continent. They were no less, indeed even more, intent on destroying British sea power, and so establishing their hegemony in both elements. No British statesman could have negotiated a peace which did not remove the mortal threat posed by the German navy. Yet there was no chance at all that the Germans would budge on that issue in 1917. The conditions for a negotiated peace simply did not exist.

Lloyd George's attitude to the Kühlmann overture was a serious aberration, and it was fortunate that his colleagues overruled him, as in effect they did. When he visited Haig's headquarters after meeting the French at Boulogne, the Field-Marshal was already aware of his state of mind. Another of Haig's visitors while the Prime Minister was at Criccieth had been Churchill, who had 'admitted that Lloyd George *and he* were doubtful about being able to beat the Germans on the Western Front'.[15] In his memoirs Lloyd George is scathing about Haig's reply concerning the possibility of

---

15. Haig diary, 13 September 1917; my italics.

victory in the West if the Russians were no longer a factor, ascribing it to 'the joyous arithmetic of the optimistic Charteris'. Yet he claims to have derived encouragement from the same reply given to him by Foch, and so to have *led* the War Cabinet in deciding to respond firmly to Kühlmann:

[Foch] confirmed the conviction I had already formed, that now the submarine peril was being mastered, a complete Allied triumph was assured notwithstanding the defection of Russia. When the Cabinet discussions on the Kuhlmann proposals were resumed, the part I took was influenced by the fact that my conclusions as to the military prospects had been fortified by the highest military opinion.[16]

This supremely misleading passage must reflect the discomfort Lloyd George later felt about the whole episode. To suggest that he was convinced of the need to take a tough line before he went to France is the opposite of the truth. He went there having persuaded his colleagues, against their better judgement, that the news about Kühlmann should not immediately be shared with all of Britain's major partners. His policy was to probe Germany's intentions in collusion with France alone,[17] and he hoped that his assessment of the overall strategic situation might receive some backing from Robertson, Foch and even Haig. When the last two failed to give him any support, he probably found Foch's response the more annoying because less expected. To imply that he welcomed it is palpably false, and anyway inconsistent with his rubbishing of Haig for expressing a similar view.

He was right to regard Haig as over-sanguine about the state of German morale on the Western front. But he himself was no less so, at this time, about the state of German civilian morale. There was certainly much hardship in Germany, and considerable discontent which even spread to the High Seas Fleet. The blockade was biting hard, and the police chief of Berlin reported that the public mood was one of 'despondency and fear for the future'.[18] Yet the enemy's home front was far from cracking. The Germans showed, in both world wars, that they were among the toughest and most disciplined

16. *WM*, pp. 2102 and 2104.

17. He might well have tried to act unilaterally, without France, but for the German approach to the French government.

18. Holger H. Herwig, *The First World War: Germany and Austria-Hungary 1914–1918* (1997), pp. 376–7. The High Seas Fleet had not put to sea for nearly a year, and the sailors were bored as well as hungry. 'The steady diet of turnips and dehydrated vegetables, inadequate shore leave, and the transfer of the best subaltern officers to the U-boats combined to create an atmosphere of distrust and anger.' Two sailors were executed and three received long prison sentences (August 1917).

communities ever known. Though many Germans wanted peace in 1917, very few of them wanted it on terms disadvantageous to Germany. Only a small minority would have settled for the *status quo ante*.[19] The high command was not imposing its will upon a people which had lost the stomach for national and imperial greatness.

Lloyd George reacted impulsively to the Kühlmann overture, and the impulse was mistaken. If it had not been checked by his War Cabinet colleagues – and by Foch and Haig – the results might have been disastrous. There was no chance of a deal, and in any case the readiness to abandon Russia was premature and wrong. However futile Kerensky was proving to be as a ruler, his regime was at least committed to democracy and to the Allied cause.

Yet Lloyd George should not, perhaps, be judged too harshly. His motive was above all to stop what he saw as the wholesale, pointless sacrifice of British lives, for which he felt responsible. He could not accept enormous casualties cold-bloodedly, as Haig did, but was emotionally involved in the process whereby, for the first time, British manhood was engaged in warfare on a massive scale. Sea power was cheap, in human terms; the numbers of men required to enable Britain to rule the waves were small. But by the time Lloyd George became Prime Minister Britain's losses, overwhelmingly on land, were 'greater than those she had sustained in the aggregate in all her wars put together since the Wars of the Roses'.[20] In September 1917 he believed correctly that Russia was collapsing, but incorrectly that the German people might be ready for a peace in the West that Britain could accept. He also believed that the German army could not be beaten on the Western front – an opinion shared at the time (it should be noted) by Churchill and Robertson. In these circumstances the Kühlmann overture tempted him. Fortunately, however, the danger passed, and the one important result of the Kühlmann episode was that Britain at last endorsed France's demand for the return of Alsace-Lorraine.

Lloyd George's trip to France in late September gave rise to a curious piece of litigation. The night of his departure the Exchange Telegraph Company put out the following report, which was published next day by the *Star* and the *Westminster Gazette*:

19. In July the Reichstag carried a resolution in favour of a compromise peace, but Matthias Erzberger, whose Centre group made this gesture possible, was 'as far from accepting the *status quo* as the end of Germany's war policy as the Emperor Wilhelm II'. The Reichstag continued to vote war credits, only the Independent Social Democrats opposing (Fischer, *Germany's Aims*, pp. 403–4).   20. *WM*, p. 2036.

Raid Item – Mr. Lloyd George's Country Retreat.

The Prime Minister spent the night at his residence at Walton Heath, Surrey, having left Downing Street about the time it first became known that the raiders were approaching London.[21]

The innuendo was unmistakable: Lloyd George had run away from central London to the relative safety of Walton Heath as soon as he heard that a German air raid was imminent.

The *Star* was owned by the *Daily News*, whose editor was A. G. Gardiner. The *Westminster*'s editor was J. A. Spender. Both men were strong Asquithians, hostile to Lloyd George. The controlling shareholder in both papers was Lord Cowdray, another Asquithian, who was serving as President of the Air Board.

Returning from abroad Lloyd George felt that he could not ignore publication of such a damaging story. He was in no danger of losing. When he left Downing Street on the 24th, after a day of intensive discussion with colleagues, he went not to Walton Heath but to Charing Cross station, where he heard of the air raid warning. Nevertheless his train left the station, only to be halted for some time on Hungerford bridge (over the Thames) while he and Hankey ate uneasily in the dining-car, 'in a momentary expectation of bombs'. When the train resumed its journey it moved 'at a snail's pace' and did not reach Dover until 11.30 p.m. As it travelled through the suburbs the sky was lit with anti-aircraft fire, and on arrival at Dover the passengers were told the cause of delay – that bombs had fallen on the line and put it temporarily out of action.[22]

These facts were given to the court which heard the case on 16 October, and Lloyd George appeared in person to explain why he had taken the unusual step of suing. 'If [he said] I started taking actions against everyone who attacked me I should have nothing else to do.' But the report in question could be harmful to national morale, so he felt obliged to ensure as much publicity for the correction as for the report itself. He received fulsome apologies and full costs from all three parties, but did not ask for damages.[23]

The story was obviously false and defamatory in relation to 24 September, but nevertheless contained a particle of more general truth. One of Lloyd George's reasons for sleeping at Walton Heath as often as he did was, undoubtedly, that he felt safer there. His fear of high explosives gave him a

---

21. Night of 24–5 September 1917.   22. Hankey diary, 24 September 1917.
23. *The Times*, 17 October 1917.

special dislike of air raids. (Incidentally, a shell had exploded a hundred yards from him during his latest visit to the BEF.)

The raid of 24 September was the first in a series on moonlit nights, which (according to the official historian) 'remained more vividly than any others in the memory of most of those who lived through the air raids on England'.[24] Among the bombs dropped on London that night one burst at the entrance to the Bedford Hotel in Southampton Row, another fell in the Thames opposite St Thomas's Hospital, another in Dean's Yard, Westminster, and another in Green Park near the Ritz Hotel. A bomb also struck Burlington House, without exploding but doing some damage to statuary. Total casualties in London were thirteen killed and twenty-six injured (most caused by the Bedford Hotel bomb). Outside London, the place worst affected was the destination of Lloyd George's train, Dover, where five people were killed and eleven injured. Bombs also fell at other places in Kent and Essex.

During 1917 the air threat to Britain from Zeppelin airships continued, though on a diminishing scale as the means to combat it improved, particularly through the use by fighters of bullets that exploded on impact. At the same time a new form of air attack, by heavier-than-air machines, was developing ominously, having previously been no more than an occasional nuisance. The first major attack by aeroplanes occurred during the early evening of 25 May, when a squadron of Gotha IVs dropped about sixty bombs on the south-east, though none on London. The worst casualties were at a Canadian military camp and at Folkestone. In all, 95 were killed and 195 injured. Attempts to intercept the raiders had little success, though one was shot down over the Channel.

On 13 June there was a Gotha raid on London, which caused more casualties than any other in the war and, as will be seen, led to a fundamental reappraisal of air policy. It began at about 11.30 a.m. and in two minutes seventy bombs fell within a one-mile radius of Liverpool Street station. Other areas hit were Albert Docks, East Ham, Southwark and Dalston. Total casualties were 162 killed and 432 injured. Eighteen children died when a school in Poplar received a direct hit. This raid stirred the country. None of the raiders was brought down.

London was attacked again during the morning of 7 July, and this proved to be the last daylight raid on the city by aeroplanes. At least one of the Gothas was destroyed in air combat. In September the Germans switched to night raids by moonlight, London being attacked during the night of 4–5 September, when considerable damage was inflicted in the Charing

24. H. A. Jones, the official history of the war, *The War in the Air* (6 vols., 1922–37), vol. v, p. 78.

Cross area. But the night offensive began in earnest with the raid on 24 September, during the period of the harvest moon. London was attacked again the following night, and on four successive nights from 28 September to 1 October, when the Gotha IVs were accompanied by two Riesen (Giant) planes.[25] The psychological effect of this series of raids was out of all proportion to the physical harm done. After the raid on the 24th a mass of people, estimated at about 100,000, rushed to take shelter in the underground, and on each subsequent night whether or not there was a raid, the numbers grew to a maximum estimated total of 300,000.

In the East End, which suffered most in the attacks, there were some signs of panic. And everywhere the instinct of self-preservation was healthily evident. On the last night of the series Hankey had supper with Mr and Mrs Lloyd George, Churchill and Kerr in the basement of the Foreign Office, where they spent nearly three hours. And before taking refuge the Cabinet secretary 'noticed many Government officials running to get into cover, before the "shower" began'.[26]

The first Gotha raids in 1917 affected the civilian population more profoundly than the Zeppelins had ever done. Attacks by aeroplanes represented a new and seemingly more deadly threat, whose impact was all the greater since it came after three years of war, when the strain on nerves was beginning to tell. (A similar impact was produced by the German V-bombs in 1944.) Lloyd George in his memoirs admits that panic at times resulted, while stressing that the raids did not create a defeatist mood:

At the slightest rumour of approaching aeroplanes, tubes and tunnels were packed with panic-stricken men, women and children. Every clear night the commons around London were black with refugees from the threatened metropolis. It is right, however, to record the fact that the undoubted terror inspired by the death-dealing skies did not swell by a single murmur the demand for peace. It had quite the contrary effect. It angered the population of the stricken towns and led to a fierce demand for reprisals.[27]

Public disquiet was reflected in, and also to some extent augmented by, the press, since reporting of the raids was not covered by the censorship that applied to other operations of war.

The country's political and military leaders reacted swiftly to the new challenge, and the first to react was Robertson, who feared that Germany

25. The Riesen aircraft carried a crew of five and a bomb load of about 1,000 kg.
26. Hankey diary, 1 October 1917.　27. WM, p. 1861.

might be gaining the upper hand in the air. When the War Cabinet met during the afternoon following the morning raid on 13 June, he proposed a large-scale increase in the production of aeroplanes, even at the expense of other weapons. The War Cabinet agreed, and it was soon decided that the establishment of the Royal Flying Corps should be virtually doubled, from 108 to 200 squadrons, and that there should be a corresponding expansion of the Royal Naval Air Service.

After the raid on 7 July an immediate secret session of Parliament was held, at which Lloyd George explained the urgent steps that were being taken to boost British air power, but emphasized that the fighting front abroad must retain a prior claim on resources. The Germans were, he said, 'trying to force us to withdraw our machines from France in order to protect our towns', and if they knew they could succeed in this nothing would encourage them more: 'If the aeroplanes can be provided for the Front and for our defence against raids, that will, of course, be done. If not, the Army must come first, and it is vitally important that the Germans should know.'[28] Two squadrons had, in fact, been withdrawn from Haig's command to reinforce home defence after 13 June, but were returned on 6 July, the day before the next big raid. After the raid they were called for again, but Haig was prepared to release only one; and a proposed retaliatory raid on Mannheim was found to be impracticable in the short term.

In any case, Lloyd George could see that it would not be enough to devise measures to meet the short-term emergency. A more radical reappraisal of air policy was also needed. A few days after the secret session – on 11 July – the War Cabinet entrusted both tasks to a committee consisting of the Prime Minister and the ubiquitous Smuts, together with representatives of the Admiralty, the army general staff, the Commander-in-Chief, Home Forces, and other experts as required. The committee's terms of reference were to examine (1) 'the defensive arrangements for home defence against air raids' and (2) 'the existing general organisation for the study and higher direction of aerial operations'. In practice, the work was largely left to Smuts, though Lloyd George's nominal participation gave the committee the necessary authority and prestige, and he 'kept in constant touch with [Smuts]'.[29]

In little more than a week Smuts produced his first report, on the subject of home defence. The most important recommendation was that a London air defence area should be established, under the executive command of a single officer. This recommendation was promptly acted on, and Major-

28. WM, pp. 1862-3.   29. WM, pp. 1863-4.

General E. B. Ashmore was appointed. Lloyd George describes him as 'a most efficient officer', and certainly under his direction much was done to improve the air defences of London. A ring of anti-aircraft guns was placed on the outer periphery, about twenty-five miles from the centre, to prevent as many attackers as possible from reaching their objective, or at least to disperse their formations. Ashmore was a gunner by origin and made the best use of his guns, with more sophisticated sound-spotting techniques and a system of numbered squares on the map, combining to enable the enemy aircraft to be met with vertical fire as they moved from square to square. When the night raids began he installed barrage balloon 'aprons' in the eastern suburbs, with balloons at 500-yard intervals connected by horizontal steel wires. Meanwhile the number of fighter squadrons available for the defence of London gradually increased; by the end of the year there were eight of them. The total effect of all the measures taken to meet the new threat was not negligible.

Yet it is an exaggeration to say, as Lloyd George does, that the city's air defences were 'rapidly transformed', and that the night raids 'grew steadily more difficult and costly'.[30] For all his resourcefulness, the success of Ashmore's efforts was necessarily limited. The bombers continued to get through until the spring of 1918, and most of them returned safely to base. Anti-aircraft fire, even with the improved techniques, remained 'less of a menace [to the enemy] than to people and property below', as the shrapnel fell to earth. The barrage balloons could only force the attackers to fly in at 10,000 feet or so – a minor inconvenience to them – and did not always work even if they flew lower. (One of the German aircraft flew right through a steel 'apron' and managed to complete its mission.) British night fighter pilots 'had little to show for their gallantry'.[31] Their task was entirely novel and it took time to learn, by trial and error, the range of skills required. Moreover, they depended heavily upon searchlights, of which even the stronger types that came into service were of diminished value when the moon was full.

During the winter months of 1917–18 the most effective deterrent was the weather, which significantly reduced the number of raids. All the same, London and other places in the south-east still had plenty to endure throughout the period. One of the worst incidents was on 28 January 1918, when Odhams' printing works in Long Acre, which was being used as a night-time shelter, was destroyed by a 300 kg. bomb dropped by one of the German

30. WM, p. 1865.
31. Jones, *War in the Air*, vol. v, pp. 91 and 111. Some French 75 mm. guns were 'particularly dangerous', because their shell-cases fell to earth intact. They were moved to Birmingham.

aircraft. The explosion was followed by fire which engulfed the building. Thirty were killed and eighty-five injured.

People nevertheless got used to the aeroplanes, as they had got used to the Zeppelins. And they could feel that the defences were gradually asserting themselves against the bombers. On 19–20 May 1918 London was attacked by a large force for several hours, but both the anti-aircraft guns and the fighters had their most successful night, with the result that this raid proved to be the last serious one by aeroplanes that the capital experienced in the First World War. The final Zeppelin attack on England, affecting only a few coastal areas, was on 5 August.[32]

In the Second World War the country was from the start equipped with an elaborate system of air raid precautions, however ill-prepared it may have been in other respects. By comparison, the precautions that were improvised during the first war were primitive. The chief common factor was the black-out, which in the first war was naturally resented, and after a time relaxed, in areas that were hardly within range of any attacking aircraft. No air raid shelters, such as the Anderson and Morrison in the second war, were produced in the first. People were merely advised to take cover in their own houses, or in other places of refuge, when they heard that enemy bombers might be approaching, or (more likely) actually saw or heard them for themselves. Systems of public alarm varied from the firing of coloured maroons to word-of-mouth warnings from policemen on bicycles. The doleful sirens that announced the imminence and ending of air raids in the second war did not feature in the First, though sirens were among a number of devices considered in 1917. None of sufficient power existed, however, and it was decided that those available would scarcely be audible above the roar of London traffic.

Smuts's report dealing with the second item in his remit – air organization and the higher direction of air operations – was delivered to the War Cabinet on 17 August. Its significance was immense. Before stating the conclusions that Smuts came to and the consequences of his report, we should look briefly at the attempts hitherto made during the war to bring the new factor of air power under some form of political control.

The inclusion of aircraft in the armed forces of the Crown dates from 1912. In that year Britain acquired two separate air forces, corresponding

32. In this attack the ace Commander Peter Strasser was killed when his airship was brought down in flames.

to the two traditional services. The Royal Flying Corps came into existence as the army's air arm, while the Royal Naval Air Service was started (by Winston Churchill when he was First Lord) as the navy's. At the outbreak of war both forces were still very small; the RFC had only about sixty effective machines, the RNAS about fifty. The latter, however, tended to have more powerful engines, because many of them were designed to carry bombs or torpedoes, whereas the army's aircraft were at first designed solely for use in reconnaissance. The French began the war with 120 battle-ready machines, the Germans with 232.[33]

For aeronautical development the war proved to be 'a forcing-house of tropical intensity'.[34] It was also bedevilled, in Britain, by inter-service rivalry. The RFC set out to be the country's only air force, with a military and a naval wing. But the RNAS was nevertheless created, and when war came it was the only force capable of providing any air defence at home, because all of the RFC's machines were needed to support the army overseas. As time went on, the demand for combatant aircraft increased relentlessly, and with it the competition between the two service departments for productive resources. There was much overlapping and inefficiency, and when the Zeppelin attacks began in 1915 there was no clear responsibility for organizing counter-measures. Criticism mounted in Parliament and in the press, and in February 1915 a committee was appointed, with Derby as chairman, to co-ordinate the supply and design of warplanes.

The Derby committee was predictably short-lived. Even if Derby had been a sufficiently imposing and dynamic personality (which he was very far from being), the committee had no power. In March public dissatisfaction was sharply manifested when an Independent candidate, Pemberton Billing, was returned at a by-election in East Hertfordshire, after a campaign devoted entirely to the need for a stronger air policy. This was the first occasion when the wartime party truce was successfully challenged, and the government could not ignore such a signal.[35] Within weeks Curzon, who had already put forward the case for a separate air ministry, persuaded his colleagues in the Asquith Cabinet to settle for an Air Board which might still, with luck, be more effective than the Derby committee. Curzon himself became President of the Board, while remaining Lord Privy Seal, but his

33. Alfred Gollin, *The Impact of Air Power on the British People and their Government, 1909–14* (1989), p. 307.   34. *WM*, p. 1845.

35. Billing, who had the advantage of being a squadron commander in the RNAS, defeated the Coalition Liberal candidate with a majority of about a thousand. Earlier, he had narrowly failed to win Mile End. In Parliament he became known as 'the member for air'. Before the end of the war he was to cause trouble on another issue.

attempt to achieve an integrated policy was frustrated by the Admiralty, whose intransigence was ably maintained by Balfour as First Lord – the same Balfour who, though ostensibly an old friend, had earlier destroyed Curzon's viceroyalty.[36] Such was the position when the change of government occurred.

Lloyd George had been one of the first British politicians to take air development seriously. In August 1909 when he had much else on his mind he witnessed the great international flying display at Rheims and came away feeling – and saying publicly – that Britain was in danger of being left behind in a vital sphere of technology. But his attention to the subject was not sustained, and as Minister of Munitions he failed to gain control of the production of aircraft, which stayed in the hands of the service departments. Some progress was made by the next two ministers, Montagu and Addison, but responsibilities were still essentially divided when the Smuts committee was set up.

Meanwhile, in forming his government, Lloyd George had kept the Air Board but appointed a new President, Lord Cowdray, to take the place of Curzon who would be busy enough as a member of the new War Cabinet. Cowdray, as Weetman Pearson, was the founder of a great contracting business. He also had many other business interests, including oil and (as we have seen) newspapers. Under his auspices, but thanks in no small measure to Curzon's earlier efforts, the output of aircraft increased dramatically, to more than treble that of 1916. By the time Smuts got to work there were 1,500 aircraft in the RFC under Haig's command, with more in reserve, and about the same number in the RNAS. Yet inter-service co-operation was still poor, with the Admiralty still the arch-offender. Moreover there were functions, such as the air defence of Britain, which seemed to lie outside the scope of inter-service co-operation, even if it had been working well. When the day raids by German planes further aroused public opinion the case for fundamental change became more pressing. Hence the question referred to Smuts, to which he gave an emphatic answer.

His report followed Curzon in proposing that there should be an air ministry 'to administer all matters connected with aerial warfare'. It should have its own staff which would 'arrange for the amalgamation of the RFC and the RNAS' into a single force, to which however those serving in them would be transferred only 'with their own consent'. It was piously hoped

36. In 1905 Curzon resigned as Viceroy early in his second term after a dispute with the Commander-in-Chief in India, Kitchener, in which the right was substantially on Curzon's side though he acted maladroitly. The home government, led by Balfour, gave him no support and can almost be said to have engineered his departure.

that there would be 'close liaison' between the army, navy and air staffs under the new dispensation.

The future of air warfare was adumbrated in prophetic terms:

Unlike artillery, an air fleet can conduct extensive operations far from, and independently of, both Army and Navy. As far as can at present be foreseen, *there is absolutely no limit to the scale of its future independent war use*. And the day may not be far off when aerial operations, with their devastation of enemy lands and destruction of industrial and populous centres on a vast scale, may become the principal operations of war . . .

Even in 1918, 'while our Western Front may still be moving forward at a snail's pace in Belgium and France, the air battle will be far behind on the Rhine, and . . . may form an important factor in bringing about peace'.[37]

In these passages Smuts gives countenance to a philosophy of air power which was to wreak havoc, while distorting strategy, in the Second World War, and whose baleful influence persists. To the extent that the creation of an independent air force helped to promote the doctrine that air power could win wars on its own, Smuts's long-range prophecies were self-fulfilling. But the one relating to 1918 was certainly not fulfilled.

The idea that there might be a new way of winning the war, avoiding further hecatombs of British lives on land, could not fail to appeal to Lloyd George (as it did, twenty-five years later, to Churchill). Nevertheless, Smuts's proposals faced strong resistance. The Admiralty continued to fight for the RNAS, under Geddes no less doggedly than under Balfour, and there was also opposition from important quarters on the military side. Though Robertson's attitude was curiously detached, Haig was opposed to merging the RFC into a single and separate air force. So, ironically, was Major-General Hugh Trenchard, commander of the RFC in France since 1915 – ironically, because Trenchard later came to be regarded as 'the father of the RAF'. Among serving officers a far stronger claimant to that title is Sir David Henderson, who played a key part in the creation of the RFC and who commanded it in France until October 1915, when he handed over to Trenchard. Since then he had occupied high staff positions in London, and in 1917, for good or ill, his advice weighed with Smuts against that of Trenchard and all other senior RFC officers. Without him, as Trenchard

37. Smuts's second and final air report, presented to the War Cabinet 17 August 1917; my italics.

himself admitted in retrospect, the RAF would probably never have come into being.[38]

When Haig was in London in June, pressing the case for his Flanders offensive, he had Trenchard's full support for the argument that the best way to counter air raids on Britain was to overrun the German air bases in Belgium. (So it would have been, if such an operation had been feasible.) Trenchard endorsed Haig's argument in person when he attended a War Cabinet meeting on 20 June. To both men, structural change seemed a pointless distraction from the work in hand. Smuts's proposals were, therefore, most unwelcome to them. At the end of August Haig noted in his diary:

The War Cabinet has evidently decided on creating a new Department to deal with Air operations, on the lines of the War Office and the Admiralty. Trenchard is much perturbed as to the result of this new departure just at a time when the Flying Corps was beginning to feel that it had become an important part of the Army. The best solution would be to have one Minister of Defence with the three Offices under him, viz., Admiralty, War Office, Air.[39]

When he recorded this interesting thought Haig clearly had no doubt that the War Cabinet had decided in favour of Smuts's recommendations. But in fact there was no firm decision until the middle of October. Lloyd George admits that acceptance in principle followed 'ultimately', and only 'after the most careful consideration'.[40] Meanwhile Smuts was made chairman of a Cabinet committee whose function was to reconcile the existing service departments to the proposed change. Its other members were the First Lord, the War Secretary and the President of the Air Board.

Once the decision was taken, the legislation to give effect to it was swift. There was no serious opposition in Parliament, and the bill to establish an air ministry received the royal assent on 29 November. But the formation of the Royal Air Force took longer. This was the first task of the new ministry, and it was completed only in April 1918, when the RAF as such came into being.

---

38. 'Henderson had twice the insight and understanding that I had. He was prepared to run risks rather than lose a chance which he saw might never come again . . . it is doubtful whether the R.A.F. or Britain realises its debt to him, which is at least as great as its debt to Smuts' (quoted in Andrew Boyle, *Trenchard* (1962), p. 233).

39. Haig diary, 28 August 1917. The set-up envisaged by Haig – clearly (in view of the context) as a 'solution' only in the longer term – was that under which the British armed forces were run during the Second World War from May 1940, when Churchill became Minister of Defence as well as Prime Minister.   40. *WM*, p. 1869.

In a sense the Air Board already had the character of a department of state, with the Liberal Cowdray as its head and a Conservative MP, Major John Baird, answering for it in the House of Commons.[41] Another Conservative MP who had a say in air matters was Lord Hugh Cecil (later Lord Quickswood), the most brilliant son of Prime Minister Salisbury, but also the oddest. He had joined the RFC in 1915 and had somehow managed to acquire pilot's wings, though only on condition that he would never again fly solo. His contribution while in uniform was certainly more political than martial. He appears to have been consulted by Smuts about his main report, in which Cecil found 'the bombing plans rather visionary', but did not 'pour cold water' on them because he was 'so anxious for a change'.[42]

Who was to be the first Air Minister? Cowdray felt that he was entitled to the job, and with some reason. He had done well as President of the Air Board, despite the limited powers attached to it. Yet it was Lloyd George's duty, as well as his undoubted right, to consider if there was anyone whose qualifications might be even greater than Cowdray's and whom it might be even more expedient to appoint, politically. Both considerations are relevant when a prime minister is selecting a person to fill a high office of state. The process is nearly always difficult and invidious, and seldom free from risk. Indeed, what may turn out to be the best appointments may also be the riskiest. Effective leaders at any level need to have a streak of the gambler, and Lloyd George had it in a very marked degree. His gambles were usually based on intelligent calculation as well as sheer instinct. But it is in the nature of gambles that they often do not come off, and the failure of some gambles may be disastrous.

It was so when Lloyd George approached Northcliffe about the Air Ministry, within a week of the press lord's return from America. According to Lloyd George, he merely 'sounded' Northcliffe over lunch at 10 Downing

41. Lloyd George's board was established under the New Ministries and Secretaries Act, passed soon after he came to power.

42. DNB and Boyle, Trenchard, p. 231. Cecil sent a copy of the report to Trenchard, who thought he might have written it. But Cecil replied that it was probably drafted for Smuts by Major Storr of the Cabinet Secretariat (though of course Smuts was well capable of drafting it himself). Trenchard had another well-connected intellectual eccentric on his own staff in the person of Maurice Baring (hence Hilaire Belloc's reference to 'wing-commander Maurice Baring' in a footnote to one of his Cautionary Tales). Baring gave Trenchard devoted service as, in effect, private secretary and courtier, compensating for his lack of education and in every way promoting his interests. Another surprising figure on Trenchard's staff in late 1917 was Sir John Simon, the former Home Secretary, who had been at a loose end in Parliament since his resignation on the conscription issue in May 1915, and so decided to join the RFC.

Street, 'without making any definite offer'.[43] But Northcliffe claimed that the post of Air Minister was offered to him, and that the offer was 'repeated'. (It does not matter much which version is right, since the distinction between a sounding and an offer is hardly substantial.) In any case, Northcliffe wrote a letter declining the post. The letter was long, and only the first few lines referred to the Air Ministry which was, he said, 'rightly to be set up'. Most of the letter consisted of attacks on various quite unrelated aspects of government policy. But the most significant words were: 'I feel that in present circumstances I can do better work if I maintain my independence and am not gagged by a loyalty that I do not feel towards the whole of your Administration.'[44]

If this letter had simply been a private and confidential response to Lloyd George's approach, it would have done no more than serve notice of impending trouble with the Harmsworth press. But Northcliffe chose to make it an open letter, by printing it simultaneously in *The Times*.[45] The result was worse than embarrassing for Lloyd George; the breach of confidence did him very serious harm. Cowdray read the letter in the paper and immediately resigned. Thereafter, he was an implacable enemy of the Prime Minister.

Lloyd George has been too severely censured for his part in this affair. The villain of the piece was, unquestionably, Northcliffe. The press lord's mission in America had been a conspicuous success, and Lloyd George could justifiably feel that his idea of sending him – denounced at the time in many quarters – had been vindicated. He could also reasonably hope that the experience might have given Northcliffe a taste for official responsibility, and that he might rise to a suitable opportunity at home. Of all posts in government, none could have been more suitable for him than that of Air Minister. His interest in aeronautics, and his imaginative grasp of all that it implied for the future, had been unmatched for nearly a decade. Ever since the Wright brothers ushered in the air age, he had been using all his resources of publicity and propaganda to make his compatriots air-minded. Early in 1916 Sir William Robertson Nicoll, editor of *British Weekly*, called for him to be appointed Air Minister, and in May of that year, when the Air Board was set up, Northcliffe himself made one of his rare appearances in the

43. *WM*, p. 1871.
44. Northcliffe to DLG, 15 November 1917. The letter also referred to 'the most efficient army in the world, led by one of the greatest generals'.
45. *The Times*, 16 November 1917. Lloyd George says that it was published before he received it, despite being dated the previous day (*WM*, p. 1871).

House of Lords, to argue that 'this somewhat shadowy Board must develop into an Air Ministry'.[46]

In 1916 Lloyd George did not warm to the thought of Northcliffe in the post, or in government at all, commenting on Nicoll's suggestion: 'Northcliffe would not be a success. He has no experience of acting with equals. He would be especially handicapped in a Cabinet of twenty-two.'[47] The following year circumstances had changed. The large peacetime Cabinet had been superseded for the duration, and Northcliffe had apparently proved, in America, that he was capable of working in harness. Lloyd George was prepared to bring him into government, not as a member of the War Cabinet, but in an executive post for which, in so many ways, he was supremely qualified. The idea was perilous but not irrational. It might have worked, and had it worked the choice of Northcliffe as Air Minister would be hailed as one of Lloyd George's brainwaves. He should be forgiven for not realizing at once that Northcliffe was in no mood to be a team player, but was itching to revert to his normal role, the exercise of power without responsibility.

The other charge against Lloyd George, that he treated Cowdray badly in not consulting him before discussing the Air Ministry with another man, is surely absurd. When a ministerial change is in contemplation, a prime minister is by no means obliged to consult or inform the incumbent. On the contrary, the public interest requires him to move, or remove, colleagues as he sees fit, and not meanwhile to alert them. A minister who knows that his time may soon be up is unlikely to give of his best, and may even cause trouble.

Cowdray had no prescriptive right to the Air Ministry, and still less to be consulted about other candidates for the post. He did, however, deserve to be kept in the government in an office worthy of his talents, and there is no reason to disbelieve Lloyd George's statement that he intended to make such an offer, once he knew that Northcliffe would take the Air Ministry.[48] He was a prime minister who recognized efficiency and liked to employ the most gifted people, whatever their personal backgrounds or affiliations. It would have suited him to retain Cowdray for his ability alone, but also because he was a press lord and an Asquithian. The suggestion that he deliberately forced Cowdray's resignation, as an act of revenge for the libels

---

46. J. Lee Thompson, *Politicians, the Press & Propaganda: Lord Northcliffe and the Great War 1914–1919* (1999), p. 93.

47. *RWD*, 11 February 1916. Lloyd George and Nicoll were lunching with Riddell at Queen Anne's Gate just after Nicoll's article had appeared.   48. *WM*, p. 1871.

in the *Star* and the *Westminster Gazette* in September, is implausible.[49] Vindictiveness was not one of Lloyd George's more obvious faults; he seldom showed it, and hardly ever for long. Besides, it was plainly not in his interest to alienate Cowdray.[50]

He deserves, therefore, little if any blame for his approach to Northcliffe, and none at all for his silence about it to Cowdray. But he is certainly open to criticism for the appointment he made to the Air Ministry when faced with Northcliffe's refusal and Cowdray's resignation. The man he chose for the post was Northcliffe's brother Lord Rothermere, who the previous year had become a wartime public servant as Director-General of army clothing. Rothermere was an outstanding business executive, but lacked Northcliffe's breadth of vision and had no aptitude at all for politics. His tenure of the job proved unhappy, and in appointing him Lloyd George gave the impression of having no other motive than to mitigate Northcliffe's hostility.

49. 'It would seem that Cowdray accidentally earned the Prime Minister's spite when his two newspapers . . . published a brief, inaccurate item on 25 September' (Boyle, *Trenchard*, p. 247).
50. Cowdray had known since June (three months before the libel incident) that his position at the Air Board was not secure, when rumours had surfaced of Lloyd George's desire to appoint Churchill to it. But he had no reason to assume, then or later, that he would not be offered another post.

15

Passchendaele

The Kühlmann affair which precipitated Lloyd George's return from Cricci-eth would have been enough to prevent any immediate decision to halt Haig's offensive in Flanders. But it would hardly have been possible, in any case, to take such a decision when the second phase of the battle there had just begun, with apparently good results. Since the end of August, and during a spell of dry weather, Plumer had been preparing to attack with more limited objectives and on a narrower front. (It will be recalled that Haig had shifted the balance of power, under himself, from Gough to Plumer, though Gough remained commander of the Fifth Army.) The task assigned to Plumer was ostensibly far less ambitious than the original battle plan. In the first instance he was to clear the Germans off the Gheluvelt plateau, and then to make further step-by-step advances. As the victor of Messines, Plumer seemed just the man for this sort of work. But in fact Haig had not abandoned his ulterior aims, and Plumer, though naturally more cautious, was too easily swayed by the Commander-in-Chief.

On 19–20 September, after an intense preliminary bombardment, div-isions from the Second and Fifth Armies advanced across the Gheluvelt plateau to an average depth of 1,250 yards, and held their new positions against repeated German counterattack. This operation is known as the Menin Road battle. On 26 September there was a further advance of similar depth, in what is called the battle of Polygon Wood. (It was on the eve of this operation that Lloyd George visited Haig's headquarters.) Polygon Wood was to the north of Gheluvelt, and Plumer's next attack, on 4 October, was further north still, against a sector of ridge named in military history after the village of Broodseinde. Here again a victory could be claimed. Though the village itself was not captured, British troops advanced to an average depth of 1,000 yards and secured their positions. At the end of the day Haig recorded the battle as 'a very important success', and Charteris thought that, to judge from the number of German regiments represented among the 5,000 prisoners, there must be few reserves left to

the enemy.[1] It was therefore decided to maintain the offensive, and the next
stage was to be the capture of the northernmost part of the ridge, defined
by the name of another village since incomparably better known than
Broodseinde, and with a mournful resonance: Passchendaele.

Plumer's three attacks to date had succeeded in their own terms, but at a
heavy coast. British casualties in the Menin Road battle had been 21,000;
at Polygon Wood, 15,000; at Broodseinde, 20,000. In relation to the amount
of ground gained the scale of loss was, indeed, more than twice that of the
first day of the Flanders offensive at the end of July; 3,800 casualties per
square mile, compared with 1,500. The difference was that Plumer had
achieved more or less what he set out to achieve, whereas Gough's more
grandiose aims, reflecting Haig's, had not been realized. But whatever the
merits of Plumer's operations so far, after Broodseinde it was time to stop.
The prospects for another attack, to capture Passchendaele, would have
been highly questionable in any circumstances. Though the Germans, too,
had sustained heavy losses, as well as significant (if limited) loss of territory,
few of their guns had been captured, and they had learnt tactical lessons
which would make their dispositions more effective in the defence of Passchendaele. Plumer, for his part, was being forced by Haig into acting out of
character; plunging into further attacks without adequate preparation, and
in a direction that hampered the work of his artillery.[2]

Above all, circumstances did not favour continuation of the offensive,
because the rain had returned. September as a whole was an exceptionally
dry month by Flemish standards, though the weather had, in fact, started
to break when the Menin Road battle was launched. (There was rain during
the night preceding the attack, and Plumer for a time considered postponing
it.) In October wet weather was to be expected and duly occurred, with its
effects aggravated, again, by the destruction of the drainage system. The
Broodseinde battle was fought in a light drizzle, and thereafter steady
rain set in. This was bound to cause special difficulty in the approach to
Passchendaele, where the ground was prone to flooding. Nevertheless Haig
was inflexibly resolved to press on, taking what Trevor Wilson describes as

1. Haig diary, 4 October 1917.
2. 'Instead of striking due east, Plumer was being called on to drive north-east into a salient.
This was diminishing the area in which to place the guns needed to overwhelm enemy artillery
and provide a substantial creeping barrage. . . . the intended direction of the British ran counter
to the emphasis on artillery dominance which had hitherto underlain Plumer's step-by-step
successes. . . . the pace of Plumer's attacks was quickening, and so telling against his forces'
preparedness' (Robin Prior and Trevor Wilson, *Passchendaele: The Untold Story* (1996),
p. 138).

'the most lamentable decision of his lengthy – and sometimes distinguished – command'.[3]

Between 9 and 12 October British troops were thrown into action again, in weather conditions which precluded aerial spotting and in every way told against effective artillery support. The result was negligible progress towards Passchendaele, at a cost in casualties equivalent to a whole infantry division. But Haig's determination and false optimism remained as steady as the rain. In retrospect, his justification was that he had to keep on attacking to spare the French, but all the contemporary evidence belies this. The French army had recovered from its troubles and was, in fact, about to launch a successful attack on the Chemin-des-Dames. Foch had always been against Haig's Flanders plan, and whatever Pétain may have earlier said to Haig (of which we have no record) he now wanted the British to halt their offensive and take over more of his line. The French attitude was made plain to Haig at a brief meeting with Poincaré: 'He [Poincaré] looked tired. I was asked by him when I thought the operation would stop! He was anxious to know because of taking over more line. I said we ought to have only the one thought now in our minds, namely, *to attack*.'[4]

Even Charteris had come to feel that the offensive should be halted. On 10 October, after witnessing 'the wounded coming back, the noise, the news of losses, the sight of men toiling forward through mud into great danger', he could think only of 'the awfulness of it all'. While Haig was 'still trying to find some grounds for hope that we might still win through here this year', in Charteris's view there were 'none'.[5] It is not clear whether he communicated his change of heart to Haig or kept it to himself while the Field-Marshal was talking. In any case, Haig was in no mood to be deflected from his purpose. He agreed with his commanders that the next phase of the battle should go ahead only when there was 'a fair prospect of fine weather'.[6] But in the event it went ahead despite the absence of any such prospect.

What, meanwhile, were Lloyd George and his colleagues doing about a campaign to which they had given only grudging and conditional assent in July? The Prime Minister's Criccieth retreat coincided with a period of relative quiescence in Flanders, and when he got back he had the Kühlmann

---

3. Trevor Wilson, *The Myriad Faces of War: Britain and the Great War, 1914–1918* (1986), p. 477.

4. Haig's diary, 11 October 1917 (his italics). The meeting took place at Lillers station, on the President's train. Haig's comment on him was: 'I thought him a humbug, and anxious to get as much as possible out of us British.'   5. John Charteris, *At G.H.Q.* (1931), p. 259.

6. Haig diary, 13 October 1917.

approach to attend to; he was also much preoccupied with the defence of London and the south-east against air raids. Besides, even though offensive action was being resumed in Flanders at the time of his return, it appeared to be less ambitious in character than the original attack. At Criccieth the direction of his thoughts, together with Hankey's and Milner's, had been towards preparing for operations against Turkey during the winter months, while trying to find the means of reducing Robertson's power without breaking the government. There seems to have been a tacit acceptance of the impossibility of stopping the Flanders offensive outright against military advice.

During the afternoon of 24 September, before the Prime Minister and Hankey left for France, the War Policy Committee reconvened for a final series of meetings. The talk that day was entirely concerned with the Middle East – not a word about Flanders – and the same subject was further discussed for a time at the next meeting on 3 October. But then attention turned, at last, to the Western front, and Lloyd George vented his feelings about Haig's offensive, comparing it unfavourably with Nivelle's:

The War Cabinet had not forced their plans on the military authorities . . . General Nivelle and General [sic] Haig had arranged their own plans for the Western Front, and the only thing that the Cabinet had insisted upon was that the two armies during the offensive must be placed under one command . . . the offensive had yielded the biggest result this year, Arras and Vimy being part of the plan . . . though the French did not accomplish all they attempted, nothing that had since been achieved had been in any way comparable to the results then obtained. He would have no hesitation in comparing the present offensive with the predictions he made about it. We had not got the Klerken ridge . . . [and] he gathered that the military authorities . . . did not expect to get the Klerken ridge this year, but thought that they might get about half-way, namely to Passchendael[e] . . . in considering the present offensive [the War Cabinet] had been guided by the very confident paper they had received [from Haig] and he thought that no one would have voted for that offensive if they had not been considerably influenced by his optimism.

At one point Curzon intervened to suggest that it was 'only fair to take the weather into account', but Lloyd George seems to have ignored the remark.[7]

At the Boulogne conference he had agreed in principle to the French request that the British should take over more of the line, which might have

---

7. WPC, 3 October 1917. According to Haig's original plan the Passchendaele and Klerken ridges should have been captured early in the campaign.

been a roundabout way of ending the Flanders offensive. Haig was incensed about this, since he had understood that there would be no discussion of such matters with the French behind his back. His anger was directed as much against Robertson as against Lloyd George, Robertson having 'quietly acquiesced' in the French demand.[8] Lloyd George tried to use it as a means of furthering his own strategic priorities, telling Robertson that he would fight the French over it if he (Robertson) would agree to send five or six divisions from the Western front to Allenby in Egypt – a proposal that Robertson, eager to make amends to Haig, promised to resist.[9]

On 11 October Lloyd George drew the War Policy Committee's attention to a note from the CIGS concluding that 'we should confine our main efforts to the Western front, that we could not take over more of the line, and that the French should be urged to fight harder'. The Prime Minister predicted that the Klerken ridge would not be taken and said that he would remind the War Cabinet of this prediction in three weeks' time. Since the immediate objective was the *Passchendaele* ridge, he was in effect conceding that the latter might be captured within the stated period, and resigning himself to what was to be the last stage of Third Ypres. Before the meeting ended he 'pointed out that if a patient was very ill no one would limit themselves to taking the advice of the family doctor. They would call in a second opinion.'[10]

Such an opinion was duly sought, and to provide it Lloyd George turned to Haig's predecessor, French (whom Haig had helped to remove), and to Henry Wilson (whom he disliked and distrusted). Of this manœuvre Duff Cooper writes with justifiable sarcasm:

Never before, perhaps, has a Commander-in-Chief, who has been superseded on account of failure, been invited by his Government to criticise his successor. If it had been proposed at the same time that the actions of the Cabinet during the last twelve months should be enquired into and reported upon by a committee consisting of Mr. Asquith and Mr. McKenna, it is doubtful whether the Prime Minister would have welcomed the suggestion.[11]

The idea was indeed absurd. Even if French and Wilson could have been persuaded to report in exactly the sense that Lloyd George and his supporters in the War Cabinet desired, it is hard to see what benefit would have accrued.

8. Haig diary, 3 October 1917.   9. Robertson to Haig, 6 October 1917.
10. WPC, 11 October 1917. This was the twenty-first and last meeting of the Committee, which had, of course, never superseded the War Cabinet. Since both the functions and the membership of the two bodies largely overlapped, the value of the Committee had always been questionable.   11. Duff Cooper, *Haig* (2 vols., 1935–6), vol. ii, p. 180.

The political problem of dealing with Haig and Robertson would have remained as intractable as ever; if anything more so. In fact, the reports that the two second-guessers delivered within a week or so were in varying degrees critical of Haig's conduct of operations (that of French intensely so), while supporting Western front strategy in principle. Neither gave any encouragement to Lloyd George's Turkish designs.[12] Meanwhile Robertson nearly resigned over the involvement of French and Wilson, and Curzon warned Hankey that if Robertson were forced out 'Robert Cecil, Balfour, Derby, Carson and he himself, probably, would leave the Government, which would then break up'.[13] But this warning was never tested, because the CIGS was persuaded to stay – for the time being.

The row with Robertson coincided with a visit to Britain by Painlevé, Foch and Henri Franklin-Bouillon, the French Minister of Propaganda, and at the weekend they joined Lloyd George for the first prime ministerial weekend at Chequers. Others present were Balfour, Smuts, Hankey, his French opposite number, Commandant Helbronner – and Arthur Lee, who was the host.

Chequers, a fine Elizabethan house in the Chilterns forty miles from London, surrounded by an estate of 1,200 acres, had been acquired by Lee through the wealth and devotion of his American wife, Ruth, and her sister, Faith. The Lees had been life-tenants of the place since 1909, but in 1917 obtained the freehold. Previously, over eight hundred years, the property had changed hands only by will or marriage.

The Lees did much for the house, removing Victorian accretions and buying, or buying back, pictures, furniture and historic objects to adorn it. One interesting feature of the house is an attic room where Lady Mary Grey, sister of Lady Jane, was imprisoned on Elizabeth I's orders. It now contains a contemporary portrait of Lady Mary, bought by Lee. There is also a link with Oliver Cromwell, since in 1715 a grandson of the Lord Protector married the then owner of Chequers. At the time of the Lees' purchase Cromwell memorabilia from the house were in the hands of a

---

12. While approving of his aim to knock Turkey out of the war, the two men regarded a major campaign in the Middle East as impossible at the time, granted the prior claims of the Western front, which they did not dispute.

13. Hankey diary, 10 October 1917. Lloyd George had already suggested inviting French and Wilson to attend a special council of war, and it was this that prompted Robertson's resignation threat. Haig counselled him against resigning unless and until his advice was rejected (Haig diary, 11 October 1917).

pawnbroker, and he moved quickly to redeem them.[14] But the most important Cromwell relic had already been discovered. When Victorian paper was being stripped from the walls in one of the rooms, an oak door was revealed leading to a small cupboard, in which a death mask of Cromwell was found. It had been missing for two hundred years.[15]

The architect chosen for the restoration of Chequers was Reginald Blomfield, who carried out much similar work on historic houses, as well as designing many new buildings ranging from Lady Margaret Hall at Oxford to the Menin Gate at Ypres. He also wrote scholarly works of art history including (relevantly) a History of Renaissance Architecture in England. Under his guidance the Victorian stucco at Chequers was stripped off to reveal the original red brick, battlements and finials were eliminated, and pseudo-Gothic windows were replaced with stone mullions. Lee was a natural aesthete, who became very knowledgeable about houses and works of art. Between them, he and Bondfield – and Ruth Lee – did a superb job at Chequers.

As they had no children, the Lees decided to offer Chequers to the nation as a country retreat for its prime ministers, after they themselves were dead. They lost no time, once the freehold of the property was theirs, in preparing a scheme for transferring the house and contents, together with the land and a substantial endowment, to a charitable trust, of which they would become life-tenants. Lee put this scheme to Lloyd George, who responded formally, at the end of August, in suitably appreciative terms:

My dear Lee,

Your offer in regard to the Chequers Estate is most generous and beneficent, and one for which Prime Ministers of England in future will have much to thank you. The gift which you are now bequeathing in advance to the nation is . . . an indication of the practical thoughtfulness which is characteristic of you. . . . Future generations of Prime Ministers will think with gratitude of the impulse which has thus prompted you . . . to place this beautiful mansion at their disposal. I have no doubt that such a retreat will do much to alleviate the cares of state which they inherit along with it, and you will earn the grateful thanks of those whose privilege it is to enjoy it.

You have my full authority to go ahead with the scheme . . .

Yours sincerely

D. Lloyd George[16]

14. Norma Major, Chequers: The Prime Minister's Country House and its History (1996), p. 85. When John Major was Prime Minister the Cromwell connection was a useful talking-point with constituents visiting the house, because he, like Cromwell, was MP for Huntingdon.
15. RWD, 30 March 1917. The story is recorded by Riddell, who had just heard it from Lee.
16. DLG to Arthur Lee, 29 August 1917.

Soon afterwards a copy of the scheme was sent to Buckingham Palace. Queen Mary responded swiftly through her private secretary, saying that she and the King were greatly interested in it, and adding that she had once admired 'a little portrait of her ancestor Charles II' at Chequers. Would the Lees consider selling it to her for the Royal Collection? According to Lee there was 'only one possible answer to this request' and the picture was presented to her with the Lees' 'humble duty', so diminishing by one item their benefaction to the nation. She rewarded them with a signed photograph of herself, framed in Indian brocade that she had bought at Benares.[17]

Legislation was needed to give effect to the scheme, and a Chequers Estate bill, introduced in late November, soon passed amid general approval. Overt criticism was limited and muted. Only Horatio Bottomley attacked the scheme outright, saying that it would have been better to make the house available to twenty holders of the Victoria Cross and their wives, prime ministers being 'already adequately housed'. There was some muttering among the local Buckinghamshire squirearchy about the potentially disturbing change of use of a historic house in the neighbourhood, particularly if its occupant were to be Lloyd George. But most people and leader-writers praised the Lees' imaginative generosity, without going quite so far as Edward Wood (later Lord Halifax, Viceroy, Foreign Secretary and Ambassador to the United States) who described it as 'the most inspiring and exalted thing that had been done in his time'.[18]

Praise was indeed deserved. Chequers has become a cherished asset to a succession of prime ministers, and through them to the state. There is no reason to doubt that the donor's principal motive was idealistic and disinterested, but there was surely a connection between Lee's scheme and his hero-worship of Lloyd George. Under any other prime minister he might not have been so quick to surrender the freehold of Chequers, anticipating what might otherwise have been a provision in his will. We can fairly assume that in a sense he did it for Lloyd George, and he may well have hoped that the weekend in October 1917 would become the pattern for the immediate future – Lloyd George combining business with pleasure under his roof. If so he was disappointed. Lloyd George quite enjoyed the weekend, but it would not have suited him to make a habit of going to Chequers as Lee's guest. When he endorsed the scheme he did not therefore expect to be its beneficiary.

Yet it was clearly Lee's intention that he should be, and two years later

17. *A Good Innings: The Private Papers of Viscount Lee of Fareham*, ed. Alan Clark (1974), pp. 171–2.   18. Ibid., p. 172.

he decided to bring the scheme into full operation without delay. He and his wife then relinquished their life-tenancies, so making the house available to the Prime Minister. They moved out at the beginning of 1921, and Lloyd George spent quite a lot of time at Chequers during the last phase of his premiership, until his fall in 1922. Old houses never really appealed to him, and Chequers had the further disadvantage of not commanding a view, an amenity that he made sure of possessing in the two houses that he built for himself, at Criccieth and, later, at Churt. But his family liked the place, and he was glad of the opportunity to entertain domestic and foreign visitors there.

The inaugural weekend in 1917 was a stag party. Ruth Lee and Margaret Lloyd George were absent and there was no other female company. Hankey occupied Lady Mary Grey's prison room where he 'slept admirably', without psychic ill effects. Soon after the party foregathered he was invested with the Legion of Honour by Painlevé, who made a graceful speech acknowledging his services as secretary to inter-Allied conferences. Lloyd George added his own praise and all the others shook his hand.[19]

Everyone could see that Painlevé was nervous and *distrait*, feeling politically vulnerable at home; and his state of mind can hardly have been improved when, at dinner, Lloyd George quoted Robertson as saying of a recent French Prime Minister, 'Well, 'e won't last long.'[20] He left at midnight to return to France in a destroyer called up by the Admiralty. Talk then continued in Balfour's room and the following morning there was a further informal inter-Allied conference by the fire in the long gallery on the idea of an Allied general staff, a subject which belongs to the next chapter. Only Lloyd George and Hankey stayed for lunch with Lee. In the afternoon they went for a walk before driving back to London.[21]

The following morning Hankey breakfasted alone with Lloyd George at 10 Downing Street, and they had a long and important conversation, of which Hankey immediately made a full record. Hankey opened with a view of the war which showed that he had reverted to support for Haig's strategy. 'The military operations in Flanders . . . must be measured not only by the military objects which they achieved, but by their general effect on Germany [and] increasing the strain on her manufacturing resources.' They weakened the morale of the German people 'by reducing their faith in their military commanders, by the loss of relatives, and by engendering a feeling of hopelessness'. Contrary to his recent line of thought in Wales, Hankey was

19. Hankey diary, 14 October 1917. He received the rank of Commandant. The day before Lloyd George had invested Helbronner, Hankey's opposite number, as CMG (Commander, Order of St Michael and St George).   20. *A Good Innings*, p. 173.
21. Hankey diary, 15 October 1917.

now opposed to an offensive against the Turks, and he was equally sceptical of 'Pétain's tactics of striking here and striking there', without any 'prolonged offensive', until the Americans arrived in strength. He therefore argued that it was 'absolutely essential to take some offensive on the Western front next year'.

Lloyd George emphatically disagreed, wishing to avoid in 1918 the 'terrific losses' inseparable from such an offensive. 'If our army was spent in a succession of shattering attacks during 1918', it would be reduced to the present condition of the French army.

He was particularly anxious to avoid a situation at the end of the war in which our army would no longer be a first-class one. He wished it to be in every respect as the American army, and possibly, a revived Russian army, so that this country would be a great military power in the world. It was not that he could not face losses, but he insisted that the losses must not be incurred without commensurate results. *A man took 21 years to make, and human life was very precious.*

Yet Lloyd George was no longer thinking that the Germans might be brought to negotiate acceptable terms without being defeated militarily. He was convinced again that their 'overwhelming military defeat' was necessary. But he believed that it would not be feasible until 1919, when Britain and America 'at full strength', and Russia and Italy 'with such as remained to them', would attack simultaneously with France. Meanwhile tactics of the sort favoured by Pétain should keep the Germans 'sufficiently occupied on the Western Front to prevent them from dealing decisive blows against Russia . . . without the great sacrifice in life involved in a continuance of Haig's operations'. At the same time every effort should be made to detach Germany's allies from her, and he mentioned specifically the need for a military campaign against Turkey.

Hankey suggested that he take an early opportunity of making these views known to his colleagues. Lloyd George did not disagree, but asked Hankey meanwhile to report the conversation to 'one or two' of them. He attached so much importance to the war policy he had outlined that he would resign the premiership rather than abandon it. Hankey saw Balfour, Curzon and Milner the same day 'and told them the whole story, but without mentioning the Prime Minister's final observation'.[22]

*

22. Maurice Hankey, *The Supreme Command, 1914–1918* (2 vols., 1961), vol. ii, pp. 703–7, where his record of the conversation on 15 October 1917 is quoted in full.

The third week of October brought a remarkable demonstration of the French army's return to full vigour after the failed spring offensive and the mutinies. The process of revival had begun much earlier and there were increasing signs of it throughout the summer. It was never true, as alleged, that the French were wholly inactive while Haig's army was attacking in Flanders. Not only was there a substantial French force involved in his offensive, which did very well, if in a relatively marginal role; there were also, in August, local attacks north of Saint-Quentin, against the Chemin-des-Dames, and above all at Verdun where significant penetration was achieved. These were not negligible operations, but the British could still complain with some plausibility that no really large-scale effort had been made by the French in support of Haig. There was talk of such an attack, but it was repeatedly postponed.

On 22 October, however, Pétain launched one of the most successful operations of the war, if also one of the least remembered. The sector that he chose was, again, that of the Chemin-des-Dames, at the western end of the ridge where the Germans had left an exposed salient. Unlike Nivelle and Haig, he had no design to achieve a decisive breakthrough; his aim was limited, in accordance with his strategic purpose for the period of waiting for the Americans. Nevertheless, his troops scored a victory which was all the more salutary for French morale in view of the painful associations of the area in which it was won. In a sense, the nightmare of the Nivelle offensive was exorcized as, within four days, the French captured more than seven miles of front to a depth of three miles, taking nearly 12,000 prisoners. In territory as much was gained as by Haig's army in the ninety-nine days of Third Ypres, and at incomparably lower cost.[23]

This impressive feat is now almost forgotten, because it was swiftly overtaken by a major German triumph in another Allied theatre, to which all eyes were turned at the time and which became a lasting memory. When Cadorna halted his offensive on 12 September the disillusionment in Italy was similar to that in France after Nivelle. A further 100,000 had been added to a toll of casualties already proportionately the largest of any belligerent. Yet the Italians had advanced only a few miles, and had been left in a position more vulnerable than before, while the enemy's resistance held. Cadorna had driven his men too hard and they were near breaking-point. Moreover his Second Army, under General Luigi Capello, had ended its advance on the far side of the River Isonzo, but too close to it for

23. John Keegan, *The First World War* (1998), p. 394; Jacques Chastenet, *Histoire de la Troisième République* (7 vols., 1952–63), vol. iv, p. 298.

safety. Capello drew his chief's attention to the difficulty of defending this bridgehead, and urged him to make it more secure by an attack on the right. But Cadorna ignored the warning and took no action.

On the Austrians' side there had, also, been heavy losses, even though they had not cracked. And we have seen that the Emperor Karl wanted to find a way of ending the war. Yet he remained tied to the Germans. When he asked them to take over part of the Eastern front, so as to release some of his forces there for a counter-offensive against the Italians, they refused to oblige him, preferring to send forces of their own to the Italian front. They had little confidence in their ally's ability to mount a successful campaign there, and anyway feared that if, by chance, the Austrians were to defeat the Italians, they would only become more inclined than ever to seek a separate peace.

The German high command therefore decided to transfer seven divisions from the East, forming a new Fourteenth Army under General Otto von Below. With artillery and air units also brought from the Eastern front, this force was to be used against the position held by the Italian Second Army, which the Germans rightly perceived as the point of greatest weakness. Meanwhile an Austrian army group would tie the Italians down along the lower Isonzo front to the east, and another would similarly tie them down to the west, in the Tyrol.

Between 20 September and 22 October this massive transfer of troops and supporting arms was achieved, in what has to be regarded as a masterpiece of efficiency and staffwork, involving the use of 2,400 military trains. During the last few days the German soldiers, specially trained for mountain warfare, approached their jumping-off points on foot, moving at night by circuitous routes, while their supplies were brought by pack animals with muffled hoofs. Over the front as a whole Cadorna had 41 full-strength divisions against the Central Powers' 33 under-strength divisions. But in the key sector the Germans, with some Austrians under command, had 100 per cent superiority.[24]

Bad weather delayed the attack for two days, and it was still foggy when, at 2 a.m. on 24 October, Below opened fire with 2,000 guns firing gas shells. The Italians' gas masks were of primitive design and gave no adequate protection. Gas was followed by alternating mortar and artillery bombardment, and by machine-gun fire directed at the Italians' first and second lines of defence. Between 8 and 9 a.m. Prussian troops spearheaded an assault in

24. Holger H. Herwig, *The First World War: Germany and Austria–Hungary 1914–1918* (1997), pp. 338–9.

which the village of Caporetto (known in German as Karfreit) was stormed and the heights commanding the area were seized. The Italian Second Army was utterly routed, while Capello, who had been seriously ill before the battle, was forced by his doctor to hand over command to another general. During the first day the Germans advanced ten miles. One young officer who distinguished himself in the fighting was Erwin Rommel, practising as a company commander a technique of infiltration with infantry that he was to develop with tanks in the next war.[25]

The full scale of the disaster was soon apparent. On 26 October Cadorna ordered a retreat to the Tagliamento. In four days he abandoned all the territory gained in thirty months. By 3 November the Italians had fallen back to the Piave, where the line was eventually stabilized. But the scale of loss in the Caporetto campaign was staggering. More than a quarter of a million Italian soldiers were lost, of whom 10,000 were killed and nearly 200,000 taken prisoner. In addition, the enemy captured a huge quantity of equipment, including 3,000 guns. The roads to the south of the front were choked with stragglers and refugees. The Italian army was for the time being in ruins, and Cadorna's attempt to restore discipline by the summary execution of deserters was largely unavailing.

The first intimations of Caporetto reached London on 26 October. The following day a French liaison officer told Hankey that his government was offering the Italians immediate help and suggested an Allied conference, to be held in Paris or London, or at Boulogne. Hankey at once telephoned Lloyd George, who was at Walton Heath (with Riddell and Kerr). He was asked to see Robertson and then come down to Walton Heath himself.

When he arrived he found the Prime Minister in Riddell's room at the golf club, with a staff officer who had just brought this letter from the CIGS:

I enclose copies of some telegrams sent and received today regarding Italy. Italy really has stacks of men of her own and there is no *military* necessity to send troops to her provided the Italian troops fight reasonably well. . . . There have been no new developments of importance in Italy since I saw you yesterday. I call your attention to the telegram sent by the French Government and ask for instructions as to whether you wish a similar telegram sent by us. If so I will send one to Cadorna. But of course if we offer troops he is bound to accept them and it is really *very* hard on our men after what they have recently gone through to send them to Italy . . . Personally I am in favour of waiting until Cadorna asks for them, unless you think that for political

25. Keegan, *First World War*, p. 374.

reasons we ought not to be outdone by the French. We must not get rattled over this business, but of course we must stop the rot if we can.

Lloyd George was not rattled, but sensed correctly that the despatch of troops to Italy was vital for military as well as political reasons. He replied promptly to Robertson:

I have no doubt we ought to follow up the French telegram at once by a proffer of assistance . . . unless the Italian morale is restored this movement may well end in an overwhelming disaster. If we mean to exercise a dominant influence in directing the course of the War we must do so in the way the Germans have secured control, i.e. by helping to extricate Allies in trouble. We cannot do so merely by lecturing them at Conferences. We must help them, then we will have earned a right to dictate to them.

Robertson accepted the instruction, and reported in a characteristic tone that it was being carried out:

Orders have been given for the despatch of . . . two divisions as early as possible. How soon they can go will depend upon the railway arrangements made by the French. . . . The French are sending four divisions. It will probably take at least ten days from now before the six divisions have all left. . . .[26]

Robertson was sent to Italy on 29 October, and on 2 November Painlevé paid a brief visit to London to concert plans with Lloyd George. The following day the Prime Minister left for the Continent, accompanied by Smuts, Henry Wilson, General Frederick Maurice, Hankey, J. T. Davies – and Frances Stevenson. They spent a day in Paris before travelling on to Italy. It had been decided that the Allied conference should be held at Rapallo (on the Ligurian coast east of Genoa). Frances Stevenson's diary briefly resumes to give an account of this trip, before going silent again until 1919. She was paying her first visit to Italy, a country with which she had strong family links, as her maternal grandfather was Italian. The Mediterranean scenery entranced her, as it never failed to entrance Lloyd George. For the first time she saw oranges and olives growing in the open, and was 'thrilled with all the surroundings'.

26. Robertson to DLG, DLG to Robertson, Robertson to DLG, 27 October 1917. The letters exchanged by the Prime Minister and the CIGS were typewritten and marked 'Secret'. Hankey made his own handwritten copy of Lloyd George's to Robertson in the Walton Heath clubhouse, taking care to destroy the blotting paper.

1. Lloyd George (with Reading) at Chequers on his first day as Prime Minister

2. Nivelle

3. Briand

4. Cadorna

5. Clemenceau

6. Geddes

7. Beaverbrook, with a revealing smile, as Minister of Information

8. US Admiral Sims, J. L. Garvin and Northcliffe at Washington Inn, London, October 1918

9. Thomas, Haig, Joffre and Lloyd George at 14th Army Corps
Headquarters, Mesulte, 12 September 1916

10. Churchill exhorts his audience at Enfield Lock munitions factory, 1916

11. Lloyd George, Milner and Kerr walking near Walton Heath, 1917

12. Riddell, Lloyd George, Masterman and Gwilym Lloyd George
at Walton Heath Golf Course

13. Lloyd George and Balfour arriving at the Hotel Crillon, 26 July 1917

14. Robertson and Maurice leaving the Allied conference, July 1917

18. The Imperial War Cabinet at 10 Downing Street, 1917. *Front*: Long, Borden (Canada), Smuts (South Africa), Lloyd George, Weston, Massey (New Zealand), Rogers (Canada), Perley (Canada), Balfour, Henderson, Hankey. *Back*: Bonar Law, Hazen, Ward, Austen Chamberlain, Carson, Bikanar (India), Curzon.

19. The Imperial War Cabinet at 10 Downing Street, 1918. *Back*: Amery fourth from left, Hankey fifth from left. *Middle*: Weymss, Ward, Dowell, Long, Barnes, Curzon, Smuts, Austen Chamberlain, Calder, Burton, Montagu, Maclay, Macdonagh. *Front*: Massey, Patiala, Bonar Law, Borden, Lloyd George, Hughes, Balfour, Cook, Lloyd.

By contrast with the beauty of the sunlit landscape, there was plenty to remind the travellers that they were entering a country in crisis. Their train moved at a crawl as it emerged from the Mont Cenis tunnel, impeded by other trains carrying British and French troops, 'passing along the line at the rate of 40 a day'. On a road winding down from the mountains they saw 'huge motor caissons' taking war supplies to the front. In Turin 'the crowd on the platform was surly and hostile'. There had been pro-German riots in the city, which was reputed to be 'full of spies'. It seemed 'a dangerous place' and left 'a very nasty impression'.[27]

Among Italian leaders the first casualty was the veteran Prime Minister, Boselli, who felt obliged to resign. His place was taken by the Minister of the Interior, Vittorio Emanuele Orlando, a younger man (born in 1860) and a strong supporter of the war. Orlando was a Sicilian, and he vowed to defend the country if necessary all the way to Sicily. Before going into politics he had been a law professor at Palermo. In his government Sonnino remained Foreign Minister, another sign that there would be no truck with defeatism.

The conference at Rapallo lasted for two days, 6 and 7 November. On the first there was a frank discussion of the military situation, of which the Italian high command had lost all control. Lloyd George 'insisted upon the immediate riddance of Cadorna', and the Italians agreed that he should be superseded, along with his Chief of Staff. In return, Lloyd George and Painlevé promised 'ample help' to Italy.[28] More troops would be sent, in addition to those already on the way. In the end there were four British and eight French divisions in Italy. Though they were not involved in the fighting until December, the presence of Allied reinforcements in the country was good for Italian morale. Lloyd George's firm line with Robertson was justified.

On the second day of the conference the leaders agreed to establish a Supreme Allied War Council, and the final session of the conference, in the New Casino Hotel, was in fact the new Council's inaugural meeting. The gestation of this idea and the significance of its implementation, will be described in the next chapter.

Before leaving Italy Lloyd George visited the King, Victor Emmanuel III, at his headquarters at Peschiera, on Lake Garda, much closer to the scene of action. With other ministers Lloyd George went there to inform the King

27. FSD, 5 November 1917.
28. Hankey diary, 7 November 1917. Hankey had visited the 'exquisite bay' of Rapallo in the battleship *Ramillies* nearly twenty years before.

of the decisions reached at Rapallo, and to obtain his formal approval. Lloyd George found him not a commanding figure physically (he was almost a dwarf), but was 'impressed by the calm fortitude he showed . . . when his country and his throne were in jeopardy'. The King expressed 'great regret' that Lloyd George's advice had not been taken at the beginning of the year, since he 'fully shared' the view that Austria might then have been crushed with Allied help. He did not, he said, 'always have the opportunity of having his own views carried out'. Lloyd George naturally said he was sorry that the King had not been present at the Rome conference.

Victor Emmanuel accepted the changes to the high command, despite some reservations about the criticisms that had been levelled at Cadorna. His chosen successor was General Armando Diaz, who had hitherto commanded nothing larger than an army corps. Foch and Robertson would have preferred the Duke of Aosta, an army commander, but as a cousin of the King he was ruled out 'for dynastic reasons'.[29]

On the return journey there was an hour's stop at Brescia, where the Italian ministers took their leave and Lloyd George went for a walk in the town. He came back 'followed by a crowd', since it was 'impossible' (Frances Stevenson noted) 'for him to go into a remote town like that without being recognised'. The French ministers travelled on to Paris, but Lloyd George's sleeping-car was detached at Aix-les-Bains, where he spent the whole of the next day, having an important speech to prepare.[30]

The dramatic events on the Italian front did not deter Haig from going through with the last and least comprehensible phase of his Flanders offensive, the battle for Passchendaele itself – a village now barely recognizable as such, on a piece of gently rising ground for which 'ridge' is really a misnomer. Though the Commander-in-Chief's thoughts were already much occupied with another offensive project in a different sector of his front, he did not feel that it was quite time to bring Third Ypres to an end. Passchendaele was still 1,500 yards ahead, and he was determined to reach it.

On 16 October he received a telegram from Lloyd George which surprised him, as it must in retrospect surprise us:

The War Cabinet desire to congratulate you and the troops under your command upon the achievements of the British Armies in Flanders in the great battle which has been raging since July 31st. Starting from positions in which every advantage

29. WM, pp. 2324–31; Hankey diary, 8 November 1917.
30. FSD, 9 November 1917; Hankey, *Supreme Command*, vol. ii, pp. 724–5.

rested with the enemy and, hampered and delayed from time to time by most unfavourable weather, you and your men have nevertheless continuously driven the enemy back with such skill courage and pertinacity as have commanded the grateful admiration of the peoples of the British Empire and filled the enemy with alarm. I am personally glad to be the means of transmitting this message to you, and to your gallant troops, and desire to take this opportunity of renewing my assurance of confidence in your leadership and in the devotion of those whom you command.

After recording the telegram in his diary, Haig commented: 'This is the first message of congratulation on any operation by the War Cabinet which has reached me since the war began! I wonder why the Prime Minister should suddenly have sent this message.'[31]

A fair question – why did he? Lloyd George had certainly not experienced a sudden change of heart. We know from his conversation with Hankey on 15 October, the day before the telegram was sent, that his view of Haig's attritional methods was the same as ever. When Hankey argued the case for them (a curious change on his part from what he had been saying in Wales), Lloyd George maintained his opinion. Haig surmised that the Prime Minister had sent the telegram because 'the question of thanks being given to the Army and Navy was [being] informally discussed' in political circles, and he wished to anticipate a possible demand for such a message to be sent.[32] This may, indeed, partly account for the unexpected gesture.

Of course he had no difficulty in paying a tribute to the troops, whose courage and devotion he admired as much as anyone, and with whom he profoundly sympathized. But expressing confidence in Haig's leadership was another matter. He had done so, personally, earlier in the year, when Nivelle had failed and Haig's Arras campaign still appeared to be going well. But to do so now, with such formality, after weeks of an offensive which had manifestly failed in its own terms, and to which he had been opposed from the start, must have been exceedingly hard for him. No doubt it would have been awkward to ask Haig to convey the War Cabinet's congratulations to the troops without including any positive reference to himself. Politically it was expedient to placate him and his many backers at a time when a showdown with Robertson seemed to be looming. Lloyd George may also have hoped that a message lauding a job well done in Flanders might encourage the Commander-in-Chief to call it a day. But if the last consideration played any part in Lloyd George's decision to send the message, Haig signally failed to take the hint.

31. Haig diary, 16 October 1917.   32. Ibid.

On 26 October the final assault on Passchendaele began. There had been several days of relatively fine weather, but it was raining again when the attack went in, spearheaded by two Canadian divisions of the Second Army, with two divisions of the Fifth Army attacking on the left, and Australians from II Anzac corps giving protection on the right. Both the flanking operations failed, but even so the Canadians managed to advance 500 yards and consolidate their positions. In the next phase of the battle, on 30 October, the Fifth Army divisions again suffered, this time so badly that Haig decided operations from that sector should be closed down. The Fifth Army commander, Gough, was no longer the man Haig had preferred to Plumer or Rawlinson for the leading role in his offensive. Experience had made him cautious, while Plumer, under Haig's immediate influence, had ceased to be his usual careful and methodical self – a strange reversal. But Plumer did not stay to see the Passchendaele battle through, since he was removed to command the troops that were on their way to Italy. His place as commander of the Second Army was taken by Rawlinson, who had hitherto been little more than a spectator of the offensive from his post on the far left of Haig's line.

Despite the weakness on both flanks, the Canadians gained another 500 yards on 30 October. They were now on the edge of Passchendaele village, or what remained of it. On 6 November – while the Allied leaders were meeting at Rapallo – the final push was made and the objective captured. In the words of a Canadian soldier who witnessed the scene:

The buildings had been pounded and mixed with the earth, and the shell exploded bodies were so thickly strewn that a fellow couldn't step without stepping on corruption. Our opponents were fighting a rearguard action which resulted in a massacre for both sides. Our boys were falling like ninepins, but it was even worse for them. If they stood up to surrender they were mown down by their own machine gun fire aimed from their rear at us; if they leapfrogged back they were caught in our barrage.[33]

There was still a section of the ridge in enemy hands and Haig ordered further attacks. But their futility was soon obvious, as the rain became torrential. On 10 November, therefore, the battle was brought to an end. Since 26 October Canadian casualties amounted to 12,000.

In Third Ypres as a whole British casualties totalled about 275,000, of whom 70,000 were killed and many permanently disabled. The Germans

33. Corporal H. C. Baker, quoted in Prior and Wilson, *Passchendaele*, p. 179.

suffered very heavily too, and there is still debate about the figures. But it seems probable that, as usual in the First World War, the defenders' loss was rather less heavy than the attackers', and a fair estimate of German casualties is in the region of 200,000.

Even if the balance of casualties had been the other way the advantage would still have lain with the enemy because for the time being *any* large toll of manpower was more perilous to Britain and France than to Germany. Between the collapse of Russia and the hoped-for arrival of the Americans, the Western Allies needed above all to husband their resources. By attacking on such a large scale, and for so long, Haig was depleting Britain's precious reserve of manpower in disregard of the grave threat that would soon have to be faced.

The previous year the battle of the Somme was justified, in principle, at the outset, because it was clearly necessary to take the heat off the French at Verdun. But by mid-September 1916 Verdun was safe, and Haig's motive for prolonging the battle into November was that he continued to believe the Germans would crack. A similar pattern is to be seen in 1917, though with important differences that count against Haig. The Field-Marshal's apologists maintain, in retrospect, that Third Ypres had to be launched for the sake of the French, though at the time this was not the determining motive (if a motive at all) and in any case the French army's troubles were well under control by the time his offensive began. In truth he attacked because he intended to cut the Germans' communications with the Belgian ports, to overrun their U-boat bases, and ultimately to liberate Belgium altogether. The case for Third Ypres was always far more dubious and speculative than the case for the Somme, and – contrary to what has been alleged – had little to do with helping the French.

As in the previous year, the fighting was agonizingly prolonged, and in reality for the same reason, that Haig persisted in believing the Germans were at their last gasp. But in 1917 the nature of the final stages of the battle was even more appalling, and the strategic risk involved far greater. The argument put forward on Haig's behalf, that the attritional fight for Passchendaele made an indispensable contribution to the eventual breaking of German resistance, assumes (incorrectly) that that was his deliberate intention in prolonging the battle.[34] Even if it had been his purpose, it was not attained. Of course, the Germans were severely affected by the battle, but

34. '. . . it is impossible to doubt that, just as the Battle of the Somme had broken the mainspring of the old German regular Army, so the autumn offensive of 1917 undermined the resisting power of the German nation' (Cooper, *Haig*, vol. ii, p. 175).

their will to resist was not undermined and the cost to them was markedly less than to the British, both in absolute terms and in relation to the overall strategic balance.

Much is made of Ludendorff's description of Passchendaele, which matches the eye-witness account already quoted:

The horror of the shell-hole area of Verdun was surpassed. It was unspeakable suffering. And through this world of mud the attackers dragged themselves, slowly, but steadily, and in dense masses. Caught in the advance zone by our hail of fire they often collapsed, and the lonely man in the shell-hole breathed again. Then the mass came on again. Rifle and machine-gun jammed with the mud. Man fought against man and all too often the mass was successful.[35]

But what the attackers achieved was a pitifully small-scale tactical success, which created another untenable salient.[36] Ludendorff was so confident that his line in Flanders would essentially hold that he was prepared to send divisions from the East to the Italian front. Both he and Haig were gambling, but while Haig's gamble on a breakthrough in Flanders failed, Ludendorff's on holding the line there and winning a spectacular victory in Italy came off.

All in all, Lloyd George's opposition to Haig's plan was surely vindicated. But should he, could he, have stopped the offensive, and if so when? In theory the War Cabinet had a perfect right to call a halt, and had given only a conditional assent to the offensive. But there was a contradiction between suggesting that it might be stopped and saying that the civilians would always, in the last resort, bow to professional advice. This contradiction was never resolved. Establishing the War Policy Committee was an attempt to resolve it in favour of the civilians, but the core of the problem remained. The term 'war policy' did not make the warriors any more willing to defer to the politicians, or the politicians any more resolute and united in dealing with the warriors.

The best moment to have stopped the offensive would have been in September, after the first month had manifestly failed to live up to Haig's expectations. But the rain provided some excuse, and besides Haig seemed to be modifying his approach, by turning to Plumer to conduct the next

35. Erich Ludendorff, *My War Memories, 1914–1918* (2 vols., 1919), vol. ii, p. 491.
36. Rawlinson, the new commander of the Second Army, commented on the position thus: 'Nothing we can hope to do can make the line now held a really satisfactory defensive position. We must therefore be prepared to withdraw from it, if the Germans show signs of a serious and sustained offensive on this front . . .' (cited in Prior and Wilson, *Passchendaele*, p. 181).

phase. It seems strange, nevertheless, that neither the War Cabinet nor the War Policy Committee (the latter holding no meetings from 18 July to 24 September) should have carried out a detailed audit of the offensive and its prospects. And it was certainly most unfortunate that Lloyd George's retreat to Criccieth removed him from the day-to-day conduct of government at a critical time. Had he stayed in London, he and Law might have decided to take a strong line before the troops were again committed to action, and before the Kühlmann overture diverted attention from military matters. All the same, it is doubtful that even their joint advocacy could have produced a united Cabinet against continuation of the offensive, granted Robertson's unwillingness to give advice in accordance with his true feelings about the Flanders offensive. Without a united Cabinet there could have been no decision to stop it, and any attempt to stop it against military advice would have divided even those who were opposed to the campaign. (Milner, as we have seen, was adamant that military opinion, having been questioned, must ultimately prevail.)

Caporetto and the need to send troops to Italy might, on the face of it, have afforded a last chance to stop the fighting in Flanders. But by then the final assault on Passchendaele had begun; it would have been difficult to halt the operation at that point. Moreover it could plausibly be argued that pressure should be maintained in Flanders to discourage the Germans from turning their victory in Italy into an all-out invasion of the country. (In fact, there was never any question of their wishing to do this.)

Lloyd George felt the anguish of Third Ypres to the end of his life. His fury and indignation against the generals reflect his own sense of personal failure, that he of all people should have presided over such a shambles. He tried to convince himself that he had done all that was humanly possible to prevent it, but doubts never ceased to haunt him. In his memoirs he writes that 'Passchendaele could not have been stopped without dismissing Sir Douglas Haig', which would have caused Robertson to resign. This could not have been done 'without the assent of the Cabinet', most of whom 'were under the spell of the synthetic victories distilled at G.H.Q.'[37] Both statements amount to a confession of political weakness. Lloyd George is admitting that he could not have won his colleagues' support for sacking Haig, and that he could not have overruled the generals without incurring a degree of political and press odium that his government might not have survived.

What he fails to say is that he had, in effect, given *carte blanche* to the generals before the offensive began (despite the conditions ostensibly

37. *WM*, pp. 2222–3.

attached to the War Cabinet's formal assent) and that afterwards he never made a straightforward attempt to rescind it and halt the campaign. Weakness was, indeed, inherent in the nature of his coalition, but in this instance it was also partly in himself.

The various factors which placed Lloyd George at a moral and psychological disadvantage in his dealings with Haig have already been described, and in the autumn of 1917 another was added to them. When he visited Haig's headquarters in September, and sought his advice about the Kühlmann overture, Haig's response was commendably robust. At that moment, and on that issue, he was right when Lloyd George was in danger of making a false move. It was an irony that the soldier's judgement should have been sounder at the time on a question of policy, while the politician's was sounder on strategy.

A fortnight after he sent the War Cabinet's cordial message to Haig and his troops in Flanders, Lloyd George moved a resolution of thanks to the armed forces in the House of Commons. It was addressed to the army, navy and mercantile marine, and Lloyd George was particularly eloquent about the courage of merchant seamen and fishermen. He went out of his way, also, to praise the medical services, with special reference to nurses.

On the Ypres battle his words could hardly be construed as an unambiguous endorsement of Haig. On the contrary, they seem bitterly ironical:

the campaigns of Stonewall Jackson fill us with admiration and wonder. How that man led his troops through the mire and swamps of Virginia! But his troops were never called upon to lie for days and nights in morasses, and then march into battle through an engulfing quagmire, under a hailstorm of machine-gun fire. That is what our troops have gone through.

Haig himself was mentioned only after Lloyd George had deprecated 'singling out individuals' prematurely. There was a salute to 'the name, the great name of Kitchener', but among living commanders the Prime Minister made only a brief reference to three names together, French, Haig and Maude. In bracketing Haig with French he was paying the former no compliment that he could be expected to appreciate, all the more so since French had been called in to assess his performance. And to bracket him with Maude (who, incidentally, had only a fortnight to live) was to put him on a par with a commander of lower rank, in a theatre that he regarded as a sideshow.

Lloyd George had glowing words for the Royal Flying Corps, 'the knighthood of this war, without fear and without reproach – the chivalry of the air'. And he ended with a tribute to the army of the bereaved, the countless families whose lives had been darkened by the arrival of dreaded telegrams from the War Office: 'this great Empire owes you gratitude for your share of the sacrifice as well as for theirs, partakes in your pride for their valour, and in your grief for their fall.'[38]

When Riddell congratulated Lloyd George on this speech, he replied: 'Not bad perhaps, considering I had no time to prepare it.'[39] It was a striking speech by any standards, and not least in its difference, so far as Haig was concerned, from the 16 October message. Since then there had been further heavy losses in Flanders, while Passchendaele was still uncaptured. At the same time the Germans had smashed the Italian front in a matter of days. Lloyd George was preparing to make another attempt to impose his will upon the military, and his speech on the resolution of thanks showed that he was in a mood to speak the unspeakable.

38. Hansard, fifth ser., vol. xcviii: Lloyd George's speech, cols. 1237-49. Lloyd George introduced no names of naval commanders, but Asquith when he spoke suggested that Jellicoe and Beatty deserved honourable mention.

39. RWD, 31 October 1917. Nowadays the job would be done by a team of speech-writers.

16

Clemenceau

*Supreme War Council – Paris speech – Advent of Clemenceau
– Bolsheviks seize power*

Lloyd George had long believed that the Allies suffered, by contrast with
the Central Powers, from a lack of coherent staff-work and decision-making.
Each country acted essentially on its own. There was little will and no
machinery for evolving an overall strategic plan. As early as February 1915
he raised this issue on a visit to Paris, in conversation with the French
President, Raymond Poincaré. He 'called the President's attention to the
advisability of setting up a Council in France, with representatives from the
French, Russian and British Commanders-in-Chief, so that the latter may
be kept informed of the intentions and operations of their colleagues, there
being at present a lack of co-ordination between the Armies of the Allies –
which is an advantage to the German commander'.[1] Poincaré seemed to
approve of the idea, but was in no position to act on it. Nothing on the lines
envisaged by Lloyd George resulted for nearly two years.

At the beginning of August 1917 the idea of an Allied general staff was
proposed by Foch, and naturally taken up with eagerness by Lloyd George at
the Anglo-French conference in London on 7th–8th of the month. He even
discussed with Painlevé the idea of creating, at the same time, an Allied generalissimo in the person of Foch, but this had to be set aside while memories of
Nivelle were so recent. He concentrated, therefore, on the joint staff project, and
received backing for it in the reports by French and Henry Wilson. Haig was
against it and so, more strenuously, was Robertson, who regarded it as a direct
and deliberate threat to his own uniquely privileged position. And, as we have
seen, he was supported by several leading Conservative ministers, muttering
threats of resignation. Nevertheless Lloyd George brought the matter up
again during the Chequers weekend in mid-October. (It was the subject of his
informal discussion with Franklin-Bouillon and others in the long gallery.)

---

1. *The Diary of Lord Bertie of Thame, 1914–1918* (British Ambassador in Paris), ed. Lady
Algernon Gordon Lennox (2 vols., 1924), vol. i, pp. 107–8. He did not refer to Italy, because
Italy was not yet in the war.

Caporetto transformed the situation to his advantage, and he seized the opportunity to force the issue of closer Allied co-operation, with suitable institutions to give effect to it. He wrote at once to Painlevé proposing a two-fold structure, political and military: a council consisting of 'one, or perhaps two, political representatives of first-rate authority from each of the Allies', and a military staff to which naval and economic staffs might be added. The council was to advise the respective governments, not to supersede them, but the functions of the staff, as proposed by Lloyd George, clearly reflected his desire to reduce Robertson's power as the sole channel of professional advice. The new Allied staff, which was 'to remain in continuous session', was to consist of men who were not chiefs of the several general staffs and, while keeping 'in the closest touch with them', would give separate advice.[2] Painlevé immediately came over to London to discuss Lloyd George's scheme, to which he gave full support. Pétain, also, gave it his approval.

So fortified, and with the added convenience that Robertson was away in Italy, Lloyd George put his proposal to the War Cabinet on 2 November. It was agreed that the Allied council should consist of the Prime Minister and one other minister from each country; and the staff of one general officer from each, who in the British case was to be Wilson. It was also agreed that Lloyd George should leave at once for Italy to attend the Allied conference on the crisis there, at which a clear Anglo-French proposal would be presented.

During a brief interlude in Paris on the way to Rapallo, Lloyd George stayed at the Crillon. Haig came to see him there, having first visited Pétain at Compiègne. Lloyd George informed Haig of the War Cabinet's decision about the Allied war council and staff, and Haig, after reiterating his objection to the idea, accepted the *fait accompli*. The Prime Minister then complained of press attacks on him which he believed to have been inspired by the military. He said that he 'intended to make a speech and tell the public what course he had proposed and how, if he had his way, the military situation would be much better'. Haig fought back and claims to have given him 'a good talking to'. At noon Lloyd George suggested that they go out for a breath of fresh air, and together the two men walked from the Place de la Concorde to the Arc de Triomphe. Haig's comment afterwards is stupefying in its condescension and banality: 'Quite a pleasant little man when one had him alone, but I should think most unreliable.'[3]

2. DLG to Painlevé, 30 October 1917.
3. Haig diary, 4 November 1917. At the morning meeting the two were not tête-à-tête. Smuts and Maurice (and another general) were also present.

Esher, a Crillon regular, had sessions with them both, and describes the scene in the tea-room, where 'All Paris' was congregated: 'L.G. came down and walked among the people. The soldiers were gathered in groups, representing different "hates". Robertson's lot. Henry Wilson's lot. D[ouglas] H[aig]'s lot. It was comic.'[4] The fact that Haig's 'lot' are mentioned as distinct from Robertson's is significant.

Lloyd George took Smuts with him to Rapallo, because Smuts was no longer on the generals' side in the argument over grand strategy. He was now effectively on the Prime Minister's side. After Caporetto he wrote to Lloyd George:

The extent of the Italian disaster is not quite clear to me . . . but must in any case be great and may assume dimensions which may well frighten the Italians out of the war . . . our General Staff was not properly informed about the troop movements from Russia to the Italian front. But late as it is, I think we should do our duty and not let the Italians entertain the despairing feeling that they are left alone to bear the onslaught of both the Austrian and the German armies . . . We must not add Italy to our Serbian and Roumanian disasters.[5]

This was Lloyd George's language.

Incidentally, Smuts wrote the letter before leaving for South Wales on one of the strangest, though also one of the most successful, of his *ad hoc* missions. There was a dangerous strike in the coalfields, caused mainly by resentment at the combing-out of manpower for the armed forces or other forms of industrial work. Moderates among the miners' leaders felt that Smuts might turn opinion round, and Lloyd George responded to the suggestion. Smuts asked Lloyd George for advice, and was merely told 'Remember that my fellow-countrymen are great singers.' He took the hint and began his short address to a mass meeting at Tonypandy:

Gentlemen, I come from far away as you know. . . . I have come a long way to do my bit in this war, and I am going to talk to you tonight about this trouble. But I have heard in my country that the Welsh are among the greatest singers in the world, and before I start I want you first of all to sing me some of the songs of your people.

Immediately somebody struck up 'Land of Our Fathers', which was sung by all present 'with the deepest fervour'. They then remained standing and Smuts 'could see that the thing was over'. He needed only to add a few words:

4. Esher to Lawrence Burgis, 5 November 1917.   5. Smuts to DLG, 28 October 1917.

284

Well, Gentlemen! You know that the front is not only in France, [it] is just as much here as anywhere else. The trenches are in Tonypandy, and I am sure you are actuated by the same spirit as your comrades over in France ... no trouble you may have with the government about pay or anything else will ever stand in the way of your defence of the Land of your Fathers.

When he arrived back in London he heard that the strike had ended.[6] Within a few days he was on his way to Italy with Lloyd George.

The Supreme Allied Council and staff plan that Lloyd George took to Rapallo, with the War Cabinet's endorsement, had been drafted in the War Office by General Maurice, in the absence of his chief and mentor, Robertson. Maurice then travelled to the conference in the Prime Minister's party. But if Lloyd George hoped that Robertson would be reconciled to the scheme by Maurice's close involvement in its preparation, he was soon undeceived. As soon as the matter was raised on 7 November, Robertson got up and left the meeting, asking Hankey to record his gesture in the minutes. For such a public display of bloody-mindedness he might have expected to be sacked on the spot, if the Prime Minister had been subject to no political constraints. But it was precisely because Lloyd George felt unable to get rid of him by direct action that the indirect device of the Allied staff, with Wilson as British representative, was being pursued.

Though it had seemed that everything about the project had been agreed in advance with the French, there was a last-minute scare when Painlevé proposed that the French representative on the Allied staff should be Foch. Since Foch was Robertson's opposite number (though without his exceptional powers), and since Lloyd George was advancing the scheme partly as a means of circumventing Robertson, the nomination of Foch threatened to negate his efforts. If, as Painlevé intended, Foch was to combine the new post with that of French Chief of Staff, this would conflict with the scheme as drafted. Lloyd George therefore firmly resisted the proposal and it was decided, instead, that France's representative should be General Maxime Weygand. He would not be an independent adviser, as Wilson was meant to be, but no more than a mouthpiece of Foch, whose Chief of Staff he had been since 1914. Italy's chosen representative would also carry little personal weight, though for a different reason. He was to be Cadorna, for whom the appointment was a consolatory and face-saving move. The Americans were not yet involved, though it was hoped that they soon would be. (Lloyd George had seen General Pershing in Paris, at breakfast, and urged him to

6. *WM*, 1373–5, quoting Smuts's report to DLG.

come to Rapallo, but the General demurred in the absence of instructions from Washington.) The outstanding figure on the Allied staff that would be established at Versailles after the conference was, therefore, Wilson.

It is time to have a closer look at this strange man, who would have stood out physically in any company on account of his tallness and ugliness. An Anglo-Irishman from Co. Longford, he held strong views on Irish politics throughout his career, and these eventually cost him his life when, in 1922, he was assassinated by Sinn Fein terrorists on the doorstep of his London house. He showed no early signs of military promise, failing twice to get into Woolwich and three times into Sandhurst. At last he was commissioned, without examination, in the Longford Militia, transferring later to the Royal Irish Regiment and then to the Rifle Brigade. His first active service was against bandits in Burma, where he was badly wounded over his right eye. While recovering he worked hard for entrance to the Staff College and was admitted in 1892.

The Boer War gave him his first opportunity to shine. He returned from South Africa with a DSO and having served as assistant military secretary to Lord Roberts. Staff appointments soon followed in the War Office, and in 1904 he was made Commandant of the Staff College, with the rank of Brigadier-General. At Camberley his gifts as a communicator were displayed. He was a natural speaker, lucid in exposition, with a quirky humour and theatricality of style that made his lectures memorable. At this time he also formed an important friendship with Foch, then holding a similar position in France, and became committed to the idea of Anglo-French military co-operation. When, in 1910, he was appointed Director of Military Operations at the War Office, he was already a well-known and influential figure. One of his admirers during the pre-war period was Winston Churchill who, as First Lord of the Admiralty, regarded him as an officer of 'extraordinary vision and faith'.[7]

Some of his characteristics were less attractive. In particular, he was much given to intrigue, and his role in the Curragh affair in 1914, when his Unionist partisanship came into play, earned him the distrust of many, including the Prime Minister, Asquith. At the outbreak of war he went to France as sub-Chief of Staff to the BEF (British Expeditionary Force). In 1915 he served for a time as chief liaison officer with the French, before being given command of a corps, in which capacity his record was undistinguished. Haig had a poor opinion of him as a field commander, and also regarded him as excessively pro-French, in a double sense: too close to French senior officers, and too close to his fellow Anglo-Irishman, Sir John French.

7. Winston S. Churchill, *The World Crisis* (single-volume edition, 1931), p. 49.

When Lloyd George became Prime Minister he sent Wilson to Russia with Milner, and the General's report on the efficiency and morale of the Russian army was ludicrously sanguine. During Nivelle's time as French Commander-in-Chief he returned to the post of chief liaison officer, but after Nivelle's fall Pétain promptly asked for him to be withdrawn. For several months he was back in England, keeping in touch with his friends in high places, among whom Law, Carson, Milner and Lloyd George were the ones who counted most. Caporetto, and the Allied staff project, signalled a new phase in his career.

His easy command of French and long-standing friendship with Foch were obvious assets in the Versailles post, as were his lively intelligence and access to political leaders at home. But on the debit side his judgement tended to be erratic, and his capacity for making friends was matched by an equal capacity for making enemies. Not only was he an intriguer, he was also two-faced, and as time went on more and more of those who had dealings with him grew to distrust him. Lloyd George was a case in point. But in 1917 Wilson was convenient to the Prime Minister as a soldier of undeniable talent who seemed to be more in sympathy with his strategic views than with Robertson's or Haig's.

After the break in his journey at Aix-les-Bains, Lloyd George arrived in Paris at 10.30 on 11 November (Sunday), and spent the rest of the day mainly talking to French politicians. Next day he delivered the speech which he had been preparing at Aix, and on which he continued to work almost up to the last minute. The occasion was a lunch in his honour given by Painlevé in the tapestry-hung banqueting hall of the War Ministry in the rue Saint-Dominique. The large company, which included many senators and deputies, sat at separate tables. At Painlevé's, Lloyd George was accompanied by Churchill, the French Foreign Minister (Louis Barthou) and an Italian minister.

Lloyd George had warned Haig, before their walk to the Arc de Triomphe, that he intended to make a fighting speech, in effect appealing to the British people over the generals' heads. He was as good as his word. His argument was that the Allies had fought the war in a piecemeal fashion, never seeing it as a whole and planning accordingly. Thus in 1915 Serbia was allowed to fall, in 1916 Roumania, and now Germany had been left free to win another southern victory, against Italy. He applied balm to the Italians' bruised feelings, blaming the system – or lack of it – for their misfortune.

It is no use minimising the extent of this disaster. If you do, then you will never take adequate steps to repair it. When we advance a kilometre into the enemy's lines, snatch a small shattered village out of his cruel grip, capture a few hundreds of his soldiers, we shout with unfeigned joy. And rightly so, for it is the symbol of our superiority over a boastful foe and a sure guarantee that in the end we shall win. But what if we had advanced 50 kilometres beyond his lines and made 200,000 of his soldiers prisoners and taken 2,500 of his best guns, with enormous quantities of ammunition and stores? What print would we have for our headlines?

And he challenged in public the arguments with which he had so often had to wrestle in private:

I know the answer that is given to an appeal for unity of control. It is that Germany and Austria are acting on interior lines, whereas we are on external lines. That is no answer. That fact simply affords an additional argument for unification of effort in order to overcome the natural advantages possessed by the foe. You have only to summarise events to realise how many of the failures from which we have suffered are attributable to this one fundamental defect in the Allied war organisation. *We have won great victories. When I look at the appalling casualty lists I sometimes wish it had not been necessary to win so many.* Still, on one important part of the land front we have more than held our own. We have driven the enemy back. On the sea front we have beaten him, in spite of the infamy of the submarine warfare.

Much had been achieved, but if the Allies had acted together, and in time, their cause might already have prevailed.

As he came to the end of the speech Lloyd George admitted that his words were risky, but pleaded necessity:

Now we have set up this Council our business is to see that the unity which it represents is a fact and not a fraud. *It is for this reason that I have spoken today with perhaps brutal frankness, at the risk of much misconception, here and elsewhere, and perhaps at some risk of giving temporary encouragement to the foe.*

When he sat down Painlevé thanked him as the man who, 'by his energy, eloquence and ever-fruitful imagination supported, developed and untiringly stimulated the splendid effort of Great Britain and the Dominions'.[8]

Lloyd George's speech was delivered in English, which few among his audience understood. But, according to Hankey, it was such 'a wonderful oratorical performance' that 'you could have heard a pin drop most of the time'. A translation was afterwards read by Franklin-Bouillon (whom

8. Report in *The Times*, 13 November 1917; my italics.

General Wilson, in his droll way, nicknamed 'Boiling Franklin') but the speech 'lost a great deal in the reproduction in French'. Nevertheless its 'dire, sombre tones made a great sensation'. Most of the comments on it that Hankey heard were favourable, though there was some doubt that the new machinery would work, and a tendency to think that the real need was for an Allied generalissimo. This view was expressed by, among others, the former Foreign Minister Gabriel Hanotaux, next to whom Hankey sat at the lunch. Lloyd George was, of course, equally keen to achieve unity of command, but for the time being could go no further than a joint staff.[9]

The speech was by no means universally well received at home, as we shall see, and its immediate effect was to aggravate Lloyd George's difficulties with Robertson and the CIGS's political supporters, though among the general British public it probably strengthened his hand. In France, reaction to the speech was overwhelmingly favourable. A day or two later Esher spoke to General Huguet, the former French liaison officer at British headquarters, who said that in his country Lloyd George's 'sort of harsh frankness' was badly needed, and had given him a position that nothing could shake.[10] We may reasonably surmise that the speech helped to precipitate a development of momentous significance, by reminding Frenchmen of the value of tough and dramatic leadership in a time of crisis.

One of the French politicians whom Lloyd George saw the day before his speech was Georges Clemenceau. He went to see this formidable veteran at his flat in the rue Franklin and stayed with him for half an hour. The day after the speech Painlevé was defeated in the Chamber and resigned. Two days later Clemenceau was asked by the President of the Republic to form a new government. There was little love lost between Clemenceau and most of his fellow politicians, and this was abundantly true of his relationship with the President. But there was a compensating bond in that both men were thorough patriots. Faced, as he saw it, with a choice between Clemenceau and Joseph Caillaux, whose attitude to the war was suspect, Poincaré did not allow his personal animus to inhibit him from doing what was right for the country. He turned to Clemenceau, who promptly accepted the charge, and on 20 November the new government received the Chamber's endorsement by an overwhelming vote (418 to 65).

Winston Churchill was in Paris that day and witnessed the scene:

9. Hankey diary, 12 November 1917.   10. Esher diary, 15 November 1917.

[Clemenceau] ranged from one side of the tribune to the other, without a note or book of reference or scrap of paper, barking out sharp, staccato sentences as the thought broke upon his mind. He looked like a wild animal pacing to and fro behind bars, growling and glaring; and all around him was an assembly which would have done anything to avoid having him there, but having put him there felt they must obey . . . The last desperate stake had to be played. France had resolved to unbar the cage and let her tiger loose upon all foes, behind the trenches or in her midst. . . . With snarls and growls, the ferocious, aged, dauntless beast of prey went into action.[11]

Clemenceau's message was simple: 'Home policy? I wage war! Foreign policy? I wage war!' It was to be Churchill's own message when his country turned to him, in comparable circumstances, two decades or so later.

At seventy-six, Clemenceau in 1917 was eleven years older than Churchill in 1940. He had been a conspicuous figure in the life of the Third Republic since its inception. At that time he was Mayor of Montmartre, and he had been in Parliament, as deputy or senator, for most of the intervening years. There was, however, a gap of nine years (between 1893 and 1902) when he was out of Parliament and somewhat under a cloud. Like Churchill and Lloyd George, he had an adventurous temperament, and like them was attracted by similar characters, some of whom might be shady and disreputable. There were scandals with which his enemies tried to associate him, in the hope of breaking him politically. But he won through by sheer force of character, and because he was able to demonstrate that he was not financially on the make.

His origins were in western France, in the Vendée, where his ancestors were Protestant, only returning to formal Catholicism after the revocation of the Edict of Nantes. They were bourgeois who developed into landed gentry, but their Protestant antecedents showed in their support for the Revolution in 1789. There was also a strong medical tradition in the family. In the seventeenth century there were apothecaries among the Clemenceaus, and Georges's great-grandfather, grandfather and father all had degrees in medicine. He himself took after his father as a passionate republican and anti-clerical, and qualified as a doctor. In his early days he practised medicine in the country and in Montmartre, though politics soon took over as his life's work. He was a man of wide curiosity and sensibility. His mother was a devout Protestant, and this may account for a certain mystical dimension to his mind, which coexisted with his rationalism and fierce opposition to

11. Winston S. Churchill, *Great Contemporaries* (1938, repr. 1990), 'Clemenceau', pp. 310–11.

priestcraft. At the end of his life he took an interest in oriental religions. Something of his mother's spirit may have worked in him to mitigate the aridity of pure atheism.

He never cut himself off from his roots in the Vendée. He spent much time there in his last years, in a small cottage, and it is there that he is buried. Yet for most of his political life he represented a quite different part of France, the Var department of Provence in the south-east. At the same time he became a quintessential Parisian, with many contacts in the literary, artistic and theatrical worlds. Among artists he was particularly close to Claude Monet, and among writers Alphonse Daudet and Anatole France were special friends. His own writing was by no means confined to politics. He wrote a novel (heavily influenced by Zola) and a play which was performed in 1901, with incidental music by Fauré. His personality combined intense metropolitan sophistication with a deep attachment to what is called *la France profonde*.

He was also more international in experience and outlook than most politicians of his time, in his own or any other country. As a young man he visited the United States, where he taught at an academy for young ladies in Connecticut. With one of them, Mary Plummer, he fell in love, and in 1869 they were married. (There were three children of the marriage, but it was not a success and ended in divorce in 1892. He cannot be described as a good husband or father.) England was the foreign country he knew best, and he had English friends among whom Admiral F. S. Maxse and his family were paramount. Maxse, whose character is depicted in George Meredith's novel *Beauchamp's Career*, was a writer as well as a sailor, and a man of idiosyncratic political opinions. His son Leo was editor of the *National Review*, and his daughter Violet, who married Lord Edward Cecil, became Lord Milner's political confidante and, eventually, his wife. Through this connection Clemenceau was well acquainted with Milner before he came to power, a fact which was to have considerable importance in the months ahead. Violet Cecil has left a vivid account of the Clemenceau she loved and admired from childhood:

[He] was a vivid, dark man of medium height; he had a heavy moustache and expressive flashing eyes. He was vital to a degree, swifter in thought, wittier in talk, more unexpected in what he said, than anyone I ever knew. He had an immense power of entertaining and of being entertained, and this made him the most enchanting company. . . . A man of profound culture and, at the same time, a sportsman and a countryman, he was as much at home walking partridges, looking at a flock of sheep, or picking a wild flower, as in a museum or a theatre, and wherever he was he saw things in an individual way and called attention to them strikingly. . . . No one was ever such fun as he was. We hung upon his every word, and while we laughed and joked – being with him seemed to make us all witty – we leaned upon his judgement and, above all, upon his glowing affection and constant kindness.[12]

There was, of course, another side to Clemenceau, the side that earned him the nickname *Le Tigre*. He was a natural fighter, and his combativeness could take the form of duelling in the strict sense, as well as conflict in the political arena. It was said that he commanded general fear by his sword, his pistol and his tongue. During the early phase of his career his hostility was chiefly directed at right-wing opponents of the young Republic, but he also made numerous enemies among fellow republicans. Remembering the Commune, he had no time at all for the ideological left, and he later fell out with Jean Jaurès when the socialist leader paid lip-service to Marxism. In the 1880s he assailed the forward imperial policy of Jules Ferry, which he regarded as wasteful and vainglorious, and a distraction from the supreme duty of keeping France secure against Germany. He was opposed to anything that smacked of Bonapartism, an aberration which he believed had done the country infinite damage under the First Empire, and which, under the Second, had given Bismarck his chance to decoy France into a calamitous war.[13]

In or out of Parliament, Clemenceau always had an alternative political weapon in his use of journalism. He wrote for a succession of newspapers, several of which he also controlled, and his articles had all the force and pungency of his speeches. He had natural journalistic flair. It was he who chose the title '*J'Accuse*' for Zola's famous article on the Dreyfus case. Clemenceau's own fierce commitment as a Dreyfusard, which did much to restore his reputation after a difficult period, was inspired above all by his high sense of the French Republic's mission to the world. Unless it stood for justice and the Rights of Man it was, he believed, betraying its trust.

In 1906 he took office as Minister of the Interior and soon afterwards became Prime Minister. His first administration lasted until 1909 – a long period by the Third Republic's standards – and proved that a man hitherto known as a scourge and wrecker of governments was well able to conduct a government himself. In domestic affairs his pre-war premiership is notable for his firmness in dealing with any strikes that posed, in his view, a threat

12. Violet Milner, *My Picture Gallery, 1886–1901* (1951), pp. 62–3. By 1917 his hair and moustache were no longer dark but snow-white.
13. This was also the view of a man who profoundly admired Clemenceau, Charles de Gaulle. Some of de Gaulle's detractors, including unfortunately Roosevelt and Churchill, mistakenly suspected him of Bonapartist tendencies.

to the state. His attitude to trade union militancy earned him the lasting hostility of the socialists, who refused to join his wartime government. Yet he showed that he was a radical reformer in proposing a progressive income tax, old age pensions, a ten-hour working day and the nationalization of the western railway.[14] In foreign affairs he was cautious, negotiating the *entente* with Russia but at the same time going to some lengths to achieve better relations with Germany. Though convinced that war was in the long run inevitable, granted the ambitions of the German Empire, he was determined to avoid provocation and, above all, to do nothing that might forfeit British goodwill.

When war came the then Prime Minister, Viviani, offered him the Ministry of Justice, but he said that he would accept office only as Prime Minister or Minister of War. Later, when Briand tried to bring him into government, he refused again, this time insisting that only the premiership would satisfy him. Out of power, he reverted to the role of savage critic by which he had made his reputation, castigating the country's political and military leaders both in Parliament and in the columns of his paper *L'Homme libre* (which he renamed *L'Homme enchaîné* when it was subjected to censorship[15]). Enemy occupation of a substantial part of north-eastern France, and the dreadful toll of life in apparently futile campaigns, stirred him to mounting indignation and prompted his most famous *mot*, that war was 'too serious a matter to be left to generals'. Nevertheless he was at one with the high command in believing that the war had to be decided on the Western front. He was opposed at this time to sideshows such as Salonica.

As a member (from 1915) of the Senate's war and foreign affairs committees he obtained a lot of privileged information, of which he made ample use in his attacks on those conducting the war. Much of what he said or wrote was unfair, and some of the ideas he put forward were crackpot. Yet his attacks never ceased to command public attention, and no one could fail to be impressed by his combative spirit and burning faith in victory. When France needed him he was ready.

Hankey thought that Lloyd George had shown 'peculiar prescience' in visiting Clemenceau before making his speech in Paris.[16] It was certainly an opportune visit, but in fact Lloyd George did not foresee Clemenceau's advent to power, still less its imminence. He hoped to see a reconstruction of the French government under Painlevé, with Thomas taking his place as

14. The tax proposal was, in fact, blocked by the Senate until the outbreak of war.

15. Under his own government the censorship was somewhat relaxed, and the paper's original name was then restored.

16. Maurice Hankey, *The Supreme Command, 1914–1918* (2 vols., 1961), vol. ii, p. 729.

War Minister and Briand as 'the French "Bonar Law"'.[17] The sole purpose
of the visit to Clemenceau was to enlist his support for the Supreme War
Council project.

The two men had known each other for some time, though without
progressing beyond acquaintance. They had met at Carlsbad in the summer
of 1908, when the impressions each had formed of the other were markedly
different. Lloyd George had written to his uncle: 'Yesterday I had a long
talk with Clemenceau. I thought him on the whole the biggest man I had
met in politics since Gladstone. He is very anti-German but he always has
been pro-British. He has an extraordinarily high opinion of John Morley.'[18]
Clemenceau, on the other hand, had reported to his acolyte Stephen Pichon
that Lloyd George's ignorance of the political state of the peoples of Europe
and America was phenomenal.[19]

Lloyd George's retrospective account of the occasion is worth quoting:

I was having tea with Mr. T. P. O'Connor in his rooms. M. Clemenceau was known
to be taking his annual cure, and T.P. arranged a meeting. Soon after I arrived there
bustled into the room a short, broad-shouldered and full-chested man, with an
aggressive and rather truculent countenance, illuminated by a pair of brilliant and
fierce eyes set deeply under overhanging eyebrows. The size and hardness of the head
struck me . . .

We were introduced and he greeted me none too genially. I . . . was doing my utmost
to urge an understanding with Germany on the question of naval construction. . . .
M. Clemenceau referred to my efforts with scornful disapproval . . .

[The] interview was not a success. He made it clear that he thoroughly disapproved
of me. . . . It was years – eventful years – after this meeting that I discovered his
real fascination: his wit, his playfulness, the hypnotic interest of his arresting and
compelling personality.

At Carlsbad Lloyd George had given an interview to the *Neue freie Presse*
of Vienna, in which he expressed his desire for an Anglo-German *entente*
subject only to Germany's willingness to accept British supremacy at sea.
This was a condition that it was idle even to contemplate. Moreover, he said
nothing of the need to guarantee France's security, and it is understandable

17. Hankey diary, 11 November 1917. Lloyd George made these suggestions when Painlevé and
Franklin-Bouillon dined with him at the Crillon (Hankey also present). Thomas had not joined
the Painlevé government, for reasons analogous to Henderson's for leaving the War Cabinet.
18. DLG to Richard Lloyd, 13 August 1908.
19. Quoted in David Robin Watson, *Georges Clemenceau: A Political Biography* (1974),
p. 226. According to Clemenceau the conversation was not 'long', but lasted only 'five minutes'.

that Clemenceau regarded him as ignorant and naïve. In the attempt to educate him Clemenceau must have spoken with his usual force, causing Lloyd George to regard him at the time as a fanatical Germanophobe. But amends are made in Lloyd George's memoirs: 'events occurred that explained to me his apprehension of the menace as well as his detestation of the arrogance of German imperialism.'[20]

By 1917 Lloyd George's knowledge of the outside world – never so limited as it had seemed to Clemenceau at their first meeting – was greatly enlarged, and his toughness in regard to Germany had been proved, first in the 1911 Agadir crisis, and above all in three years of war. After brief initial hesitation he had thrown himself into the struggle and had since been the most dynamic figure in the British war effort. Clemenceau and he were like-minded in their pursuit of victory, and brought to the leadership of their respective countries a similar excitement and panache.

They had much else in common. Both were born rulers, and also born gamblers. Both had spent many years as Parliamentary *frondeurs* before gaining the chance to demonstrate their fitness to exercise power. Though Lloyd George was more than twenty years younger, and had reached the top more quickly, he too had arrived there after a longish period of political conflict and controversy, including some brushes with scandal. Both were genuine men of the left who were, however, resolutely opposed to socialism and, even more, to syndicalism. They were both patriots who felt that the authority of the state must be made to prevail over all sectional interests.

Both men were capable, when necessary, of great ruthlessness, but also had the saving graces of humour and simplicity. Both were at once formidable orators and men of action, who used words as accessory to deeds. Neither had any undue respect for the military or any other kind of supposed experts. Both had independent and imaginative minds, which could lead them astray but more often gave them a rare clarity of vision.

With so many affinities they might, in other circumstances, have become friends as well as working partners, but unfortunately their relationship never achieved that degree of closeness. Each recognized the other's exceptional qualities, and they found much to enjoy in each other's company. But there was never a perfect understanding between them, mainly because their national interests, as they perceived them, diverged.

In his memoirs Lloyd George pays Clemenceau a strong tribute: '[He]

---

20. *WM*, pp. 2678–9. Lloyd George came to Carlsbad after a visit to Germany, during which he combined a study of Bismarckian social insurance with a little freelance diplomacy. The latter aroused as much anxiety in Grey, the British Foreign Secretary, as in Clemenceau.

was the greatest French statesman – if not the greatest Frenchman – of his day.' He also says that the many exchanges of view he had with the French leader were 'amongst the most delightful and treasured memories' of his life. But he is unjust to Clemenceau on two crucial points. The first concerns his anti-clericalism. He was indeed a secularist (as was Lloyd George, at heart). He rejected Roman Catholic doctrine and asserted the supremacy of the French state against the pretensions of the clergy, as against those of any other 'trade union' (actual or metaphorical). But it is quite wrong to suggest, as Lloyd George does, that he was prejudiced against Roman Catholics in the public service or in the armed forces; specifically, that he was prejudiced against Foch. On the contrary, during his first premiership he made Foch head of the École Supérieure de Guerre, and later gave him plenty of support during the war. His post-war quarrel with Foch was on issues quite unrelated to religion.

More serious is Lloyd George's statement: 'He [Clemenceau] had no real interest in humanity as a whole. His sole concern was for France.' In saying this in his memoirs Lloyd George is almost paraphrasing J. M. Keynes's epigram, more often quoted: 'He had one illusion – France; and one disillusion, mankind, including Frenchmen and his colleagues not least.' Both comments depict Clemenceau as a narrow-minded Frenchman with no awareness of the outside world, and as a cynic about human nature. The description is grossly unfair.

Of course it is the primary duty of any national leader to uphold the interests of his own country, and Clemenceau did so with all his mind and heart. Whatever their rhetoric, Woodrow Wilson and Lloyd George did the same. Clemenceau was deeply patriotic, as they were, but he knew far more about their countries than they did about his, and in other ways, too, his outlook was far from narrow. France was rightly his first concern, and France, like other nations of long pedigree and splendid achievement, was no 'illusion', but a fact of enduring significance. As for 'humanity as a whole', Clemenceau's view of it was realistic but definitely not cynical. His love of country was combined with a belief in the civilized and humane values for which, he felt, the French Republic stood. At the same time he believed in power, without which – experience had taught him – fine sentiments were worthless.[21]

21. Lloyd George's quoted comments on Clemenceau are from WM, pp. 2683, 2686 and (for his alleged hostility to Foch on anti-religious grounds) 2871. The Keynes quotation is from Essays in Biography, p. 6 (in essay on 'The Council of Four'). This book was published in 1933, the volume containing Lloyd George's comments in 1936. To Keynes and other members of the Bloomsbury group patriotism was a vulgar emotion with no basis in reality.

Since France had suffered so much, and was so vulnerable, Clemenceau had to concentrate upon removing the invader from her soil and then insuring her future against the threat of a German revival. His principal partners could afford to entertain apparently more spacious and generous visions – Lloyd George of a world developing in peace and unity on the model of a liberal British empire, Wilson of a *pax Americana*. But the nature and quality of the man himself should not be misrepresented.

Like Painlevé, Clemenceau held the War Ministry as well as the premiership, but brought to both a personal authority of which Painlevé was incapable. He entirely dominated his government, appointing to it men of competence who were no threat to him politically and could be relied on to follow his lead. His private office was at least as important as the Cabinet itself. The key members of it were General Jean Mordacq for military and Georges Mandel for civil affairs. Mordacq was an officer who had kept him supplied with secret information since before the war; Mandel had come to his notice as a journalist on *L'Homme libre*.

Clemenceau continued to live at his flat in the rue Franklin, to which he nearly always returned to lunch and dine as well as to sleep. He regularly saw old friends and members of his family, either at home or in his office, but otherwise avoided all social activity. He had never had much taste for large parties or meeting strangers, and now more than ever felt the need to ration his time and protect his privacy. Like Lloyd George, he went to bed early and woke early. His day began working on papers between 5.30 and 7.30 a.m., when a physical training instructor arrived to put him through a routine of exercises and massage. He was at his desk in the War Ministry by 8.45 a.m.

Though his power was ostensibly less circumscribed than Lloyd George's, he felt the need to pay more attention to Parliament, visiting the Chamber or the Senate for an hour or so most afternoons. He also kept in closer touch with the army at all levels, above all by frequent visits to the front.

The change of leadership in France was preceded by a more dramatic change of regime in Russia, which was to overshadow world politics for decades to come, and whose consequences were acutely troublesome to Russia's Western allies. On 7 November (25 October in the Russian calendar), while the Allied leaders were meeting at Rapallo, the Bolsheviks seized power in Petrograd. Within three weeks the new rulers had applied to the German high command for an armistice. Lenin was convinced that Russian soldiers were no more willing to fight an international war for him and his cause than for the Tsar or Kerensky. His aim of world revolution remained constant, but the first priority was to take Russia out of the war. He was well aware that this would not give the Russians peace, since a bitter internal struggle was bound to follow, and he also knew that the Germans would exact a heavy price for leaving him free to impose his dictatorship at home. But, unlike some of his colleagues, he saw that the war with Germany must at all costs be brought to an end. A delegation was, therefore, sent to negotiate with the Germans at their headquarters at Brest-Litovsk.

To Lloyd George the fall of Kerensky and the collapse of Russia as a fighting partner came as no surprise. Since the failure of the July offensive he had discounted Russia's further effective participation in the war, and had even toyed with the idea of abandoning his Eastern ally if a satisfactory basis could be found for peace with Germany in the West. From this momentary lapse of judgement and conscience, precipitated by the Kühlmann overture, he had been saved by Balfour and the War Cabinet. Now, faced with the disappearance of Kerensky and Lenin's initiative in seeking a separate peace, Prime Minister and Foreign Secretary were from the first in close accord, though they had some difficulty in persuading colleagues to endorse their realistic response to a complex situation.

One matter of concern was that the British diplomatic mission and other British nationals should be protected, if only by the avoidance of any action which might make them a target for Bolshevik violence. It was also necessary to prevent the very large stores of equipment held up *en route* from Britain to Russia, mainly at the ports of Murmansk and Archangel, from falling into enemy hands. But above all it was vital that the Germans should not become free to transfer the bulk of their forces from East to West, and that they should not gain control of Russia's vast material resources, especially wheat and oil, so enabling them to break the Allied blockade.

At first Lenin's grip on power was largely confined to the Petrograd area – where it had come to him by default, Kerensky having dismissed and imprisoned the army commander, Kornilov, who alone might have provided a government strong enough to stop the Bolsheviks. Lenin needed time to consolidate and extend his power. He also hoped that revolution would soon spread to countries more 'ready' for it (according to the Marxist analysis) than Russia; in particular, to Germany and Britain. He therefore instructed Trotsky, leader of the Bolshevik peace delegation, to spin out the negotiations at Brest-Litovsk by seeking a general peace between all belligerents. This delaying manœuvre suited the Western Allies and gave them, paradoxically, an immediate common interest with a regime dedicated to their subversion and overthrow. Having obtained an armistice, Lenin was in no hurry to sign a peace with Germany which was bound to be truly Carthaginian; and the Allies, for their own reasons, were keen that the Brest-Litovsk bargaining should be indefinitely prolonged. In the event it lasted until March 1918, but meanwhile the armistice alone enabled the Germans to transfer ten divisions to the Western front.

There could be no question of granting the Bolshevik government even *de facto* recognition in the early stages. Quite apart from its ideologically aggressive attitude, its effectiveness and durability were highly doubtful. But Lloyd George favoured informal dealings for practical purposes, and also took the view – which Balfour, though by no means all of his colleagues, initially shared – that overt hostility would merely help the Bolsheviks to consolidate their power. His policy was adopted, and as a small gesture two Bolsheviks detained in Britain were returned to Russia.

Lloyd George was, of course, no friend to Bolshevism. Opposed to social-ism in any form, he naturally objected to it most strongly in the extreme and tyrannical form that Lenin represented. But he was well read in the history of the French revolutionary period, and had learnt from it that foreign attempts to scotch the Revolution in France only aggravated it and turned it into a greater menace. While he never ceased to keep a wary eye on potentially dangerous trends in the British labour movement, he had confidence in its fundamental good sense and patriotism, and rightly felt that its leaders would be more, rather than less, resistant to Russian revolutionary influence now that Kerensky had been superseded by Lenin. The Labour Party, not yet committed to socialism even in theory, remained part of his coalition, and Henderson, despite his resignation, could be depended upon to stand firm against Bolshevism.

The position in France was different. Much of the French left was *marxis-ant*, and the Socialists refused to serve in Clemenceau's government. More-over, the French bourgeoisie was more sensitive than the British to developments in Russia, since the French had a much larger financial stake in that country. (In 1914 French loans accounted for 80 per cent of Russia's external debt, and nearly 28 per cent of French overseas investment was in Russia, mainly in the form of state bonds.[22]) Clemenceau, for his part, was above all alarmed by the military implications for his country of a separate Russian peace with Germany before the Americans could arrive in strength. His diplomatic line with the Bolsheviks was, therefore, ostensibly harder than Lloyd George's, in that he regarded their armistice as a betrayal and insisted that they were precluded by treaty from negotiating a separate

22. Niall Ferguson, *The Pity of War* (1998), pp. 43–4.

peace. But this difference of approach was of limited significance and had little effect on the course of events. Realist that he was, Clemenceau could see the advantages of the Brest-Litovsk negotiations, while denouncing the Bolsheviks for entering into them.

17

The 'House Party'

The 'House Party' – Political challenge – Cambrai

Back in the summer, at Great Walstead, Lloyd George had devoted much labour to composing, with the assistance of Hankey and Kerr, a long letter to President Wilson, to be delivered personally by Reading. The letter was intended as an alternative to the face-to-face meeting that Lloyd George would have preferred. Granted the imminence of 'a very difficult period' and the need 'to take far-reaching decisions', the Prime Minister began by stating his view that it was essential for the heads of the British and American governments to understand one another. Seeking a personal relationship, he said that he did not wish his remarks 'to have an official character'.

After reviewing the recent course of the war and noting that the Germans were 'in possession of more and not less Allied territory', he discussed the reasons for this state of affairs. The main one, he admitted, was the collapse of Russia, but experience had convinced him that another was the lack of 'real unity' among the Allies. While Germany had established a 'practically despotic dominion' on the enemy side, among the Allies direction of the war had 'remained in the hands of four separate Governments and four separate General Staffs'.

He went on to develop his familiar argument that the strategy of mounting large-scale offensives on the Western front was no longer justified (though he oddly conceded that it might have been 'a sound policy at the outset'). The Central Powers were effectively besieged, and in a siege 'you do not seek out the strongest part of the enemy line but the weakest'. The weakest part of the enemy line was now 'unquestionably the front of Germany's allies' which were 'weak not only militarily but politically'. Moreover, since campaigning in the West was anyway possible only 'for six or at most seven months of the year', it was lamentable that no adequate effort had been made to 'achieve decisive results' in south-eastern Europe and Turkey during the period when Allied forces could not be employed on the main fronts.

To avoid further 'wasted effort and wanton loss of life' an improved system of war direction had to be found. In his view it would be 'necessary to establish some kind of Allied joint Council, with permanent military and probably naval and economic staffs attached, to work out the plans for the Allies, for submission to the several Governments concerned'.

This brought him to the role of the United States, a subject which he approached with care:

I fully appreciate the objections which the American people feel to being drawn into the complex of European politics. The British people have always attempted to keep themselves aloof from the endless racial and dynastic intrigues which have kept Europe so long in a state of constant ferment, and even today their main desire is to effect a settlement which will have the elements of peaceful permanence in itself, and so free them and the rest of the world from the necessity of further interference. These feelings must naturally be far stronger in America. I have not, therefore, the slightest desire that the United States should surrender the freedom of action which she possesses at present.

All the same, he felt that there were 'very strong reasons why the United States should consider whether they ought not to be represented at the Conferences of the Allies'. Such conferences would 'vitally affect the American army in Europe', but another reason weighed, he said, even more with him.

I believe that we are suffering today from the grooves and traditions which have grown up during the war, and from the inevitable national prejudices and aspirations which ... influence the judgment of all the nations of Europe. I believe that the presence at the deliberations of the Allies of independent minds, bringing fresh views, unbiassed by previous methods and previous opinions, might be of immense value in helping us to free ourselves from the ruts of the past ...

Yet another reason for American involvement in Allied councils was that people were increasingly thinking of peace and how to give it an enduring basis in the post-war world. In Lloyd George's view, two powers should accept and carry together the prime responsibility both for winning the war and for making the world safe afterwards:

If [victory] is to be obtained, it will only be because the free nations exhibit greater moral unity and greater tenacity in the last desperate days than the servants of autocratic power. The preservation of that moral unity and tenacity will be our principal task during the forthcoming winter, and I believe that it depends more and more upon the British Commonwealth and the United States. This does not mean, of course, that our Allies are not fighting as vigorously and valiantly as ever. It rather means that for one reason or another they have mobilised their national resources to the utmost point of which they are capable without having overthrown the enemy, and that consciously or unconsciously they rely upon the British and the Americans to supply that additional effort which is necessary in order to make certain of a just, liberal and lasting peace.

He ended by complimenting Wilson on his war speeches, which had been 'not the least important' of America's contributions to the cause of human freedom.[1]

Readers in the early twenty-first century will perceive in this letter the germ of what was to become a potent and pernicious theme in British foreign policy – the search for a 'special relationship' with the United States, or the assumption that one already existed. Lloyd George suggests to the President that they should correspond as though they were personal friends, rather than merely as heads of government. In showing his appreciation of America's reluctance to be 'drawn into the complex of European politics', he claims that it has also been Britain's traditional policy to stay 'aloof' from Europe. He looks forward to a peace based upon close Anglo-American co-operation.

No American president would have been likely to respond positively to such an approach. The American Republic existed by virtue of its rejection of all things European, and in particular British imperial power. Americans could not regard Britain as separate from Europe; to them it was pre-eminently involved in the Old World machinations that Lloyd George affected to spurn. Only America was, in that sense, regenerate. Against this basic prejudice even the common language and (for Americans of British descent) other shared traditions could not ultimately prevail. Besides, there were many Americans whose ethnic background was not British, in some cases instinctively anti-British in the present conflict. Above all, America was another continent, three thousand miles away, with an ideology and interests of its own.

Like any American president before or since, Woodrow Wilson had a world view which ruled out any arrangement such as that proposed by Lloyd George. It was unthinkable for him to treat Britain as an exclusive partner,

1. DLG to Woodrow Wilson, 3 September 1917. The letter was typed and signed in Downing Street, but composed at Great Walstead on 28–30 August. It went through many drafts; 'before we had finished one . . . [Lloyd George] would invariably get a "brainwave" and want a new one' (Hankey diary, 28 August 1917). Hankey was 'appalled' by one of Kerr's drafts (ibid., 30 August). In its final form the letter was approved by the War Cabinet.

and any policy that might help the British Empire even to consolidate, let alone expand still further, was in principle repugnant to him.[2] He would do nothing to encourage operations in the Middle East which were merely designed, as he thought, to promote British power in the area. His country was not at war with the Turks and he had no intention that it should be.

The prejudices Wilson shared with nearly all his compatriots were reinforced by his own character. He was a naturally autocratic man, who did not take kindly to the idea of working on equal terms with anybody. Least of all was he disposed to enter into a special relationship with a British prime minister of whose motives he was suspicious and whom he regarded as a potential threat to his own authority, even at home. Lloyd George had demonstrated that he was too like an American politician for comfort, with a capacity to appeal directly to American public opinion.

No reply was sent to the letter on which the Prime Minister and his aides had expended so much labour. But Wilson's reaction to it was expressed soon afterwards to his closest adviser on foreign affairs:

The President thought he could not go much further toward meeting Lloyd George's wishes than to express a feeling that something different should be done in the conduct of the war than had been done, and to say that the American people would not be willing to continue an indefinite trench warfare. . . . The difficulty is, Lloyd George's methods and purposes are not always of the highest. It is unfortunate not to have a government there composed of such men as Grey, Balfour and Cecil.[3]

2. American and Wilsonian double standards are drily remarked upon by the American historian David R. Woodward: 'The president's enthusiasm for Anglo-Saxon political and legal institutions did not imply a similar affection for the far-flung British Empire with its millions of subject African and Asian peoples. As opposed to that of the British, American leaders viewed their country's expansion from coast to coast and overseas in the Philippines and elsewhere as the fulfilment of America's civilising mission rather than conquest' (*Trial by Friendship: Anglo-American Relations, 1917–1918* (1993), p. 93). He might have added that the expansion from coast to coast had involved the virtual genocide of the American Indians.

In the Second World War Winston Churchill carried on a famous correspondence with Franklin D. Roosevelt, but he received no endorsement from Roosevelt when he proposed (at Harvard, in September 1943) that there should be a common Anglo-American citizenship after the war, with 'British and Americans moving about freely over each other's wide estates'. Roosevelt was, in fact, even more hostile to the British Empire than Wilson had been, and Britain's 'wide estate' was soon to go into liquidation.

3. House diary, 16 September 1917. The final remark reads oddly, because Balfour and Cecil were, of course, prominent members of Lloyd George's government. Presumably House was reflecting Wilson's regret that the British government did not consist exclusively of gentlemen-politicians, without the hustling Lloyd George at its head. (In reality Balfour was as ruthless as Lloyd George, if not more so.)

It was, to put it mildly, somewhat premature of Wilson to insist that the American people would not be willing to continue trench warfare. At the time there were still only about 80,000 American troops of all ranks in France, none of them as yet in the trenches. Even by the following spring only about 150 Americans had been killed on the Western front. It was not until September 1918 that the American Expeditionary Force (AEF) began to make a really substantial contribution to the fighting there, and by then the war was nearly over. Meanwhile the value of American military participation was psychological but little else.

The commander of the AEF, General John Pershing, would not allow any American units to be brigaded with British or French units in the lines. They had to form part of a separate, entirely independent American army. In this policy he had the full backing of his Commander-in-Chief, the President. (Pershing was a martinet and a man of rigid views, whose career had been helped by a politically advantageous marriage.) There was certainly a case for keeping American troops, like British and French, in their own national army, but only if the build-up could be rapid. In fact, it was unbelievably slow. If Wilson's intention had been to leave his European associates to carry on fighting while he conserved American strength and awaited the moment to impose a 'peace without victory', his actions – and inactions – would hardly have been different. Perhaps that was his intention, or perhaps he was merely a hopeless war leader. The truth may lie somewhere between the two explanations.

In the autumn of 1917 there were about a million conscripts under arms in the United States. But their equipment and training were inadequate and there was an acute shortage of officers. Even if the mass of conscripted manpower had been ready for action, the United States government was doing nothing about producing ships to transport the men to Europe. The assumption in Washington was that Britain, on top of all its other burdens, would provide the necessary shipping. Enemy ships in American ports had been impounded, as had the ships under construction for Britain in American yards. But these and other merchant vessels were not being mobilized for war purposes, and there was no plan to boost American shipbuilding to meet the demand for troop transports. Wilson 'was much more motivated by commercial considerations in questions of shipping than was the prime minister'.[4]

---

4. Woodward, *Trial by Friendship*, p. 117. This comment is important as that of an American historian, but is, surely, an understatement. Lloyd George subordinated commercial considerations almost totally to the requirements of war.

When his letter to the President was silently rebuffed, Lloyd George decided to try an indirect approach through House. At the end of September he asked Reading and Sir William Wiseman, the British intelligence chief in Washington, to propose to House that an initiative be taken on the American side to bring about closer co-operation across the Atlantic:

Would the President consider the advisability of sending plenipotentiary envoys to London and Paris, with the object of taking part in the next great Allied Council, bringing their fresh minds to bear on our problems . . . and also to arrange – if that be possible – for some machinery to bridge over the distance between Washington and the theatre of war?[5]

The response to this roundabout overture was positive, and a formal invitation was then sent by Balfour. In consequence, a high-powered American mission left for London at the end of October. Nine strong, it consisted of experts in all the principal fields of war activity, with a State Department official as secretary. The United States navy was represented by the chief of naval operations, Admiral W. S. Benson (the man who had said that his country might as well be fighting the British as the Germans), and the military member was the army Chief of Staff, General Tasker H. Bliss. The mission was led by Colonel House.

We must now take a closer look at this dapper, soft-spoken operator from Texas, whose role as presidential surrogate in foreign affairs anticipated that of Harry Hopkins or Averell Harriman in the Second World War. House's father was a self-made plutocrat, based in Houston but with wide-ranging interests. His ancestry was Dutch (the original form of the name was Huis) and he came to Texas when it still belonged to Mexico. During Edward's childhood the family lived for a time in England, and the boy attended a school at Bath – which must have been rather different from his next one, in Virginia, where he needed a pistol and a knife to hold his own with his contemporaries. His academic career ended with some time at a northern university, Cornell, prematurely curtailed when his father died and he felt obliged to return to Texas.

Politics was always his passion, but he did not seek to become a politician in the ordinary sense, allegedly for reasons of health but as much, perhaps, for reasons of temperament. Instead, he became a king-maker and power

5. Wiseman to Col. E. M. House, 26 September 1917. Wiseman was close to House, and often more concerned to keep in with him than to give faithful service to his own government. He was hostile to Lloyd George, and made considerable mischief about him with House and other leading Americans.

behind the throne, first in Texas and then at the national level. (A grateful governor of Texas bestowed on him the rank of Colonel, which stuck to him for the rest of his life.) In 1912 his party, the Democrats, had not held the Presidency since 1897, mainly because it had been dominated by the charismatic orator, William Jennings Bryan, whose cranky economic views did not appeal to the business community. Looking around for a candidate who might bring the party back from the wilderness, House decided – without having met him – that the Governor of New Jersey, Woodrow Wilson, was the man. When they met, a political alliance was forged which helped to win the Democratic nomination, and then the Presidency, for Wilson. It also made House a figure of national and, particularly after 1914, international importance. Wilson liked to conduct foreign affairs himself, with scant regard for the State Department. During the war, while America was still neutral, House visited Europe on his behalf, with a remit transcending that of any ambassador. In October 1917 House was Wilson's natural choice to head the mission to London.

The British government gave the 'House party' (as it was nicknamed) treatment befitting a state visit. The Colonel and his colleagues docked at Plymouth on 7 November, and when their train reached London (Paddington) at midnight Balfour was on the platform to greet them. Lloyd George was abroad until the 13th, but he dined with House alone on the evening of his return. Meanwhile House had been busy seeing important people in and out of the government, and other members of the mission had been meeting their opposite numbers in the various war-related departments. While he was in London, House stayed at Chesterfield House in Mayfair, which was put at his disposal by the Duke of Roxburghe, and where he was waited on by the Duke's cockaded servants. The others stayed at Claridges. On 11 November House lunched with the King at Buckingham Palace.

On the 20th there was a joint session of the 'House party' (minus, for some reason, House himself) and the War Cabinet, with the British chiefs of staff and other experts from the home side also present. Because of the size of the meeting, it was held not in the Cabinet Room but in the grander and more spacious Treasury Board Room. The main purpose of the occasion was to enable Lloyd George to expound to the visitors the British government's thinking on the war, with special reference, of course, to the American dimension. Before the meeting he discussed what he should say at breakfast with Milner, Smuts, Kerr, Reading and General Swinton (Hankey's assistant). The result was a powerful statement.

He began by noting a fact which 'lent an added interest to the gathering'. From the room in which they were meeting 'Lord North had decided and directed the policy which drove the Americans to revolt against the British Crown'. This he described as, from the British point of view, 'a cardinal error', from which, however, lessons had been learnt, bearing fruit in 'the British empire such as it is'. He then set about indicating ways in which, judging from 'three and a half years of war experience', America could best contribute to victory.

Vital and related spheres were manpower and shipping. It was most urgent that as many American troops as could be spared should be sent to Europe 'next year, and as early next year as possible . . . to enable us to withstand any possible German attack' – quite apart from the chance of defeating the enemy. They might think that they could 'work up' their army at leisure, and that it did not matter whether the troops arrived in 1918 or 1919. But he had to tell them that 'it might make the most vital difference'.

On the subject of shipping, he explained how stretched British resources already were:

Sixty percent of our shipping is engaged on . . . purely war service, for ourselves and our Allies. 2,600,000 tons of our shipping is devoted exclusively to helping the Allies . . . and half the time another 2,300,000 tons of shipping as well is directed to the same purpose. Now, we are a country more dependent upon imports than probably any other great country in the world. It is a very small country, as you have probably observed in crossing it, and a very thickly populated country. We only grow about one-fifth of the wheat we consume . . . Taking the barest essentials not merely of life, but of war, we have also to import a good deal of our ore and other commodities essential to our war equipment. Our exports have almost vanished, except war exports. I should like our American friends to realise what this means to us . . . we have stripped to the waist for war.[6]

From the ensuing discussion it was clear that the Americans did understand how much Britain was contributing, and that their own country was not doing anything like enough. All that the members of the 'House party' saw and heard in Britain made 'a deep impression' on them. Even the anglophobe Benson, while still viewing British sea power as 'a threat to American interests', did not dissent from the main thrust of the mission's report to

6. WM, pp. 3004–12; Charles Seymour, *The Intimate Papers of Colonel House* (4 vols., 1926–8), vol. iii, p. 248; Hankey diary, 20 November 1917. It was in the Treasury Board Room that Lloyd George had negotiated, in March 1915, an agreement with (most of) the leaders of organized labour, for the wartime acceptance of compulsory arbitration as an alternative to strikes, and the temporary suspension of restrictive practices, so permitting dilution.

Washington, to the effect that 'Germany might win the land war in 1918 unless America did more'.

Wilson appeared to agree, but in fact took no appropriate action. He did not give high priority to the building of ships in America, with a view to transporting troops to Europe. And he failed, as Commander-in-Chief, to accelerate the build-up of the AEF and so ensure that American troops were ready to play their part in resisting any large-scale German attack in the spring of 1918. Pershing was left, in effect, to carry on doing things in his own slow way.[7]

When Lloyd George and House dined together on 13 November, the Prime Minister asked the Colonel what, if anything, the President had in mind for American representation on the Supreme War Council. House immediately cabled Washington and the President replied: 'Please take the position that we not only accede to the plan for a single war council but insist on it, but think that it does not go far enough.'[8] What exactly he meant by this is not at all clear. To be really effective, the Council needed full American participation. But Wilson was not, and never intended to be, a proper ally of his European co-belligerents. The Council would, in his eyes, have gone 'far enough' only if it had become an instrument under his total control. Since it could obviously not develop thus, he was determined that America's share in its activities should be limited. He appointed Bliss as American military representative at Versailles – an excellent choice – but at the political level made no comparable appointment. He merely asked House to represent him at the first meeting of the Council, not on a permanent basis.

Wilson's reply to House's cable was helpful to the Prime Minister to the extent that it reinforced his defence of the Supreme War Council project at home. Pershing had declined to come to Rapallo in the absence of instructions from the President. At that stage, and until Wilson replied to House, America was in no sense a party to the project, a fact which could be used to discredit it. Lloyd George was under attack both for the scheme itself and for his speech commending it in Paris. He faced, as he later told C. P. Scott, 'an unholy alliance of the Generals' press and the partizan [i.e. Asquithian] Liberals'; or, as L. S. Amery put it, a 'Cocoa and Old Port cabal'.[9] Hostility in the press was reflected in Parliament, where opposition Liberals and the

7. Woodward, *Trial by Friendship*, pp. 119–22.
8. Wilson to House, 16 November 1917. The President's reply was paraphrased by House in a statement released for publication (*The Times*, 19 November 1917).
9. Scott diary, 16–19 December 1917; Amery diary, 16 December 1917. Lloyd George was grateful to Scott for not joining in the hue and cry against him.

sort of Conservatives always resentful of political interference with the military formed an anomalous front against Lloyd George. On his initiative, the matter came to a head in a short but significant Commons debate on 19 November (the day before the War Cabinet and the House mission held their joint meeting). Though Asquith opened the debate, it took place not on an opposition motion but on the adjournment, and was not followed by a vote. It was, however, seen as a trial of strength.

The strength proved to be on Lloyd George's side, not least because he made a highly effective, if disingenuous, speech. Asquith's was far from being the wounding challenge that his supporters – and Robertson – would have wished. Riddell described the speech well, in lawyerly terms: 'Mr. A. opened the case like a counsel who says in consultation, "we will open tenderly, and wait and see what the other side do and how the judge and jury take the opening statement".' That kind of speech was, in Riddell's view, 'useless'.[10]

Lloyd George was on the front foot throughout. He noted that Asquith accepted the need for greater co-operation between the Allies, and was complaining only of details in the proposed new machinery, while denying that the Allies had suffered 'substantially' from the previous inadequate system – for which he acknowledged his share of responsibility. But he insisted that a heavy price had been paid, and defended the instances he had given in Paris. At the same time he made a clever debating point to counter the (well-founded) accusation that his scheme was designed to undermine the existing military chiefs:

May I just point out that the illustration upon which I dwelt most is . . . Serbia. That took place in 1915. Sir Douglas Haig was not then commander-in-chief; Sir William Robertson was not chief of the staff . . . I was simply using the illustration in order to show the same common defect . . . without any reference to individuals, but purely in order to prove that the lack of coordination amongst the Allies had brought disaster . . .

Meeting the demand addressed to him (in the *Star*) 'Hands off the British Army', he claimed to have given the generals consistent backing. 'No soldiers in any war have had their strategical dispositions less interfered with by politicians.' He had backed them with deed rather than with speeches, because speeches were 'no substitute for shells'. Only twice had he acted against the soldiers' advice:

10. *RWD*, 24 November 1917.

The first occasion was with the gun programme. I laid down a programme which was in advance of the advice of soldiers and against it. They thought that I was manufacturing too many and was extravagant . . . I took a different view, and there is not a soldier today who will not say that I was right. . . . The second case . . . was in the appointment of a civilian to reorganise the railways behind the lines – my right hon. friend [Sir Eric Geddes, now First Lord of the Admiralty] – and I am proud to have done it. There is not a soldier who will not say that he is grateful that I pressed my advice . . .

Justifying the tone of his speech in Paris, he argued that public opinion had to be aroused in support of the Supreme War Council, and arousing public opinion was never easy:

I may know nothing about military strategy, but I do know something of political strategy, and to get public opinion interested in a proposal . . . is an essential part of political strategy. That is why I did it . . . I might have gone over there and delivered a speech – passing eulogies upon the armies, upon generals, upon governments, and upon peoples; and they would have said – probably civility would have made them say it – 'That is a very fine and eloquent speech'. But it would not have had the slightest effect. So I set out to deliver a disagreeable speech, that would force everybody to talk about this scheme. They have talked about it, throughout two or three continents, and the result is America is in, Italy is in, France is in, and Britain is in – and public opinion is in . . . That is all I wanted.[11]

In a rather scrappy debate that followed the oddest feature was a long, and apparently unpremeditated, speech by Carson, in which he said that Lloyd George was 'absolutely right' in his main object, but 'absolutely wrong in some of the arguments to prove its necessity'. Despite this unhelpful intervention by a War Cabinet colleague, Lloyd George had by general consent scored a triumph with his speech. Sitting beside him on the bench afterwards Addison congratulated him and remarked that he had never shown to greater advantage. With his 'usual skill' he had been careful not to 'emphasise the points of his speech that were most open to criticism'. Addison expressed admiration for what he had said 'and, even more, for what he had *not* said'. Lloyd George 'turned round with a twinkle in his eye, and said: "Yes, the camouflage wasn't bad, was it?"'[12]

11. Hansard, fifth ser., vol. xcix; report of the whole debate, cols. 883–971; Lloyd George's speech, cols. 893–906.
12. Addison diary, 19 November 1917.

The camouflage consisted of pretending that the Supreme War Council was not a new proposal by him, but the resurrection of one first made by Kitchener (in Tory eyes, a totemistic figure);[13] that he had no intention of pursuing the idea of an Allied generalissimo; and that he did not regard the British military representative at Versailles as a rival to, or substitute for, the CIGS. On the last point, he had faced a threat of resignation by the whole army council, including the Secretary of State, which he had averted only by agreeing (with some amendments) to terms set out in a letter to him from Derby on the eve of his Commons speech. The terms were these:

1. All questions [changed by Lloyd George in pencil to 'proposals'] to be discussed at a Supreme General Council will be initiated by the respective Governments, and will not be put before the Supreme Council until, in our case, the War Cabinet has had it in front of them, and heard the opinion of the CIGS on the proposal.
2. The Allied Staff shall have no power of initiation of ['independent' inserted] proposals unless ordered to do so by the Supreme Council themselves, and any ['such' inserted] proposal they may wish to make should follow the same procedure as in (1).
3. The CIGS will accompany you to any meetings of the Supreme Council whenever a decision has to be arrived at on military matters.
4. The Allied General Staff will give their advice as a whole, and not as individuals.[14]

A threat of resignation by Derby alone would not have needed to be taken too seriously. His threats to go were almost routine, and anyway he said that on this issue he would accept the ultimate decision of the War Cabinet. But the possibility of a walk-out *en bloc* by the military members of the army council could not be ignored. The effect of such a development on Conservative back-benchers, and even some Conservative ministers more resolute than Derby, was incalculable. Lloyd George was, therefore, probably right to feel that he had to make some gesture to Robertson, via Derby. It did not amount to much. The terms accepted in the letter added very little to the limitations imposed on the Allied staff, and in particular its British

13. This was true in a sense – Hankey had made a last-minute discovery in the records – but Kitchener's conception of an Allied war council would have been very different from Lloyd George's. He would have wished it to be a means of extending his own control of strategy, rather than an alternative source of advice to the civilian leadership.
14. Derby to DLG, 18 November 1917. The points are ticked and initialled by the Prime Minister, as amended.

member, under the Rapallo agreement, and Robertson's position was only marginally enhanced. On balance, Lloyd George emerged the winner from what was to be only the first round in a prolonged contest with Robertson and his political friends. He had gone as far as he could, at the time, towards establishing improved machinery for Allied co-operation, and in doing so he had carried public opinion and, more grudgingly, majority opinion in Parliament with him.

The day of the Anglo-American business meeting in Whitehall was also a notable day on the Western front. Since September Haig had been planning an attack different in kind from Third Ypres and in a different sector of his line. On 20 November he launched what is known to history as the battle of Cambrai. Needless to say, no advance notice of this was given to Lloyd George and his colleagues; still less were they asked to rule on its expediency. Even Robertson heard about it only on the last day of October, and of course he did not see fit to share the information with the War Cabinet. That the nation's constitutional leaders should be so treated, and so taken by surprise, is hardly to be wondered at, granted the ingrained habits of the high command. What is far more remarkable is that the attack totally surprised the enemy.

It took place in the Somme sector, south of Arras, where the line was held by the Third Army under the command of Sir Julian Byng. Byng had led the Canadian corps in its brilliant feat of arms at Vimy in April, and had soon afterwards been appointed commander of the Third Army in succession to Allenby. For the Cambrai operation he had at his disposal the Tank Corps, which had been in existence (in fact though not in name) for just over a year, and whose Chief of Staff was an officer of exceptional talent and imagination, Colonel (later General) J. F. C. Fuller. Byng's plan was to use massed tanks and six divisions of infantry to break through the Hindenburg defences, five and a half miles deep, and then to bring five divisions of cavalry forward to capture Cambrai and fan out beyond to the north and east.

Fuller thought the plan far too ambitious. He favoured a mere raid in strength to show that the Hindenburg line was not impenetrable and to take as many prisoners as possible, so shaking German morale. Even Haig suggested an advance only to Bourlon ridge, not to Cambrai and beyond. But characteristically he did not impose his thinking on Byng, just as he had failed to back his own view, before the battle of the Somme, that the British attacking troops should not go forward in line abreast, and just as he had failed, before Third Ypres began, to press on Gough his fears about enfilade from the Gheluvelt plateau. He was always too reluctant to modify an army commander's plan, particularly when it erred on the optimistic side. There was a persistent tension in him between shrewd practical intelligence and reckless temperament, in which his temperament usually prevailed. So, in this case, the Byng plan went ahead, subject to the proviso, reminiscent of Nivelle, that it would be stopped if it did not succeed within forty-eight hours.

Tanks had already been used, prematurely in the Somme battle, and in hopelessly unsuitable conditions in Flanders. But in the Cambrai area the ground was hard and not, as yet, cratered by endless shelling. The weather also was good for the time of year. Under cover of darkness a great force of 476 tanks mustered in Havrincourt wood, a convenient feature enabling the vehicles to escape detection. At the same time a thousand guns, equally unobserved, moved into position. At 6.20 a.m. the guns opened a sudden, brief, terrific barrage of smoke, high explosive and shrapnel. The tanks then trundled into action, with infantry in close support. The thick new barbed wire of the Hindenburg defences was crushed, and the specially wide trenches were crossed with the help of fascines (bundles of brushwood) lowered into them from the tanks.

Formidable as it was, the German line was lightly held by troops not expecting any blow to fall on them. At first the attack was almost entirely successful, only faltering where one divisional commander sent his men forward in line abreast, ignoring Fuller's request that they should advance in single file. By early afternoon on the 20th the Hindenburg defences were breached to a depth of four and a half miles, with two German divisions routed and many prisoners taken, at the cost of 4,000 British casualties. But 179 tanks were lost, mainly through mechanical breakdown, and above all the British victory was not exploited. The cavalry did not arrive before nightfall, and would in any case have soon run into trouble, because mounted troops were inappropriate to the conditions of war on the Western front. Byng's army needed infantry reserves, but these did not exist because of the heavy losses in Flanders and the despatch of divisions to Italy.

The Germans rushed reinforcements to the scene, and within forty-eight hours Haig halted the advance towards Cambrai on the right. But he could not bring himself to abandon the attempt to capture Bourlon ridge, which like another ridge (Passchendaele) came to obsess him. The battle was therefore disastrously prolonged until 7 December.

Meanwhile the Germans delivered effective counterattacks from the south and north of the salient created by the British advance. When the battle ended British casualties had multiplied more than tenfold from the first day, to 45,000, for the gain of only a small salient – which did not even include Bourlon ridge – and with the offsetting loss of some ground to the south.

German casualties were on roughly the same scale as British, but in the end Cambrai turned out more satisfactorily for the enemy.

Disappointment at home in Britain was acute, and all the more so because first news of the battle had been greeted with excessive rejoicing. The Bishop of London, Dr A. F. Winnington-Ingram, a militantly patriotic prelate, ordered that the bells of St Paul's should be rung, and the cathedral's example was followed by other churches in London and throughout the country. When the outcome of the battle was known it served not to repair the effects of Third Ypres on national morale, but to compound them.

Byng's plan was certainly defective, but Haig cannot escape ultimate responsibility for the failure at Cambrai. To have any chance of achieving a big result the battle should have been fought earlier (as Fuller wished), when infantry reserves would still have been available. In late November it was a doomed enterprise. The idea of exploiting a breakthrough with cavalry was absurd, and it is a sadly apt irony that the only contribution made by the cavalrymen to the battle was dismounted, helping the infantry to resist German counterattacks.

It was, of course, encouraging to know that the Hindenburg defences could be breached, and the new artillery techniques employed at Cambrai proved their worth. Accurate, unregistered bombardment by massed guns was, indeed, even more of a potential war-winner than the tank. But the demonstration of it at Cambrai was of double-edged significance. Whereas the Germans had no tanks, and could therefore learn no lessons in the offensive use of them, there was no shortage of guns in the German army, and in that respect the enemy undoubtedly benefited from the experience of Cambrai. Ludendorff says in his memoirs that the battle provided him with 'valuable hints for an offensive battle in the West, [should he wish] to undertake one in 1918';[15] and he probably had in mind the nature of the preliminary British barrage as well as the counterattacking methods used by his own infantry.

Lloyd George was understandably furious about Cambrai, and he was not alone. Haig had sought to justify his prolonged attritional campaigning in Flanders by repeated assurances that the German army was on the point of collapse. Cambrai dramatically and comprehensively belied such claims. Lloyd George asks a pertinent question in his memoirs:

The German Army whose divisions, we were assured, had all been used up by the great offensive, was able to muster 14 divisions to overwhelm our scattered and tired

15. Erich Ludendorff, *My War Memories, 1914–1918* (2 vols., 1919), vol. ii, p. 497.

troops. Five of these divisions had been transferred from the Flanders battle area, and nine from other portions of the Western Front. These they could spare in addition to the six divisions that had already gone to Italy and the five divisions that had captured Riga. How could they have raked up three separate striking forces of 25 effective divisions . . . after a battle of 14 weeks' duration, which we were assured had shattered their Army in the West and destroyed their reserves?

And he argues that Haig's strategy had queered the pitch for 1918:

Had there been adequate reserves to throw in, Cambrai would have been captured, the German defence system would have been dislocated, a new retirement would have been imposed on the enemy, and the time and strength he devoted to prepare his [1918] offensive . . . would have [had] to be spent in reorganising his own defences. One-fourth of the men flung away so profligately at Passchendaele would have sufficed to win this signal victory, and to exploit it.[16]

Such a hypothesis can never be proved, and, however accomplished, the eventual defeat of the German army was bound to involve heavy cost. But Lloyd George's contention that Haig's strategy in the latter part of 1917 made the cost heavier than it need have been, while placing the British at a disadvantage for the next phase of the struggle, has undeniable force.

There is, indeed, corroboration of Lloyd George's argument in a letter written at the time by Robertson to Plumer:

The Germans have brought down 19 [Lloyd George's later figure was 14] divisions to the Cambrai front since Haig attacked and as you know *his troops were pretty well used up in the Ypres salient and therefore he is rather hard put to it to hold his own.* As a matter of fact the incident is not altogether without value for *I think it has taught the people in France that the German still has a good deal of fight in him. The diminution of German morale has been greatly overdone at General Headquarters.*[17]

Since the supposed destruction of the German army's fighting spirit was the principal argument used by Haig to justify his persistence with Third Ypres, Robertson's comment could hardly be more damning.

One important side-effect of Cambrai was that it ended Northcliffe's love affair with Haig and the high command, which already showed some signs of cooling. Though still ready to attack the government on many counts,

16. WM, pp. 2255-6.   17. Robertson to Plumer, 10 December 1917; my italics.

the press lord was now prepared to support it against the commander whose devoted champion he had formerly been. He gave qualified backing to Lloyd George's Supreme War Council initiative, and after Cambrai wrote to Haig's secretary, Sassoon, that the question was being asked 'what [was] the use of sending out men to be Cambrai-sed?'[18] For the Prime Minister, Northcliffe's support was a mixed blessing, and for a time it seemed that Robertson might be saved by a Northcliffe vendetta, as Kitchener had been in 1915. But on balance the press lord's change of heart was a bonus, all the more so as it reflected the change in public opinion which Lloyd George's Paris speech had helped to create.

Robertson's reprieve was temporary, but two factors combined to save Haig. The first was that he allowed drastic changes to be made in his headquarters staff, his loyalty to subordinates proving in the end less strong than his instinct for survival. The first casualty was Charteris, his Director of Intelligence, who had long attracted criticism for the oversanguine content and tone of his reports. When it became apparent that almost everyone was against him, not only Lloyd George and the War Cabinet, but Robertson, Derby and Haig's Chief of Staff, Kiggell – who said that Charteris was 'much disliked in Corps and Armies'[19] – Haig at length accepted his resignation, though he stayed on at GHQ as an adviser and companion. By the end of January 1918 Kiggell too had gone, and his deputy as well. Kiggell's replacement as Chief of Staff was Sir Herbert Lawrence, who had briefly succeeded Charteris as Director of Intelligence. In addition, new appointments were made in the posts of Quartermaster-General, Engineer-in-Chief and Director-General of Medical Services in Haig's command. It was virtually a clean sweep.

Yet the man at the top remained. Though he often insisted that he was responsible for his subordinates, and for any advice of theirs that he chose to take, he did not ultimately act on the principle. They went; he stayed. However much he may have believed in them, he believed in himself more. After Cambrai he challenged Lloyd George, through Robertson, to back him or sack him: 'I gather that the P.M. is dissatisfied. If that means that I have lost his confidence, then in the interests of the cause let him replace me at once. But if he still wishes me to remain, then all carping criticism should cease, and I should be both supported and trusted.'[20] Lloyd George would

18. Northcliffe to Sassoon, 13 December 1917. Northcliffe's conversion cost him the services of *The Times*'s famous military correspondent, Charles à Court Repington, who resigned in January 1918.
19. Haig diary, 9 December 1917. Yet another critic of Charteris was Lady Haig.
20. Haig to Robertson, 9 December 1917.

have liked to replace him, and the Field-Marshal's stock was certainly lower than it had ever been. But who was to succeed him? Early in the New Year Smuts and Hankey were sent on a visit to the front, partly to make discreet enquiries and form a view as to who might take Haig's place. They returned without any plausible candidate. Even if a name had been produced, it would have been very hard to make the change. But no name was offered to the Prime Minister, and he had no hunch of his own.

In fact, it was probably just as well that Haig kept his job at the beginning of 1918. He had done his worst in the months just past; in the months ahead he would appear at his best.

18

Allied Conclaves

Allied conclaves – Lansdowne letter – Mensdorff

Colonel House and his mission left London on 22 November, to arrive in Paris a week before the two major Allied conferences scheduled to take place, there and at Versailles, at the end of the month. The Americans were keen to show that, far from being in exclusive cahoots with the British, their relationship with France was at least as 'special' as with Britain. House in particular wanted to establish a good personal rapport with the new French leader, and in this he succeeded. The two men immediately got on and the bond of affectionate regard between them proved enduring. (Clemenceau later described the Colonel as 'a super-civilized man escaped from the barbarism of Texas'.[1])

Before Lloyd George arrived, nearly a week later, House had several meetings with Clemenceau, at which the French leader stressed the critical need for more fighting men on the Western front in the coming year. Only the Americans were in a position to make good the Allies' manpower deficiencies, and he urged House to persuade the President at all costs to expedite the training and despatch of United States troops. House undertook to do this, but his ability to influence Wilson's actions was by now more limited than Clemenceau knew, or than he himself realized.

At one meeting House asked Clemenceau and Pétain how far they accepted the organization of the Supreme War Council as devised by Lloyd George. Both replied that they were against it, and put forward instead the idea of a council composed of the national commanders-in-chief and chiefs of staff, with a single executive to give effect to its decisions – in other words, an Allied generalissimo. When General Bliss suggested that this role might belong to a chairman of the Council chosen by the Council itself, Pétain agreed, but with the proviso that 'there might be emergencies' in

1. 'Un surcivilisé échappé des sauvageries du Texas' (Georges Clemenceau, *Grandeurs et misères d'une victoire* (1930), p. 124). In fact, House remained more Texan at heart than Clemenceau supposed.

which the chairman would have to act more or less independently, with only the briefest consultation with other members. Both he and Clemenceau indicated that their plan would eliminate the level of political control.[2] Clemenceau at this stage was apparently prepared to make a big sacrifice of his own authority in the military sphere, in order to secure the prize of a unified command to be exercised, in all probability, by a Frenchman (and he may have been counting, as well, on his personal capacity to influence a French generalissimo).

Lloyd George left Charing Cross at 8.25 a.m. on 27 November, with a party of more than a hundred. As well as a British contingent including (among others) Balfour, Milner, Reading, Maclay, Geddes, Robertson, Henry Wilson and Northcliffe, there were also various foreigners: Admiral Sims and other representatives of the United States navy, some Japanese soldiers and diplomats, and a Greek delegation led by Venizelos. Northcliffe was invited to come along partly because of his knowledge of America and friendship with House, but also no doubt partly to keep him out of trouble at home.

In Paris the British delegation stayed at the Crillon, on the same floor as the American. House lost no time in tackling Lloyd George about the matters he had discussed with Clemenceau, but the Prime Minister was adamant that the military representatives at Versailles should not be the chiefs of staff, and that for the time being there could be no question of a generalissimo under any guise. At his first talk with House, the evening of his arrival, Lloyd George seemed to the American more flexible on the subject of political control, but in fact he was only willing to consider *ad hoc* meetings of heads of government as an alternative to regular meetings on set dates. In principle he stood firm on the terms of the Rapallo agreement, among which political control was an essential item. He made it clear that unless the agreement were implemented he would leave Paris at once.[3]

House claims to have persuaded Clemenceau next day to fall in with Lloyd George's wishes 'because of his difficulties at home', but we may be sure that Clemenceau would have done so in any case. Whatever his reservations about the War Council scheme as agreed to by his predecessor, he cannot for a moment have regarded it as a good issue on which to have a serious quarrel with the British Prime Minister. Britain was France's principal, and for the time being only effective, ally. Without the British

2. Conversation of House and Bliss with Clemenceau and Pétain, 25 November 1917 (recorded in a memorandum by House).

3. Hankey diary, 27 and 28 November 1917; Henry Wilson diary, 27 November 1917.

army France could not have held the Germans for the past two years or more, and in the dangerous months ahead, while America was only a token presence, the British army would be more important than ever. Clemenceau might find House easier to deal with than Lloyd George, but House was not a head of government or even a representative with full powers. The most that could be said of him was that he was a glorified listener and observer, reporting to a distant potentate who would not delegate any part of his political authority. (House had none of the freedom, in the political sphere, that Wilson as Commander-in-Chief allowed Pershing in military matters.) Lloyd George on the other hand was, like Clemenceau himself, a head of government, and one whose exigencies were of cardinal and immediate relevance to France. Besides, Clemenceau could not object to Lloyd George's motives at Rapallo, and understood well enough that he was moving as far and as fast as he could towards unity of command.

The first conference to be attended involved representatives of all the Allies, great and small. This omnium gatherum had been in contemplation for some time, and had been postponed at least twice. The countries represented at it were France, Britain, the United States, Russia, Italy, Japan, Belgium, Serbia, Montenegro, Greece, Roumania, Portugal, Brazil, China, Siam, Cuba and Liberia. Not all of those present could expect to carry much weight. The Russian delegation was led by an ambassador appointed by Kerensky, whose credentials had never been accepted. Some of the countries were playing so small a part in the war, either intentionally or through force of circumstances, that their opinions hardly counted. The main purpose of the conference was to show the world that a large and diverse league of nations was already in existence, committed to defeating the Central Powers and (perhaps) creating a better world. It thus anticipated the plenary side of the Peace Conference in 1919, just as the Supreme War Council anticipated the Council of Four.

The international conference met in plenary session at the Quai d'Orsay (French foreign office) at 10 a.m. on 29 November. The weather was cold, but there was 'quite a crowd' outside and 'the watchers raised discreet cheers when men like Mr. Lloyd George, M. Clemenceau and General Foch passed, men whose features had become familiar through the Press'.[4] Inside, in the Salle de l'Horloge, 120 people assembled, 'of every imaginable race and colour'.[5] Clemenceau was in the chair and opened the proceedings. Had this task fallen to Briand, the audience would have been treated to a speech of considerable length and high eloquence, but Clemenceau was determined

4. *The Times*, 30 November 1917.   5. Hankey diary, 30 November 1917.

to get through the general meeting as quickly as possible and then break the conference up into working committees. His speech was short and to the point, ending: 'The noble spirit which animates us must be translated into action. The order of the day is work. Let us get to work (*Travaillons*).'

The work of the resultant committees was, however, of limited interest to Clemenceau and the other leading Allied figures, whose thoughts were now turning to the Supreme War Council, due to meet at Versailles two days later. In preparation for this Lloyd George had a discussion with the French leader, which turned out exceptionally well from his point of view. Since to Clemenceau, as to Lloyd George, victory now seemed out of the question in 1918, the two men were able to reach a large measure of agreement on strategy for the coming year. Clemenceau had modified his opposition to sideshows, provided they did not drain forces from the defence of France. (He was doubtless also influenced by British success against the Turks, which will be described in the next chapter.) He now accepted the need to maintain the Allied presence at Salonica, granted the new threats in Eastern Europe, and he favoured the policy of trying to eliminate Turkey from the war. Looking to the political future in the Levant, he gave Lloyd George a free hand to negotiate with the Turks, and agreed that Palestine should not be restored to them. So far as France was concerned, he would not refuse a protectorate over Syria 'as it would please some reactionaries', though he was personally indifferent.[6] Thus spoke the opponent of Jules Ferry's colonial expansionist policy in the 1880s; he had not changed.

The Supreme War Council met at Versailles on Saturday, 1 December, at the Trianon Palace Hotel. Again, Clemenceau presided, and he began by announcing that the opening statement he was about to make had been written in consultation with Lloyd George. In fact, he had asked Lloyd George to write it, and the actual drafting was done by Hankey. Clemenceau delivered the text substantially as drafted.

According to the statement, the Council's first task was 'to consider the nature of the military campaigns to be undertaken in 1918'. The permanent military advisers should be asked to study the whole situation and make recommendations, each government having ensured that its own general staff should transmit its views to the military advisers. Certain recent changes should be borne particularly in mind: the collapse of Russia, the 'grave reverse' in Italy, and the 'gradual maturing of the American army in Europe' ('gradual' an obvious euphemism for 'slow'). Shipping would have a vital bearing on 'the intensity of military operations', and these in turn would

6. Hankey diary, 28 November 1917.

react upon the amount of shipping available for bringing reinforcements. 'For example, a prolonged operation of the character attempted on the Somme in 1916, and in Flanders in 1917, involved an expenditure of matériel far greater than defensive operations, or than offensive operations of the type of the recent attacks on the Chemin des Dames or in the region of Cambrai.'

The key passage in the short address was this:

I would propose to invite our permanent military advisers . . . not to forget that the war has become largely one of exhaustion. It may be that victory will be achieved by endurance rather than by a military decision. Russia has already collapsed . . . but it must be remembered that Turkey and Austria are neither of them very far from collapse. The final objective is [still] the overthrow of Prussian militarism, but I would ask the military advisers to weigh carefully whether possibly that object may not be brought nearer final achievement by the overthrow, first of all, of Germany's allies, and the isolation of Germany.

A proper subject for enquiry would be 'whether the Allied forces in the Balkans [at Salonica] are so disposed, and in such strength, that they may be expected to hold their own against any force which can reasonably be brought against them'. Finally, Clemenceau insisted that the advisers' function was 'to advise the Supreme War Council as a whole and not merely as the representatives of their respective nations'; and he trusted that their advice would, as often as possible, be unanimous.

The speech was translated by Spears, who sat on Clemenceau's left. During the rest of the day many topics were covered and resolutions carried. According to L. S. Amery, who attended as a member of the British staff, 'L.G. was the most effective talker, and his effectiveness was doubled by having Hankey at his side ready to draft a resolution at five seconds' notice while also taking notes of the whole discussion'. About 120 people attended the meeting (the British forming the strongest contingent), and others were brought in as and when required. Venizelos was there when Salonica was being discussed, and 'with voluble earnestness talked down everyone else', saying that he could mobilize up to twelve Greek divisions if he could count on food for them. Such was his eloquence that everyone stood up at the end of his speech. Robertson attended throughout, and because he was there Foch was summoned by telephone and arrived half-way through the meeting.[7]

The Council remained in session for another day, but Lloyd George left

7. Amery diary, 1 December 1917.

after the first day, having a plausible reason for returning to London. He could feel some satisfaction with the way his project had been launched. Clemenceau, despite his initial hostility, had played up well. Though he naturally expected reciprocal favours – that Haig would take over more of the line in France, and that British shipping would do much to accelerate the arrival of American troops – Lloyd George appreciated his support. 'He is a fine old boy,' he said to Riddell on his return.[8]

The British had been the quickest to establish themselves at Versailles and it was they who picked the Trianon Palace Hotel as headquarters for the SWC. This 'magnificent building in its own small park' was commandeered by them on behalf of the Allies. The second and fourth floors were divided between the British and French, the first and third between the Americans and the Italians. The nearby Villa Romaine was secured as a residence for Henry Wilson and his immediate entourage, including his Chief of Staff, Colonel Charles Sackville-West (nicknamed 'Tit Willow') and his ADC, Lord Duncannon.[9] Wilson was a good organizer and lost no time in setting up various groups to work on specific problems, such as manpower and materials, and strategic prospects considered from both the Allied and the enemy point of view. Before long a naval liaison committee and other comparable inter-Allied bodies were functioning at Versailles, and Wilson kept in close touch with them.

Colonel Lancelot Storr was temporarily seconded from the War Cabinet office to act as secretary to Wilson's team. He was a man of diverse interests. After Sandhurst and the Indian staff college he had taken a course in economics and political science, and he contributed occasional articles and verse to Indian newspapers. Before joining Hankey in 1916 he had been on Kitchener's personal staff. Amery, too, was brought over from London to work with Wilson during the early months. Multiple linguist, fellow of All Souls and Conservative MP, he was put in charge of the political section at Versailles, and also acted as liaison officer with the War Cabinet. Hankey's willingness to help was not confined to lending two of his key assistants; he also provided clerks and typists.

Robertson and the War Office showed no such goodwill. Indeed, an attempt was made to deny Wilson the services of Sackville-West and Duncannon (in the latter case ostensibly because Duncannon had close links with the Irish National Party: an absurd reason, granted that the arch-Unionist Wilson had no objection to his politics). The War Office also

8. *RWD*, 3 December 1917.
9. L. S. Amery, *My Political Life* (3 vols., 1953–5), vol. ii, p. 128.

tried to block Wilson's promotion to the rank of acting full general. But on these petty issues, as on much else, decisions went in his favour, because he had the backing of higher authority.

The other national components gradually took shape. Cadorna was an intelligent man but, as a defeated general representing an army that was holding its own only with the direct support of allies, he could hardly expect to carry much weight. All the same, the Italians were next only to the British in the speed with which they established a working presence at Versailles. General Maxime Weygand represented the largest army in the Alliance, which had come through the severest tests. He was also a highly efficient and professional soldier. But his standing was necessarily diminished by his subordination to Foch, which was emphasized by the fact that the best room in the French quarters at the Trianon Palace Hotel was reserved for the use of the Chief of Staff. It was obvious that Foch was, in reality, the leading French member of the supreme advisory body, even though Lloyd George's unwillingness to appoint Robertson made it impossible for him to hold the position formally. Despite this anomaly the system up to a point worked, mainly because Wilson and Foch were old friends.

Wilson also got on well with his American opposite number, General Bliss, who was a wise and scholarly man. Son of a classics professor, he himself was well versed in history and the arts, and a student of geology. As a linguist he was almost in Amery's class, speaking French and five other European languages. He was senior to Pershing in the United States army, and had been Chief of Staff for a short time before being assigned to the post at Versailles. He was also a man of broader outlook than the commander of the AEF. Unfortunately he could not match Pershing's authority in the European theatre, which resulted from the more or less free hand given to him by the Commander-in-Chief in Washington. And Bliss's urgent, enlightened arguments could not prevail against the President's obstinate self-righteousness and administrative weakness. On his way back to America with House and other members of the 'House party' Bliss sent Woodrow Wilson a grave warning:

A military crisis is to be apprehended culminating not later than the end of next spring, in which, without great assistance from the United States, the advantage will probably lie with the Central Powers.

To meet [this crisis] we must meet the unanimous demand of our allies to send to France the maximum number of troops as early in the year 1918 as possible. There may be no campaign of 1919 unless we do our best to make the campaign of 1918 the last . . .

To transport these troops before it is too late we should take every ton of shipping that can possibly be taken from trade . . . Every branch of construction which can be devoted to an extension of our shipbuilding programme . . . should be so devoted in order to meet the rapidly growing demands for ships during 1918 . . .[10]

In fact, during the very month in which Bliss was addressing this appeal to the man who, above all, had the responsibility for mobilizing his country's war effort, the target for American shipbuilding was reduced from six million to two million tons. It was not until the last months of 1918 that America was producing ships at an adequate rate. Meanwhile the war had been won, largely through the efforts and sacrifice of America's fellow democracies who were not even dignified with the title of allies.

Bliss returned to Versailles in the New Year with an excellent staff and the American contribution to the work of the SWC was, at the military level, all that could be desired. But at the political level there was a vacuum until House returned in the autumn of 1918. At meetings of the prime ministers or their deputies (Lloyd George's deputy, when he could not be present, was Milner) the United States was represented by the counsellor at the Paris embassy, A. H. Frazier.

At the closing plenary session of the inter-Allied conference on 3 December, House paid a warm tribute to France: 'Ever since our government was founded there has been a bond of interest and sympathy between us – a sympathy which this war has fanned into passionate admiration.' And Clemenceau in his speech on the same occasion said: 'In the past we were the friends of America and the enemies of Great Britain . . . the two peoples are today united in community and friendship.'[11] Both speakers were reminding each other, and anyone who chose to listen, that there was a special relationship between the United States and France, which had originally been at Britain's expense.

The morning that the inter-Allied conference first met (29 November) a letter appeared in the London *Daily Telegraph* from the veteran Unionist statesman Lord Lansdowne. In it he made an appeal for a negotiated peace on the lines of his memorandum to the Cabinet a year earlier, when he was a member of the Asquith coalition. The underlying assumption on both occasions was that victory on the battlefield was unattainable and that the

10. Bliss to Woodrow Wilson, from USS *Mount Vernon*, 14 December 1917.
11. *The Times*, 4 December 1917.

war had to be brought to an end before European civilization was completely destroyed. Lansdowne's plea also assumed that the ruling forces in Germany were interested in a compromise peace, but in fact they were not. The military leadership which controlled the government and the country still believed that it could achieve total victory, East and West.

The appearance of such a letter at such a time was bound to be, at the very least, embarrassing to British ministers in Paris. But just how much trouble did it cause? According to one contemporary but second-hand witness, Lord Crawford, its effects were nearly disastrous:

Lloyd George told Jack Poynder [Lord Islington] that Lansdowne's letter very nearly broke up the Paris conference. Nobody among the allied representatives could or would believe that such a document, coming from so cautious and so experienced a man, could have been made public without the tacit consent of his old colleagues. Fortunately Lloyd George was not alone. Had he been by himself he says publication would have defeated him: but he had four or five colleagues all of whom spent the whole day in visiting people, and giving assurances . . .[12]

Crawford is unlikely to have misunderstood Islington, or Islington to have misreported Lloyd George.[13] On the other hand, there is no other evidence of the feverish damage-control activity here described. Hankey, for instance, makes no reference to anything of the sort. Perhaps Lloyd George was exaggerating a little as he told the story. A firm statement was, however, immediately issued on behalf of the government:

Lord Lansdowne in his letter spoke only for himself. Before writing it he did not consult nor, indeed, has he been in communication with any member of the Government, His Majesty's Ministers reading it with as much surprise as did everybody else.

The views expressed in the letter do not in any way represent the views of his Majesty's Government, nor do they indicate in the slightest degree that there is any change or modification in the war policy of this country.

This is still what it has always been described to be by the Prime Minister, Mr. Asquith, Mr. Bonar Law, and Mr. Balfour. This war policy has been spoken of in different words, but perhaps is best summed up in the recent utterance of M. Clemenceau, 'the war aims for which we are fighting are victory'.[14]

12. Crawford diary, 6 December 1917.
13. Islington, at the time under-secretary for India, was a straightforward man, a good listener and not given to exaggeration (personal knowledge).   14. *The Times*, 1 December 1917.

The background to the letter was, in fact, a good deal more complicated than the statement implied. There is no reason at all to doubt that Lloyd George and most of his colleagues read the letter with surprise, though to those of them, including the Prime Minister, who had been members of the previous government, Lansdowne's views were familiar from his secret memorandum of November 1916. Balfour, however, knew about the letter itself in all but the most technical sense, and his role in the affair deserves careful scrutiny.

Lansdowne had entered politics as a Whig-Liberal, but his allegiance had been changed by Gladstone's espousal of Irish Home Rule, mainly for the obvious reason that he was a large Irish (as well as English and Scottish) landowner. When he returned to home politics after ten years as, success-ively, Governor-General of Canada and Viceroy of India, he served as a Unionist minister: at the War Office during the Boer War, and as the Foreign Secretary who negotiated the Anglo-Japanese treaty and the Entente Cordiale. (He was, incidentally, on his mother's side a great-grandson of Talleyrand). In the Asquith coalition he held purely ornamental office as Minister without Portfolio.

Meanwhile he had led the House of Lords in its reckless rejection of Lloyd George's 1909 budget, and had done so under strong pressure from his party leader, Balfour. At Eton he had been Balfour's fag-master, but in politics the roles were reversed. He was in the habit of deferring to a man who was his junior in years but his superior in intellect. Most regrettably, Balfour failed to capitalize on this advantage in November 1917, when Lansdowne consulted him about going public on the subject of a negotiated peace.

Lansdowne's first intention was to raise the matter in the House of Lords, but Balfour dissuaded him from doing so, asking instead for a memorandum setting out his views, to which Balfour then replied in characteristic style. He began with a general, but hardly emphatic, statement: 'I don't know that this is a very suitable time for discussing peace matters. I rather think not.' He went on to deal with Lansdowne's detailed suggestions for making the government's position on peace terms known to the world. The Allies did not 'desire the destruction or dismemberment of Germany, if by "Germany" is meant that part of Central Europe which properly belongs to the German people'. This did not include Alsace-Lorraine or that part of 'historic Poland as is really Polish'. There was no intention to 'paralyse' enemy powers as 'trading communities', but nothing should be conceded that would 'hamper the attack on Germany as a *war* measure', or 'the threat of post-war action in case Germany shows herself to be utterly unreasonable'.

In response to Lansdowne's proposal concerning freedom of the seas (that it should be up for discussion) Balfour said that the government would be prepared 'to examine in concert with other nations the great group of international problems . . . connected with the question of "freedom of the seas" '; but this was an 'extremely vague' concept, and anyway neutrals would have to be involved as well as belligerents. Balfour ended by asserting that the government's territorial aims had already been stated 'in broad outline', though there had been no corresponding statement from the enemy.[15]

Despite this letter Lansdowne still itched to make his views publicly known, and his thoughts turned to writing to the press. But Balfour had a chance to deflect him again. According to a note found among Lansdowne's papers after his death, he and the Foreign Secretary met by chance outside St Margaret's, Westminster, on 26 November:

I [Lansdowne] proposed to put my view before the public in the form of a letter. *He* [Balfour] *did not dissuade me.* I said I was anxious not to publish anything misleading . . . that I would gladly have shown him my draft, but that was impossible, as he was leaving [for Paris] . . . Did he object to my showing the draft to Hardinge [permanent under-secretary at the Foreign Office] . . . ? *He assented, adding: 'Hardinge knows my thoughts.'* I showed my letter to Hardinge. He made one or two suggestions not touching questions of principle. *He observed that it was 'statesmanlike' and 'would do good'.*[16]

Lansdowne then saw Geoffrey Dawson and offered him the letter for publication in *The Times*. Dawson asked for time to consider it and next day urged Lansdowne strongly to withhold it, fearing that it would be used by the Germans for their own purposes and would discredit the author. Dawson's motives were those of a friend and patriot, but hardly those of a cut-throat journalist. He thought his arguments had prevailed, but was mistaken; Lansdowne promptly offered the letter to Burnham (whom he met in the House of Lords) and so it appeared in the *Daily Telegraph*. Northcliffe, absent in Paris, was incensed that a rival newspaper had been allowed to obtain such a scoop. His own decision would have been to publish the letter in *The Times* to the accompaniment of 'a stinging leader'.[17]

15. AJB to Lansdowne, 22 November 1917.
16. My italics. The full text of this note first appeared in *Nineteenth Century*, March 1934, after Lansdowne and Balfour were dead.
17. J. Lee Thompson, *Politicians, the Press & Propaganda: Lord Northcliffe & the Great War 1914–1919* (1999), p. 176.

Balfour's conduct seems rather odd, especially in view of the hard line he had taken in the Kühlmann affair only two months before. If, when he and Lansdowne met outside St Margaret's, he had stamped firmly on the idea of a letter to the press, it is more than likely that Lansdowne would have abandoned, or at least delayed, his proposed step. Instead the Foreign Secretary reacted in a way that Lansdowne could legitimately interpret as permission, if not encouragement, to go ahead. The official statement from Paris, in which it was said that Lansdowne had written his letter without consulting *any* member of the government, may well have been issued without Balfour's knowing its precise terms. But he must obviously have been made aware of them soon after he got back to London, when Lansdowne was being vilified for the views he had expressed and also, scarcely less, for making them public without warning the government. Yet Balfour never corrected the mistake. The fact that the long-standing friendship between the two men was resumed after the war says much for Lansdowne's charitable and forgiving nature.

To Lloyd George the letter (though not the author's opinions) certainly did come as a surprise, but his objection was more to the timing than to the contents, as he made clear to Riddell the day after his return from Paris:

The letter was ill-advised and inopportune . . . Of course the time will come when it will be necessary to open the question of peace, but the moment is unfavourable. When the time arrives . . . a section of the public will no doubt want to fight on in a blind unreasoning way without any proper conception of the attainable. The point is that at the moment we could not secure favourable terms. That being so, the letter is harmful.[18]

Lloyd George also said that he had reason to think Colonel House 'was cognisant of and approved the letter'. Essentially he was right. House saw Lansdowne while he was in London and was given, in effect, a preview of the letter. He found himself in almost total agreement with Lansdowne's ideas, and was much impressed by the man himself, who was the sort of gentleman-politician he instinctively admired:

He believes that definite war aims should be set out – aims that are moderate and that will appeal to moderate minds in all countries . . . strangely enough, Conservative that he is, we scarcely disagreed at all. [He advocated] a more liberal sea policy, bordering on the plan for the freedom of the seas, which indeed he was good enough to say he had obtained from me during my last visit here . . .

18. *RWD*, 3 December 1917.

Lansdowne is a great gentleman . . . not merely in intellect and character, nor from having for a background an ancient and distinguished lineage, but in manner and in that intangible and indefinable air which comes as a gift from the gods.[19]

No doubt Lansdowne was flattered by House's attention. For the past year he had been out of office, having not been invited to join Lloyd George's government. In the irreverent view of a fellow-aristocrat he was suffering from 'vexation and annoyance' at being out of things after holding 'high or responsible positions for thirty years on end'.[20] It must have been most encouraging to him to know that his opinions were shared by a man so close to the President of the United States.

In favouring Lansdowne's initiative House knew that he was reflecting the President's own thinking, for which there was, indeed, strong support among sections of his compatriots. One private correspondent described the letter as 'the most noteworthy and noblest utterance that has come out of England', which seemed 'to run with [the President's] purpose', adding that Lloyd George and (Theodore) Roosevelt were 'dangerous leaders in the present emergency'.[21] Nevertheless *The Times* reported from Washington that the letter was 'fiercely resented by the bulk of the American people',[22] and Northcliffe himself wrote in a message to the *Daily Mail* staff that 'virile people like the Americans' did not understand 'our "lack of backbone" in these matters'.[23]

How 'virile' was the reaction of press and public in Britain? There was a striking division of opinion between the national and the provincial press, the former – apart from the *Daily News* and *Star* – almost solidly condemning Lansdowne's plea, the latter – including the *Manchester Guardian* – tending to support it. According to Lansdowne's biographer, he was subjected to 'a flood of invective and an incredible mass of abusive correspondence'. But he himself wrote at the time to his daughter, the Duchess of Devonshire, that he had been 'snowed under with letters from all manner of folk – a few hostile, but mostly in complete sympathy'.[24]

Certainly there was considerable support for Lansdowne in high quarters,

19. Col. E. M. House diary, 14 November 1917.   20. Crawford diary, 1 December 1917.
21. Harry Augustus Garfield to Woodrow Wilson, 30 November 1917.
22. *The Times*, 1 December 1917.   23. 15 December 1917.
24. Lord Newton, *Lord Lansdowne: A Biography* (1929), p. 472; letter quoted, 10 December 1917. Perhaps we should accept Newton's statement, as being the less liable to subjective distortion.
   Incidentally, the Duchess did not agree with Lansdowne on the issue, and Lord Kerry, his son and heir, publicly distanced himself from his father (*The Times*, 11 December 1917).

which did not appear on the surface. Among those who wrote him sympathetic letters were Esher, Haldane and the Archbishop of Canterbury, Randall
Davidson. A former permanent under-secretary at the Foreign Office, Lord
Sanderson, also wrote expressing substantial agreement, though he 'did not
think the time very wise'.[25] McKenna and other Asquithian ex-ministers
tried to persuade their leader to come out in favour of the letter, but Asquith
would not be budged from his admirably consistent line.[26] One American
observer reported from London to House:

The pessimistic views to which the Prime Minister gave utterance in his Paris speech
have contributed no less than the Cambrai check to produce a frame of mind
favourable to the reception of Lord Lansdowne's letter. I was surprised to find, at a
luncheon party ... the day after the letter was published, only one person out of
four inclined to criticise it.[27]

In the upper reaches of the Conservative Party there may have been some
covert sympathy for Lansdowne, but the party leader showed just how
well he understood the ordinary membership when he addressed a party
conference the day after the letter appeared. Law's dismissal of it was blunt
and unqualified: 'I disagree absolutely not only with the arguments, but
with the whole tone of the letter. I think it is nothing less than a national
misfortune that it should have been published, now of all times.' Lansdowne
had lost one son in the war, but Law had lost two, and 'so powerful and
unambiguous a rejection of Lansdowne's sentiments must surely have been
magnified in its effect by his hearers' awareness of his own recent losses'.[28]

As for Balfour, his curious conduct in the affair was perhaps influenced
by the amount of time he had been spending with House while the Colonel
was in London. We have seen that House admired Balfour, as did President
Wilson, and Balfour to some extent reciprocated the feeling. In any case his
mission to the United States had left him very sensitive to American opinion,
particularly in Washington. One of his reasons for objecting to Lloyd
George's proposed handling of the Kühlmann overture was that it would
have involved keeping the Americans in the dark, at least for a time. One
way or another we should probably look to the American connection for an
explanation of his markedly less tough and hawkish attitude in November, in
so far as it can be explained.

25. Newton, Lord Lansdowne, p. 478.
26. John Turner, British Politics and the Great War: Coalition and Conflict, 1915–1918
(1992), pp. 250–51.   27. William Hepburn Buckler to House, 30 November 1917.
28. R. J. Q. Adams, Bonar Law (1999), p. 263.

Not many people identified themselves openly with Lansdowne, but those who did included pacifists and regular opponents of the war, mainly on the left and therefore most unlikely allies. Only a few years back such people would have regarded Lansdowne as the supreme embodiment of archaic privilege and reaction, and the idea of marching under his banner would no more have entered their heads than it would have occurred to him that he could ever become their leader. Yet a Lansdowne Committee was formed, with the support of some businessmen and also 'labouring men throughout the country'. Its first meeting was held at the end of February 1918, and the following month Ramsay MacDonald said that he would welcome a Lansdowne government.[29] When the Germans attacked in the West the movement, such as it was, soon petered out, and the German collapse later in the year made nonsense of Lansdowne's premise that the war could end only in a stalemate.

Lloyd George's first public speech after the letter appeared was at Gray's Inn on 14 December, and he chose to handle Lansdowne with gentle irony, in an attempt to separate him from his potential supporters in the country:

Recently a highly respected nobleman ... startled the nation by a letter ... but I now understand that [he] had not at all intended to convey the meaning which his words might reasonably bear ... I was attending the Allied conference in Paris at the time his letter appeared. It was received there with painful amazement. However, it is satisfactory to know that he was misunderstood.

I shall therefore pass on to the view which [the letter] was supposed to advocate ... to the opinions which are held and expressed by a number of people in this country. It is true that they are in a minority, but they are a very active minority ... The Lansdowne letter brought them out into the open. They thought that at last they had discovered a leader ... with a view to forcing this country into a premature and vanquished peace. The danger is not the extreme pacifist. I am not afraid of him. But I warn the nation to watch the man who thinks that there is a halfway house between victory and defeat ... who thinks that you can end the war now by ... setting up a League of Nations with conditions as to arbitration ... That is the right policy after victory. Without victory it would be a farce.[30]

29. Newton, *Lord Lansdowne*, p. 474.

30. Lansdowne had protested that he agreed with President Wilson, and this was enough for Lloyd George to suggest, tongue in cheek, that he had not meant what people took him to mean.

The speech was made at a dinner given by the Gray's Inn benchers in honour of the Prime Minister and leaders of the air services. He was introduced by the Treasurer of the Inn, his colleague and old Tory friend, F. E. Smith. Rothermere, the Air Minister, also spoke.

In his memoirs, where most important events are described in detail, Lloyd George never explicitly mentions Lansdowne's letter, and therefore says nothing of its effect upon the statesmen assembled in Paris. But there is an implied reference to the letter in a passage showing how seriously he took the body of opinion of which Lansdowne became the accepted protagonist:

The desire for peace was spreading amongst men and women who, although they were convinced of the righteousness of the War, felt that the time had come for putting an end to its horrors in the name of humanity, if it could be done on any terms that were honourable and safe. Lord Lansdowne constituted himself the spokesman of this sentiment. He represented a powerful and growing section of the people not only in social, but also in industrial circles.[31]

Lloyd George was no stranger to the discussion of war aims, and he had never sought the destruction of Germany as a nation. But he was convinced that there could be no honourable or durable peace with Germany until the Prussian-directed military machine was knocked out. His only wobble on this point (in September) had been occasioned by a momentary fantasy that the Germans might abandon all their gains in the West in return for a free hand in the East. But he had returned to his settled belief that the German army had to be beaten and its control of the German state broken. He wanted a change of regime in Germany, and regarded this as the only guarantee of security for the future. He also wanted proper compensation for the damage inflicted in Allied countries. His views on war aims had been given an airing in June, at Glasgow. Soon he would feel moved to develop them further in a speech of even greater impact. Meanwhile he genuinely felt that any talk of negotiations with Germany was premature and, as he told Riddell, 'harmful'. At the same time he had not abandoned his persistent dream of detaching Austria-Hungary and so accelerating the collapse of Germany.

The latest and last peace approach from Austria before the final cataclysm began with intimations to the British government that the Austrian Foreign Minister, Count Czernin, was prepared to send an emissary to meet a representative of the War Cabinet in Switzerland. The proposed emissary was well chosen. He was Count Albert Mensdorff who – like Kühlmann – had been in London before the war. As Austrian Ambassador he had been

31. WM, p. 2483.

greatly liked and trusted. He had taken part in the London conference of ambassadors which, under Edward Grey's chairmanship, had resolved the Balkan crisis of 1912–13. In August 1914 he had privately deplored the German invasion of Belgium, which he felt had 'ruined everything'. Grey quotes in his memoirs a despatch from Mensdorff to the then Austrian Foreign Minister, Count von Berchtold, which shows how strongly he sympathized with Britain's attitude at the time, as expressed by Grey.[32] Among leading individuals on the enemy side few could be more acceptable as a man of understanding and goodwill.

During the Allied conference in Paris preceding the SWC meeting Lloyd George sought the agreement of his leading partners to pursue the Austrian approach. The matter was discussed 29 November, which was not the happiest of days, with the Lansdowne letter just published. Lloyd George was nevertheless given the go-ahead. Only the Italians were seriously minded to block him, and they were hardly in a position to dictate to their allies. Clemenceau thought the whole exercise a waste of time, but did not join the Italians in trying to veto it. House supported it. Since his prime objective at the conference, to secure an agreed Allied statement of war aims, could not be achieved, he was content for Lloyd George at least to explore the possibility of a separate peace with Austria.

Soon afterwards, and before the encounter with Mensdorff took place, the United States acquired, as it were, a share of the action by belatedly declaring war on Austria-Hungary. Wilson proposed this step in his annual State of the Union address and, while admitting that the same logic 'would lead to a declaration of war on Turkey and Bulgaria', refrained from making a similar proposal in their case, because they did not stand in America's 'direct path'.[33]

Who was to represent the War Cabinet in the talks with Mensdorff? Lloyd George's first idea was to send Reading, but he was unwilling to go, for the quaint reason that 'everyone would wonder what the Lord Chief Justice was doing in Switzerland'.[34] (Since the mission was to be top secret hardly anybody would have known about it, whereas Reading's manifold non-judicial activities since 1914, in America and at home, were public knowledge. Did it not concern him that people might wonder about them?) When Lloyd George returned to London on 2 December, missing the last session of the SWC, his excuse to his colleagues was that he needed to

---

32. Mensdorff to von Berchtold, 7 August 1914 (quoted in Edward Grey, *Twenty-Five Years, 1892–1916* (2 vols., 1928), vol. ii, pp. 233–4). 33. 4 December 1917.
34. House to Wilson, 1 December 1917.

expedite the Mensdorff meeting. During a rough Channel crossing he talked to Hankey about sending him to Switzerland, and for the next week Hankey's bag was 'ready packed'.[35] But Lloyd George eventually decided that he could not be spared, and the task fell instead – as so many tasks did – to Smuts, who was accompanied by Kerr. They arrived in Geneva on 18 December, nearly three weeks after the mission had received Allied authorization in Paris.

During 18–19 December Smuts had four talks with Mensdorff in 'a quiet suburb on the outskirts of Geneva'. In one sense Clemenceau's scepticism was fully justified. From the first Smuts and Mensdorff were at cross-purposes, the former having instructions only to discuss a separate peace with Austria, the latter being expressly forbidden to discuss any such thing. Nevertheless their conversations, as reported immediately afterwards by Smuts, have a melancholy interest.

Lloyd George's aim was to assure Austria of Britain's support if she would detach herself from Germany and also liberalize the Habsburg Empire on the lines of the British. In this respect Smuts was just the man to represent the Prime Minister's views:

I assured him that . . . our object . . . was to assist Austria to give the greatest freedom and autonomy to her subject nationalities. . . . We had no intention of interfering in her internal affairs, but we recognised that if Austria could become a really liberal Empire . . . she would become for Central Europe very much what the British Empire had become for the rest of the world . . . now that Russia had disappeared as the principal military danger upon her flank, there was no reason why she should not adopt this policy and lean more and more towards the British Empire and dissociate herself from German militarism.

Mensdorff replied that these views would 'appeal very deeply' to the Emperor Karl and to Czernin (who was 'a young statesman descended from the Royal House of Bohemia, full of lofty idealism'). But first there had to be a general negotiated peace. When Smuts insisted that this was out of the question for the time being, because Germany was a menace 'no less grave than that of Napoleon and . . . meeting with an even more determined temper on the part of the British people', Mensdorff said that to prolong the war would be 'the end of Europe'. Like Lansdowne, he was convinced

---

35. Maurice Hankey, *The Supreme Command, 1914–1918* (2 vols., 1961), vol. ii, p. 736. Lloyd George also claimed to Riddell that he 'read a French novel' during the crossing and 'almost forgot he was at sea' (*RWD*, 3 December 1917).

that the German army could not be defeated. If the Allies were to state their terms for ending the war, he 'did not anticipate that the Germans would be unreasonable'. Belgium would be evacuated, 'provided German economic and industrial interests . . . were not injured or hampered'. He did not think that any parts of Russia would be annexed, though 'could not say this for certain'. There were, he knew, 'great difficulties' about Alsace-Lorraine, but did France want 'the whole of Alsace-Lorraine back'? The Germans would demand the return of some, at least, of their colonies, or 'heavy compensation' if they were not returned. He had nothing to say about any compensation due from the Germans for the immense damage they had inflicted.

At one point Mensdorff tried to drive a wedge between Britain and France, by suggesting that British war aims had already been achieved: 'while the Germans had been successful in Central Europe, the British Empire had gained far more lasting and far-reaching victories over the whole world, and was now in complete control of everything outside Central Europe.' Back in the spring, when the approach was made through Prince Sixte, the Austrians had tried at first to play the French off against the British. Now, through Mensdorff, they were trying to play the British off against the French. The difference was that on the earlier occasion they had been acting without the Germans' knowledge, and so making proposals that disregarded German interests. In December 1917 Czernin, whatever his private feelings, was so conscious of the Habsburg Empire's weakness that he had no choice but to inform Germany of the overture he intended to make, and to act as a cat's-paw for Germany. Smuts appears to have had no suspicion that he was talking to a man who, willy-nilly, was speaking for the Germans. He concluded his report by saying that he had no doubt the talks would 'prove most useful and fruitful'. Austria would 'strain every nerve to induce Germany to accept moderate terms', and would 'thereafter strive to recover and assert her political independence of Germany'.[36]

Such a view of the situation was totally unrealistic and out-of-date. The time for salvation of the Habsburg Empire through internal reform was long past, and the Empire's fate was sealed in 1914, when its rulers allowed themselves to be pushed into war with Serbia to serve Germany's larger ambitions. The Emperor Karl and his circle – including Czernin, whom he had appointed – were not in control in Austria, and Austria was anyway a German dependency.

Nevertheless the exchanges begun in Geneva did not end there. As with the Sixte affair, the process associated with the name of Mensdorff dragged

36. Smuts's report to War Cabinet, 20 December 1917.

337

on for several months, while Lloyd George clung to the vain hope of a separate peace with Austria. The process ended in April, when Czernin made a crazy speech asserting that Clemenceau had sabotaged the chances of peace by demanding the return of Alsace-Lorraine. Clemenceau instantly countered by leaking Karl's letter to his brother-in-law (Sixte), in which he had said, among other things, that he favoured the return of Alsace-Lorraine and would use his influence to bring it about. Karl was reduced to putting the blame on Czernin, while also describing the letter as a forgery. Even so he had to travel to German headquarters to apologize for his actions. It was the ultimate humiliation, and the final proof that attempts to detach Austria from Germany were futile.

While Smuts was talking to Mensdorff, Kerr was talking, in Berne, to a Dr Parodi, on the subject of a separate peace with Turkey. Parodi was said to be in close touch with Turks 'disposed towards the Entente and especially Great Britain'. They were still a minority, because whereas Germany was committed to restoring the Turkish Empire the Entente was committed to its dismemberment. After listening to Parodi, Kerr arranged for an outline of possible Allied terms for Turkey to be conveyed to the peace faction there. The communication would be made through the British minister in Berne, Sir Horace Rumbold, and would be subject to confirmation from London.

The suggested terms were that the Turks would remain in Constantinople, but with the Straits neutralized; that they would surrender all 'executive authority' over Armenia, Arabia, Syria, Mesopotamia and Palestine, though in the last three they might retain a nominal suzerainty; and that they would be relieved of debt in respect of those territories, and offered 'liberal' economic assistance 'to make a fresh start'. But these terms were available only 'in the event of an immediate peace'.[37] With some amendments requested by the Foreign Office the message was transmitted at the end of the year, but no immediate peace followed. It was still too early for the changes in Constantinople that would lead to the acceptance of such tough terms. But the fact that they could even be demanded was a reflection of Britain's growing strength in the area, resulting from events which must now be described.

---

37. Philip Kerr to DLG, 19 December 1917. Rumbold was later High Commissioner and Ambassador in Constantinople (1920–24) and signed the treaty of Lausanne with Turkey on behalf of the British Empire (1923).

19

The Balfour Declaration

Jerusalem by Christmas – Balfour Declaration

We left General Allenby on the Egypt–Palestine border, improving his lines of communication and imposing his personality on the troops under his command. At the time of his appointment in June Lloyd George had charged him in person with the mission of capturing Jerusalem 'as a Christmas present for the British nation', and had told him to read Sir George Adam Smith's *Historical Geography of the Holy Land*, remarking mischievously that it probably contained more of practical value than could be found in War Office surveys. Unlike many in his profession, Allenby formed a liking for the Prime Minister. Years later, when asked to join in protesting against Lloyd George's criticism of Haig in his war memoirs, Allenby refused to do so, saying: 'Attack Lloyd George? But I like the little man. He won the war, though for Heaven's sake don't tell him so.'[1]

Robertson had recommended Allenby for the Egyptian command, but his support for an autumn offensive against the Turks in Palestine was grudging and dubious. From the first he insisted that any divisions to reinforce Allenby must either come from Salonica or be created from scratch in the Middle East. None could be spared from Britain or the Western front, even if the shipping could be spared to transport them. Robertson was more helpful with guns and aircraft, but his letters to Allenby were full of 'ifs' and 'buts'. At the beginning of August he wrote:

---

1. Archibald Wavell, *Allenby: A Study in Greatness* (1940), pp. 186 and 223 n.; Lawrence James, *Imperial Warrior: The Life and Times of Field-Marshal Viscount Allenby, 1861–1936* (1993), p. 114. *WM*, p. 1835. Lloyd George had been given the Adam Smith book by Sir William Robertson Nicoll, editor of the Nonconformist *British Weekly*, and was struck by the author's 'detailed survey of the country from the point of view of the geographical difficulties it presented to an invader'. James states that the Prime Minister *gave* Allenby his copy of the work, but Lloyd George does not claim to have done so. According to Wavell, Allenby needed no introduction to the book, because it was his 'invariable practice on going to a new country to obtain and study the best books available on it'. Allenby's goodwill towards Lloyd George was doubtless assisted by his lack of warm feelings towards Haig.

The Turk has never had a good shelling I imagine. At the same time, and with reference to the general situation, we need to be careful as to the extent to which our commitments are increased . . . I am therefore taking the line at present that it will be a good thing to give the Turk in front of you a sound beating, but that the extent to which we shall be justified in following him by an advance into Northern *and* *Central* Palestine is a matter which for the moment must be left open. The further we go north the more Turks we shall meet; and the greater will be the strain upon our resources.

In a PS he added:

I . . . ask you not to take too definitely what I have said about the advance into Palestine. As you know the Prime Minister is very much in favour of it . . . The only point I wish to make is that in deciding to go forward we have to bear in mind what the situation will be after we have gone forward and whether we can, having regard to all the circumstances of the war, maintain ourselves after going forward . . .[2]

It is clear that Robertson was arguing against Lloyd George's instruction, while pretending to defer to his authority. The suggestion that it might be dangerous to advance into central Palestine was tantamount to calling into question Lloyd George's explicit objective: Jerusalem. In fact, the Prime Minister believed that if Allenby were to attack at the earliest possible moment he might be able to occupy the whole of Palestine and advance still further, knocking Turkey out of the war. In view of what we now know, he may well have been right. But the attack was delayed from September until the end of October, and might not have gone ahead at all but for the firm line taken by Lloyd George and the War Cabinet.

Allenby was a commander of spirit and ambition, but also (like Montgomery) cautious and thorough. He wanted to attack, but only if he could be sure of doing so with superior, and preferably overwhelming, force. He acquired one division from Salonica, and was able to form another in Egypt, giving him a total of ten divisions. But the intelligence he received locally, and even more from the War Office, tended to make him overrate the strength of the opposition. He was told that the enemy forces confronting him consisted of twenty divisions, two of which were German. In fact, there were no German divisions (only three battalions) and the Turkish divisions could hardly be described as such, since their numbers were so reduced that they hardly amounted to brigades.

2. Robertson to Allenby, 1 August 1917; my italics.

This scare caused Allenby to put in a request for thirteen divisions – to give him superiority – which obviously could not be conceded. The suspicion must be that this unrealistic request was deliberately provoked as a means of demonstrating that the planned offensive was not feasible. Robertson also took the step of bringing to the War Policy Committee General Lynden-Bell, whom Allenby had replaced as his Chief of Staff. In reply to a direct question from Lloyd George, Lynden-Bell said that 'he did not anticipate that it was possible to secure very rapid results in the Palestine theatre'.[3] His pessimism was disregarded, and the policy of attacking in Palestine was maintained despite all attempts to scupper it. But the price was delay, which limited the time available for operations before the rains were due in the latter part of November.

The delay was full of risk for another reason: that the German commander in the theatre, General Erich von Falkenhayn, might have gained from it the time to concentrate his forces against Allenby.[4] Falkenhayn was expecting a British attack, but was at first undecided whether it would be in Mesopotamia – where Maude had been achieving such success – or in Palestine. When he arrived at the correct conclusion the British delay would, in normal circumstances, have still left him time to make the necessary dispositions. But he was then frustrated by the incompetent and primitive state of Turkish logistics. This was one great piece of luck for the British, and another – perhaps even greater – resulted from the mere fact that the Turkish forces were under German control. The local command of them in Palestine was offered to Mustapha Kemal (Atatürk), the Turkish hero of Gallipoli and future ruler of the country. But he declined, because he did not wish to serve under a foreign commander and staff. The difference that he might have made in the coming campaign is beyond reckoning.

Allenby was aware that he had a significant asset in the progress made by the Arab Revolt, mainly through the collaboration of the Emir Feisal, a son of the Sherif of Mecca, and the young British scholar-adventurer T. E. Lawrence. Allenby recognized the value of Lawrence's raids on the railway into Arabia, which caused disruption and tied down a considerable number of Turkish troops. And he was even more impressed by the capture of Aqaba, the Ottoman Empire's last remaining outlet to the Red Sea – a remarkable exploit, involving a 600-mile camel ride through the desert in

3. WPC, 8 October 1917.
4. Falkenhayn was a major figure, though his career had its ups and downs. In September 1914 he succeeded Moltke as Chief of Staff of the German army, but was sacked after the failure to capture Verdun in 1916. Since then his reputation had been revived by his important and successful share in the campaign against Roumania.

the hot season. Allenby met Lawrence and assured him of support for the movement with which he had identified himself, and for the operations that he would in future conduct as an adjunct to his own. Though Lawrence was to emerge from the war with a legendary status that Allenby could not hope to match, in reality the defeat of the Turkish Empire owed far more to the General and his army than to the Arab Revolt or Lawrence's personal contribution to it. The Revolt's military impact was on the whole marginal, but Allenby made the most of the advantages it brought him, particularly on the political side – though in this respect it also caused him difficulties with the French over Syria.

By the end of October he was at last ready to attack. His army was divided into three corps, one of which, the Desert Mounted Corps, consisted predominantly of Anzac troops and was commanded by an Australian, General Harry Chauvel. The 60th (London) division, transferred from Salonica, was an all-volunteer force forming part of XX Corps, and XXI Corps included the 75th division, recently put together in Egypt. With a total of about 80,000 men Allenby's army outnumbered the enemy directly opposed to it by almost two to one.

Instead of making Gaza his first objective, he decided to go for Beersheba, twenty-five miles to the south-east, while leading the Turks to expect an attack on Gaza. His deception plan was cleverly devised and well executed, and his command of the air enabled him to concentrate against Beersheba without being observed by enemy reconnaissance. On 27 October he opened a heavy barrage on Gaza, with assistance from the guns of an Anglo-French flotilla. The Turks were thus confirmed in their belief that an assault on the town was imminent. But four days later the bulk of Allenby's army captured Beersheba after a cavalry charge by the 4th Australian Light Horse. Air photographs had shown that the Turkish trenches were not protected by wire or forward anti-cavalry ditches, and the charge took the enemy by surprise. The British forces then advanced northwards from Beersheba, while keeping up the bombardment of Gaza. The combined effect of accurate, sustained shelling and the threat of encirclement made the place untenable, and the Turks abandoned it on 7 November. As they retreated along the coast towards Jaffa they were strafed by British aircraft. Despite determined rearguard actions, not least by German and Austro-Hungarian units, by 16 November Jaffa was captured and links between Jerusalem and the coast were cut.

Rain and cold now set in, as a prelude to a winter of exceptional severity. But Allenby, with the War Cabinet's continued support, advanced into the Judaean hills. His men were ill-equipped for such conditions, wearing summer uniforms and without greatcoats, but they were fired by the prospect of victory and had the advantage of numbers. Allenby was warned by the government to avoid fighting in Jerusalem itself, for fear of damage to the holy places. After a fortnight or so of fighting around the city, it was evacuated by the enemy on 9 December and its Mayor came out under a white flag to surrender it to the British. He had some difficulty in accomplishing his mission. He offered the keys of the city to some cooks of a London regiment, to a sergeant on outpost duty, and to some artillery officers who were busy training their guns on Turkish rearguards; but none felt 'quite equal to so historic an occasion'. Eventually he found a taker in General John Shea, commander of the 60th division, who accepted the keys on Allenby's behalf.[5]

Two days later the General entered the city, and the occasion was most fittingly and imaginatively choreographed. By contrast with the Kaiser, who in 1898 had ridden into Jerusalem wearing a white cloak and plumed helmet, Allenby entered the city on foot, accompanied by French, Italian and (surprisingly) American representatives, as well as a few of his own senior officers – and Lawrence. At the Jaffa gate he was received by guards representing England, Scotland, Ireland, Wales, Australia, New Zealand, India, France and Italy. He wore ordinary khaki service dress.

In his presence a proclamation of martial law was read out at the citadel in seven languages, in which it was emphasized that his sole aim, apart from military security, was to protect the holy places and to enable the citizens to pursue their normal business without fear of interruption. He decided that no Allied flags should be flown over the city, and he showed special sensitivity to Muslim feelings, in a situation which could too easily have lent itself to Christian triumphalism. Indian Muslim guards were posted around the Mosque of Omar, and no non-Muslim was to pass the cordon without permission from the military governor.

Similar feeling for Islam was not shown at home, where the capture of Jerusalem was greeted with Christian as well as patriotic fervour. Church bells were rung – this time justifiably – and *Te Deum*s were sung at St Paul's and Westminster Cathedral. A Bernard Partridge cartoon in *Punch* depicted Richard the Lionheart looking down on the city that he had failed to seize from the infidel more than seven hundred years previously, with the caption 'The Last Crusade'. (The Crusader motif did not at all appeal to Allenby.)

Lloyd George would naturally have liked to announce the city's fall to

5. Wavell, *Allenby*, p. 229. A picture was, however, taken of the Mayor and his party with men of the 60th Londons.

the House of Commons himself, as he had a right to do. But he was out of action with one of his feverish colds, and the announcement was made by Law on 10 December.[6] Two days later the Prime Minister was back and read to the House Allenby's telegram describing his entry into Jerusalem.[7]

Curiously, Lloyd George had nothing to say about the capture of Jerusalem in his Gray's Inn speech a few days later. But in his end-of-the-year report to the House of Commons on 20 December (other aspects of which will be referred to later) he devoted a resonant and most revealing passage to what Allenby's army, and also Maude's in Mesopotamia, had accomplished:

The capture of Jerusalem has made a most profound impression throughout the whole civilised world. The most famous city in the world, after centuries of strife and vain struggle . . . has fallen into the hands of the British army, never to be restored to those who so successfully held it against the embattled hosts of Christendom. The name of every hamlet and hill occupied by the British army . . . thrills with sacred memories. Beersheba, Hebron, Bethany, Bethlehem, the Mount of Olives are all names engraved on the heart of the world, and although not in the main theatre of war I venture to say that the achievements of British troops in . . . Mesopotamia and Palestine, which have been the cradle and the shrine of civilisation, will remain for many ages to come.

So far the Crusader theme is clearly to the fore, and of course it was bound to play well with Lloyd George's fellow Nonconformists, and with Christians generally, in Britain and elsewhere. At the same time, by bringing Mesopotamia in, he evokes non-Christian and pre-Christian cultures. Yet it is in the words that follow that his own personal vision and sense of priorities are authentically expressed:

I know there is a good deal said about 'side-shows', and that, after all, these [campaigns] were only side-shows. The British empire owes a great deal to side-shows. During the Seven Years' War, which was also a great European war – for practically all the nations now engaged . . . were then interlocked in a great struggle – the events which are best remembered by every Englishman are not the great battles on the Continent of Europe, but Plassey and the Heights of Abraham; and I have no doubt at all that, when the history of 1917 comes to be written, and comes to be read ages hence, these events in Mesopotamia and Palestine will hold a much more conspicuous place in the minds and in the memories of the people than many an event which looms much larger for the moment in our sight.[8]

6. Hansard, fifth ser., vol. c, col. 875.   7. Ibid., cols. 11180–81.
8. Ibid., col. 2211.

It has been an argument of this life of Lloyd George that he was consist-ently, from the beginning of his career, imperialist in outlook. While Clemen-ceau was heartily opposed to the expansion of French power, Lloyd George was no less heartily a believer in Britain's imperial destiny. His reputation as a Little Englander derived from a complete misreading of his attitude to the Boer War, which he had denounced as a crime and also an act of folly, injurious to the British Empire's best interests. He believed, certainly, in the largest possible measure of local home rule within the Empire, and was happy to see the white Dominions, at any rate, emerge as effectively sover-eign nations under the common Crown, acting together freely on the world stage. But he had no *mauvaise honte* about Britain's enormous dependent empire, where power was exercised over what were then regarded as back-ward peoples, not yet fit for self-government. Indeed, he aimed to acquire new spheres of direct or indirect rule, not least in the Middle East. Milner regarded him as 'the greatest war minister since Chatham',[9] and his reference to empire-building exploits in the Seven Years War surely indicates that in another sense as well he was conscious himself of the Chatham analogy.

Allenby's victory in Palestine was a powerful vindication of Lloyd George's faith in attacking the Turks from Egypt, and his contention that the results might have been decisive if the campaign had been launched sooner is tenable, to say the least. At the cost of 18,000 casualties – a heavy toll by normal standards, though certainly not by comparison with Third Ypres – a victory was gained which had a double importance. It was of substantial strategic value, in that it prevented Falkenhayn from counter-attacking in Mesopotamia (where Maude, after his remarkable successes, died in November). It also created a front in Palestine from which the total defeat of the Ottoman Empire could be undertaken the following year.

Yet the moral significance of the victory far transcended the strategic. The capture of Jerusalem provided 'a glowing finale to the year's endeav-ours'.[10] As Lloyd George justly claims in his memoirs, it 'cheered our own people at a critical time, when defeatist elements were making their influence felt among us'.[11] Napoleon's well-known maxim is applicable: 'In war, three-quarters turns on personal character and relations.'[12] What Wavell's victories over the Italians did for British morale in the winter of 1940, Allenby's did during a similar period of gloom in 1917. The difference was

9. Thomas Jones, *Lloyd George* (1951), p. 283.

10. Trevor Wilson, *The Myriad Faces of War: Britain and the Great War, 1914–1918* (1986), p. 501.   11. WM, p. 1838.

12. *A la guerre, les trois quarts sont des affaires morales* (Napoleon's *Correspondance*, as translated in *The Oxford Dictionary of Quotations*).

that Allenby's were won against a more formidable enemy, and proved lasting. Allenby's army was not driven back (as Wavell's was in the Sec nd World War, when Rommel's Afrikakorps appeared on the scene), and the Turks never regained Palestine. But British rule there did not have the permanence of which Lloyd George dreamed. It lasted just over thirty years, and then ended in circumstances of violence and bitter recrimination resulting from a policy conceived by his own government, which was finally brought forth, after long gestation, at the time Allenby's Palestine campaign was launched.

This was the policy of providing a 'national home' for the Jews in Palestine. It was agreed at a meeting of the War Cabinet on 31 October and then incorporated in a letter from Balfour as Foreign Secretary to Lord Rothschild in his capacity as the nominal leader of British Zionists. The letter, somewhat misleadingly known to history as the 'Balfour Declaration', was dated 2 November and published six days later. The key passage reads:

His Majesty's Government views with favour the establishment in Palestine of a national home for the Jewish people, and will use its best endeavours to facilitate the achievements of this object, it being clearly understood that nothing shall be done which may prejudice the civil and religious rights of existing non-Jewish communities in Palestine, or the rights and political status enjoyed by Jews in any other country.

The policy might just as well be identified with the name of Lloyd George, since it was the policy of his government and he was strongly committed to it. There is, however, some justice in linking it to Balfour's name. He was dedicated to Zionism as a movement in a profound philosophic sense not matched by Lloyd George or any of his other colleagues. A strange feature of Balfour, normally so cool, sceptical and detached, was that he was capable on rare occasions of succumbing to the force of an idea, of which he then became a quietly impassioned exponent. The first instance was his commitment to the cause of public education, which was due largely to the influence of a civil servant of genius, Robert Morant. The second (and perhaps only other) instance was his commitment to Zionism, in which his guru was a research chemist at Manchester University, Dr Chaim Weizmann.

Weizmann was Russian-born but partly educated in Germany and with a doctorate from the Swiss University of Freiburg. In 1904, when he was just thirty, he settled in England, having obtained a job at Manchester through an introduction from his Freiburg professor. In 1910 he became a British subject and thereafter retained a genuine loyalty to his country of adoption. Yet he always described himself as a Jew and was from the first a wholehearted Zionist, with no desire to join the assimilated Anglo-Jewish community.[13]

Balfour's government at the beginning of the twentieth century enacted legislation to curb the entry into Britain of 'aliens', most of whom were in practice East European Jews. Nevertheless his personal attitude to the Jews was unusually understanding and sympathetic for a Briton of his period and class, even before he met Weizmann. He was conscious of the debt owed by Christianity to Jewry, which had, in his view, been shamefully ill-requited. His first meeting with Weizmann occurred during the general election of 1906, when he was defending his East Manchester seat (unsuccessfully, as it turned out). His constituency chairman was a Jew who knew Weizmann, and Balfour asked him to arrange a meeting. The two met at Balfour's campaign headquarters, and their conversation, meant to last a quarter of an hour, extended to an hour and a quarter. A deep impression was made on both sides. After listening to Weizmann Balfour was convinced that 'the Jewish form of patriotism was unique', and that it could be satisfied with nothing less than a return to Palestine.[14]

At this time Weizmann was a marginal figure in the Zionist movement, whose central direction was on the Continent, particularly in Berlin. But the outbreak of war, and above all the Ottoman Empire's involvement, gave him an opportunity that he was swift to seize. On the assumption that the Turks would be defeated, it seemed to him likely that Britain would be the principal agent of their defeat, and so might well emerge as the occupying power in Palestine. He also regarded Britain as the power under whose auspices the Jewish people would have the best chance of returning to their ancient homeland. He therefore started to promote this idea in influential circles, and his remarkable talents as a political lobbyist were reinforced by his wartime value to Britain as a chemist, since his original method of producing acetone became indispensable in the manufacture of cordite.

After 1914 he had further meetings with Balfour, who at one of them

13. The aspiration to return to Zion (Jerusalem) had been cherished in a vague way by Jews of the Diaspora (Dispersion) over the eighteen centuries or so since the Roman Emperor Titus destroyed Jerusalem and drove their ancestors out. But the modern Zionist movement that Weizmann joined dates from the late nineteenth century. Its founder, Theodor Herzl, was a highly assimilated Viennese theatre critic who became a fervent Zionist in horrified reaction to the Dreyfus case in France. The movement swiftly gathered strength as Jews fled in large numbers from persecution in Eastern Europe.
14. Blanche E. C. Dugdale, *Arthur James Balfour* (2 vols., 1936), vol. i, p. 435. Weizmann was entirely opposed to the idea of Jewish settlement in East Africa, discussed by Herzl and the Colonial Secretary, Joseph Chamberlain, while Balfour was Prime Minister.

said: 'You know, Dr. Weizmann, if the Allies win the war you may get your Jerusalem.'[15] But Balfour was not, at first, very keen that this should happen under exclusively British control. While certainly wishing to keep the French at arm's length, he feared that Britain might be suspected of territorial aggrandizement. He therefore suggested that American sponsorship might be preferable, or at any rate an Anglo-American condominium in Palestine.[16] But circumstances were to rule these options out. Besides, Weizmann did not at all favour the idea of dual control in the country, and Lloyd George had none of Balfour's inhibitions about British rule there.

Lloyd George found Weizmann's proposal attractive before he met the man himself. It was put to him early in the war by C. P. Scott, whom Weizmann had recently converted to Zionism. At about the same time Scott introduced Weizmann to Herbert Samuel, the only Jewish member of the Asquith Cabinet, who was fired by the proposal and raised it with his colleagues. Lloyd George discussed it with Samuel *à deux*, and was 'astonished to find how that cold and dry person suddenly kindled' (as he told Scott). He made two other significant points about the conversation. He and Samuel 'had sympathised on the common ground of the small nationality', and he (Lloyd George) 'was interested at the suggestion of a partly Jewish buffer state, but thought France would have strong objections, [while] as to Russia she might prefer Jews to Catholics in the Holy Places'.[17]

Grey was at first sympathetic to Weizmann's project, as presented by Samuel, and Haldane also showed some interest. But Asquith was against making any addition to Britain's responsibilities and Grey came round to his view. Among leading members of the Liberal Cabinet only Lloyd George was firmly in favour. Asquith commented on his attitude in a letter to Venetia Stanley:

Lloyd George who, I need not say, does not care a damn for the Jews or their past or their future . . . thinks it would be an outrage to let the Christian Holy Places – Bethlehem, Mount of Olives, Jerusalem &c – pass into the possession of 'Agnostic Atheistic France'! Isn't it singular that the same conclusion shd be . . . come to by such different roads?

He was contrasting Lloyd George's approach with Samuel's, while in the same letter describing Samuel's uncharacteristic fervour on the subject much

15. Dugdale, *Balfour*, vol. ii, p. 226.
16. Max Egremont, *Balfour: A Life of Arthur James Balfour* (1998), p. 264.
17. Scott diary, 27 November 1914.

as Lloyd George did: 'It is a curious illustration of Dizzy's favourite maxim that "race is everything" to find this almost lyrical outburst proceeding from the well-ordered and methodical brain of H.S.'[18]

Not for the only time, Asquith got Lloyd George rather wrong (though too much should never be made of throwaway remarks in private conversation or correspondence). Whatever argument Lloyd George may have used to win support for the Weizmann/Samuel scheme, his own primary reason for championing it was that he thought it would serve the interests of the British Empire. Though not on the whole Gladstonian in his Liberalism, he did share Gladstone's detestation of the Ottoman Empire, regarding it as cruelly oppressive and a blight on its subject peoples. He looked forward to its dismemberment as a result of the war, and to Britain's assumption of an altogether more benevolent paramountcy over some of its provinces. In particular, he had Mesopotamia and Palestine in mind, the latter because it could serve, as he told Scott, as a protective 'buffer' (no doubt for the Suez Canal and the British position in Egypt).

The French, though now allies, were traditional rivals in the Levant, and Lloyd George's desire to keep them out of Palestine was prompted by considerations of worldly power, not by any feeling that they were metaphysically disqualified from acting as custodians of the holy places. He knew that Christian piety was still very strong in France, scarcely less so (if not more so) than anti-clericalism. In any case, he was very far from being a religious bigot, and only religious at all in the loosest sense. Though on some political issues he was obliged to strike Nonconformist attitudes, in reality he was crypto-secularist rather than sectarian. He could appreciate a good sermon and good singing in any place of worship, and even Roman Catholic ritual held a certain fascination for him. But he would have been the last man to lose sleep because a freethinker might be in charge of the Mount of Olives. It may nevertheless have suited him, when discussing the future of Palestine with anti-imperialist Liberal colleagues, to disguise his true motive for seeking to exclude the French.

Was it true that he did 'not care a damn for the Jews or their past or their future'? Substantially, it was untrue. He had been brought up on the Bible, and the story of the ancient Jews was as familiar to him as the history of England. He was a romantic nationalist, and on that account the idea of reuniting the Jewish people with the land of their forefathers appealed to him. The best historian of Zionism acknowledges that his romanticism

18. Asquith to Venetia Stanley, 13 March 1915. The exact words that Disraeli puts into the mouth of his character Sidonia in *Coningsby* are: 'All is race; there is no other truth.'

about recreating a Jewish national home in Palestine was 'too simple (in so complex a man) to have been anything but sincere'.[19] But unlike Balfour, he could not divorce the Zionist project from his ambitions for Britain in the area. His conception of the Jews in Palestine was that they would form a lively, distinct community within the British Empire. There was never any contradiction in his mind between his form of nationalism and his form of imperialism. He cared for the interests of nations, especially small nations, but he cared still more for the interests of the British Empire, which he saw not as a static institution to be defended, but as a dynamic and life-giving force to be promoted. He counted on the Zionists to show, in Palestine, a spirit akin to his own Welsh patriotism, proud and assertive yet subordinate to a larger loyalty.

In Lloyd George's day anti-Semitism was quite prevalent in Britain, and he was by no means free from it himself. His casual talk and writing contains not a few disparaging references to Jews, as individuals and as a people, which would now be condemned as racist. The same could be said of other politicians, including Balfour. For the most part the degree of prejudice and malice involved was no greater than in comparable gibes about other ethnic groups, such as the French, English, Scots, Irish – or Welsh. (Lloyd George himself was throughout his career a prime butt for anti-Welsh racism.)

Yet the Jews were a special case, because of the long tradition of anti-Semitism in Europe, of which the Dreyfus affair and the pogroms in Russia were only the latest manifestations. Britain was perhaps the least anti-Semitic of the major nations, but even in Britain some anti-Jewish comment reflected truly virulent racial feeling. It was not so with Lloyd George, but in the post-Holocaust era remarks such as he was apt to make seem a good deal less innocuous than they would have seemed at the time.[20] The main thing, however, is that he had much admiration for the Jews, whatever he might say in passing, and his support for Zionism was genuine in its own terms.

While he was at the Ministry of Munitions Weizmann earned his gratitude by finding an answer to the acetone problem. But the suggestion in his memoirs that the Balfour Declaration was the form his gratitude took is, of course, a charming fantasy. According to Lloyd George, he asked Weizmann how his own and the nation's appreciation could be shown. By some honour?

19. David Vital, *Zionism: The Crucial Phase* (1987), p. 210.
20. Since the Holocaust even the mildest of anti-Jewish remarks can only safely be made by a Jew, and any criticism by non-Jews of Zionism as a concept, or of the conduct of the state of Israel, has been open to denunciation as anti-Semitic. Such taboos are undesirable and will, one hopes, disappear with the passage of time.

[Weizmann] said: 'There is nothing I want for myself [but] I would like you to do something for my people.' He then explained his aspirations as to the repatriation of the Jews to the sacred land they had made famous. That was the fount and origin of the famous declaration about the National Home for Jews in Palestine.[21]

Humbug, alas. Lloyd George already knew all about Weizmann's project, and had, as we have seen, espoused it for reasons unrelated to acetone or any desire to reward Weizmann for his scientific services. (It was also, incidentally, untrue that Weizmann was indifferent to honours. He much resented not being elected a fellow of the Royal Society, and after the war was disappointed at not receiving a knighthood. Perhaps Lloyd George took him at his word when he said that he wanted nothing for himself.)[22]

During the latter part of 1915 and throughout 1916 the Zionist project had no place on the British government's agenda. The Prime Minister (Asquith) was opposed to it, as were most of his colleagues, and the way the war developed did not favour it. The Ottoman Empire, far from collapsing, inflicted severe defeats on the Allies; on the British and French at Gallipoli, and on the British alone in Mesopotamia. Though Egypt did not fall, Palestine remained in Turkish hands. There were, however, political developments that had a crucial bearing on the future course of events. The Arab Revolt began, with British help and encouragement. And a secret agreement was entered into by the British and French, with Russian approval, to determine post-war spheres of interest in the Levant.

This agreement is known by the joint names of the two men who did most of the negotiating, Georges Picot and Sir Mark Sykes. Picot was a former Consul-General in Syria, Sykes a politician of varied gifts, hard to categorize. Still under forty, as a younger man he had travelled extensively in the Near East, and had published amusing, idiosyncratic books on the subject. His formal education had been limited, but he made up for it by curiosity and imagination. He was a Roman Catholic who became an enthusiastic Arabist and also – while engaged in his negotiation with Picot – an equally enthusiastic Zionist: evidence of a sanguine, ecumenical outlook. He spoke excellent French.

Under the terms of Sykes–Picot the French would control what are now Syria and Lebanon, and the north of Palestine. The British would control southern Mesopotamia and much of the Palestine coast, including Haifa and Jaffa. Between the British and French spheres there would be an area of Arab sovereign territory, under British protection. Jerusalem and central

21. WM, p. 586.   22. Vital, *Zionism*, pp. 158–9.

Palestine would have a special status, the details of which would have to be worked out later. No Jewish national home in Palestine was envisaged in the agreement.

When Lloyd George took over as Prime Minister the direction of Britain's Near Eastern policy became at once more purposeful and sharply focused. He was intent on defeating the Turks, and insisted that Britain should gain control of Mesopotamia and Palestine when the Turks were evicted, regardless of the niceties of Sykes–Picot. In Palestine, he wished to see British paramountcy reinforced by a strong and growing Jewish presence. Zionism thus returned to the agenda, and Lloyd George's appointments gave it a powerful impulse. Balfour as Foreign Secretary was obviously a priceless asset to the Zionist cause, but scarcely less helpful were Lloyd George's two political appointees to the War Cabinet secretariat, Amery and Sykes, both Conservative MPs and both committed Zionists. (Amery was also Jewish on his mother's side, a fact which he chose to conceal.)

Maude's victories in Mesopotamia during the early months of 1917 strengthened Britain's hand, and Allenby's victories at the end of the year gave Britain the physical control of Jerusalem and a large part of Palestine. Meanwhile the political process leading to the Balfour Declaration went ahead. Of special importance was a diplomatic coup achieved principally by Sykes, working again with his old negotiating partner Picot, and wisely giving a prominent role in the talks to a Zionist leader associated with Weizmann, Nahum Sokolov. The result of Sykes and Sokolov's efforts was that by June the French government was tacitly reconciled to the idea of British paramountcy over the whole of Palestine when the Turks were gone, and sympathetically disposed to the Zionist project. In the course of this effective revision of the original Sykes–Picot Agreement, Sokolov was asked to visit Italy (where Sykes had prepared the way), because the French government felt that Italian, and still more Vatican, support might be helpful to them. It says much for Sokolov's own gifts as a diplomat that he succeeded in this mission. The Italian government's goodwill was obtained at least partly because he first secured the Pope's. At a private audience Benedict XV expressed his approval of 'the British interest in Palestine and Zionism', and said that he believed Roman Catholics and Zionists would be 'good neighbours' in Palestine.[23]

Soon afterwards the new Anglo-French solidarity on the Levant was strikingly demonstrated when Weizmann and a French Jewish colonel were

23. Vital, *Zionism*, pp. 247–9. It is interesting, in view of later controversies, that Monsignor Pacelli, the future Pius XII, was involved in the Vatican's friendly reception of Sokolov.

sent to counter a potentially dangerous initiative by the American President. Henry Morgenthau, a former American Ambassador to Turkey, was asked by Wilson to explore the possibility of peace with the Ottoman Empire. His mission was ill-defined even in private, and the formal pretext for his journey was merely that he would be discussing the welfare of Palestinian Jewry. But the British and French governments were suspicious, because America, not at war with Turkey, was known to be hostile to their aspirations in the area. And Weizmann was thoroughly alarmed, because Morgenthau was a leading American Jew opposed to Zionism. Aided perhaps by divided counsels in Washington, or in President Wilson's own mind, the move to head off Morgenthau was a total success. Weizmann and the French Colonel held talks with him at government house, Gibraltar, and as a result he decided that the time was not ripe to open negotiations with the Turks. Instead of travelling to the eastern Mediterranean, he saved face by visiting Pershing in France before returning home.

Even so the Zionist project did not go through without serious challenge. In mid-1917 two big questions continued to trouble even some politicians who were broadly favourable to it. Was Zionism supported by a majority of world Jewry, and would its realization prove, on balance, to be a boon or a curse? On the first question there was palpably a division of opinion among Jews. In Russia, where half of the world's twelve million Jews lived, Zionist feeling was certainly strong, though as yet only to a very limited degree organized. Even after the Revolution the movement numbered fewer than 200,000, whose leadership was more concerned with establishing equal rights for Jews within the new Russia than with any specific plan for a return to Palestine. Indeed, it maintained a neutral stance between the belligerents, since there were Jews and Zionists in all the countries that were at war – notably in Germany. There could be no question at this stage of endorsement for Weizmann's project from the Russian Zionists as a body.

In America the division of Jewish opinion on the subject of Zionism was broadly between Jews whose families had emigrated earlier from Western European countries and the recent flood of emigrants from Eastern Europe. The former, of whom Morgenthau was an example, tended to be anti-Zionist, though there were many exceptions. The new arrivals were overwhelmingly Zionist, though without any clear idea of how the Jews were to return to Zion, and in any case busy finding their feet in their actual country of refuge, which was a long, long way from Palestine.

Jewish opinion in Britain was similarly divided. It was natural that the most effective lobbyist for Zionism should be a first-generation immigrant of Russian provenance. Among the settled élite of British Jewry the division of opinion was quite close, and epitomized in the contradictory views of two cousins, Herbert Samuel and Edwin Montagu. Samuel, as we have seen, had become an out-and-out Zionist under Weizmann's influence, and was convinced that the establishment of a Jewish national home in Palestine under British auspices was the right policy for Britain as well as for Jewry. Montagu regarded the whole idea as disastrously flawed. In his view it would damage Britain's relations with other national and religious groups, particularly the Arabs, and would also have calamitous consequences for the Jews themselves.

In July 1917 he had returned to office as Secretary for India in Lloyd George's government, whereas Samuel had been out of office since its formation (having refused Lloyd George's invitation to serve in it as Home Secretary). Montagu lost little time in making his objections to Zionism known to his colleagues in a powerful memorandum entitled 'The Anti-Semitism of the Present Government'. He was not, he explained, suggesting that those proposing the policy were anti-Semitic, but that anti-Semitism would inevitably be boosted by it, because it would prove 'a rallying ground for anti-Semites in every country in the world'. He denied the existence of a Jewish nation, in the political sense, and argued that the attempt to recreate one in Palestine would undermine the position of Jews in other parts of the Near and Middle East, and cast doubt upon the allegiance of Jews who, like himself, were the loyal citizens of Western countries.

I claim [he wrote] that the lives that British Jews have led . . . that the part that they have played in our public life and our public institutions, have entitled them to be regarded not as British Jews, but as Jewish Britons. I would willingly disenfranchise every Zionist. I would almost be tempted to proscribe the Zionist organisation as illegal and against the national interest. But I would ask of a British government sufficient tolerance to refuse to endorse a conclusion which makes aliens and foreigners by implication, if not by law, of all their Jewish fellow-citizens.

A national home in Palestine could not in any case accommodate the whole of the Jewish people, or even a majority of them.

If my memory serves me right, there are three times as many Jews in the world as could possibly get into Palestine if you drive out all the population that remains there now. So that only one-third get back at the most, and what will happen to the remainder?[24]

24. Memorandum circulated 23 August 1917.

Lloyd George was already aware of the last point. He had been rather disconcerted to learn some time earlier from Samuel the limits to potential Jewish absorption into Palestine. But Montagu's memorandum brought the point home to him more forcibly, and altogether the case made by the Indian Secretary could not be ignored. Moreover, he had an ally in the War Cabinet in Curzon, who had the advantage of knowing the area. Curzon asked what was to become of the existing population of Palestine, which had been there for 1,500 years.[25]

The counterattack led by Montagu delayed the Balfour Declaration by several months, but failed to stop it. He was invited to address the War Cabinet on 3 September, and succeeded in getting the issue postponed until President Wilson's view was ascertained. At first Wilson's response was non-committal, since he was influenced for a time by House's arguments against it. But he also listened to others besides the anti-Zionist House, in particular to the eminent jurist Louis D. Brandeis, who was a leading figure among American Zionists. Even House, moreover, may have been a little swayed by an argument used by Balfour at this stage, that the Zionist project had to be adopted at once, with Allied and American backing, or it would be pre-empted by the Germans. The evidential basis for Balfour's argument was dubious, to say the least, but it was certainly effective.[26] In mid-October Wilson gave his approval.

Meanwhile the War Cabinet had been subjected to an anti-Montagu memorandum from Weizmann, and to another one from Montagu himself, as well as numerous letters from him. At the beginning of October he attended the War Cabinet again, and Balfour was there to answer him, maintaining that the Zionist movement was opposed only 'by a number of wealthy Jews', but had 'behind it the support of a majority . . . at all events in Russia and America'. He did his best to reply to Montagu's argument that the position of Jews in Britain and elsewhere would be compromised by the national home policy. He saw nothing inconsistent between the establishment of a Jewish national focus in Palestine and the complete assimilation and absorption of Jews into the nationality of other countries. Just as English emigrants to the United States became American nationals,

25. But apart from their agreement on the subject of Zionism, Curzon and Montagu 'agreed on little else' (David Gilmour, *Curzon* (1994), p. 483).

26. 'That the Germans would wish, or feel free, to go beyond an anodyne expression of sympathy for the Jews was inherently incredible: the territory in question was Turkish, the Turks were their allies. The most they could promise the Zionists was an effort to press the Turks to soften their position. There was no hard evidence that they had attempted to do so' (Vital, *Zionism*, p. 287). Balfour had had two long conversations with Brandeis during his mission to America earlier in the year.

so, in the future, should a Jewish citizenship be established in Palestine, Jews would become either Englishmen, Americans, Germans, or Palestinians. Zionism, he said, represented 'the intense national consciousness held by certain members of the Jewish race'. They regarded themselves as 'one of the great historic races of the world, whose original home was Palestine', and they had 'a passionate longing to regain it'.[27]

When the War Cabinet at last reached its decision at the end of the month, Montagu was out of the country. He had left for India, where he was to spend the next six months. Wavering members of the Cabinet were influenced by President Wilson's endorsement of the policy, itself clearly a reflection of the force of Zionist sentiment in America (since it cannot have been easy for him effectively to give his support to an extension of British imperial power). Even Curzon, while restating his objections to the policy, came round to agreeing that 'some expression of sympathy with Jewish aspirations would be a valuable adjunct to our propaganda', and admitted that 'the bulk of Jews held Zionist rather than anti-Zionist opinions'.[28] For the Cabinet as a whole – as distinct from Lloyd George, Milner and Smuts, whose motive was primarily imperial – the factor that counted most was the need to appeal to Jewish opinion throughout the world, and above all in America, together with Balfour's argument that unless Britain moved the Germans might get in first.

The Declaration finally agreed by the War Cabinet made some concessions to critics and doubters. In the first draft Palestine was to be 'reconstituted' as 'the' national home of the Jewish people. In the final version 'reconstituted' became 'constituted' and the indefinite 'a' replaced the definite 'the'. Reassuring words were also added about the rights of non-Jewish Palestinians, and Jews living outside Palestine. (Amery claims to have been the author of the final text, but there are difficulties about his claim.[29]) Semantic

27. War Cab., 4 October 1917. The word 'race' is notoriously hard to define, but on any definition the Jews are not a separate race. Their identity, miraculously preserved, is religious and (now increasingly) cultural. So far as race is concerned they and the Arabs are fellow Semites, though the Semites in turn are part of the Caucasian, or Indo-European, racial group. Palestine was not the Jews' 'original' home. Abraham and his followers came from Ur of the Chaldees (Mesopotamia).

28. War Cab., 31 October 1917.

29. In his autobiography he states that when the matter was to come up for definite decision early in October Milner asked him to produce a new text 'half an hour before the meeting' and he 'sat down and quickly produced' the final agreed version (L. S. Amery, *My Political Life* (3 vols., 1953–5), vol. ii, p. 116). But the matter came up for decision late, not early, in October, and Amery's contemporary diary does not corroborate his version of events. All the same, he is likely to have played a part in the drafting process, along with others.

tinkering could not, however, affect the perceived meaning of the Declaration, or its actual consequences. To most Zionists it meant that a Jewish state would once again be created in Palestine, and to most Arabs it meant the same. Both were right.

Lloyd George had been sufficiently impressed by Montagu's arguments to allow time for further consideration of the policy before the eventual decision. Though Montagu irritated him, he could never be wholly indifferent to a case argued with logical coherence and passion. Besides, the Jew he knew and liked best, Reading, was also at heart anti-Zionist, though careful not to antagonize American Zionists by making his attitude publicly known. But in the end Lloyd George stuck to his concept of a British Palestine, to which (as he believed) the Zionist experiment would be accessory. Though he also took seriously the anticipated short-term benefits to the Alliance, it was above all for the sake of his own country and its empire that he promoted one of the most fateful decisions of his premiership.

From the imperial point of view it proved to be a complete disaster, even during his own lifetime. After the war Britain duly became the mandatory power in Palestine, and introduced the policy of systematic Jewish settlement. Before long Jews and Arabs were in conflict, and both were turning against Britain. The situation in Palestine was getting out of hand even before it was further complicated, and immeasurably aggravated, by the Nazi persecution of Jewry. Soon after Lloyd George's death Britain abandoned its mandate in tragic and humiliating circumstances. As the Jewish national home became the state of Israel (with Weizmann as its first President), the swift disintegration of the British Empire was beginning. Since then, and into a new century, the problem created by the Balfour Declaration has remained one of the most intractable in the world. For Jewry the policy may have been a great boon, though not without countervailing loss (much of it predicted by Montagu). For Britain, except in the very short term, it was an unmitigated curse, as it has been, of course, for the Palestinian Arabs.

20

Manpower

*Ecclesiastical row – Working breakfasts – Manpower
committee – Removal of Jellicoe*

When Lloyd George forced a change in the system of government in
December 1916, what he sought was a free hand to run the war, though not
necessarily the actual office of Prime Minister. In many ways he would have
preferred the arrangement that he proposed, under which Asquith would
have remained head of the government in a role analogous to that of the
chairman of a company, with himself as a dynamic managing director. The
arrangement would have had little chance of working, and it was probably
just as well that in the end Asquith turned it down (though most unfortunate
for the country, and still more for the Liberal Party, that he refused to serve
in Lloyd George's government). But there is no reason to doubt the genuineness of Lloyd George's indifference to the prime ministerial title, or of his
reluctance to be saddled with the incidental chores that went with the office.

One of these was the duty to advise the sovereign on senior appointments
in the Church of England. Tidy routine administration was never to be
expected of Lloyd George, and in any case he was hardly likely to apply his
thoughts with much diligence to a sphere of patronage far removed from
the war. Moreover, his important role in the affairs of the Church of England
was, in one sense, uniquely anomalous. He was the first Prime Minister to
be a Nonconformist. All of his predecessors had been, at least formally,
members of the Church of England or (in one or two cases) of the Church
of Scotland, which was also established.[1] But he had been brought up in a
tradition that rejected ecclesiastical establishments, and to a Welsh Nonconformist of his generation the Church of England was associated with
England's political as well as religious domination of the Principality. Disestablishment of the Church in Wales had been an obligatory cause for him
to espouse, and he had devoted to it much time and eloquence. In reality he
was a sectarian *malgré lui*. Denominational conflicts as such bored him, and
he could only enter into them cheerfully if they had a political dimension,

---

1. Asquith had started life as a Congregationalist, but gravitated into formal Anglicanism.

or if they enabled him to assert the freedom of personal and lay opinion against priestly authority. His true position was that of a secularist with a sentimental colouring of Christianity. While leading the fight against the Church of England on the issue of Welsh disestablishment, he had long been eager, privately, to find a way of resolving the matter. He was on the friendliest of terms with Bishop Edwards of St Asaph, with whose help, after the war, he finally achieved a satisfactory settlement.

His Nonconformist background was, therefore, no barrier to the exercise of Church patronage in a proper spirit and he did the job with commendable impartiality, if not always with promptness. It did not fall to him to recommend appointments to the highest posts of all. The two archbishops had been appointed before the war, and outstayed him in office. (Randall Davidson had been Archbishop of Canterbury since 1903, and his exceptionally long tenure of the post ended only in 1928. Cosmo Lang was Archbishop of York from 1909 until he succeeded Davidson at Canterbury.) But Lloyd George was responsible for the appointment of a number of bishops and deans, many of them distinguished men; and the most interesting of all his recommendations, made in December 1917, was that of Herbert Hensley Henson for the bishopric of Hereford.

Henson was one of the best-known clerics of his time, and one of the most gifted. He came from Broadstairs in Kent. His father was a Nonconformist businessman of narrow outlook, but when his mother died during his early youth he had the good fortune to acquire a German stepmother who encouraged him to read and gave him the ambition to cultivate his mind. At her suggestion he was sent as a non-collegiate student to Oxford, where he gained a first in modern history and then a fellowship at All Souls. After some heart-searching he took Anglican orders, and spent seven years in arduous parish work as Vicar of Barking. In 1900 his career took a decisive turn when he was appointed to the rectorship of St Margaret's, Westminster, with a canonry at Westminster Abbey. St Margaret's is the parish church of Parliament, and moving there brought Henson into contact with the political world. Already admired as a preacher, at St Margaret's he drew a large congregation of influential people. In 1912 he became Dean of Durham on Asquith's recommendation.

In character, Henson had a rebellious and combative streak. At the private school he attended he had 'a difference of opinion with his headmaster which led him to leave school abruptly'.[2] Throughout his life he revelled

2. *DNB* (Supplement 1941–1950), entry on Henson by A. T. P. Williams (Bishop of Winchester).

in differences of opinion. Originally Anglo-Catholic, his churchmanship broadened to a position which the High Church regarded as heretical. Actually his theological stance was still essentially conservative, though it did not seem so to his critics. He was also a firm defender of the establishment, until in the late 1920s Parliament rejected the revised Prayer Book. But he never had any patience with the sort of opaque discourse that enables difficult issues to be fudged. A brilliant arguer, expressing himself with clarity and wit in the written or spoken word, he often gave needless offence to opponents whose minds were less luminous than his. Though he had a generosity of spirit that they often lacked, and though he was liked or loved by most of those who knew him well, he could not resist the lure of debate and took a mischievous delight in scoring points. He admitted himself that the 'extravagance' of his language sometimes so infuriated his antagonists that they 'absolved themselves from the effort to understand his meaning'. He had been 'perilously, perhaps indefensibly, reckless', and so 'garnered a rich harvest of superfluous resentments'.[3]

Such a man was bound to appeal to Lloyd George. In their different spheres they obviously had much in common. The letter that the Prime Minister wrote to Henson on 6 December is unmistakably his own: it cannot have been drafted by a secretary:

My dear Dean of Durham,

The Bishopric of Hereford is vacant and I should be glad if I may submit your name to His Majesty the King . . .

It is not quite the diocese I should have chosen for you, if there had been any choice, as I should prefer to see you grappling with the needs of some large and industrial population. Such a vacancy . . . may arise in due course; if so I trust you will have proved your powers of governance and guidance in such a way that I may have the privilege of suggesting your translation. In the meantime . . . the Diocese of Hereford will give you an insight into the quiet needs of a rural population, and will enable you to bring your mind to bear on the many problems which confront the Episcopate at this time.

> With all good wishes,
> Yours very truly
> D. Lloyd George.

Henson accepted without much hesitation. He could not, he said, 'rightly refuse' in view of 'the difficult and embarrassing circumstances in which the

3. H. H. Henson, *Retrospect of an Unimportant Life* (1943), p. 213.

Church of England now stands'.[4] He did not elaborate on these, but the row that ensued was certainly difficult and embarrassing, prompting Lloyd George perhaps to reflect that the acrimony of political warfare could be at least matched, if not surpassed, by ecclesiastical controversy. Though Henson's appointment as a dean seems to have caused no disturbance, the idea of his becoming a bishop – with authority over parishes and clergy, and in the Apostolic Succession – provoked outrage.

The first to protest were representatives of the High Church, who may have had a special prejudice against Henson as a renegade from Anglo-Catholicism. They objected to his views on the Virgin Birth and the Resurrection, in which they perceived the taint of heresy. Henson's position was that he had no difficulty in proclaiming these doctrines, along with all others in the creeds, *ex animo* (in spirit), while insisting upon liberty of interpretation. His position was, he maintained, in the true tradition of the Church of England, which it was his duty to uphold quite apart from the nuances of his own conscience.

The leader of the High Church party was Bishop Charles Gore of Oxford, whose personal affection for Henson in no way diminished his zeal in opposing him. The organization which mobilized the campaign against Henson's appointment was the English Church Union (ECU). Its views were faithfully reflected in the *Church Times*, which ran leaders entitled 'Unhappy Hereford' and 'The Hereford Scandal'. By chance, the editor of the paper lived in Hereford, and through his influence the local *Hereford Times* also came out against Henson. Two veteran High Church noblemen, Lords Halifax and Selborne, wrote to the press deploring the proposed appointment, as did numerous less known or unknown citizens. The High Church party was joined by Evangelicals, and the campaign was more than just a war of words. Its purpose was to persuade the Chapter of Hereford to take the unprecedented course of rejecting the Sovereign's *congé d'élire*, a formality required to give effect to Henson's nomination. If this were to happen, a crisis would be precipitated in the relations between Church and State.

The controversy dragged on until early February and, as chronicled in Henson's diary, reads as pure Trollope. Archbishop Davidson was no theologian, but instinctively closer to Henson than to his critics. At the same time he was naturally concerned about division within the Church. Henson sensed that the Archbishop had been opposed to his appointment, and would have been happy for him to withdraw. 'I came away from [Lambeth] Palace

4. DLG to Henson, 6 December 1917; Henson to DLG, 9 December 1917.

with an uncomfortable suspicion that the Archbishop would like to throw me over, if he decently could! . . . I suspect that [his] *amour propre* has been wounded by his own arrangements having been more or less set aside.'[5]

The Hereford Chapter was unusually large and Henson feared that a majority of its members might be against him. To encourage them to vote in this sense the ECU hoped to hold a large public meeting in the town, but an important local layman blocked their plan. 'The Mayor of Hereford writes very properly repudiating the agitation in the city, and announcing that he and his municipal brethren had refused the use of the Town Hall to the agitators.'[6] Since there was no available alternative, the planned mass protest had to be abandoned. The ECU then switched to another tactic. The Vicar of Leominster, clearly a Henson sympathizer, sent him a printed postcard which had been circulated among the clergy of the diocese. It said that the protest meeting had had to be scrapped, but that 'a Celebration of H.C. [would] take place at All Saints, Hereford' on 2 January 'with special intention for the peace of the Diocese . . . a very nauseous piece of quite gratuitous hypocrisy' (Henson's comment).[7]

In the event the ECU's hopes, and Henson's fears, of opposition to him in the diocese proved exaggerated. When the Chapter met on 4 January 1918 to receive the *congé d'élire*, he was duly elected. But he was not yet out of trouble. He had still to be confirmed as Bishop at a ceremony in London at the end of the month, and then consecrated in Westminster Abbey. Meanwhile letters for and against him continued to flow into newspapers and there was a lurking danger that his enemies might try to prosecute him for heresy. He did not take part in the public correspondence, taking his stand on the 'what I have written I have written' principle, and allowing others to defend him.

Bishops and other senior clergy were divided on the issue, and he was well aware of their reservations, which in some cases (as he thought) were less than spiritual in character.

My letters included congratulations from the Archbishop of York (Dr. Lang) and the Bishop of Peterborough (Dr. Woods). The first was embarrassed and lukewarm, evidently scenting trouble ahead. The last was cordial but cautious. I get the impression that their lordships are waiting to catch the direction of the wind, and that they would find little difficulty in lining up against me.[8]

5. Henson diary, 18 December 1917.   6. Ibid., Christmas Eve, 1917.
7. Ibid., 29 December 1917.   8. Ibid., 20 December 1917.

At his club, the Athenaeum, friends and enemies alike were encountered. At lunch there 'Sir Walter Raleigh joined me. He was very emphatic in his support. Henry Newbolt also came to my table in order to assure me of his goodwill. But there were divers Bishops who looked away, or cast down their eyes, when they saw me coming!'[9] Henson also met Asquith at the Club, who was 'quite kind'.[10] In the government he was warmly supported by Prothero (a parson's son), who said that he thought the bishops had 'behaved abominably'.[11] Another valuable sympathizer among senior ministers was the high Tory Walter Long.

Eventually the storm blew itself out. Davidson drafted an exchange of letters between himself and Henson, and Henson signed the one prepared for him. This expressed astonishment that anyone who had 'knowledge of [his] public ministry' could doubt his sincere acceptance of the creeds. Some of his opponents chose to regard this as a recantation, which it clearly was not. He never departed from his insistence on the right to freedom of interpretation. On 23 January his appointment was confirmed at Bow Church, and on 2 February he was at last consecrated. Apart from Davidson, fifteen bishops were present in the Abbey, a turn-out which more than satisfied canonical requirements. And nothing happened 'to mar the function'.[12]

While the row was gathering force Lloyd George breakfasted at Derby's London house to meet Conservative colleagues in his government, and he took the opportunity to talk to them about the Henson affair. A junior minister, Sir Arthur Griffith-Boscawen, was asked what he thought of Henson's appointment, and replied that he 'thoroughly disapproved'. Lloyd George then defended his choice. In making it

he had the support of Dr. Burge the Bishop of Southwark (a very sane and sensible prelate). With the Church an established body it [was] essential that all aspects should be reflected in its government: were the Church merely a sect, or a private and unofficial corporation, it would be possible and it might even be right that aspects such as those which Henson reflect[ed] should be excluded or suppressed. The little man stated his case with incomparable lucidity and humour, carrying the sympathy of those who heard him . . .[13]

Henson's performance as a bishop justified his appointment. Though he stayed only a short time at Hereford, he won over most of those who had objected to

9. Ibid., 9 January 1918.   10. Ibid., 22 January 1918.   11. Ibid., 4 February 1918.
12. Ibid., 2 February 1918.
13. Crawford diary, 18 December 1917. Most Nonconformists regarded the Church of England as 'the great sect' and would have been scandalized by Lloyd George's suggestion that their own churches were 'mere' sects.

his coming, including the editor of the *Hereford Times*. In 1920 the see of Durham became vacant and Lloyd George was able, sooner than expected, to give him the chance to minister to a 'large and industrial population'. It was a diocese where he already had many friends and admirers, and he remained there for nearly twenty years. When he left the clergy of the diocese recorded their 'affectionate gratitude for a great and generous episcopate'.[14]

The breakfast at which Lloyd George spoke, incidentally, about Henson's appointment was a more or less regular fixture on Tuesdays or Thursdays when Parliament was sitting, to enable the Prime Minister to keep in touch with Unionist members of his government. Derby was normally the host, and his fine London House made an agreeable venue.[15] Similar breakfast parties for Liberal and Labour colleagues (together) were held on Wednesdays, or occasionally on a Monday. These gatherings were organized by Lloyd George's chief whip, Captain Frederick (Freddie) Guest, whose official residence, 12 Downing Street, provided the usual meeting-place, though sometimes the breakfasts were held at Number 10.

Even with the new ministries that Lloyd George had set up, his government was still small by comparison with governments since the Second World War. The main reason was that the ministerial strength of each department was normally just two, a senior minister and a single junior minister. The hypertrophic growth of ministerial establishments, with an intermediate layer of ministers of state and multiple under-secretaries, was a thing of the future.[16] The number attending Lloyd George's breakfasts was, therefore, never so large as to preclude intimacy; as a rule, about twenty-five could be expected to attend. When he was abroad the breakfasts might take place without him, but his presence was their principal *raison d'être* and he tried not to miss them, because they were useful to him as well as to his colleagues. Since he visited Parliament so seldom, and had so little contact with back-benchers, it was all the more important that he should have a direct line of communication to lesser members of his government.

Talk at the breakfasts was not unduly stage-managed, though Lloyd George naturally took advantage of them to put across any themes of policy that were uppermost in his mind. He spoke with candour and his usual light touch, attuning himself to the different political cultures within his coalition. On the

14. *DNB* entry on Henson.

15. In Stratford Place, off Oxford Street: now (2002) the Oriental Club.

16. His appointment in September 1917 of a secretary for overseas trade within the Board of Trade may be seen as a portent of the ministers of state to come. But this post remained as an exception to the general rule until, in 1943, a minister of state was appointed at the Foreign Office.

day that he raised the subject of Henson, his remarks were chiefly devoted to the problem of manpower, which (as we shall see) was very much in his thoughts. He complained of the obstructiveness of skilled artisans, 'notably the highest grades of skilled labour such as the engineers – "The House of Lords of Labour" as he slyly called them'.[17] He was simultaneously appealing to the employer-orientated prejudices of his Tory colleagues, and pulling their legs about a 'trade union' and vested interest of their own. The following day the same subject was discussed at a Wednesday breakfast for Liberal and Labour colleagues, but there is no evidence that he used the House of Lords analogy with them.

As well as the large breakfasts for ministers, Lloyd George very often had individuals or small groups to breakfast at Number 10, when they would be joined by any members of his family who happened to be there. Breakfast was his favourite meal for entertaining, though he also frequently had people to lunch, which again was likely to be a family occasion. In the evening he preferred to eat early and go to bed early, because it was his habit to wake early in the morning. He was therefore reluctant to give or attend dinner parties, though obviously there had to be some exceptions to this rule. His avoidance, so far as possible, of social activity late at night, and his consequent ability to start work long before breakfast time, contributed greatly to his effectiveness during the day.

He would wake not later than 6 a.m. and then work on papers until about 7.30, when tea and fruit would be brought to him. Hankey emphasizes the importance of his early morning reading:

It was believed at the time that Lloyd George read nothing, and he seemed almost to encourage that idea at times. In fact he was an omnivorous reader . . . His official papers were placed by his bedside overnight, and at an early hour he would apply himself to them. If one wanted to ensure that he read a particular paper, this could be put beyond doubt by persuading his private secretary to place it high up among the documents on his bed table. By breakfast the Prime Minister had mastered the contents of a mass of official and unofficial documents, and had skimmed through the whole of the London Press as well as a good many provincial newspapers . . . and was ready to begin – what was really his main fount of knowledge – sucking the brains of the best men he could get on every subject.[18]

17. Crawford diary, 18 December 1917.
18. Maurice Hankey, *The Supreme Command, 1914–1918* (2 vols., 1961), vol. ii, pp. 575–6. Hankey adds that Lloyd George 'rarely held official meetings late at night, which wears most people out quicker than anything else'. Very different from Churchill.

After drinking his early morning tea, Lloyd George would get up, have a bath and shave. His cleanliness and healthy appearance struck everybody he met. Almost until old age he retained the smooth skin and glowing cheeks of a child. Clemenceau described him as 'fresh and pink, with a joyous smile', but also 'clenched fists'.[19] It was after his ablutions that he read the papers. By breakfast time he had been going for at least three hours and was thoroughly well briefed.

For those of his colleagues who were accustomed to start the day in a more leisurely fashion, allowing time for postprandial digestion, his working breakfasts were accepted as a penance. One who found them hard to bear was Austen Chamberlain, who wrote: 'Breakfasts are the devil. Destructive of the digestion and the temper! And nothing disturbs me more . . . than the matutinal habits of the Prime Minister.'[20] Robertson was another who found them objectionable. When Hankey tried to improve relations between him and the Prime Minister by starting a weekly breakfast, the experiment failed and was soon discontinued. The CIGS could not tolerate Lloyd George's habit of extending talk 'for a long time after breakfast', to which his (Robertson's) 'digestive apparatus could not adapt itself '.[21]

On 6 December (the day he wrote to Henson) Lloyd George proposed to the War Cabinet that it should set up a committee to consider all aspects of the manpower problem and recommend priorities for the coming year. Like the War Policy Committee before it, the manpower committee would be little different from the War Cabinet itself, since it was to consist only of War Cabinet members: the Prime Minister (presiding), Curzon, Carson, Barnes and Smuts. Other ministers and miscellaneous experts would be summoned to attend, and Hankey would act as secretary.

One minister who attended every meeting, without being formally a member of the committee, was Auckland Geddes, who in August had succeeded Neville Chamberlain as Minister of National Service. Geddes was the son of an Edinburgh civil engineer whose progeny achieved much distinction. Auckland was the second son. His elder brother was First Lord of the Admiralty; his younger brother was for many years chairman of the Orient shipping line; and one of their sisters was the first woman to be

19. 'Et voici Lloyd George, frais et rose, qui s'avance éclairé d'un joyeux sourire à poings fermés' (Georges Clemenceau, Grandeurs et misères d'une victoire (1930), p. 124).
20. Charles Petrie, Life and Letters of the Rt. Hon. Sir Austen Chamberlain (2 vols., 1940), vol. ii, p. 160. (Chamberlain was in office through most of Lloyd George's time as Prime Minister, though his over-punctilious resignation in July 1917 kept him out for nine months.)
21. Hankey, Supreme Command, vol. ii, pp. 775–6.

awarded a doctorate of medicine by Edinburgh University. Auckland also started his career as a doctor, and before the war was, like Addison, a professor of anatomy. At the same time he took a deep interest in military matters and contributed ideas when the Territorial Army was being created by Haldane (to whom he was distantly related). On the outbreak of war he joined the Northumberland Fusiliers, but was soon made unfit for combatant duty by a riding accident, and was then posted to GHQ in France as assistant adjutant-general. In 1916 he was appointed director of recruiting at the War Office, and his manifest efficiency in this post led to his appointment as Chamberlain's successor the following year. A Parliamentary seat was found for him at Basingstoke, and he showed more natural aptitude for politics than his brother Eric, while sharing his talent for administration.

During his first four months at the Department of National Service he transformed its character and gave it an authority that it had previously lacked. His department took over the task of recruiting for the army and, though it could not similarly control the recruitment of men for civilian work, Geddes established good working relations with the other departments concerned, Labour and Munitions, while accumulating an 'array of administrative talent' in his own Ministry.[22] Thus he gradually acquired a dominant influence in the distribution of manpower on the home front.

He was quite capable, when necessary, of standing up to Lloyd George, but of doing it so artfully that the Prime Minister's goodwill was not forfeited. When Geddes was appointing regional directors of recruiting, Lloyd George took particular interest in the appointment for the Welsh region and wanted his former private secretary, John Rowland, to be given the job. Geddes did not oblige but appointed instead Lord Treowen, Lord-Lieutenant of Monmouthshire, partly because he thought it a wise policy to exploit the historic connection of lords-lieutenant with the army. Treowen, formerly Sir Ivor Herbert, was a retired major-general and a large landowner, who had served as a Liberal MP until recently ennobled by Lloyd George: hardly a man to whom the Prime Minister could object.[23]

Geddes was asked to sit on the War Cabinet's war priorities committee, but since the needs of the army were outside the committee's purview it could not arrive at a comprehensive judgement on priorities for the use of manpower. On 3 December Geddes submitted a memorandum which led to the decision, three days later, to set up a manpower committee to review

22. Keith Grieves, *The Politics of Manpower, 1914–18* (1988), p. 152. One of the men brought in by Geddes was Philip Lloyd-Greame; later came Cunliffe-Lister and Lord Swinton.
23. Geddes offered Rowland another post, which he refused (A. Geddes to J. T. Davies, 19 October 1917).

the whole subject. Geddes showed that of 3,600,000 men of military age in civilian life only 100,000 were fighting fit (category 'A') and between the ages of eighteen and twenty-five. Nearly all the older men who could be conscripted for the army were already doing vital war work. Only about 100,000 in the lower categories were available. It was obvious that hard decisions had to be taken between the competing claims of army, navy and war industry.

The manpower committee met for the first time on 10 December, at Curzon's London house, 1 Carlton House Terrace. Lloyd George presided, as he did at the four remaining meetings, which were held at 10 Downing Street. At the first the committee questioned two generals, Sir Nevil Macready, Adjutant-General to the forces, and Sir George Macdonogh, chief of military intelligence, who were summoned to attend along with Derby. Lloyd George pointed out that, according to the figures supplied by the generals, there was a present Allied superiority of nearly 400,000 men on the Western front. When he asked how much German strength could be transferred from the East if the Russians made peace, Macdonogh replied that it would certainly be more than Haig's estimate of 250,000. He estimated the army's total manpower requirement over the next twelve months at 1,304,000. When Lloyd George asked what rate of casualties this estimate assumed, Macdonogh said that it would be the same as 1917, regardless of whether the army would be attacking or defending. Lloyd George challenged the statement, remarking that useful information on the subject could be obtained from Pétain. Later in the meeting he asked Hankey to send a telegram to Clemenceau, requesting that 'a competent French officer' be sent over to report on Pétain's methods.

The Prime Minister insisted that the country would not stand for a repetition of the human toll of 1917. 'If the Government was responsible for making a further call on the manhood of the country it was equally [responsible] to see that when these men had been handed over to the Army every care was taken . . . that human life was not wasted.' And he mentioned the reference to casualties in Lansdowne's letter, which 'had made a profound impression upon the country, and was being very freely discussed'.[24]

The following day Lloyd George made a vain attempt to secure Derby's co-operation in finding a way to remove Robertson and Haig. He suggested, at a private meeting, that Haig should be kicked upstairs as overall

24. Manpower committee minutes, 10 December 1917. The French were slow to respond, but when officers were eventually sent their testimony did not help Lloyd George, since they insisted that lower French casualties, compared with British, were merely proportionate to the scale of operations.

Commander-in-Chief, in the manner of Joffre, and that a new commander should be found for the army in France. He seems to have been less clear how to save Robertson's face. In any case Derby, predictably, would not co-operate. In a long letter written the same day he attributed all recent failures in Haig's command to the Field-Marshal's excessive trust in subordinates, and the net result of Lloyd George's *démarche* was the purge (already described) of Haig's staff officers.[25]

Quite apart from his determination to deny Haig any more men than he strictly needed, for fear that he would throw them away in more Passchendaeles, Lloyd George 'had no doubt that merchant shipbuilding and all its adjuncts came absolutely first'. More ships would mean more American troops brought to Europe, and a proportionate reduction in the drain on British manpower. He also pressed the case for following the example of the Germans and French in reducing the infantry component of divisions and substituting more mechanical power: machine-guns, mortars and light artillery.[26]

There was much discussion in the manpower committee of means to make better use of men already in uniform. The cavalry in Haig's army should, it was felt, largely be used in unmounted roles, and the size of home forces and the army in Ireland seemed excessive. But the suggestion that conscription should be applied to Ireland met with strong resistance from the Prime Minister. This could not be done, he said, without 'raising a tremendous storm', which would have repercussions in partner countries, especially the United States. An alternative idea that Ulster alone might offer to accept conscription was rejected by Carson as 'impracticable'.[27]

When the committee completed its work, Hankey produced a report based upon its minutes, which the War Cabinet discussed over Christmas and into the New Year. The decision that emerged was in line with the Prime Minister's thinking. Top priority in the allocation of manpower was given to shipbuilding and naval escorts, while the army's claim was ranked below tank and aircraft production and all civilian industries upon which the country's life depended. The army was required to make better use of

25. Derby to DLG, 11 December 1917. While reasserting his faith in Haig as 'the best man we have got for Command in the Field', he mentioned as the only conceivable replacement Munro (Commander-in-Chief in India) or Rawlinson: not Plumer, who was 'sound' but lacked the necessary imagination. Derby defended Robertson rather less robustly than Haig, but declared his total opposition to Wilson as CIGS. The letter contained the usual threat of resignation.
26. Manpower committee, third meeting, 11 December 1917. (This was in the afternoon, the committee having held its second meeting in the morning).
27. Manpower committee, fourth meeting, 15 December 1917.

its existing resources. Home forces were to be cut from eight divisions to four, so making about 40,000 men available for service in France. The divisional establishment in Haig's army was to be nine rather than twelve infantry battalions, and the cavalry was to be substantially reduced in favour of dismounted service. Only 150,000 new recruits were to be drawn from civilian life, compared with the 600,000 demanded by the army.

Nevertheless, a large number of men, hitherto protected, had to be 'combed out' of civilian work which could no longer be regarded as vital. In his Commons speech on 20 December Lloyd George warned that the schedules of protection would have to be revised. He did not deny that pledges had been given, to which he was party, but a new situation had been created, he said, by the collapse of Russia and the crisis in Italy. The pledges had been right at the time and given in good faith, but he now had to ask that they 'be either altered or cancelled' as a result of the 'changed conditions'. He was able to quote Henderson as having refused at the time (April 1916) to give an absolute guarantee that, whatever happened, the pledges would remain sacrosanct. When questioned by a trade union leader, Henderson had stated firmly that changes might have to be asked for in the light of 'changing circumstances', but that any proposals for change would be discussed with the unions before being implemented or – if legislation were needed – submitted to Parliament. Lloyd George stuck by what Henderson had said, and announced that Geddes would be summoning a conference of trade unionists the following week.[28] (It was, in fact, held early in the New Year, and was twice addressed by the Prime Minister, as we shall see.)

Meanwhile Geddes received new powers under the Defence of the Realm Act, to close or restrict non-essential industries and thus to channel labour into the civilian war work that really mattered. Industrial conscription remained taboo, but direction of labour was in large measure achieved by the use of Geddes's regulatory powers. As for military service, to change the schedules of protection and exemption a bill was needed, and Geddes introduced one after the trade union conference. But the engineers (ASE) would not agree to the recruitment of skilled men before all dilutees had been withdrawn. Despite the opposition of this powerful union, the bill became law in early February.[29]

The age-span of liability for compulsory service remained eighteen to forty-one, and the minimum age for combatant service stayed at nineteen. Moreover, for the time being Lloyd George had his way in preventing the

28. Hansard, fifth ser., vol. c, cols. 2213–17.
29. Grieves, *Politics of Manpower*, pp. 182–3.

extension of conscription to Ireland. But all this would soon be changed under the impact of tremendous events on the Western front.

As the end of 1917 approached Lloyd George had the mortification of knowing that he had failed, during his first year as Prime Minister, to remove either Robertson or Haig, despite his strong desire to be rid of both of them. On the naval side, however, he was more successful, though only just. With a week to spare he was able to rid himself of the First Sea Lord whom he had long regarded as pessimistic and obstructive. Before Jellicoe left for home on Christmas Eve he received a letter from the First Lord, Eric Geddes (Auckland's brother), relieving him of his post. Two days later his departure became public knowledge, and it was also announced that he would be raised to the peerage as a viscount. His place as First Sea Lord was taken by his deputy, Sir Rosslyn Wemyss.

Jellicoe was a distinguished officer and a fine man, commanding much affection and loyalty in the service. In his early years his most memorable experience of fighting was, paradoxically, on land, when he acted as Chief of Staff to Admiral Sir E. H. Seymour in an attempt to rescue the foreign legations at Peking in the Boxer Rising of 1900. Jellicoe was severely wounded during the expedition, which never reached its objective (though the job was eventually done by an international force).

A favourite of Admiral Jacky Fisher, Jellicoe was given an important position at the Admiralty when Fisher became First Sea Lord a few years later. He did good work on gunnery and arranged for the output of naval ordnance to be transferred from the War Office to the Admiralty. In 1910 he was appointed to command the Atlantic fleet, and on the outbreak of war was made Commander-in-Chief of the grand fleet. Fisher was soon back for another term as First Sea Lord, recalled by Churchill, and he supported Jellicoe's cautious view of the grand fleet's function, that at all costs its control of the North Sea must not be risked.

During the titanic quarrel between Fisher and Churchill over Gallipoli, which resulted in the departure of both men from the Admiralty, Jellicoe's sympathies were naturally with his patron, to whom he wrote at the time: 'We owe you a debt of gratitude for having saved the Navy from a continu-ance in office of Mr. Churchill, and *I hope that never again will any politician be allowed to usurp the functions that he took upon himself to exercise.*'[30] The idea that the political head of a service department was a usurper if he presumed to have a mind of his own, independent of his chief professional

---

30. Ruddock F. Mackay, *Fisher of Kilverstone* (1973), p. 505; my italics.

adviser, was exactly that of Robertson; and it was, of course, to remain Jellicoe's when he became First Sea Lord. With Balfour he had little difficulty in maintaining his dominance, and with Carson none at all. But when Lloyd George made Geddes First Lord a clash was inevitable.

Meanwhile Jellicoe had come through the biggest test of his career. The battle of Jutland (May 1916) might have destroyed him and the country as well. In fact, though not a great victory – and hardly a victory at all in the ordinary sense – it proved strategically decisive. British losses in the battle exceeded the Germans', and Jellicoe failed to prevent the imperial High Seas Fleet from running the gauntlet and returning safely to its bases. Nevertheless, it did not again mount a comparable challenge to the grand fleet, which remained in effective control of the North Sea. The Nelson touch was absent, but if Jellicoe had tried to act like Nelson the result might have been a Trafalgar in the Germans' favour.

As First Sea Lord he was seriously miscast, and it was most unfortunate that he was appointed just before Lloyd George took over as Prime Minister. In one respect he was worse than Robertson, having more in common with Kitchener as an obsessive centralizer. His pessimism when faced with the Germans' unrestricted U-boat campaign, and his conservatism on the subject of convoy, have been described and are clear from the record. The attempt of his official biographer to present him as the man who mastered the U-boats is absurd. The fight against them was, indeed, effectively won while he was First Sea Lord, but most of the credit is due to others. It is also rather ludicrous to suggest that a viscountcy was inadequate recognition for him.[31] Fisher was never more than a baron, and French at the time was still a viscount. Jellicoe already had the Order of Merit, awarded to him by the King after Jutland. (Later, after a successful term of office as Governor-General of New Zealand, he was advanced to an earldom.) On the whole his services were well requited.[32]

Yet the manner of his dismissal as First Sea Lord was clumsy, to put it

31. Sir R. H. Bacon, *The Life of John Rushworth Earl Jellicoe* (1936), chapter XXIII. Bacon was commanding the Dover Patrol when Jellicoe was dismissed, and soon afterwards was replaced himself by Roger Keyes, a change that Geddes would have liked to make earlier.

32. One should mention, too, that in June 1918 Lloyd George put his name forward for the post of supreme Allied naval commander in the Mediterranean. The question arose because there was a danger that the Russian Black Sea fleet might be used by the Germans, which made the creation of a stronger and more integrated Allied naval presence in the eastern Mediterranean an urgent necessity. The idea of Jellicoe as admiralissimo was acceptable to the French, but came to nothing because the Italians insisted on retaining command in the Adriatic. The Mediterranean was, therefore, reinforced, but did not come under united command on the analogy of the Western front.

mildly. Geddes felt that he had to convey such an important decision in writing, but it was hardly the sort of letter that even an Admiralty clerk would expect to receive at the end of the day on Christmas Eve. The letter itself was courteously expressed, and Geddes said in it that he was still in the building and available to talk about it if Jellicoe so wished. But Jellicoe spoke only to another admiral (Halsey, Third Sea Lord) and then wrote to Geddes saying that he would do what was best for the service. Geddes replied in another letter suggesting that he go at once on leave and that Wemyss would assume his duties.

Why was Jellicoe's removal so long delayed and why, in the event, was it executed so precipitately? Lloyd George certainly hoped that Carson's departure from the Admiralty would make it easier to accomplish, but it was impossible in July, because any addition to the trouble caused by bringing Churchill back into the government, which occurred at the same time, would have been fatal to the Prime Minister's position. During August and September he was preoccupied with the military side of the war, while Geddes was trying to reform the naval staff despite the incompatibility of outlook between himself and Jellicoe. An opportunity to remove the First Sea Lord seemed to arise in late October after the loss of a Norwegian convoy. An enquiry found that Jellicoe had failed to act on 'secret, but absolutely reliable' information pointing to the likelihood of an attack on the convoy. The question of replacing Jellicoe was then discussed by Geddes with his two immediate predecessors as First Lord, Balfour and Carson, in Lloyd George's presence.[33] But the crisis on the Italian front, followed by the business of establishing the Supreme War Council, again distracted the Prime Minister from bringing matters to a head at the Admiralty.

Geddes meanwhile was increasingly restive, showing a strong desire to leave the frustrations of his job and return to controlling transport behind the line in France. He made several attempts to escape but Lloyd George would not let him go. By late December it was obvious to the Prime Minister that action would have to be taken about Jellicoe or he would lose Geddes. In any case, his own determination to have a new First Sea Lord was unchanged. When Parliament rose before Christmas the moment at last was opportune, but the blow had to be delivered without delay, because the political consequences would need careful handling and other important business awaited Lloyd George early in the New Year. Hence Geddes's letter on Christmas Eve.

It was suggested at the time that he acted independently, and it must have

33. Hankey diary, 26 October 1917.

suited the Prime Minister to have it believed that he (Lloyd George) was not an accessory before the fact. But it is surely inconceivable that Geddes would have taken a step which was bound to have serious political repercussions without consulting the Prime Minister and securing his support. Moreover, since he sat in Parliament (for Cambridge) as a Conservative, it would have been natural for him also to seek the backing of his party leader, Bonar Law. There is good reason to believe that he did, in fact, write his letter to Jellicoe with the knowledge and acquiescence of both Lloyd George and Law.

The evidence is to be found in the Commons debate on the naval estimates on 6 March 1918, when Jellicoe's dismissal was brought up. In his speech in the debate Geddes gave the show away, deliberately or accidentally. 'I have been accused,' he said, 'of conveying *the decision of the Government* to Sir John Jellicoe in a way that hurt his feelings . . .' Questioned by opposition MPs on the words he had used he gave a rather laboured explanation: 'When I said that I conveyed the decision of the Government, I thought that the advice I gave, and which was accepted by the Prime Minister, then became the decision of the Government.'

Law also spoke in the debate and admitted that he had prior knowledge:

my right hon Friend [Geddes] says that some of his colleagues, *in addition to the Prime Minister*, knew of [what was to happen]. I was one of those who did know . . . My right hon Friend the Prime Minister sent a messenger to me – we are in the same building – and asked me to come into the Cabinet Room. I came there and [Geddes] said that he had come to the conclusion that it was in the public interest there should be a change . . . I believe that the Prime Minister sent for me, not because I was the Leader of the House, but because I was available, and he told me. I feel sure that if [Carson] had been available he would have told him also.[34]

That there would be trouble with Carson was only to be expected, and Law's suggestion that the former First Lord would have been given advance notice if he had been 'available' must have been made tongue-in-cheek. Lloyd George was in no hurry to tell him, and never, in fact, put the question of removing Jellicoe to the War Cabinet. The decision was Lloyd George's own, and we can reasonably assume that the way of carrying it out was concerted by him with Geddes, probably during the afternoon of 24 December. The idea of sending for Law may well have been proposed by

34. Hansard, fifth ser., vol. ciii: Carson's speech, cols. 2023–6; Geddes's, cols. 2029–31; Law's, 2033–8 (my italics).

Geddes, for the reason suggested, or it may have been Lloyd George's. Either way, it was a good idea.

All the same, things were difficult, if never quite critical, for over a week after Geddes wrote his letter to Jellicoe. The government had certain advantages, one of which was that Parliament had just gone into recess. In that respect the stroke was well timed and of course deliberately so. Whatever protests and mischief-making might result, there could be no immediate question of a confidence vote in the House of Commons. Another helpful factor was that the army top brass was not actively engaged on Jellicoe's behalf. Indeed, it will be recalled that in June Haig had aligned himself firmly with Lloyd George and Geddes about the need for changes at the Admiralty (where Geddes at the time was Controller), and had discussed the possibility of Carson's place being taken by Robertson.

During the Christmas holiday further advantages were sought and secured. On Christmas morning Geddes motored to Sandringham – probably at Lloyd George's suggestion – and was asked by the King to stay to lunch. He explained the changes he wished to make and received the King's assent to them. After lunch the King wrote a letter in his own hand to Lloyd George, sending Christmas greetings and confirming his approval of the Admiralty changes. On Boxing Day Geddes travelled overnight to Rosyth, accompanied by Wemyss, where the following day he gave Beatty a confidential briefing. Beatty had read of Jellicoe's dismissal in the morning papers, and had written him 'a strong letter saying that he was filled with dismay', promising to write again after his talk with Geddes. Significantly he did not write again for a month, and then only in anodyne terms.[35] In fact he had no serious objection to the deed itself, but felt that it should have been done less brutally.

Geddes had more trouble with the sea lords (other than Wemyss), which he compounded by inept handling. Though Jellicoe, to his credit, advised them to stay at their posts, their mood was at first mutinous. Somewhat rattled, Geddes talked to them and unwisely referred to the meeting at the end of October, at which he and Lloyd George had discussed Jellicoe's position with Balfour and Carson. Whatever he actually said, he managed to convey the impression that the two former first lords had then agreed to the removal of Jellicoe. When consulted by the sea lords they denied that they had done so, though Balfour's denial was markedly less emphatic than Carson's. On 31 December Geddes was faced with a threat from the sea lords that they would resign unless the matter were cleared up. But it proved

35. Jellicoe's contemporary note, quoted in Bacon, *Life of Jellicoe*, p. 380.

to be an empty threat. 'After interminable argument [they] decided to remain.'[36]

The toughest problem was Carson. Lloyd George was prepared for him to leave the War Cabinet, while preferring him to stay, if only for his symbolic value. But it would have been dangerous if he had resigned at once, and explicitly on the Jellicoe issue. Lloyd George managed to avert both dangers. When Carson did resign, towards the end of January, he gave (as we shall see) a different reason for going, and his subsequent protests about the removal of Jellicoe, as in the debate on 6 March, carried little weight. By then the issue was virtually dead.

After Jellicoe's departure Geddes was content to see the war through at the Admiralty, and the new arrangements that he set in place worked well. Jellicoe had conspicuously failed to share decision-making with Wemyss, though Geddes had created the post of deputy First Sea Lord with that end in view. Wemyss, on the other hand, was a good delegator. Without being as big a figure in the navy as Jellicoe, he had a record of thoroughly efficient service. At Gallipoli he had played a key part in the landings, and above all in the evacuation of the troops, which was a triumph of organization. Recently, before being recalled to the Admiralty, he had covered Allenby's advance into Palestine. He was a genial colleague, who got on well with both politicians and his professional colleagues. A further asset was that he spoke fluent French.

36. Contemporary note by Admiral Duff (Bacon, *Life of Jellicoe*, p. 383).

21

Speeches

Working New Year – War aims speech – King and Prime Minister – New Year honours

Lloyd George again spent Christmas and the New Year in London, where he had much to occupy him. The War Cabinet met during the morning of Christmas Eve, though apparently nothing was said about the impending *coup* at the Admiralty. Hankey was allowed Christmas Day and Boxing Day off. Lloyd George presumably had the company of Frances Stevenson (though we cannot be sure in the absence of her diary, which does not resume until March 1919.) It is just possible that Megan was with him, though there is no evidence. Margaret was at Criccieth, awaiting the birth of two grandchildren. She stayed there for several months, with only brief and infrequent visits to London. He wrote to her quite often, and it is clear that he missed her. His letters at this time are rushed, but intimate and affectionate. When the arrival of the first grandchild is imminent he writes: 'Tell them to hurry up as I want my old pal back.'[1]

On Christmas Day Riddell was with Lloyd George at 10 Downing Street from midday until 10 p.m. While he was there Geddes telephoned to report on his visit to Sandringham. Riddell gathered that Jellicoe had been 'asked to resign', and Lloyd George commented that this was 'a good thing' because Jellicoe had 'lost his nerve'. The Prime Minister was clearly not yet prepared to take even Riddell wholly into his confidence about the sequence of events at the Admiralty.[2] Incidentally, when Churchill lunched with Riddell on New Year's Day he was vehement against the changes, describing the replacement of Bacon in particular as 'madness'.[3] But by the time he wrote *The World Crisis* he had evidently changed his mind, since in that work he remarks that the new barrage placed across the Dover Straits (by Bacon)

---

1. DLG to MLG, 7 February 1918.
2. *RWD*, 25 December 1917. According to A. J. Sylvester (talking to the author) the house contained only one telephone throughout the war.
3. *RWD*, 1 January 1918. Churchill also said that he wished he were in opposition, and would resign when the war was over. Yet he admitted that he was 'miserable' while unemployed. Perhaps he was in a bad mood because he had not been consulted about the changes.

had utterly failed to stop the passage of U-boats from the Flanders ports into the Atlantic by the much shorter Channel route, but that when Keyes replaced Bacon he 'revolutionised the situation'.[4]

Lloyd George had an uninvited but welcome visitor during the morning of 1 January. Addison called to wish him a happy New Year, and was asked to accompany him for 'a walk and a quiet talk' in St James's Park. They were out for three-quarters of an hour and Lloyd George used the time to share some thoughts with Addison, whom he trusted and whose opinion he respected.

British diplomacy needed to be stiffened with 'new and bolder men'. What about bringing Balfour into the War Cabinet and making Smuts Foreign Secretary? He would be the 'ideal man', but it would be difficult to get South Africa to agree. And how could Derby be eased out of the War Office, where he was 'not very keen' (an understatement) on changing the army staff? Lloyd George suggested that he might be sent to Paris, since Bertie was about to retire as Ambassador there, and his place could then be taken by Milner, who was entirely sympathetic to staff changes.

Still apparently hopeful that the Irish Convention would come up with some worthwhile proposal, the Prime Minister wondered how he could find 'a loyal Tory who wanted an Irish settlement' and who would 'carry more weight with the rank and file of the Tories than Duke'. In any case, H. E. Duke, Chief Secretary since December 1916, might be interested in a high legal office that would soon become vacant. Lloyd George mentioned no potential successor to Duke as Chief Secretary, but expressed his desire to keep Carson in the government if he possibly could, because outside he might well be 'captured by the Ultra-Ulstermen'. He was also 'personally very loyal' to himself (a somewhat mistaken view).

Another matter of concern to Lloyd George was that Law's workload did not leave him enough time for the War Cabinet. Perhaps Austen Chamberlain might relieve him at the Treasury, so that he would be free to concentrate on the War Cabinet and the House. Addison's only criticism of the Prime Minister's speculative proposals – some of which were to bear fruit – was that if Milner and Smuts were removed from the War Cabinet it would be 'seriously weakened'. Lloyd George finally told his colleague that he had 'decided to make a clear and determined statement on War Aims, if possible by the end of the week'.[5]

Preparing his speech on this subject was, indeed, his principal task over

4. Winston S. Churchill, The World Crisis, p. 759 (single-volume edition, 1931).
5. Addison diary, 1 January 1918.

the New Year. The necessity to do it caused him some irritation, since he felt that he had already defined the purposes for which Britain was fighting fairly comprehensively in his Glasgow speech at the end of June. The only important subsequent addition was Britain's endorsement of France's claim to Alsace-Lorraine. Nevertheless he was under pressure from many quarters to state, or restate, the British Empire's war aims, and he realized that such a statement might have a good effect on morale at home, while serving to counteract enemy mischief-making and propaganda. The yearning for peace was profound, and he could not ignore the fact that it was, in a sense, uniting two such disparate characters as Lansdowne and Mac-Donald. He had to respond to a mood which was war-weary and confused, though still in the main resolute. It was time to articulate and justify the will to win.

Since Parliament was in recess, he chose to deliver the speech to the conference of trade unionists. This was anyway a most suitable audience, at a time when Bolshevik and pacifist influences were at work in the labour movement. He took enormous trouble over the speech. Drafts were provided by Smuts and Robert Cecil and others had their say. But of course he selected from and adapted the material supplied to him, as well as contributing passages of his own. If the text was more composite and less personal than his speeches normally were, it was because he wanted it to be far more than a declaration by the Prime Minister, or even the government. His intention was that it should be an authoritative statement on behalf of the whole British nation and Empire, and he left little to chance in ensuring that such was its character.

The text was exhaustively discussed at several meetings of the War Cabinet before being finally approved on the eve of delivery. At the same time the Dominion governments were informed of the proposed contents of the speech, and gave their general approval. Lloyd George also had the support of Asquith and Grey, though this was only obtained after elaborate diplomacy in which C. P. Scott was the prime mover.

The intermediary was Lord Buckmaster, who had been Lord Chancellor for the eighteen months of the Asquith coalition, and whom Scott regarded as 'the best and strongest' of the Liberal ex-ministers.[6] Scott saw Buckmaster and brought him round to the view that there should be a meeting between Lloyd George and his predecessor. About a week later the two men breakfasted with Lloyd George, who said that he would like to see Asquith together with Grey, who was 'a great figure' and whose 'influence would be

6. Scott diary, 16–19 December 1917.

valuable'. He also said that his difficulty was 'not with Asquith, but with the smaller men about him, and pre-eminently with McKenna'.[7] Buckmaster then set about trying to persuade Asquith, which was not easy, and when Asquith agreed Grey proved even harder to get. But eventually Asquith saw Lloyd George twice, on his own for lunch on 3 January, and with Grey on 5 January (the day Lloyd George was to speak) for breakfast. Both meetings took place at Asquith's house, 20 Cavendish Square.

According to Lloyd George he 'got on all right' with his former colleagues, who were 'very friendly'. The war aims statement was read to them in its entirety and received their approbation.[8] But afterwards Margot Asquith did her best to make it seem that the hated Lloyd George had, as it were, gone to Canossa, writing to A. G. Gardiner, editor of the *Daily News*: 'Don't fail to let the political world know that Ll.G. went to *my* husband – Asquith did not go to 10 Downing Street ... My husband said he was amazed at Ll.G.'s deferential manner to him!'[9]

Lloyd George delivered his speech the day after the meeting with Asquith and Grey, and the day after the final text had been approved by the War Cabinet. The conference of trade unionists which provided the immediate audience was held at the Caxton Hall, not far from the Houses of Parliament whose members were in recess. It was 'a crowded gathering of delegates and thoroughly representative'.[10] Lloyd George began by emphasizing the representative character of what he would be saying:

... although the Government are alone responsible for the actual language ... there is national agreement as to the character and purpose of our war aims and peace conditions, and in what I say to you today, and through you to the world, I can venture to claim that I am speaking not merely the mind of the Government but of the nation and of the Empire as a whole.

And he mentioned specifically that he had had 'an opportunity of discussing this same momentous question with Mr. Asquith and Viscount Grey'.

Before turning to positive war aims, he explained what the British Empire was 'not fighting for'.

We are not fighting a war of aggression against the German people ... Most reluctantly, and indeed quite unprepared for the dreadful ordeal, we were forced to

7. Scott diary, 28 December 1917. This breakfast meeting lasted until nearly lunchtime.
8. Ibid., 7–8 January 1918; DLG to MLG, 5 January 1918.
9. Margot Asquith to A. G. Gardiner, 7 January 1918.   10. WM, p. 2486.

join in this war in self-defence, in defence of the violated public law of Europe, and in vindication of the most solemn treaty obligations . . . we had to join in the struggle or stand aside and see Europe go under . . . [But] Germany has occupied a great position in the world. It is not our wish or intention to question or destroy that position for the future, but rather to turn her aside from hopes and schemes of military domination and to see her devote all her strength to the great beneficent tasks of humanity. Nor are we fighting to destroy Austria-Hungary or to deprive Turkey of its capital, or of the rich and renowned lands of Asia Minor and Thrace, which are predominantly Turkish in race.

He denied that Britain had entered the war to force a change in the German constitution, though he repeated the view expressed at Glasgow that 'the adoption of a really democratic constitution by Germany would be the most convincing evidence that . . . the old spirit of military domination had indeed died'.

Looking to the future of Europe, Lloyd George proclaimed that 'the days of the Treaty of Vienna are long past'. The new Europe must be 'based on such grounds of reason and justice as will give some promise of stability'. Britain felt that 'government with the consent of the governed must be the basis of any territorial settlement in this war'. The 'first requirement', therefore, must be 'the complete restoration, political, territorial and economic, of Belgium and such reparation as can be made for the devastation of its towns and provinces'. There was no question of any 'war indemnity such as that imposed on France by Germany in 1871', or of shifting 'the cost of warlike operations from one belligerent to another'. But reparation was essential; 'the great breach in the public law of Europe must be repudiated and, so far as possible, repaired.' Unless international right was recognized by insistence on 'payment for injury done in defiance of its canons' it could 'never be a reality'.

What was true of Belgium must also apply to 'Serbia, Montenegro, and the occupied parts of France, Italy and Roumania'. He repeated the new commitment (since October) that 'Britain would stand by the French democracy' in the demand for the return of Alsace-Lorraine, 'two French provinces' incorporated in the German Empire in 1871 'without any regard to the wishes of the population'.

As for Russia, he would 'not attempt to deal with the question of the Russian territories now in German occupation'. The 'present rulers of Russia' were engaged in separate negotiations with the common enemy. No one who knew Prussia could 'for a moment doubt her ultimate intention' to attach the occupied territories of Russia to Germany. Britain would be 'proud to fight to the end side by side with the new democracy of Russia', as would America, France and Italy. But if the Bolsheviks persisted in acting independently the Allies could do nothing 'to arrest the catastrophe which was assuredly befalling their country'.

Britain believed, however, that an independent Poland comprising all 'genuinely Polish elements' was 'an urgent necessity' for the stability of Europe. Similarly, while agreeing with President Wilson that 'the break-up of Austria-Hungary [was] no part of our war aims', Britain felt that 'genuine self-government' had to be 'granted to those Austro-Hungarian nationalities who have long desired it'. Britain also regarded as 'vital' the reunion of all Italians 'with those of their race and tongue'.

Outside Europe 'the same principles should be applied'. Subject peoples of the Ottoman Empire were 'entitled to a recognition of their separate national conditions', though the precise form it would take 'in each particular case' could be discussed later. The German colonies would be held 'at the disposal' of the peace conference, and their future 'must have primary regard to the wishes and interests of the native inhabitants'.

Reverting to the subject of reparations, he said that the peace conference 'must not forget our seamen and the services they have rendered to, and the outrages they have suffered for, the common cause of freedom'.

He ended with an appeal for the creation of a new international order:

So long as the possibility of dispute between nations continues ... and war is the only means of settling a dispute, all nations must live under the burden not only of having to engage in it, but of being compelled to prepare for its possible outbreak. The crushing weight of modern armaments, the increasing evil of compulsory military service, the vast waste of wealth and effort involved in warlike preparation, these are blots on our civilisation of which every thinking individual must be ashamed.

For these and other similar reasons we are confident that a great attempt must be made to establish by some international organisation an alternative to war as a means of settling international disputes. After all war is a relic of barbarism and, just as law has succeeded violence as the means of settling disputes between individuals, so we believe that it is destined ultimately to take the place of war in the settlement of controversies between nations.[11]

Albert Thomas heard the speech as a fraternal delegate to the trade union conference, and afterwards lunched at 10 Downing Street. Others at the lunch were the Winston Churchills, Reading, Riddell, J. L. Garvin (editor

11. Caxton Hall, 5 January 1918.

of the *Observer*) and Paul Mantoux (scholar and interpreter). Thomas reported Henderson as having said to him, presumably after the speech, that 'L.G. now stood stronger with the Labour Party than he had done for some time'. Garvin 'took the view that L.G.'s terms, if accepted, would leave the Germans stronger than when they entered the war', and Churchill agreed. Lloyd George said that his purpose was to appeal to the German people over the heads of their rulers, and to detach Austria from Germany (an incurable obsession of his). He pleased Thomas by promising that Britain was 'with France to the death'.[12]

Thomas was an old friend and his support was welcome, but he was no longer in office, much to Lloyd George's regret. The following day he was, therefore, pleased to receive a telegram from Clemenceau expressing wholehearted agreement, which he naturally regarded as 'most important'.[13] President Wilson also largely agreed with what he had said, but was annoyed that he had said it. The President was himself preparing an address to Congress on the same subject, and was afraid that Lloyd George might have stolen his thunder. When the text of the Caxton Hall speech reached Washington during the afternoon of 5 January, Wilson seems to have considered abandoning his own address. But House dissuaded him (according to the latter's account):

When Lloyd George's speech came out . . . the President was depressed. He thought the terms which Lloyd George had given were so nearly akin to those he and I had worked out that it would be impossible for him to make the contemplated address before Congress. I insisted that the situation had been changed for the better rather than for the worse. I thought that Lloyd George had cleared the air and made it more necessary for the President to act. I also insisted that after the President had made his address, it would so smother the Lloyd George speech that it would be forgotten and that he, the President, would once more become the spokesman for the Entente, and indeed . . . for the liberals of the world. [He] was greatly heartened by this opinion, and set to work again with renewed zest.[14]

House's competitive approach may jar, but his judgement proved correct. Wilson's address, delivered on 8 January and incorporating the famous Fourteen Points, certainly did 'smother' Lloyd George's speech three days earlier, both in contemporary coverage and in the attention of posterity. But were its merits superior? Was it indeed, in substance, so very different?

12. *RWD*, 5 January 1917.　13. *RWD*, 6 January 1918.
14. House diary, 9 January 1918 (covering a period of several days, including 5 January).

Wilson himself had admitted that his ideas and Lloyd George's were 'nearly akin', and before enunciating his Points he acknowledged that Lloyd George had 'spoken with admirable candor and in admirable spirit for the people and government of Great Britain'. He was implying, perhaps, that he would be speaking for liberal-minded people throughout the world, transcending nationality. But he had no more right than Lloyd George to speak for the human race, and his general idealism was, like Lloyd George's, rooted in national self-interest. It was unfortunate that he had the delusion of seeing himself as a world saviour, and that so many came to share his delusion.

When his speech and Lloyd George's are compared, it may seem to any fair-minded critic that the differences are, on the whole, in Lloyd George's favour. The first of Wilson's Fourteen Points calls for an entirely new form of international relations: 'Open covenants of peace, openly arrived at, after which there shall be no private international understandings of any kind, but diplomacy shall proceed always frankly and in the public view.' Such a procedure would make diplomacy impossible. 'Open covenants' is a reasonable concept, but 'openly arrived at' reduces it to absurdity. Lloyd George also envisages a new world order, but one based upon government by consent and the sanctity of treaties, both rational objectives.

Wilson demands (Point II) 'absolute freedom of navigation upon the seas, outside territorial waters, alike in peace and in war', but qualifies the demand with the words 'except as the seas may be closed in whole or in part by international action for the enforcement of international covenants' – so making nonsense of the word 'absolute'. Lloyd George says nothing about freedom of the seas, knowing that untrammelled sea power is a vital British interest. (It is also incidentally taken for granted in the Monroe Doctrine, which is hardly an 'international covenant'.)

Point III, calling for 'equality of trade conditions among all the nations', is courageous coming from the leader of a protectionist country. But Lloyd George, as the leader of a free trade country, does not need to reassert the principle. On the need for disarmament there is little to choose between the two speeches. Wilson's demand (Point IV) that armaments should be 'reduced to the lowest point consistent with national safety' matches Lloyd George's remarks about the burden and wastefulness of modern armaments. The two speeches also substantially agree on Italy, Austria-Hungary, the Ottoman Empire and Poland (Wilson's Points IX, X, XII and XIII). Both stand for concessions to Italy, but only on lines of nationality; for the maintenance of Austria-Hungary, with the maximum local autonomy for its component parts; for the Turks to be assured of sovereignty within their own territory, but not over the rest of the present Ottoman Empire; and for

20. Lloyd George conversing with the officers of the Guard of Honour, Birkenhead, 7 September 1917

21. The Western front: a line of men blinded by tear gas at an Advanced Dressing Station, Béthune, 10 April 1918

22. *(left)* Lloyd George, Foch and Wilson en route to the Supreme Allied War Council, 1918

23. *(below)* Haig and Clemenceau at Doullens station, 26 March 1918

INTERLUDE.

Dr. Plunket: "THAT'S NOT THE WAY I DEALT WITH POISONOUS REPTILES. WHAT'S THE GOOD OF TRYING TO CHARM IT?"

Mr. Lloyd George: "I'M NOT TRYING TO CHARM IT. I'M JUST FILLING IN THE TIME."

24a. *Punch*'s attitude to the Irish Constitutional Convention, November 1917

DAVID IN RHONDDALAND.

David: "I'M OFTEN AWAY FROM HOME. HOW DO I GET SUGAR?"

The Mad Grocer: "YOU DON'T, YOU FILL UP A FORM."

David: "BUT I HAVE FILLED UP A FORM."

The Mad Grocer: "THEN YOU FILL UP ANOTHER FORM."

24b. Rhondda's system of sugar allocation as seen by *Punch*, December 1917

25. Lloyd George and his wife attending a flower show in Trafalgar Square, July 1918

26. Rhondda and Lady Rhondda at a communal kitchen in Silvertown,
East End of London, January 1918

27. Curzon and Milner leaving the memorial service for Rhondda, July 1918

28. Lloyd George speaking at an unidentified meeting, 1918

29. Lloyd George being greeted by women munitions workers at the end of the war

30. Colonel House and President Wilson, 1 December 1918

31. Lloyd George, Smuts and Hankey in Paris, November 1918

32. The railway carriage in the forest of Compiègne, 7.30 p.m., 11 November 1918.
1. Foch. 2. Weymss. 3. Weygand. Foch holds the text of the Armistice, just signed,
in his case and is about to leave for Paris to put it before the French government

the establishment of an independent Poland, whose population would be all-Polish.

On Belgium, France, Roumania, Serbia and Montenegro (Points VII, VIII and XI) Wilson's policy is that these countries should be freed and 'restored', and he endorses France's claim to Alsace-Lorraine. But what does he mean by 'restored'? Unlike Lloyd George, he does not explicitly demand full reparation for damage and loss, and he is totally silent on the subject of compensation for British losses at sea. On the colonial issue he is vague, calling for a 'free, open-minded and absolutely impartial adjustment of all colonial claims' (Point V). He seems to be treating German claims on a par with others, while Lloyd George virtually rules out the return of Germany's colonies. Both men pay lip-service to the interests of indigenous populations. There is, however, agreement on establishing an international organization to uphold the new world order (Wilson's Point XIV and Lloyd George's peroration).

The most striking difference between the two speeches is on Russia. Lloyd George may justly be criticized for professing more loyalty to a democratic Russia than he had actually shown at the time of the Kühlmann overture, or was prepared to show in the absence of military effectiveness on Russia's part. But Wilson's commitment to the Russians, apparently regardless of the character of their regime or their willingness to fight, is surely indefensible in principle and an insult to fellow democracies which had made, and were still making, enormous sacrifices for the common cause.[15]

Lloyd George spoke again to trade unionists, at Auckland Geddes's request, on 18 January. This time the meeting was at the Central Hall, Westminster, and after a fighting speech which was manifestly his own, fresh-minted, not a carefully prepared and agreed text, he answered numerous questions from delegates. In his speech he tackled the peacemongers head-on, pointing to the example of Russia:

You have either got to put your whole strength into [the war] or just do what is done in the Russian army and tell those brave fellows that they can go home whenever they like . . . There is no other alternative. Believe me, if there are men who say that they will not go into the trenches, then the men who are in the trenches have a right to say, 'Neither will we remain here'. Supposing that they did it, would that bring the war to an end? Yes it would, but what sort of an end? When the Russian soldiers ceased fighting and fraternised, and simply talked great ideals and principles to the German army, what did the Germans do? Did they retreat? No, they took Riga and the islands . . . and if Petrograd had been nearer they would have taken that too. The

15. Wilson's address to joint session of Congress, 8 January 1918.

Channel ports are not so far from the fighting line, and unless we are prepared to stand up to the whole might of the people who are dominating Germany now – and will dominate the world tomorrow, if we allow them – you will find that Britain and British democracy and French democracy are at the mercy of the cruellest military autocracy that the world has ever seen ... My own conviction is this, the people must either go on or go under.

Asked by a delegate if he shared President Wilson's views on freedom of the seas, he replied:

I want to know what 'freedom of the seas' means. Does it mean freedom from [misprint for 'for'?] submarines, does it mean starvation for this country? After all, we are in a very different position from America or Germany or France, or any other Continental country. We are an island, and we must scrutinise with the greatest care any proposal which might impair our ability to protect our lines of communication across the seas.

Another delegate asked if he would undertake to bring compulsory military service to an immediate end if a settlement were reached on the lines he had indicated. His reply was carefully qualified:

It is my hope, and that is really what we are fighting for, that we will establish conditions that will make compulsory service unnecessary, not merely in this country ... It is not a question of whether you are going to stop it in this country. You must stop it in other countries, otherwise you cannot stop it here. We must put an end to militarism throughout the world.

He dealt with a variety of questions, some on labour-sensitive issues such as attendance by trade unionists at international conferences on peace. In reply to one of these he explained his reasons for opposing such attendance:

after long consultation with the leaders of other democracies we came unanimously to the conclusion that it was a very dangerous experiment to begin. You cannot confine it, you must remember, to one section. If you begin permitting one section to meet, you must permit another section to meet. For instance, it was said we were permitting financiers to meet in Switzerland. It was not in the least true, but if you do permit one section to meet, you must allow financiers to meet ... and so you would get a sectional discussion which did not represent the nation as a whole ... It is far better, from the point of view of establishing a righteous peace, that you should mould the views of your own governments to begin with. You mould the opinion of our government, the German labour people mould the opinion of theirs, and then, when the governments meet, they will do so having first of all had their ideas fashioned by public opinion in their own countries. That is far and away the most effective way of doing it . . .[16]

As usual, Lloyd George was asserting the right of governments, and of governments alone, to speak and negotiate on behalf of nations.

His two meetings with representative trade unionists during the month of January, and the effort he put into both, show how seriously he took the need to carry labour opinion with him at a critical stage in the war. His speeches and answering of questions constitute a feat of leadership which no other British politician at the time would have been likely to attempt, still less to perform with success.

After the meeting on 18 January (a Friday) he drove with Riddell to Barnes, and then walked through Richmond Park to Kingston, where the car picked them up and took them on to Walton Heath. Lloyd George admitted that he had had 'a very hard week' (which also included a secret session of Parliament), and that he was 'longing for a sleep'.[17]

Over the New Year direct relations between George V and his Prime Minister were exceptionally good. The King's letter written on Christmas Day, already quoted, was couched in very warm terms, and Lloyd George replied in kind. Still more noteworthy was the King's telegram on 17 January, Lloyd George's fifty-fifth birthday:

I wish to send you my hearty congratulations on your birthday and to express my entire confidence in you and am convinced with your help we shall bring this war to a victorious conclusion. The Queen joins me in sending her good wishes, George R.I.

To this Lloyd George replied:

I am deeply touched by Your Majesty's message & by Her Majesty the Queen's good wishes. Such expressions of confidence & goodwill give me renewed strength and courage to face the terrible responsibilities of my task. I share Your Majesty's assured hope of a victorious conclusion to the War.

Despite their many differences of outlook and temperament the two men had, indeed, a growing regard for each other, and a degree of affection that

16. Report in *The Times*, 19 January 1918.   17. *RWD*, 18 January 1918.

no amount of mutual exasperation could ever quite remove. All the same, trouble often arose and cloudless interludes were of short duration. On petty issues Lloyd George usually managed to avoid becoming directly involved, leaving his rather ignorant and cavalier private secretary, J. T. Davies, to reply on his behalf to letters from the King's private secretary, Stamfordham. At this level such matters as Lloyd George's dilatory attention to the appointment of new lords-lieutenant were discussed. But there were some royal grouses which had to be dealt with by the Prime Minister himself, either in private audience or, less frequently, in the form of a letter.

A case in point resulted from Lloyd George's decision in February 1918 to make Beaverbrook responsible for propaganda. Beaverbrook agreed to do the job but only on condition that he was given a place in the government as Chancellor of the Duchy of Lancaster. To Lloyd George and Beaverbrook this was merely a convenient ministerial sinecure, but to the King it was an office whose holder had access to an important part of his personal estate. He anyway disapproved of Beaverbrook, to whose peerage he had objected in the early days of Lloyd George's regime. Now he tried to block the proposed appointment, but Lloyd George insisted on it, maintaining that Beaverbrook was a 'first-rate business man' who would administer the Duchy well.[18] In fact, there is no evidence that he took the slightest interest in its affairs, but he was a good choice for the real job he was offered, which had the Orwellian title Minister of Information.[19]

The New Year honours for 1918 elicited no murmur of dissent from the King. In the top awards numbers were up only slightly on the 1917 Birthday honours list: five peers, six privy counsellors, twenty baronets and fifty-three knights.

The first category included a step to viscount for Lord Furness, whose father had made a great fortune in shipping and received a barony from Asquith. The new peerages went to sitting or former MPs, two each for the Unionist and Liberal parties. One of the Unionists was the man who had resigned the Cambridge seat to make way for Eric Geddes.

Among the privy counsellors two stand out as deserving figures who were also strikingly contrasted: Lord Hugh Cecil and Tom Richards. Cecil was an intellectual maverick, brother of Lord Salisbury and of Lord Robert, the Minister of Blockade. Though one of the finest Parliamentary speakers of

18. DLG to Stamfordham, 9 February 1918.
19. He held it until the end of the war, thus establishing a department which was recreated under the same name (though not under him) in 1939.

his day, Lord Hugh was also capable, before the war, of displays of partisan-ship so intemperate that the nickname 'Hughligans' was inspired by him. He resembled his father, the Prime Minister, not in having any interest in, or aptitude for, the exercise of power, but as a High Churchman who revelled in paradox and in comments calculated to shock the simple-minded. He would say, for instance, that a world war was far less challenging philosophically than a cold in the head.[20] He sat in the House of Commons as one of the Oxford university burgesses from 1910 until 1937 (having previously represented Greenwich for fifteen years). In 1941 he went to the House of Lords as Lord Quickswood, on the recommendation of Winston Churchill (at whose wedding he had been best man). In 1918 he was, as we have seen, somewhat incongruously combining his Parliamentary duties with service on the air force staff.

Tom Richards had worked in a coalmine at the age of twelve and had been Labour MP for West Monmouthshire (which became Ebbw Vale) since 1904. He had also been general secretary of the South Wales Miners' Federation for the past thirty years. He was a moderate and a Lloyd George loyalist. When he retired from politics in 1920 Ebbw Vale was held, though for a much shorter time, by another moderate. It 1929 it was won by the young Aneurin Bevan, who in his own way proceeded to radicalize Welsh politics as Lloyd George had done in the 1890s.

The new baronets included three of Lloyd George's cronies: Riddell, the Unionist F. E. Smith, who was Attorney-General in the government, and Henry Dalziel, Liberal MP and proprietor of *Reynolds' News*, who had been close to Lloyd George since their early days together in Parliament. All three were to be ennobled during Lloyd George's premiership. Another Welsh Parliamentarian who received a baronetcy was Ellis Griffith, but he was not one of Lloyd George's favourites and was not in the government (though he had held junior office under Asquith). A more significant figure among the baronets was James Craig, the future Lord Craigavon and Prime Minister of Northern Ireland. For some years he had been the true organizer of Ulster Unionism, while Carson had supplied the charisma.

There were not a few political hacks in the list of new knights, but also some more interesting names. One was the novelist John Galsworthy, but he had, in fact, refused the honour and his name should have been removed. (Later he accepted the Order of Merit.) A less eminent but certainly popular

20. Personal recollection. In a rather similar vein his father would stand a cliché on its head by saying that he 'never doubted Christ's divinity' but that his 'private judgement revolted' at Christian ethics (*Letters of Conrad Russell, 1897–1947*, ed. Georgiana Blakiston (1987), p. 124).

writer was Anthony Hope Hawkins, author, as Anthony Hope, of *The Prisoner of Zenda*. He was also a lifelong Liberal and had recently been doing war work in the propaganda department, which became the Ministry of Information. Among others who were knighted were the painter John Lavery, the journalist and constitutional historian Sidney Low, the architect Edwin Lutyens, and the cartoonist Leslie Ward (the 'Spy' of *Vanity Fair* from 1893 to 1909, who had depicted Lloyd George as 'A Nonconformist Genius').

Finally, as an example of Lloyd George's freedom from rancour, there was a knighthood for Kingsley Wood. As a young solicitor Wood had caused Lloyd George no end of trouble when he acted, before the war, as principal adviser to the industrial insurance combine, to which many concessions had to be made before the great 1911 National Insurance Act could pass. Though Wood acted most effectively for his clients, Lloyd George realized that he did not ultimately want to wreck the scheme, as many of them did. Lloyd George was anyway impressed by his ability and harnessed it for his own purposes later. Meanwhile he gave him the title under which he became a major politician during the inter-war period and a figure of historic importance in 1940.[21]

The Times again deplored the continuation of political honours, but in less strong terms than the previous year, affecting to believe that criticism had 'produced a certain effect'.[22] In February, when Parliament reassembled, there was an exchange at Question Time initiated by the Independent MP, Pemberton Billing, who asked the leader of the House 'whether his attention had been called to a statement by Mr. Oswald Stoll to the effect that he had been repeatedly approached by political touts of the Liberal Party, who claimed to be vendors of knighthoods at prices ranging from £10,000 to £12,000 . . . and whether . . . he would consult with the law officers of the Crown as to the desirability of instituting proceedings against Mr. Oswald Stoll for statements calculated to hold up to ignominy the ancient and honourable order of knighthood.' Law's deadpan reply provoked some amusement in the House: 'I naturally have no information on this subject, but I cannot imagine that there is any foundation for the allegations.'[23]

Margaret was annoyed that some names that she had put forward for New Year honours, including Dick's father-in-law Robert McAlpine, had

21. At the time of the Norway debate in May 1940, Wood, who had been one of Neville Chamberlain's closest colleagues, transferred his allegiance to Churchill and advised him on no account to agree to serve under Lord Halifax. He became Chancellor of the Exchequer in Churchill's government, but died in 1943.
22. *The Times*, leader, 2 January 1918.
23. *The Times*, 21 February 1918 (reporting proceedings the previous day).

not appeared in the list. Lloyd George replied promptly: 'I know nothing of your suggestions for the Honours List for you never said a word to me about them. Macalpine [*sic*] had better wait as there have been some parliamentary attacks on him because of his connection with me. He will be alright [Lloyd George's invariable spelling].'[24] It seems more likely that he had conveniently forgotten what Margaret said than that she had not said it. Anyway McAlpine did not have long to wait. He became a baronet in the next list.

24. DLG to MLG, 2 January 1918.

22

Rhondda and Rationing

*Rhondda and rationing – What would the enemy do? – Irish
Convention fails*

For the political leaders of France and Britain the winter of 1917–18 was a
testing time. Their countries and empires had been carrying the principal
burden of war in the West for more than three years, and seemed likely to
have to carry it for many months longer. The United States was as yet
sharing in the ordeal to only a minuscule degree in Europe, and at home not
at all. The war had brought boom conditions to the American economy,
but so far no daily heartbreak to American families in the form of telegrams
announcing the death of sons, husbands and fathers. On the military side,
the British and French had recently been further burdened by having to
support their Italian ally in a critical situation, and had now had to face the
even graver implications of Russia's total collapse. Their civilian populations
had shown remarkable stamina, but signs of strain and uncertainty about
the future were increasingly apparent. The Germans too, of course, had
suffered heavily in battle, and the blockade was hitting them very hard. But
their immediate prospects were more promising, not least because the
collapse of Russia might well mean that the blockade would soon be broken.
Moreover, they were ruled by a military oligarchy, whose dictates they were
prone to accept, whereas the nations whose morale Lloyd George and
Clemenceau had to sustain were democracies.

Clemenceau's policy for the home front was to make sure that it was
purged of treasonable or defeatist elements, and the distinction between the
two tended to become blurred. Actual enemy agents, such as the dancer
Mata Hari, were executed, while two politicians were deprived of their
liberty on dubious grounds. One was Louis Malvy, the former Minister of
the Interior, whom Clemenceau had accused in the Chamber of betraying
France's interests. At his own request he was tried by the Senate, and when
no evidence of treason could be found he was convicted on a different charge
and sentenced to five years' exile. The more important victim was Joseph
Caillaux, who had been Finance Minister in Clemenceau's first ministry and
later Prime Minister during the Agadir crisis. At that time Clemenceau

began to feel that his attitude to Germany was insufficiently robust, a feeling that grew over the ensuing years. Poincaré was even more hostile to Caillaux, and one of the President's motives for calling on Clemenceau in November 1917 was the fear that Caillaux might be the only alternative. In December the Chamber voted, on Clemenceau's initiative, to remove Caillaux's Parliamentary immunity, and soon afterwards he was imprisoned for the rest of the war. (Indeed, his trial was delayed until 1920, when he was found guilty of treason, though with 'extenuating circumstances', and immediately released.) The proceedings against him were a travesty of justice, though in a long-established French tradition of arbitrary action in defence of the state.

Clemenceau's tough measures had the support of public opinion, and this was reflected in the Chamber, where even the socialists did not vote against the withdrawal of Caillaux's immunity (they merely abstained). The need to eliminate defeatism on the home front had been recognized by Painlevé, and he began the process which was completed by Clemenceau with his enhanced authority. France had endured more than any other Western ally, and was therefore bound to be most susceptible to siren voices advocating a premature peace. Much German money had been spent in France subsidizing defeatist elements. A further danger was that the French left, with its Marxist tendencies and memories of the Commune, would succumb to the appeal of Bolshevism. Clemenceau did his best to keep the trade unions out of politics, and to avoid any discussion of war aims with their leaders. At the same time he went some way towards modifying their view of him as an enemy of the workers by showing open-handedness in response to wage demands.

Lloyd George had less power than Clemenceau to deal with dissidents on his home front. He could not have acted against Lansdowne or MacDonald as the French premier acted against Caillaux, even if he had wished to do so. But he had the advantage of a civilian population which had suffered less than the French, and of a trade union movement which was still, despite the Russian Revolution, largely free from Marxist ideology, and far more patriotic than internationalist in outlook. Morale on the British home front was therefore, as in the army, relatively high.

All the same, Lloyd George knew that he could not afford to be complacent, and he remained very sensitive to grievances and shifts of opinion at home. Hence the trouble he took to identify and tackle the causes of the industrial strikes in May, and his recent efforts to explain the government's war aims to the leaders of organized labour. In appealing to them to accept further sacrifices he treated them as partners, as he had done when he negotiated the original compact with them (the so-called Treasury Agreement) in March 1915.

His New Year message to the nation was aimed, above all, at the home front, and ended with a reminder to civilians that whatever they might be experiencing was hardly comparable with the soldiers' lot:

To every civilian . . . I would say: 'Your firing-line is the works or the office in which you do your bit; the shop or the kitchen in which you spend or save; the bank or post-office in which you buy your bonds'. To reach that firing-line and to become an active combatant yourself there are no communication trenches to grope along, no barrage to face, no horrors, no wounds. The road of duty and patriotism is clear before you; follow it, and it will lead ere long to safety for our people and victory for our cause.[1]

The biggest domestic problem at the time was the food queue, which resulted not from any general shortage of food (though there were temporary shortages of some items), but rather from a reluctance on the part of government to control food distribution by a system of rationing. Until the queues appeared the idea of rationing was opposed, by labour in particular, and it is probably fair to say that unless there had been queues it would have been hard to implement. Fortunately Lloyd George's second Food Minister, Lord Rhondda, had been preparing for such an emergency and was able to cope with it when it arose. Meanwhile the queues were a manifestation of anger, but certainly not of hunger. Bread consumption in 1917, for example, was half a pound per head above the pre-war level. Indeed, the diet of ordinary British people improved during the war, not least because workers in war industry had more money to spend.

Rhondda's original name was D. A. Thomas. As such he was very well known to Lloyd George during his early years in Parliament, when they were fellow back-benchers; but in their case familiarity did not make for friendship. They clashed on at least two major Welsh issues, the home rule movement (Cymru Fydd) and Balfour's 1902 Education Act. Antagonism and rivalry between them sprang partly from their personalities, both strong and ambitious, and partly from the differences which anyway existed between North and South Wales. Thomas was from the South and represented its interests. Son of a Merthyr Tydfil grocer who speculated in colliery shares, he himself became the dominant figure in the South Wales coal industry, and for twenty-one years Liberal MP for Merthyr. He was

1. *The Times*, 1 January 1918.

first elected in 1888, two years before Lloyd George, to whom he was also senior in age. But he was no match for Lloyd George as a speaker or Parliamentarian, and while the younger man's political career prospered Thomas's languished. Despite his outstanding gifts as an entrepreneur and manager of men, he received no ministerial appointment when the Liberals returned to power, and in 1910 he decided to leave politics and concentrate on business.

Some aspects of his upbringing and way of life were further barriers to intimacy with Lloyd George. As a boy he was sent to an English school at Clifton (not Clifton College), from which he won a scholarship to Caius College, Cambridge. Though a brilliant mathematician, he was more drawn to sport than to academic work, excelling as oarsman, boxer and long-distance swimmer. He loved the atmosphere of the university and enjoyed his time there. In his mid-twenties he married Sybil Haig, from a Radnorshire family apparently linked with the future Field-Marshal's (the Haigs of Bemersyde). Soon he took a lease of a large period country house, Llanwern, on the Welsh side of the Bristol Channel, within easy reach of his office in Cardiff. The Thomases had one child, a daughter, Margaret.

Lloyd George was brought up to disapprove of anglicized Welshmen, and he would not have been in his element at an ancient English university. He recoiled from the atmosphere of old institutions and old houses. A Welsh bourgeois who seemed to be adopting the English squirearchical style naturally irritated him. Nevertheless he and Thomas had much in common beneath their differences. Both had adventurous spirits and questing minds. Both were born to lead. Both, though nourished in the Welsh Nonconformist tradition (Thomas as a strict Congregationalist), developed as essentially free-thinking agnostics. Above all, both were social reformers and patriots.

During the years immediately preceding the war Thomas was taking an increasing interest in the New World, particularly in the Canadian North-West. In 1915 Lloyd George, ever respectful of talent, and never one to be deflected on personal grounds from choosing the best man for a job, asked Thomas to undertake a mission to the United States on behalf of the Ministry of Munitions. He agreed to go, though as a recent survivor of the sinking of the *Lusitania* he can hardly have relished so early a return to transatlantic travel. His mission was a success, and soon afterwards he received a peerage. But until Lloyd George became Prime Minister he was still offered no post in government.

When the new administration was formed he was at once given high office as President of the Local Government Board, in which position he devoted himself to planning the creation of a Ministry of Health. For this reason alone he would have been most reluctant to move to another job in June 1917, even one far less difficult and demanding than the Food Ministry. But in the end he agreed to do it, though with much misgiving and against medical advice. (His heart had been weakened by attacks of rheumatic fever when he was a young man, and cannot have been helped by a phase in middle age when he smoked fifteen cigars a day and drank nearly a whole bottle of port at dinner. Though he was now a non-smoker and total abstainer, the effects of the past could not be undone.)

Unlike his predecessor, Rhondda had no prior knowledge of the food business. But he had what Devonport lacked – and what mattered far more – the qualities needed for running a department of state. He began by laying down his conditions for acceptance in a letter to Lloyd George:

My dear Prime Minister,

Confirming the conversation I had with you this afternoon I am prepared to undertake the duties of Food Controller on the understanding that I am given a free hand, and that I may count on the support of the War Cabinet should I find it necessary

(1) to take over the whole food supplies of the Country,
(2) to reduce the price of the necessaries of life although it may involve an expense of many millions to the Exchequer,
(3) to utilise the Local Authorities for the purposes of food distribution, and
(4) to take strong measures to check profiteering . . .

I wish to repeat that it is with very great reluctance both that I leave the Local Government Board and that I take up a task of such difficulty as that of the Food Controller in the present critical times; and that I only do this because I feel that it is my duty to help you by carrying out your strongly expressed wish.

Yours very faithfully
Rhondda.[2]

The War Cabinet granted the powers that he requested and he was then free to tackle the job in his own way.

An excellent picker of men, he chose as his permanent secretary U. F. Wintour, whose work as director of army contracts had impressed him.

2. Rhondda to DLG, 14 June 1917. A passage omitted in the middle of the letter referred to Rhondda's understanding that early steps would be taken to introduce a Ministry of Health. Unfortunately he did not live to see his pioneering work on this project come to fruition. The Ministry of Health was brought into being in 1919, by Lloyd George's peacetime government.

Wintour fully justified his choice, and Rhondda worked well with him and other civil servants in the department. One of the most valuable, Beveridge, found him as satisfying to work for as he had found Devonport frustrating. Rhondda also made good use of experts and businessmen whom he brought in from outside. Like Maclay at the Ministry of Shipping, he fused the governmental and non-governmental elements into an effective team. His director of statistics, Professor Gonner, attributed his success as head of 'a huge department created in a hurry' to his 'remarkable powers of organisation and wide views', combined with 'the strong affection felt for him' and 'a peculiar sense of security due to his soundness of judgment and loyalty to the staff'.[3]

When he took office the May strikes were in everyone's mind, and the price of food had been identified as one of the working-class grievances that had led to them. In any case, Rhondda had his own passionate belief that food prices should be kept at moderate levels in wartime. But it was clear to him that it would be impossible to control prices unless he were also controlling supplies. Before him only an exiguous proportion of food supply was under the direct control of his ministry, but he at once set about effecting a drastic change, using the authority that he had obtained from the War Cabinet. The result of his work was that ultimately 85 per cent of all food consumed by civilians in the United Kingdom was bought and sold by the Food Ministry. In this process he left the wheat and sugar commissions undisturbed in the exercise of their semi-autonomous functions, while ensuring close co-ordination and his own predominance on questions of policy.

To facilitate the huge task involved, and to bring administration as close as possible to the people, he invited local authorities to set up food control committees in their areas, which came to number nearly 2,000. As a link between the Ministry and the committees about a dozen regional commissions were established. The committees and commissions were manned by people of experience and high local standing. The pattern of organization so created was similar to that established by Prothero at the Board of Agriculture.

With the necessary machinery of control Rhondda was able to tackle prices, and his first target was the price of bread. In August it was fixed at ninepence for a standard loaf, thanks to a subsidy from the Treasury of £50 million a year. The subsidy covered the increasing cost of imported and homegrown wheat. Cheap but nutritious bread thus remained in unlimited supply for the rest of the war.

3. E. C. K. Gonner, 'Lord Rhondda at the Ministry of Food', in D. A. Thomas, Viscount Rhondda by his daughter and others (1921), p. 256.

For other foodstuffs Rhondda fixed maximum prices while controlling the supply. This was not an activity that he took to with enthusiasm, because it offended his instincts as a Liberal businessman. But nevertheless, recognizing its necessity, he devoted himself to it with immense care and conscientiousness, studying all the relevant evidence in each individual case, listening to expert advisers, and, not least, drawing upon his resources as a mathematician. Gradually the point was reached where 94 per cent of all food and drink consumed in the country was subject to fixed maximum prices. The effect of his policy is graphically stated by Beveridge:

In the three years from July 1914 to the time of Lord Rhondda's appointment the prices of bread, beef, butter and milk increased more rapidly in the United Kingdom than in any other important belligerent or neutral country except Austria; from that time to the cessation of hostilities they increased far less rapidly than elsewhere.[4]

While attending to the problems of supply and price, Rhondda did not neglect the problem of distribution, and so went far towards anticipating the challenge of the autumn and winter queues. In all that he did to control distribution, both before and after the decision to introduce rationing, his flexible and in-depth system of administration proved invaluable. When the local food control committees were set up they were immediately called on to put into force a scheme, approved by the War Cabinet, for the distribution of sugar. This was simply a distributive scheme; it did not amount to rationing, but provided a useful basis for rationing when it came. Every household in the country was registered at one particular shop, and the supply of sugar to each shop was calculated in relation to the number of persons registered, at a given rate per head. The scheme worked smoothly within its limits, but it soon became clear that more was needed than a loose system of distribution based on a register of households. Rhondda then decided that sugar should be rationed. A scheme was prepared and came into force on New Year's Day.

Meanwhile, in September and October 1917 there was a shortage of tea resulting from shipping losses, and soon afterwards Danish bacon and Dutch butter supplies failed. Action was taken to increase bacon purchases from America, and to replace butter by boosting the production of margarine. But Rhondda decided that there had to be a general system of rationing, and the War Cabinet's authority to establish one was sought. He further asked the local food committees to deal with queues in any way that might

4. William Beveridge on 'The Ministry of Food under Lord Rhondda', in *D. A. Thomas*, p. 225.

suit their circumstances. This was a most fruitful initiative, which led to the evolution of rationing schemes in various parts of the country. The first and most striking of these was in Birmingham, where by the end of the year ration cards for tea, sugar, butter and margarine had been issued and queues for those commodities had been eliminated.

During the winter meat supply became an acute problem. The problem would have existed anyway, because of the inevitable difficulty of maintaining the level of meat imports, and because the government's corn production policy was reducing the area of grazing for cattle. But Rhondda undoubtedly aggravated the problem by enforcing a descending scale of cattle prices, which encouraged formers to fatten, slaughter and sell their stock early. This was, perhaps, his only serious mistake, and its result was that reserves of meat were more depleted than they need have been in the early months of 1918.

Rhondda's preparations were, however, soon adapted to meet the new challenge. A rationing scheme already planned for the London area, but originally intended to cover only butter and margarine, was amended to include butchers' meat as well. It came into force at the end of February and 'had a dramatic and almost instant success'. In the week before rationing 1,339,000 people were counted in food queues in the London area. In the first week the number fell to 191,000, and by the end of the fourth it had fallen to 15,000. Queues for unrationed articles such as cheese, lard and fish fell in the same proportions.[5] Before long the food queue had ceased to be a significant feature of life in London.

Indeed it was already on the way out in the country as a whole, as local schemes proliferated. The experience gained through them was collated for the benefit of the national system on which Rhondda and his department were working. A national system of meat rationing was introduced in early April, and a comprehensive system with a single ration book in July.

Lloyd George had picked the right man. But did he give Rhondda unwavering support throughout his year of office? Sadly, not quite. During the early months there were no complaints. On the contrary, Lloyd George gave full backing to the Food Minister and his work in a letter from Criccieth in September.[6] But a list of names submitted by Rhondda for honours in the New Year list was totally ignored and he had to protest about this to the Prime Minister[7] – who for his part was becoming anxious about the queues. He had the idea of appointing a director of distribution and rationing to

5. Ibid., pp. 241–2.   6. DLG to Rhondda, 15 September 1917.
7. Rhondda to DLG, 1 January 1918.

make up for the supposed administrative weakness of Rhondda's department in those respects. The analogy in Lloyd George's mind must have
been that of Lee as Director-General of food production at the Board of
Agriculture. But the analogy was not at all apt. Prothero was admirable on
policy, but did not regard himself as a dynamic administrator, and therefore
welcomed Lee's appointment. Rhondda was equally strong on policy and
administration. His plans for rationing were well in train, and he resisted
the appointment of a new man for the job, using delaying tactics.

Early in February Lloyd George wrote to him in a tone of the sharpest
impatience:

I was anxious to see you this afternoon about the Food situation, which I consider to
be dangerous. I was sorry to find that you had left for Newport before settling the
appointment of the new Food Distributor. There is no time for delay and it ought to be
done immediately. Your present staff is quite inadequate to the gigantic and difficult
task with which you are confronted . . . the matter ought to be put right at once, and I
am sorry that you should have left for a weekend before finding time to do so.[8]

One can hardly doubt that Lloyd George lived to regret having written this
letter. Rhondda's staff was by no means inadequate, and he was quite right
to resist the Prime Minister's unhelpful and unnecessary proposal. The
suggestion that he was neglecting essential work by leaving early for a
weekend at home (Newport being the station for Llanwern) was grossly
unjust. Rhondda always went there with a load of urgent papers and spent
his weekends hard at work. But it was a comfort to him to work in his
familiar surroundings, because he was mortally ill: a fact of which Lloyd
George was not yet aware.

As the various local rationing schemes developed, and the queues began
to shorten – well in advance of the general unified system – Rhondda's
reputation soared. He acquired in the eyes of the British public the status
accorded to his successor as Food Minister during the Second World War,
Lord Woolton. He was trusted for his efficiency in keeping the nation fed,
and above all for his fairness. When, towards the end of April, he wrote
tendering his resignation, pleading that he was 'fast losing grip' of his
functions,[9] the Prime Minister did not at all wish him to go, since his name
alone was of increasing value to the government. A few days later his Labour
junior minister, J. R. Clynes, wrote expressing the hope that he would be
dissuaded from resigning, because 'the public mind [would] be disturbed' if

8. DLG to Rhondda, 8 February 1918.   9. Rhondda to DLG, 23 April 1918.

he were to go. A fortnight or so later, after seeing Rhondda, Clynes wrote again to say that his chief would be willing to stay on if he were given two months' leave of absence. But he would do so only on the understanding that the powers of the Ministry as agreed when he took office would remain 'intact'.[10] Lloyd George was happy to accept this arrangement.

In the Birthday honours Rhondda became a viscount, with special remainder to his daughter. He had requested this favour of Lloyd George, who had won the King's acquiescence to it, as he explained to his now dying colleague:

My dear Rhondda,

I am very glad to be able to tell you that at the audience which the King has just given me he agreed that the Remainder of your Peerage should be settled upon your daughter. He is always very reluctant to make these special arrangements, and as he explained to me yesterday he only assents in cases where the service rendered to the state is very conspicuous. That is why in your case he was prepared to depart from precedent.

In my judgment there has been no case during the King's reign where it was better justified than in yours. You undertook the most difficult and thankless task which could be entrusted to a Minister. To undertake it required great courage. It required not merely courage, but great ability and especially judgment and untiring effort to carry it out. There is but one opinion about your efforts – that they have been one of the most distinguished triumphs of the war. No Food Controller in any belligerent country has won such unanimous encomiums and no one has better deserved them.

I am sincerely sorry that the very hard work and the constant anxiety . . . have temporarily affected your health, but I am glad to learn that with some weeks of rest your medical advisers are confident that you will be able to continue your valuable labours for the state.

Ever sincerely,
D. Lloyd George.[11]

In fact, Rhondda died on 3 July, and his viscountcy then passed to his daughter Margaret. She had always been close to him and was a fellow survivor of the *Lusitania* sinking.[12]

Lloyd George deserves much credit for appointing Rhondda, for giving

10. J. R. Clynes to DLG, 26 April 1918, 13 May 1918. When Rhondda died, Clynes succeeded him as Food Controller.

11. DLG to Rhondda, 18 June 1918.

12. In 1920 she founded the weekly magazine *Time and Tide* which flourished (though at her expense) for nearly four decades. Her marriage to a hunting baronet produced no offspring, so at her death in 1958 the Rhondda peerage became extinct.

him the necessary powers, and for showing at the end a suitably warm appreciation of his services, which was perhaps a conscious *amende honorable* for the momentary lapse in February. Rhondda's view of Lloyd George was well expressed to one of his experts at the Food Ministry:

when he had been speaking of his many relations with the Prime Minister and criticising his attitude with his usual frankness, he said suddenly . . . 'Yes, it's all quite true, but we must back him for all we are worth. He is the one man who can win the war, he has plenty of drive and he's an optimist. No one but an optimist can win a war of this magnitude'.[13]

Until the middle of March 1918 there was room for great uncertainty about the Germans' intentions. Of course it was highly possible that they would try to knock Britain and France out while the Americans were still, as a fighting force, insignificant on the Western front. On the other hand there were also good reasons for doubting that they would launch another all-out offensive in the West. So far, in every year of the war, the defending side had ultimately prevailed there over the attackers. Hugely costly attempts had been made by both sides to achieve a decisive result, but always in vain. Why should the Germans suppose that they would do any better in 1918 than in 1914 or 1916, or than the Allies had done in 1917?

The new factor favouring them, which for the time being, at any rate, more than balanced the entry of America into the war, was the collapse of Russia. This was enabling them to transfer troops and matériel *en masse* from East to West, and so would give them the chance to attack with an initial preponderance that might be overwhelming. But hitherto the problem had always been to sustain momentum after initial success. Could the Germans be confident that their advantage in numbers would at last carry them through to total victory in the West?

An alternative strategy was open to them. They could decide to stand firm on the Western front, retaining all the territory they had occupied, while avoiding the risk of an offensive in 1918. Reinforcements from the East would make their position there stronger than ever; so strong that even a trained American army poised for action (as yet not in sight) might never be able to tilt the scales against them. Meanwhile they would be obtaining food and other vital supplies from East European sources, above all Russia, so countering the effects of the blockade. Civilian morale in Germany would rise, while rifts might begin to appear among the

13. Gonner in *D. A. Thomas*, p. 257.

associated powers, leading to renewed pressure for a negotiated peace. But the German warlords had no interest in such a strategy. Their plan was to destroy all their enemies in the shortest possible time, and they still regarded Britain as the principal enemy. They were confident that their gamble would succeed.

No Allied leader failed to recognize the danger of an early and formidable German attack in the West. But not all of them regarded it as a certainty, and some, including Lloyd George, remained hopeful that it might not occur. Among British military leaders, Robertson was firm in his belief that the Germans would attack; Haig, until a late stage, tended to believe that they would not. Towards the middle of February H. A. L. Fisher visited Haig's headquarters and sat next to him at dinner. While discoursing on a variety of matters the Commander-in-Chief said that, in his view, the Germans had 'nothing to gain by trying the offensive' in the current year.[14] Clemenceau and the French generals were from the first more apprehensive – naturally enough, since their country was immediately at risk. Henry Wilson's team of planners at Versailles, divided between groups looking at the war from the Allied and enemy standpoints, concluded that the Germans would attack. But Wilson's own judgement of the likely course of events was less clear.

A disproportionate amount of Lloyd George's time during the first two months of 1918 was spent in machinations concerning Robertson. It was not just a struggle between civilian and military power. No less important was rivalry amongst the soldiers themselves, in particular within the Robertson–Wilson–Haig triangle.

In early January the CIGS made a remarkable proposal to Lloyd George, using the faithful Maurice as intermediary. Breakfasting with the Prime Minister, Maurice suggested the appointment of an Allied generalissimo in the person of Marshal Joffre, to whom Robertson would act as Chief of Staff, with Italian and American staff officers under him.[15] The idea was that the generalissimo would control, in particular, the new Allied reserve which it was hoped to bring into being. It is inconceivable that Maurice would have made this proposal without Robertson's knowledge, and Robertson's motive for authorizing it can hardly have been a sudden conversion to the policy of unity of command, for which he had never previously shown any enthusiasm. This had been Lloyd George's policy, not his, and

14. Fisher diary, 11 February 1918. Haig also 'grumble[d] at politicians and decisions of the Versailles conference', and said that 'we [had] been far too considerate to the French and . . . ought to take a higher hand with them'. At the same time he expressed 'a very high regard' for his French opposite number, Pétain. 15. Maurice diary, 10 January 1918.

anyone of moderate intelligence would have had his suspicions when the CIGS advanced it. To imagine that it could fool Lloyd George was naïve indeed.

To the Prime Minister its true motivation was instantly apparent and he reacted accordingly. Robertson was clearly seeking to outflank Wilson and the joint staff at Versailles. Clemenceau wanted a French generalissimo and had been reluctant, at the outset, to endorse the Versailles project. He might therefore have been expected to welcome Robertson's idea in principle. As Chief of Staff to the generalissimo the CIGS could hope to acquire a new dimension of power for himself while sidelining Wilson and Versailles.

Lloyd George amended the proposal in such a way as to defeat its author's intent. By all means let there be a French generalissimo, but with Wilson rather than Robertson as his Chief of Staff. No more was heard of the proposal from the CIGS or Maurice. When the idea was mentioned to Wilson, he made the counter-suggestion that the reserve should be put under Versailles, which would have 'most of the advantages of a generalissimo and . . . few of the disadvantages'.[16] Wilson would certainly have been more qualified than Robertson to be Chief of Staff to a French generalissimo. But he was close to Foch, not to Joffre, whose name was presumably raised by Robertson (via Maurice) for that very reason. At any rate it was never seriously discussed; however unfairly, Joffre was now regarded as a man of the past.

Robertson's proposal of a French generalissimo was not only futile as an attempt to bypass Lloyd George's creation at Versailles, and thereby diminish Wilson. It was also a very false move from the point of view of his relations with Haig. The Commander-in-Chief, already dissatisfied with Robertson's attitude towards Third Ypres (of which he was much better aware than the War Cabinet), was bound to be further alienated by the CIGS's espousal of an idea to which he had the strongest objections.

At the end of January the Supreme War Council reconvened at Versailles, with most of the Allied top brass, including Robertson and Haig, in attendance. The Americans were represented by Pershing and Bliss, with Frazier in his nebulous role as political observer. Lloyd George, Milner and Hankey stayed with Wilson at the Villa Romaine. At first Hankey was full of complaints (to his diary) about Lloyd George's state, describing him as 'impossible to work with . . . petulant, irritable . . . suspicious, sly, and dog-tired but refusing to rest'. There was nothing new in this sort of private moan, which was usually of short duration. It was so in the present case.

16. Wilson to Milner, 14 January 1918 (letter sent on by Milner to Lloyd George).

Two days later Hankey was praising Lloyd George's 'great skill' in handling the conference.[17]

The Supreme War Council had received two reports from the permanent military representatives, submitting advice on strategy for 1918. They advised that the Allies should stand on the defensive in the West, until the Americans were there in strength. This entirely chimed with Clemenceau's thinking, and no less, of course, with Lloyd George's. But the French leader was not at all pleased that the joint staff endorsed Lloyd George's plan for an early renewal of the campaign against Turkey. In Clemenceau's view every available man should be brought to France to guard against the threatened German onslaught. Far from accepting the advice that operations should resume in the spring against Turkey, he wished to see troops temporarily withdrawn from Palestine and Mesopotamia, and also, if possible, from Salonica.

On this issue Lloyd George gave some ground but seemed essentially to have got his way. He conceded that operations against Turkey should be delayed by two months, to allow more time for German intentions in the West to become apparent, and he undertook that in no circumstances would any British troops be withdrawn from the Western front. But subject to those concessions, the renewal of offensive action against Turkey was endorsed by the Supreme War Council. (In practice, the plan was overtaken by events and troops from Allenby's army had to be transferred to France before he could make any further move against the Turks.)

The general reserve proposal resolved itself into two questions: of what should the force consist and who would control it? The Versailles staff had recommended a force of up to twelve divisions, but Clemenceau insisted that it should be much larger, about forty divisions. Both figures turned out to be academic, because the commanders-in-chief were unwilling to part with any of their own divisions to constitute a reserve. Haig maintained that by the autumn the strength of his army was likely to fall from fifty-seven to thirty divisions, and Pétain was even more alarmist, stating that his army would be down by twenty-five divisions even if there were no fighting, and by fifty divisions if it were actively engaged. Lloyd George expressed astonishment at these figures, and did not accept them, but in the end the commanders-in-chief prevailed and no general reserve was in existence when the Germans attacked.

The question of control was, therefore, as academic as the discussion of numbers, though it had an important bearing on the future command structure in Britain and France, and between the Allies. Robertson argued

17. Hankey diary, 31 January and 2 February 1918.

that the reserve should be controlled by the chiefs of staff, while Wilson said that it should be under Versailles. Lloyd George was determined that on no account should Robertson gain control, even in partnership with Foch, and Clemenceau did not regard the existing set-up at Versailles as suitable to exercise command. The result was a compromise which Lloyd George successfully put to the Supreme War Council on 2 February. The putative reserve was to be controlled by a new body, called an executive committee or war board, which was to consist of Cadorna, Bliss, Wilson and Foch (not Weygand), with Foch as chairman.

This arrangement marked a distinct revival in Foch's standing relative to Pétain's and anticipated events the following month. At the turn of the year Clemenceau had tended to lean towards Pétain. Though always appreciative of Foch's optimistic spirit and flair for action, he felt that the Chief of Staff was rather too keen on pre-emptive, if limited, attacks at a time when French manpower needed above all to be conserved and cherished. Pétain's view was that the role of the French army was to prepare against a major German offensive, and to do so in a strictly defensive mode. As the defender of Verdun he seemed the appropriate man to give effect to such a strategy.

On the other hand, Clemenceau naturally responded to the idea of unity of Allied command under a French general, even when the force to be commanded was an as yet non-existent reserve. Lloyd George's proposal seemed to represent a big step towards the creation of an Allied generalissimo and to provide a less anomalous and more focused role for the Versailles establishment.

In making the proposal Lloyd George was acting with full authority from the War Cabinet which had given him and Milner freedom to negotiate. But he was going against his undertaking to Parliament in November, that Versailles would have no executive functions. The spectacle of Foch, the French Chief of Staff, presiding over an executive war board was bound to cause trouble. Lloyd George argued that no other Chief of Staff could be spared for such work, for logistical reasons. Foch was in a position to react quickly to an emergency, being only a few miles from Paris, whereas in such a case the British Chief of Staff would have to cross the sea and be absent from his duties in London for an indefinite period. But Lloyd George's true motive for keeping Robertson out of the picture was, manifestly, absence of trust. At the Versailles conference Robertson angered Lloyd George by making a forceful statement of his opposition to any further action against Turkey, and by showing his disapproval of the conclusions reached by the SWC. The final showdown between him and the Prime Minister was approaching.

*

As if Lloyd George did not already have enough to cope with in the early weeks of 1918, the Irish Question returned to plague him and he had to devote a lot of time to it. Carson's resignation in January was a disturbing symptom. Though it was a relief that he had delayed his departure and then not given the dismissal of Jellicoe as his reason for going, the reason that he actually gave was scarcely less troublesome. In his letter to the Prime Minister he wrote:

> When I joined your Cabinet . . . I did not anticipate that the question of the Irish government would be reopened during the war. Subsequently, when the Convention was proposed, I thought it right to use any influence I had in inducing my Ulster friends to take part in the effort to come to some settlement . . . It is, however, apparent that whatever the result of the Convention may be, its proceedings may lead to a situation demanding a decision by the Government . . . After anxious consideration, I feel certain that it will be to the advantage of the War Cabinet to discuss this policy without my presence having regard to . . . the pledges by which I am bound to my friends in Ulster.[18]

At the same time James Craig, Carson's ostensible lieutenant but in fact the real power in Ulster Unionism, resigned his post as a government whip.

As a device for buying time the Convention had served Lloyd George well, but it was now nearing the end of its usefulness. Carson and Craig were reacting to a development from which optimists, including the Prime Minister, at first derived some hope, but which soon led to disillusion and greater difficulty for the government. At the end of 1917 Lord Midleton (earlier, as St John Brodrick, a Conservative Cabinet Minister, and now leader of the Southern Unionists) offered a 'compromise' under which an Irish Home Rule Parliament would control internal taxation and excise, but customs would be reserved to the Imperial Parliament. Redmond, after at first insisting that customs must also be under Dublin, was finally converted to the plan for the sake of a deal with the Southern Unionists. His only condition was that the British Parliament must immediately act to give effect

18. Carson to DLG, undated but from circumstantial evidence 22 January 1918. Carson had been an unsatisfactory and at times disloyal colleague, but shortly before he resigned he spoke of Lloyd George in glowing terms to Riddell: 'He is a wonderful man. How he accomplishes so much and stands so much strain, I do not know. When I look round, I do not see who could replace him. His courage, power of work, power of decision, and urbanity are remarkable' (*RWD*, 11 January 1918). Lloyd George for his part accepted Carson's resignation 'with the deepest and most unfeigned regret', also with understanding.

to it. (No doubt he had in mind the fatal delay over the deal negotiated by Lloyd George after the Rising in 1916.)

But the state of Ireland had undergone further profound change, and there was now no hope at all that a scheme such as Midleton's would be accepted. To Sinn Fein, which was boycotting the Convention and whose fortunes were rising at the expense of Redmond's party, any Home Rule scheme was out of the question, while the Ulster Unionists' attitude was the same, though from the opposite viewpoint. Sinn Fein wanted nothing less than effective independence for the whole country; the Ulster Unionists were determined to keep control in their own part of the island and to maintain the union with Great Britain. They regarded Midleton and those Southern Unionists who went along with him as traitors. On 19 January the chairman of the Convention, Plunkett, had to report to Lloyd George that it was making no serious progress and might soon break up.

Lloyd George knew that he would have to try, and be seen to try, to salvage something from the wreck. He did not need to be jogged on this point by Northcliffe, who wrote to him at the time: 'I appeal to you to consider the far-reaching effects upon ... the United States, upon our Dominions, especially Australia, and upon our enemies, if the world knows that the Convention has failed.'[19] During February the Prime Minister held a succession of meetings with members of the Convention, but he soon found that there was no scope for a negotiated settlement. It was too late for a Home Rule solution involving the whole of Ireland, and too early for anything more drastic. The Nationalists and Southern Unionists told him that even temporary partition was unacceptable, and expected him to coerce the Ulster Unionists. Lloyd George shared their belief in a united Ireland, but made it clear that without Ulster Unionist assent no scheme could be said to command the 'substantial' support needed to justify legislation by the Imperial Parliament.

Even before the war he had taken the view that Ulster would have to be persuaded, and could never be coerced, into a united Ireland. (In the Asquith Cabinet only he and Churchill had argued thus.) How, therefore, could he reasonably be expected to attempt coercion of the Ulstermen at the height of a world war, when British forces might be about to face their supreme test on the Continent, and when his government anyway depended upon the Unionists?

19. Northcliffe to DLG, 20 January 1918, enclosing a report from the *Times* Washington correspondent, Willert, that there was 'something like consternation' there at the news that the Convention might fail.

At the end of February he wrote Plunkett a long letter, in which he set out the government's ideas for a possible interim settlement. Much would have to be left for determination after the war. On the fiscal side, while 'the control of all taxation other than Customs and Excise could be handed over to the Irish Parliament', those two functions would have to be reserved for the duration. So would control of the police and postal services.

On the constitutional issue dividing north and south, he mentioned with approval various constructive proposals that had emerged from the Convention. There might be 'additional representation [of Ulster] by means of nomination or election'. There might be an Ulster committee within the Irish Parliament, 'with power to modify, and if necessary to exclude, the application to Ulster of certain measures'. The Parliament might meet alternately in the two principal cities, and the head office of 'an Irish department of manufacturing industry and commerce' might be located in Belfast. He ended by appealing for a settlement which 'would give to Irishmen the control of their own affairs, while preserving the fundamental unity of the United Kingdom'.[20]

As soon as he received this letter Plunkett read it out to the Convention, 'stressing its main points and driving home the view that the limitation of the powers of the Irish parliament was . . . temporary'.[21] The letter was then discussed over two or three days. The Archbishop of Dublin, John Bernard, asked the leader of the Ulster Unionist delegation, Hugh Barrie, if Ulster would accept a single Irish Parliament granted that customs and excise would be outside its control. Barrie did not answer, but it soon became apparent that Ulster's opposition to a single Parliament remained implacable.[22]

Lloyd George's efforts in February may have been just enough to satisfy outside opinion that he had done his best to secure an Irish settlement in peculiarly difficult circumstances. The failure of the Convention was due to the new political dynamics of Ireland, as the relentless rise of Sinn Fein hardened Ulster Unionist intransigence. All too soon, events would force him into a decision which would make Ireland even harder to handle. Meanwhile he had gained a little more time.

20. DLG to Plunkett, 25 February 1918. Various advisers had a hand in the composition of the letter, of whom the most influential was, perhaps, W. G. S. Adams, head of Lloyd George's special secretariat or 'Garden Suburb'. He was Gladstone Professor of Political Theory at Oxford, and had earlier worked as a civil servant in Ireland.

21. R. B. McDowell, *The Irish Convention, 1917–18* (1970), p. 166.

22. Ibid., p. 168. Barrie was himself conciliatory but had no freedom to negotiate. All questions of principle had to be referred to Belfast.

LLOYD GEORGE

The fundamental change that was occurring in the South is well illustrated in the story of two funerals. In September 1917 Thomas Ashe, an associate of Michael Collins in the Irish Republican Brotherhood (IRB), went on hunger strike in Mountjoy gaol while serving a sentence for sedition. After being forcibly fed he fell ill and died. He was then buried on the last day of the month in Glasnevin cemetery. Up to 40,000 people followed his coffin through the streets of Dublin, and the hearse was flanked by armed volunteers in uniform. At the cemetery three volleys were fired over the grave, and Collins gave a short but menacing address.[23]

On 6 March Redmond died in London, but for him there was no triumphalist funeral when his body was brought back to Ireland. His coffin was 'hurried by night through Dublin on its way to his native Wexford, where esteem for him survived political repudiation'.[24] He had served his country devotedly according to his lights, but his services now counted for nothing. Together with his party he was despised and rejected. The future belonged to Sinn Fein and the men of violence who marched under its banner and would increasingly determine its course.

23. Robert Kee, *The Green Flag* (1976), pp. 607–8.
24. Nicholas Mansergh, *The Unresolved Question: The Anglo-Irish Settlement and Its Undoing 1912–72* (1991), p. 106.

23

Robertson Goes

Fall of Robertson – Grandfather – An evening with
Beatrice Webb

The fortnight after Lloyd George's return from Versailles in early February was dominated by what he hoped would be his final and decisive joust with Robertson. Though he had Ireland, air raids, food queues and much else on his mind, his time was largely consumed in the intricate process of removing the CIGS.

He would, of course, have liked to rid himself of Haig as well, and for that reason had sent Smuts and Hankey to France in January to find a replacement for the Commander-in-Chief. Haig may have guessed the true purpose of their mission, but if so gave no hint of it even in his diary. He arranged for them to spend a night at each advanced army headquarters, and found them 'anxious to help and friendly'.[1] Their reconnaissance was entirely fruitless and left Lloyd George with no choice but to make a virtue of necessity, so far as Haig was concerned. Moreover, as the showdown with Robertson progressed he had reason to be grateful for the Commander-in-Chief's accommodating attitude.

It would be tedious to describe in detail all the manœuvrings that led, in the end, to Robertson's fall. But the principal stages in the drama need to be explained and the underlying issues discussed. Lloyd George was convinced that his enemies were out to destroy him, using Robertson as their instrument, and the belief gathered strength with the passage of time. In his memoirs he writes that 'a very determined effort' was made 'to form a cabal which would overthrow the existing War Cabinet and especially its Chief, and enthrone a Government which would be practically the nominee and menial' of the military, as in Germany. He quotes a top secret memorandum addressed to Ludendorff at the time and published by him after the war, showing that the Germans were hopeful that 'the *English military party* [would] come forward and try at last to get rid of the Lloyd George they loathe[d] so heartily'.[2]

1. Haig diary, 21 and 22 January 1918.
2. *WM*, pp. 2785–6 (italics in the original German).

German hopes were exaggerated, as was Lloyd George's conspiracy theory. In fact there was nothing remotely deserving the description of a military party, but rather a hotchpotch of disparate elements opposed to Lloyd George, whose intent actually to replace him and his government varied in seriousness from group to group and from person to person. His political enemies were no more united than his military enemies. Among most of the politicians opposed to him there was a proper reluctance to substitute military for civilian control of the nation's affairs, while few senior officers were prepared to carry their contempt for politicians, or their specific hostility to Lloyd George, to the point of challenging a government responsible, through Parliament, to the country.

Yet Lloyd George was not entirely wrong in the fears he entertained at the time or even in his subsequent view that a threat to civilian supremacy existed. Robertson was in close touch with Asquith and backed by newspapers whose influence with dissident MPs, particularly on the Tory right, was considerable. Northcliffe's loss of faith in the military, and the attacks on them mounted in his papers, were worse than unhelpful to the Prime Minister; they were a boon to Robertson. Moreover, Northcliffe's new position had caused a break between him and *The Times*'s military correspondent, Charles à Court Repington, who was now working for the *Morning Post*. Repington was a journalist whose ability to reveal inconvenient facts and create a political crisis had been demonstrated in May 1915, when a report from him about the shell shortage in France, written in collusion with Sir John French, helped to end Asquith's Liberal government and bring about the formation of the first wartime coalition.[3] In February 1918 he reported that the 'decisions of the recent Inter-Allied War Council regarding the control of British troops in the field [were] of such a strange character that Parliament ... should examine them at once and take the opinions of our General Staff concerning the new arrangements'.[4] This report was published in defiance of the War Cabinet's ruling that the decisions of the SWC should be kept secret. As the crisis developed Repington carried his defiance further, expanding his revelations and demanding the Prime Minister's removal from office.

Understandably, Lloyd George assumed that Robertson had planted the

3. See my *Lloyd George: From Peace to War 1912–1916* (1985), p. 244. At the same time Northcliffe's attack on Kitchener in the *Daily Mail* had rallied public opinion behind the warlord and so made it impossible to get rid of him – a precedent whose relevance to the current situation was obvious.

4. *Morning Post*, 8 February 1918 (the report's dateline was Versailles, 5 February).

story, and was incensed by what he regarded as an act of treason. It is possible, however, that the story may have come initially from a French source. Clemenceau was not happy about the Versailles compromise, and was still leaning towards Pétain rather than Foch. He himself, or people close to him, may have given Repington the hints he needed at the outset. But thereafter he must surely have received fuller briefing from British sources. Robertson's attitude to what was happening was hardly that of a pure professional, aloof from politics. Before retreating to Eastbourne, ostensibly to recover from an attack of bronchitis, he wrote to the *Morning Post*'s editor, H. A. Gwynne:

I am just off for 2 or 3 days. The little man [Lloyd George] is all out for my blood, & is trying to isolate me . . . Keep your eye on things while I am away. My intention is to see him out. If he wants me to go, he should *tell* me so. But he daren't. He is trying therefore to make my position impossible. And all the trouble is that I am trying to see that the fine British Army is not placed at the mercy of irresponsible people – & some of them foreigners at that. . . . The general situation is – I have tried to insist upon the right things being done. L.G. is sick of me because I would not give in and trim to his ideas. The country always claims that the soldier should 'stand up' to the politician. I have stood up. What will the country do?[5]

Lloyd George was certainly determined that Robertson should cease to be CIGS. The idea of his remaining in the post, even with reduced powers, was no longer tolerable. Yet in spite of everything the Prime Minister felt grudging respect and some affection for the old soldier, and had no desire to humiliate him, quite apart from all the good prudential reasons for handling him carefully. To succeed him Lloyd George's preferred choice was Wilson, though he knew that Wilson was disliked and distrusted by many senior officers, and he himself may already have had some reservations about him. Wilson, for his part, had no lack of ambition and was eager to strengthen his own hand, but felt that he might have better scope for doing so at Versailles than in London, on the assumption that Robertson would be replaced by a less potent CIGS.

On 9 February, while Robertson was at Eastbourne, Lloyd George proposed that there should be a simple switch: Wilson to become CIGS, Robertson to take his place at Versailles. He made the proposal first to Milner, the most hawkishly anti-Robertson of his colleagues, arguing that if the CIGS refused the offer 'he would put himself in the wrong and nobody would have any sympathy with him'.[6] Later in the day he put the idea to Haig, whom he had asked to come to London to see him 'if possible alone, without Robertson'.[7] The Commander-in-Chief was met at Victoria station by Derby, with whom he drove to Downing Street 'by a circuitous route' so that the situation could be explained to him by the War Secretary. He heard that Robertson 'had lately become most difficult to deal with and lost his temper quickly'. At the meeting, which Derby and his under-secretary, Ian Macpherson, also attended, Haig made no serious attempt to block the proposed new arrangement, though he said that the army 'might be very shocked' by the appointment of Wilson, and insisted that only the army council or a field-marshal senior to himself could give him orders. A document recording what had been agreed was signed by Derby, and Macpherson was given the task of driving to Eastbourne the following day 'to communicate the news to Robertson'.[8]

But Macpherson never made the trip. Robertson refused to see him, having already heard the news from another source, who may well have been Maurice (Derby could have spoken heedlessly in the War Office after the Downing Street meeting). At any rate, the CIGS promptly returned to London and soon made it clear that he would not budge an inch from his original position. Having stated from the first that the British military representative at Versailles should be the CIGS and none other, it followed that he would not go there himself except as holder of his present post.

The military members of the army council backed his stand, but the man on whose support he had most reason to count did not. On 11 February (Monday) Haig visited Robertson in his room at the War Office and told him bluntly that 'it was his duty to go to Versailles or anywhere else if the Government wished it'. In his diary the Field-Marshal commented that he was afraid Robertson resented Wilson's appointment and meant to 'embarrass the Government to the utmost of his power'. From the War Office Haig went to Buckingham Palace. Robertson had done his best to secure royal support, and the King undoubtedly sympathized with the line he was taking. But Haig did nothing to increase the King's sympathy, urging him 'to insist on R. going to Versailles'.[9] This advice may not have been acted on at once, but ultimately Haig's influence with the King was greater than Robertson's and what he said must have carried weight. The same evening the Commander-in-Chief left for France.

6. Milner memorandum, 9 February 1918.   7. Haig diary, 7 February 1918.
8. Ibid., 9 February 1918, and DLG to Milner, same date.
9. Haig diary, 11 February 1918.

Why did Haig so signally fail to requite the slavish loyalty that Robertson had shown him for so long? As must already have been obvious, he was not the paragon of personal loyalty that his admirers have made him out to be. He was loyal to his family and, according to his lights, to three great causes: the Christian religion, the British Empire and the British army. But these loyalties were inseparable from his faith in himself. In the pursuance of his own destiny he would, if necessary, sacrifice fellow professionals at all levels. Even staff officers most devoted to him might, like the men in the trenches, have to be treated as expendable, so long as he and his vision survived.

Besides, his confidence in Robertson had been ebbing since Third Ypres. He no longer regarded the CIGS as a true ally. In a letter to his wife he said that Robertson had 'not resolutely adhered to the policy of "concentration on the Western Front"', but had 'allowed all kinds of resources to be diverted to distant theatres at the bidding of his political masters'.[10] He believed, most unjustly, that Robertson had been a wholehearted backer of Allenby's campaign in Palestine, whereas in reality he had dragged his feet about that enterprise and tried hard to frustrate Lloyd George's promotion of it. But one must suspect that Robertson's real offence was not any lack of commitment to the Western front, but rather one that Haig could not bring himself to admit to his wife or even, perhaps, to himself: that the CIGS had shown fundamental doubts about the Third Ypres strategy. The doubts had not been conveyed to Lloyd George or the War Cabinet (his 'political masters'), but had been intimated to Haig in letters quoted earlier. Such backsliding was unforgivable and unforgiven.

The loss of Haig's support was, of course, a severe blow to Robertson. Nevertheless he still felt that his position was strong and had no intention of giving up without a fight. Indeed he had some reason to hope that with the combined support of the army council, a powerful section of the press (reinforced by the counterproductive hostility of Northcliffe), and the various anti-Lloyd George elements in Parliament, his cause would prevail. By coincidence (or was it coincidence?) on 11 February, the day that he formally rejected the Prime Minister's proposal, a long article by Repington appeared in the *Morning Post*, in which the nature of the Allied executive war board was described in detail, including the fact that Foch would be its chairman. This was particularly awkward for Lloyd George, because when the SWC was set up he had made a promise to Parliament that the military staff at Versailles would be advisory, not executive. The war board was a new body, and the state of the war had changed significantly since November. All the

10. Haig to Lady Haig, 5 February 1918.

same, there were bound to be many who would argue that the Prime Minister had reneged on his promise behind Parliament's back.

Though Lloyd George wanted to arraign Repington and the *Morning Post* for high treason, it was decided on legal advice that such action might not succeed and was anyway likely to help the Germans by seeming to validate the disclosures, while making a martyr of Repington in the eyes of his sympathizers. Consequently he and Gwynne were merely charged with a technical breach of the Defence of the Realm Acts, for which a fine of £100 plus costs was imposed. The hearing (at Bow Street Magistrates' Court on 13 February) brought Repington all the publicity he could desire. He attended in uniform, and the occasion drew a large crowd, including representatives of the military and the London social world. Most notably, Maurice was there, and Lady Robertson, though Robertson himself stayed away.

Meanwhile Lloyd George had a bad day on 12 February. Derby, as ever susceptible to military pressure, proposed that Robertson should remain as CIGS, though without the special powers conferred on him in 1916. This solution appealed to three of the Prime Minister's most important colleagues, Curzon, Balfour and Law, though Milner and Barnes continued to argue that the CIGS should either change places with Wilson or be sacked. Lloyd George fully shared their anger and would have liked to do as they wished. But his political instincts, more sensitive than theirs, told him that the moment was not right for forcing the issue, and he postponed a decision. No doubt the onset of a feverish cold did nothing to boost his fighting spirit, but his reluctance to act was due to politic caution rather than pusillanimity.

In the afternoon he faced Asquith in the House of Commons and handled the encounter badly, by suggesting that his predecessor's probing of the new arrangements at Versailles was tantamount to asking for information 'which any intelligence officer on the other side would gladly pay large sums of money to get'. The following exchange ensued:

Mr. ASQUITH: I am sorry to interrupt, but I must protest in the strongest terms against the insinuation made. [HON. MEMBERS: 'Withdraw!'] . . . I made it perfectly plain that I asked for no information of that kind. My question was, In what respect have the functions of this council been permanently enlarged?

The PRIME MINISTER: I apologise to my right hon. Friend. If he thinks I have made any insinuation against him, not only do I regret it, but I withdraw any possible suggestion of it. It was far from my mind to suggest. [An HON. MEMBER: 'You did pretty well!'] I say it was far from my mind to make any insinuation against my right hon. Friend or any other Member of this House. I suggest to him . . . that to give information as to the decisions at Versailles would be unwise . . .[11]

But the mood of the House was against him and he knew it. Next day he wrote to Margaret:

Trying to throw off a bad chest cold whilst settling three or four bad crises. Yesterday in the House was unpleasant & I was not at my best. The Asquithites mean mischief. I have always thought they would when they had a chance. It will take me all my strength to fight them. But I mean to do it.[12]

Robertson had wondered, in his letter to Gwynne, what 'the country' would do. Lloyd George was confident that the general public was on his side, but had reason to fear a possible upset in Parliament. It was true that Asquith meant mischief, in the sense that he wanted to wound Lloyd George. But had he any stomach for trying to regain the premiership himself, and even if he had was there a majority in Parliament ready to support him? The answer to the first question is probably no, to the second certainly no. All the same, Lloyd George was well aware that if the various opposition groups were to combine to vote against him some new prime minister might emerge.

The Prime Minister's delaying tactics were rewarded when the CIGS made a false move which played into his hands. On the day of the Bow Street hearing Robertson, misled perhaps by the superficial appearance of popular support, indicated that he would remain as CIGS, without the 1916 powers, provided he also had a seat on the executive war board at Versailles, where Wilson would act as his deputy whenever he had to be absent. This was an arrangement that Lloyd George had from the first ruled out, and he dismissed it again when Derby resurrected it, with Robertson's approval, on 13 February. To have accepted it would clearly have been to negate his original purpose of making Versailles an independent source of advice, bypassing Robertson.

Next day Lloyd George shrewdly asked Balfour to see Robertson and try to persuade him either to remain as CIGS on 'traditional' (i.e. pre-1916) lines, or go to Versailles as military representative, but not to hold out for both positions. The Foreign Secretary had been wobbly about Robertson, but during their meeting was shocked by his intransigence. In vain Balfour

11. Hansard, fifth ser., vol. ciii: Asquith's speech, cols. 14–21; Lloyd George's, 21–30.
12. DLG to MLG, 13 February 1918. It was most unusual for Lloyd George to admit in a letter home that he had failed to shine in debate.

argued that 'the responsibility of refusing a great position at the most critical moment of the War was one which he was hardly justified in taking'. Robertson was unmoved, and the discussion cost him Balfour's goodwill.[13]

Breaking the CIGS's overweening power mattered far more to Lloyd George than promoting Wilson. The proof of this is that when it seemed that Robertson might after all agree to go to Versailles on Lloyd George's terms if Plumer, rather than Wilson, were to become CIGS, the Prime Minister immediately offered the post to Plumer, of whom, anyway, he had a good opinion. But Plumer refused it, and the way was then open for Wilson. (What would have happened to him if Plumer had accepted is an interesting question.) Robertson was given a last chance to accept the original proposal, and his continued refusal was treated as resignation, though he never actually resigned. In effect he was sacked, and Wilson was then appointed in his place.

At a long audience with the King on 16 February Lloyd George explained the situation and obtained royal acquiescence to what was now the settled policy of the War Cabinet. That evening Haig was back in London, and next day (Sunday) he visited Lloyd George at Walton Heath. The house reminded the Field-Marshal of 'summer lodgings at the seaside', and he noted that 'a sort of maid-of-all-work opened the door'. He found the Prime Minister 'anxious to deal generously with Robertson'. But Haig himself showed no gratitude to the man who had been his unwavering champion against the civilians. When Lloyd George suggested that Robertson might be sent as Commander-in-Chief to India – a post for which, with his Indian experience, he was well qualified – Haig protested at the idea of moving the existing occupant (Monro) and had nothing better to propose for Robertson than the Irish command, a most difficult assignment for which he would not have been specially qualified.[14] In the event he was given the Eastern command in England, to which Wilson had been relegated in mid-1917 and which had remained vacant since his move to Versailles. This was a humiliation that Lloyd George had not intended, and fortunately it was of short duration. In June Robertson was transferred to the command of home forces, a post worthier of his talents.[15]

Haig was accompanied to Walton Heath by Derby who, for the umpteenth time, had submitted his resignation, 'out of loyalty to the men with whom

13. AJB to DLG, 15 February 1918. The talk with Robertson had occurred the previous afternoon.   14. Haig diary, 17 February 1918.
15. At the end of the war he received the thanks of Parliament and a grant of £10,000, together with a baronetcy. In April 1919 he became commander of the British army of occupation on the Rhine, and in 1920 was promoted Field-Marshal.

he had worked at the War Office'. Lloyd George made sure that the Field-Marshal was aware of this fact, concerned that it might affect his attitude. But there was no need to worry: 'so far from the news disturbing [Haig], he sniffed it aside with an expression of contempt.'[16] He had even less of a sense of obligation to the War Minister than to the CIGS, and far less respect for him as a character. It was Haig who described him as 'like the feather pillow [bearing] the marks of the last person who sat on him' – an image more typical of Lloyd George, to whom it is often attributed.[17] The Prime Minister was ready, if necessary, to replace Derby, and arranged with Law on the telephone that the War Office should be offered to Chamberlain. But the need did not arise, because once again Derby withdrew his resignation. For the time being this suited Lloyd George, because the War Minister's departure simultaneously with that of the CIGS would have been politically awkward, and his decision to stay helped to deter other members of the army council from resigning.

The Parliamentary threat remained, but on 19 February Lloyd George appeared in the House of Commons again, in better health and altogether better form. This time he spoke first, and made a good case both for the new arrangements at Versailles and for his handling of Robertson. The speech was not without its disingenuous moments, but on the whole it was convincing and the atmosphere in the House was very different from a week earlier.

The policy decided on at Versailles was not, Lloyd George said, 'merely the policy of this Government, [but] the policy of the great Allied Governments in council'. It was 'based on the assumption that the Allies [had] hitherto suffered through lack of concerted and co-ordinated effort', from which the enemy had benefited. In the light of the Italian defeat and Russia's collapse it had become apparent that there should be a central Allied authority, and at the last meeting of the SWC it was agreed that for some purposes it needed to have executive powers.

Without going into details Lloyd George managed to seem more informative than before, and certainly was careful to avoid any suggestion that the House's desire to be informed was irresponsible, not to say treasonable. He dwelt at length upon the consensual nature of the plan adopted by the Allies, while skilfully exploiting the difference between Haig and Robertson:

I was specially anxious that the Commander-in-Chief, who is more directly concerned in the matter than even the Chief of Staff . . . should be satisfied that the arrangements

16. *WM*, p. 2821.   17. Haig to Lady Haig, 14 January 1918.

that were made were such as would be workable as far as he was concerned. Therefore I invited him to come over here. I had a long talk with him and *he said that he was prepared to work under this arrangement* [on condition that the British military representative at Versailles became a member of the army council].

The formula that Haig was 'prepared to work' the new machinery, with one apparently technical proviso, masked the fact that he regarded the machinery as basically flawed. But the agreed form of words was just enough for Lloyd George. It left a vital gap between Haig and Robertson, since the latter was not prepared to work the machinery on any terms and was carrying his objection to it to the point of open defiance of War Cabinet and Allied policy.

Lloyd George was prodigal in praise of the departing CIGS, while at the same time defending his own delay in bringing matters between them to a head:

He has great capacity and great strength of character . . . and, if I may say so, as one who has been associated with him for two or three years . . . a most attractive personality. During [those years], so far as our personal relations are concerned, not merely have they been friendly, but cordial. During the whole of this final controversy not a bitter word has been said on either side, and at a final interview – when I did my best to urge Sir William Robertson to take one or other of [the] alternatives – we parted with expressions of great kindliness . . . *All the hesitation that has taken place has [been] because the Government were trying this and trying that, in order to secure Sir William Robertson's acceptance; and although I knew it was laying the door open to the criticism that the Government did not know its own mind, I preferred that to anything which would lay us open to the charge that we were in the least hustling Sir William Robertson.*

The speech ended on an ostensibly humble note, which made it all the more effective:

If the House of Commons tonight repudiates the policy for which I am responsible, and on which I believe the saving of this country depends, I shall quit office with but one regret . . . that I have not had greater strength and greater ability to place at the disposal of my native land in the gravest hour of its danger.

Asquith, replying, soon showed that he was no longer intent to kill, if he had ever been. He paid Lloyd George an oblique compliment: 'I cannot help wishing that the speech which we have just heard from the Prime Minister had been delivered a week ago.' He also announced that he would not be calling for a division. Yet he could not refrain from going over some controversial ground, which only served to indicate how much he and Robertson had been in touch. It was now his turn to incur the House's displeasure. An exchange with Lloyd George led him into trouble:

Mr. ASQUITH: . . . may I ask is it not a fact that on the Monday Sir William Robertson intimated that he could not possibly assent to the proposals which were then put forward, and that Sir Henry Wilson had already been sent for, with a view to succeeding to his place?

The PRIME MINISTER: That was only a proposal made on the Saturday, when Sir Douglas Haig came over . . . I believe that Sir Henry Wilson was seen by the Secretary of State on Monday. I knew nothing about that interview until a day or two afterwards, but that was the proposal.

Mr. ASQUITH: Of course, I know nothing of these matters . . . [but] the impression on my mind and on the mind of the House, and on the mind of the country . . . was, when the right hon. Gentleman made his speech on Tuesday last, that there was complete agreement between him and the military advisers of the Government. Am I to understand that to have been the case?

The PRIME MINISTER: I have really stated the whole of the facts. We really thought, when we met the Army Council on these technical and constitutional points, that the last difficulty had been removed, and it was a great surprise to me that resistance developed rather on the ground of policy . . .

Mr. ASQUITH: I will come to that presently. My right hon. Friend said on Tuesday last that he had complete agreement.

Mr. G. FABER: *You are not a cross-examining counsel.*

Mr. O'GRADY: *Men are dying at the front while this is going on.*

Asquith was followed by Chamberlain, who made the speech of a man who knew that he could not be ignored and was ready to return to government after a period of self-inflicted exile on the back benches. He welcomed the Prime Minister's statement, but agreed with Asquith that he should, the previous week, have 'taken the House more fully into his confidence'. He also deplored the inclusion of newspaper owners in the government, and attacks in the press 'upon distinguished officers serving the State'. But he balanced this criticism with a comment most helpful to Lloyd George:

The House has asserted that a civilian Minister must take the responsibility for accepting the advice which the military officers give, and it is not sufficient, if that advice is subsequently disapproved by the House, to say that he acted upon military advice. [But] . . . he is entitled to reject the advice . . . *The Government is entitled to reject it. I think they will not ever do it lightly, but they are entitled, if any soldier or sailor, however high his position, however great his service, is unable willingly to accept and loyally to pursue the policy which they think necessary, to dispense with his services.*

Political leaders should not seek to undermine their professional advisers by means of leaks to the press. But, he insisted, there was a corresponding obligation upon the soldier and the sailor:

I do not want to hear rumours started at the expense of some high officer, which public report attaches in some way to Downing Street . . . *But neither do I want to hear rumours that military officers disapprove the policy of the Government.*

Nobody, he thought, could have listened to Asquith's speech, 'and the particularity and the persistency with which he questioned the Prime Minister, without wondering where [he] got his information, and whether such a brief ought ever to have come into his possession'.[18]

As he listened to this speech Lloyd George must have felt that he had been right to suggest to Law that Chamberlain be approached to take over the War Office, should Derby for once make good on a threat to resign. Instead, Chamberlain was quite soon (April) asked to join the War Cabinet, where the vacancy created by Carson's resignation had not been filled. Lloyd George's preferred candidate for the War Office was Milner (as we have seen from his New Year's Day conversation with Addison). But Milner was not really a politician, and in the political crisis resulting from Robertson's defiance, and the press campaign associated with it, a major Unionist politician would have been needed to offset the loss of Derby. The ending of the crisis left Lloyd George free, in his own time, to make the appointment of his choice.

If there had been a vote in Parliament on 19 February, and it had gone against the government, Lloyd George would have had to resign. In that event no alternative leader might have been able to command a Parliamentary majority, and the indispensability of Lloyd George might thus have been demonstrated. Yet it is also surely possible that his enemies in his own party and on the left might have been prepared to join with right-wing dissidents in sustaining a Unionist leader, as the only means of bringing him

18. Hansard, fifth ser., vol. ciii: Lloyd George's speech, cols. 633–46; Asquith's, cols. 646–54; Chamberlain's, cols. 654–8; my italics.

down. That leader might have been Balfour, Chamberlain or Carson, and under any of them the service chiefs would have been likely to gain in power. The regime thus established would still have been very different from the effective military dictatorship that existed in Germany. But it would, nevertheless, have represented a significant shift away from civilian and towards military control of the nation at war. To that extent Lloyd George may have been justified in regarding the issue between him and Robertson as vital for the British constitution.

As it turned out, Robertson and his supporters were worsted, and for the time being Lloyd George's dominance was restored. But within a few months it was to be challenged again in a crisis again involving Robertson, though by proxy. Meanwhile it was not only the Prime Minister who emerged triumphant. An even bigger winner, within his own sphere, was Haig. After Cambrai the Commander-in-Chief's position had never been weaker, and if an obvious substitute had then been available a change of Commander-in-Chief could probably have been made without any serious political trouble at home. Moreover, Haig's record suggests that he would have gone quietly, because he accepted, however grudgingly, the supremacy of civilian power. Two months after Cambrai his position was transformed, not least by his own canny behaviour in the crisis leading to Robertson's removal.

After his last talk with Lloyd George during the crisis, at Walton Heath, Haig returned to his own house at Kingston, where he was visited the same evening by Henry Wilson. Haig was confident that he could handle the new CIGS, and he was right. Wilson had no wish to quarrel with the Commander-in-Chief, whose sense of superiority to politicians he secretly shared (nicknaming them, in a vaguely derogatory way, 'Frocks'). He was keen to have Haig's goodwill and invited him to propose a successor to himself (Wilson) at Versailles. Haig nominated Rawlinson, on whom he felt he could rely to cause him no trouble. Wilson, now that he was CIGS, was well content that the British military representative at Versailles should be less self-assertive than he himself had been. When, in the near future, Rawlinson was recalled to an army command, the Versailles job was given to Wilson's own man, Sackville-West ('Tit Willow').

Robertson deserved to go. Indeed his departure was long overdue. He had many fine qualities, but not enough tolerance, adaptability or humility. In the end he was too obstinate for his own or the nation's good. Wilson was quite as much the self-conscious member of an exclusive military caste, and as a character definitely less admirable. All the same, he was more suited to acting as chief military adviser to a democratic government, and his understanding of the French was, in the circumstances, a crucial asset. His good relations with Milner and Churchill were also of special value. He had imagination, revelled in argument, and was a good talker (in two languages). Beneath his bantering manner he was properly deferential to politicians, whatever his private opinion of them. For all his faults, of which Lloyd George soon became better aware, his appointment on the eve of decisive events was, on the whole, advantageous.

While he was still physically under the weather, and politically bruised by his poor performance in the House of Commons on 12 February, Lloyd George was pleased to hear three days later that Roberta Lloyd George had given birth to a daughter. Roberta was living at the time at a house in Llanystumdwy, Plas Hen, just up the road from her mother-in-law at Criccieth. Her husband, Richard, was serving in France.

The child was named Valerie, apparently because she was born on St Valentine's Day – though if she had been a boy she would have been called not Valentine, but David.[19] As the Lloyd Georges' first grandchild she was naturally a source of delight to them both. On receiving the news the embattled grandfather scribbled a line to his wife. 'So glad to get news. Wel Wel Taid & Nain.' He also told her that he had been congratulated by Derby and D. R. Daniel (a friend of his youth whose opposition to the war had divided them, though not to the point of total estrangement).[20]

Olwen's expected child was born over two months later, on 25 April, when Lloyd George was preoccupied with a still graver emergency. This child, too, was a daughter. At the time of her birth Olwen was living under her mother's roof at Brynawelon, Criccieth. Lloyd George had ideas about a suitable name for the child:

Have you fixed upon your name for the little one? Ask Llwydyn [Olwen] to give her a pretty Welsh name. [He suggested Gwifid=honeysuckle.] When there are so many pretty Welsh names it is a pity to go on with Margarets & Ellens & Elizas . . .

News from France mixed.

Love to all –

Give the little one a sweet and tender kiss & another for its mother.

from

Taid.[21]

19. MLG to DLG.
20. DLG to MLG, 15 February 1918 (Taid and Nain are Welsh for grandfather and grandmother). 21. DLG to MLG, 26 April 1918.

ROBERTSON GOES

His wife may have been somewhat nettled by this reflection on her own name, and Olwen may have wished to assuage her sore feelings. In any case Lloyd George's suggestions were ignored and Margaret was the name chosen for the child.[22] The Prime Minister had no opportunity to give either of his granddaughters 'a sweet and tender kiss' in person until he was at Criccieth in August. Meanwhile he had to rely on news of them conveyed to him by letter or word of mouth.[23]

As Prime Minister Lloyd George kept in touch with his former colleague Lord Haldane, who was, however, in one sense politically untouchable. Since May 1915 he had been out of office, and there was no prospect of his returning to any government depending upon Conservative support. Asquith, his oldest friend in politics, had found it expedient to leave him out of the first wartime coalition, and any attempt to bring him back would have been strongly resisted by many Conservatives, who perversely held it against him that he had once described Germany as his spiritual home (having studied German philosophy at Göttingen), while choosing to forget all that he had done, as a great reforming war minister, to prepare the country for war. Lloyd George never suspected him of pro-German sympathies so far as the war was concerned, and had a very high regard for him as a public servant. But understandably he did not feel inclined to stake the survival of his government on his behalf, as he did in the case of Churchill, to whom he was closer and whose talents he valued even more.

Instead he employed Haldane in tasks outside government, such as the chairmanship of an important committee on the machinery of government, and also consulted him privately from time to time. For instance, he asked his opinion of Plumer's fitness for the post of CIGS, when his appointment to it as a compromise alternative to Robertson was being mooted.[24] Haldane appreciated the Prime Minister's confidence and, for his part, did his best to help him in various ways.

A case in point was a small dinner that he gave, at Lloyd George's request, on 1 March 1918, to enable the Prime Minister to have a confidential

22. Margaret Carey Evans was, like her mother, sent to school at Roedean, and in 1948 married Michael Barrett, a fellow adherent of Moral Rearmament.
23. He was amused to hear that his five-year-old nephew William had remarked of Olwen's baby: 'I don't think much of it. Her face is red. Evidently she has been drinking!' (*RWD*, 11 May 1918).
24. Haldane advised against it since, though he acknowledged Plumer's 'fighting qualities', he doubted his 'intelligence'. Lloyd George did not take the advice, but anyway Plumer 'settled the matter by declining the post' (*WM*, pp. 2820–21).

discussion with Beatrice and Sidney Webb, the only other guests. Haldane had known the Webbs for some time. In 1902 he was a leading member of the Coefficients, a dining club which they founded to bring together people from different parties with a shared interest in social reform. In *The New Machiavelli* by H. G. Wells (himself a member), the Coefficients appear as the 'Pentagram Circle'. Beatrice Webb's contemporary account of the occasion is of such interest that it deserves to be quoted almost in full:

Prime Ministers usually excite, in all but the most sophisticated minds, a measure of awe and instinctive deference. No such feeling is possible with Lloyd George. The low standard of intellect and conduct of the little Welsh conjurer is so obvious, and withal he is so pleasant and lively, that official deference and personal respect fades [*sic*] into an atmosphere of agreeable low company – but low company of a most stimulating kind, intimate camaraderie with a fellow adventurer. We talked about reconstruction, current politics, the late crisis, the personal traits of generals and Ministers, the Russian revolution, the terms of peace and the prospects of the next election. His object in meeting us was, I think, to find out whether any co-operation with the Labour Party was practicable – or at any rate how the land lay with regard to the Labour Party and the Asquithian Liberals. It was, in fact, a counter-thrust to the Asquith touting for coalition with the Labour Party. He could not approach Henderson, so he approached Sidney. Like many other persons who have known Henderson as a Cabinet Minister, he thinks that all the recent success of the Labour Party must be due to someone else . . . 'I know Henderson', he laughingly remarked. 'It is not Henderson who has made the *réclame* – all the distinction comes from' . . . and he waved his hand towards Sidney. He made distinct advances, pressed us repeatedly to come and dine with him and meet Milner, apparently to discuss the terms of peace. But I was not responsive. I don't want to go to Downing Street. In fact, I had told Haldane when I accepted the invitation that we would not go to 10 Downing Street. But we parted with cordiality.

Coming up to date, she recorded:

The PM re-seen (we have not seen him for three or four years) did not impress me favourably, in spite of his flattering friendliness. He is a blatant intriguer, and every word he says is of the nature of an offer to 'do a deal'! He neither likes nor dislikes you: you are a mere instrument, one among many, sometimes of value, sometimes not worth picking up. He bears no malice for past opposition, he has no gratitude for past services. He is no doubt genuinely patriotic and public-spirited, but all his ways are crooked and he is obsessed by the craving for power. His one serviceable gift is executive energy. He sees that things are done and not merely talked about.

Unfortunately, he does not care whether or not they are thought about. He is the best of boon companions: witty, sympathetic, capable of superficial argument and quick retort, and brilliant in his observations on men and things.

What was clear from our talk is that the P.M. and Milner are thinking of a peace at the expense of Russia. He repeated with more frankness and emphasis what he has said publicly – that the Russians must lie in the bed made by the Bolsheviks, that neither France nor England would fight to restore Courland and Lithuania, leave alone to restore the lost Poland. I interposed 'Would Wilson and the U.S.A. agree?' 'The U.S.A.', he almost snapped out, 'would not go on with the war if England and France refused to do so.'

I am not at all sure whether his desire to meet us and his desire that we should meet Milner is not connected with this possible sacrifice of Russia and her revolution. He wants to know how the Labour Party would take such a peace – whether it would be considered a betrayal of the cause of democracy ... With Russia to cut up, the map of the world is capable of all sorts of rearrangements which give all the more powerful and ambitious belligerents an opportunity to expand their jurisdiction over the more helpless races – not only the German empire, but the empires of Great Britain, of France of Italy and of Japan. But would the one disinterested power, the U.S.A., agree to such a peace, and would the democracies of the powers look benignantly on the victory of the Junkers of all countries?[25]

This diary entry provides a vivid portrayal of Lloyd George. It is also highly revealing of the author. Mrs Webb's intellectual snobbery, her priggishness, her imperfect sense of humour, and the streak of naïvety in her (seen, not least, in her reference to the United States as 'the one disinterested power') are all manifest. So is the conflict, which makes her so fascinating, between her governessy sense of *comme il faut* and the lust for adventure that she could never quite control. Ruthless pursuit of power attracted as much as it repelled her, and in spite of herself she was drawn to men of action. After all, she had been in love with Joseph Chamberlain. Chamberlain had also been much admired by Lloyd George, until the Boer War came between them. In social policy they had much in common, and they had a similar impatience with out-of-date party doctrines. Both were politicians who 'made the weather'. But Lloyd George's style was more light-hearted than Chamberlain's. Without being any less consistent in his fundamental aims, he seemed less rigid.

25. *The Diary of Beatrice Webb*, ed. Norman and Jeanne MacKenzie (4 vols., 1982–4), vol. iii, pp. 299–301. The dinner took place at Haldane's London House, 28 Queen Anne's Gate, where in 1911 he had given a small lunch party for the Kaiser (an occasion inevitably held against him later).

Mrs Webb's description of him is honest and perceptive, but also reflects her confused emotions and values. She bestows great praise, but balances it with severe and not always just criticism. The positive qualities that she observes in Lloyd George might seem to cover much, not to say most, of what is required in a national leader: 'genuinely patriotic and public-spirited', possessing 'executive energy', seeing that 'things are done and not merely talked about', bearing 'no malice for past opposition' – with wit, sympathy and brilliance thrown in. Yet she has to say that he does not impress her favourably. His standard of intellect is 'low', as is the atmosphere that he creates, however 'agreeable'. He is a 'blatant intriguer', always looking 'to do a deal'. He has 'no gratitude for past services', and treats people as mere instruments, neither liking them nor disliking them. His ways – all his ways – are crooked, and he is 'obsessed by the craving for power'. His arguments, for all their sparkle, are 'superficial'.

It is certainly true that Lloyd George often took loyal service for granted, that he did not allow personal affection to hinder his progress. He believed that his life's work was the highest priority. Such an attitude is surely normal among major creative artists. The exceptions are remarkably few. It is also true that Lloyd George could be devious in pursuit of his objectives, especially when he felt that a direct approach had no hope of succeeding. But most of his crookedness, even where money was concerned, was practised not from low motives, but to assist him in achieving results that transcended his own self-interest. Similarly, he craved power not for its own sake, but for what he could do with it.

Like most outstanding men of action, he was not an intellectual. He acted intuitively rather than through a process of deep and systematic thought. But Mrs Webb was quite wrong to describe his standard of intellect as low. Not only did he have a wide-ranging intelligence, combined with the rarer quality of imagination; he also had a profound respect for people of intellect and habitually sought their company. Why otherwise would he have been dining with Haldane for the purpose of talking to the Webbs, at a time when the demands on him were so many and pressing?

We can sense that Mrs Webb was on her guard against him partly, if not mainly, because he made such a strong appeal to one aspect of her own nature. She shrank from being drawn into 'intimate camaraderie with a fellow adventurer'.

24

Before the Storm

Brest – Litovsk – Before the storm – 21 March 1918

At Haldane's dinner party it was clear to Mrs Webb that Lloyd George was thinking of a peace at Russia's expense, and wanted to know whether 'this possible sacrifice of Russia and her revolution' would be regarded by the Labour Party as 'a betrayal of the cause of democracy'. On her own admission the Prime Minister had already stated publicly (to the trade union conference in January) that if the Bolsheviks made a separate peace they would automatically forfeit any right to support from the Western Allies. Two days after the dinner, on 3 March, a separate peace was signed at Brest-Litovsk. This represented a triumph for the German warlords, whose extreme demands were met, and also a triumph for Lenin's policy of peace at any price.

Negotiations had effectively broken down at the beginning of the year, when the military lost patience with the civilians, Kühlmann and Czernin, the foreign ministers of Germany and Austria. Czernin was in a hopeless position, because the Habsburg Empire was no longer fit for war. When he threatened that the Empire would not take part in any resumption of fighting on the Eastern front, the German military responded brutally that that would enable them to reclaim the use of twenty-five divisions currently employed in propping up the Austrians. Kühlmann, reluctantly abandoning his hopes of a general settlement, was now concerned that the ruthlessness of the high command's plans in the East would show the Western Allies what they could expect in the event of a German victory and so stiffen their resistance to the forthcoming offensive. He was right, but his advice was ignored.

A wave of strikes in Germany during January had the perverse effect of strengthening the hand of the military, who attributed them to the influence of Western money and Bolshevik propaganda, and pointed to the need for tougher measures. The strikes were suppressed and a 'victors' peace' in the East became the established policy. On 9 February a deal was struck with nationalist leaders in Ukraine, which turned the province into a German protectorate and increased the Bolsheviks' isolation. Four days later, at a Crown Council at Bad Homburg, the Kaiser, expressing the will of the military, spoke of dismembering Greater Russia, placing its component parts under German rule, and destroying the Bolsheviks in a manner 'akin to a tiger hunt'.[1]

Meanwhile the Bolshevik leadership was split three ways. The largest faction, led by Bukharin, was for maintaining the revolutionary struggle and wholly opposed to accepting any help from the capitalist West. The second largest group, Trotsky's, doubted the capacity, or even willingness, of Russian peasant bands to resist a German onslaught, but shared Bukharin's hope that revolution would soon spread to the enemy. Trotsky was ready to accept Entente help. Lenin, at first in a small minority, was becoming sceptical both of effective resistance and of salvation from abroad in any form, whether military aid or early revolution. In his view, there was no alternative to accepting German terms if the Bolshevik regime were to have any chance of surviving.

In January Lloyd George decided to establish contact with the Bolshevik leaders through an unofficial emissary. This was Robert Bruce Lockhart, just turned thirty, who for six years had been Vice-Consul in Moscow until a sexual indiscretion (one of many in his life) led to his recall in September 1917, ostensibly on health grounds. But earlier in the year he had impressed Milner during the latter's mission to Russia on the eve of the first Revolution, and had himself fallen under Milner's spell. At the time of the Bolshevik Revolution he was at home and out of a job, but with the advantage that a member of the War Cabinet was aware of his special knowledge and ability, and keen to bring him to the notice of senior colleagues.

Lockhart was entirely Scottish, inheriting Lowland characteristics from his schoolmaster father, but with a temperament chiefly reflecting his mother's Highland (McGregor) ancestry. He was a born adventurer, with courage, imagination and flair. In addition he was a natural linguist, with a capacity for insight into the affairs of foreign countries. During December he had many talks with Milner, through whom he met Carson, Curzon and Smuts, and who in due course introduced him to Lloyd George. We have Lockhart's own description of the scene:

A Cabinet meeting had just ended. Mr. Lloyd George, his pince-nez in his hand, was standing by the window, talking and gesticulating to Lord Curzon. My sponsor, Lord Milner . . . came in . . . and took me up to Mr. Lloyd George.

1. Holger H. Herwig, *The First World War: Germany and Austria-Hungary 1914–1918* (1997), p. 383.

'Mr. Lockhart?' he said. He shook hands and stepped back in order to scrutinise me more carefully. '*The* Mr. Lockhart?' . . . Then, having made me the centre of attraction, he continued very slowly, so that everyone could hear: 'from the wisdom of your reports I expected to see an elderly gentleman with a grey beard.' He patted me on the back, asked me my age, muttered something about youth and Pitt being Prime Minister at twenty-four, and we sat down to business . . . [He was] remarkably active and adroit in his handling of the meeting. He asked me a few questions about Lenin and Trotsky. A fresh question followed almost before I had time to answer the previous one . . . the questions ended, [he] stood up, referred briefly to . . . the necessity of getting into touch with Lenin and Trotsky, emphasised the need for tact . . . and finished up by stating that Mr. Lockhart was obviously a man whose right place at that moment was in St. Petersburg and not in London. I was then told I could go.[2]

After spending Christmas with his parents, Lockhart was back in London at the New Year to prepare for his mission. At a Lyons corner house near Charing Cross he met Maxim Litvinov, the Bolsheviks' representative in London – as unofficial as himself – who gave him a letter of recommendation to Trotsky. (Litvinov noticed 'pouding diplomate' on the menu, and thought it a suitable dish to order, only to be told by the waitress that it was no longer available. 'Not recognised even by Lyons' was his felicitous comment.)[3]

Lockhart also received briefings from the Foreign Office, where his appointment was viewed with covert disapproval as an act of prime ministerial intrusion, and with considerable scepticism as to its utility, notably on the part of Lord Robert Cecil. Nevertheless he was given ciphers and, having assembled a small staff (not including any member of the diplomatic service), left from the Firth of Forth on 13 January. He travelled to Petrograd via Norway, Sweden and Finland, then in the grip of a civil war between Whites and Reds. The last stage of his journey – by train across Finland from the north end of the Gulf of Bothnia – was consequently full of danger, since he had to cross the line between the combatants. But he reached his destination safely on 27 January, and the following day had his first interview with G. V. Chicherin, who was in charge of the Foreign Ministry while Trotsky was away at Brest-Litovsk.[4]

2. R. H. B. Lockhart, *Memoirs of a British Agent* (1932, repr. 1974), pp. 199–200.

3. Ibid., p. 204. Litvinov was later Foreign Minister, until his supersession by Molotov in May 1939. In 1941 he was for a short time Ambassador to the United States.

4. Chicherin was the grandson of a nobleman and had started his career as a Tsarist official. But he was a convinced revolutionary, who had given up his fortune before the change of regime.

Lenin did not bother to see him until a month later, but Lockhart soon realized that anything said to him by Chicherin was dictated by Lenin. The line was that the negotiations at Brest were going badly and that the moment was opportune for Britain to make 'a friendly gesture' to Bolshevik Russia. In fact, Lenin's policy was 'to play off the Germans against the Allies and the Allies against the Germans'.[5]

The cruiser which took the Lockhart party to Bergen collected the home-coming British Ambassador, Sir George Buchanan (who breakfasted with Lloyd George on his return). But the rest of the embassy staff remained in Petrograd, and Lockhart found that a number of them favoured recognition of the new regime. One was Rex Hoare, with whom he stayed until he acquired a house for his mission. Another kindred spirit was Raymond Robins, head of the American Red Cross in Russia, who had been Theodore Roosevelt's running mate in the latter's 'Bull Moose' campaign in 1912 (when his intervention only helped to win the presidency for Wilson). Robins had a role in Petrograd similar to Lockhart's, though even less clearly defined. He too wanted his country to recognize the Bolsheviks.

What did Lloyd George hope to achieve through the Lockhart mission? Ideology had nothing to do with his calculations, one way or the other. He simply wanted to reactivate Russian participation in the war against Germany. Failing that, he would feel free to abandon Russia to the fate that its rulers, right and left, had brought upon it. As a keen amateur student of the French Revolutionary period, he was prepared to imagine that the Bolsheviks might prove more effective in motivating resistance to the foreign enemy than Kerensky had been. And what he had heard from Milner about Lockhart, as well as what he had read in Lockhart's reports, encouraged him to think that the young Scot might help to influence the Bolshevik leaders, especially Trotsky, in the desired direction. He was struck by Lockhart's knowledge and independence of mind, and an adventurous character naturally appealed to him.

There could be no question of according official recognition to a regime which was openly fomenting revolutionary activity in all other states, including those which had been Russia's allies and were still providing the only brake upon German power. But Lloyd George could justifiably feel that by sending an unofficial emissary who clearly had his confidence, and by allowing Litvinov to stay in London on the same footing, he was giving the Bolsheviks a limited form of *de facto* recognition, which was the only 'friendly gesture' he could offer in the circumstances, and more than they

5. Lockhart, *Memoirs*, pp. 221-2.

had any right to expect. Further gestures would be possible only if they made an effective stand against the Germans and put a stop to their subversive propaganda among those whose help they needed. Lloyd George's move was carefully judged and the War Cabinet backed it. But it went against the opinion of important colleagues, such as Cecil, who regarded the Bolshevik leaders as German agents, and Lloyd George was suspected by some of having a degree of sympathy for their ideas, even Hankey describing him one day, absurdly, as 'half a Bolshevik himself '.[6]

On the day that Kühlmann signed a separate peace with the Ukrainian nationalists (9 February), the German Foreign Minister also presented – under orders from the Kaiser, expressing the will of the military – an ultimatum to Trotsky. If the German terms were not accepted and peace signed the following day, war would be resumed. Trotsky then left Brest-Litovsk, refusing to sign but at the same time declaring that Russia was no longer in the war. His deluded hope was that the spectacle of German troops attacking revolutionary Russia would precipitate revolution in Germany. On 15 February, back in Petrograd, he gave his first interview to Lockhart. During two hours of talk he told the British agent that he did not know how the Germans would react to his 'no peace and no war' declaration, but 'had a shrewd idea that it would be unpleasant'. He was full of 'belligerent fury' against the Germans, but seems to have made no specific request for Allied aid.[7]

Trotsky was certainly right in fearing that the German reaction to his declaration would be unpleasant. Three days after his talk with Lockhart hostilities on the Eastern front were fully resumed and within a week the Germans had advanced 150 miles. They encountered hardly any resistance and there was, of course, no sign of miraculous deliverance in the form of a German revolution. Petrograd itself was under imminent threat. Then at last Lenin's policy was accepted by the Bolshevik central committee, though only by the narrowest of votes.[8] It was too late to settle for the extremely onerous and humiliating terms presented to Trotsky in early February. The final terms demanded and agreed to were even more drastic. Neither Lenin nor Trotsky, nor any other leading Bolshevik went to Brest to sign the treaty, but a delegation of minor figures led by Chicherin. Russia's honour and vital interests were comprehensively sacrificed in order to save the Bolshevik regime.

6. Hankey diary, 8 February 1918.   7. Lockhart, *Memoirs*, pp. 226–7.
8. Seven votes to five: at the last moment Trotsky switched to Lenin's side, which made the difference. When the peace proposals were later put to the larger Soviet executive, the vote in favour was 116 : 85.

Under the treaty of Brest-Litovsk Germany acquired all the territory occupied during the war, right up to the last few days. Finland, the Baltic provinces and Ukraine were to be German protectorates, though nominally independent. Poland was to be separated from Russia, with a view to its division between Germany and Austria. In the south, German power extended to the River Don and took in the Crimea. If the treaty were to go the way of the guarantee to Belgium, and prove nothing more than a piece of paper, the Germans were poised to advance to Murmansk, to Moscow, into the Caucasus – and beyond. Meanwhile the Russia of 1914 was to lose 34 per cent of its population, 32 per cent of its agricultural land, 54 per cent of its industry and 89 per cent of its coal-mines; reducing it, as has been said, to 'a status on a par with seventeenth-century Muscovy'.[9] Aptly, at about this time the seat of Bolshevik government was transferred from Petrograd to Moscow.

The Bolsheviks had come to power because they offered the Russian people peace, and external peace they delivered, but at a terrible price and soon to be followed by the conquerors' oppression and an escalating civil war. Moreover the price of peace with Germany was even worse than it need have been, because of Trotsky's irrational behaviour when the Germans presented their ultimatum. He did not have the excuse of sharing Bukharin's belief that Russian soldiers might be stirred to action in defence of the Revolution. It was clear to him that they were through with fighting the German army on behalf of the Russian state, whoever was in power. His delaying tactics were based only on the fatuous hope that the Germans themselves might be made to stop fighting by revolution at home. Yet his remarks to Lockhart at their first meeting suggest that he did not hold that hope very strongly.

When they met again after the debate in which Lenin's will eventually prevailed, Trotsky complained that the British government had been 'indecisive and vacillating', and that Lloyd George in particular was 'like a man playing roulette and scattering chips on every number'.[10] In his blind fanaticism Trotsky could not see that the Prime Minister had gone as far as he could possibly go without some evidence either of a Russian military revival or of diminished Bolshevik-inspired subversion, preferably of both. Far from scattering his chips, Lloyd George may more justly be criticized for putting too many of them on Trotsky, whom he described in December as 'the biggest man the revolution had produced'.[11] Lockhart, from whose

9. Orlando Figes, *A People's Tragedy: The Russian Revolution 1891–1924* (1996), p. 548.
10. Lockhart, *Memoirs*, p. 231.
11. Scott diary, 12 December 1917. He made the remark at a weekly breakfast for Liberal ministers.

reports this opinion must have derived, seems to have felt that the British government could have done more to help and encourage Trotsky. But it is hard to see how. Lloyd George believed that the Bolsheviks needed 'a great general'[12] and Trotsky certainly showed military talent of a high order when, after Brest-Litovsk, he became War Commissar and created the Red Army. His contribution to Bolshevik victory in the civil war is indisputable. But Lloyd George could not have foreseen this, and it would have made no difference if he had, because the Russians were in no mood for further fighting against the Germans and Trotsky made no serious attempt to rally them for this purpose.

On the face of it, the treaty of Brest-Litovsk was an overwhelming triumph for Germany. Yet in the wider context of the war it turned out to be almost the equivalent of a defeat. Kühlmann had been right: for Germany to emerge victorious from the whole war the pursuance of a *Drang nach Osten* in early 1918 was inexpedient and premature. All that was needed, as the warlords prepared for the supreme struggle in the West, was that Russia should present absolutely no military threat, enabling the maximum transfer of troops and equipment from the Eastern front; also that Russia should, by free and fair commercial processes, contribute an abundance of food for the German people and raw materials for German industry. Instead, the military became committed to a policy of unlimited conquest in the East before the war was won in the West. The opportunity to exploit the national and ideological divisions in Russia was squandered, while intense popular hostility to Germany was aroused. At the same time the Western Allies were left in no doubt what would be in store for them if they allowed the Germans to win.

The way Ukraine was mishandled was typical. Under the treaty granting Ukrainian 'independence' 300 truckloads of grain were to be despatched daily to Germany, as the price of German 'protection'. The peasants soon began to hide their grain rather than pay this tribute, and German troops were then sent into the villages to collect it. Their heavy-handed methods drove the peasants to revolt and sabotage. The puppet nationalist government was in due course replaced by one largely consisting of landowners and former Tsarist officers, which was even more subservient to the Germans and Austrians. (The latter, despite having opposed further action on the Eastern front, established a conspicuous presence in occupied Ukraine, and an Austrian Archduke had his headquarters at Kiev in the hope of becoming King.) The very large German and Austro-Hungarian armies of occupation

12. *R WD*, 20 January 1918.

consumed almost as much food as was meant to be reaching the underfed population at home. As a result only one-tenth of the expected volume of grain left Ukraine.[13]

In May the Germans imposed another harsh treaty, on the Roumanians, under which the country was to be occupied for an indefinite period and was to pay all the costs of occupation. A ninety-nine-year monopoly of Roumanian oil was established under German control and all Roumanian agricultural surpluses were to go to the Central Powers. This treaty (of Bucharest) was, like the treaty of Brest-Litovsk, approved by the German Reichstag. The main opposition socialist party abstained, but only the small independent socialist party voted against the treaties.

To enforce Germany's expansionist and (in all but name) annexationist policies in the East, at least a million men in total were kept there, most of whom might otherwise have been transferred to the West. These men might have decided the issue had they been available as reserves for Ludendorff's offensive in France. In effect, he and his fellow warlords continued to operate in force on two fronts, when events had given them the freedom to concentrate on a single front. This was a capital error, providential for the Allies.

It was hardly surprising that Lloyd George seemed to Beatrice Webb to be willing to 'sacrifice Russia and her revolution' in order to reach a peace with Germany based on the war aims that he had stated to the trade unionists. (But one has to wonder if she was right in thinking him indifferent to the fate of Poland, for whose restoration he had specifically called.) He had been willing to sacrifice Kerensky's Russia when it became apparent that military resistance was collapsing under his leadership; how much more so when the country was under leaders who were clearly not transforming themselves into patriots capable of inspiring a national stand against the Germans, and who also made no demands at all upon his loyalty as a fellow democrat. (In early January Lenin had closed down the constituent assembly elected to give Russia a democratic constitution, and had ordered his troops to shoot people demonstrating against its closure.) The question of peace with Germany was in any case quite unrealistic at the time, so far as the West was concerned. The leaders of Germany were bent on total victory.

Russia's formal exit from the war was the occasion for the withdrawal of all regular Allied diplomats from Petrograd. But Lockhart stayed on for

13. In the Second World War the Germans similarly antagonized the Ukrainians, who at first welcomed them as liberators. Neither side had learnt from experience.

some months in an increasingly precarious situation. In October, after a month in prison, he was released in exchange for Litvinov. Though he had continued to advocate recognition of the Bolsheviks, they rewarded him by permanent exclusion from Russia on pain of death.

In February–March 1918 Lloyd George had no doubt at all that the climacteric of the war was approaching. Towards the end of his Commons speech on 19 February, when he reasserted his authority in the House, he said:

We are faced with terrible realities. Let us see what is the position. The enemy have rejected . . . the most moderate terms ever put forward . . . Why has he done it? It is obvious. He is clearly convinced that the Russian collapse puts it within his power to achieve a military victory, and to impose Prussian dominancy by force upon Europe. That is what we are confronted with.

And when he addressed a Nonconformist audience a week before the German offensive he began his speech with the words that he had come 'in an hour of grave national emergency'.[14]

But what form would the emergency take? How would the Germans choose to exploit the enormous advantage they had gained? On this point neither the Prime Minister nor his colleagues had a clear view. Until almost the last moment there was uncertainty as to German intentions. The massive transfer of force from East to West during the winter was well observed, but did not necessarily mean that the enemy would try to win the war on the Western front in the spring. He might be strengthening his position there to guard against renewed Allied offensive action and to counter the American build-up, while his top priority might still be to seize the strategic opportunities presented by total victory in the East. Further prizes beckoned there, notably the oil of the Caucasus and the chance to threaten Britain's position in the Middle East and India. The latter hypothesis was of special concern to the War Cabinet's two most imperial-minded members, Curzon and Milner, and the Prime Minister largely shared their concern, as did the new CIGS. Much time was therefore devoted to considering how to establish a defensive front against the Germans in the East (only possible with Japanese and American co-operation), while the storm was about to break in the West.

14. Speech to National Free Church Council, City Temple, 14 March 1918. In the same place, in November 1914, he had made a powerful appeal to his fellow Nonconformists to support British intervention in the war.

If Lloyd George erred at the time, it was in attributing too much rationality to the German warlords (as he later did to Hitler). It was rational to assume that they would not try to win the war outright in two main theatres simultaneously, and equally rational to judge that the East was the more promising from their point of view. But reason was not the determining factor. Others made a shrewder judgement of their mentality. Haig, who had shown earlier that he was not blind to the logical arguments for doubting their intention to attack in the West, came to regard them as power-crazy, and therefore unpredictable. Before the SWC met in London in mid-March he had a long talk with Lloyd George and Law at 10 Downing Street, and recorded that they 'did their best to get [him] to say that the Germans would not attack'. But he replied that the German leaders seemed 'drunk with their success in Russia', so that it was 'impossible to foretell what they [might] not attempt'. He was anyway insistent on the need to prepare 'to meet a very strong attack indeed on a 50-mile front', which meant that drafts were 'urgently required'.[15]

Two days later Wilson and Foch discussed what the Germans would do and were clearly as unsure of the answer as Lloyd George and Law. 'I think [Wilson noted] the Boche ought to threaten us on our front and the French, and fall on the Italians about May or June. He [Foch] does not think the Boche will try Italy because it would be too advantageous for the Austrians. He thinks the Boche will threaten, as I do, and then turn all his attention and energy to the East.'[16] The shattering rebuttal of such speculations was less than a week away.

Despite his reluctance to believe that the Germans would attack on the Western front, Foch was none the less eager to give effect to the previous SWC's decision that a general reserve should be created under the control of his executive war board. But this project was sabotaged by Haig, Pétain and Clemenceau, acting more or less in collusion.

Clemenceau was confidently expecting the German attack, and still inclined to support Pétain as the man best fitted, with his Verdun experience, to defend France in another mortal crisis. He therefore preferred French reserves to be under Pétain than under Foch, and took his side when he refused to contribute any divisions to Foch's general reserve unless Haig also did so. Haig absolutely refused, so enabling Pétain to keep all his divisions, and Clemenceau was well content. When Foch protested at the SWC meeting in London, Clemenceau silenced him. In the end the principle of a general Allied reserve was maintained by a formula, devised by Hankey,

15. Haig diary, 14 March 1918.   16. Wilson diary, 16 March 1918.

that British and French divisions remaining in Italy should be deemed to constitute the reserve: obviously no more than a face-saving fudge.[17]

The case for Haig's bloody-mindedness was that the German build-up was preponderantly on his part of the front, that his forces were below strength, and that he had nevertheless taken over twenty-eight miles more of the Allied line (as agreed between Lloyd George and Painlevé the previous year, with Robertson's assent). Clemenceau had been pressing for a greater extension, on the argument that Britain's share of the line was much shorter than France's. But the British could with justice reply that some French sectors were strategically unimportant and habitually quiet, whereas the British army was responsible for territory all of which was vital. Moreover it was demonstrably true that Britain was carrying a heavier burden in various other ways, above all in the maritime war effort. Lloyd George found himself obliged to support Haig in resisting French pressure, not least because the Commander-in-Chief had been so helpful in the showdown with Robertson.

Was the Prime Minister wrong to keep British manpower reserves under his own hand in Britain, so giving Haig an excuse to withhold divisions from the proposed Allied general reserve in France? His experience of 1917 had bred in him a firm resolve that the Commander-in-Chief should be denied the wherewithal to launch more attacks such as those that had drained his armies the previous summer and autumn. Even after Cambrai he was still talking on offensive lines until warned by Robertson that in doing so he was fatally weakening his case for more drafts. In the light of experience Lloyd George's unwillingness to entrust him with Britain's ultimate reserves is surely understandable. At home the men were near enough to the front to be sent there quickly in any emergency. Meanwhile the Prime Minister preferred to keep them under his own control. If, as a result, the crisis that arose when the enemy attacked was more acute than it need have been, one can argue that a temporary crisis was anyway unavoidable and that the extent of the Germans' initial success was, in the event, to prove disastrous for them.

By March 1918 they had 192 divisions in the West, compared with the Allies' 178. This gave them a clear numerical superiority in the theatre as a

17. Maurice Hankey, *The Supreme Command, 1914–1918* (2 vols., 1961), vol. ii, pp. 781–2. The executive war board's original plan had been to form a reserve of twenty divisions, of which only two would be British. (Twelve would be French and six Italian.) In the event two British divisions were ordered back from Italy, but to rejoin Haig's army, and a similar withdrawal was made by the French for Pétain's benefit. A committee was to be sent to Italy to determine how many Italian divisions could be spared for the general reserve.

whole, which could be made overwhelming for a time at any point chosen for concentrated attack. Moreover, many of the German divisions transferred from the East came flushed with triumphs recently achieved almost without effort, whereas Pétain's and Haig's forces had endured a year of dour and costly struggle with little to show for it. The French army had regained its morale after the shaky period following Nivelle's failure, and the spirit of the BEF had not been broken by the prolonged misery and frustration of Third Ypres, or the disappointment of Cambrai. Nevertheless, the Germans had the edge in self-confidence, as well as in numbers, as they prepared for their big effort.

In other respects they did not have the edge. The Allies had more guns, more aircraft and a virtual monopoly in tanks. They could also look forward to the growing participation of America, with its vast resources, if only they could hold out in the short term. The Germans knew that they had to win quickly if they were to win at all; and Ludendorff judged that his first objective must be to defeat the British. He therefore decided in January on an operation codenamed Michael, which would involve a massive attack in the Somme area, at the southern end of the British line. His aim was to break through and then drive the British back towards the sea, forcing them to abandon their position in Flanders and separating them from the French. Thus he hoped to gain a comprehensive victory which would leave the French at his mercy and soon persuade the United States to accept the *fait accompli* of German hegemony in Europe. On 10 March the final plan, endorsed by Hindenburg, fixed the launch of the operation for eleven days later. After a five-hour bombardment the attack was to go in at 9.40 a.m. on the 21st.

Haig was given fair warning of enemy intentions. At a conference of army commanders on 2 March his new chief of intelligence, Brigadier-General Cox, gave reasons for believing that the Germans were 'preparing to attack on the fronts of our Third and Fifth Armies' (the two armies at the southern end of the line). Haig's composure seems to have been in no way disturbed by this information. He told his commanders that he was 'very pleased' with the defensive arrangements that were in hand, which he described as 'sound and thorough'. His only fear was that the enemy would find the British front 'so very strong' that he would 'hesitate to commit his Army to the attack with the almost certainty of losing very heavily'.[18]

The two British armies facing the likely German onslaught (the Third and Fifth) were commanded by, respectively, Byng and Gough. Between them

18. Haig diary, 2 March 1918.

they were responsible for well over half of the entire length of the British line: 70 out of 126 miles. Yet they were allotted only 29 of the 57 divisions in the BEF. Byng's army was the less deprived of the two, containing 14 divisions for a front of 28 miles; but Gough's army consisted of 15 divisions (three of which were cavalry) for a 42-mile front.

Haig's dispositions were partly based on the reasonable assumption that Flanders was the area of greatest risk, since it was nearest to the coast and so offered the least room for defensive manœuvre. He must also have been determined, if possible, to hold on to all the ground so painfully won the previous autumn. He underrated the threat to Gough's army, since he regarded the stretch of country behind it, adjoining the old Somme battlefield abandoned by the Germans in early 1917, as of no strategic value. He also counted on Pétain to give prompt assistance from the right if Gough's army came under serious pressure, though Wilson warned him (Haig) against over-reliance on Pétain.[19]

Granted the intelligence reports, the position of the Fifth Army would have been unduly vulnerable whoever had been leading it. But Gough was in any case not the right man. He never had been suitable for command at that level. As one eminent military historian has written: 'Officers who served under him formed the opinion that lives were lost in the battles he organised because he failed to co-ordinate artillery support with infantry assaults, failed to limit his objectives to attainable ends, failed to curtail operations that had patently failed and failed to meet [Plumer's] standards of administrative efficiency.'[20] Yet Haig had delayed his Flanders offensive by giving Gough rather than Plumer the principal command at the outset, with the dire consequences already recorded. If Lloyd George had had his way Gough would have been removed during the winter, and even Derby expressed doubts about him as late as 5 March.[21] But Haig's obstinate partiality left him in command of the Fifth Army as it faced, this time, a supreme defensive test.

According to John Terraine, Haig was 'distinctly uneasy' after visiting Gough's army in early March, and ordered a division to be moved to it from the Fourth Army.[22] But uneasiness does not seem to have been the prevalent feature of his state of mind as he awaited the German attack, and his

---

19. In a private talk with Haig during the SWC meeting in London, Wilson impressed on the Commander-in-Chief that his refusal to contribute any divisions to general reserve would force him 'to live on Pétain's charity [which] he would find very cold charity' (Wilson diary, 13 March 1918).   20. John Keegan, *The First World War* (1998), p. 424.
21. Derby to Haig, 5 March 1918.
22. John Terraine, *Douglas Haig: The Educated Soldier* (1963), p. 411.

equanimity was enhanced by the news, in mid-March, that his wife had given birth to their first and only son.[23] On the eve of the attack he wrote to her explaining that he would have to postpone coming over to see her and the child by a week, until the 29th, because if he came at once 'it might lead to "talk"', adding: 'not that my actual presence in France at the moment of attack is necessary because all Reserves and other questions . . . have been settled.' 'Everyone', he assured her, 'is in good spirits and only anxious that the enemy should attack.'[24] The enemy was about to oblige.

The night of 20 March was spent by Winston Churchill as the guest of General Henry Tudor, whom he had known since they were young officers together in India. Tudor was now commanding the 9th division in Byng's army. The Minister of Munitions had been visiting Haig's headquarters, and the previous day had received a private briefing from the Commander-in-Chief. Before he went to bed Tudor told him that the German attack was now certainly imminent, because trench raids that evening had identified no fewer than eight enemy battalions on a single half-mile of the division's front.

Shortly after 4 a.m. Churchill woke up and lay for a while musing in complete silence. Then:

The silence was broken by six or seven very loud and very heavy explosions several miles away . . . And then, exactly as a pianist runs his hands across the keyboard from treble to bass, there rose in less than one minute the most tremendous cannonade I shall ever hear . . . Far away, both to the north and to the south, the intense roar and reverberation rolled upwards to us . . .

I dressed and went out. On the duckboards outside the Mess I met Tudor. 'This is *it*', he said. 'I have ordered all our batteries to open. You will hear them in a minute.' But the crash of the German shells bursting on our trench lines eight thousand yards away was so overpowering that the accession to the tumult of nearly two hundred guns firing from much nearer to us could not be even distinguished. From the divisional Headquarters . . . one could see the front for many miles. It swept round

23. George Alexander Eugene Douglas, the future 2nd Earl Haig, born 15 March 1918, known to friends not by any of his four first names, but by the courtesy title, Dawick, assumed when his father became an earl.
24. Haig to Lady Haig, 20 March 1918. Haig's carefree tone to his army commanders and to his wife is, of course, partly attributable to a proper sense of the need to keep their spirits up. All the same, in expressing such eagerness to be attacked he was surely admitting by implication that on the Western front defence was likely to prevail: a view that he had hitherto conspicuously spurned.

us in a wide curve of red leaping flame stretching to the north far along the front of the Third Army, as well as of the Fifth Army on the south ... There were still two hours to daylight, and the enormous explosions of the shells upon our trenches seemed almost to touch each other, with hardly an interval in space or time. Among the bursting shells there rose at intervals, but almost continually, the much larger flames of exploding magazines. The weight and intensity of the bombardment surpassed anything which anyone had ever known before.[25]

To produce this awesome preliminary barrage Ludendorff had concentrated 6,600 guns and 3,500 mortars against the forward positions of the Third and Fifth Armies, so achieving overwhelming local superiority, only 2,800 guns and 1,400 mortars being immediately available to the defenders. In carrying out a relatively short but intense bombardment he was employing a tactic which had already worked for his own side at Riga and Caporetto, and on the Western front, for the British, at Cambrai. High explosive was combined with gas shells – chlorine, phosgene, mustard and tear gas – and the total effect was to leave survivors in the advanced area in no state to resist when the German assault troops went in. They were further handicapped, and the Germans helped, by a mist which hung over the battlefield for the first two days, enabling the attackers to form up unobserved and cross no man's land unharmed, emerging out of the mist with hand-grenades ready to throw at the bewildered and shell-shocked British troops. Within an hour and a half the whole of the Fifth Army's advanced area, and much of the Third Army's, had been overrun.

Throughout the day matters went from bad to worse. The mist which favoured the Germans' initial assault also favoured their tactics of infiltration. Points of resistance in the so-called battle zone, behind the advanced area, were swiftly bypassed as enemy detachments pressed forward. There was great confusion and a fair amount of panic among the defenders, particularly in Gough's army. Some units held out and inflicted heavy casualties, but the general picture was of retreat, if not of rout. By the end of the day ninety-eight and a half square miles of territory had fallen into German hands, and a further forty square miles were being evacuated. Penetration was to a maximum depth of four and a half miles, as much as was achieved by the British and French during the entire Somme campaign of 1916.

In another way comparison with the earlier Somme battle vividly illustrates

25. Winston S. Churchill, *The World Crisis* (1927), part II, pp. 410–11. At 10 a.m. Churchill took his leave of the 9th division 'with mingled emotions' and was driven away from the scene of the action.

the enormity and humiliating character of the British defeat. On 1 July 1916, generally regarded as the worst day in the history of the British army, 20,000 British soldiers were killed and a further 40,000 wounded, but almost none was taken prisoner. On 21 March 1918, 7,000 were killed and 10,500 wounded, but these figures were far exceeded by the figure of prisoners – a staggering 21,000. German casualties on the day amounted to about 40,000, but of these two-thirds were wounded and therefore included many who would be able to return to action later. On the British side 28,000 were totally lost.

Haig's diary entry at the end of the day is worth quoting:

Before 8 a.m. General Lawrence [Chief of Staff] came to my room while I was dressing to tell me that the German attack had begun.

At 4.43 a.m. enemy opened a heavy bombardment on the Fifth Army front ...

Very severe fighting on the Third and Fifth Army fronts continued well into the evening. Our men seem to be fighting magnificently.

About mid-day Byng seemed very anxious because reports showed that the enemy had ... penetrated into the 'Battle Zone'. But by 2 p.m. he found that the enemy had not got as far as had been reported at first.

By evening Byng had his troops ... generally on the rear line of the 'Battle Zone' and (with my approval) ordered the withdrawal of the 5th Corps back from the Flesquières salient to the Battle Zone ... during the night. This gives us an extra Division in Reserve.

With my approval, Gough decided to withdraw from the sector between La Fère and the Somme to the St. Quentin Canal. I asked the French to place some troops on Gough's right here in the Oise Valley. Two Divisions and one dismounted Cavalry Division were ordered to the Noyon area.

Having regard to the great strength of the attack (over 30 extra Divisions having reinforced those holding the original German front line for the battle) and the determined manner in which the attack was everywhere pressed, I consider that the result of the day is highly creditable to the British troops; I therefore sent a message of congratulation to the Third and Fifth Armies for communication to all ranks.[26]

Though one cannot but admire Haig's imperturbable tone, it is clear that he had no idea of the extent of the disaster that had occurred. It is surely rather astonishing that the first he knew of the attack was more than three

26. Haig diary, 21 March 1918. Haig fails to mention (presumably through inadvertence) that the bombardment also covered the whole of the Third Army's front, referring only to its impact upon the Fifth Army.

hours after Churchill had personally witnessed its opening phase. Someone at GHQ must have heard about it earlier. Was there no instruction that Haig should be woken up as soon as news was received of the beginning of an offensive which, by then, was precisely anticipated as to time and place? The decision to withdraw from the Flesquières salient should have been taken before the battle; but the salient was all that remained of the ground gained in the ill-judged Cambrai operation, and this probably explains Haig's reluctance to shorten his line – as the Germans had shortened theirs, on a much larger scale, before the Nivelle offensive. The withdrawal was decided on only in the stress of battle, and on Byng's initiative. It was very lucky that the British troops in the salient were not cut off as they might have been, with incalculable consequences, and adding to the bag of prisoners, if enemy progress on the Third Army's front had been as rapid as on the Fifth Army's. As for Haig's message of congratulation, John Terraine admits, with some understatement, that it was 'premature'.[27]

Wilson, in London, recorded at the end of the first day:

The Boches started their big attack this morning. Two hours intense artillery, and then infantry attack on an 85 kilometre front from the Scarpe to the Oise. This is a big affair. We seem to have fallen back ... from our outpost line to our battle position, and the Boches appear to have got a lodgment in about five places in our battle position. We ought to kill them all off.[28]

Dependent upon information from GHQ, he did not realize what was happening to the Fifth Army and so took an over-sanguine view of the immediate prospects.

Lloyd George, reflecting what he heard from the CIGS, wrote the following day to Margaret:

We are all here full of anxiety about this terrible battle – undoubtedly the greatest the world has ever seen. So far nothing much has happened. We have been forced to retire from our front lines but that always happens in an attack of this kind. It will go on for weeks & might well end the war.[29]

The battle would last for months rather than weeks, but Lloyd George's intuition about its outcome was correct. It would, indeed, be decisive.

---

27. Terraine, *Haig*, p. 416.   28. Wilson diary, 21 March 1918.
29. DLG to MLG, 22 March 1918.

25

Ludendorff's Offensive

Crisis measures – Doullens – Help from the enemy –
Appeal to Americans

Haig had told his wife that he had to be in France when the Germans
attacked, for form's sake and to avoid adverse comment, but that he might
just as well be in England for all the difference it would make. During the
first forty-eight hours this was almost literally true. He remained at his
headquarters at Montreuil without even attempting to make contact with
his most threatened army commander. He spoke to Gough only when the
latter telephoned him to say that enemy assault troops were through his
third, so-called reserve, line of defence. The Commander-in-Chief then
'concurred on [*sic*] his falling back and defending the line of the Somme and
to hold Péronne Bridgehead in accordance with his orders'.[1] At the same
time Haig sent a message to Pétain asking for his support, though without
explaining the gravity of Gough's plight, which he still failed to understand
himself.

In the early afternoon of the next day he did meet the Fifth Army commander at Villers-Bretonneux, and was 'surprised to learn that his troops
[were] *now behind* the Somme'. While appreciating their exhaustion 'after
two days' fighting and long march back' (also that on the first day they had
had to wear gas masks, which was 'very fatiguing'), he could 'not make out
why the Fifth Army [had] gone so far back without making some kind of a
stand'.[2] The truth was that the men of the Fifth Army had fought just as well
as their neighbours in the Third Army, but they were too thin on the ground
and the arrangements for reinforcing them were inadequate. When the battle
began their strength was far below the Third Army's in relation to the length
of front they had to defend, and as it developed fewer reserve divisions were
allotted to them than to the Third Army. All things considered, the extent

1. Haig diary, 22 March 1918. The entry begins: 'All reports show that our men are in great
spirits.' The previous night Gough had spoken to GHQ, but not to Haig himself. The Chief of
Staff, Lawrence, to whom he spoke, 'did not seem to grasp the seriousness of the situation' and
expressed the view that 'the Germans would not come on again the next day' (Sir Hubert
Gough, *The Fifth Army* (1931), p. 271). 2. Haig diary, 23 March 1918.

of their retreat – an average distance of eight miles and a maximum of fourteen – should hardly have been a matter for surprise.

By now Haig had moved to his advanced headquarters at Dury, three miles south of Amiens. Returning there from his meeting with Gough he received a visit from Pétain. The French Commander-in-Chief said that he had arranged to put 'two Armies under General Fayolle on [Haig's] right to operate in the Somme Valley' and emphasized the importance of keeping their forces 'in touch with one another'. But he also said that he expected the enemy to attack him in Champagne.[3] We can only surmise what Haig told him about the state of the Fifth Army, but it cannot have been reassuring.

The following morning the two men met again at Dury, when Pétain struck Haig as 'very much upset, almost unbalanced and most anxious'. While undertaking to give Fayolle 'all his available troops', Pétain said that 'in the event of the German advance being pressed still further' Fayolle had orders 'to fall back south westwards . . . in order to cover Paris'. When Haig asked if this meant that the French would abandon his right flank, Pétain 'nodded assent and added "it is the only thing possible, if the enemy compelled the Allies to fall back still further".' Haig gathered from him that he was under orders from his own government to cover Paris at all costs. Alarmed by what he saw as a crucial change in French strategy, Haig lost no time in communicating his alarm to London, accompanied by an appeal to the CIGS and the War Secretary to come at once to France.[4]

Haig was right to fear above all a breach between the Allied armies, and it is also fair to note that he had taken over more of the front on the understanding that he could count on French help in an emergency. Pétain did provide help, though not enough in strength or speed to save Gough's army. In fairness to Pétain, however, it should be observed that Haig was as surprised as he was by what happened to the Fifth Army, though with less reason. We should remember, too, that French fears at the time were by no means irrational. The Germans had been bombing Pétain's headquarters, and had started to bombard Paris with long-range ('Big Bertha') guns. Before long they would indeed attack in Champagne. Meanwhile they were occupying ten French departments and were within striking distance of the French capital. Even Clemenceau felt obliged to give contingent orders for the possible transfer of ministries and their staffs to Tours, and he was the least defeatist of men.

The British army in France was in danger, and if it were decisively separated from the French the potential threat to Britain itself might soon

3. Ibid. (Saturday).   4. Ibid., 24 March 1918 (Sunday).

become as acute as it had been the previous year, at the height of the U-boat campaign. But meanwhile France had every reason to feel more immediately threatened.

Lloyd George's reactions to the crisis were far swifter than Haig's, despite his distance from the battle and the patchiness of the information that reached him. (Wilson told the War Cabinet that the German attack 'might only develop into a big raid or demonstration.)[5] When Lloyd George wrote to his wife on the second day he still thought that the Germans' initial success was no greater than might have been expected. But by the following morning he knew, or sensed, that the peril was of a quite different order. Before driving into London from Walton Heath he told Riddell that the news was very bad and he feared it meant 'disaster'.[6]

On arrival at 10 Downing Street he decided that the War Cabinet should not meet until the afternoon and that meanwhile he would spend the morning at the War Office questioning the military and taking whatever urgent action might seem necessary. Before going there he spoke to Maclay and asked him to work out a programme for transporting reserves to France in the minimum time. At the War Office he was told that 170,000 men could be moved at once, if the shipping were available. These included 50,000 aged between eighteen and a half and nineteen, whom the government was pledged not to send overseas unless there were a national emergency, such as now existed in the Prime Minister's view. He found to his astonishment that 88,000 men from the BEF were currently on leave, though the Germans had stopped all leave weeks before the attack, and leave was normally postponed by the British high command before one of its own offensives. Some of the men in question were not from fighting units, but many were, and their absence in the opening phase of the battle undoubtedly contributed to the weakness of the defence. As to speed of cross-Channel movement, Lloyd George found that the routine rate was 6,000 a day, but after further discussion with Maclay this was increased at once to 20,000, which was raised to 30,000 reached within a few days.

Sunday the 24th brought more bad news and a clearer picture of the developing crisis. Lloyd George decided to send Milner at once to France to deal with the French government on behalf of the War Cabinet. It had been a question whether he himself or Milner went, but his own presence in London was judged to be essential, to co-ordinate all the emergency measures that had to be taken. In any case, Milner was the Prime Minister's deputy on the SWC and a thoroughly suitable emissary, as events were to

5. War Cab., 21 March 1918.   6. *RWD*, 23 March 1918.

prove. Lloyd George would never have considered sending Derby, the minister asked for by Haig.

At midday on the 24th Churchill returned from France (having spent the whole of the previous day at the chemical warfare school near Saint-Omer). At the War Office Wilson showed him the latest telegrams, and then the two of them walked across Whitehall to 10 Downing Street. What followed should be read in Churchill's own words:

It was a bright crisp day, and Mr. Lloyd George was seated in the garden with Lord French. He seemed to think that I had news at first hand, and turned towards me. I explained that I knew nothing beyond what he had already read in his telegrams, and had seen nothing but the first few hours of the bombardment in a single sector. After some general conversation he took me aside and posed the following question: If we could not hold the line we had fortified so carefully, why should we be able to hold any positions further back with troops already defeated? I answered that every offensive lost its force as it proceeded . . . It appeared that he had already despatched Lord Milner to France, though I was not aware of this. The Chief of the Staff said that he himself intended to go over that night. We [Churchill, Lloyd George and Wilson] arranged to dine together at my house in Eccleston Square before he left . . . I never remember in the whole course of the war a more anxious evening. *One of the great qualities of Mr. Lloyd George was his power of obliterating the past and concentrating his whole being on meeting the new situation.* There were troops in England that could be swiftly sent. What about munitions and equipment? Wilson said, 'We might well lose a thousand guns', and that mountains of ammunition and stores of every kind must have been abandoned. *I was thankful to be in a position to say that about these at least there need be no worry. Everything could be replaced at once from our margins without affecting the regular supply.* Presently the Chief of the General Staff went to catch his train, and we were left alone together. *The resolution of the Prime Minister was unshaken under his truly awful responsibilities.*[7]

After dining with Churchill, Lloyd George drove to Walton Heath, arriving at 10.30 p.m. There he told Riddell that things looked 'very bad'. But Riddell comments in his diary:

Notwithstanding the news, the P.M. was firm and cheerful. Although very anxious and much worried, he did not fail to have a good laugh as usual. His courage is

7. Winston S. Churchill, *The World Crisis*, part II, pp. 432–4; my italics. Clementine Churchill was hostess at the dinner, but probably took little part in the talk and withdrew at the earliest opportunity. Churchill refers to 'a bright crisp day' and it was true that the alarming news from France was accompanied, in Britain, by a spell of lovely spring weather.

remarkable. His work and anxieties are always with him, but he mingles them with bright and amusing conversation which lightens the burden.[8]

If a leader's performance in a crisis is to be judged by his ability to sustain his own and other people's morale, Lloyd George scores heavily for his response to the crisis of spring 1918. It was generally agreed at the time that the challenge brought out the best in him, and most historians have endorsed the contemporary view. Trevor Wilson, for instance, who never errs on the side of over-indulgence towards him, says that he 'rose heroically to the occasion'.[9] Both in the actions he took and the optimistic mood he inspired, he showed the qualities of a true leader.

Churchill's impression of him at a particularly bad moment is, of course, of special interest in view of the many similarities between the two men, and of the role the younger was to play in the next war. Though his observation of Lloyd George as Prime Minister taught him some negative lessons – mistakes that he should try to avoid – above all he saw an example of how to lead a government and nation at a time of supreme crisis. The assurance that he was able to give about the replacement of losses in equipment was an indirect tribute to Lloyd George, in that it reflected his achievement, before he was Prime Minister, in creating the Ministry of Munitions from scratch. Though his successors as head of the department, not least Churchill himself, all carried on the good work, none could fail to recognize Lloyd George's paramount contribution, which was one of the greatest of all that he made to victory.

Lord Milner crossed the Channel during the night of 24–5 March. On arrival at Boulogne he was driven first to British GHQ at Montreuil, where he received a briefing of sorts from Brigadier-General John Davidson (who had been lucky to survive the post-Cambrai purge as Haig's director of military operations). From Montreuil Milner went to the Villa Romaine at Versailles, which he reached at 2.30 a.m. after a six-hour journey. Nevertheless he rose early the following morning and had time for a talk with Rawlinson before leaving for Paris at 9 a.m. to meet Clemenceau at the War Ministry.

The two already knew each other well and were linked by a shared affection for Violet Cecil, daughter of Clemenceau's old friend Admiral Maxse, who was also Milner's closest confidante and soon to become his wife. The French Prime Minister's later description of Milner shows remarkable insight into his character:

8. *RWD*, 24 March 1918.
9. Trevor Wilson, *The Myriad Faces of War: Britain and the Great War, 1914–1918* (1986), p. 565

a luminous intelligence, crowned with a high culture completed by an inner sentimentality. Extreme gentleness, extreme firmness. A man with a poetic streak, who in moments of great difficulty ... could pause to speak of the beauty of moonlight or the grass in spring.[10]

To contemporaries who saw him only from afar Milner could appear stern, aloof, almost heartless; and many historians continue to depict him as an arch-bureaucrat and ideologue of Empire, concerned with humanity in the mass though not with individual human beings. Had it been so, he could never have inspired the devotion that he did, not only among his band of disciples (his so-called Kindergarten in South Africa, and later the Round Table group), but also among numerous others, such as Lockhart, who encountered him casually. Though his mind could be hard and unyielding, his heart was tender. Far from lacking personal sympathy, he possessed it to a degree unusual among busy and successful public men.

The meeting at the War Ministry was brief, but Clemenceau 'showed not the slightest sign either of despondency or confusion' and was adamant that a connection between the British and French armies must be maintained. He had heard that Wilson would be arriving to meet Haig, and was trying to arrange for them to come on to Pétain's headquarters at Compiègne. Unfortunately the arrangement miscarried and the British soldiers did not attend, but conferred separately at Montreuil, while Milner went on his own to Compiègne, where Clemenceau, Poincaré, Loucheur (Armaments Minister), Pétain and Foch were assembled. Pétain gave his view of the situation, in a tone which struck the politicians as 'pessimistic', and Foch then spoke. 'While not differing from Pétain's strategic plans', he seemed more willing to take risks in giving effect to them and made a 'very energetic statement'. Milner proposed another meeting to be held the following day, at which, he hoped, the present company would be joined by Wilson and Haig. The French readily agreed to the proposal. Before leaving Compiègne, Milner (according to his own account) had a few private words with Clemenceau, in which he expressed some doubts about Pétain's sense of urgency. Clemenceau defended Pétain up to a point, but agreed 'in sympathising with the attitude of Foch'.[11]

10. Clemenceau, *Grandeurs et misères d'une victoire* (1930), p. 124 (my attempted translation of a passage typical of Clemenceau's idiosyncratic style). Incidentally, what he says of Milner bears a marked resemblance to what Lady Milner says of *him* (see pp. 291–2).

11. Milner's memorandum for the War Cabinet, 27 March 1918. Amery attributes the muddle about Wilson and Haig to inefficiency in Clemenceau's office. 'Someone on [Clemenceau's] staff ... arranged over the telephone that Haig, Wilson and Weygand met at Abbeville, and

When Milner got back to Versailles at 9 p.m. he was pleased to find that the CIGS had arrived there. Much talk ensued, in the course of which a curious idea was discussed. This was that Clemenceau should be made co-ordinator of the Allied armies, with Foch as his technical adviser. Whose idea was it? Milner says that it was Wilson's, but that he thought it 'a good one'. Wilson does not exactly claim authorship, though Amery describes it as 'Henry's suggestion, which Haig apparently agrees to'.[12] At any rate Wilson paid an immediate nocturnal visit to Foch in the hope of winning him round to the idea, but without success. Foch dismissed it as unworkable, giving as his reason that Clemenceau 'might be drawn in opposite directions by Pétain and himself', with the result that 'there would be no unity of control'. For himself, he 'did not wish to command anything' but was evidently keen 'to try and get the British and French to work more closely together'.[13]

The idea of Clemenceau as the Allies' military co-ordinator was indeed undesirable and unworkable, though Foch's argument against it was not the most compelling. It had been a great mistake, a year earlier, to give the role to Nivelle, while he was at the same time French Commander-in-Chief. Quite apart from his own defects, there was bound to be an appearance, if not the reality, of conflicting interests. Clemenceau was far more suited than Nivelle to supreme command, despite being a civilian. Nevertheless the same consideration applied to him. As the political leader of one nation in the Alliance he could not have acted convincingly on behalf of other nations as well. Though he was a loyal ally and a sincere believer in unity of command, it would have been invidious for him to assume formal responsibility for exercising it. It would also have strained even his astonishing powers beyond the limit. No more was heard of the idea, and rightly so.

The Allied meeting next day took place at Doullens, about fifteen miles north of Amiens, where Haig had arranged to meet his army commanders. The French party arrived first, but Milner and Wilson were there just after midday. Movement on the roads was impeded by the flow of military traffic and, in the opposite direction, of refugees. When the conference began, Clemenceau at once startled Milner by telling him that Haig had spoken of abandoning Amiens and falling back on the Channel ports. After an urgent discussion with the Commander-in-Chief and three of his army commanders,

---

the others went to Compiègne. And this is on the most critical day of the whole war . . .' (Amery diary, 25 March 1918). Wilson, it seems, thought that *he* had arranged for Clemenceau and Foch, though not Pétain, to meet him at Abbeville at 4 p.m. (Wilson diary, same day). There must have been misunderstandings on both sides.   12. Amery diary, 25 March 1918.
13. Milner memorandum.

Plumer, Horne and Byng, Milner was able to assure the French that there had been a complete misunderstanding. Haig had no such intention, and there was no doubt in his mind 'as to the supreme importance of Amiens'.[14]

This misunderstanding having been cleared up, the leading figures soon reached agreement on the question of closer Allied operational unity. Clemenceau and Milner came with their minds predisposed towards choosing Foch as the man to give effect to it. The French premier had been disturbed by Pétain's tone at Compiègne, and his concern was increased by the few words he exchanged with him at Doullens before Milner arrived. Of this conversation he spoke afterwards to Poincaré: 'Can you imagine what he [Pétain] said to me . . . ? It is this: "the Germans will defeat the English in open country, after which they will defeat us". Should a general talk, or even think, like that?'[15] Any disillusionment with Pétain was bound to improve Clemenceau's view of the optimistic Foch. On his way to Doullens Milner, for his part, had become convinced that 'Foch possessed in a quite exceptional degree the promptitude, energy and resource necessary to get the most done to the time available, the whole question being evidently a race for time'.[16]

Pétain's contribution to the general discussion at Doullens created, again, a negative impression. To Haig he 'had a terrible look – the appearance of a Commander who was in a funk'.[17] Foch said nothing, but his looks were eloquent in the opposite sense. Before long Milner asked to speak to Clemenceau alone, and suggested to him that Foch should 'be placed by both the Governments in a position of general control'. Clemenceau, whose mind, Milner believed, 'had been steadily moving in the same direction', agreed at once but asked to speak to Pétain. Milner at the same time spoke to Haig, and then, with the concurrence of both commanders-in-chief, a document was signed by the two statesmen charging Foch to 'co-ordinate the action of the allied armies on the Western front'.[18]

Doullens was of vital significance politically and psychologically, re-asserting the Allies' unity and will to win at a moment of perilous uncertainty. For this it fully deserves its place in history. In the strictly military sense, however, its importance should not be exaggerated. The agreement did not create an effective supreme command in the field, nor was Foch ever put in the position of Eisenhower in the Second World War. The Doullens formula was soon slightly amended to give him 'the strategic direction of military operations' in the West, and the new agreement – at Beauvais in

14. Ibid.
15. Raymond Nicolas L. Poincaré, *Au service de la France* (11 vols., 1929–74), vol. x, p. 88.
16. Milner memorandum.   17. Haig diary, 26 March 1918.
18. Milner memorandum.

early April – had the further advantage of being signed by Pershing and Bliss. But this was little more than a formal gesture. The Americans, as will be seen, had no intention of surrendering their essential independence, and the Beauvais agreement provided that all national commanders-in-chief, including Pétain, should have the right of appeal to their own governments if an order from Foch seemed to them to put their forces in danger. Moreover he was to work with only a small staff; no attempt was made to form a mighty integrated machine such as Eisenhower's Supreme Headquarters Allied Expeditionary Forces (SHAEF) was to be (and it would have been hard to form one in the absence of a common language). Foch made no use of Versailles for operational purposes, and Versailles anyway included the Italians on whose front his writ, such as it was, did not run. Foch's personality ensured that he was not a negligible figure in the months ahead, for good or (sometimes) ill. But any control he had depended far more on personality than on actual powers.

It is tempting to see in Pétain's attitude in March 1918 a foreshadowing of the future, and in 1940 the story of Doullens was, indeed, recalled by British commentators. Yet his record on the earlier occasion should not be judged anachronistically. In 1918 he was still a very competent commander, whom Clemenceau, whatever his doubts, never seems to have thought of dismissing. Though Pétain lacked the faith, and therefore the recklessness, of a Foch or a Haig, his contribution to ultimate victory was at least as valuable as theirs. The allegation that he failed to come to the help of the British is largely unfair. His 'charity' may have been 'cold', because he was understandably anxious about his own front, but it nevertheless took the form of substantial intervention, without which the developing battle for Amiens would probably have been lost. Failures of anticipation and planning there were, but Haig has to share responsibility for them, as for the decision that he and Pétain took together to sabotage the project for an Allied reserve agreed on by the SWC.

Gough was not among the army commanders present at Doullens. What remained of his army was already operating under the orders of the French General Fayolle, and would soon be absorbed into the Fourth Army under Rawlinson, recalled from Versailles. For Gough himself the role of sacrificial offering was being prepared. After the Doullens meeting Wilson spoke to Haig about his future. According to the CIGS: 'I discussed removal of Gough, and told Haig he could have Rawly [Rawlinson], and Rawly's old Fourth Army staff from Versailles, to replace Gough. Haig agreed to this.'[19] Haig does not record having agreed, but claims to have defended Gough: 'I

19. Wilson diary, 26 March 1918.

said that whatever the opinion at home might be ... I considered that [Gough] had dealt with a most difficult situation very well. He had never lost his head, was very cheery and fought hard.'[20]

We see here the familiar Haig 'loyalty' routine, which invariably resulted in the departure of anybody but himself. In fact, he had not been greatly impressed by Gough's conduct of the battle, and on the 29th he took the General and his staff out of the line, with a vague instruction that they should 'reconnoitre the Somme Valley from [i.e. behind] Amiens and prepare a system of defence'.[21] Yet Haig's official attitude was that the German break-through was due to the shortage of men under his command, for which the politicians were entirely to blame, rather than to any failure of generalship by Gough or (by implication) himself. When Lloyd George was in France for the Beauvais conference he told Haig that Gough must no longer be employed, mentioning that he had failed to destroy the Somme bridges as he retreated. Haig (according to his diary) replied that if Gough was to be suspended the Prime Minister must send an order to that effect.[22] The order duly came through (from Derby), and, in conveying it to the General, Haig emphasized that it did not come from him. In saying goodbye he told Gough: 'You will have every chance to defend yourself, Hubert. There will be a court of enquiry.'[23] Two months later Haig was writing to his wife: 'As regards Gough, I am sorry that he is talking stupidly ... I am doing all I can to help him, but, *as a matter of fact, some orders he issued and things he did were stupid – and anything in the nature of an enquiry would not do him any good.*'[24]

In the harsh circumstances of war Gough had to go. He may have been unlucky, but in a leader luck is scarcely less necessary than talent, efficiency and flair. Gough had many good soldierly qualities, which he displayed not least in March 1918. But the fact remains that he was over-promoted. Command of an army is a big job, to which he was simply not equal. Granted that the Fifth Army was being treated as the poor relation in Haig's plan of defence, Gough should have made sure that his advanced area was very lightly manned. As it was, he had too many men in forward positions, a high proportion of whom were either killed or taken prisoner on the first day. He should have pressed Haig for as many reserve divisions as possible in close support. Yet the one additional reserve division obtained for his

20. Haig diary, 26 March 1918.   21. Ibid., 29 March 1918.

22. Ibid., 3 April 1918. In the same entry he says that Lloyd George 'looked as if he had been thoroughly frightened, and he seemed still in a funk'. This conflicts with all other evidence on Lloyd George's demeanour at the time.

23. Anthony Farrar-Hockley, *Goughie: The Life of General Sir Hubert Gough* (1975), p. 312.

24. Haig to Lady Haig, 16 June 1918; my italics.

army before the battle was granted on Haig's initiative, not under pressure from him; and he did not insist upon its being capable of giving him rapid support. (It was on twenty-four hours' notice to move and then needed a further thirty-six hours to be in action – far too long.) Gough was also sketchy in his joint planning with the French, which was obviously vital. He counted on Pétain to help him swiftly in an emergency, but did not see his French neighbours often enough to make detailed contingency plans. Finally, his preparation of defence in depth was conducted in a somewhat amateurish spirit. Sundays continued to be rest days, and on the Sunday before the blow fell – which also happened to be St Patrick's Day – there was 'a show-jumping competition for officers' chargers', in which he entered both of his and 'took first place on one of them out of 120 entries'.[25] The only comment has to be: 'C'est magnifique, mais ce n'est pas la guerre.'

Any criticism of Gough is, however, inescapably a criticism of the man who insisted on his appointment. Haig was right to leave the Fifth Army relatively weak, though in doing so he needed a commander for it with outstanding qualifications for preparing to fight a defensive battle under the most disadvantageous conditions. For such a role Gough was particularly unfitted. Haig gravely underrated the short-term consequences of the situation in which the Fifth Army and its commander were placed, and he made inadequate provision, at his level, for what was likely to happen. For instance, he must share responsibility for the absence of any plan to blow the Somme bridges. After the battle began he was extraordinarily slow to grasp the reality of the Fifth Army's plight, and even when he did grasp it gave Gough less moral and practical support than he should have done. Despite his show of loyalty, he acquiesced in Gough's being made the only scapegoat for a disaster of which he was at least the part-author; and in private he condemned him only less acerbically than he condemned Lloyd George.[26] Himself, of course, he could never blame.

*

25. Farrar-Hockley, *Goughie*, p. 269.
26. As scapegoats go, Gough turned out to be one of the more fortunate. Though he was never given the chance to clear himself before a court of inquiry, his disgrace was far from complete and anyway of limited duration. Lloyd George gave him military employment soon after the war, and in 1922 he retired from the army with the rank of full general. In 1937 his own and the Fifth Army's honour were fully restored when King George VI invested him with the GCB in a special ceremony. Meanwhile Lloyd George had made amends in his *War Memoirs* – partly, it must be said, as a means of getting at Haig. After dining with Lloyd George at the Reform Club Gough said: 'I see now why [he] was so successful as our prime minister. He has many remarkable qualities which must have been invaluable in carrying us through the critical days of the war' (Farrar-Hockley, *Goughie*, p. 358). Gough lived on until 1963, dying at the age of ninety-three.

The Germans' success on 21 March was devastating and over the next fortnight they continued their forward drive at a rate unheard-of since 1914. By 4 April they had advanced forty miles and occupied 1,200 square miles of territory. They had inflicted nearly 200,000 casualties on the British and 80,000 on the French (a figure hardly compatible with the idea that the French did little to help their allies). Among the British casualties, 90,000 were prisoners. At the same time more than 1,000 guns had been lost. On the face of it, Ludendorff had scored an immense triumph and was well on the way to achieving decisive victory in the West.

Yet all was not quite as it seemed. German casualties also were very heavy – 250,000 – and they were virtually irreplaceable, since Ludendorff had left so many men in Russia pursuing his policy of conquest and repression there. Britain was far better placed to make good its losses in men, and still more in matériel. For all his complaints, Haig had much to be thankful for (and Lloyd George deserved his special thanks). Pétain, too, had substantial reserves to meet the apprehended onslaught on his front, even after about twenty divisions had been diverted to support the British. And of course the Americans constituted a vast, if as yet minimally committed, reservoir of manpower.

Much of the territory occupied by the Germans had been evacuated by them the previous year, precisely because they regarded it as of little strategic value. Moreover they had difficulty in supplying their advancing troops, since their transport was much inferior, both in quantity and quality, to the Allies'. (They had 23,000 largely iron-rimmed trucks, whereas the Allies had 100,000 rubber-wheeled vehicles.) A further serious problem was a breakdown of discipline, as underfed German troops found themselves in a position to plunder British army stores. According to one observer, the momentum of advance suffered as 'entire divisions . . . gorged themselves on food and liquor'.[27]

Yet the most serious flaw on the German side after a fortnight of the campaign was that Ludendorff was allowing his strategy to become blurred and diffused. The aim of Operation Michael was to destroy the British army in France, or at any rate to separate it from the French and drive it back to, and preferably across, the Channel. To achieve this Ludendorff needed to break both the Fifth and Third Armies and then concentrate upon pushing northwards with the utmost speed, so 'rolling up' the rest of Haig's forces. The Fifth Army was effectively broken, but the Third Army, though severely

27. Quoted in Holger H. Herwig, *The First World War: Germany and Austria-Hungary 1914–1918* (1997), p. 410.

battered, was not. Albert and Bapaume soon fell, but the fate of Arras was crucial, and Arras held. Haig was right to give priority to blocking the Germans' northward drive and, for that reason, to giving the Third Army all the support he could. On 28 March Ludendorff mounted a heavy attack in the direction of Arras, which 'failed conclusively'. Trevor Wilson describes this as 'one of the decisive days of the Great War'.[28]

Amiens was another key objective and its capture would have been disastrous for the Allies. But the move towards Amiens involved shifting the prime axis of advance from north to west. This might not have mattered so much if Ludendorff had been single-minded in his determination to capture Amiens. But he was goaded by the French operating on his left into deploying excessive strength against them. Perhaps the lure of Paris had also begun to seduce him. Whatever the reason, he ordered two of his armies to attack the French, one of which was to have Compiègne as its objective. Thus, instead of merely holding the French while concentrating upon the capture of Amiens, he embarked upon serious offensive action against Pétain's forces, sending one whole army in a south-westerly direction. Not only was he trying to do too much, he was losing the plot of Operation Michael. Having already divided his forces between East and West, he was now dispersing his effort in the West as well.

Nevertheless, the battle for Amiens was a close-run thing. On 27 March Lloyd George wrote to his wife: 'Next three days – in fact next week – most critical. If they get Amiens we shall be in the tightest place we have ever yet been in.' The following day (Good Friday) he wrote to her in Welsh: 'Great worry continues. No light yet. An occasional break in the clouds & then they close. I shall have a tiresome & troubled Easter.'[29] That afternoon he went with Hankey to St Anne's church, Soho, to hear 'Bach's Passion music' (the *St John* or *St Matthew Passion*),[30] and on Easter Saturday he and Philip Kerr lunched with Riddell, the talk turning to religion:

R.: Many great military commanders have been famed for their piety. It is a very appropriate military accoutrement. If you are always risking sudden death, you want to dig yourself in.

L.G.: That is a very practical, business-like view!

R.: Most of the Indian Mutiny generals were very religious – Havelock, Nicholson, etc. Stonewall Jackson is another instance. Lord Roberts was inclined that way, but it must be admitted that there are many illustrious instances to the contrary.

28. Wilson, *Myriad Faces*, p. 564.   29. DLG to MLG, 27 and 29 March 1918.
30. Hankey diary, 29 March 1918.

L.G.: Don't forget Oliver Cromwell.

R.: Religious politicians are more difficult to find. Mr. Gladstone is the only one I can remember.

Kerr: Abraham Lincoln.

L.G.: He was not devout.

Kerr: He had the religious sense strongly developed.

L.G.: Well, I claim to have that, but I do not claim to be religious in the sense we have been discussing.[31]

In what sense could he claim to be religious? Like Lincoln (a special hero of his) he was certainly not devout, and his mind rejected most of the doctrinal side of Christianity. In particular, the Nonconformist culture and ethos in which he had been bred was in many ways uncongenial to him. Yet Christianity of a kind was a vital part of his life, from which he derived inspiration rather than consolation. When he attended a place of worship, as he often did, it was not really for worship, and still less for intercession, but for the uplift that good religious music or a good sermon could provide. He did not believe in Christ's divinity or the afterlife or the efficacy of prayer. He believed in God as the indefinable sovereign force without which there could be no sense or purpose in the universe, and his belief in God was, like Haig's, closely allied to his own self-belief (though in other respects very different from the Field-Marshal's). He looked to Jesus as a human being who was the supreme example that humanity should follow. In commending one of his own measures of social reform he had claimed to be doing the work of Jesus, but called him 'the man of Nazareth', not the Son of God.

Soon after Easter Ludendorff further extended the scale of his operations by attacking the British in a sector he had deliberately ruled out when he chose Operation Michael – the Flemish sector south of Ypres. This was another instance of the loss of focus which was to prove fatal to his strategy. The original plan for a Flanders offensive had been code-named George; now, undertaken in a somewhat reduced form, it was known as Georgette. All the same, though less than it might have been, it was still a formidable threat. Haig was given ample warning of it by his air reconnaissance but did not take it seriously enough, because he was convinced that Arras and Amiens remained the Germans' prime targets and that anything else would be in the nature of a diversion.

Consequently defensive preparations in the threatened area were inadequate. A Portuguese corps, about to be relieved, was at the centre of the

31. *RWD*, 30 March 1918.

eleven miles of front, between Armentières and Béthune, where the Germans attacked in the early morning of 9 April. Again they had overwhelming local superiority in men and guns, and again they had the advantage of mist hanging over the battlefield. The Portuguese gave way under the impact of bombardment with high explosive and gas shells, followed by German shock troops with grenades, and soon the British division to the right of the Portuguese gave way too. The attackers advanced three miles on the first day, at one point crossing the River Lys (after which the battle came to be named), until they were checked by depleted divisions recently transferred from the Somme front. Though the flank divisions were not forced into any precipitate withdrawal, the enemy breakthrough in the centre necessitated a fighting retreat. By the end of the following day Armentières had fallen, and the Germans had retaken a part of the Messines ridge. They were also within ten miles of the important railway junction of Hazebrouck.

During the third day of the offensive they strengthened their bridgehead west of the Lys and the whole Allied position in northern France began to seem acutely dangerous. That day Haig sent his uncharacteristically dramatic message: 'With our backs to the wall, and believing in the justice of our cause, each one of us must fight on to the end. The safety of our Homes and the Freedom of mankind alike depend upon the conduct of each one of us at this critical moment.'[32] Over the next fortnight two choices had to be considered by the British high command. If the enemy advance in Flanders could not be held, should the BEF fall back upon the Channel ports, even at the price of losing contact with the French, or should it retreat westwards, maintaining a continuous Allied front? The Admiralty at one point was asked if the army could still be supplied even if Calais and Boulogne were lost. The reply was that it could, and a hypothetical decision was therefore taken, in the spirit of Doullens, that Allied unity should at all costs be maintained.

In fact, the situation never arose, because the German offensive was halted a long way short of most of the Channel ports. Dunkirk was the only one at serious risk, and orders were given (though ineffectively executed) to flood the surrounding land. A lot of territory was evacuated for good tactical reasons, including Passchendaele ridge and most of the other ground captured, at terrible cost, the previous autumn. To his credit, Haig's 'backs to the wall' message was not reflected too literally in his conduct of the battle. In any case, the symbolic ruined city of Ypres remained in British hands and so, more importantly, did Hazebrouck.

32. To all ranks of the British Forces in France, 11 April 1918.

Foch gave some help to the British in the Lys battle, but not very much. He regarded the defence of Amiens as the top priority. Haig, essentially agreeing with him on this point, was also unwilling to commit too many of his reserves in Flanders. On 24 April the Germans made a last thrust towards Amiens, and Villers-Bretonneux, a few miles east of the city, briefly fell to them. But it was soon retaken, and by the end of the month Ludendorff's attempt to win the war by destroying the British army in France was tacitly abandoned. Months of peril still lay ahead, while he turned the heat on the French; but his best chance of total victory in the West had gone.

Operations Michael and Georgette had cost him, in all, nearly half a million casualties. They had also, of course, exacted a very heavy toll of British manpower, and the French, who had their biggest test yet to face, had been hard hit as well. Yet the Germans, for the reasons explained, were far less well placed than the Allies to sustain such a scale of damage to their war machine. Ludendorff had weakened his forces in the West to a disastrous degree, while his only strategic achievement was negative, the creation of two large and highly vulnerable salients.

What was the American Expeditionary Force doing in the crisis of spring 1918? It already numbered about 250,000 men, but its organized strength amounted to only four divisions, whose fighting potential was limited by deficient training and equipment and by the total absence of artillery. During the winter vain attempts had been made to secure the 'brigading' of American troops (four battalions to a brigade) in British divisions, for training and, if necessary, action. This was a policy in which Lloyd George supported Robertson, and they thought it had won the backing of the House mission. But it was never realistic. The placing of any American troops under British command was bound to be a sensitive matter, and this was particularly true of smaller units, whose national identity was the more likely to be submerged. Pershing took the line that nothing less than a division could be placed with the British for training, but he must have known that this was unrealistic for another reason, that Haig could not spare the resources for training such large units. In any case, Pershing's consistent aim was the creation of an independent American army, which would be ready to play a decisive part in the defeat of Germany – in 1919.

President Wilson gave Pershing virtual *carte blanche* because he, too, was fundamentally averse to any dilution of American independence on the battlefield. Moreover in early 1918 his thoughts were much less of battle than of peace. Far from expecting the Germans to attack in the West, he was hopeful that the Central Powers would make peace on his terms. Just as Trotsky was under the illusion that German workers would never permit their rulers to attack a Bolshevik-led Russia, so Wilson was under the illusion that the people of Germany and Austria were so entranced by his liberal programme that they would insist upon an early peace with a view to its implementation. Despite the warning of Brest-Litovsk he was still clinging to this hope up to 21 March, when the proof that he had been utterly mistaken came as a severe shock to him, and not least to his pride. Though he was converted overnight to the Entente view of German motivation in the war, he could never bring himself to admit as much. While denouncing, from then onwards, Germany's pursuit of world domination, he continued to give little if any credit to those who had been aware of it since 1914 and whose nations had been resisting it at enormous cost.

Ludendorff's offensive brought home to the American public not only the extent of the danger that had to be faced but also the inadequacy of America's war effort to date. In particular, Wilson's shortcomings as a war leader came under scrutiny, and there was much criticism of him in the press and in Congress. Lloyd George had been rebuffed when he tried the previous year to open a personal correspondence with Wilson. His dealings with the President could only, therefore, be through diplomatic channels. But he knew that a direct appeal from him to the American people would not go unheard, and when the British Ambassador, Reading, asked him for a message to be read out at a dinner at the Lotus Club in New York on 27 March he responded without hesitation. In the message he said:

We are at a crisis in the War. Attacked by an immense superiority of German troops our Army has been forced to retire. The retirement has been carried out methodically . . . the situation is being faced with splendid courage and resolution. The dogged pluck of our troops has for the moment checked the ceaseless onrush of the enemy and the French have now joined in the struggle.

But this battle, the greatest and most momentous in the history of the world, is only just beginning. Throughout it French and British are buoyed up with the knowledge that the great Republic of the West will neglect no effort which can hasten its troops and its ships to Europe. In war, time is vital. It is impossible to exaggerate the importance of getting American reinforcements across the Atlantic in the shortest possible space of time.

These words received wide coverage and undoubtedly enhanced American public consciousness of the crisis.

Wilson, however, was furious at what he chose to regard as a breach of protocol, even suggesting to House that it was enough to justify asking for

Reading's recall. Since the Ambassador was due to see him 'within the hour', the Colonel's presence was opportune. He managed to 'smooth the matter over, both as to Lloyd George and the Ambassador'.[33] He told the President that 'George had been requested to send the cable because of Reading's proposed speech'. The Ambassador had 'no diplomatic experience', but was 'America's sincere friend and doing the best he knew'.[34] Wilson was probably not much mollified, but at least refrained from showing Reading how he felt. In any case he could not ignore the intensity of American public opinion, to which Lloyd George's message can only have contributed.

While Wilson was complaining to House, Lloyd George addressed a long message to the President, via Reading, in which he mentioned the agreement reached at Doullens and stressed the 'paramount importance' of the despatch of more American troops 'with the utmost speed possible'. He also again appealed for the brigading of American units with British or French divisions. 'We most earnestly trust that he will agree,' the Prime Minister said in conclusion, because there was 'no other way of utilising this splendid material . . . this summer when the whole war [might] be decided one way or the other'. The Prime Minister sent an even longer message through the same channel the following day, making the same urgent appeal.[35] In reply Wilson conceded the 'principle' of brigading, but left the details of implementation to his 'military chiefs'. At the same time he undertook to 'direct that 120,000 infantry should be embarked for transport to Europe in each of the months of April, May, June and July . . . always provided that the ships and necessary equipment would be available'.[36] In fact, more than half the troops would be transported in British ships, involving the temporary drastic curtailment of imports of food and other raw materials.

When the news from Washington reached Lloyd George at Walton Heath, he at once telephoned the CIGS and Hankey to share it with them. To Henry Wilson he began: 'Well, General, I have some good news for you. Your cousin has agreed to send 120,000 men per month . . .'[37] (It was a characteristic joke of the CIGS to refer to the President as his cousin.) In return for Wilson's equivocal gesture Lloyd George, acting on a hint from House, issued a tongue-in-cheek statement that the President had done 'everything possible to assist the Allies', and had 'left nothing undone which could contribute thereto'.[38] But would Wilson make good on his latest commitment? Lloyd George had his doubts:

33. House diary, 28 March 1918.   34. Ibid.
35. DLG to Reading, 28 and 29 March 1918.   36. Reading to DLG, 30 March 1918.
37. RWD, 31 March 1918 (Easter Day).
38. House diary, 29 March 1918; statement published in the British press, 2 April 1918.

We have so often had large promises in the past which have invariably been falsified in result that I am sincerely apprehensive that this last undertaking may not be carried out in practice. In the circumstances [he told Reading] everything depends upon your going beyond the ordinary province of an Ambassador and exercising personal supervision over carrying out of pledge. War Mission of which you are the head will enable you to find out where delays are occurring. Immediately a hitch does occur we rely on you to bring pressure to bear in right quarter to secure its immediate removal.[39]

In the event the troops did come, but Pershing saw to it that there was no brigading.

After his exchanges with Washington Lloyd George attended the Allied conference at Beauvais, where he heard the American Commander-in-Chief proclaim that the American army would 'soon be ready to function as such and should be included as an entity like the British and French armies'. Meanwhile Pershing's best division was moved from Lorraine to Picardy, though no American combat units were committed to action there. Two American engineer companies working on railways behind the British front were, however, overtaken by the German advance and suffered seventy-nine casualties.[40]

39. DLG to Reading, 2 April 1918.
40. David R. Woodward, *Trial by Friendship: Anglo-American Relations, 1917–1918* (1993), p. 152.

26

Extending Conscription

*Extending conscription – Irish consequences – New
appointments – Family solidarity*

When the German offensive began Parliament was about to adjourn for the
Easter recess, and Lloyd George was well content that it should do so. It
suited him to be free to concentrate on executive measures to deal with the
crisis, without the distraction of Parliamentary questioning and (from his
inveterate critics) sniping. At about 8.15 p.m. on 21 March Law made a
brief statement in the House of Commons, the tone of which was unduly
reassuring. The government was still largely in the dark about what was
happening, but he wanted, no doubt, to forestall any demand that the House
should remain in session over Easter. While admitting that the attack was
'on a larger scale than any that ha[d] been made at any stage of the war on
any part of the front', he insisted that it had 'not come as a surprise', that
'those responsible for our forces' had foreseen it, and that there was no
cause for undue anxiety.[1] With that, MPs dispersed until the second week
of April.

While they were away Lloyd George issued a statement to the press,
which corrected the unintentionally misleading effect of Law's Commons
statement:

For the first few days after the German army had launched upon our lines an attack
unparalleled in its concentration of troops and guns, the situation was extremely
critical. Thanks to the indomitable bravery of our troops, who gradually stemmed
the enemy advance until reinforcements could arrive and our faithful Ally could
enter into the battle, the situation is now improving. The struggle, however, is still
only in its opening stages, and no prediction of its future course can yet be made.

From the first day the War Cabinet has been in constant session and in communication with Headquarters and with the French and American Governments. A
number of measures have been taken in concert . . . to deal with the emergency.

The enemy has the incalculable advantage of fighting as one army.

---

1. Hansard, fifth ser., vol. civ, cols. 1292–3.

To meet this the Allies have, since the battle began, taken a most important decision.

With the cordial co-operation of the British and French Commanders-in-Chief, General Foch has been charged . . . to co-ordinate the action of the Allied armies on the Western front.

In addition to the action needed to meet immediate needs . . . it will be necessary to bring into operation certain measures which have long been in contemplation should a situation such as the present arise.

It is clear that, whatever may happen in this battle, the country must be prepared for further sacrifices to ensure final victory. I am sure that the nation will shrink from no sacrifice which is required to secure this result, and the necessary plans are being carefully prepared by the Government and will be announced when Parliament meets.[2]

Lloyd George also sent a message for publication to the prime ministers of Canada, Australia, South Africa, New Zealand and Newfoundland.

When MPs reassembled on 9 April, they were immediately presented with a piece of draconian legislation framed in response to the crisis that had been developing in their absence. This was a military service bill, following Auckland Geddes's first measure enacted as recently as February. The terms of the new bill were made public on 7 April, and two days later Lloyd George personally introduced it in the House of Commons. The upper age of liability for military service was to be raised from forty-two to fifty, or even (for certain specialist categories, including doctors) fifty-five. Exemption of younger industrial workers in protected jobs was withdrawn on the 'clean cut' principle up to the age of twenty-three and, if necessary, beyond. In any case, for those above twenty-three the process of selective combing could continue.[3]

But the most controversial feature of the new bill was that it extended the principle of compulsory service to Ireland, hitherto exempt. Lloyd George embraced this proposal with extreme reluctance, since he was well aware that it was militarily futile and politically lethal. But he had no choice. Not only were most Conservatives adamant that the Irish must be conscripted; he also had to reckon with the attitude of British labour, whose support for other provisions of the bill was indispensable. 'Organised labour had intimated that it would bitterly resent the pressing through of a measure

2. 30 March 1918 (Saturday). The statement appeared in the daily papers on 1 April.
3. The 'clean-cut' principle was established in the February Act, but only implemented in the new measure, under which it was to apply at once to men under twenty-three, with power to raise the level of block withdrawal to twenty-five.

which combed out thousands more of the members of Unions which had already contributed millions to the fighting forces, whilst we exempted the Irish peasantry which had done well out of the war and had given us nothing but trouble in return.'[4]

On 6 April he held a meeting at Downing Street at which members of the War Cabinet were joined by ministers who would have been in the Cabinet in peacetime. For the latter's benefit he gave a fairly detailed account of the recent fighting and the reasons for the Germans' initial success, before explaining why a new manpower bill was necessary. 'We must raise hundreds of thousands of men more than we contemplated, because we cannot take any risks in this matter.'[5] In his Commons speech introducing the bill he amplified the case for raising the maximum number of men for the armed forces, now that the Germans had revealed their intention of seeking a military decision during the current year, whatever the consequences to themselves:

The enemy has attacked at the height of his strength. We have been deserted by one powerful Ally. Another, and a more powerful, Ally is not yet ready to put forth one-tenth of his might. But, on the other hand, this battle must exhaust the German reserves. The enemy's last call must be thrown in before this battle is over, and America is only now putting in the first instalment of her first call. If we wish to avoid a war lasting for years, the battle must be won now, and to win it we must be ready to throw in all our resources . . . we have no fear of the ultimate issue.[6]

The speech was not one of Lloyd George's best Parliamentary performances. H. A. L. Fisher, a particularly loyal and admiring colleague, found it 'rather ineffective', and to Addison it seemed 'possibly a little too long'.[7] He may have been thinking of the opening section, in which Lloyd George spent too much time giving a tendentious recapitulation of events preceding the crisis, including statistics of relative strengths on the Western front that were soon to be a source of trouble to him. He said that there were more British troops on the Western front in January 1918, and that there were only three white divisions in Egypt and Palestine in March 1918. At the end of the speech he became, perhaps inevitably, embroiled with Irish MPs and their sympathizers. (The impact of the bill upon the Irish issue will be considered separately.) Whatever the weaknesses in its presentation the

4. WM, p. 2668.   5. War Cab., 6 April 1918.
6. Hansard, fifth ser. vol. civ, 9 April 1918: Lloyd George's speech, cols. 1337–66.
7. Fisher diary, 9 April 1918; Addison diary, same date.

new military service bill was swiftly enacted, receiving the royal assent on 18 April.

In Great Britain the mood at the time was intensely patriotic, and the reaction of most people to the crisis at the front was to close ranks at home and co-operate with the government. This was particularly true of labour, whose attitude was transformed by the German offensive. In January Lloyd George's speeches to the assembled trade unionists had already done much to reconcile labour to the need for victory as the precondition of an acceptable peace, and since then the spectacle of Brest-Litovsk had served to validate his argument in their eyes. Even so, there was resistance on the part of important unions, above all the miners and the engineers, to Geddes's first Military Service Act as it affected workers in protected occupations, and it seemed that the 'clean cut' policy could be implemented only at the risk of large-scale strikes. After 21 March the same unions were prepared to accept the even more stringent demands of his new measure. (Miners indeed were so eager to enlist that many came forward above the age of the clean cut, so creating the temporary threat of a labour shortage in the mines.) Henderson spoke in the spirit of the hour just before the new bill was introduced: 'The latest act of aggression on the part of the German government . . . threatens everything that counts in the development of national and international life.'[8]

The solidarity of labour behind the government did not last until the end of the war; cracks in it began to appear quite soon. But it lasted for as long as the British army seemed to be in supreme peril, and it enabled Lloyd George to obtain the necessary control of the nation's manpower resources. In the last eight months of 1917 only 68,000 munitions workers had been recruited for the army; in the first three months of 1918 the figure was 32,000. But in the five *weeks* following 1 April 40,000 were recruited, and by mid-July the figure had risen to 100,000.

What was achieved did not show that the War Cabinet's priorities for the use of manpower set at the turn of the year had been wrong but, on the contrary, that they had been right, for the war effort no less than politically. The case is well stated by David French:

The events of March to June demonstrated that the War Cabinet had been right to try to conserve British manpower. Only by pouring so many men into the BEF that the domestic economy would have been crippled could they have forestalled a major German success in the spring. And, had they done so, they would have played into

8. Address at London Wesleyan Mission, 8 April 1918.

Ludendorff's hands, undermining Britain's staying power and bringing about the very collapse of British morale which Ludendorff sought. As it was, by being seen to conserve manpower until the crisis broke, they were able to mobilize the last dregs of patriotic self-sacrifice. They could scrape the bottom of the manpower barrel without destabilizing the industrial economy by igniting a series of protest strikes.[9]

The government's intention in taking the power to call up older men was chiefly prudential and psychological. Those liable to be called up would represent only a small proportion of the age-group, and they would certainly not be sent wholesale to fight in France. Lloyd George was aware that many men in their forties had not only family dependants, but people depending upon them for work in small businesses. In his speech introducing the bill he tried to give reassurance:

When you come to the question of raising the age up to fifty, it does not mean that men between forty-two and fifty are necessarily to be taken, in order to put them in the fighting line. It may be that there are men of that age who are just as fit as men of twenty-five, but I am sorry to say they are the exception ... There are a good many services in the Army which do not require the very best physical material, and it would be very helpful to get men of this age to fill those services, in order to release younger and fitter men ... There is also to be borne in mind that we have to prepare for Home defence, so as to be able to release men from this country, and to fill their places by men between forty-two and fifty, who, I have no doubt, will fight very tenaciously for their own homes should there be ... an invasion. The proportion of men from forty-two to fifty whom we expect will be available is not very high – something like 7 per cent ...

When he set up the Irish Convention Lloyd George undertook (it will be recalled) that his government would seek to legislate into being any scheme emerging from it which could be said to command the 'substantial agreement' of its members. During February he spent a lot of time talking to members of the Convention and trying to resolve their differences. As a result of those exchanges it became obvious to him that nothing that could pass for 'substantial agreement' was attainable and that the Convention would not, in itself, produce a solution of the Irish problem. Nevertheless, it remained in existence and on 9 April finally approved a report by 44 to 29 votes, with no Ulster Unionist voting in the majority. The report envisaged Home Rule for Ireland as a whole, still within the United Kingdom.

9. David French, *The Strategy of the Lloyd George Coalition, 1916–1918* (1995), p. 230.

Nationalists voted more than two to one in its favour, and it also had the backing of the Southern Unionist and labour representatives. But Sinn Fein, of course, had boycotted the Convention and was even less compromising in its attitude than the Ulster Unionists. Moreover, among those who voted for the report there were many reservations and nuances. The majority was substantial neither in size nor in coherence.

As the report was being produced the new manpower bill was being introduced, raising the emotive issue of conscription for Ireland. This united nationalists of all descriptions, and the Irish Roman Catholic hierarchy, in passionate opposition to the measure, a reaction which came as no surprise to Lloyd George. He knew perfectly well that it would be impossible to apply conscription to Ireland without a diversion of force which would be tantamount to opening another military front. In the bill he therefore asserted the principle of conscription through taking power to apply it, if necessary, by Order in Council. But he did not intend to apply it and it was never, in practice, applied.

At the same time he felt obliged to make another gesture. While Conservative, military and labour opinion was forcing him to put Irish conscription into the bill, he was also under strong political pressure to bring in, immediately, another Home Rule bill, as a means (it was thought) of making conscription more palatable to Irish nationalists. His Liberal and Labour colleagues, and the Asquithian Liberals, all felt that a Home Rule measure had to be introduced, and the report of the Convention was looked to hopefully as a basis on which to proceed. Lloyd George decided that the dual approach had to be attempted, though he did so without illusions.

His difficulties are plainly visible in this extract from the minutes of the full Cabinet meeting on 6 April:

Prime Minister: . . . our proposal is to bring in a Conscription Bill, which will include Ireland, but . . . provide for the application of Conscription to Ireland by Order in Council. We propose to bring in simultaneously our Home Rule Bill . . . It will take time to put Conscription into force in Ireland. We have not the machinery, we shall have to improvise a register with the aid of the police. There is no reason why the preparation of the necessary machinery should be delayed . . .

Bonar Law: Suppose we start with trying to force both Bills through and then find that Members of all kinds are opposed to the Home Rule Bill. How can you possibly carry it through?

Prime Minister: It is not necessary to decide that today. Why should we . . . anticipate that the Irish will refuse Home Rule when we have . . . had the Report of the Convention? It is absurd to decide what we can do before the crisis arises.

Churchill: The two measures should be regarded as independent and be simultaneously introduced . . .

Barnes: . . . I cannot assent to apply conscription willy-nilly without any guarantee of Home Rule . . .

Bonar Law: You do not ask your colleagues to commit themselves today to the form of the Home Rule Bill.

Prime Minister: That would be hardly fair.

H. A. L. Fisher: Has not the Government given a pledge to proceed if there was substantial agreement at the Convention?

Prime Minister: I do not think you can say that 44 to 29 is substantial agreement. We are now going on the other line: that failing substantial agreement the Government will produce a Bill and in that Bill we must make provision for Ulster.

Bonar Law: It is absurd to ask ministers to commit themselves now.

Churchill: . . . It is hard that we should commit ourselves to Conscription unless we can count on cordial agreement among our Unionist colleagues that they will go forward in support of Home Rule with equal energy.

We see here Lloyd George playing for time on the Irish Question. While seeming to take conscription seriously as a means of recruitment in Ireland, he explains that there has to be delay in giving effect to it. On Home Rule he pre-empts the report of the Convention by proposing another government initiative to find a constitutional solution.

The initiative took the form of appointing a Cabinet committee to formulate a new policy for Ireland, which held its first meeting on 15 April. Its chairman was Walter Long, the Colonial Secretary, who earlier in his career had served briefly as Chief Secretary for Ireland. He had since been prominent as a spokesman for Unionism, though by 1918 there were reasons for regarding him as essentially a pragmatist. The other members of the committee were Duke (the actual Chief Secretary), Curzon, Smuts, H. A. L. Fisher, Barnes, Cave (Home Secretary) and Gordon Hewart (Attorney-General). Of these, only Fisher and Hewart were Liberals in the British party sense, though Smuts could be seen as liberal on the Irish issue and Barnes, the Labour member, was a Home Ruler.

As a playing-for-time exercise the committee, like the Convention before it, served its purpose. With some changes of personnel it sat for weeks trying to work out a scheme that would pass the House of Commons. Long and some other Unionists were convinced that only a federal scheme involving the whole United Kingdom would be acceptable. This was the policy once advocated by Lloyd George as 'Home Rule all Round'. But such a scheme no longer had any hope of being acceptable to nationalist Ireland, even if

Parliament could be persuaded to vote for it. By early June a member of the committee was saying with resigned pessimism: 'Nobody believes we ought to introduce a Home Rule Bill now. We must go on drafting and say we have not finished.'[10]

Meanwhile the ill effects of the conscription proposal in Ireland were increasingly manifest. John Dillon, who had succeeded Redmond as leader of the Irish National Party, was a constitutionalist but more hardline than his predecessor. He hated the landlord class in Ireland, and in his youth had been very active in the agrarian movement, for a time flirting with the idea of physical force (which, however, he soon abandoned). He had come to believe that only self-government such as that enjoyed by the overseas Dominions would satisfy nationalist Ireland. In his view Gladstonian Home Rule, or any variant of it, was now out of date. He regarded the Irish convention as futile and would have nothing to do with it.

When the new manpower bill included conscription for Ireland he became obsessed with the belief that Lloyd George had introduced it with the deliberate intention of destroying the Irish National Party and setting up a direct conflict between the British government and Sinn Fein, which would help him to impose an anti-nationalist policy. Dillon's own sympathetic, but balanced, biographer can only dissent from this conspiracy theory and in the process, defend Lloyd George against a thoroughly unjust charge:

if [Dillon] had been able to lift his eyes from what lay immediately before him, he might have seen that Lloyd George's primary objective, after all, was the prosecution of a great war and that, by comparison with the destruction of the German armies the destruction of the Irish parliamentary party occupied only a very small part, if any, of his attention.[11]

C. P. Scott tried to rid Dillon of his demonizing obsession about Lloyd George, asking him to bear in mind:

(1) His love of, and exaggerated belief in, the use of force. (2) His eagerness for more men – conscription would at least give him 4 or 5 divisions from Ulster. (3) His conviction that only by imposing conscription can he carry his govt. for Home Rule. (4) His belief that the Home Rule movement has developed, or is developing, into a

10. Thomas Jones diary, 4 June 1918. The remark was made by Edward Shortt, who had replaced Duke on the committee. Jones took the committee's minutes.
11. F. S. L. Lyons, *John Dillon: A Biography* (1968), pp. 435–6.

definitely separatist movement and that the question of . . . the control of the Imperial Parlmt. of the armed forces of the Crown (which includes the raising as well as the use of them) is the touchstone of this.[12]

On 16 April Lloyd George spoke again in the House of Commons, and far more effectively than a week before. He concentrated upon the Irish aspect of the military service bill, and replied specifically to arguments put forward by Dillon:

One is his reference to the American precedent, when a government of this country endeavoured to tax the American Colonies against their will. I think my hon. Friend [Dillon] must see that there is a very substantial difference between the two cases. The case against the Government of that day . . . was that it was taxation without representation . . . the opposition was based entirely on the fact that the American Colonies had no representation.

Mr. PRINGLE: No.

The PRIME MINISTER: There is no use in rudely interrupting. The opposition was based, at any rate in the main, upon the argument that the American Colonies were not represented in the Parliament that sought to tax them.

Dillon had also argued that Ireland, as a nation, should have been consulted before any 'forcible measures' were taken to recruit its sons for service in an imperial army. In reply to this argument Lloyd George cited the example of other Celtic nations:

The same argument would apply to Wales and to Scotland. I certainly claim that Wales is a nation, and it has at least one characteristic which Ireland has not. It has a language of its own. [Hon. MEMBERS: 'Whose fault is that?'] That is certainly not the case in the country from which I come. I am perfectly certain, if I said that Scotland were not a nation, I should be interrupted by Members from across the border . . . [Yet] Scotsmen would never contend that the question of the method of raising forces for the defence of the Empire should be purely a Scottish question . . . although there is no nation in this Kingdom or in the Empire that has a greater reason to be proud of their nationality than Scotland, they do not think there is anything which derogates from their national pride or from the pride of a great race that they should delegate to the Empire . . . the right to enforce any measure, in the name of the Empire and through imperial machinery, for the raising

12. C. P. Scott to John Dillon, 26 April 1918. The first point is unfair to Lloyd George, who had no love of force. How, if not by force, was the German army to be resisted and defeated?

of forces for defence. Therefore when my hon. Friend says that there is something which is insulting to Ireland, I would point out that it is something which is not considered insulting to a proud nation like Scotland, or to a very ancient race like the race to which I belong, just as ancient a race as the one to which my hon. Friend belongs.

Having dealt so far as he could with Dillon, Lloyd George turned to Carson, who had also spoken. He had to meet the argument that the government was breaking a pledge in proposing to implement Home Rule before the war was over. Lloyd George appealed to Carson to consider the quite unforeseen length of time that had elapsed since the pledge was given:

how many were there in this House, or out of this House, who contemplated at the beginning of the War that it would go into four years? If it had been a matter of a year or two, it is possible that no grave consequences would have arisen had you suspended legislation of that character for Ireland. But . . . when the War came to be prolonged, a continuation of that state of suspense was one of peril . . . Therefore, it was obvious to every man who had anything to do with the running of the war that it was important, if not essential . . . to get the Irish question settled at the earliest possible moment.

That was why attempts had been made, in which Carson had 'taken an honourable part', to find a settlement. The first (in 1916) had failed 'through no fault of his'. Then he had 'agreed to the setting up of the Convention'. Carson intervened to remind Lloyd George that he had agreed only with the proviso that 'unless there was absolute agreement there was not to be legislation'. Lloyd George replied that if conscription for Ireland were to be Britain's only answer to the Convention, the feeling that it was inadequate and unfair would not be confined to Ireland.

He made much of the American factor:

American opinion, so far as I have been able to judge it . . . supports the justice of the Manpower Bill, provided self-government is offered to Ireland.

Mr. HODGE: Only offered?

The PRIME MINISTER: That is American opinion so far as it has reached us, and it is vital to us at the present moment. I wish I could tell the House how vital it is.[13]

13. Hansard, fifth ser., vol. cv: Lloyd George's speech, cols. 340–50. William Pringle and James Hodge, whose interruptions are recorded here, were enemies of the Prime Minister (critics would be too soft a word). Both were opposition Liberals representing Scottish constituencies, and both were anti-conscriptionists on principle. Pringle was also an anti-coalitionist, having

In fact, Lloyd George had less reason to be anxious about American opinion than a year previously, when he had recourse to setting up the Convention. The alarming developments on the Western front had drastically changed the American sense of priorities. The public in the United States was now far more concerned about the struggle in France than about Irish grievances and ambitions. In saying that conscription for Ireland would be accompanied by a new Home Rule bill the Prime Minister was doing more than enough to satisfy the Americans and their President.

Nevertheless, in Roman Catholic Ireland resistance to conscription was all the rage. When the manpower bill was passed the Irish Party withdrew from Westminster and in the last week of April a conference representing all shades of nationalist opinion was held at the Mansion House in Dublin. Dillon attended the conference along with Joseph Devlin, the Nationalist leader in Ulster, and Arthur Griffith and Éamon de Valera from Sinn Fein. It was decided to launch a national defence fund to finance the resistance movement, and the Lord Mayor of Dublin was to be sent to America, 'where, of course, it was particularly important, *but also peculiarly difficult*, to explain the reasons for this great upsurge of feeling'.[14]

In mid-May the government rounded up the leaders of Sinn Fein, alleging a treasonable conspiracy between them and the Germans. A former associate of Casement had been shipwrecked off Galway and was found to be carrying a message pledging German support for another rising in Ireland. The message was addressed to the leaders of Sinn Fein, some of whom, notably de Valera, had taken part in the 1916 Rising. All the same, the government's action was of value only for propagandist purposes outside Ireland. In Ireland its effects were entirely helpful to Sinn Fein, all the more so as Michael Collins got wind of it in advance and successfully avoided arrest.[15] He and other members of the secret, terrorist group within the republican movement were thus free to lay their murderous plans for the future, while the electoral fortunes of Sinn Fein candidates, in or out of prison, received a powerful boost. Griffith was the first to benefit, since his incarceration

been 'a savage critic' even of Asquith's coalition (John Turner, *British Politics and the Great War: Coalition and Conflict, 1915–1918* (1992), p. 186). Neither man missed an opportunity to harry Lloyd George.

In Ireland only 11 per cent of those eligible had enlisted voluntarily, and in the South recruitment had almost dried up since 1916. By contrast, in Scotland 27 per cent of men up to the age of forty-nine had volunteered for service by December 1915 (Niall Ferguson, *The Pity of War* (1998), p. 199). 14. Lyons, *John Dillon*, p. 434; my italics.
15. Robert Kee, *The Green Flag* (1976), pp. 621–2.

ensured victory for him in the East Cavan by-election held in June. (Ironically, though still the leader of Sinn Fein, he was not even a republican, favouring a dual monarchy on the Habsburg model.)

It was understandable that Dillon should be bitter since there had been some signs of reviving support for his party before the conscription issue was raised. He was, however, quite wrong to suspect Lloyd George of raising it in order to destroy the Home Rule Party and provoke a straight fight with Irish separatism. Lloyd George had no desire at all to fight the Irish, least of all when British resources were stretched to the limit in the war against Germany. He was, in any case, a sincere Home Ruler, who knew that Gaelic-Irish nationalism was a fact of life. But unlike Dillon and other Nationalist leaders he also knew that Ulster Unionism was equally so. He will always be open to criticism for having failed, with Asquith, to push through the settlement that he negotiated in 1916, which might just possibly have worked. But in 1918 he was faced with a choice of evils, and cannot fairly be blamed for choosing the lesser evil. Having chosen it, he defended his enforced position robustly in debate, concealing his private chagrin.

Two days after his second and more successful Commons speech on the military service bill, Lloyd George made a new appointment to the War Cabinet, and at the same time effected a long-desired change at the War Office. Austen Chamberlain had been outside the government since his typically over-punctilious resignation as Secretary for India when the Mesopotamian Report was published in July of the previous year. But he was a natural insider, and his recent speech after the sacking of Robertson had been unmistakably that of a man ready to return. Along with some criticism of the government he had made comments which seemed calculated to assist Lloyd George, and were no doubt interpreted as such. At any rate on 18 April he was appointed to the War Cabinet as Minister without Portfolio, so in a sense filling a place which had been vacant since Carson's departure in January.

Like Carson, his value to the Prime Minister was chiefly political, since he was a man respected in Parliament and with a significant following in the majority party supporting the government. Though he had experience of high office, above all as Chancellor of the Exchequer in the last two years of the Balfour government, he was hardly a brilliant man, and could hardly be described as a dynamic head of department. His qualities of mind were only moderately distinguished, and he was a good linguist. But had he not been Joseph Chamberlain's son and political heir he would never have risen as far or as fast as he did.[16] Among politicians he was exceptional above all for his character, which was straightforward and honourable to a fault.

There was something faintly absurd about him. Physically, and even more sartorially, he seemed a clone of his famous father, with the same features, the same build, the same hair parting, the same eyeglass and the same orchid buttonhole. Yet in other respects, as Roy Jenkins has well observed, the two men could hardly have been more different. Joe Chamberlain had gone into business at the age of sixteen and made a large fortune before entering local politics and transforming Birmingham as its Mayor. His memorable career in Parliament did not begin until he was forty. Austen, by contrast, did little apart from attending Rugby and Trinity College, Cambridge, before entering Parliament under his father's aegis while still in his twenties. He entirely lacked Joe's 'ruthless flair', and was 'condemned by a combination of paternal force and filial piety to adopt the appearance and to attempt to fulfil the role of his father'. As time went on he 'became like a beached whale of Edwardian formality', one of the last MPs habitually to wear a top hat in the House of Commons.[17]

Lloyd George had much in common with Joseph Chamberlain, whose social reforming programme had many attractions for him in his early years, and whom he never ceased to admire despite their mutual antagonism during the Boer War. He and Joe were both outsiders who had forced their way into the citadel of British power; alike in their combativeness and disregard for established conventions. Of course, there were also important differences, partly ethnic and partly in cast of mind. Lloyd George was far more sensitive to the thoughts and feelings of other people, and not prone, as Joe Chamberlain was, to monomania. But they were both politicians of whom it could be said that they made the weather, and there was a temperamental affinity between them that did not exist between either of them and Austen.

All the same, Lloyd George's appointment of Austen proved to be well judged. For the rest of his time as Prime Minister he had no more loyal colleague (which is more than could be said of Carson). When in 1921 Austen Chamberlain replaced Law – temporarily as it turned out – as leader of the Conservative Party, at a time when the Conservative rank-and-file were growing increasingly restive, his loyalty did not weaken but became, if anything, even stronger. As second man in the government his support

16. He was the only son of Joseph Chamberlain's first marriage. Neville was the only son of their father's second marriage, and not for many years seen as a potential high-flyer. Yet he was the only Chamberlain to become Prime Minister.

17. Roy Jenkins, chapter on Austen Chamberlain in *The Chancellors* (1998), pp. 112–13.

for Lloyd George was then as solid and dependable as Law's had been, though there was never the same personal closeness.

During their walk in St James's Park on New Year's Day Lloyd George had spoken to Addison of his idea that Derby should be sent to Paris as Ambassador, to succeed Bertie who was due to retire, and that Milner should be given the post of War Secretary. These changes now at last occurred, though not without some preliminary complications.

The removal of Derby presented, in itself, no serious problem. He had been made War Secretary when the government was formed, mainly as a gesture to Robertson with whom at the time Lloyd George could not afford to quarrel. But now Robertson was out, and Derby had forfeited respect in military and political circles by failing either to defend him or to show solidarity by resigning, as he said he would. To Lloyd George it was convenient that he did not resign with Robertson, but by mid-April he had finally outlived his usefulness at the War Office and the time was ripe for him to go. He accepted the Paris embassy 'with great reluctance', but bowed to the Prime Minister's request, supported, as it was, by Balfour as Foreign Secretary, merely stipulating that he should be accorded powers analogous to Reading's in Washington. While admitting that the ways of diplomacy were strange to him, he hoped that he would still be able to 'render service to the Army'.[18] If he genuinely doubted his own fitness for a major diplomatic post, he was in good company; many shared his doubt. But in fact he was better suited to being an ambassador than a minister of the Crown, and he did quite well in France, partly for a reason that Lloyd George gives in his memoirs: 'His beguiling geniality and forthrightness of manner concealed valuable powers of observation which were really serviceable to those who had to transact business amid the rapid and baffling fluctuations of French politics.' To Frenchmen who dealt with him as ambassador it was less obvious than to his fellow politicians in Britain that 'his bluffness was only bluff'.[19] He was a good host and the presence of a *grand seigneur* at the magnificent embassy in the rue du Faubourg Saint-Honoré seemed appropriate. His guests had the satisfaction of eating off his own family gold and silver plate, and he had a remarkable gift for placing them at meals as they entered the dining-room, without the need for name-cards, his apparently casual arrangement of people nearly always proving felicitous.[20]

Who was to succeed him at the War Office? Lloyd George did not,

18. Derby to DLG, 16 April 1918.   19. WM, p. 3406.
20. DNB, and personal information from the author's mother, who stayed at the embassy in Derby's day.

after all, decide at once to appoint Milner, but first considered two other possibilities. One was Hankey. The idea of appointing him was put to Milner, specifically as an alternative to himself, and Milner wrote about it in terms artfully favourable to his own claims:

Hankey or I. There is a good deal to say for both ... H. has, of course, in some respects far greater qualifications. On the other hand, I should, I think, be more generally acceptable to the Army, could, if necessary, take drastic action with greater resolution and authority, and would be more easy to move, if ... I was wanted back in the Cabinet or not wanted at all. H. would not, I think, be a good man in the Commons, and he might not care to be forced into the Lords *nor would he be as acceptable there as I might be* [the italicized words scratched out, but legible].

Personally I have absolutely no feeling one way or the other. I only want the best thing done.

But if you decide to have Hankey, I strongly urge you to have a word with Wilson first. I don't think he would object, but clearly it might be a bit of a shock to him and to others ...[21]

Whether or not this letter influenced him, Lloyd George abandoned the idea of appointing Hankey. His next idea was that like Clemenceau, he should take over the War Office himself. From this idea, or even intention, he seems to have been dissuaded above all by the King, whose annoyance at the way the whole matter was being handled was conveyed in a letter from Stamfordham to J. T. Davies, dated 16 April:

Your telephone message asking for the King's permission for the Prime Minister to announce tomorrow certain changes in the Cabinet has greatly surprised His Majesty. The King saw the Prime Minister on Saturday last (13th) and I saw him yesterday morning, and on neither occasion did he refer to these or any alterations in the Government. Weeks ago, at the time of Sir William Robertson's resignation, the Prime Minister *did* mention to His Majesty the possible change of Lord Derby from the War Office to the Embassy in Paris, and that Mr. Austen Chamberlain might be asked to join the War Cabinet. Since then no allusion to these changes had been made by the Prime Minister to the King.

I cannot disguise the fact that His Majesty is not only surprised, but hurt, that the ordinary procedure of consulting the Sovereign with regard to such important changes in his [NB pronoun] Government has not been followed on this occasion ...

As to the appointment of Lord Derby to the Embassy in Paris ... His Majesty

21. Milner to DLG, 13 April 1918.

cannot give his approval until he knows that the proposed change has been submitted to, and approved by, the French Government.

Lloyd George replied the following day, through Davies:

the Prime Minister . . . desires me to say that he was under the impression that when he mentioned the matter to the King some time ago His Majesty had approved of the changes which are now proposed . . .

The situation at the Front has developed so rapidly during the week that Mr Lloyd George came to the conclusion that this was the moment to make the necessary changes. When he saw you on Monday he had meant to discuss them with you, but as you recollect your conversation had to be interrupted on account of the War Cabinet.

[The change in Paris] at this moment becomes imperative in view of the fact that there is no one of very high standing in Paris . . . in touch with M. Clemenceau, who understands thoroughly the military situation. In consequence of this it has been necessary, as you know, to keep sending Lord Milner back and fore to discuss matters of high military policy with the French Government, at a time when he can be ill spared from the deliberations of the War Cabinet. That is why the Prime Minister, after consultation with his colleagues (including Mr Balfour who thought the change was to the public advantage) decided to ask Lord Derby to take Lord Bertie's place. Of course there was no intention of announcing the appointments before the President of the Republic gave his consent . . .

With regard to filling the vacancy at the War Office, Mr Lloyd George had of course in mind the fact that M. Clemenceau is President of the Council and Minister of War, but as you point out in your letter the Prime Minister's labours and responsibilities at the present time are heavy and arduous, and he wishes me to assure you that he would not wish to add to them by becoming responsible for the administration of a big Department like the War Office, unless he thought that by doing so he would be acting in the highest interests of the State. But he thinks there is great force in His Majesty's objections and he is considering alternative proposals for submission to the King. The best alternative in his opinion is Lord Milner who is now in France, but I understand is returning to London this afternoon when this question will be considered further . . . [22]

By the time Milner returned from France Lloyd George's mind was, in fact,

22. Stamfordham to J. T. Davies, 16 April 1918; Davies to Stamfordham, 17 April 1918; my italics. The correspondence ended with a friendly note of acknowledgement from Stamfordham, sent on the 18th.

already made up. A message was sent to Milner offering him the War Office. He accepted and his appointment, together with Derby's and Austen Chamberlain's, was announced the following day (18th).

Lloyd George's memoirs are completely silent on this curious episode. The narrative contains no record of the appointments on 18 April 1918, let alone any indication of Lloyd George's alternative ideas for the War Office before appointing Milner. (The comments on Derby as Ambassador occur incidentally in an appendix.) More surprising is the absence of any mention of the correspondence between Stamfordham and Davies in biographies of King George V, though it surely deserves to be highlighted as a rare case of royal influence over a modern prime minister on an issue of the first importance. It is quite clear that Lloyd George was intending to announce the changes on the 17th, and that they would have included his own appointment as War Secretary (while remaining Prime Minister). It seems equally clear that the King's strong argument against the latter course at the very least helped to persuade him to reconsider it, and may have been decisive in changing his mind. The only other people who, to our knowledge, were aware of his intention were Hankey and Law. On the day the announcement was to have been made Law told Hankey that Lloyd George was 'flirting' with taking the War Office himself.[23] He appears to have said nothing of Stamfordham's letter, of which Lloyd George may not have chosen to inform him or Hankey. But it is more than likely that the Prime Minister discussed his idea with the colleague whose support mattered most to him, and that Law reacted to it in the same way as the King, though without necessarily being made aware of the King's opinion.

Credit for deflecting Lloyd George from an unwise step may therefore be due in some measure to Law as well as to the King. But Lloyd George's own words leave us in no doubt of the King's influence. According to Davies's letter, which must essentially have been dictated by the Prime Minister, the King's objections had 'great force' and he would, therefore, be considering other options, among which Milner was the preferred. The letter shows that the example of Clemenceau may have given him the idea of becoming his own War Minister, and his recent visit to the War Office may also have suggested to him that the two jobs could usefully be combined. (Asquith as Prime Minister had twice taken charge of the War Office: from the Curragh crisis in spring 1914 until the outbreak of war, and towards the end of 1915 when Kitchener was abroad. But the tenure on both occasions was *ad hoc* and temporary.)

There are good reasons for believing that it would have been a serious

23. Hankey diary, 17 April 1918.

mistake for Lloyd George to become War Secretary in 1918. One, certainly, was that put forward by the King. As Prime Minister his workload was already heavy enough. He had created a War Cabinet on the principle that its members would be free from departmental duties, and it would have been odd for him to depart from the principle himself. (Law was the only exception, and he was grossly overworked.) As for the post in question, it was one that he had held (from July to December 1916), and it had been his least happy ministerial experience. He was not at home at the War Office. Moreover, it would have been wrong for the Prime Minister to be the head of one service department when there were (now) two others. In France the army was so preponderant that Clemenceau's dual role was, in that sense, less anomalous than Lloyd George's would have been. Churchill in the Second World War was Minister of Defence, which gave him an equivalent relationship to all three service departments (in which, however, his effective control of them was limited, since the fact that there was no integrated Ministry of Defence severely limited his real power). Altogether it was probably fortunate that Lloyd George did not act on his sudden impulse.

Was the appointment of Milner also a mistake and did Lloyd George have an inkling that it might be? Despite what he had said to Addison, he was bound to be reluctant, when it came to the point, to lose Milner's services as a member of the War Cabinet, which had been outstanding.[24] But was there more to it than that? Did the Prime Minister perhaps sense that Milner as War Secretary might not so much take over the military establishment as be taken over by it? He was very close to Wilson, of whose defects Lloyd George was becoming daily more aware (while still regarding him as a big improvement on Robertson), and there was a danger that Milner's zeal for War Office reform might not survive absorption into the department. Hitherto he had operated exclusively within the Prime Minister's magnetic field. At the War Office he would be within another, and there would be a competitive pull.

Whether or not these thoughts were in Lloyd George's mind, they were to prove justified. No significant changes in the high command, or working

24. The King also seems to have had much to do with Milner's appointment to the War Cabinet when the government was formed. Lloyd George had decided in any case to give him a big position in it, but his original idea was to appoint him First Lord of the Admiralty and to put Carson in the War Cabinet (since he rightly doubted Carson's fitness for a major administrative post). But the King argued firmly and, it would seem, persuasively that Carson should be sent to the Admiralty, and Milner's appointment to the War Cabinet thus came about. Lloyd George's explanation is different, but the evidence clearly suggests that he deferred to the King's view (see my *Lloyd George: From Peace to War* (1985), pp. 483–5).

practices of the War Office, were brought about by Milner. At the same time his move there unquestionably damaged his relations with the Prime Minister. The process was only gradual; at first Lloyd George tried to retain the benefits of his membership of the War Cabinet, by having regular meetings with him before the Cabinet met (see below p. 525). But before long differences were beginning to show, and the old intimacy was never quite restored.

According to Hankey, Milner asked him to come to the War Office as his under-secretary, saying that Lloyd George had 'strongly pressed' him to make the request. But Hankey refused outright, giving as his reason that he had no wish to defend the War Office 'in either House'. Milner accepted his decision with apparent equanimity, adding that his 'encyclopaedic general knowledge of the war' and capacity to influence the Prime Minister made him 'irreplaceable' where he was.[25] It is interesting that Lloyd George tried to promote this move, having abandoned the idea of making Hankey Secretary of State. Did he regard it as the next best thing, and also, perhaps, a means of keeping Milner out of the generals' power?

On 25 April there was another ministerial change, forced upon Lloyd George by Rothermere's resignation as Air Minister. As we have seen, the press lord was appointed when his brother, Northcliffe, refused the post in a manner which caused the Prime Minister much embarrassment and anger. From the first controversial, Rothermere's appointment did not work. His attempt to house his Ministry in the British Museum aroused much indignation. It was strenuously opposed in the War Cabinet by Curzon, and outside the Cabinet by the Education Minister, Fisher, who was also a trustee of the Museum. But the occasion for Rothermere's departure was a row with Trenchard, whom he had chosen as Chief of Air Staff. Disagreeing with the Minister on air policy, Trenchard walked out, and the row between them was played up in Parliament and the Tory press. Rothermere felt that a lot of mischief was caused, in particular, by the two notable MPs attached to the air staff, Lord Hugh Cecil and Sir John Simon. A further complication was that the Conservative under-secretary at the Ministry, John Baird, warned that he would not defend his chief's position in the Commons. Anyway Rothermere resigned,[26] and Lloyd George appointed as his successor Sir William Weir, a Scottish industrialist whom he had recruited in 1915 to be director of munitions for Scotland, and who had recently been serving as the Ministry's director-general of aircraft production. He proved

25. Hankey diary, 22 April 1918.
26. To ease Rothermere's departure the Prime Minister tried to obtain a step in the peerage for him, but the King objected and the matter was not pressed. Rothermere did not have to wait too long, however, receiving his viscountcy the following year.

a competent Air Minister and held the post until the end of the war. His party allegiance was, like Rothermere's, Liberal.

In early May the two senior political office-holders in Ireland were changed. On New Year's Day Lloyd George had told Addison that he would like to replace the Chief Secretary, Duke, with another 'loyal Tory who would carry more weight with the rank and file'. But now that Walter Long was presiding over the committee charged to find a formula for Irish settlement, it was no longer so necessary for the Chief Secretary to be a Tory, though the Tory Lord Advocate, James Clyde, was approached before the post was offered to two Liberal ministers, Addison himself and H. A. L. Fisher. After they too had prudently refused it, a Liberal back-bencher, Edward Shortt, agreed to take it, on the understanding that he had Long's support. Unlike Duke, he had some Irish blood (Protestant ancestry in Co. Tyrone) and the fact that he had voted against the Irish clauses of the new Military Service Act might, it was hoped, recommend him to moderate nationalist opinion. But such opinion was by now fast disappearing, and when his first action as Chief Secretary was the arrest of the Sinn Fein leadership his chances of gaining any nationalist goodwill became even slimmer. At the same time neither this show of toughness nor Long's support was enough to earn him the confidence of Unionists. His record as a Home Ruler inevitably made him suspect in their eyes.

As for the lord lieutenancy, Lloyd George asked the incumbent, Lord Wimborne, to resign at the end of April to make way for a commission in which judges, chosen to create a sense of impartiality and balance, would predominate. But this scheme soon proved unworkable, and a new lord lieutenant was therefore appointed, in the person of Field-Marshal Lord French. He too was of Irish extraction, but his personality was more likely to provoke than to appease Irish nationalists (like Gough, he was a lucky survivor of the Curragh affair in 1914). His attitude as he took up the job was that both conscription for Ireland and Home Rule in any form were non-starters until authority in the country had been re-asserted. As he put it to Lloyd George, his appointment signalled the establishment of 'a quasi-military Government in Ireland with a Soldier as Lord Lieutenant'.[27] A long, hard and painful period lay ahead before there could be any further movement towards a settlement. Ludendorff's offensive may ultimately have had the effect of harming Britain more profoundly in Ireland than on the Western front.

*

27. French to DLG, 5 May 1918.

During the anxious days of April Lloyd George wrote frequent snatched letters to his wife at Criccieth. It must have helped him to share with her his doubts and fears, as well as his hopes, while to the world at large he maintained a consistently cheerful front. But the correspondence seems to have been one-sided:

Not heard a word from Brynawelon for days. In the battle we are holding our own better. But we are not out of it yet. I am getting America at last to do something. Hope [to] God it is not too late.[28]

Before leaving for the Beauvais conference he writes (in Welsh):

Am starting for France. Expect to come back tomorrow night or Thursday. Things are fairly quiet today but it is the peace before the storm. The best thing that has happened so far is the arrangement with America that we shall have 300,000 or 400,000 men perhaps to help us between now and July – the battle will last till then.[29]

And on his return:

Back from France. Arrived about 2 this morning. Met the French Generals, Clemenceau and Haig. The French much more confident about the situation on their side. Haig more anxious. I am still more anxious after seeing Haig and his Chief of the Staff [Lawrence] – both of them very second rate men.[30]

(The day before Haig had described the Prime Minister in his diary as an 'impostor' and a 'cur'.[31] He and Lloyd George were fated to underrate each other.)

Preparing to make his first Commons speech in the new military service bill he wrote: 'I'm busy with my speech for tomorrow. A most critical speech.'[32] And the day after it has been delivered:

Had a hard task yesterday. We shall have great difficulties with the Bill in the House & after. If we fail to carry it we should have to resign or dissolve – the latter is very difficult in the middle of a great battle.

Things are not going well in France – but they may improve . . .[33]

28. DLG to MLG, 1 April 1918.   29. 2 April 1918.   30. 4 April 1918.
31. Haig diary, 3 April 1918.   32. 8 April 1918; first sentence in Welsh.
33. 10 April 1918.

A day later:

Military – & political – situation still anxious.
[And as PS] Have you heard anything as to whether Dick is near this fighting?[34]

The question seems an odd one for *him* to have had to ask *her*.

In the middle of the month he has the welcome company of Megan: 'She is here expanding with consequence playing the hostess! . . . things very anxious in the House.' 'Megs & I driving down to Walton. Situation a little better in France.'[35] Then Megan leaves for Criccieth:

I am sad & forlorn today at the departure of my little girl who has been so sweet to me during the 4 or 5 days she 'housekept' for me. She wrote me a most inspiring letter before I went to the house yesterday [for his second speech on the military service bill]. I was in a tight place & animated by Megan's letter I charged into my foes & scattered them. I really made one of the speeches of my life.

News is better today . . .[36]

Megan was on holiday from Garret Hall School, Banstead. Soon after leaving her father she celebrated her sixteenth birthday at Criccieth (22 April). A year earlier Frances Stevenson had written of her as 'an amusing little person', getting rather selfish but nevertheless 'wonderfully unspoilt, considering the way she ha[d] been brought up'.[37] In 1918 she and Frances were close friends and were to remain so for two more years. It was because of Megan that Frances had become part of the Lloyd George family circle. She had been engaged as a holiday governess for Megan at Criccieth during the summer of 1911. The romance that had since developed between her and Lloyd George was in no way suspected by Megan. (In those days teenage girls had an innocence now scarcely imaginable, and in any case there were many older people around Lloyd George who regarded Frances as no more than a trusted private secretary.) It was not until the Lucerne conference in 1920 that the scales fell from Megan's eyes, and her affection for Frances then turned to lifelong hatred and enmity.[38]

Lloyd George's letters to Margaret reflect the ebb and flow of the battle in France:

34. 11 April 1918.   35. 12 and 13 April 1918.   36. 17 April 1918.
37. FSD, 29 April 1917.
38. Private information from Megan's friend Thelma Cazalet. It is very much to Margaret Lloyd George's credit that she clearly did nothing to prejudice Megan against Frances, though she knew well enough – and resented – what was going on.

News better these last two days . . . & every day now counts in our favour. Saturday and Sunday's fighting saved us [the days immediately following Haig's order of the day, when the German advance towards Hazebrouck was held]. But we are by no means through. We have anxious days & weeks in front.[39]

Nearly ten days later:

French news not quite so good. We have had just a little 'biff' south of Amiens. Had it not been so near Amiens would have had no importance.[40]

But on the last day of the month:

News from France of last battle excellent.[41]

This refers to the recapture of Villers-Bretonneux, and the lifting of the imminent threat to Amiens.

While in France at the beginning of May he saw 'a good deal of Dick' (of whose whereabouts he had earlier been uncertain), finding him 'fat sleek & prosperous looking'.

He is a changed man. Never saw him look better. Full of enquiry about the youngsters – & about Olwen. I only heard from him that Olwen had a bad time [giving birth to her first child]. I was very distressed.[42]

At the same time Gwilym was in England, on instructional duties at Lydd. But 'I have no doubt that he will have to go soon & he is keen to go – & he ought to go'.[43] At the end of April he stayed a couple of days at 10 Downing Street, 'in great form'. 'He is not off to France just yet as he has no men in his battery. They will come in soon but they will take a month or six weeks to train.'[44] In fact, it was several months before Gwilym was able to return to France, but he was there again for the final campaign. He and Dick both ended the war with the rank of Major, respectively in the Royal Artillery and the Royal Engineers.

39. DLG to MLG, 15 April 1918.   40. 24 April 1918.   41. 30 April 1918.
42. 30 April 1918.
43. 15 April 1918. A week after the outbreak of war in August 1914 Lloyd George had written to his wife urging her to make sure that Gwilym was not 'bullied into volunteering abroad', though soon afterwards he was invoking the spirit of sacrifice in a famous speech at the Queen's Hall. In the crisis of 1918 it was obvious to him, as national leader, that his sons had to be *seen to be* running the same risks as so many other fathers' sons.   44. 30 April 1918.

Megan was at Downing Street again when Lloyd George got back from his visit to France in early May. But she had to return to school and anyway he evidently felt the need for her mother's company, because on 4 May he ends a short letter to Margaret with the underlined words 'When are you returning?' and 'Do come soon' added in Welsh. Understanding him better than anyone, and sensing the earnestness of his appeal, she responded to it at once and came to London in time to be with him as he faced the most serious political challenge of his wartime premiership.

27

The Maurice Affair

General Maurice's letter – The Maurice debate –
Rights and Wrongs

On 7 May a sensational letter appeared in four London newspapers, *The Times*, the *Morning Post*, the *Daily News* and the *Daily Chronicle*. (It was also offered to the *Daily Telegraph* which, however, decided not to publish it.) The author was a senior serving army officer, Major-General Sir Frederick Maurice, until recently director of military operations (DMO) at the War Office. The letter accused Lloyd George of having misled the House of Commons in his speech on 9 April, and Bonar Law of having done so in reply to questions on 23 April. The alleged misstatements by Lloyd George concerned the relative British and German numerical strength on the Western front in January 1918 compared with a year earlier, and the number of white divisions under British command in the Middle East; Law's related to the taking over by the BEF of part of the line in France previously held by the French army. The clear intention of the letter was to suggest that the government, through its action and inaction, had made the BEF vulnerable to Ludendorff's assault, and that it was now trying to conceal the fact by giving false information to Parliament.

General Maurice ended with an explanation of his motives and an attempt to justify, in somewhat rhetorical language, his flagrant breach of military discipline:

Now, Sir, this letter is not the result of a military conspiracy. It has been seen by no soldier. I am by descent and conviction as sincere a democrat as the Prime Minister and the last thing I desire is to see the government of our country in the hands of soldiers.

My reason for taking the very grave step of writing this letter is that the statements quoted above are known to a large number of soldiers to be incorrect, and this knowledge is breeding such distrust of the Government as can only end in impairing the splendid morale of our troops at a time when everything possible should be done to raise it.

I have therefore decided, fully realising the consequences to myself, that my duty as a citizen must override my duty as a soldier, and I ask you to publish this letter in the hope that Parliament may see fit to order an investigation into the statements I have made.

Maurice's name has already cropped up more than once in this narrative, but the man himself now needs to be introduced. He was the third Frederick Maurice in line. His father, another Sir Frederick and also a general, was the eldest son (and biographer) of the eminent Victorian divine and social reformer, Frederick Denison Maurice. On his mother's side he had an Irish connection, reflected in his second name, Barton, and he was born in Dublin. After St Paul's School he went to Sandhurst and followed his father into the army. As a young officer he served overseas and did well in the Boer War. Back in England he graduated at the staff college and then worked under Haig at the War Office before returning to the staff college, where the commandant was Robertson. The close friendship there formed between the two men determined most of Maurice's future military career – and its premature end. When, in January 1915, Robertson became the BEF's Chief of Staff, he put Maurice in charge of the operations section; and at the end of the year, when he became CIGS, he took Maurice with him to the War Office as DMO. Though much liked and respected for his own qualities, Maurice was also clearly identified as Robertson's man.

He married the sister of Edward Marsh, noted aesthete, Edwardian social-ite and Churchill's private secretary. The Maurices had four daughters and a son, and a fifth daughter who died in infancy on 16 March 1918. One daughter became, as Joan Robinson, a famous Cambridge economist, and the eldest, Nancy, married (as his second wife) Edward Louis Spears, whom we have also encountered. Years earlier Spears wrote this vivid description of the man who was to become his posthumous father-in-law:

As imperturbable as a fish, always unruffled, the sort of man who would eat porridge by gaslight on a foggy morning in winter, looking as if he had enjoyed a cold bath, all aglow with soap and water, just as if he were eating a peach in a sunny garden in August. A very tall, very fair man, a little bent, with a boxer's flattened-out nose, an eyeglass as flat and not much rounder than his face, and a rather abrupt manner. A little distrait owing to great inner concentration, he simply demolished work, never forgot anything, was quite impervious to the moods of his chief, the accurate interpreter of his grunts and groans, and his most efficient if not outwardly brilliant second. No man ever wasted fewer words or expressed himself when he spoke with greater clarity and conciseness.[1]

1. E. L. Spears, *Prelude to Victory* (1939), pp. 35–6. Spears married Nancy Maurice in 1969, after the death of his first wife, the American-born novelist Mary Borden. Nancy had long been his devoted personal assistant and mistress. Reproducing his description of Maurice in the 'Appreciation' that he contributed to Nancy's book, *The Maurice Case*, he added that he could hardly improve on it after a 'long lapse of time'.

THE MAURICE AFFAIR

Spears well conveys the appearance and manner, though perhaps not the inner complexity, of the man. The character of Maurice's grandfather, F. D. Maurice, was marked by a certain tension between an instinctive desire to conform and an uncontrollable streak of rebelliousness. This resulted in a theological controversy which aroused strong passions at the time and caused him to resign his chair at King's College, London. His grandson may have inherited the same trait, and the resultant controversy in his case was political.

How did his letter come to be written? When Henry Wilson took Robertson's place as CIGS he lost no time in appointing a new DMO. He told Maurice that he needed 'a man from the trenches' for the job, and that Haig had promised to give him (Maurice) command of a division. The new DMO was to be Major-General P. de B. Radcliffe, but impending and actual events at the front delayed his arrival at the War Office until 11 April, and even then Maurice did not go on leave or take up a new post, but remained technically in charge of the military operations department for about another week. During this time he visited Haig's headquarters and was offered by the Commander-in-Chief, not a divisional command, but a senior post on the staff of the new army which was being constituted from the wreck of the Fifth. Maurice must have declined the offer though he never says so or explains why; but he does record that while at headquarters he found people there 'very dissatisfied with LG's speech of 9 April'.[2]

The next month found him, therefore, without military occupation. But he certainly busied himself in other ways, above all in talking to critics of the government. On 9 April Lloyd George had told the House of Commons that the army in France was 'considerably stronger' on 1 January 1918 than on 1 January 1917. He had also said that there was only one white division in Mesopotamia, and only three in Egypt and Palestine, the rest of the British forces in that area being 'either Indians or mixed with a very, very small proportion of British troops'. According to Maurice, he did not notice the inaccuracies in the speech until his attention was drawn to them by officers at Haig's headquarters, but he then 'undertook to go into [it] carefully' on his return to London, and 'to see what steps were necessary to correct' the mistakes.

On 18 April a Liberal back-bencher asked in Parliament if the figure of relative strength on the Western front given by the Prime Minister represented truly combatant strength, or if it included labour battalions and other non-combatant units. Ian Macpherson, under-secretary at the War

2. Maurice diary, 15 April 1918.

491

Office, confirmed Lloyd George's figure, armed with statistics supplied by the Adjutant-General's department and sent to Downing Street by Colonel Walter Kirke, deputy to the DMO – who was still, technically, Maurice.[3] Nevertheless, four days later a weekly summary prepared by the DMO's office stated that the Germans currently had a rifle-strength superiority of 333,000 in the West. And the following day a question was put to Law about extension of the line, by three MPs of the awkward squad type. He replied that the extension to Barisis was agreed between Haig and Pétain, and not imposed by the SWC at Versailles.

By now Lloyd George and indeed the whole War Cabinet were beginning to suspect that a campaign was being orchestrated by the government's enemies in Parliament, the press and the higher ranks of the army, with a view to forcing it out of office. There was a growing buzz of anti-Lloyd George talk, and the *Morning Post* was openly calling for a change of government. But what was Maurice doing? On 29 April he saw his mentor, Robertson, who had already told him that action was necessary. At this meeting he put 'proposals' to Robertson: evidently (from the context) to write to the CIGS about what he believed to be the misleading statements by Lloyd George and Law, and, if he received no satisfactory reply from Wilson, then writing to the press. Robertson agreed that he should write to Wilson, but suggested that before raising the issue publicly he should first talk to Asquith. Had he done so, the probability is that Asquith would have advised him against taking the ultimate step he proposed. But we shall never know, because Maurice decided not to see him and to take 'sole responsibility for action' himself.[4]

He did so with Robertson's approval, if not at his instigation, since in the course of the same day the former CIGS changed his mind about the desirability of seeing Asquith:

I have been thinking further and am not sure that I like the Asquith idea after all. The case is rather one for your own judgement. *The thing is to decide irrespective of what the results may be, unless you feel sure that the results will certainly be nil.* I shall be interested to know what reply, if any, you get to your letter to the CIGS . . .[5]

Maurice's letter to Wilson, also sent that day, received no reply. On 2 May Maurice composed his letter for the newspapers, but still delayed sending

3. He handed over to Radcliffe on the 20th.
4. Robertson to Maurice, 29 and 30 April 1918. Robertson also was under-employed, in the military sense, as GOC Eastern Command. Both men had time on their hands.
5. Robertson to Maurice, 30 April 1918; my italics.

it. Robertson, however, wrote again in terms manifestly calculated to stiffen his resolve:

Everyone I see swears that the days of LG are numbered but I don't attach much confidence to these statements. The point of this is to repeat what I have said already, namely, be quite sure of your facts and do not say a word that cannot be conclusively substantiated or that can be twisted to your disadvantage.

You are contemplating a great thing – to your undying credit.[6]

Maurice's letter to the press was then despatched and duly appeared. Reading it, Lloyd George and his colleagues were convinced that they were facing a conspiracy. They could no longer doubt that an attempt was being made to fasten blame on them for the disaster of 21 March and the ensuing crisis, with the aggravating offence of lying to Parliament to evade their own responsibility and foist it instead upon the high command. Lloyd George's immediate response was that the threat must be countered by a statement from him in the House of Commons, followed by a vote of confidence. There was only one dissentient in the War Cabinet – Law – but he was too important to be ignored. He was not happy that the matter should be settled by a political vote, either of the whole House or of a select committee, but wanted a judicial inquiry to clear the honour of ministers, especially his own. His colleagues agreed that a select committee would be unsuitable (it would split on party lines), but regarded a judicial inquiry as even more so, since it would be inappropriate for the honour of ministers to be submitted to the arbitrament of judges. Nevertheless Law insisted, and when Asquith put a private notice question to him on the evening of the 7th he offered a judicial inquiry, with Asquith free to choose the judges if he wished. MPs were by no means unanimous in support of the offer, and in any case Asquith turned it down, demanding instead a select committee of the House to investigate Maurice's charges. It was then arranged that a motion by him to that effect, opposed by the government, would be debated in two days' time.

Asquith, as we have seen, had not been visited by Maurice (whom he knew quite well) to read or discuss his letter in advance. On the other hand he was seeing Robertson, who is likely to have told him something of Maurice's agonies of conscience. The day before his letter appeared Maurice wrote to Asquith:

6. Robertson to Maurice, 4 May 1918; my italics.

I have today sent to the press a letter which will, I hope, appear in tomorrow's papers. When I asked you to see me ... I had intended to consult you about this letter, but on second thoughts I came to the conclusion that, if I consulted you, it would be tantamount to asking you to take responsibility for the letter, and that I alone must take responsibility. I ask you to believe that in writing the letter I have been guided solely by what I hold to be the public interest.[7]

During the next forty-eight hours Asquith was under considerable pressure to show his willingness to resume the premiership if Lloyd George were brought down. On the morning of the debate he received an astonishing letter from the editor of the *Morning Post*:

It seems to me that the almost immediate effect of General Maurice's letter and your motion must be the dissolution of the present government and the disappearance from it of Mr. Lloyd George and Bonar Law. A consequent change will, in all likelihood, be your accession to power.

The editor admitted that he had been a political opponent of Asquith 'of many years' standing', and that he had advocated his supersession by Lloyd George. But he now felt (as one could paraphrase his words) that anything would be preferable to the existing regime. The letter concluded: 'We are in a very sad case ... But the nation is all right. It means to win or die, and if you can guide and lead this spirit of victory to its goal, then you will find an ample reward in duty done ...'[8]

Lloyd George rightly sensed that Asquith, while harbouring deep resentment, had lost the will to rule. He also sensed, equally rightly, that Parliament, reflecting the popular mood, would not vote to bring the former Prime Minister back. He therefore approached the debate with confidence, and gave Hankey the task of preparing a brief for him. So far as the issue of relative strength in the West was concerned, he decided to take his stand on the figures supplied by the War Office for Macpherson's reply in Parliament on 18 April, choosing to disregard the very different figures produced by the DMO's office on 22 April (which had anyway since been substantially amended) and even a last-minute set of figures sent from the same office on 8 May. His mood was supremely combative, and his aim was to defeat what he regarded as an essentially political challenge with his full armoury of political ruthlessness and skill.

On the eve of the debate he received this message from a mass meeting of

7. Maurice to Asquith, 6 May 1918.   8. H. A. Gwynne to Asquith, 8 May 1918.

1,500 workers at Woolwich Arsenal: 'Hold fast! We are with you because you are the people's Prime Minister and our symbol of victory ... Your enemies are our enemies. Damn them all! God save England!' He may also have read that day the report of a speech by the Labour politician and former trade union leader G. H. Roberts (who the previous August had succeeded Hodge as Minister of Labour) in which he said that no government could do its job if it was subject to constant 'sniping'.[9] The final word may have caught Lloyd George's eye as he prepared his own speech. It was to appear in his peroration, to great effect.

At about 3.45 p.m. on 9 May Asquith rose to move 'that a Select Committee of this House be appointed to inquire into the allegations of incorrectness in certain Statements of Ministers of the Crown to this House, contained in a letter of Major-General Maurice, late Director of Military Operations, published in the Press on the 7th day of May'. The former premier began with a laboured explanation of what his motion was not. It was not, he said, 'either in intention or effect', a vote of censure on the government. And it was not, he strongly implied, a move aimed at bringing about his own return to power:

I know that there are people ... gifted with more imagination than charity, and with more stupidity than either, who think of me as a person who is gnawed with a hungry ambition to resume the cares and responsibilities of office. I am quite content to leave foolish imaginations of that kind to the judgment of my colleagues in this House and of my countrymen outside.

He was one of those who did not think that it was Parliament's business in wartime to be 'constantly inquiring' into the conduct of the war 'by committees or by any other instrument of investigation'. But the government itself had raised the issue of looking into Maurice's allegations when Law offered a judicial inquiry. He (Asquith) had rejected this offer because as an old Parliamentarian he was 'jealous' of Parliament's honour and did not believe that the correctness or otherwise of ministerial statements should be submitted 'to any other tribunal' than a Parliamentary tribunal. What was the alternative to a select committee? To this unwise question Asquith received a prompt answer from the Independent Labour MP for Merthyr Tydfil, C. B. Stanton, 'Get on with the War' – which according to Lloyd George was greeted with a cheer such as he had 'rarely heard in the

9. Reports in *The Times*, 9 May 1918.

House'.[10] Asquith compounded the damage to himself by describing the intervention as 'very irrelevant'.

The mood of the House was, therefore, potentially favourable to Lloyd George when he got up. By the time he sat down it was overwhelmingly so. He dealt briskly with the rather difficult question why the government had changed from offering a judicial inquiry to seeking, now, to resolve the issue by a Parliamentary debate followed by a vote of confidence (the course which, though he did not say it, he had always preferred). An investigation of Maurice's charges might have been worthwhile if it could have been strictly objective, 'short and sharp', and leading to an 'immediate decision'. A panel of judges might have produced such a result. But a Commons select committee was 'not the best tribunal for investigating facts when passions were aroused'. The House itself had come to the same conclusion in matters such as election petitions, and Asquith had not set up a Commons select committee to conduct the Mesopotamia inquiry. In the present affair, circumstances had changed since a judicial inquiry had been offered and turned down:

it is perfectly clear, from the action of the Press, which is egging on my right hon. Friend [Asquith], prodding him and suggesting that he ought to do this and the other to embarrass the Government, that no statement, no decision of any secret tribunal, would ever be accepted . . . We have therefore decided to give the facts in public and to let the public judge.

Lloyd George's presentation of the 'facts' was selective but extraordinarily telling. He concentrated his fire on Maurice, despite regarding him as no more than the tool of others who were his real enemies:

What is the present demand? A general, a distinguished general, who has ceased to hold an office which he has occupied for two years, challenges, after he has left office, statements made by two Ministers during the time he was in that office. . . . he never challenged those statements, when he had not merely access to official information, but when he had access to the Ministers themselves. . . . was it not his business first of all to come to the Cabinet, or, at any rate, to come to the Minister whom he impugned, and say to him, 'You made a mistake in the House of Commons on a most important question of fact'? He might have put it quite nicely. He could

10. WM, p. 2988. Stanton had been a miner and a docker. Among his activities listed in *Who's Who* was 'backing the War to a finish'. His recreations were said to include painting in oils and violin music.

have said, 'I daresay you were misled, but you can put it right.' Never a word was said to me! Never a syllable until I saw it in the newspapers!

On the question of relative strengths on the Western front, Lloyd George chose to rest his case on the figures given to him before his speech on 9 April and on those given to Macpherson for his Parliamentary answer on 18 April. If those figures were incorrect, Maurice was 'as responsible as anyone else', since they came through his department. The question to Macpherson had concerned combatant as distinct from non-combatant strength, but Lloyd George did not accept the distinction:

Are the men who are under fire every day, making and repairing roads ... and railways, and who suffer severe casualties, combatants or non-combatants? ... Does anyone mean to tell me that they are not part of the 'fighting strength' of the Army? Take the men who, when the British Army retreated, and had to abandon trenches ... and who had to improvise defences under shell fire to relieve the Infantry – are those men no part of the fighting strength of the Army?

Yet even on the narrow definition of 'combatant' the figures given to Macpherson showed that the strength of the British army was up in January 1918 compared with the previous January and March.

Maurice was also, he said, the official primarily responsible for reporting the number of divisions in other theatres of war, and it was therefore through him that the information about divisions in Egypt and Palestine had come. When he (Lloyd George) had said on 9 April that there were only three white British divisions in that theatre, he was relying on 'the statement ... made at a Cabinet meeting' at which Maurice was present, and of which he received a note for correction. But no corrections were made by him or anyone else. In fact, a change was being made in Allenby's forces at the time, but 'the change was not complete' and Lloyd George claimed to have been unaware of it when he spoke.

On the extension of the British line question he rebutted Maurice's allegation, while pointing out that *he* was guilty of *suggestio falsi*. Maurice had implied that he was present when the SWC 'decided' the question, by saying that he was 'at Versailles' at the time:

I think anyone reading that would say that General Maurice was present at the meeting. He was at Versailles, it is true, but the implication is that he was in the Council Chamber.... As a matter of fact, the extension of the front of General Gough's Army – the extension to which allusion has been made, the extension which is supposed to be responsible . . . for the disaster, though I do not accept that – was never discussed at that Council at all. There was a demand for a further extension [but] that particular extension [to which Law referred in his answer] had taken place before the Council ever met. It had been agreed to between Field-Marshal Haig and General Pétain . . .

Lloyd George was at his deadliest as he considered the effect of Maurice's letter on army morale, and the inevitable political consequences of a vote for Asquith's motion. On the second point he was emphatic:

if this Motion be carried, he will again be responsible for the conduct of the War. Make no mistake! This is a Vote of Censure upon the Government. If this Motion were carried, we could not possibly continue in office, and the right hon. Gentleman, as the one who is responsible for the Motion, would have to be responsible for the Government.

Noting that Asquith had admitted Maurice's breach of discipline, Lloyd George suggested, with cold politeness, that he ought also to have deprecated it:

What does it mean? It is not merely a flagrant breach of the King's Regulations. . . . Supposing a regimental officer had done this. After all, they have their views about their superiors. . . . They might even challenge the accuracy of statements made by their superiors. Are they to write to the papers and say, 'Grave statements have been made. It is my duty, not as a soldier but as a citizen, because I am a democrat, and because my grandfather was a democrat, to forget the King's Regulations'? I wonder what would be said if a poor ordinary soldier acted in that way! . . . Is this the time for such an example by a distinguished soldier, who has held some of the most confidential positions in the Army?

In his peroration, the Prime Minister set the debate in the context of repeated attacks on him by certain elements, military and civilian:

I wonder whether it is worth my while to make another appeal to all sections of the House and to all sections of the country. These controversies are distracting, they are paralysing, they are rending, and I beg that they should come to an end. It is difficult enough for Ministers to do their work in this War. We had a controversy which lasted practically for months over the unity of command. This is really a sort of remnant of it . . . Days have been occupied in hunting up records and minutes and letters and *procès verbaux* . . . in raking up a whole twelve months in the War

Cabinet. And this at such a moment! I have just come back from France. I met some generals and they were telling me how now the Germans are . . . preparing perhaps the biggest blow of the War . . . and they asked me for certain help. I brought home a list of the things they wanted done, and I wished to attend to them. I really beg and implore, for our common country, the fate of which is in the balance now and in the next few weeks, that there should be an end of this sniping [G. H. Roberts's word].

After Lloyd George's speech the debate staggered on for another hour or so, but the result was a foregone conclusion. The most significant intervention was by Carson. The day before the debate he had tried to persuade Unionist back-benchers to support neither Lloyd George nor Asquith, but found that anti-Asquithian feeling was too strong for such a tactic to be acceptable. Willy-nilly, therefore, he made a speech which was helpful to the government and its leader, ending:

We are bound to accept the statement of the Government, unless we are prepared to challenge them as a Government. Therefore, I say in the interests of the War, in the interests of the dignity of this House, in the interests of the relations between the civil and military powers, and above all things as an example to the people of this country who are going through a very trying time, let us close up our ranks.

As the debate neared its end there were impatient cries of 'divide, divide', and would-be orators took the hint. The House then voted, and Asquith's motion was defeated by 293 votes (including Carson's) to 106, a majority of almost three to one. Yet the number supporting the government was less than half of the total membership of the House. Even when one allows for the absence of eighty-odd Irish Nationalists, the size of the vote is scarcely impressive, suggesting that the result is more to be seen as utter rejection of Asquith than wholehearted endorsement of Lloyd George. Outside Parliament his position was, in all likelihood, much stronger, though until the age of opinion polling there could be no proof of a leader's popular following. In any case, the Parliamentary vote on 9 May ensured Lloyd George's immunity from further challenge until the war was won.[11]

Two days later Maurice heard that he had been put on half-pay, and soon afterwards his retirement from the army was announced. But he was even less of a martyr than Gough, because as his career in uniform ended he received, simultaneously, a new job as military correspondent of the *Daily Chronicle*. Far from being threatened with penal sanctions, he was treated

11. Hansard, fifth ser., vol. cv, cols. 2347–406: Lloyd George's speech, cols. 2355–73.

with studied courtesy. With Lloyd George's approval, Milner wrote him a letter asking him, in the politest terms, to exercise discretion and a degree of self-censorship as a military journalist, granted that he was 'the depository of the most intimate details of the Allied military position'. He replied in a thoroughly accommodating tone.[12] After the war he tried to secure official vindication of the line he had taken in his letter, though without success. All the same, many years of fruitful activity remained to him. He wrote numerous books and held various academic posts. For a time he was Principal of the Working Men's College which his grandfather had founded, and in 1927 he became Professor of Military Studies at London University. From 1933 to 1944 he was Principal of the East London College, later Queen Mary College. He died in 1951.

If there was a serious casualty of the Maurice affair it was not Maurice himself, but rather Repington, who made the mistake of attacking Milner as well as Lloyd George. Milner had devotees to whom any reflection on his honour was almost tantamount to sacrilege. On 12 May a two-page editorial in the *Observer* delivered a counterattack on Repington from which the Colonel's anyway somewhat brittle reputation never recovered.[13]

Now that we have seen what, in essentials, happened in the Maurice affair – how it originated, how it developed and how it ended – it is time to consider the rights and wrongs of it. Did Lloyd George deserve his triumph of 9 May, or was it a case of barefaced mendacity and roguery prevailing over truth and decency? Was Maurice a hero, or was he at best a high-minded fool allowing himself to be used by others for their own dubious purposes? How should the conduct of Law, Asquith, Wilson and Robertson be rated? Were genuine principles at stake in the controversy, or was it no more than a squalid power struggle between individuals? Was the Commons' vote at the end of the debate a vindication of the British Parliamentary system or a disturbing example of its fallibility? These are important questions, to which there are no simple answers. But an attempt must be made to give a balanced assessment.

Law's part in the affair was limited to his reply about extension of the line in France and his insistence upon offering a judicial inquiry to clear his name. In the process, he caused unnecessary embarrassment to his

12. Milner to Maurice, 16 May 1918; Maurice to Milner, same date.
13. The demolition of Repington was the work of the *Observer*'s editor, J. L. Garvin, acting willingly on a suggestion from the proprietor, Waldorf Astor. The incident is amusingly described by A. M. Gollin (*Proconsul in Politics: A Study of Lord Milner in Opposition and in Power* (1964), pp. 514–17).

colleagues, partly because the offer of an inquiry applied to the whole of Maurice's letter, and therefore exposed Lloyd George as well as himself to the hazard of condemnation by judges. It also implied that Maurice's charges were of sufficient gravity to warrant independent investigation, which in turn made the government's rejection of a select committee harder to justify. The argument that such a committee was bound to be partisan, and to divide accordingly, was perfectly valid, but could be made to seem an insult to Parliament and anyway stirred memories of the Marconi inquiry in 1913 which Lloyd George would have preferred to lie dormant.

In his Commons reply on 23 April Law said that the question of extending the line had been settled between Pétain and Haig, and in a further reply to a supplementary from the ever-troublesome Pringle said that '*this particular matter* [my italics] was not dealt with at all by the Versailles War Council' – on which Maurice commented in his letter that he 'was at Versailles when the question was decided by the Supreme War Council to whom it had been referred'. The exact truth was not quite as either Law or Maurice represented it. In fact, the decision to extend the British line had been agreed in principle between Lloyd George and Painlevé the previous September, and the following month Haig had grudgingly agreed with Pétain to take over the French line as far as Barisis. At the end of the year the British came under heavy pressure from the French to take over more of their line, which Lloyd George as well as Haig resisted. The matter was referred to the SWC in January, with a recommendation from the military staff at Versailles that the British should take over about half of what the French were demanding. But Pétain did not press Haig to act on this recommendation and, when the Germans attacked, Barisis was still the southernmost point of the British line (and of Gough's army front).

It was therefore strictly true that the only extension that had actually occurred had been agreed between Haig and Pétain, and that the SWC had not discussed 'this particular matter'. But in suggesting that the SWC had not discussed the extension issue at all, Law's words were misleading. Indeed they provided another Marconi echo, Rufus Isaacs having notoriously told Parliament that he and his friends had no shares in 'that company', referring to English Marconi but implying that they had no Marconi shares of any kind, when in fact they had taken shares in the associated American Marconi company. Law was perhaps guilty of a similar *suggestio falsi*, though in his case with the justification that to have told the whole truth would have been to reveal matters that needed to be kept secret. Lloyd George was similarly inhibited in defending his position, but had none of Law's shame when avoiding total truthfulness for a good cause. As he put it engagingly (to

Stanley Baldwin, of all people): 'Poor old Bonar, he felt it very much. He doesn't like being called a liar. I don't mind. I've been called a liar all my life.'[14] Law's 'quaint honour' (the poet Marvell's phrase, used by him in a non-political context) was in this instance a liability to the government and its chief, whom he normally served so well.

Asquith's conduct over Maurice was much the same as in the crisis leading to the fall of Robertson, though with one crucial difference. As before, his raw grievance against Lloyd George, constantly inflamed by his wife and political associates, made it impossible for him to keep entirely aloof from machinations against his successor. Yet he was a true patriot, whose instinct was to support the country's government in times of danger; and he was a constitutionalist, to whom the idea of using extra-Parliamentary forces to destroy a British administration was repugnant. Moreover, when invited – as by Gwynne – to resume the leadership of the country, he was conscious not only of the lack of support for him in Parliament and outside, but also of his own diminished energy and will to rule. His infirmity of purpose can be seen in the confused guidance given by the *Westminster Gazette*, edited by his friend and future co-biographer, J. A. Spender. At first the paper was calling on the House of Commons to pursue Maurice's allegations whatever the consequences, but on the eve of the debate it emphasized the need for unity 'at a moment of unparalleled danger' and said that the situation 'must give every patriotic man occasion for the most severe self-examination and discipline'.[15] Readers of those words can hardly have been surprised at the unmenacing tone of Asquith's speech opening the debate. Yet he went beyond what he had done in the Robertson affair by dividing the House at the end. This was, surely, a calamitous error.

Wilson's part is hard to explain, and he seems, to say the least, guilty of some negligence. Did he see the revised Western front figures before they were sent from the DMO's department to Downing Street on 22 April? If so, did he seek any explanation of their gross incompatibility with figures previously given? And if not, why not? Lloyd George wrote Milner a furious letter about the figures, describing them as 'extraordinarily slipshod' and asking how they came to be prepared. But there is no evidence of any advice about them having been given either to him or to Milner (just installed as Secretary of State) by the government's chief military adviser.

There is also the curious matter of Maurice's letter to the CIGS, and Wilson's failure to reply to it. Did he mention it at once to Milner, or to Lloyd George and Law, the two ministers accused of misleading Parliament? Again,

---

14. R. J. Q. Adams, *Bonar Law* (1999), p. 268.   15. 8 May 1918.

there is no evidence that he did. He referred, almost casually, to having heard from Maurice, when the War Cabinet met on the morning the General's letter to the press appeared. But he said nothing of the contents of the personal letter received by him over a week before, nor did he mention that it had been left unanswered. Admittedly Maurice had given the CIGS no reason to suspect that he would go public with his complaint unless he received a satisfactory reply. But Wilson should have been alert to any sign of potential trouble-making from a man whom he had recently sacked, and who was so close to Robertson. It was surely most unwise, as well as rude, to ignore his letter.

Robertson is the person who comes worst out of the affair. He told Maurice that action was necessary, and then effectively endorsed the action that he proposed to take. Though for a moment he advised that Asquith's opinion should be sought before Maurice wrote to the press, he quickly thought better of this advice and urged his acolyte to go ahead on his own responsibility, unless he felt sure that the results would 'certainly be nil': an absurd qualification, which can hardly have been intended as a deterrent. As a former professional head of the army he might have been expected to discourage a brother-officer from breaking King's Regulations, and as a friend it would have been natural for him to argue strongly against a course likely to prove disastrous to Maurice himself. Instead, he seems to have been prepared to use Maurice as an instrument for wreaking vengeance on Lloyd George, while perhaps at the same time creating the conditions for his own reinstatement as CIGS. In a remarkable, if flawed, career this was the ignoblest episode. Whether or not there was any credit in what Maurice did, Robertson's manipulative conduct stands to his eternal discredit.

Maurice was certainly naïve in allowing himself to be so exploited by his former chief. Naïvety was a feature of his character, as was apparent again in 1939 when, as President of the British Legion, he broadcast an appeal to the German army not to invade Poland three days before the invasion occurred. But Maurice was not merely an ingénu, a holy fool. He was a clever man, and there was a disingenuous side to him as well. His letter to the press in 1918 was far from being that of a simple soldier, puzzled and pained by the obliquity of politicians. Both the letter itself and his account of the circumstances in which it was written contain statements just as questionable, and innuendoes just as artful, as any that he could impute to Lloyd George or Law.

The last three paragraphs of the letter are especially open to criticism on this score, and were in fact sharply criticized in a *Times* leader the following day: 'His whole peroration is far too suggestive, not indeed of a "military conspiracy", but of one of those disingenuous Parliamentary answers which

GENERAL MAURICE comes out to condemn.'[16] He stated, for instance, that the letter had been 'seen by no soldier'. There is no reason to doubt that this was technically true – as was Law's statement that the 'particular matter' of the extension of the British line to Barisis had not been discussed by the SWC. But it was, surely, in the same way a *suggestio falsi*. The substance of the letter, if not the precise text, was well enough known to Robertson, who was indeed the principal moving spirit in the whole affair. The only difference was that Law was prevaricating in order to avoid revealing that there had been Anglo-French discord about further extension of the British line, whereas Maurice was doing so to protect Robertson. Which was the more honest and patriotic motive?

In the rhetorical part of his letter Maurice claimed to be writing for the sake of army morale, impaired by distrust of the government. But how can he have believed that a remedy for the condition lay in greatly increasing the distrust? If such was his honest belief, he was capable of self-deception far transcending the normal bounds of naïvety. The alternative explanation is that he was being deliberately hypocritical to justify a proposal whose true intention was to destroy Lloyd George and his ministry. On the whole, the second seems the more plausible hypothesis.

Lloyd George could fairly ask why Maurice had waited so long to make his complaints, and why he had not made them first privately to the ministers concerned, whom he was seeing almost daily. In his letter to the press he used the time-honoured formula that his 'attention' had been 'called' to Law's answers in the Commons, implying that he had been unaware of them at the time; and in his secret apologia dated 22 May 1918 (but only published many years later in his daughter's book on the affair), he makes a similar claim about Lloyd George's speech on 9 April:

I had no leisure to read through the full report of the Prime Minister's speech until I left the War Office on 20 April . . . On 13 April I went to France, returning later on the 16th, and while there I heard from a number of officers in important positions grave criticisms of some statements which the Prime Minister had made on 9 April, and I was informed that these statements were having a bad effect on the Army . . . I undertook to go into the Prime Minister's speech carefully on my return, and to see what steps were necessary to correct these statements.[17]

16. *The Times*, 8 May 1918.
17. 'The Story of the Crisis of May, 1918', published in Nancy Maurice, *The Maurice Case* (1972), pp. 91–116.

It defies rational belief that the statements in question by Lloyd George and Law were not noticed earlier by Maurice, since they were widely reported and discussed at the time. What Lloyd George said about the relative strengths on the Western front was singled out for publicity and comment in the press. Even if Maurice had been a retired man living in the remote countryside, he could hardly failed to have at least a vague awareness of the statements. Living and working at the heart of things he must have known about them in detail from the moment they were made. If Lloyd George's 9 April speech was the subject of discussion and criticism at Haig's head-quarters, it must have been no less so at the War Office where Maurice spent his days. His excuse for failing to speak out earlier, in private confrontation with the ministers, is therefore simply not credible.

He was, no doubt, upset about losing his job as DMO. Like Robertson he had a personal grievance, and such grievances can too easily be sublimated as concern for the higher interests of the state. He was offered alternative employment, though his hopes of a field command were dashed – by Haig, not Lloyd George. There is some evidence that he saw Hankey very shortly before writing the letter, and that Hankey told him he was '*bien vu* by Lloyd George', suggesting 'several appointments'.[18] (Whether or not these included the staff appointment he was offered by Haig we cannot know.) In any case, his army career was not being brought to an end. He alone was responsible for that outcome.

Finally, it is surely right to take note of the illness and death of Maurice's youngest child in the spring of 1918. Elizabeth Olive, known as Betty, was nearly eight years younger than the next youngest, and still not quite one year old, when she died on 16 March of 'tubercular peritonitis wasting'. How much, if at all, the anxiety that preceded, and the grief that followed, the child's death may have affected Maurice's judgement at a critical period in his life can only be a matter of speculation. But it is rather odd that Nancy Maurice does not even mention Betty's existence.[19]

We come, now, to Lloyd George. Of course he has been in the picture all

18. The source is Hankey, talking in 1932 to Liddell Hart ('Talk with Sir Maurice Hankey at United Services Club 8th Nov. 1932', quoted in Stephen Roskill, *Hankey: Man of Secrets* (3 vols., 1970–74), vol. i, p. 539). It is possible that Wilson, having received Maurice's personal letter, may have suggested to Lloyd George or Hankey that a friendly word to him might be prudent. If so, criticism of Wilson's failure to reply to Maurice would need to be qualified.

19. She may have felt that even to hint at any factor that could have had an adverse bearing on her father's state of mind might be damaging to her pious defence of him.

For information about Betty, and other matters relating to the case, the author is much indebted to Christopher Graham, a great-nephew of Maurice.

along, since the way others behaved in the affair is of obvious relevance to any appraisal of his conduct. But we have now to consider his part in it directly, and a good point of departure is to emphasize his conviction that his enemies were out to get him. He regarded the Maurice letter as a put-up job, and Asquith's motion in Parliament as a collusive move. Behind both Maurice and Asquith he saw the implacable figure of Robertson, with his network of military minions and his array of supporters in Parliament and the press. He felt threatened and was profoundly indignant about the nature of the threat. In his speech of 9 May he was fighting for his political life, and his whole approach was suitably combative. Yet it reads not only as the speech of a man who intended to survive, but as that of a man who believed himself to be essentially in the right.

He was surely justified in feeling that the blame for any weakness in the BEF, as it faced a much reinforced German army on the Western front, lay chiefly with Haig, who had squandered so much of his manpower the previous autumn. The War Cabinet's decision, under Lloyd George's leadership, to hold the bulk of the reserves in England rather than entrust them to Haig was soundly based. If more drafts had been sent to Haig early in the year he might have used them for offensive rather than defensive purposes. A major German attack in the spring was bound to achieve some initial success, and it is probable (though improvable) that a period of crisis would have ensued even if there had been many more divisions in France at the outset. Haig's defensive priorities, in principle correct, would still have exposed Gough's army to disaster, though the scale of the actual disaster, and the extent of Ludendorff's advance after 21 March, took Haig, quite as much as Lloyd George, by surprise.

The Prime Minister had a good overall case, though it could not be stated in full to the public. Perhaps for this reason he made the mistake of quoting figures in his speech on 9 April. The figures came from the War Office, and it was doubtless tempting to avert criticism by pointing to the simple 'fact' of superior British numbers on the Western front at the beginning of the year. But even if January had been the appropriate month for comparison (rather than March), he would have been wise to keep clear of statistics. They were never his strongest point, and besides they are seldom reliable and nearly always lead to controversy. In this instance, his critics were soon asking if the figures he had given were for combatant strength. Though he regarded the distinction as largely spurious, he had reason to feel satisfaction when the War Office produced figures for a Parliamentary answer by the under-secretary, Macpherson, on 18 April, showing that in January the BEF had possessed a superiority in combatants.

One can sympathize with Lloyd George's wrath when, four days later, the War Office came forward with new figures showing an inferiority in rifle-strength of 330,000. As a result of his angry letter to Milner the figures were re-examined and the deficit was reduced to 262,000. The original error had been due, it seemed, to the inclusion of 86,000 British troops in Italy in the Western front tally. On 7 May a further revised estimate was sent to Hankey, according to which the rifle-strength of the BEF was 100,000 below that of the Germans in January.

At the best of times Lloyd George had little confidence in figures supplied by the War Office, and had often suspected, with reason, that they were cooked by the military to suit themselves and bamboozle the politicians. His scepticism was shared by Hankey, who wrote in his diary the previous December:

The fact is . . . that the War office figures and statements are utterly unreliable, and their facts are twisted to support their arguments. If they want men they make out that they can hardly hold the line . . . If they want to do an offensive they make out that the enemy is exhausted and demoralised, and that they have lots of men.[20]

The figures produced by the War Office after Maurice's letter were doubly suspect in Lloyd George's eyes. He was sure that a deliberate attempt was being made by the Robertson camp to destroy his credibility as national leader and encompass his downfall. He may or may not have been right about the motivation of those in the Adjutant-General's department who produced the figures. What is certain is that the latest figures, sent to Hankey on 7 May, were still defective, in that they treated artillerymen, machine-gunners and tank men as non-combatants and did not include them in the BEF's fighting strength.

Lloyd George did not know this, but he anyway decided to disregard all statistics that came from the War Office after 18 April, when Macpherson gave his answer about combatants. Regarding all figures emanating from that quarter as likely to be bogus, and never more so than in the existing circumstances, he chose to follow the generals' example by using the figures that suited him best. In his speech on 9 May he therefore took his stand on the figures used in his 9 April speech, and on those given to Macpherson for his 18 April reply.

Of course he was entirely aware of the 'corrected' figures that had since come through. He made a row, as we have seen, about the first lot on 22 April, and we have Hankey's evidence that he knew about the final lot on 7

May. In his diary two days later, after listening to Lloyd George's speech from the gallery, Hankey wrote:

It was not the speech of a man who tells 'the truth, the whole truth, and nothing but the truth.' For example, while he had figures from the D.M.O.'s Dept. showing that the fighting strength of the army had increased from 1st Jan. 1917 to 1918, he had the Adjutant-General's figures saying the precise contrary, but was discreetly silent about them. This knowledge embarrassed me a little when M.P.s of all complexions kept coming to the official gallery to ask me what was the 'real truth'.[21]

He may have been 'a little' embarrassed, but not remotely to the extent of turning against Lloyd George or feeling that the speech – which he described as 'a superb parliamentary effort' – was fundamentally false. It would be difficult, indeed, to think of any fighting speech by a politician based upon the truth, the whole truth and nothing but the truth. In politics a speech can be sufficiently honest without being strictly truthful, and Lloyd George's in the Maurice debate was a case in point.[22]

Fine distinctions between honesty and truthfulness were clearly not on his mind, however, when he had breakfast with Conservative colleagues on the morning of the speech. He was 'in excellent spirits' and 'talked so much and with such animation that he let his cigar out a dozen times'. He reviewed the whole Maurice affair and as he walked back to Downing Street said to George Younger, 'This time I have been caught out telling the truth' – the sort of reckless, unpompous remark that was typical of him.[23] He was in the right mood for a virtuoso performance in the afternoon.

21. Hankey diary, 9 May 1918.
22. On the lesser issue of troop strength in the Middle East he admitted that he had been inaccurate in his speech on 9 April, but claimed to have been misinformed. This was true at the time. He had been told by Wilson that Allenby had three all-white divisions under his command, though the correct figure at the time was seven. A month later he was probably aware of the mistake, but then mentioned that orders had been given for a change, which was not yet complete. He must have been referring to the transfer of Indian units from Mesopotamia, but this was only to a very limited degree relevant, because few had been moved before the German attack in the West. Most were moved after the attack, to take the place of white British troops switched to the Western front.
23. Crawford diary, 9 May 1918. The Tory breakfasts were no longer taking place at Derby House, because Derby was now in Paris. They had moved to St Stephen's Club, where Lord Edmund Talbot, the Unionist chief whip (later Lord Fitzalan of Derwent), acted as host.

Another example of Lloyd George's refusal to talk in the manner of a grave statesman was a remark he once made to Lee: 'I have an instinctive sympathy for criminals. I could so easily have been one myself!' (*A Good Innings: The Private Papers of Viscount Lee of Fareham*, ed. Alan Clark (1974), p. 155).

The speech treated Maurice roughly, and in some ways unfairly. It was wrong to suggest that War Office figures came from the DMO's department. In fact, they came *through* it, but were prepared by the department of the Adjutant-General. The figures provided for Macpherson's answer on 18 April were not even seen by Maurice (who was away at the time) but were initialled by his deputy. This Lloyd George had to admit, in response to an interruption.

Even when the crisis had passed he did not relent towards Maurice, whose efforts to obtain official vindication came to nothing. In his memoirs Lloyd George wrote of him no more charitably than he had spoken of him in the famous debate. He did not forgive what he still saw as the General's bad behaviour towards him. And he was not prepared even then to come clean about his selective use of figures, which no doubt he regarded as merely fighting his enemies with their own weapons.

It was while he was writing his memoirs that Frances Stevenson made a curious entry in her diary, which first came to light in Beaverbrook's *Men and Power*:

Have been reading up the events connected with the Maurice Debate in order to help Ll.G. and am uneasy in my mind about an incident which occurred at the time & which is known only to J. T. Davies & myself. Ll.G. obtained from the W[ar] O[ffice] the figures which he used in his statement on April 9th in the House of Commons on the subject of manpower. These figures were afterwards stated by Gen. Maurice to be inaccurate. I was in J. T. Davies' room a few days after the statement & J.T. was sorting out red dispatch boxes to be returned to the Departments. As was his wont, he looked in them before locking them up & sending them out to the Messengers. Pulling out a W.O. box, he found in it, to his great astonishment, a paper from the D.M.O. containing modifications & corrections of the first figures they had sent, & by some mischance this box had remained unopened. J.T. & I examined it in dismay, & then J.T. put it in the fire, remarking, 'only you & I, Frances, know of the existence of this paper'.

There is no doubt that this is what Maurice had in mind when he accused Ll.G. of misstatement. But the amazing thing was that *the document was never fixed upon* ... They argued round & over the point, but never did one of them put any finger on it. I was waiting for the matter to be raised, & for the question to be asked: 'Why did D. not receive these supplementary figures? Or did he?' But the questions never came & I could not voluntarily break faith with J.T., perhaps put D. in a fix, & who knows, have brought down his Government! The only explanation is that Maurice & Co. were relying on getting their judicial Committee where every point would have been thrashed out in detail. When the judicial committee was turned down, it was by that time too late to bring up details again, & by that time also Maurice was beaten.

I suppose it is too late now for the matter to be cleared up . . . And as the Official Statistics since compiled seem to justify D.'s statement at the time, it were better perhaps to let sleeping dogs lie.[24]

Beaverbrook's book appeared in 1956. By then Maurice was dead, but Frances Stevenson was alive and became involved in controversy as a result of reviews of the book, particularly one in the *Spectator* by Samuel Hoare, Lord Templewood. This prompted her to write to the *Spectator* stating that the incident had occurred not before the Maurice debate but *'some time afterwards'*.[25] In her autobiography, published in 1967, she says that when she made the diary entry she telephoned J. T. Davies, who told her that 'he had no recollection of the incident'.[26] Nancy Maurice speculates that Davies 'staged the discovery of the War Office document he destroyed, and made Frances Stevenson his innocent accomplice'.[27]

Such speculations need not detain us, because the whole story – though naturally fun for Beaverbrook and his readers – is quite irrelevant, even if we overlook its obvious inaccuracies. It is irrelevant, because the major 'correction' by the War Office was made on 22 April, causing Lloyd George to react strongly in a letter to Milner. We also know that he saw the last-minute figures sent on 7 May. What Davies may or may not have done about a paper found in a red box, and when he did or did not find it, has absolutely no bearing upon the case.

Milner annoyed Lloyd George by suggesting, soon after the debate, that the figures given in good faith by Macpherson should be corrected in the light of the later figures. Since Lloyd George had used them in his speech it would have been political madness to do so, and granted that the later figures were themselves inaccurate and misleading, whether intentionally or through incompetence, even the ethics of the matter are confused. Milner did not press the point, but the fact that he raised it at all contributed to the Prime Minister's gradual loss of confidence in him as War Secretary.

Hankey, despite knowing all about Lloyd George's selective use of War Office figures, seems to have felt that this was justified in the circumstances, and took pride in the brief he had prepared, on which the speech was substantially based. He, too, did not forgive Maurice and may well, in 1925,

24. FSD, 5 October 1934; Lord Beaverbrook, *Men and Power, 1917–1918*, pp. 262–3.
25. *Spectator*, 23 November 1956; her italics.
26. Frances Lloyd George, *The Years that are Past*, p. 133.
27. Maurice, *Maurice Case*, p. 174.

have used his influence to prevent the General becoming Chichele Professor of the History of War at Oxford.[28]

The most significant comment on the affair was that of Balfour, who was approached by Maurice, whom he liked personally, at the beginning of 1920 with a request for help in resolving the statistical dispute. In his reply Balfour wrote:

It is evident that I cannot approach this problem in an attitude of abstract impartiality. The Prime Minister is my colleague and my friend. Together we have gone through most difficult times ... I could not but deplore, both on public and on private grounds, anything which should damage his position in the country.

May I, however, make one observation ... You believe, rightly or wrongly, that the Prime Minister's statement gave a wholly false impression of your case, and you assume that this was done deliberately by the Prime Minister, who was prepared to sacrifice your character in the interests of political expediency. Now I am quite confident that this view is most unjust. The Prime Minister no doubt felt very strongly upon the subject, and it is possible, as sometimes happens in the heat of controversy, that he may not have measured his language ... but of one thing I am quite confident, which is that he thought *you* were the doer of a wrong, and that *he* was the victim of it.[29]

It would be hard to imagine a gentler or more effective put-down. Moreover, despite Balfour's confession of partiality, more than eighty years later the comment seems not far from an objective judgement on the real, as distinct from the technical, merits of the case.

Principles *were* involved in it. Far more than the survival of the government was at stake, because on its survival depended the country's ability to come through the last phase of the war, which was full of difficulty and peril. Of course Lloyd George had plenty of faults, and his government was far from perfect. But since December 1917 the record of achievement was, on balance, impressive, and a change of political leadership in the spring of 1918 would have been of advantage only to the enemy. It would certainly have done immense harm to national morale, including that of the army for which Maurice claimed to speak.

The damage to the country would have been compounded by the way the change came about. It is impossible to read Robertson's words at the time without feeling that the principle of civilian control was under threat. In the

28. Roskill, *Hankey*, vol. i, pp. 550–51; Maurice, *Maurice Case*, pp. 149–50.
29. AJB to Maurice, 7 January 1920.

Maurice affair, if not before, Lloyd George's idea of a military conspiracy was surely not entirely fanciful. The vote of the House of Commons on 9 May was therefore a victory for Parliamentary government, as well as for the actual government and its leader.

28

The Germans Advance Again

Encouragement from the navy – Lloyd George at Edinburgh –
German threat to Paris – Americans in action

During the anxious days of April, while the BEF was struggling to hold the line in France, the spirits of the British people were cheered by a spectacular naval exploit. The raids on Zeebrugge and Ostend, carried out on St George's Day (23 April), had a powerful effect on home morale, comparable with the capture of Jerusalem by Allenby's army the previous December. There was, it is true, an important difference. Allenby's was a complete victory, a victory of substance, whereas the raids turned out to be victories only in the moral sense. This was not known at the time, however; the general belief was that they had succeeded brilliantly. In any case, moral victories can often be of great value in war.

The raids on the Flemish ports resulted from the appointment of Admiral Roger Keyes as commander of the Dover Patrol, in the Admiralty shake-up following the departure of Jellicoe. Keyes's varied service had established his reputation as an officer whose instinct, like Nelson's, was always to attack. Yet while resembling Nelson in valour and pugnacity, he was not quite his equal in intelligence. An eminent naval historian has described him as 'one of the most attractive of men, warm-hearted and full of boyish enthusiasm – a born leader with few brains'.[1] Yet his admirers included Churchill, who rightly considered that he 'revolutionised the situation' when he assumed command of the Dover Patrol.[2] There his main task was to fight the U-boats based in Flanders, which were responsible for about one-third

---

1. Arthur J. Marder, *From the Dreadnought to Scapa Flow* (5 vols., 1961–74), vol. v, pp. 39–40.
2. Winston S. Churchill, *The World Crisis* (1927), part II, p. 370. Churchill's high opinion of him was doubtless influenced by his very positive attitude during the Dardanelles campaign. Before the evacuation Keyes argued strongly that the navy should make another attempt to force the Narrows, but the idea did not find favour with his superiors. In the Second World War, as an admiral of the fleet and (since 1934) a Conservative MP, he was Churchill's first choice as Chief of Combined Operations. He held the post until October 1941, but was then removed to make way for Lord Louis Mountbatten.

of the sinkings of merchant ships. Their principal base was at Bruges, eight miles inland. From there they reached the sea by way of two canals, debouching at Zeebrugge and Ostend. Keyes's bold plan was to block these two exits by sinking superannuated naval vessels, loaded with rubble and cement, in the mouths of the canals, so making the ports unusable. At both ports he had to contend with powerful shore batteries, but at Zeebrugge there was the added complication of a heavily fortified mole protecting the harbour.

Keyes envisaged dealing with the shore batteries by fire from 15-inch naval guns, but he decided that the German guns on the mole would have to be put out of action by a landing party. At the same time submarines would blow a gap at the landward end, to deny the Germans reinforcements during the battle. When the defences of the mole were neutralized three blockships would be sailed round it and scuttled in the harbour entrance. Survivors from the mole, the submarines and the blockships would be taken off by small craft, but the enterprise was so hazardous that heavy casualties were expected and only unmarried men were allowed to take part.

For complete success the attackers needed to approach their objective under cover of darkness or smoke. By the time weather and tide conditions seemed favourable there was a full moon, which made the use of smoke all the more essential. At first the wind was blowing in the right direction to carry the smokescreen inland, but at a late stage it swung round and revealed the approaching force to the enemy. As a result the landing on the mole was achieved only with great difficulty and to a very limited extent. The German guns there continued to fire, and the success of the submarines in blowing a gap was wasted, since the Germans on the mole did not need to be reinforced. Even so, two of the three blockships managed to penetrate the harbour and were duly sunk by their crews. But unfortunately they settled on the sea-bed in positions that did not effectively block the canal, and the U-boats remained free to come and go (the smaller ones at once, the larger after a short interval).

At Ostend, which had seemed the easier proposition, failure was in fact total, because the markers laid to guide the blockships were destroyed by German gunfire, and the ships ended on sandbanks well clear of the harbour entrance. To whose who took part in this operation it must have been obvious at the time that it had failed, though an optimistic view was understandable in the case of Zeebrugge. The cost to the attackers of about 700 casualties may be considered light, granted the difficulty of what was attempted and the absence of smoke cover when the attack went in.

At any rate, Keyes's exploit was immediately hailed as a triumph, both at home and by Britain's allies. The Admiral himself was promptly knighted, and also received high awards from France and Belgium. Lloyd George wrote to Geddes, congratulating him and all concerned, and in his reply the First Lord said that later reports showed the operation to have been 'as fully, if not more' successful than at first supposed.[3] Zeebrugge soon entered the sphere of national mythology, and after the war Churchill helped to sustain the myth, writing in *The World Crisis*: 'It may well rank as the finest feat of arms in the Great War, and certainly as an episode unsurpassed in the history of the Royal Navy.'[4] In a new sort of conflict, which contained little romantic derring-do but all too much unspectacular heroism on land and sea, Zeebrugge was a story to capture the imagination.

At a more humdrum level Keyes achieved real success against the Flanders-based U-boats. For about a year the Admiralty had been trying to make it impossible for them to reach the Atlantic through the English Channel, by means of a barrage of mines and other obstacles laid in the Straits of Dover. But this barrage had so far been almost totally ineffective. As director of plans at the Admiralty from October 1917, Keyes had argued that the area needed to be lit up at night to force the U-boats to dive to a depth at which they would encounter the mines etc.; but Admiral Bacon, then commanding the Dover Patrol, did not accept his argument. The contest between these two men reflected the deadlock between Geddes and Jellicoe, and when Jellicoe was pushed out Keyes took Bacon's place. He was then free to put his theory into practice.

It turned out to be correct (so perhaps he had more brains than have been credited to him). When the area of the barrage was lit up U-boat losses rose to a point that forced the Germans to abandon the Channel and send the Flanders flotillas through the North Sea and round the north of Scotland, cutting ten days from their three to four weeks' operational time. The illuminated barrage was not the only deterrent – sea and air patrols contributed to closing the Straits – but the barrage was the decisive factor.[5]

---

3. DLG to Geddes, 24 April 1918; Geddes to DLG, same date.

4. Churchill, *World Crisis*, part II, p. 371.

5. Lighting up the barrage area involved a large number of small craft, including trawlers, for which it was, of course, a hazardous process, since they were themselves highly visible to the enemy while operating searchlights and sending up flares. A foray by German destroyers on 14 February resulted in the sinking of eight of these small vessels, and severe damage to seven more. Altogether eighty-nine seamen were lost in the incident, which for a time cast a shadow over Keyes's reputation. But Zeebrugge more than restored it, so enabling his less glamorous good work to continue.

Of no comparable value was a barrage laid across 240 miles of sea between Scotland and Norway. Keyes had nothing to do with this, except in so far as the success of his barrage created an illusory belief that the same trick could work on a much larger scale. In fact the northern barrage was crucially unlike the one in the Channel, since it could not, obviously, be illuminated. And there were other differences. Laying the northern barrage was a task largely performed by the United States navy, which laid 56,000 mines compared with 15,000 laid by the British. The American mines were of imperfect design and tended to explode prematurely. Another problem was that at the Norwegian end there was neutral water which the Germans used to circumvent the barrage. For all the effort put into it, the barrage probably cost the enemy no more than six U-boats.

Yet the anti-submarine war was being won. In May the Germans tried to regain the initiative by concentrating on the south-western approaches to Britain. They hoped to demonstrate that the convoy system could be broken, but the attempt served only to prove its effectiveness. During the period they had as many U-boats at sea as during the most destructive period in 1917. Nevertheless thirty-six convoys passed through with only three ships lost, while 10 per cent of the patrolling U-boats were sunk. In April and May the mass transfer of troops from Britain to reinforce the BEF was accomplished without the loss of a single ship or a single British life. Now the ferrying of hundreds of thousands of American troops across the Atlantic was to be achieved with a similar safety record. At the same time the building of new merchant ships was outstripping the losses caused by U-boat action.

The Grand Fleet, for its part, had no opportunity to win a glorious old-style victory during the last phase of the war. Beatty, despite his swash-buckling temperament, was obliged to be no less cautious as Commander-in-Chief than Jellicoe had been, if only because so many of his ships had to be diverted to convoy duty. There was, however, one moment at the end of April when a major fleet action seemed to be imminent. Admiral Scheer made a sortie in strength in the hope of intercepting a British convoy, escorted by battle-cruisers, off Scandinavia, and Beatty responded by ordering his fleet to sea. But no battle ensued. Scheer, finding that he had been misinformed about the convoy, immediately returned to base, while Beatty, partly on account of signalling errors, failed to arrive in time to engage his force. The German High Seas Fleet made no further significant move during the rest of the war, and British domination of the North Sea was quietly maintained.

*

Lloyd George had much to say about the naval war when he spoke at Edinburgh on 24 May. He dwelt upon the success achieved against the U-boats, and naturally extolled the raids on the Flemish ports:

... you would like to know what has been accomplished. The Navy (cheers). Give them another, they deserve it all (another round of ringing cheers). ... looking back upon it now – knowing our fears, our legitimate apprehensions, a year ago – it is to me incredible how with skill, with ingenuity, with resource, above all with invincible valour, the sailors of the navy and of the mercantile marine (cheers) have overcome these difficulties ... They had to protect our ships ... [and] then to make difficult the nefarious work of the submarine ... they never ceased until, at last, thank God, they conquered this pest (cheers). They worried their nests (cheers) and they blocked two of them – Zeebrugge and Ostend (cheers). These are thrilling deeds that give new heart to a people, not merely for the hour but, when they come to be read by our children, and our children's children, for ages to come (cheers) ... The submarine is still a menace ... as a means of inflicting injury, as a means of absorbing energies which might be better devoted to other purposes ... but as a danger which could cause the winning or losing of the war you can rule out the submarine (loud cheers).

Accompanied by his wife, Lloyd George was in Edinburgh to receive the freedom of the city and an honorary doctorate from the University. His big speech was made at the freedom ceremony in the Usher Hall, to an audience of 4,000. The Lord Provost welcomed him as 'the man called for by the stern necessities of the times, rooted in the public confidence, unifying and inspiring the ... people, bracing them to their full energies and efforts, and galvanising their reserve of moral and physical strength'. The Prime Minister made no specific reference to the recent threat to his leadership in Parliament, but strongly asserted his legitimacy as an exponent of the popular will:

When attacked, I have appealed to the judgment of the vast majority of my fellow-countrymen, and I have never yet appealed in vain (cheers). They have called me to this colossal task; they have generously supported me in its discharge, making just allowance for its terrible, terrible, terrible difficulties. I do not propose, neither now nor later on, to defend myself against personal criticisms ... but there is one thing I want to say, and say it here in Scotland – that no mere intrigue or cabal would place at the head of ... the greatest Empire in the world, and in the greatest days of its history, an ordinary man of the people, without rank or social influence or special advantage, and with no party organisation behind him. I was put here, by the will of the people of the country, to do my best to win the war (cheers). And as long as I continue to do my best I feel I shall have behind me men of all parties and creeds, who place the honour of their native land and the freedom of mankind above the triumph of any faction (loud cheers).

While disclaiming self-defence he was, of course, defending himself most artfully and effectively. By implication he was rejecting the Asquithian charge that he had usurped the throne, as it were, by means of a palace revolution. Though in a more than technical sense he had become Prime Minister by the will of Parliament, he was daring to suggest that the true source of his power was the will of the people. And there was, beyond doubt, something in the suggestion. A Parliamentary majority supported him because most MPs recognized not only his qualifications for war leadership, but also the extent of his appeal to the general public. Since the beginning of the war and for some years before he had been the politician most representative of the British democracy, and he was the one most in touch with the mass of hitherto disfranchised citizens (40 per cent of men and all women) who were now coming into their own as they contributed ever more vitally to the war effort.

There was always a touch of demagoguery in his man-of-the-people rhetoric, but it was never entirely spurious. The same could be said of his claim to transcend the traditional party system. Even before the war he had secretly tried to promote a coalition, and despite his record as a barnstorming party warrior his underlying belief in national government was genuine. He was demonstrating it in the composition of his own ministry, with men of talent picked regardless of party and, indeed, from outside politics.

In emphasizing his wish to speak as he did in Scotland, he was not merely flattering his immediate audience. It must have seemed to him appropriate to proclaim the simplicity of his background in the land of Robert Burns, author of the most eloquent lines rejecting social hierarchy. He did not, in fact, quote 'The rank is but the guinea's stamp;/The man's the gowd for a' that', but the words must have been in his mind. And he did quote Burns in another context, that of national unity:

> Oh, let us not like snarling tykes
> In wrangling be divided;
> Till, slap, come in an unco loon
> And wi' a rung decide it.

. . . I believe the poet Burns wrote that for the Dumfries volunteers. General Ludendorff is reported to have said that the effect of the offensive is not to be measured by results in territory gained, and in captures made, but by its effect on the spirit and *moral* [morale] of the enemy's civil population . . . we must not disappoint him (cheers).

Lloyd George rested his appeal to the people on his and their patriotism and willingness to sink sectional differences for the sake of a much larger cause. He also asked them to make allowances for the difficulty of his task. His threefold repetition of the word 'terrible' must have struck home.

On the next phase of the land war he spoke gravely, but with measured confidence:

we must not underrate the formidable character of the attack. We have to bridge the chasm between Russia and America . . . There are still several spans which have to be constructed, and we are building under the heaviest fire of the war . . . Britain, France and Italy have to defend the gap. This is not a time for boasting. I have been rebuked for being unduly optimistic, but . . . what is the good of any man in the direction of affairs if every time there is any difficulty or any reverse he puts his heart down? That is the time to keep it up. But . . . we are on the eve of a very great attack, and no man who enters into battle ought to boast about its result . . . [Nevertheless] I have the right to tell you that those who know best what the prospects are feel the most confident about the result (cheers).

There were, as usual, no compliments for Haig, but a superabundance of them for Foch:

The commander at the head of the Allied forces . . . is one of the brilliant strategists of the day – a man who combines . . . dynamic energy with imagination and a profound knowledge . . . Now that we are approaching the [next] stage of the greatest battle ever fought on earth, for the greatest cause for which battles have ever been fought . . . I am glad that we have at the head of the forces of freedom a man of General Foch's commanding genius (cheers). For all that until the American army arrives in strength we shall have a time of great anxiety.

At the lunch that followed the freedom ceremony Lloyd George spoke of Ireland:

I wish I could say the contribution of Ireland to this struggle for human liberty was equal to that of Scotland. Irish regiments have fought valiantly, as Irishmen always do . . . but the bulk of the young manhood of Ireland has unfortunately held aloof, and it is not relevant to say that England has treated Ireland badly in the dim past.

This is not England's struggle; it is the struggle of Belgium, Serbia and Poland . . . it is the struggle of France, the truest . . . friend that Ireland has ever had [surely a dubious statement].

He referred to the alleged conspiracy with the enemy, on the basis of which the leaders of Sinn Fein were being detained:

The whole story, a sad, unpleasant and painful story to every friend of Ireland, will be complete in the course of the next few days. I have seen the evidence and, after perusing it, there can be no doubt . . . as to the duty of the Irish government. Much of it cannot be published without endangering public safety . . . and no taunts will drive us to publication of that part of the evidence.

But, he said, he did not despair of Irishmen realizing soon that they were 'not doing well for the credit of their great race'. An opportunity would be given to them 'to come forward of their own accord' and he was hopeful that the response would be worthy of their 'best and highest traditions'. This remark provided a strong hint that the government would soon be abandoning any attempt to conscript the Irish, and would be falling back on a variant of the Derby scheme, a last chance for voluntarism, which had failed in Great Britain two years earlier and was, therefore, obviously doomed in the Ireland of 1918. In fact, conscription for Ireland was tacitly dropped the following month.[6]

The Lloyd Georges returned from Scotland on Sunday the 26th. The following day the Prime Minister was 'in high spirits' at Walton Heath, playing 'remarkably well' in a round of golf with Riddell, Kerr and the club professional, James Braid. But at the same time events were unfolding in France which he had reason to regard as 'most serious'.[7]

Paris was already threatened as a result of the way Ludendorff had allowed the direction of Operation Michael to veer westwards when his advance towards Arras was checked. Now he turned against the French army though without ceasing to regard the destruction of the BEF as his principal

6. Report of Lloyd George's speeches in Edinburgh, *The Times*, 25 May 1918.
7. *RWD*, 'May 1918', but from the context clearly the 27th. The game must have been a foursome rather than a four-ball, because Riddell says that 'they were out in 36, a score with which Braid himself might well have been satisfied'. We do not know who partnered Lloyd George. If it was the professional or Kerr (a scratch player) the score is rather less remarkable, though still very creditable to the Prime Minister. Since Riddell says that 'they' were out in 36, it seems that he was not Lloyd George's partner.

objective. He hoped that his attack on the French would draw reserves away from the British front as the threat to Paris developed, and that he would then be able to renew his operations against the British with the prospect of total success. The strategy was rational, but depended upon a swift collapse of the French, since he no longer had the resources – if he ever had – for a long campaign. Though he attacked, again, with overwhelming local superiority, aided by gross errors of generalship on the Allied side, his three army commanders in the operation knew that his reserves were 'at full ebb', and one of them said that unless the offensive achieved 'truly decisive success' they would be 'stuck'.[8]

The chosen sector for the new offensive (code-named Blücher) was the Aisne front west of Rheims, including the Chemin des Dames. This was where Pétain had been expecting an attack in March. But two months later the French Commander-in-Chief had no such fears. Like Haig, he was expecting Ludendorff's next move to be on the Arras front, reverting to the original concept of Operation Michael. Meanwhile Foch was absorbed in the task of building up reserves for a counter-offensive in the Amiens sector. With this end in view, he took French divisions out of the line in Champagne, arranging with Haig that they would be replaced by British divisions exhausted in the recent fighting and in need of a rest. By a cruel irony it was thought that the Chemin des Dames was a quiet sector where they could gradually recover.

The French command did not lack warnings of what was to come. In the middle of the month Pershing's intelligence branch came to the conclusion that Ludendorff was preparing an attack in Champagne. At first there was the excuse of the Americans' supposed ignorance (and undeniable inexperience) for failure to take their assessment seriously. But when Pétain's own intelligence officers were converted to the American view, it should have been taken very seriously indeed. In fact it continued to be scouted, as was the evidence obtained from German prisoners on 19 and 22 May, and from several escaped British prisoners. On the 26th men captured from a German patrol confirmed that there would be a great attack on the Aisne front, and gave the precise time that it would be launched – 1 a.m. the following morning.

By then it was too late to avert the impending disaster, even if the French had been willing to reconsider their plan of defence. But General Duchêne, Commander of the French Sixth Army upon which the blow was about to

---

8. Holger H. Herwig, *The First World War: Germany and Austria-Hungary, 1914–1917* (1997), p. 415.

fall, had learnt nothing from recent British experience. He was a former Chief of Staff to Foch, and a faithful exponent of his doctrine that every inch of territory should be defended. Accordingly he made Gough's mistake of having too many of his troops in the forward area, instead of leaving it very lightly manned and organizing a proper defence in depth. He failed to have the Aisne bridges prepared for demolition, repeating Gough's mistake in the case of the Somme bridges. Duchêne worked on the assumption that his army could not be pulverized and overrun as the British Fifth Army had been.

One has to ask why the prudent Pétain, who believed in defence in depth, should have allowed Duchêne to make his dispositions on the opposite principle. The Commander-in-Chief did make his views known, but did not impose his will. Since he was disregarding the advice of his own intelligence branch, and therefore still not expecting the enemy to attack in Champagne, he may have preferred to avoid an unnecessary quarrel with a subordinate close to Foch. It is hard to think of any more plausible explanation of his strange failure to assert his authority. There were protests from the British divisional commanders who, most unfortunately, found themselves under Duchêne's command. But he was hardly likely to pay any attention to them and three of the five 'resting' divisions were in fact placed in the front line.

Ludendorff was not only given the gratuitous advantage of surprise, and of masses of men in forward positions waiting to be killed or captured. He also had, as on 21 March, the benefit of mist on the battlefield when he attacked. Nevertheless, it is only fair to say that his extraordinary success at the outset was due above all to the phenomenal efficiency with which the attack was planned and carried out. Sixteen assault divisions, 4,000 guns and two million shells were brought forward without being detected by air reconnaissance, at a time of growing Allied air superiority. Twenty more divisions were concentrated in reserve. All movement was by night; every wheel, every horse's hoof was muffled. The guns were placed in camouflaged sites during the night of the 25th and moved to their firing positions the following night. The infantry moved forward by nightly stages from the 16th, hiding in woods by day and reaching their starting line during the night of the 26th.

The attackers faced a daunting task. Most of the ridge had been recaptured by Pétain's men the previous October, when they avenged Nivelle's failure. Before attempting to storm it the Germans had to cross a relatively small river, the Ailette, which involved bringing foot-bridges (twenty-four per division) to the river-bank, and concealing them there, before the operation:

a difficult manœuvre assisted – another stroke of luck – by a nightly caco-
phony of frogs in the river. The actual bridging was effected only after
the preliminary bombardment had begun.

This surpassed in ferocity even the bombardment of 21 March, according
to British witnesses with experience of both. It lasted from 1 a.m. to 5 a.m.
and reduced the defenders to a state in which they could offer no serious
resistance, except in isolated pockets.[9] The Germans swiftly gained the
ridge and reached the Aisne, with its undemolished bridges, by 10 a.m. At
the end of the day they had advanced twelve miles and reached another
river, the Vesle. For four more days the tide swept on, covering in all
thirty miles and reaching Chateau-Thierry on the Marne, thirty-seven
miles from Paris. Duchêne's army was virtually wiped out, and 50,000
Allied troops were taken prisoner. On the left of the line Soissons fell to the
enemy, but on the right there was at least the comfort that Rheims was
holding out.

Clemenceau's reaction to the crisis was entirely characteristic of him.
Paris was under long-range artillery bombardment and attack by Gotha
bombers. About a million of its inhabitants were soon leaving the city to
find refuge in the country. (A similar number had left two months before,
but most had since returned.) Clemenceau also left Paris – for the front.
From early morning on the 28th he spent the best part of four days in the
field, visiting the commanders and seeing for himself what was happening.
As on many previous and subsequent occasions he showed a reckless disregard for his own safety, narrowly avoiding death or capture. He was taking
a big risk with his political position as well, since behind him defeatism was
spreading among the politicians and his enemies scented the chance to bring
him down. But perhaps he was right to make his presence felt where the
military threat was developing, before tackling problems behind the front.
His companion as he drove around was General Mordacq, to whom at one
point he exclaimed: 'Yes, the Germans might take Paris, but that will not
prevent me from waging war. We will fight them on the Loire, then on the
Garonne . . . even in the Pyrenees. If . . . we are driven from the Pyrenees,
we will continue the war at sea. But make peace, never!'[10]

9. Among the British troops two units, the 2nd Devons and the fifth battery of the 45th Field
Artillery, sacrificed themselves almost to a man. They were collectively awarded the Croix de
Guerre by the French command, a gracious acknowledgement and a mark of sincere regret that
they had been placed in such a situation while supposedly recuperating from the ordeal of
March–April on their own front.
10. General Jean Mordacq, *Le Ministère Clemenceau: journal d'un témoin* (4 vols., 1930–31),
vol ii, p. 54 (describing events of 31 May 1918).

Back in Paris he saw Churchill, who was there on munitions business, and who later recorded the old man's words: 'I will fight in front of Paris; I will fight in Paris; I will fight behind Paris.' The words obviously stayed in Churchill's mind and, like Clemenceau's speech from the tribune of the Chamber the previous November – which he had also heard – provided him with inspiration in similarly desperate times.[11] Again Clemenceau subdued the politicians, though they gave him a rough time with demands for scapegoats. As War Minister he felt a special responsibility for any failure by the army, but was determined on no account to part with Pétain or Foch, whose complementary abilities he regarded as vital for France. On 4 June he faced a hostile Chamber and, after a stormy debate, won by a majority of 377 to 110. While defending the army's leaders, robustly in a general way, he wisely saw that changes had to be made. Among those sacrificed the most prominent was Duchêne, who shared the fate of Gough. Pétain made a Haig-like protest on Duchêne's behalf, but allowed himself to be overborne by Clemenceau.[12] The crisis marked a change in the Prime Minister's attitude to the two principal French soldiers. Whereas hitherto he had tended to lean towards Pétain, he now shifted the balance towards Foch. In the course of June it was established that Pétain would in future be straightforwardly under Foch's orders, waiving his right of appeal to the government as agreed at Beauvais. The face-saving reason given for this was that, since they were both Frenchmen, the need for such a right scarcely existed. But Pétain still had the advantage of a proper staff, which Foch continued to lack.

One helpful by-product of the German attack was that a wave of politically motivated industrial action, particularly at Saint-Etienne, at once came to an end. The aim of the militants had been to bring about a negotiated peace on terms which Clemenceau could never have contemplated. Though he was confident that French public opinion as a whole was with him, the action was most damaging to the war effort and absorbed much of his attention during the days before the attack. In France, as in Britain, the patriotism of labour was powerfully stimulated by Ludendorff's threat to national survival.

Milner was in Paris on the 27th and saw the French premier that morning,

11. Winston S. Churchill, *Great Contemporaries* (1938, repr. 1990), 'Clemenceau', p. 312. Churchill adds his own comment: 'Happy the nation which when its fate quivers in the balance can find such a tyrant and such a champion.'

12. In the early days after the attack Clemenceau had shown sympathy for Duchêne, visiting him, and giving him encouragement, before Pétain did. But, like Gough, Duchêne was not up to the job, and in any case became a necessary sacrificial victim.

within hours of the offensive's shattering start. He found that Clemenceau did not take 'a very gloomy view of [it] and . . . intimated that he was glad the Germans had attacked and . . . not compelled the French to do so'. But he referred to the recent strikes which he said, were 'definitely anti-war' in character. Milner felt that he was more concerned about the possible effect on civilian morale than about the military threat.[13]

The following morning Foch gave Clemenceau his preliminary assessment, when the premier visited his headquarters at Sarcus, a small village between Beauvais and the coast. This was an appropriate location for supervising the earlier campaign, but remote from the immediate battle, and the remoteness clearly influenced Foch's view. He saw no reason, at present, to draw on his strategic reserves, which were chiefly held in Flanders and the Somme region. The Chemin-des-Dames attack might well be no more than a feint. He was right up to a point; Ludendorff had not abandoned his original aim of destroying the BEF and was hoping to create the conditions for fulfilling it. But in the process he found himself changing course, as he had done before – tactical success again luring him into a different strategy. Clemenceau doubted that the attack could be held without any call on outside reserves, and his doubt became a certainty when he reached the battle area and saw how chaotic the situation was. Foch soon moved his headquarters nearer to the scene of action, establishing it at Bombon, south-east of Paris and in the neighbourhood of Melun, where it was to remain until October. And he also decided that reserves must be brought from the north to cover the defence of Paris. He did not meet all of Pétain's demands, but gave orders for the movement of the French divisions behind Amiens,[14] and he warned Haig that he might have to call upon some of his reserves. He also arranged with Pershing that five American divisions training with the BEF should take over quiet sectors of the French front, so releasing French divisions for the battle.

How did Lloyd George react to the news from France? At Downing Street on 27 May, after returning from Scotland, he held a meeting of the X Committee at 11 a.m. before the War Cabinet at noon. The X Committee had been set up mainly as a device for keeping Milner as a *de facto* member of the inner circle of decision-making, when he left the War Cabinet to

13. Milner's report to War Cabinet, X Committee, 29 May 1918.
14. Most of these orders had been pre-empted by Pétain in his capacity as French Commander-in-Chief, but Foch, as it were, ratified them when he became better aware of the situation. Pétain could be excused for not consulting him while his headquarters were so far away. Clemenceau may well have known what Pétain was doing and approved of it.

become War Secretary. The Committee consisted of Lloyd George, Milner, Wilson and Hankey, with Amery taking the minutes (and also occasionally contributing to the discussions).[15] But on the 27th Milner and Amery were in France, so that only the Prime Minister, Wilson and Hankey attended. Since all three knew what there was to know about the attack after only a few hours, Wilson was free to muse about the implications for the future. There would be two months of 'real anxiety', he said, followed by two more of 'serious, though diminishing, anxiety'. By the end of September anxiety on the Western front might have 'practically disappeared', and it would then be necessary to build up strength for 'a tremendous and crushing blow at the enemy'. But this would 'take much time', and meanwhile there must be 'no operations of the Passchendaele type'. Lloyd George remarked that the Germans could not allow the Turks to be knocked out, and Wilson agreed, adding that one of the objects of campaigns in 'outlying theatres' should be to draw enemy reserves away from the Western front.

At the War Cabinet meeting that followed Wilson briefed on the attack, and in particular on the British divisions caught up in it, saying that they seemed to have been driven off the Chemin-des-Dames ridge. There was much talk about the availability of American reinforcements for the *British* line, and Wilson was asked to report how much help would come from the brigading of US battalions with the BEF. Two days later Milner told the X Committee that he had inspected Americans training in Rawlinson's army and had found them 'fine men, very keen, but also very raw'. Though he was not much impressed by the senior officers, the young ones 'seemed very intelligent'. He thought they needed 'at least a month or six weeks' more training', and he understood from Haig that they were to be trained by the cadre divisions and then 'attached, first by battalions, and afterwards by regiments (brigades), to our fighting divisions'. Wilson,

15. 'By far my most interesting task . . . was in connexion with the little triumvirate of Lloyd George, Milner and Henry Wilson, known as the X Committee, which really ran the war during the critical spring and summer months of the German offensive. Hankey was . . . indispensable . . . for the purpose of keeping its work in touch with that of the War Cabinet. But he deputed to me the actual taking of the minutes and looking after the conclusions. We met almost daily . . . at 10 Downing Street. Most days it was fine enough to allow the meeting to take place walking up and down the flagged terrace outside the Cabinet room. This was just wide enough for five to walk abreast. I wish I had a photograph of the group: Lloyd George and Henry for ever gesticulating and laughing, Milner serene but serious, Hankey attentive on one flank, myself on the other with a pad in my left hand on which to jot down arguments and decisions. No easy task, for much of the talk was discursive . . . But many of the decisions were momentous, and the men who took them worthy of their great responsibilities' (L. S. Amery, *My Political Life* (3 vols., 1953–5), vol. ii, pp. 157–8).

however, suggested that this plan might have been changed – as indeed it had.[16]

The idea of brigading American troops in the BEF died hard in the minds of Lloyd George and other British leaders, but it was never a realistic proposition. Pershing had no intention of allowing his men to be drawn into battle piecemeal under British command. More than that, his private desire was to be as little involved with the British as possible. His aim was to establish an independent American army in part of the existing French front, and on 19 May, even before the German offensive was launched, he reached an agreement with Pétain, behind Haig's back, that at the earliest opportunity his divisions training in the British zone would be transferred to a sector in Lorraine, which would then become exclusively American. The implementation of this plan was accelerated, at least partially, as a result of the offensive, since (as we have seen) Foch soon arranged for five American divisions in the British zone to be moved to the French.

Pershing had a strong, if not altogether attractive, character. His family was of Alsatian extraction (originally named Poersching or Pförschin), but his grandfather emigrated to America and Pershing himself was born in Missouri. Though he was certainly an efficient officer, with the temperament of a martinet, he owed his exceptionally rapid promotion to friendship with Theodore Roosevelt and marriage to the daughter of an influential Republican politician, chairman of the Senate military affairs committee. In 1906 he was advanced from Captain to Brigadier-General over the heads of 862 brother-officers, many of whom later served under him in France. In 1915 he won President Wilson's good opinion, despite his Republican connections, by his conduct of a punitive expedition into Mexico. During his absence his wife and three daughters died in a fire in San Francisco, only his son surviving: a tragedy that may have further hardened an already hard personality. In 1917 Wilson appointed him Commander-in-Chief of the American Expeditionary Force, giving him no guidance about co-operation with the Allies but saying: 'General, you were chosen entirely upon your record and I have every confidence that you will succeed; you shall have my full support.' The President was as good as his word and Pershing rightly sensed that he had *carte blanche* to deal with the Allied leaders as he saw fit.

His nickname 'Black Jack' was not a comment on his character, but

---

16. X Committee, 29 May 1918. Milner began by reporting on his meeting with Clemenceau the day of the attack, as quoted above. During the afternoon after the War Cabinet meeting that followed Lloyd George must have gone to Walton Heath and played the round of golf recorded by Riddell.·

derived from the fact that he had once commanded a black cavalry unit. All the same, he was never a popular figure in the AEF. He inspired respect and fear, but not warmth. Having an obsession about venereal disease, he did his utmost to prevent his men from consorting with the natives, particularly of the opposite sex. Even in what were supposed to be rest camps they were given little time to themselves, but were kept busy with organized games, training or drill. They resented his attitude and would doubtless have done so even more had they known that he was paying frequent visits to his mistress in Paris, Micheline Resco, a Roumanian artist, naturalized French (whom he eventually married when he was eighty-five, two years before his death in 1948).

Pershing may have lacked the flexibility and imagination of a great general, but he was a formidable exponent of American power, who asserted from the first his own and his army's independence. This was what mattered most to him; defeating the Germans was important but secondary. He had the common American attitude of moral superiority to the Old World, and of special hostility to, and suspicion of, the British Empire. He was opposed to Lloyd George's aims and impervious to his charm. Relations between the two men were never good, and the Prime Minister's mishandling of Pershing's personal liaison officer with the War Office, Major Lloyd Griscom, did nothing to improve them. In May the Prime Minister had Griscom to tea at 10 Downing Street and, after complaining to him about Haig, went on to attack Pershing for not sending American troops to reinforce hard-pressed British divisions. When Griscom said that Pershing had explained where he stood on the issue and regarded it as settled, Lloyd George replied: 'Yes, but I don't.'[17] It was most unsuitable to disparage Haig to a middle-ranking officer from the army of another country, but even worse to speak as he did about the American Commander-in-Chief to 'a trusted member of the relatively small squad of Pershing admirers'.[18] At about the same time Griscom reported to House that American troops did 'not like being with the British or in fact with anybody else but their own people'.[19]

Nevertheless there was a shade of preference for the French. It was not just that they shared America's republican ideology, or that their ancestors (under the Bourbon monarchy, and for the sake of France's national self-interest) had made a vital contribution to American independence. More to the point, France was not a rival for the superpower status to which America

17. Gary Mead, The Doughboys (2000), p. 221, quoting from Griscom papers in US Army Military History Institute.   18. Ibid., p. 465 n. 26.
19. David R. Woodward, Trial by Friendship: Anglo-American Relations, 1917–1918 (1993), pp. 164–5.

was aspiring. The obstacle to American ambitions in that respect was the British Empire, the world's first superpower, which was striving under Lloyd George's leadership to maintain its position. Of course, language was a barrier between the Americans and the French, and superficially a bond with the British. But the difficulty of communication with the French had one big advantage for the Americans, that it made the substantial integrity of the AEF a practical necessity. By the same token, the bond of a common language could be seen as potentially a menace in their dealings with the British, in that it removed one good argument against the effective absorption of American battalions and brigades into the BEF. Moreover, the ability of Americans and British to understand each other did not always make for understanding in the deeper sense. On the contrary, it brought out the differences between them and often acted as a goad and an irritant. (Even the way the British officer class spoke was bound to grate on American ears, and minister to traditional prejudice.) Whatever the reasons, it was significant that the AEF's first experience of serious action in the First World War was in support of the French rather than the British.

Before describing how this came about we must see what had been happening to Ludendorff's attack. As in March–April, initial triumph was followed by a gradual loss of momentum and increased vulnerability. With every day that passed the task of supplying his advanced formations became more difficult, and again the discipline of his troops often succumbed to the temptation to plunder captured stores of food and drink. There was, moreover, a sinister new factor. The epidemic of influenza, called Spanish but probably of South African provenance, which was to become far deadlier in the autumn, was beginning to affect all combatants, but the Germans suffered from it disproportionately, because they were weakened by poor diet.

The advance to the Marne had created another large salient and a considerable extension of the German line. Paris was tantalizingly close, but the French were regrouping and Pétain was organizing defence in depth behind the river. On 9 June Ludendorff launched another attack, on the River Matz between Montdidier and Noyon, intended to threaten Paris from another angle. But in this case he did not achieve surprise and after two days of relatively modest progress the attack was halted. Indeed, the French delivered a successful counterattack, which was carried out by five divisions under General Charles Mangin. Mangin had been under a cloud since the Nivelle offensive, in which he was prominently involved, but had just been brought back in the changes following the shock of 27 May. He was one of the best attacking commanders in the French army, but Pétain wisely kept him on a tight rein and did not allow his counterattack to be pressed too far.

In objective reality the defence of Paris and the Allied fight-back were largely conducted by the French themselves. All the same, the part played by the Americans was of distinct military value and, above all, of immense value symbolically. The first engagement was in the Montdidier sector at the end of May, when an American regiment recaptured the small village of Cantigny, taken by the Germans in April. This operation was overshadowed by Ludendorff's Aisne offensive, with which it had the misfortune to coincide. But it was planned by Pershing earlier, as a way of testing and demonstrating the AEF's battle-readiness, and as such it served its purpose. More conspicuous were the exploits of an American division at Château-Thierry and of American Marines at Belleau Wood, both actions which contributed to the frustration of Ludendorff's attempt to break through towards Paris in early June.

The good showing of the Americans in action was not lost on Lloyd George, who on 5 June drew his colleagues' attention 'to the fact that the American troops, in spite of their lack of training, had apparently met the new German style of fighting very well'. This style, he said, 'was practically the old Boer method of individual stalking with the substitution of the machine-gun for the rifle, and in dealing with it troops who were used to open country and not trench-stale had an advantage'. The analogy with the war in South Africa was far-fetched and false, but he was surely right to suggest that too much was being made by the British high command of the need for prolonged training, and that 'the Americans could be put into the line more quickly than had been contemplated'.[20] They were now proving his point, in co-operation with the French.

The one Allied leader who was able to establish a good relationship with Pershing was Pétain, and the results were extremely helpful to the French in the crisis of May–June and subsequently. With Foch and Clemenceau the American Commander-in-Chief got on less well, though he accepted Foch's role with the limitations defined at Beauvais. When the SWC met at Versailles on 1–2 June there was an exchange which shows that Pershing could be as tough with the French as with the British on the key issue of his own and his army's independence:

Foch to Pershing: 'You are willing to risk our being driven back to the Loire?'
Pershing: 'Yes, I am willing to take the risk.'

20. X Committee, 5 June 1918.

Lloyd George to Pershing: 'Well, we will refer this to your President.'

Pershing: 'Refer it to the President and be damned. I know what the President will do. He will simply refer it back to me for recommendation and I will make to him the same recommendation as I have made here today.'[21]

Pershing was asserting a principle, while at the same time acting in support of the French on his own initiative. He recognized the threat to Paris and was prepared to commit some of his troops to the battle. But intervention had to be on his terms, and he correctly judged that his own Commander-in-Chief – the President – would not overrule him.

By the end of May 1918 the total of American troops in France and Britain was nearly half a million, most of them brought over in British ships. From this mass of men 290,000 or so had been formed into eleven combat divisions, each 25,000 strong: about twice the size of the average French or British and three times the size of the average German division. Lloyd George and Clemenceau had wanted the (at last) accelerated flow of American troops to Europe to consist mainly of infantry battalions and machine-gun units, which could be quickly trained and used as reinforcements for their own battered and struggling armies. But Pershing was adamantly opposed to this process, for the reason already explained. Whatever might appear to be agreed with other leading American leaders, such as House, Bliss or the War Secretary, Baker, Pershing always succeeded in undermining or modifying the arrangement to conform to his own *idée fixe*. There were compromises – another was negotiated with him at the beginning of June – but in the end his will essentially prevailed.

Lloyd George can be criticized for not grasping sooner the extent of Pershing's power, though he grasped it sooner than most. He may also have shown too little understanding of the American's mental furniture. But it remains true that Pershing showed extreme cussedness. He wanted American troops to be transported to Europe as complete, fully equipped, divisions, rather than in the form that the Allies, and Lloyd George in particular, desired. He made no allowance for the logistical difficulties and waste of resources involved. If a given amount of shipping 'had to bring over the full personnel and equipment of divisions intact . . . and all the paraphernalia with which a wealthy country could load up its forces, then the actual number of combatant troops which could be brought to France within a given period was drastically reduced'.[22]

In fact the Americans were not able to send over fully equipped divisions,

21. Donald Smythe, *Pershing: General of the Armies* (1986), p. 135.   22. WM, p. 3015.

because of the lamentable failure of American industry to produce guns, just as it was failing to produce ships. Until the end of the war the AEF was dependent on the French for its light and medium artillery, and on the British for its heavy artillery. Pershing was not to blame for Wilson's inability or unwillingness to mobilize his country's vast industrial resources for war. But he was to blame for showing more concern to build up a great American army, with which to achieve a largely American victory in 1919, than for responding on anything like an adequate scale to British and French needs in 1918. Granted the sacrifices the Allies had made, and his dependence on them for the means to fulfil his ambition, he did not, perhaps, choose the best way of displaying his country's moral credentials.

At the beginning of June, when America had been a belligerent for well over a year, the first list of United States war casualties to date was announced:

Killed in action	800
Killed accidentally	261
Died from disease	1,122
Lost at sea	291
Other causes	84
Wounded	3,598
Prisoners	99
Missing	208
Total	6,463[23]

This list appeared as Pershing was, for the first time, starting to commit American troops to battle. But the scale on which he was doing so was still not remotely proportionate to the combat strength he possessed, and it was not for several months – until the enemy was visibly cracking – that he allowed the AEF to punch its full weight.

23. *The Times*, 1 June 1918.

29

The Imperial War Cabinet Reconvenes

Friction with Clemenceau – Empire leaders reconvene –
Ludendorff's gamble fails

Lloyd George and Clemenceau had a lot in common (as we have seen). Their many affinities of outlook and temperament made for a relationship that transcended mutual respect; they often found stimulus and fun in each other's company. In May 1918 Lloyd George described the French leader to Riddell as 'a wonderful old man . . . full of humour' and the following month as 'full of vitality and energy', governing 'in the old-fashioned way', giving no quarter and expecting none. At the same time Clemenceau was telling Violet Cecil that Lloyd George was 'the one European statesman who was *à la hauteur des grands évènements* and capable of speaking *des grandes choses grandement*'. These were no idle compliments, but paid spontaneously in private conversation with intimates.[1]

Yet it was inevitable that two such mettlesome men would quite often quarrel, and that the stress of events and divergent national interests would provide frequent occasions for friction between them. Before Ludendorff attacked in the West they were at odds about the length of line to be taken over by the BEF, and after the crisis of March–April Clemenceau felt strongly that the British were not doing enough to make good their losses and restore their complement of divisions on the Western front. In his view, Lloyd George's emergency measures were insufficiently drastic, and in mid-May he wrote the Prime Minister a strong letter on the subject. Noting that Haig had 57 divisions before the attack, and that four had been brought from Italy and Palestine soon after, Clemenceau based his argument on the assumption that an establishment of 61 divisions was the minimum needed. But, he pointed out, the losses suffered since 21 March had reduced the effective number of Haig's divisions to 52; and, since the forecast average monthly figure of reinforcements for May, June and July was to be no more

---

1. *RWD*, 4 May and 30 June 1918; Fisher diary, 7 June 1918. Clemenceau's remark, though quoted at second hand, is surely authentic, since Violet (Maxse) Cecil was a close friend of Clemenceau and Fisher a great historian.

than 34,000 men, it was obvious that the deficit of nine divisions could not be met. More men had to be found, Clemenceau said, and he was sure that they should be looked for principally among the category B troops in home forces. The definition of such troops was that they were fit to defend the country against invasion, but not to fight outside the United Kingdom. Clemenceau reminded Lloyd George that French front-line troops included 160,000 men aged over forty-two, and 110,000 from the auxiliary service. Only a similar trawl by Britain of men for combatant duty in France would enable the Allies 'to emerge victorious from the most redoubtable, but also the most decisive, test of the war'.[2]

Clemenceau was giving a new twist to a grievance long held by the French, that the United Kingdom's contribution to the war on land was far less substantial than their own, though the United Kingdom's population was significantly larger than France's. Moreover, the BEF included powerful contingents from the self-governing Dominions, to which there was no analogy in the French Empire. Yet in spite of these France was still manning a disproportionate length of line and incurring, overall, heavier losses. It cannot be denied that the scale of French sacrifice far exceeded the British. At the end of the war the British Empire had lost 920,000 men killed, whereas France and its colonies had lost 1.4 million.

The British answer to French complaints emphasized the vital importance of the British contribution at sea, in particular that of the merchant service, and also maintained that throughout the war the British economy had carried far more than its share of the general Allied burden. It could be argued, too, that whatever the relative national strengths on the Western front, the BEF had done more fighting than the French in 1917, and that between March and May of the current year three British soldiers had been killed for every *poilu*. A further consideration was that the French army was fighting on and for its own territory, and that this naturally gave it a motive lacking in the men of the BEF, whose distance from home also involved fewer opportunities for home leave. Another relevant factor was that France as a nation was familiar with the experience of military conscription and *levées en masse*, which to the British was as strange as it was odious.

Lloyd George was incensed by Clemenceau's demands, because he felt that he had done his utmost to find reinforcements for the BEF in response to the crisis on the Western front. Nevertheless he allowed a French officer, Colonel Roure, to be sent to investigate the distribution of British man-power, seeing perhaps a potential advantage from his own point of

2. Clemenceau to DLG, 16 May 1918.

view, should Roure detect weaknesses in War Office procedures. In fact Roure did criticize the army's use of its available manpower, and some of the criticism struck a chord with Lloyd George. But its value to him was undermined by the insolence of its tone, which he felt obliged to condemn.[3]

In any case, there was a fundamental conflict between him and Clemenceau on the appropriate level of British fighting strength in France. Lloyd George's idea was that, once the immediate threat there had passed, reinforcement of the Western front should be the task, above all, of the Americans. He did not want the British army to be over-committed in the West, and so denied the resources for operations in other theatres, notably the Levant. While acknowledging the supremacy of the Western front, and the necessity of securing total victory there, he believed that it would not be possible until 1919 at the earliest, by which time the Americans should have provided a decisive numerical margin. Clemenceau, however, felt that, if the French and British had to rely too much upon America for the defeat of Germany, they would be abdicating the prime role to which they were entitled in the post-war settlement.

After 27 May French pressure on the British naturally increased, and Lloyd George began to complain that Foch was acting less as an Allied generalissimo than as a French general taking his orders from Clemenceau. This was, on the whole, unfair to both men, who had proved their Allied credentials at Doullens. Both were well aware of the continuing threat to the BEF, so long as the German army group facing it still had a reserve of almost fifty divisions. Both were prepared to resist excessive demands from Pétain even when the threat to Paris seemed most acute. Nevertheless, Foch was certainly tactless and high-handed in moving French and American divisions from Haig's command without consulting the Field-Marshal, and when in addition he gave orders for three British divisions to be moved south to the Somme area Haig made a formal protest, with full support from the War Cabinet. A little later Lloyd George gratuitously urged Haig to exercise his right of appeal to the British government whenever he felt so inclined: some irony, granted the Prime Minister's normal attitude to Haig, and his persistent advocacy of unity of command.

Inevitably, Lloyd George and Clemenceau fell out over relations with the Americans. First, Clemenceau felt that the British were trying to establish a virtual monopoly in the use of United States troops, and then, after the withdrawal of five American divisions from the British sector, Lloyd George

3. X Committee, 12 June 1918, but also Committee of Prime Ministers, 6 August 1918.

was 'convinced that he been done' by Foch and Clemenceau.[4] In fact, Pershing was adept at playing the Allied leaders off against each other, and for his own reasons (already explained) chose to be closer to the French than to the British.

There was a short but exceptionally sharp dispute when, in early July, Clemenceau abruptly changed his policy on Salonica. He decided that there would be an Allied offensive there, and appointed a new commander, Franchet d'Esperey, without a prior word to his British colleague. This was the more curious, in that Clemenceau had always strongly opposed the Salonica expedition; and the reasons for his sudden change of mind remain obscure. In the event it proved to be a good decision, and his choice of commander also was vindicated. But Lloyd George's wrath at the time is understandable. He should obviously have been consulted, and the change should not have been decided on without his agreement. At the SWC he attacked Clemenceau, though more for the appointment of Franchet d'Esperey than for the strategic change. Since he was the originator of the Salonica strategy, Clemenceau's belated espousal of it could not, in itself, be condemned by him.

Another cause of friction between the two prime ministers was the position of the Czechoslovak legion in Russia. Before the war thousands of Czechoslovaks had migrated to Russia, as part of the pan-Slav movement, leaving an empire in which the Slavs were second-class citizens. During the war many of them enlisted as a distinct formation in the Russian army which was swelled by deserters and prisoners-of-war to the dimensions of a corps. As such it fought well in Kerensky's disastrous offensive in 1917 (one of the few units that did). After the Bolsheviks seized power the Czechoslovak leader, Thomas Masaryk, decided to transfer the corps to France, and agreed that it should be under French command. Its attitude at first was pro-Ally rather than anti-Bolshevik; indeed, it joined with the Bolsheviks in resistance to the Germans in Ukraine before, as it hoped, being transported to France by way of the trans-Siberian railway and Vladivostok. But when the Bolsheviks obstructed the trains carrying it the mood of the Czechoslovak troops changed, and soon they were controlling most of the railway in defiance of the Bolsheviks.

After 21 March Clemenceau was more than ever keen to have the Czechoslovaks in France, but Lloyd George, Balfour and the War Cabinet took a different view. They did not want to use British ships for the long journey from Vladivostok, which was much less economical than bringing Americans

4. X Committee, 17 June 1918.

across the Atlantic. In any case they believed that the Czechoslovaks could be more advantageously employed in protecting Allied stores in the northern Russian ports and perhaps helping to form a front against the Germans. It was proving difficult to persuade the Japanese or the Americans to intervene in Russia, whereas the Czechoslovaks were already there and, as fellow Slavs, less likely (the British thought) to offend Russian susceptibilities. The argument went on for weeks, but to no avail until it was resolved by events. When Ludendorff's bid for victory in the West ultimately failed, Clemenceau no longer felt the need for the Czechoslovaks, while they, for their part, had by then acted as the catalyst for bringing the Japanese and Americans into Russia. (The fateful story of Allied intervention there belongs in the next chapter.)

Despite their various rows, there was enough fellow feeling between Lloyd George and Clemenceau to make their working relationship as war leaders effective and often congenial. On 4 July they witnessed, side by side, a parade in honour of American independence, and Lloyd George murmured to Clemenceau: 'Do you realize, dear friend, that you have asked me to join in celebrating Britain's greatest defeat?' To which Clemenceau replied: 'Yes, but after all do you really regret American independence? What harm has it done you? Besides, Britain and France have often fought each other, and yet you saw just now with what respect soldiers of our two countries saluted each other's flag.'[5] Later the same day there was a meeting of the SWC at Versailles, which leaders of the British Dominions were invited to attend.

It was over a year since the Imperial War Cabinet (IWC) had been set up and held its first series of meetings. Much had happened since May 1917, particularly on the Western front, where Dominion troops had been more prominent than ever in the costly operations of the British army. The new series of meetings, which began on 11 June, was more fully representative than the first, since the Prime Minister of Australia, W. M. (Billy) Hughes, attended – though he arrived a week late, having travelled to England via the United States. His presence brought to the Imperial conclave a strong and singular personality, who could be difficult and quirky, but whose contributions could never be ignored.

Hughes, like Lloyd George, was from north Wales. Though also not strictly a native of the Principality (he was born in London, Lloyd George in Manchester), he spent five of his childhood years with an aunt at

5. General Jean Mordacq, *Le Ministère Clemenceau: journal d'un témoin* (4 vols., 1930–31), vol. ii, p. 102.

Llandudno, not far from Llanystumdwy and very close to Conwy, one of the boroughs forming Lloyd George's constituency. As a young man he emigrated to Australia where, after doing odd jobs in the Queensland outback, he settled in Sydney and became active in the labour movement. His political career started in New South Wales but after federation in 1901 was elevated to the national level, where it lasted for over half a century, ending only with his death in 1952. He led Australia through most of the First World War, and might have led the country again in the Second, had he not been narrowly defeated in a leadership contest by Robert Menzies. His period of supreme power almost coincided with Lloyd George's; he was Prime Minister from 1915 to 1923. But unlike Lloyd George he was frequently in government during the rest of his career.

As political characters the two men were in many ways similar. Both had a legal training (Hughes after he entered politics) and both were brilliant orators. Both were men of the left whose distaste for ideology and, above all, concern for national defence forced them into alliance with the right. Even before the war Hughes was advocating compulsory military training in Australia, while Lloyd George was secretly proposing an armed militia of half a million supplementary to the regular British army. During the war both men were convinced of the necessity for conscription, which in Britain was at length introduced, though in Australia twice rejected in plebiscites despite Hughes's best efforts. Both men were strong imperialists: patriotic adventurers impatient of party restraints.

Their many shared opinions and traits did not, however, exclude serious differences, which became more apparent when the war was over and the enormous task of peacemaking began. Of all the Dominion leaders Hughes was the one who gave Lloyd George most trouble. His natural acerbity was aggravated by chronic dyspepsia and deafness.

Robert Borden, still Prime Minister of Canada, had since the 1917 meetings introduced conscription there, but the measure aroused bitter controversy. Canada had its own 'Ireland' in the form of the province of Quebec, and the Quebecois did not take kindly to conscription. Indeed the leader of Quebec nationalism, Henri Bourassa, had even opposed Canadian participation in the war. It may seem odd that a community of the French-speaking diaspora should have shown so little enthusiasm for a war in support of France. But French Canadians had the social and religious ethos of the *ancien régime*; Clemenceau's France was not theirs. As a would-be unifier of his country Borden may have done more harm than good by the step he took in October 1917. Though he was unusual among British Canadians in speaking French well and having a genuine fondness for the French cultural tradition, by introducing conscription he widened the ethnic divide in Canada. At the same time he formed a coalition government in which, apart from himself, the Liberals were equally represented with his own Conservative Party. But the Liberal leader, William Laurier, a staunch supporter of the war, felt unable to join it because he could not risk losing the support of his fellow French Canadians. In the ensuing general election Borden and his coalition won overwhelmingly; but Quebec voted with Laurier. In March 1918 four were killed in anti-recruiting riots in Quebec City.[6] Conscription helped to keep the Canadian divisions on the Western front up to full strength for the rest of the war. Even so, Canada's conscripted rate of enlistment (7 per cent) was still lower than Australia's voluntary rate (7.5 per cent).[7] Borden brought three colleagues with him to London in June. He remained Prime Minister until 1920, and died in 1937.

W. F. Massey, Prime Minister of New Zealand, who also led a coalition government, was accompanied by the Finance Minister, Sir Joseph Ward, his principal coalition partner. Massey outlasted Lloyd George in office, resigning in 1923 and dying soon afterwards. He was not a native New Zealander, but an Ulster Protestant from Co. Londonderry, whose parents moved to New Zealand after his birth. He joined them there at the age of fourteen, having been at school in Ireland. Newfoundland had a new Prime Minister since the previous year: W. F. Lloyd, a barrister, who had replaced E. P. M. Morris, now ennobled. As the spokesman for a very small community, Lloyd was suitably sparing in his interventions. South Africa was again represented by Smuts, though he was joined by Henry Burton, Minister of Railways and Harbours, the Prime Minister, General Louis Botha, being still unable to make the journey. The only change in the trio representing India was that a new Maharaja, of Patiala, took the place of the Maharaja of Bikaner.

The Dominion leaders were considerably fêted while they were in London, but did not allow themselves to be dazzled by the metropolitan glitter. On the contrary, the attitude in council of some of them – Borden and Hughes in particular – was that of men who felt that their countries had a lot to teach the mother-country. Smuts, as a non-British ex-enemy, who was a member of the War Cabinet as well as the IWC, had his own unique position, which he used to promote the interests of white South Africa, while also taking a lordly

6. Though French Canadians constituted 35 per cent of the country's population, they provided only 5 per cent of those who served in the Canadian Expeditionary Force. In the Second World War the Liberal Prime Minister, Mackenzie King, never introduced conscription.

7. Robert Holland, 'The British Empire and the Great War', in *The Oxford History of the British Empire*, vol. iv (1998), p. 128.

philosophical view of world affairs. Lloyd George presided over all the meetings, but was careful to behave only as *primus inter pares*.

In his opening statement on 11 June he gave a self-defensive exposition of the course of the war since mid-1917. The crisis on the Western front was, he argued, due to the collapse of Russia, the slow development of the American war effort, the advantages to the enemy of a single command – only recently acquired by the Allies – and the exhausting effect on the BEF of its costly operations during the previous summer and autumn. On the credit side he pointed to the failure of the U-boats to bring Britain to its knees, and to the victory in Palestine which, he thought, presaged the elimination of Turkey from the war.

Two days later Borden made a general statement reviewing Canada's war effort in all its aspects. At the end he said that he was convinced the BEF's lack of military success was 'largely due to lack of foresight and preparation, and to defects in the organisation and leadership of our forces'. He urged the 'imperative necessity of putting aside every consideration in appointments except efficiency'. In this context he drew attention to the 'high degree of organisation' attained by the Canadian forces 'under officers of whom only a small proportion were professional soldiers', suggesting that if it were true that in the British army only professional officers had the chance to rise above the rank of brigadier-general 'that was equivalent to a wholesale scrapping of the brains of a nation in its struggle for existence'. He also suggested that the Canadian army might be 'specially utilised in helping with the training of the American forces, whose problems were identical with those . . . they had themselves solved'.[8]

According to Hankey, Borden's 'plain speaking' had been prompted by Smuts. Lloyd George of course welcomed it wholeheartedly, and arranged for the report of the 1917 War Policy Committee to be made available to the Dominion leaders, showing the efforts he had made to dissuade Haig from his offensive plan in Flanders. After the meeting he also told Borden that the 'vital issues' he had raised must be thoroughly probed, but suggested waiting until Hughes arrived in a few days' time.[9] At the first meeting the Australian premier attended he gave his full backing to Borden, but went further. It was futile, he said, to express an opinion without 'much fuller information as to what had actually happened' and as to why the previous year's operations had occurred 'with very heavy casualties'. Australia had 'poured out its men . . . but had

---

8. IWC, 13 June 1918. At the same meeting Massey expressed appreciation of Lloyd George's and Borden's frankness, and gave his own review of New Zealand's achievements to date.

9. Maurice Hankey, *The Supreme Command, 1914–1918* (2 vols., 1961), vol. ii, pp. 815–16.

never had a scratch of a pen to explain what had really happened'. He wished to be sure that men were not being 'wasted for want of proper leadership and strategy'. As he saw it, the position of the Allies was now the same, if not worse, than 'before the battle of the Marne'.

Lloyd George, riding the punch, said that what Hughes was saying was really a continuation of the point raised by Borden, and suggested that the whole matter be referred to a committee of the IWC consisting of the prime ministers alone, plus Milner and, when necessary, the CIGS.[10] This proposal was agreed to, and the new body held its first meeting the following day.

Between late June and mid-August the Committee of Prime Ministers (as it was called) met eleven times, usually in the afternoon or evening, but occasionally at noon. All but one of the meetings took place at 10 Downing Street, and at all of them Lloyd George presided, though he was careful to do so in a collegiate spirit. Because of its composition it tended to overshadow not only the British War Cabinet but even the IWC. Every important operational question that arose while it was in existence was discussed by it, and it took many decisions without reference to the two larger bodies, whose supreme responsibility it was temporarily usurping in an unconstitutional but commonsensical way.

Before its first meeting, the IWC as a whole, including Hughes, had met in the CIGS's room at the War Office for a briefing by Wilson on the general state of the war and future prospects. This lasted an hour and ten minutes and gave Wilson a chance to deploy his remarkable talents as a communicator. With the help of a large map and a stick, he impressed upon his audience the global character of the war. His argument was that victory on the Western front would not be enough; Germany's allies had to be defeated, and so did the Germans themselves in the East, where they had scored their greatest successes.

It is very nearly fair, and it is very nearly true to say . . . when we took Bullecourt, a little village at the end of the Somme fight, the Boche took Roumania; when we took Messines, they took Russia; and when we took Passchendaele, they very nearly knocked out Italy . . . No military decisions . . . that we can get here [in the West] now will settle the East.[11]

Three days later, at the first meeting of the Committee of Prime Ministers,

---

10. IWC, 14 June 1918. At the same meeting Smuts gave an account of South Africa's contribution, and Montagu spoke of India's. Lloyd said that he would be circulating a 'brief statement' on Newfoundland's.   11. IWC, 18 June 1918.

the same theme was pursued by Smuts, who pointed out that the British forces too had been most successful outside Europe. Would Foch ever agree to sending troops back to Palestine? In the discussion that followed, however, it was generally felt by the Dominion leaders that if the BEF were smashed on the Western front 'we should not be able to maintain our position anywhere'.

At the same meeting the leaders discussed further the question about the higher direction of the war originally raised by Borden. They felt that the Dominions should have 'a direct voice' in plans of campaign, to the same extent as the War Cabinet (which was not saying all that much). They were reminded that the IWC had shared in decisions in 1917, apart from the regrettable absence of Hughes.[12] At a later meeting Lloyd George made a strikingly candid statement about his own and the War Cabinet's responsibility for Third Ypres:

the Government could have stopped it *if they had had the moral courage to do it*. Had they done so, however, the Military Authorities would have insisted that they had been on the point of breaking through, that the enemy was demoralised, and at the last moment they had been stopped by civilian politicians.

Hughes said that if Australia had been consulted, he would have opposed Passchendaele. He wished to emphasize that 'if the British Empire won a victory in the field of battle, but bled to death in the process . . . we should have gained the shadow but lost the substance'.[13]

The demand for a more direct voice in the conduct of affairs led to an important political evolution. The Imperial War Cabinet was presented with two resolutions by the Imperial War Conference (the larger body of representatives which met to consider post-war problems):

(1) that the development which has taken place in the relations between the United Kingdom and the Dominions necessitates such a change in administrative arrangements and in the channels of communication between their Governments as will bring them more directly in touch with each other.

(2) that the Imperial War Cabinet be invited to give immediate consideration to the creation of suitable machinery for this purpose.

When these resolutions were discussed by the IWC Hughes said it was

12. Committee of Prime Ministers, 21 June 1918.   13. Ibid., 31 July 1918; my italics.

'generally agreed that the time had come when the self-governing Dominions should be in direct touch with the Prime Minister of the United Kingdom'. The present system was suited to the old colonial days, but was no longer appropriate. The prime ministers were in touch when the IWC was in session, but when they separated would again 'have to meander through the indirect channels of the colonial office'. In his view, the Colonial Office should cease to exercise 'powers of administration as regards the Dominions'. He did not want another 'subsidiary department', but 'a real recognition of the fact that the Dominions were participants in the councils of the Empire on a footing of equality'.

Borden supported Hughes, while paying a gracious compliment to the three colonial secretaries with whom he had to deal. The change suggested was 'an inevitable consequence of the step taken by [Lloyd George] in December 1916 in summoning the Imperial War Cabinet'. The Dominions had come into the war 'voluntarily' (morally, if not technically, true), but the British government 'could not call upon Canada to come into another war with regard to the causes of which she had no voice'. He put it still more bluntly: if she could not have an independent voice in Imperial foreign relations, 'she would before long have an independent voice . . . outside the Empire'. At present the IWC met for only two months in the year, but it was 'essential that there should be means of constant consultation'. Massey agreed, adding that each Dominion should maintain a resident minister in the United Kingdom through whom it could communicate with the British government.

Smuts agreed with the general principle, but thought that the practical devising of new machinery should be held over until it could be done properly, and with due deliberation, after the war. (Meanwhile, of course, the problem did not exist for him, because he was firmly established at the heart of Imperial government – a point he neglected to mention.) Balfour suggested that there had to be a single imperial foreign office, but a way had to be found for the Dominions 'to exercise a share in the control of it'. Montagu touched on a vital point when he said that whatever was done for the Dominions should also be done for India. Lloyd George asked if 'all that they contemplated was that there should be the same communication between the different Prime Ministers of the Empire as . . . between himself and M. Clemenceau and M. Orlando', on the question of peace or war. Hughes replied that it was essential anyway for war, because peace might come suddenly. Law thought that 'at this juncture' it would be 'a fatal mistake' to transfer the work of the Colonial Office to the Prime Minister. Routine work was much better done by a minister 'specially devoted to the task'. On the other hand it should always be possible, on a matter of sufficient importance, for a Dominion prime minister to communicate directly with the Prime Minister of the United Kingdom.[14]

The discussion was resumed at the next meeting of the IWC. Churchill attended it by invitation, and said that he hoped 'the larger question of Imperial reconstruction would not be regarded as unattainable or not worth discussing at the present moment' (the view Smuts had expressed). It was, on the contrary, 'an urgent and vital necessity'. Lloyd George considered that the debate was one of the most important ever to occur at an IWC meeting. He 'entirely agreed' with Borden that the Empire could not continue to work on the old basis. He thought there should be 'the same communication between the Prime Ministers of the Empire as between the Prime Ministers of the Alliance', and he did not think they should separate without adopting some measure for securing 'continuous consultation'. As for the larger question of creating permanent machinery for a more effectively united Empire, he agreed with Churchill that it should not be postponed until after the war. It was easier to get things done in wartime. He invited his colleagues to think out the best method of investigating the problem. It might be possible, he suggested, to set up a committee of 'men of knowledge and experience' who might produce a report in time to send it out to the Dominion leaders before the next session.

Hughes welcomed what Lloyd George had said about direct communication. On Massey's idea of resident ministers from the Dominions he thought the snag was that 'no one could speak with final authority except the Prime Minister'. On Lloyd George's suggestion of a committee of wise men to be set up in the United Kingdom to consider future machinery for the Empire, he declared flatly that 'Australia would not have anything to do with it'.[15]

When the same subject was discussed yet again at the IWC it was immediately apparent that Hughes's view on the proposed committee was shared by the other Dominion leaders. Lloyd George put forward three resolutions: the first about direct communication between prime ministers, the second about resident ministers, and the third about the committee to produce a blueprint for the future. Borden said he was quite happy about the first and second, but could not agree to setting up even an informal committee for the purpose suggested. Smuts and Lloyd endorsed his opinion, and so did Massey, who said that such a committee would raise the spectre of Imperial federation, to which he was opposed precisely because he was an ardent Imperialist. Any attempt to impose a federal system on the Empire would 'only involve a repetition of the Boston Tea Party'.

14. IWC, 23 July 1918.　15. IWC, 25 July 1918.

Faced with such unanimous opposition, Lloyd George gave way with a good grace, saying that he 'quite understood the difficulties which the Dominion representatives had experienced with regard to the third proposal'. He would not therefore press it, though he had to say that there was 'no real danger' of the British government repeating the mistake of the Boston Tea Party, having learnt its lesson on that occasion. The first two resolutions were passed, the third dropped.[16]

Loyalty to the Empire was very strong in the Dominions, and the war further strengthened it. But Dominion nationalism was even stronger, and gained still more from the experience of war. Lloyd George helped greatly to make Imperial unity more effective, while on the whole welcoming the spirit of Dominion independence. He would carry the process further during the rest of the year and at the Peace Conference. Rightly believing that change could more easily be accomplished in wartime, he was prepared to go along with Churchill to the extent of proposing a committee to advise on longer-term change for the Empire. But when he saw that even the existence of such a committee would arouse suspicion throughout the Dominions that their independence might be threatened by some centralizing federal scheme, he swiftly withdrew. At heart he sympathized with Dominion nationalism, as Churchill never did.[17]

After Ludendorff struck against the French on 27 May it seemed for a short time possible that the French army might disintegrate and the BEF be left fighting alone in France against overwhelming odds. General Sir John Du Cane, head of the British mission at Foch's headquarters, took the view that 2.5 million British troops might be trapped in France, and Haig's Chief of Staff, Lawrence – though not, it would appear, Haig himself – argued that the Channel ports might have to be abandoned and the BEF retreat behind the Somme. When Hankey reported these baleful thoughts to Lloyd George,

16. IWC, 30 July 1918.

17. The interesting point about non-professional Army officers, also raised by Borden (though it had been exercising some people in Britain, notably H. A. L. Fisher), was discussed by the Committee of Prime Ministers at its first meeting (21 June). It was felt desirable that educated men who had held high responsibility in other professions, and who had 'by now acquired great military knowledge and experience', should as a matter of policy be given more chance to be promoted to high command. But the CIGS gave the idea short shrift. The government, he said, should appoint the Commander-in-Chief, 'who alone was in a position to select his subordinate commanders'. As a result, no British non-professional army officer was promoted to a fighting command above that of a brigade in the First World War. (More surprisingly, the same virtual monopoly of the highest positions by professional officers was also maintained during the Second.)

the Prime Minister was 'very indignant' at the idea of abandoning the Channel ports.[18]

Fortunately the more nightmarish speculations were short-lived, because within a fortnight or so the German advance was held. Indeed, Mangin's counterattack showed that the French army was still full of fight, as was also apparent in the fact that Rheims was holding out. Meanwhile the reinforcements received by the BEF had raised its strength to a level higher than in March. Nevertheless the German army group commanded by Crown Prince Rupprecht of Bavaria, with nearly fifty (admittedly depleted) divisions in reserve, continued to pose a heavy threat to the northern part of the Allied line, mainly held by the British.

Between mid-June and mid-July there was a period of relative quiet on the Western front. But there could be no quiet in the minds of Allied leaders. The Germans were still within striking distance of Paris and the Channel ports. They were bound to strike again. The only questions were, when and where.

Foch regarded the defence of Paris and the Channel ports as of equal importance, and maintaining the link between the Allied armies as more important than either. In this he showed excellent judgement. He was building a reserve to be used wherever it might be needed, and by early July his personal hunch was that the next German attack would be against the French alone. Wilson's appraisal was different. He expected the next attack to be in the north, and was concerned about the length of line to be defended there. He therefore advocated a limited withdrawal on the coast, flooding the land around Dunkirk and holding the town with a small garrison as a separate operation. He was even prepared to contemplate the abandonment of Ypres. Lloyd George thought this idea 'too serious to be settled without a formal decision'. It would have to be decided, first, by the War Cabinet, and then by an Allied council of war.[19] The idea was also strongly opposed by the Admiralty as a potential threat to the efficacy of the Channel barrage. Wilson continued to press for it, but in the end it came to nothing, because events vindicated Foch.

Even before this happened, a good relationship was developing between the generalissimo and Haig. At the end of May, in the crisis precipitated by the Aisne offensive, Foch had angered the Field-Marshal – as well as Wilson and Lloyd George – by moving French and American troops, and even British divisions, from his command without consulting him. But by the middle of June Foch was taking trouble to see Haig and agree with him

18. Hankey diary, 31 May 1918.   19. X Committee, 5 June 1918.

ground rules for the future. They met twice at a chateau belonging to the Duchesse de Mouchy, a granddaughter of Napoleon's marshal (and brother-in-law) Murat, and the room where they talked was dominated by 'a great picture of Murat looking like a half-caste but beautifully dressed!' At this first meeting the two men discussed 'the principles of defence and how to meet German methods of attack', in a 'most friendly' atmosphere. At the second meeting they got down to details and arrived at an understanding about the movement of reserves in hypothetical situations.[20]

Not long afterwards, at the end of the next SWC meeting in early July, Lloyd George had a blistering row with the generalissimo about his position *vis-à-vis* the staff at Versailles. Foch threatened to resign, and Lloyd George told Clemenceau that 'generals were too fond of talking of resignation . . . if a *poilu* talked of resigning he would be stuck against a wall and shot'. 'But you know you do not want to shoot him!' replied Clemenceau, doubtless amused that Lloyd George should be quarrelling with the man whose office he had worked so hard to establish. Nevertheless Clemenceau supported Lloyd George on the substance of his argument with Foch, thus proving that the Prime Minister was wrong to suspect the two men of being in cahoots to promote French as distinct from Allied interests. Clemenceau said that his wrath was often aroused by the obstinacy of generals, who made him '*fou*'; and when he was *fou* (he added in English) he usually tried to kill someone – 'a general, if possible'. 'Whereat' (Hankey, who witnessed the scene, records) 'the old boy of 78 began to chase Wilson round the room like a schoolboy.'[21]

The row with Foch occurred on 4 July, the day of the American Independence Day parade that the two prime ministers attended together. It was also the day when a small but highly significant operation took place at Le Hamel, between Villers-Bretonneux and the River Somme. Le Hamel was occupied by the Germans in a salient overlooking British positions, and Rawlinson, commanding the British Fourth Army, had decided to use the 3rd Australian division, under General Sir John Monash, to attack the place, with some companies from the American 33rd division. Monash, a Jewish Australian, was a remarkably gifted officer, who before the war had been a leading civil engineer as well as a part-time citizen soldier. Independence

---

20. Haig diary, 18 and 20 June 1918.
21. Hankey diary, 4 July 1918. The joint staff at Versailles, which was also largely Lloyd George's creature, was a natural complement to the unified command. But Foch pig-headedly held aloof from it, using only Weygand and his own very small staff, which many – including Haig – regarded as inadequate.

Day was deliberately chosen by Rawlinson as an appropriate date for 'the first American offensive action in the British zone'.

When Pershing heard that American soldiers were to be involved, he was furious and insisted that they be withdrawn. But Monash did not receive an order to this effect until 3 p.m. on 3 July. He then told Rawlinson that if the order were carried out the operation would have to be cancelled, since there would be no time for him to fill the gaps. Rawlinson gave him permission to go ahead, and the attack was an outstanding success. In an hour and a half its objectives were completely attained, and at relatively low cost (the Australians losing 51 officers and 724 other ranks, the Americans 6 officers and 128 other ranks; while in prisoners alone the Germans lost 41 officers and 1,431 other ranks). Next day Lloyd George and Milner, on their way home from Versailles, visited some of the American troops who had taken part. After saluting the American flag, the Prime Minister addressed them from a car, speaking of the new world-wide British-American alliance: 'American flags flew in Toronto, Sydney and Wellington in recognition of America's Independence Day.' But Pershing did not rejoice. On the contrary, he 'seethed', since in his view 'the United States was still struggling for its independence from the British'.[22]

At this time Lloyd George did not share the common opinion that the next German blow would necessarily fall on the Western front. Of course he could not fail to recognize the danger, but he thought that other possibilities should be considered, while in the West he counted on the growing American presence to secure the Allied position. At a meeting of the X Committee he asked if the general staff was sure that the Germans were 'not going to break off operations on the Western front and go elsewhere, for example to Russia, just as Napoleon after concentrating his forces at Boulogne had diverted them eastwards' (when he decided against attempting to invade Britain). Wilson's deputy, General Charles Harington, replied that this possibility had not been overlooked, and that elaborate railway programmes were being worked out. The Prime Minister said that 'if the Americans concentrated a great army on the Western front next year, it might be possible for our army to follow out its traditional role of operating on the outskirts of the war area'. Was anybody studying the implications for manpower, equipment, lines of communication, and so on? Harington assured him that a great deal of work had been put into lines of communication. And so it went on: question after question, each met with a tactfully

22. David R. Woodward, *Trial by Friendship: Anglo-American Relations, 1917–1918* (1993), pp. 181–2.

stonewalling answer.[23] Any good war leader is entitled to ask such questions, but in this instance they were wide of the mark. The German leadership had no intention of abandoning its conquests or its ambitions in the West. Despite the appalling casualties in Ludendorff's army (over 200,000 in June alone), and despite the growing strength of the Allies, with the American build-up now at last providing an almost limitless reservoir of manpower, the rulers of Germany continued to believe in outright victory on the Western front. One more heave, they felt, and the enemy coalition would collapse. At a war conference at Spa on 2-3 July, at which the Kaiser presided, Germany's war aims in the West were reasserted. Absent from the conference was the Foreign Minister, Kühlmann, who had been forced out after a speech in which he dared to say that Germany could not achieve a satisfactory peace by military means alone. He resigned formally on 8 July (to be succeeded by an admiral who could be relied on to act dutifully in the spirit of Spa).

There were few other dissident voices in Germany. A few days later the Reichstag approved war credits of 13,000 million marks, before going into recess until the end of October. As in the vote on Brest-Litovsk, the only opposition came from the Independent Socialists. The Liberal Nationalist Gustav Stresemann (later joint architect of the Locarno treaty, in which Britain by implication placed Weimar Germany on a par with France) said at the time: 'Never had we less cause than now to doubt in Germany's victory.' The utter repudiation of any policy that could have brought peace in the West was not imposed upon Germany by the country's rulers; it reflected (in the words of the most eminent German revisionist historian of the post-1945 era) 'exactly the ambitions and political philosophy of the overwhelming majority of the German people'.[24]

From 6 July Haig took a week's leave in England. Before the German attack in March he had felt obliged to stay at his post for fear of creating the wrong impression, but four months later he felt confident enough to give himself a break, not least to make the acquaintance of his infant son. He gave Lawrence authority to act for him in his absence.

Ludendorff still meant to deliver his war-winning blow against the British in Flanders, but regarded their present position there as too strong to tackle unless and until substantial reserves were drawn off to the south. He therefore decided to attack, first, in Champagne, so justifying Foch's intuition. In early July French intelligence produced accumulating evidence

---

23. X Committee, 1 July 1918. Harington, formerly Chief of Staff to Plumer, later proved himself 'a diplomat as well as a soldier' (*DNB*, Supplement 1931-1940) in his handling of the Chanak crisis in 1922, when he was Allied Commander-in-Chief in Turkey.

24. Fritz Fischer, *Germany's Aims in the First World War* (1967), pp. 621-4.

to support it, and on the 5th Foch asked Pétain to reinforce the Rheims sector. Six days later he authorized him to move reserve divisions southwards from the Amiens sector, asking the British to replace them with four divisions from the north. Lawrence gave qualified assent on Haig's behalf, and the Field-Marshal confirmed his full approval when he returned from leave on the 14th.

He was less accommodating, however, when he received the same day a request from Foch to send the four British divisions straight to Champagne, and to replace them by sending four more to the Amiens sector. He agreed to send only two divisions to Champagne, and arranged to see Foch on the 15th. It was at this point that Lloyd George and the War Cabinet reminded him of his rights under the Beauvais agreement, and he could hardly complain of such support from the government, though it happened to be misplaced. When he and Foch met on the 15th (again at the Duchesse's chateau), the Germans had already launched attacks east and west of Rheims. Haig then agreed to send the two additional divisions, on the understanding that they would be returned to him at once if the BEF were attacked.

The Kaiser came to witness the launching of what he termed the 'peace battle'. So it turned out to be, though not in the sense he intended. The French were not only ready for an attack in Champagne, but aware in advance of the precise timing (betrayed to them, suitably, by Alsatian deserters). There was no repetition of the French collapse following 27 May. On the contrary, the attempt to capture Rheims failed within forty-eight hours, and within seventy-two hours a French counter-offensive began, in which the tide of the war finally and irreversibly turned. Two French armies, under Generals Mangin and Degoutte – nineteen French divisions in all, together with four American divisions (the equivalent in size of eight French) – attacked the west side of the Marne salient, with the assistance of 750 tanks and over 2,000 guns. In the air, where the British contribution was most marked, the attack was aided by more than a thousand planes. The Germans carried out a fighting retreat to the line of the Vesle, reducing the length of their front but abandoning most of the Marne salient and leaving behind 25,000 prisoners. What is known as the second battle of the Marne had the same effect as the first; it saved Paris.

But that was not its only effect. The day before the counter-offensive (originally planned by Foch as a pre-emptive strike) was launched, Ludendorff travelled north to Mons and gave orders for artillery to be moved from Champagne to Flanders, in preparation for an attack in the Ypres sector to drive the BEF into the sea. Some of Haig's reserves had, after all, been drawn off. But news of the French success forced the warlord to cancel the orders and hurry back to the Aisne front. On 29 July he admitted that the attack in the north, which had remained his ulterior purpose, would probably never occur. But still he would not admit that the war was as good as lost, though there were others who did not share his reluctance to face unpleasant facts. General von Lossberg, for instance, a senior staff officer, begged him to withdraw at once to the Siegfried (or Hindenburg) line, and Crown Prince Rupprecht informed the high command that morale in his army group was deteriorating steeply, with up to 20 per cent of reserves sent to the front failing to report for duty.[25]

At the end of the month the Committee of Prime Ministers discussed the future course of the war in the light of Ludendorff's failure and the French victory. The CIGS had produced a memorandum in which, to Lloyd George's annoyance, he emphasized the supremacy of the Western front. He still did not, however, expect the Germans to be defeated there until 1919 at the earliest.[26]

Milner spoke first, and questioned the Allies' ability to win on the Western front even then. He said he would like to see the French and Americans providing the bulk of the forces there, 'with considerable assistance from us [but] leaving a margin of some 10 or 15 divisions with which we could operate in other parts of the world'. Hughes, though equally sceptical of an early end to the war, 'asked his colleagues not to overlook the fact that the Powers that had the largest forces on the Western front at the end of the war would probably exercise the greatest influence on the terms of peace'. From that point of view it was, he suggested, 'very undesirable to leave France and the US to finish the war on the Western front'. He also wondered if Milner had 'given enough consideration to the factor of the waning *moral* of the Germans'.

After a somewhat equivocal intervention by Borden, Smuts said that he regarded Italy as 'the most promising theatre'. But on the whole he agreed with Milner. He did not question that the Western front was the decisive front, but from the beginning of the war it had always proved 'the fatal front'.

25. Holger H. Herwig, *The First World War: Germany and Austria-Hungary 1914–1918* (1997), p. 418.

26. Wilson's memorandum caused Lloyd George to describe him as '*Wully redivivus*' since its purely Western front attitude reminded him of Robertson (Hankey diary, 30 July 1918). When, a few days later, Hankey mentioned to Wilson how the Prime Minister felt about his paper, the CIGS 'admitted he was dominated by the idea of not quarrelling with our Allies and more especially with Foch, but explained a scheme he had for concentrating twelve divisions [during the war] on the Italian front' (ibid., 2 August 1918).

Summing up, Lloyd George said that he was 'not too impressed by what was said about German morale, because he had heard it all before'. But he agreed with Hughes that 'unless peace was preceded by military victory, the position would be unsatisfactory'. He recalled having been 'taken to task for a sporting expression that he had made use of earlier in the war, namely, the "knock-out blow"'. Nevertheless, 'in substance he had not altered his opinion'.[27]

There was a certain unreality about the politicians' palaverings. The military side of the war was now, more than ever, in the hands of the soldiers. The day after the discussion just summarized, Borden told his colleagues that he had heard the previous evening, 'in confidence and great secrecy, that the Canadian Army Corps, which had lately been in the region of Arras, was now being moved forward into another region, and he had reason to believe that the intention was to use them offensively'. It seemed that 'the operation for improving our front might be about to commence'.[28] Thus the British Prime Minister received, indirectly, his first intimation of a battle which was to begin in a week's time and was to prove one of the most momentous in the history of the British army.

27. Committee of Prime Ministers, 31 July 1918. Lloyd George was referring to the interview he gave to the American journalist Roy Howard in September 1916.
28. Ibid., 1 August 1918.

30

The Russian Dimension

Haig's hour – The Russian dimension – Educational reform

Any good that Haig may have done himself in Lloyd George's eyes by his helpful attitude during the removal of Robertson was soon undone by the events of late March. The Prime Minister deeply resented the suggestion that the German breakthrough was due to his refusal to put Britain's ultimate reserves of manpower under Haig's control. He attributed the disaster above all to what he saw as the Field-Marshal's relentless squandering of lives during the previous summer and autumn, particularly in the battle for Passchendaele, and he also felt, with less justification, that Haig's dispositions to meet the German spring offensive had been basically faulty. There are, of course, many things to be said on both sides, but on the whole the balance of argument may reasonably be said to lie with Lloyd George. In any case, and whatever the respective merits, the Prime Minister was once again eager to be rid of Haig.

The problem was how to do it, and this problem proved as intractable as ever. It would have been hard enough to make a change at the top at such a critical moment even if there had been an obvious successor, but it remained true that no obvious successor to the Commander-in-Chief existed. Haig was well aware of this and, as usual, exploited the advantage with ruthless skill. As we have seen, he acquiesced in the sacrifice of Gough as a symbolic victim after going through the motions of defending him. A few days later he wrote a cleverly worded letter to Derby:

It is the duty of everyone to do his utmost in his own particular line to help the State to weather the storm. Personally, I have a clear conscience, and feel that I have done the best with the means at my disposal and am prepared to continue here as long as the Government wish me to do so. But, *as I have more than once said to you and to others in the Government, the moment they feel that they would prefer someone else to command in France, I am prepared to place my resignation in your hands.*[1]

1. Haig to Derby, 6 April 1918; words underlined by Haig.

He was not actually resigning, but saying that he would resign *if* . . . He thus challenged the government to sack him, in the unlikely event of finding an acceptable alternative. He was also disclaiming any responsibility for the recent débâcle, and implying that the government itself was responsible.

Meanwhile he had strengthened his hand at the Doullens conference. Despite his record of aversion to the idea of a unified command, he went out of his way to be co-operative about the appointment of Foch, even insisting that his powers should be wider than originally proposed. His own explanation of this remarkable change is that only Foch could control Pétain, and he therefore felt that Foch should co-ordinate all the armies on the Western front, and not just the operations around Amiens.[2] No doubt this was one of his motives, and a good one, but it was also, surely, convenient to him to remove a major excuse that the government might have had for dismissing him.

His letter to Derby was read to the War Cabinet, though not mentioned in the minutes. Immediately afterwards Lloyd George discussed it with Curzon, Law and Hankey. Should Haig be taken at his word? No member of the group could suggest a replacement. Hankey (who after his visit to France, with Smuts, in January, had been able to come up with only the unknown name of General Claud Jacob) records that no name could be produced – 'Plumer, in whom the troops are said to have confidence, being about as stupid as Haig himself '.[3] Later the same day Lloyd George put the same question to Wilson, who advised that no action should be taken against Haig 'failing some really outstanding personality', adding that in his opinion none was available.[4]

During the Maurice affair the Commander-in-Chief was careful to avoid any personal involvement in the vendetta against the government. Having refrained from backing Robertson in February, he was hardly likely to lend any support, in May, to Robertson's acolyte and stalking-horse. Though the story of Maurice's letter to the press begins with his visit to Haig's headquarters and the talk he heard there, there is no evidence that Haig himself had anything to do with the General's decision to write to the press, a course which he privately deprecated. In letters to his wife he condemned the General's breach of discipline, while showing his usual contempt for politicians, and Lloyd George in particular:

2. Haig diary, 26 March 1918.
3. Hankey diary, 8 April 1918. When Lloyd George praised Plumer in a speech as 'doughty', the General remarked that he supposed that was better than being called dotty.
4. Wilson diary, 8 April 1918.

Reuter states Gen. Maurice has written to the papers. This is a grave mistake. No one can be both a soldier and a politician at the same time. We soldiers have to do our duty and keep silent, trusting to Ministers to protect us.

And four days later, after the debate:

Poor Maurice! How terrible to see the House of Commons so easily taken in by a clap-trap speech by Lloyd George. The House is really losing its reputation as an assembly of common-sense Britishers.[5]

At about this time the CIGS, contradicting his advice the previous month, suggested that Haig should be brought back to fill the home forces command, which had been kept vacant since the appointment of French as Viceroy of Ireland. He told Haig that he had made the suggestion, eliciting no response from the Field-Marshal.[6] According to Wilson's biographer he now favoured Plumer as Haig's successor[7] – though he knew that others did not consider the General up to the job. In any case, he might well have refused to step into Haig's shoes, as he had refused to step into Robertson's. Nothing came of the idea, and at the end of the month, the command of home forces was given to Robertson (a more dignified billet for him than the Eastern command). Soon afterwards Haig received an explicit assurance from Wilson that the government had 'no wish at all to replace [him] as C in C in France'.[8]

Nevertheless Lloyd George continued to hope that an alternative might somehow turn up. In the latter part of July his hopes were momentarily fixed on the Earl of Cavan, who had succeeded Plumer as commander of the British force in Italy. Cavan was an Irish Guards officer, who had previously commanded the Guards division and an army corps on the Western front. He had a more than adequate record, and later played an important part in the victorious advance of the Italians at the end of the war. But when he reported to the Committee of Prime Ministers he could offer no immediate prospect of a breakthrough on the Italian front, and this disappointed Lloyd George.[9]

5. Haig to Lady Haig, 7 and 11 May 1918. Haig was, of course, most adroit politically, not least in knowing how to cover his tracks.
6. Wilson diary, 11 and 20 May 1918. The proposal came as no surprise to Haig, who heard rumours of it from his wife.
7. Charles Edward Callwell, *Field-Marshal Sir Henry Wilson: His Life and Diaries* (2 vols., 1927), vol. ii, p. 100.   8. Haig diary, 17 June 1918.
9. 23 July 1918. The Dominion leaders may have reflected that an hereditary aristocrat like Cavan was a rather surprising person to be even considered by Lloyd George for the top command in the modern British army.

Milner as War Secretary was also a disappointment, not least in his acceptance of the inevitability of Haig. Shortly before Cavan's report to the prime ministers Milner told his colleagues that 'short of heroic remedies all that was possible was being done to improve the organisation of the army', and that the question of 'making a change in the chief command had been repeatedly discussed, but he was not yet clearly convinced that a better substitute could be found'.[10] With the tacit elimination of Cavan, Lloyd George made no further effort to disprove this statement, and in a few weeks' time Haig was as unsackable as, in the next war, Bernard Montgomery was to become from the battle of Alamein onwards.

On 17 July Haig informed Foch that he was preparing secret plans for an offensive 'north of the Luce, direction east'. This fitted in with Foch's own 'long-cherished desire' and he was 'prompt in approving it'.[11] A few days later the Field-Marshal's diary records:

As we are fairly well prepared to meet an attack by Rupprecht upon my Second Army [in the north], it is most likely that the attack won't be delivered. So I am prepared to take the offensive and have approved of an operation taking place on Rawlinson's [Fourth Army's] front and steps have been taken to make preparations very secretly in order to be ready, should the battle being fought on the Marne cause the situation to turn in our favour.[12]

The Luce is a river running south of Amiens, parallel with the Somme. The immediate object of the attack now proposed by Rawlinson, and endorsed, in turn, by Haig and Foch, was to put Amiens, and the railway between Paris and the Channel ports that ran through the city, out of range of German bombardment. Both Amiens and the railway had been kept out of enemy hands during the desperate fighting in the spring, but they were still not entirely out of danger or out of trouble. The British plan aimed to push the Germans back on the front to the east of Amiens, in the process inflicting maximum damage and advancing as far as possible.

The operation at Le Hamel on American Independence Day, whose depressingly negative political significance has been indicated, was no less significant militarily, but in a positive way. Le Hamel demonstrated the value of tanks in the initial stage of an attack, in giving protection to infantry advancing towards the enemy line. The lesson was applied on a much larger

10. X Committee, 16 July 1918.
11. Basil Liddell Hart, *Foch, the Man of Orleans* (1931), pp. 341–2.
12. Haig diary, 23 July 1918.

scale in the Amiens offensive. Whereas the force employed in the Le Hamel attack consisted only of 10 battalions of infantry and 64 tanks, at Amiens 18 infantry divisions, 3 cavalry divisions and about 450 tanks took part, supported by 2,000 guns and 800 aircraft. An outstanding feature of preparations for the attack was the secrecy stressed by Haig in his diary, combined with elaborate deception ploys which seem to have worked. The Canadian corps, commanded by Sir Arthur Currie, was brought from the Arras area without its move being detected by the Germans, though the fact that it was being moved was told 'in confidence and great secrecy' to the Canadian Prime Minister, as we have seen, more than a week before the attack, and he then mentioned it at a meeting of the Committee of Prime Ministers, saying that it 'looked as if an operation for improving our front might be about to commence'. But he did not say into which sector the corps was moving, either because he had not been told or because he thought it best for his colleagues not to know. Wilson, who was present at the meeting, said that 'he knew nothing of any forthcoming operation', and may well have been telling the truth.[13] (Haig had often kept Robertson in the dark about operations, and is unlikely to have been any more confiding to Wilson.)

Foch – who had been made a marshal of France after the Marne victory – told Clemenceau on 4 August that Haig was ready to launch an offensive 'in Picardy and Flanders': information vague enough to be of little use to the enemy even if it had leaked through indiscreet members of the Prime Minister's entourage.[14] On the eve of the attack the King visited Haig's headquarters and received a detailed briefing from the Field-Marshal, who no doubt trusted his friend and sovereign to keep absolutely quiet about it

13. Committee of Prime Ministers, 1 August 1918. General Currie was almost certainly Borden's informant, though he may have drawn the line at telling even his Prime Minister where the offensive was to take place.

He was anyway a notable example of what Borden had in mind when he spoke of the need to promote non-professional officers to higher command. Like Monash, Currie was only a part-time soldier before the war, his main activities being, first, school-teaching and then insurance broking. In 1914 he volunteered for service overseas and was given command of a brigade. Thereafter he rose steadily, commanding a Canadian division on the Somme and at Vimy, and the Canadian corps in the last stages of the fight for Passchendaele. Haig thought highly of him, but he seems not to have been considered for the command of an army, though he surely deserved to be.

14. General Jean Mordacq, *Le Ministère Clemenceau: journal d'un témoin* (4 vols., 1930–31), vol. ii, p. 161. The marshal's baton for Foch also had the desirable effect of removing the anomaly that his military rank had been inferior to Haig's.

until the following morning.[15] Meanwhile, among many devices used to keep the enemy guessing, two Canadian battalions were sent to the northern part of the front, where their presence was noted by the Germans; the main body of Canadians being kept out of the line in front of Amiens until the last moment.

One way and another, perfect surprise was achieved when the offensive opened on a thirteen-mile front at 4.20 a.m. on 8 August. There was no preliminary bombardment and the weather, for a change, favoured the Allies, a mist covering the battlefield as the tanks and infantry moved forward behind a creeping barrage. In a few hours the Germans were driven back seven miles along most of the front, but what mattered more was the low quality of resistance encountered. The day cost the Germans 27,000 casualties, of whom 15,000 were prisoners. British casualties amounted to 9,000. Ludendorff in his memoirs describes it as 'the black day of the German Army in the history of this war', giving his reasons:

Our war machine was no longer efficient. Our fighting power had suffered . . . [and] the 8th of August put the decline of that fighting power beyond all doubt and in such a situation, as regards reserves, I had no hope of finding a strategic expedient whereby to turn the situation to our advantage. On the contrary, I became convinced that we were now without that safe foundation for the plans of G.H.Q., on which I had hitherto been able to build . . .

He asked Hindenburg to replace him, but the offer was refused. The Kaiser, too, gave him 'quite special proofs' of confidence in the days that followed. He was 'deeply moved, but remained anxious as to whether His Majesty really read the whole situation aright'. (The Kaiser later told him that 'after the failure of the July offensive and after August 8th', he himself 'knew the war could no longer be won'.)[16]

The ground gained in the battle of Amiens was not, as at Cambrai, lost in counterattacks. All the same, the momentum of the attack was much slower the second day, partly because most of the tanks were either destroyed or out of action. In the centre the Canadians and Australians, star performers in the battle, advanced a further three miles, while on the left flank the British III Corps, and on the right Debeney's French divisions, consolidated their positions. But enemy resistance was clearly stiffening.

15. Haig diary, 7 August 1918. The King brought a message from Lloyd George, who was now (the King said) talking of the excessive length of line that 'poor Haig' had to hold.
16. Erich Ludendorff, *My War Memories, 1914–1918* (2 vols., 1919), vol. ii, pp. 679–85.

At this point a crucial difference arose between Haig and Foch. The generalissimo wanted the attack to continue without interruption, and Haig at first agreed. But within a few days he changed his mind, reaching the uncharacteristic view that to go on attacking on the same line without a pause would be unduly costly. He thus showed that he was a late convert to Rawlinson's doctrine of 'bite and hold', itself the product of harsh experience. And his conversion was assisted by advice that came to him, at the time, from Currie. While sharing to the full Foch's eagerness to exploit the Amiens success, he thought that the enemy should now be attacked from other directions so far as the BEF was concerned, and was prepared to use Byng's Third Army for the purpose.

On 14 August he and Foch met at the latter's old headquarters at Sarcus, when Haig spoke to Foch 'quite straightly', hinting that he might, if necessary, have to appeal to his own government (as he had so recently been encouraged to do). Foch not only bowed to *force majeure* but seems to have been genuinely convinced.[17] The method of alternating attacks then became his own and contributed greatly to the speed and effectiveness of Allied operations in the months ahead. Haig 'had at last divined the manner of proceeding on the Western Front: that he should not seek a strategic triumph but should deliver a sequence of limited, tactical but ultimately mortal hammer blows'.[18]

Immediately after the Amiens victory Clemenceau visited Rawlinson's headquarters and was lavish in his praise for all concerned. A week later he presented France's highest military award, the Médaille Militaire, to Haig. The ceremony (at Amiens) was followed by a 'more than cordial' lunch, after which, at Clemenceau's request, there was a visit to the battlefield. During this Haig suggested a review of the 4th Canadian division, which the French Prime Minister gladly carried out. Before his departure, Haig assured him that the Third Army would soon be launching an attack.[19]

There was no visit to the BEF by Lloyd George, though the CIGS was present when Clemenceau came to Rawlinson's headquarters. And the following day the Committee of Prime Ministers instructed Wilson to convey congratulations, in the name of the Imperial War Cabinet, 'to Field Marshal Sir Douglas Haig and the troops under his command, for the brilliant

17. Haig diary, 14 August 1918; Liddell Hart, *Foch*, p. 352.

18. Trevor Wilson, *The Myriad Faces of War: Britain and the Great War, 1914–1918* (1986), p. 595.

19. Mordacq, *Le Ministère Clemenceau*, vol. ii, pp. 173–4 and 185–8 (11 and 18 August 1918). The Médaille Militaire was awarded to private soldiers and top commanders alike. Pétain received it a few days after Haig.

operation just completed'.[20] The same day Lloyd George broke his normal habit of not mentioning Haig by name in any public speech when he referred to him, along with others, in a speech at Newport, Monmouthshire. The recent victory, he said, was 'due undoubtedly to the brilliant qualities of our troops, and of the French troops . . . [and] to the very courageous leadership of Sir Douglas Haig and General Rawlinson and of the French generals'. This was a very diluted tribute, and Lloyd George diluted it further when he said: 'I must say I think a large share of the triumph is to be attributed to the unity of command . . . Everybody has combined, and you have had one great directing mind.'[21] In view of his actual opinion of Foch at the time, one can only marvel at the lengths to which he was prepared to go to avoid any unqualified acknowledgement of Haig's personal success.

If there was one directing mind in planning the Amiens offensive, it was not Foch's. Credit for the plan is due above all to Rawlinson, but Haig had much to do with it as well as being the man ultimately responsible for all that the BEF undertook, for good or ill. Moreover, he played a vital role, as we have seen, in persuading Foch to modify his thinking about the form of future offensive action, having just modified his own to most salutary effect. In mid-August Haig deserved praise as never before; it was his hour. And he grasped the implications of the battle more swiftly than any other leader on the Allied side. Lloyd George, his civilian colleagues and the CIGS still believed that the Germans would hold out until 1919, if not longer. So did Clemenceau, and even Foch did not immediately think otherwise. But after Amiens Haig was quite sure that the war could be won by the end of the year, and this time he was right.

If we look at the situation in Russia after the treaty of Brest-Litovsk as it appeared to British statesmen at the time, without allowing our judgement to be distorted by hindsight, we shall have no difficulty in understanding their anxieties. The collapse of the Russian army under the Tsarist regime, and the failure of the Provisional Government to revive it as a fighting force, had already brought about a change in the balance of the war gravely detrimental to the Western Allies. After the Bolsheviks seized power Lloyd George had been encouraged by Lockhart to hope that the new regime,

20. Committee of Prime Ministers, 12 August 1918.

21. Speech in the town hall at Newport, at a gathering organized by Comrades of the Great War, same date. In his memoirs Lloyd George devotes the minimum of space to the battle of Amiens, in which, however, he manages to criticize Haig for failing to exploit the victory with sufficient boldness and dash (WM, p. 3127). In fact, his new-found caution was one of the best features of his conduct of the battle.

however uncongenial in other respects, might have the will and the capacity to organize effective resistance to the Germans. The precedent of Revolutionary France stimulated this hope, and Lloyd George looked in particular to Trotsky as the man who might inspire the Russian people to fight in defence of their homeland. But the historical analogy was flawed. Though revolution, extreme and doctrinaire, was certainly a common factor, the crucial difference was that in 1792 the French people had not been through over three years of futile, exhausting war. They were in a mood not only to defend the soil of France against foreign invaders (*qu'un sang impur abreuve nos sillons*), but soon afterwards to embark upon a war of foreign conquest. Such was not the case with the Russians in the spring of 1918, as Lenin clearly perceived. And Lenin, not Trotsky, was the Bolshevik leader who really mattered.

If Brest-Litovsk had only made the Bolshevik regime neutral in the struggle against the Central Powers, it would have been bad enough in Lloyd George's eyes. But the Bolsheviks could not be regarded as neutral. As well as being the sworn enemies of 'capitalism' and 'imperialism', eager to foment social revolution in Britain and rebellion by all subjects of the British Crown, they were now so dependent upon Germany that their neutrality seemed unlikely to prove a reliable barrier against further German encroachment. As a result, it was inevitable that Lloyd George's attitude to the Bolshevik regime should change to outright hostility, though he remained above all concerned by the implications of Brest-Litovsk for the war against Germany and the survival of British power in the world.

Other members of the War Cabinet, and the CIGS, fully shared his concern. There was, it appeared, a more serious risk than ever that the huge stores of military equipment that had accumulated at the northern Russian ports of Murmansk and Archangel, and at the Far Eastern port of Vladivostok, might fall into German hands. And fear of this was linked to another: that the host of German and Austrian prisoners-of-war in Russia – up to a million of them – might be rearmed and brought back into active service. But to British minds the worst danger was that the Germans would now be free to dominate and exploit the whole Eurasian land-mass north of the Himalayas, and so threaten India. Even before Brest-Litovsk, they had established their control over Ukraine, and their scope for further eastward expansion now seemed almost unlimited. Curzon, the former Viceroy and exponent of the 'Great Game' (of defending Britain's Indian Empire against the supposed threat to it from Imperial Russia), was especially sensitive to the new peril. In his view, German ambitions had 'received an immense impetus' from Brest-Litovsk, and he drew attention to the potential line of enemy advance towards India through Persia and Afghanistan.[22] Another, but related, preoccupation was that there was no longer any Russian front against the Turks, who might therefore also pose a threat to India by an appeal to Muslim solidarity both inside the subcontinent and among Islamic peoples of the former Russian Empire.

Curzon was right about German ambitions. As we have seen, the rulers of Germany intended to combine their fight to a finish in the West with an aggressively forward policy in the East. After Brest-Litovsk the Germans took control of the Crimea, occupied the lower Don area, including Rostov, and unofficially supported the anti-Bolshevik Cossacks between the Don and the Volga with money and arms. Germany controlled the Black Sea and hoped to establish a protectorate over the whole of Caucasia, with its precious resources of oil and other minerals. Such a protectorate was also intended to serve as 'a bridge to Central Asia and a threat to England's position in India'.[23] But the Turks were equally active in the area, and they were acting as rivals rather than allies of Germany. In the end the Germans had to settle for control only of Georgia and the dream of more far-reaching dominion evaporated.

The truth is that Ludendorff's army of occupation in the East was much too large in relation to what he was attempting to achieve on the Western front, but not nearly large enough to enable a Teutonic empire to take over from that of the Tsars. Because of his oppressive policy in the already vast areas occupied by German troops, most of them were needed to hold the increasingly hostile native population down; and there were none to spare for further extending German power. Two divisions might have been enough to give the Germans control of Caucasia, but not even two divisions could be spared.

The limits on German power in the East were even more strikingly demonstrated when the German Ambassador in Moscow, Count von Mirbach, was assassinated on 6 July. Though the assassins were Social Revolutionaries, enemies alike of Germany and of the Bolsheviks, Lenin feared that the crime would give the Germans a perfect pretext to overthrow his regime and assume control of the Russian heartland. There were indeed many in the German leadership who saw the opportunity and would have been glad to seize it; but they lacked the strength to do so. Lenin and the Germans, despite their mutual antagonism, had a common interest in maintaining the

22. IWC, 25 June 1918.
23. The Kaiser's view at the end of June (Fritz Fischer, *Germany's Aims in the First World War* (1967), p. 560).

Brest-Litovsk arrangement for the time being – a sign of weakness on both sides. At least they were not fighting each other, while they had much else on their hands.

The day of Mirbach's assassination also witnessed the beginning of Western intervention in Russia on a serious scale, as Murmansk and Vladivostok passed under Allied and American protection. Hitherto anything that had happened on land had been militarily negligible and without American involvement. A detachment of 130 British Marines had been put ashore at Murmansk in early March, and in May the force was increased to 600. The British presence there was annoying to Germany, though secretly condoned by the Bolsheviks, who regarded it as preferable to occupation by the Germans or counter-revolutionary forces operating, with German backing, from nearby Finland. But when, on 6 July, Britain, France and the United States reached an agreement on joint defence of the area against the Germans, the Bolshevik leaders denounced the imperialist invasion and disowned the local Soviet leader who was a party to the agreement. In the state of panic following the Mirbach incident they could have done no less.

At Vladivostok, the eastern terminus of the trans-Siberian railway, there had been a brief intervention in April by 50 British and 500 Japanese Marines, when local Bolsheviks seized key points in the city. But the situation was soon defused and the Marines were withdrawn. Lloyd George and his colleagues always realized that substantial action to block apprehended German designs in Siberia could be taken only by the Americans or the Japanese, or preferably both. The Japanese had been in the war on the Allied side since August 1914, but their only significant contributions had been the capture, with token British assistance, of Tsingtao, the German fortress and naval base on the coast of China, and their seizure of three groups of islands belonging to Germany, the Marianas, Marshalls and Carolines. Their interest in the war was exclusively to strengthen their own position, and from that point of view a move into Siberia had its attractions for them. But they had no desire to quarrel with the United States, and they therefore insisted that they would do nothing in Siberia without American assent.

President Wilson was for months implacably opposed to American involvement in Russia, believing that the disadvantages would far outweigh any possible benefit. But he was under strong pressure from Britain and France, whose very natural anxieties have been explained. The Allies particularly regretted his negative attitude to the idea of joint action with the Japanese, and so did some powerfully placed compatriots of his. Hughes told the Imperial War Cabinet that, while he was in Washington on his way to London, he had found members of the Senate foreign affairs committee 'distinctly in favour of intervention, provided the operation was a joint one and not conducted by Japan alone'.[24] When the Dominion leaders attended a meeting of the SWC in early July they lent their weight to a renewed appeal to Wilson to intervene in the Far East. But by now he had overcome his profound reluctance, and on 6 July American, Japanese, British and French representatives (among others) in Vladivostok announced that the port and surrounding area were to be temporarily under the protection of the Allied and associated powers.

About 9,000 Japanese landed there and were joined before long by roughly the same number of Americans. Within two months the Japanese force in Siberia had grown to 70,000. Its presence there had none of the miraculous effects that Hankey, for one, had in mind when he expressed the hope that the 'vitalising rays' of the Japanese sun might 'revivify what remain[ed] of life in the frozen steppes of Russia, recreating for Germany an eastern front'.[25] The re-creation of a front against Germany proved a mirage, and the Japanese stirred in the racist Russians a degree of hostility even greater than that felt towards other foreign interventionists. (Kerensky had warned Lloyd George that it would be so when they talked in London in late June.[26]) By this time the civil war was beginning to take shape, though 'shape' is a questionable term granted the confusion of events in European and Asiatic Russia over the next two years. In the south a movement of anti-Bolshevik volunteers had come into existence under the leadership of Generals Kornilov and Alexeyev. When Kornilov was killed in April General Anatol Denikin succeeded him as military leader, and on Alexeyev's death later in the year Denikin became, as well, political leader of the volunteer movement (soon a misnomer, as voluntary recruitment gave way to conscription). Denikin was an able man, though without charisma. So long as the Germans were dominating Ukraine and the Crimea there was, in any case, limited scope for his small army, which was based upon the Kuban area east of the Sea of Azov and north of the Caucasus mountains. There was also a serious political difficulty. His movement sought to restore the old order in all its aspects, including the imperial power of Great Russia, but the Don Cossacks, with whom he needed to co-operate, had declared their own independent republic. In their fight against the Bolsheviks they were prepared to accept help from the Germans, given (unofficially and deniably)

24. IWC, 20 June 1918.   25. Hankey, 'general impressions', 19 July 1918.
26. Hankey diary, 24 June 1918. Lloyd George said that Kerensky had 'the most piercing eyes' he had ever seen, and found him 'an attractive personality', but was confirmed in his view that he was not a man of action (R WD, 29 June 1918).

in return for wheat. Denikin's movement was as anti-German as it was anti-Bolshevik, and had absolutely no sympathy for the self-assertion of subject peoples within the former Russian Empire.

Partly because of these cross-purposes a big opportunity was missed in June, when Denikin refused to join with the German-armed forces under General Peter Krasnov, leader of the Don Cossacks, in a move to capture Tsaritsyn (the future Stalingrad, now Volgograd), centre of Red power on the Volga. Had this move been effected, and had the volunteer army and the Don Cossacks then made contact with the growing anti-Bolshevik movement in the upper and middle Volga region, with a view to advancing together on Moscow, the Leninist regime might (according to at least one authority) have been overthrown.[27] But the vital element of political solidarity was lacking; Denikin stayed in the Kuban.

The Volga anti-Bolsheviks had, in early June, proclaimed a government at Samara (which, as Kuibyshev, was to become for a time the Soviet seat of government during the Second World War). The Samara rebels were Social Revolutionaries, to whom Denikin's reactionary aims and the nationalism of the Don Cossacks were equally repugnant. They regarded the Bolsheviks as usurpers, since Lenin had dissolved the constituent assembly in which they (the Social Revolutionaries) were the majority party, having obtained 38 per cent of a large popular vote compared with the Bolsheviks' 24 per cent. In fact, the issue was not quite as clear-cut as they made out, because the left wing of the party had supported the Bolshevik seizure of power, but too late for the ballot papers to be reprinted. Had left and right Social Revolutionaries been separately listed the overall proportions would certainly have been different, though the Bolsheviks' claim to be ruling by the will of the people would still have been spurious.

In any case, the Brest-Litovsk treaty had turned the left Social Revolutionaries against the Bolsheviks. After the assassination of Mirbach, which was their doing, they attempted an uprising in Moscow. This might well have succeeded if they had been less incompetent, but they were only good for violent gestures, not for practical planning. Lenin was given time to reimpose his mastery, using to the full the weapon of terror which was to be the hallmark of the Soviet regime throughout its horrible history. The ultimate left Social Revolutionary gesture was the attempt on Lenin's life by Dora Kaplan at the end of August. He survived this, but even if he had died the regime would have been unlikely to fall. As it was, all over Russia suspected anti-Bolsheviks were rounded up and shot, and the only result was to make

27. Orlando Figes, *A People's Tragedy: The Russian Revolution 1891–1921* (1996), p. 566.

the Red terror even more effective. The Tsar and his family had already been massacred, along with countless anonymous victims.

Nine days after the murder of the Imperial family, on 25 July, the city where it occurred, Ekaterinburg, was captured by Czech troops. The presence of a large Czechoslovak legion in Siberia was mentioned earlier, as a cause of friction between Lloyd George and Clemenceau. The situation had now changed, in that the French leader accepted that the legion could not, for logistical reasons, be brought to France. The Czechs controlled most of the trans-Siberian railway, and in western Siberia about 50,000 of them had become loosely allied with the so-called people's army based on Samara. Though originally their object had been to fight the Germans and Austrians, willy-nilly they had been drawn into fighting the Bolsheviks. They could, however, hope that they would become part of a strong front against the Germans, and they were encouraged by rumours that there would soon be a massive landing of Allied troops at Archangel.

The rumours were grossly distorted and exaggerated. There was indeed to be an Allied landing at Archangel, and one of its purposes was to make contact with the Czechs and Russian resistance groups. But far from being a great army, the Allied force that landed at Archangel on 2 August consisted of one British battalion, one French colonial battalion, a few Royal Marines and fifty American sailors: in all, 1,500 men. News of the mere fact of the landing preceded information about its size, and aroused wild hopes on the Volga. Disillusionment when the truth got through was therefore all the more bitter.

Nevertheless, while morale was still high, a mixed Czech–Russian force captured Kazan (6 August), and with it the Imperial gold reserve, which the Bolsheviks had sent there for safety from Petrograd. But this was the high-water mark of anti-Bolshevik success by the Samara regime and its Czech champions. Trotsky immediately left Moscow in his famous armoured train and began to organize a fight-back. In little more than a month Kazan was retaken (though not at first the bullion, which was recaptured later). In October Samara itself fell to the Bolsheviks. Resistance to them was then maintained from bases further east, but the threat to Moscow was averted.

Like other Allied leaders, Lloyd George was largely in the dark about Russia after Brest-Litovsk. His ideas on the subject were as confused as the situation itself, but it is clear from what he said at the time that he found his desire to protect Allied stores and keep the Germans out of Asia drawing him into conflict with the Bolsheviks. He wanted to use the Czechs 'as a nucleus of a democratic anti-Bolshevist movement in Siberia' which would form a government and invite the Japanese in to help. 'What was needed was somebody to help organise and inspire such a movement, someone like Chinese Gordon, with a streak of genius in him.'[28] The analogy was false. When the young Charles George Gordon (not yet General) was making his name in China in the early 1860s, the 'ever victorious army' that he commanded was a Chinese force with a few British officers, used by the established Chinese authorities to suppress a rebellion. There was no world war to complicate the issue, and the Western powers, however resented by the Chinese, were unquestionably in the ascendant. None of these conditions applied in the Russia of 1918. There was no scope for a man like Gordon, even if one had been available.

The commander of the Allied force at Archangel, and formerly at Murmansk, was certainly no Gordon. General Frederick Poole was a narrowminded soldier, whose sense of his own importance was in inverse ratio to the force at his disposal. He was ideologically anti-socialist and anyway devoid of political flair. Though it was obviously essential for him to work well with the local Social Revolutionaries and make them feel that they were in charge, if with Allied support, in fact he treated Archangel and its vast hinterland as a colonial territory. At the same time his military impact was negligible. Even when 4,000 American troops joined his command in September he could make very little headway, partly because hundreds of them were confined to their ships with flu. The only value of the American presence was that it enabled Wilson to insist that Poole change his attitude to the local Social Revolutionary government, under threat that the American troops would otherwise be withdrawn. In October Poole was recalled to London, and then sent, more appropriately, as head of a mission to Denikin. At Archangel he was succeeded by his Chief of Staff, General Edmund Ironside, Russian-speaking and a future CIGS. But by then the original purpose of the Allied landings had been largely stultified by events.

At the time of the landings Lockhart was living dangerously in Moscow. He had been converted, though with extreme reluctance, to the idea of Allied intervention to save the Czechs and the Volga line. But in his messages to London he emphasized that it had to be on a large scale. When he heard of the landings at Archangel he was thinking in tens of thousands. As he wrote later:

For forty-eight hours I deluded myself with the thought that the intervention might prove a brilliant success. I was not quite sure what we should be able to do when we reached Moscow. I could not believe that a bourgeois Russian government could be

28. X Committee, 19 June 1918.

maintained . . . without our aid. Still less did I believe that we could persuade any number of Russians to renew the war with Germany . . . But, with the adequate forces which I assumed we had at our disposal, I had no doubt of our being able to reach the Russian capital.

When the exiguous size of Poole's force became known to him, he felt that a blunder had been committed 'comparable with the worst mistakes of the Crimean War'.[29]

There was no way the British and French could have intervened effectively in Russia in 1918. Like the Germans they lacked the resources for a war on two fronts, and did not even have the Germans' advantage of interior lines. Britain's weakness was well illustrated by an operation at about the time of the Archangel landing, though far removed from it geographically. A column of armoured cars was sent north from Mesopotamia to the Caspian, with a mission to gain control of the oil centre Baku and to hold it against both Germans and Turks. The leader was General L. C. Dunsterville, a spirited and enterprising character (Kipling's model for Stalky). But, though he did his best, 'Dunsterforce' was just not equal to the task assigned to it. In September it was driven from Baku by the Turks.

Only Japan and the United States were capable at the time of large-scale intervention in Russia, and both (as we have seen) decided after some delay to send large numbers of men, the Japanese a particularly large number. But their motives were not such as to make their presence of much value to the Allied cause. The Japanese came to Siberia to promote their own interests, and not, as Lloyd George hoped, to help the Czechs or Russian resisters. Wilson was, indeed, to some extent influenced by the plight of the Czechs in reaching his decision to intervene. But he adamantly refused to support them in western Siberia, and was not even prepared to assist their departure from Russia through the northern ports.[30] He insisted that they should leave,

29. R. H. B. Lockhart, *Memoirs of a British Agent* (1932, repr. 1974), pp. 310–11. The day after the attempt on Lenin's life Lockhart was arrested and held first in the Lubianka, then in the Kremlin. In October he and others were allowed to return to Britain via Finland, in an exchange involving Litvinov.

30. Archangel was icebound during the winter months, and could therefore have been used for evacuating Czechs in 1918 only if the means had existed for moving them there with reasonable speed from the Volga. In fact, the logistical and military difficulties precluded any such move. Besides, now that the Germans were in retreat on the Western front, the need for them to be moved was no longer what it had been. Murmansk was a product of the war, created as an ice-free port all the year round, to enable supplies from the West to reach Russia (though many never reached the Russian army). As a port of potential egress for the Czechs it was, of course, far more remote even than Archangel.

if at all, from Vladivostok, and his support for them was confined to the Far East, at a time when most of them were either in the West or moving to central Siberia.

As for the Bolsheviks, after a short period of panic following the Archangel landing – when they too expected a march on Moscow by a large Allied force – they were able to turn the intervention greatly to their advantage. Even while it was limited to Murmansk they were blaming the 'capitalists' and 'imperialists' for most of their problems. Now they had a more plausible basis for their propaganda, without the inconvenience of a serious military threat.

The day the battle of Amiens began, a quiet ceremony in London marked another major British achievement of a very different kind. In his diary for 8 August H. A. L. Fisher records that in the House of Lords that day his education bill received the royal assent.

His appointment as President of the Board of Education (as the Minister responsible for education was then called) was one of Lloyd George's happiest inspirations. When Fisher accepted the post he was serving as Vice-Chancellor of Sheffield University, having previously been a history don at New College, Oxford, for over twenty years. His basic formation was in the classics, but he switched to modern history, which he studied in France and Germany before returning to teach it at Oxford. During the pre-war period he wrote a number of books, including the best short life of Napoleon. He was a lifelong Liberal, whose social conscience and willingness to do public work were already apparent before he entered politics as a minister.

Above all, he was an outstanding product of the Victorian intellectual aristocracy, one of the greatest and most fruitful élites ever known. His mother's family was close to Tennyson, Gladstone and George Eliot. His parents were painted by G. F. Watts. His uncle-by-marriage, Leslie Stephen, was a powerful influence in his life, as was the eminent historian F. W. Maitland, who married his eldest sister. Another sister married Ralph Vaughan Williams, and Stephen's daughters Vanessa (Bell) and Virginia (Woolf) were, of course, his first cousins. His father-in-law, Sir Courtenay Ilbert, clerk of the House of Commons, provided a link with the Parliamentary world.[31]

31. He met Lettice Ilbert when she came to him from Somerville as a history pupil – clearly an apt one, as she got a first. They were married in 1899.

An august, though hardly intellectual, connection was with Edward VII, who was Fisher's godfather because at the time of his birth (in 1865) his own father was private secretary to Edward, then Prince of Wales.

Fisher accepted the job after asking for, and receiving, an explicit assurance from Lloyd George that there would be 'money for educational reforms and improvements'. On this issue the Prime Minister, a schoolmaster's son, was 'as good as his word'. According to Fisher, his 'strong and constant support ... ensured the acceptance of every plan' that he (Fisher) put forward. In Balfour, too, who had introduced the last major educational reform in 1902, he had 'an enlightened and powerful friend'. Though he regarded the Balfour system as being very far from the kind 'which it would have occurred to any statesman to construct as a *tabula rasa*', it had, in his view, 'two great advantages': that it was a going concern and 'clearly one that could be developed'.[32] His own approach, like Balfour's, was both idealistic and pragmatic.

As a departmental chief he proved effective, and was well served by a team of officials of high quality. The permanent secretary was a fellow Wykehamist, Sir Amherst Selby-Bigge, who had also been an Oxford don before entering the public service. W. N. Bruce, of whom Lloyd George had a particularly high opinion, was head of the secondary schools department, and four scholarly men of letters – Gilbert Murray, J. W. Mackail, E. K. Chambers and O. M. Edwards – were among those who served the Ministry in Fisher's time. As private secretaries he chose Frank Oates, cricketer and squire, endowed with 'saintly character and sagacious judgment', if not with 'intellectual brilliance', and Alan Kidd who, Fisher believed, would have risen much higher in the civil service had his career not been blighted by ill-health.[33] In June 1917 the Ministry was moved from Whitehall to temporary accommodation at the Victoria and Albert Museum. (Fisher seems to have raised no strong objection to this, as he later, as we have seen, did to the occupation of the British Museum by the Air Ministry.[34])

As his junior minister he inherited Lloyd George's old friend Herbert Lewis, who had been Parliamentary secretary since 1915 and an MP since 1892. He was kindly, knowledgeable, amenable and skilled in committee work. But Fisher needed little guidance in his new sphere. He took naturally to politics and Parliament. In February he circulated two memorandums to the Cabinet: one on the need to increase state subsidy of teachers' pay, the other on his general plans for improving the educational system. His proposals were considered by the War Cabinet (the first he attended) and

32. H. A. L. Fisher, *An Unfinished Autobiography* (1940), pp. 92 and 96.

33. Ibid., pp. 99–101. Murray was Fisher's closest friend.

34. The difference was that the Air Ministry was a service department, which made the British Museum, with those of its contents that could not be moved, a potential target for enemy bombers.

endorsed in less than half an hour. In April he made his maiden speech presenting the educational estimates. He spoke without notes for over two hours, a feat earning him much admiration and the special interest of Law, who had an equally phenomenal memory. He secured a supplementary estimate of nearly £4 million, enabling the Board of Education to meet three-fifths of the cost of teachers' salaries, the local authority finding two-fifths. As a result, the average wage of every elementary (primary) school teacher was doubled, and under a superannuation measure that he put through later in the year teachers' pensions were trebled. His comment on this transformation of the status of teachers in the public sector, making them 'one of the liberal professions', can only be read with a sense of rather cruel irony in the early twenty-first century: 'The young should not be entrusted to the care of sad, melancholy, careworn teachers. The classroom should be a cheerful place. The state which values harmony should begin by making its teachers happy.'[35] After the war Fisher appointed a committee under Lord Burnham to work out a progressive system of salary awards for teachers, standardized across the country. The resulting 'Burnham scales' lasted almost to the end of the century, and Fisher deserves the credit for them.[36]

His general scheme of educational reform had four main features. The school-leaving age of fourteen, permissive since 1900, was to be made compulsory, with permission for local education authorities (LEAs) to extend it to fifteen. All forms of paid employment for children under twelve were to be abolished absolutely, and for those over twelve before 6 a.m. and after 8 p.m. For children between fourteen and eighteen attendance was to be mandatory at 'continuation schools' for 320 hours a year, to ensure that education would not come to an abrupt end when they left school. The LEAs were to remain responsible for co-ordinating all local schemes of education, but in future the Board would pay at least half the cost. The Parliamentary timetable became clogged in 1917 by the franchise and other complex measures, and not least by Fisher's own superannuation bill. His first comprehensive measure had, therefore, to be deferred until the following year, and meanwhile some concessions were made to various interest-groups which had objected to particular aspects. The 1918 bill was introduced as a new measure, but in essentials it was not changed. Unfortunately one of the main provisions, for continuation schools, was

35. Ibid., pp. 104–5.
36. '[He] was certainly their godfather, for he had to sponsor them in a Cabinet of imported business men whose views on public education were often pre-twentieth-century' (G. A. N. Lowndes, *The Silent Social Revolution* (1937, 2nd edn., 1969), p. 126).

not implemented, because it fell victim to the post-war economy drive. In any case it would have taken time to train the necessary number of teachers. But the provision remained on the statute book as a pointer to the future.

As well as what he achieved by legislation, Fisher made important changes through the exercise of his administrative powers. He produced the money to make possible a big increase in the secondary school population. His aim was to raise the number attending such schools from the pathetic figure of 30,000 to 600,000, and by the Second World War it had, in fact, reached half a million, thanks largely to his initiative. At the same time, for the fifty-five different types of test which secondary school pupils might be asked to take he substituted a single, national examination for school certificate, the forerunner of GCSE. He also turned his attention to university education, which of course meant much to him. When the war ended he made £8 million available for the purpose of sending ex-servicemen to British universities, and 27,000 benefited from the opportunity. In obtaining more funds for higher education he was careful to safeguard academic freedom; the system of distribution through an independent university grants committee was his creation.

While he was Minister there was profound popular interest in education, to which he responded by speaking throughout the country as a missionary for the cause. At Bristol he addressed a meeting of dockers organized on a Sunday morning by the young Ernest Bevin, and was astonished when the audience rose to its feet two or three times during the speech, cheering and waving handkerchiefs. The occasion was described to Lloyd George in a letter from Herbert Lewis, who accompanied Fisher to Bristol and in a subsequent tour of Wales. Later, when Lloyd George wrote to Lewis to congratulate him on his share in bringing the education bill through to third reading, Lewis in thanking him added this tribute to Fisher: '[He] has been wonderful. It was a happy day for me when you sent him to the Board of Education. He has been a magnificent Minister ... & deserves every encouragement.'[37] Lloyd George needed no reminder of Fisher's merits. The Education Minister was one of his favourite colleagues, having the quality that he most valued in a departmental chief, of being able to decide for himself what needed to be done and then to get on with doing it subject only to prime ministerial and Cabinet backing. He did not wait for instructions on how to tackle his job. Moreover, despite the heavy demands of his programme at the Board of Education, Lloyd George did not hesitate to consult

37. Fisher, *Unfinished Autobiography*, p. 106; Herbert Lewis to DLG, 17 October 1917 and 17 July 1918.

him on other matters and he was willing to take on other work. He was often brought into the discussion of problems relating to foreign affairs and Ireland, and he accepted a watching brief at the India Office during Montagu's long absences. For his part, his admiration for Lloyd George as head of the government, and his pleasure in working under him, are well expressed in this estimate written at the end of his life:

His animated courage and buoyancy of temper, his gift of witty speech and uncon-querable sense of fun, his easy power of confident decision in the most perilous emergencies, injected a spirit of cheerfulness and courage into his colleagues which was of extraordinary value during those anxious years. He mastered all the business, he showed a power of resource in counsel which can rarely have been equalled, and he so handled his distinguished and highly varied team that, when the Government finally broke up in 1922 Balfour observed that he never remembered a Cabinet which had worked together in greater harmony . . . During the War [Lloyd George] was at the summit of his brilliant powers.[38]

Yet it was not only as colleagues that the two men got on well. They also became friends and the friendship lasted. As an Oxford classical scholar Fisher had, on the face of it, more in common with Asquith, and he was indeed on excellent terms with the former Prime Minister. (Having never served in Asquith's government he could not be regarded as one who had gone over to the enemy.) But in fact his personal relations with Lloyd George were closer. No doubt his cool, disciplined intelligence responded to the gusto and genius of Lloyd George's, and vice versa. Fisher the historian revelled in the company of a maker of history, and Lloyd George the ever-curious savoured contact with a mind that was imaginative as well as academic. The two men became Surrey neighbours when Lloyd George built a house at Churt and Fisher acquired one at nearby Thursley. During the inter-war years the Fishers were frequent, not to say regular, visitors for Sunday lunch at Churt, and after Fisher became warden of New College in 1925 Lloyd George occasionally stayed there at the lodgings.

38. Fisher, *Unfinished Autobiography*, p. 135. Fisher had completed ten chapters of his autobiography when he died in April 1940, after being knocked down by a lorry as he was walking along Millbank, Westminster. Soon afterwards the Archbishop of Canterbury officiated at a memorial service for him at St Margaret's, Westminster, which many leading politicians were unable to attend, because the Norwegian campaign was at its height. But Lloyd George attended.

3 1

The Police Strike

*Interlude in Wales – Police strike – Speech and collapse
at Manchester*

Lloyd George spent, in total, more than half the month of August in Wales. Early in the month he went there on a speaking tour, which included traditional attendance at the National Eisteddfod. From the middle of the month until near the end of it he was at Criccieth for his usual sort of holiday, combining pleasure with much business – though the distinction in his case was blurred, because he always injected fun into any work he was doing or making others do.

He left for South Wales on 8 August, the day when, unknown to him, Haig's army was going into battle at Amiens. (Though alerted by Borden that something was in the wind, he had heard nothing from the military, and anyway had no idea of the precise time or location of the attack.) Before leaving he had issued, on the anniversary of the outbreak of war, a message to the people of the British Empire:

We are in this war for no selfish ends. We are in it to recover freedom for the nations which have been brutally attacked and despoiled, and to prove that no people, however powerful, can surrender itself to the lawless ambitions of militarism without meeting retribution . . . at the hands of the free nations of the world. To stop short of victory for this cause would be to compromise the future of mankind. I say 'Hold Fast' . . .[1]

Little did he realize how near the Allies were to victory, or how soon the alleged British unselfishness would have to be tested.

His first destination was Neath, where the National Eisteddfod was being held. He travelled there with Margaret and Megan, and they were met by the Mayor and Corporation before driving to the Gwyn Hall in procession. After accepting the freedom of the borough, he gave a speech of thanks, recalling that Neath had been a Roman garrison city and mentioning the ruined abbey which he had seen the night before:

1. Message for general release, 4 August 1918.

574

That ruin suggests to me that those old monks could teach us a lesson today. They never set up a building which was out of keeping with the beauty of this exquisite valley. There is nothing more distressing when one goes through the beautiful valleys of South Wales than to see how they have been disfigured by the mad lust for wealth. In the hour of restoration which is coming we shall owe it to this valley to see that the houses which are constructed, the workshops, factories and buildings set up there, are in conformity with the beautiful picture which God has painted on the canvas of South Wales.

On the war he said that, while recognizing from the start (actually from September 1914) that it would be 'a long job and a terrible job', he had 'always been confident we should get through'. He had some appropriately glowing words for Britain's principal ally. To cheers from the audience he proclaimed his 'unbounded admiration for France', which was 'one of the great gallant nations of the world'. Though possessing 'the greatest army next to Germany', France was 'less inclined for war in August 1914 than she had ever been'.

The freedom ceremony was followed by lunch, and then the Lloyd Georges visited the Eisteddfod. They were given an enthusiastic welcome and Lloyd George 'joined heartily in some of the choral numbers'. In the evening he attended a 'sacred concert' and made a speech in the soulful manner he reserved for such occasions. It was delivered in Welsh and he spoke of the hymns that had been sung:

It is only Welsh people who have been exiled from their native land for a generation who appreciate their full value. I do not think there has been a Sunday since I have lived in London when some of those charming hymns have not been sung on my hearth. . . . Every one of those hymns is full of meaning for men in times of stress. I am glad to be here to listen to their rendering by thousands of my fellow-countrymen, and I will go back imbued with a new spirit to face new trials. (Cheers.)[2]

What he said was largely true. Though much of the content of the hymns meant nothing to him in the literal sense, he loved the tunes and derived emotional uplift from singing them.

Two days later, at the end of his short tour, he had heard the news from Amiens and in a speech at Newport, paid the tribute already quoted to Haig (among others). In the same speech he again made a warm reference to France, while appealing to the coalmining industry to do its utmost to help her:

2. Report in *The Times*, 10 August 1918.

France has for the moment lost practically all her best mines, and France is a very gallant country. There is not a land under the sun that has suffered more for human liberty ... Go now to those districts which have been liberated, and you will find them shattered, torn, rent, bleeding. That is the beautiful land of France. I do ask the miners of this country, the colliery managers, the proprietors and everybody who has anything to do with producing coal all to do their best to get more coal to France.

He urged the miners to 'hurl coal' at the enemy.[3]

There had been a serious drop in coal production resulting from the call-up of miners for the army during the spring crisis on the Western front, which was combined by a surge in voluntary recruitment of miners not obliged to go, depleting the workforce beyond expectation. But as the military threat receded the War Cabinet decided that the withdrawal of category 'A' men from vital war industries should cease, and in the remaining months of 1918 'coal mining had a higher priority than military recruitment'.[4] It was in these circumstances that Lloyd George made his vehement appeal at Newport. (The situation had been further aggravated by the incidence of flu among miners, which in July alone cut output by nearly three million tons.)

Returning to London on the 12th he held a meeting of the Committee of Prime Ministers in the afternoon, from which, as earlier mentioned, congratulations were sent to Haig and his troops. Over the next few days there were two more meetings of the Committee,[5] and much discussion of the report of its proceedings, drafted by Hankey. The talks took place first in London and then at Danny Park, the country retreat organized for Lloyd George that summer by Riddell. Hankey's work was much praised, but in the event Hughes did not agree to all of the report and even Lloyd George could not be pinned down to signing it. In any case, it became 'rather out of date owing to the rapid course of events'.[6] Borden left for Canada on the 16th, and Massey for New Zealand a few days later. Hughes stayed on in London until the peace conference, and Smuts remained at his post in the War Cabinet.

On the 17th Lloyd George left for Criccieth, where he spent the next eleven days surrounded by his family and a shifting cast of colleagues and advisers. Megan had two school friends staying. Philip Kerr was in attendance throughout the visit. There were picnics and expeditions, but

3. *The Times*, 12 August 1918.
4. Keith Grieves, *The Politics of Manpower, 1914–18* (1988), p. 197.
5. 15 and 16 August 1918.
6. Maurice Hankey, *The Supreme Command, 1914–1918* (2 vols., 1961), vol. ii, p. 832.

most of the time was devoted to planning home policy with an eye to the next election; also to the timing and mechanics of the election itself, which had been in Lloyd George's mind for some weeks. His idea was to go to the country quite soon and certainly before the end of the year, which he still assumed would be before the end of the war. Though his preference was for fighting in partnership with Law, he was prepared to fight on his own if no programme acceptable to himself and his fellow Coalition Liberals could be agreed with the Conservatives.

Before leaving for Criccieth he talked about the election to Riddell, saying that he would discuss reconstruction during his time in Wales, and then make a speech at Manchester which would, in effect, open his campaign. He would deal with Free Trade and Protection 'only very generally' but would concentrate upon the state of the working class:

The statistics given me by Sir Auckland Geddes are most disquieting. They show that the physique of the people of this country is far from what it should be, particularly in the agricultural districts where the inhabitants should be the strongest. That is due to low wages, malnutrition and bad housing. It will have to be put right after the war. I have always stood during the whole of my life for the underdog. I have not changed, and am going still to fight his battle. Both parties will have to understand that.[7]

He said that the organizer of his campaign would be Sir Henry Norman.

Norman was the Coalition Liberal MP for Blackburn. According to Lloyd George, he 'started life as a cobbler', a fact not mentioned, however, in his exceptionally long *Who's Who* entry. Certainly he was 'very ambitious', and had covered a lot of ground in his life, both literally and metaphorically. He was very widely travelled, in North America, the Far East, Russia, Egypt and the Balkans, and he had turned his hand to numerous forms of employment. As a young man he had been a journalist, and he had been in Parliament since 1900. He first worked for Lloyd George as honorary secretary of the (1909) Budget League, and had worked for him again as a liaison officer at the Ministry of Munitions. During the war Norman was in the army and reached the rank of Major, accumulating a variety of foreign decorations. He seems also to have accumulated over the years a considerable fortune, and he married, as his second wife, a daughter of Lord Aberconway. He was knighted in 1906, became a baronet in 1915, and was made a Privy Counsellor in 1918. Lloyd George thought that he 'ha[d] his

7. *RWD*, 13 and 14 August 1918.

price' and would be 'entitled to his peerage' if he did the election job well.[8] In August 1918 he took a house in the neighbourhood of Criccieth and came over for many of the political discussions.

The principal colleague summoned to confer about home policy and electoral matters was Addison. He travelled on the 20th to Bangor with the junior Coalition Liberal whip, Dudley Ward, who made the train journey agreeable by bringing 'an excellent basket of provisions'. They spent the night at the Railway Hotel and were collected next morning by Lloyd George's car, arriving at Brynawelon about midday 'after a glorious drive'. Addison was put up in the house, while sleeping accommodation was found for Ward at Harlech.

That evening there was a far-reaching discussion of general politics, with special reference to a possible election in the fairly near future. The question was considered: what should be Lloyd George's relations with the Tories, and what terms should he make with them, with a view to a joint appeal to the country that Liberals could support? Among the many issues that had been engaging Addison's attention as Minister of Reconstruction, none was more important to him than the establishment of a ministry of health. He had been working hard on this ever since his appointment the previous year, but he had encountered many obstacles, among which one of the most intractable was the attitude of the Tory president of the local government board (LGB), Hayes Fisher. Whereas the previous occupant of the post, Rhondda, had been fervently committed to creating a health ministry, Hayes Fisher was very much against it.

All the same Addison had been making progress, through patient negotiation with the various interested parties. (One name that cropped up was that of Kingsley Wood, with whom Lloyd George had to bargain so hard over his pre-war health insurance scheme.) Moreover, Addison was helped in his tussle with Hayes Fisher when a group of influential back-bench Unionists, headed by Waldorf Astor (known as a close aide of the Prime Minister), wrote to *The Times* early in 1918 calling for a health ministry on the lines favoured by Rhondda and himself, and attacking Hayes Fisher for his obstructionism.[9] On 2 August the idea was approved in principle by the recently constituted home affairs committee, over which the Tory Home Secretary, George Cave, presided. Another advantage was that the joint committee of the Royal Colleges (of Physicians and Surgeons) was well

8. *RWD*, 29 July 1918; *Who's Who*. Norman's 'recreations' are listed as 'farming, shooting, fishing, automobilism, mechanics, electricity, wireless telegraphy'. Not even the name of his first wife is recorded, let alone any other details. If it was his ambition to become a peer, he did not attain it. 9. *The Times*, 10 January 1918.

disposed to the project, and Addison was therefore delighted when Lloyd George, late in the first evening's talk at Criccieth, said that he would like to discuss the matter with the joint committee's moving spirit, Sir Bertrand Dawson. Immediately, Dawson was contacted by telephone and asked to come to Criccieth the following day.

He arrived in the evening, with Milner and Hankey, and did all that Addison could have wished, talking in a way that commanded Lloyd George's enthusiastic interest, insisting that the health ministry should be quite separate from the LGB, and showing that his colleagues had no time for Hayes Fisher. Milner also made useful contributions. Dawson stayed over the weekend (23–4 August) and took part in further detailed discussion of the health project.

Meanwhile a good deal of time was given to the electoral talk. It was clear that the Asquithians were against an early election, as were a few leading Tories, notably Walter Long and Hayes Fisher, but that Law, Balfour, Carson, Milner and others were on the whole inclined to go for it. On these assumptions, the working party at Criccieth drew up an outline programme emphasizing welfare, with health the central theme, which was to be sent to the Unionist programme committee under the party chairman, Sir George Younger. Matters of inevitable discord were to be either fudged (as in the case of tariffs) or completely ignored (as in the case of Ireland). The tone for the election, whenever it might be – and whether or not fought in concert with the Tories – would be set by Lloyd George in his speech at Manchester scheduled for 12 September. Campaign fund-raising was already being actively pursued.[10]

Milner wrote to Violet Cecil (who had been in Paris and seeing Clemenceau):

Criccieth has again been rather amusing . . . The two first days were among the most beautiful I have ever known. Since yesterday we have a deluge. I am staying longer than I expected . . . I am very well, rather exhausted mentally by the effort to keep my nimble-minded host from skipping too rapidly all over the universe. Bertram [sic] Dawson is here – an interesting man on his own subjects – also Amery [again

10. For instance, Riddell's diary entry for 15 August 1918 (omitted from RWD): 'I met William Sutherland . . . at the Carlton . . . He was engaged as usual in supping and wining, being entertained to dinner by a Tory magnate who is coming over to L.G. A few days ago Sutherland dined with Lord Charles Beresford, who has £100,000 for party purposes and proposes to utilise it for L.G.'s campaign . . . I gave him some likely names, including Sir Howard Spicer, who came to me the other night to say that he and nineteen friends of his can put up £250,000. The Asquithians are busy hunting for cash and the Tories are doing the same.'

self-invited], Kerr, Hankey &c, & all sorts of odds & ends of politicians & wire-pullers come prancing in & out.[11]

The final dismissive category presumably included Addison, a politician of real stature. But to Milner democratic politics was a low business for which he had nothing but contempt – though his current position of high authority was due to, and dependent upon, one of its arch-practitioners.

The Criccieth party was diverted one evening by a charity concert in the village hall at Llanystumdwy (built from the proceeds of Lloyd George's successful libel action against the *People* in 1909). Addison described it as 'a capital performance', while regretting that 'there was not enough Welsh music in it'. The star turn was the musical-comedy actress Lily Elsie, whom Lloyd George had long admired. (During the record-breaking run of *The Merry Widow* at Daly's Theatre before the war it was said that he 'formed a habit' of watching her from the wings.) At the end of the concert Milner made 'a charming little speech' of thanks to the performers.[12]

One rather ominous feature of the Prime Minister's break at Criccieth was the intensity of press coverage: harmless enough, no doubt, by modern standards, but a warning of things to come. According to Addison, members of the party were 'persistently followed about by photographers – especially near the house'. But the photographers missed one big opportunity. The afternoon before the concert Lloyd George had wandered down to the river with Milner and Kerr, where they

found themselves in difficulties in an attempt to get across. Finally L.G. took his trousers off on a stone mid-stream and paddled up to his middle in his shirt and pink pants, Milner doing the whole business in his trousers. They both arrived across wet up to the middle [Kerr having apparently avoided the immersion]. They had previously been followed by a photographer, but managed to shake him off before this choice moment, which would have made his reputation. We were all of opinion that L.G.'s pink pants – suitably touched up on the cinematograph – would have been a gold mine . . .[13]

During the visit the war and foreign affairs were also, of course, discussed, and Hankey records one outburst by Lloyd George which caused him some uneasiness:

11. Milner to Violet Cecil, 25 August 1918. He said of Clemenceau that without him 'France at any rate would have collapsed, & though we & America might still have gone on, a decisive victory over the Central Powers would have become impossible'.
12. Addison diary, 23 August 1918; Hankey diary, same date; *DNB* (Supplement 1961–1970), entry on Lily Elsie.   13. Addison diary, 23 August 1918.

At dinner we had a discussion of war aims, and Lloyd George, under the stimulus of our present remarkable military successes, showed a very hard attitude talking of judgments and penalties. I fear he may overrate our power and miss securing a good peace which would as far as possible remove the bones of contention.

[He] is out for blood, and wants to give Germany a thorough hiding – in fact he actually used the term 'destroy Germany' – as a punishment for the atrocities by land and sea.[14]

Hankey's own ideas for a good peace, as expressed at the dinner, were of breathtaking naïvety. He proposed that two new federated states should be brought into being on either side of Germany, one to consist of Switzerland, Alsace-Lorraine, Luxemburg, Belgium and possibly Holland, the other of 'greater Serbia', Roumania, Poland and perhaps the Baltic countries. Both were to be 'under the suzerainty of the League of Nations'. Without wasting any time on such absurd fantasies, we are surely bound to share his regret that Lloyd George spoke as he did about Germany, even on a private occasion and in the company of friends. Perhaps he was misunderstood, or just carried away on the spur of the moment, since he had never spoken of destroying Germany as a nation, only of removing the Prussian military autocracy. This may have reflected an oversimplified view of the German problem (which Churchill was to carry into the next war[15]), but nevertheless showed an essential moderation, which was, indeed, to be the prevalent feature of his attitude to Germany during the peace conference. Though he certainly felt, and with reason, that Germany should make amends for the immense damage and suffering she had caused, he never consciously sought to destroy the German nation or to punish the German people, as distinct from their rulers, in a spirit of primitive retribution. All the same, just a little of it may have lurked in him below the level of consciousness.

Addison was not present at the dinner in question. He had left Criccieth that day. Two days later, on the 28th, Lloyd George and the rest of the party returned to London.

Hardly was the Prime Minister back than he had to deal with a bizarre and wholly unforeseen crisis, which took all Londoners by surprise and affected them acutely. It also had the potential for developing into a much larger

14. Hankey diary, 26 August 1918.
15. At the Tehran conference in 1943 Churchill proposed that Prussia should be detached from the rest of Germany, regarding Prussia as the source of all German evil – though Hitler was an Austrian, and the resistance to him, such as it was, most marked among Prussian Junkers.

crisis, in which the rest of the country might have been involved. With extreme suddenness most of the metropolitan police failed to report for duty, leaving the streets of the capital, including Downing Street, devoid of the familiar men in blue.

What had happened was technically a mutiny rather than a strike, because the police were a disciplined force serving under oath, like the armed forces. But they were also meant to be part of the civilian community, and were naturally not immune to influences bearing upon the rest of the civilian population, such as trade unionism. Shortly before the war a metropolitan police union was founded, which soon spread to other forces throughout the country, and to the prison officers, to form a national union of police and prison officers (NUPPO). Membership was illegal and, until 1918, very small, but the union published its own journal which circulated clandestinely. By the last year of the war genuine grievances about police pay were boosting support for the union, and at the same time links were established with the London trades council, on which six NUPPO men were chosen to serve.

Meanwhile those at the top of the metropolitan force were becoming increasingly out of touch with the rank and file. The minister directly responsible was the Home Secretary, Sir George Cave, a distinguished Tory lawyer, who was appointed to the job by Lloyd George on the understanding that he would be relieved of it to fill the 'first high judicial vacancy'.[16] (He had been Solicitor-General in the Asquith coalition, and was later Lord Chancellor under Law and Baldwin.) In his dealings with the metropolitan police he depended largely on the commissioner of the force, Sir Edward Henry, who had held the post since 1903, having already served for two years as assistant commissioner: in all, seventeen years at Scotland Yard. He was a decent and in many ways admirable man, but his background in the Indian civil service gave him a tendency to paternalism which was not altogether appropriate in wartime Britain. And his superintendents, most of them chosen by him, failed to keep him informed of what was going on in the union, mainly because they were unaware of it themselves.

Police pay had fallen behind the wages of even unskilled workers, and there was a delay in announcing new rates for 1918, because the deal was to include a pension for widows – on which Henry, to his credit, insisted, but for which the actuarial calculations were not yet ready. Nobody bothered to explain the position to the men, whose sense of grievance naturally rose to new heights. This was reflected in a rapid surge in recruitment to the union, and on 25 August a martyr was created when a popular Hammersmith

16. *RWD*, 10 December 1916.

constable, Tommy Thiel (a Boer War veteran and former Brigade of Guards drill sergeant), was dismissed from the force for his work as a union organizer, about which he was quite unrepentant.

Two days later the union executive drew up an ultimatum, which included a detailed pay claim together with demands for both recognition of the union and the immediate reinstatement of constable Thiel. Non-compliance by midnight on the 29th would result in the withdrawal of labour. The ultimatum reached Scotland Yard during the afternoon of the 28th, where the assistant commissioner, Sir Frederick Wodehouse, was in charge, in the absence of Henry, who was on holiday in Ireland. Wodehouse took the letter straight to the Home Office. Cave was there, but not his permanent under-secretary, Sir Edward Troup, who was also on holiday. His deputy, Sir Ernley Blackwell, was the senior official of the department in London, as he was to remain until Troup's reluctant return late on the 30th. Meanwhile Wodehouse, having been reassured by his superintendents, duly reassured Cave. Only a few policemen would answer the union's call, he said, and their action would provide a good excuse for cracking down on them. The union's letter would be passed at once to the director of public prosecutions. Cave accepted Wodehouse's bland assessment and left at once for his country house in Somerset.[17]

The strike was well organized. Before the ultimatum expired a packed meeting was held at Pimlico Mission Hall with the union's chairman, the determined (if not very clever) constable James Marston, presiding. Headquarters were then established in basement rooms in Cadogan Place, from which throughout the night messengers cycled with orders to the various divisions. With the help of purposeful picketing the stoppage achieved was on a massive scale. Though the response was patchy at first, by early evening on the 30th the *Daily News* estimated that 12,000 men were out. Only the CID and the special constabulary were not involved.

For Lloyd George the 30th would have been a busy day in any case, but it became busier than he could have imagined, and the next day even more so. After a War Cabinet meeting in the morning he had to speak at a lunch at the Carlton Hotel in honour of the American labour leader, Samuel Gompers. He did not refer to the embarrassing fact that industrial action

17. Gerald W. Reynolds and Anthony Judge, *The Night the Police Went on Strike* (1968), chapter 4. Before leaving, Cave authorized a statement to the press that police pay was under active consideration, on the strength of which the *Daily Chronicle* published a rumour that an increase had been granted. Instead of letting the report go unchallenged, an official correction was issued by Scotland Yard, 'one of the major blunders made by Wodehouse during the crisis' (p. 42).

was being taken by the bulk of the capital's police, which must have been all too apparent to the American visitors. (Just about the only policeman they would have seen was the Prime Minister's detective, who as a member of the CID was able to accompany him.) Already he had, of course, turned his mind to the developing crisis, and had sent Smuts to the Home Office to see what could be done about it. Smuts's presence there had a steadying effect on Blackwell whose nerves were becoming frayed, and Smuts helped to arrange with the GOC London District for 600 guardsmen to be posted at important public buildings (apart from the Admiralty, for whose protection Marines were used). He was also prepared to open negotiations with the strike leaders, and Marston came to the Home Office. But when the constable was told that there could be no recognition of the union, he left without seeing Smuts to attend a mass meeting on Tower Hill, where he received the welcome news that the separate City of London force had joined the strike.

At an emergency meeting of the War Cabinet at 5.30 p.m. the crisis was discussed, but Lloyd George could see that he would have to handle it himself, using all his resources of conciliation and guile. Later in the evening he talked to Smuts, Cave (who had hurriedly returned from the country) and the junior minister at the Home Office, William Brace, a Labour man. They all agreed that the men must be got back to work quickly, and that the union must not be recognized. But how was this miracle to be accomplished?

Lloyd George sensed that an intermediary was needed, and that a suitable man for the task might be the Labour MP Charles Duncan, who was chairman of the general workers' union and also honorary president of NUPPO. Brace was sent to fetch him at once to Downing Street, and when he arrived Lloyd George enlisted his help in arranging an early meeting with the strike leaders. They were to come to Downing Street at noon the following day. Duncan told Lloyd George that the strike action had been taken against his advice.[18]

Next morning (Saturday) Whitehall and Downing Street were full of policemen – in plain clothes. They were there to show the union's strength and to give their leaders moral support. The demonstration was on the whole good-natured with plenty of cheering and singing but little sign of anger or menace. Despite the inconvenience caused to the public, ordinary Londoners felt considerable sympathy for the strikers and few showed any hostility towards them. Even soldiers on duty at key points tended to treat the 'mutineers' with geniality. There were cheers for the union leaders as they arrived, particularly for the burly Marston and Tommy Thiel. Duncan

18. Hankey diary, 30 August 1918.

came on his own in a taxi and was also cheered, as was James Carmichael, leader of the London trades council, attending by invitation. At twenty minutes past midday an official car brought Cave and Henry (back at last from Ireland) to Downing Street. They were greeted with ironic cheers rather than boos. The besieging crowd then waited while the crucial meeting took place in the Cabinet room.

It lasted an hour. Lloyd George faced the police representatives across the Cabinet table, with the Home Secretary on his right, the commissioner on his left. On condition that the men would return immediately to work, he offered an attractive pay deal, which he had personally fine-tuned, and agreed that Thiel should be reinstated. But when asked about recognition of the union he gave an answer that was open to more than one interpretation. Though he had no doubt (he said) that the union leaders represented the men's views, the police *in wartime* were in the same position as the armed forces, and in neither case could the government recognize a union. This was taken by the men opposite him to mean that unionization would be permissible when the war ended, and they undertook to commend the settlement to their members. But Lloyd George had not said so explicitly, and had only committed himself to making sure that the police had a representative system for airing and adjusting grievances. As the leaders left he assured Marston that he would always be ready to see them if any similar trouble were to arise in future.

Carmichael was the first to emerge, and he announced to the enthusiastic crowd in the street: 'You have been received by the prime minister of England. Certain proposals have been made . . .' He announced that there would be another mass meeting on Tower Hill that afternoon to consider the government's terms. The crowd then dispersed and made its way to Tower Hill, where the leaders had a heroes' reception. The pay deal was warmly endorsed, and Thiel – introduced as 'Still one of us, Constable Tommy Thiel' – was cheered with fervour. But in reply to questions about recognition Carmichael was as equivocal as Lloyd George:

the prime minister, when he received your executive, gave you that recognition (loud cheers). Your executive, with the Home Office, are going to have meetings in order to draw up on your behalf the rules to apply to *an authorised organization* (cheers) . . . And during the war this authorised organization which *is framed on* your present union in concession to your demands, will deal with every grievance you have got.[19]

19. Reynolds and Judge, *The Night the Police Went on Strike*, pp. 70–71; my italics.

This was good enough for the overwhelming majority. The deal was accepted on a show of hands and the strike was at an end.

But at Downing Street there was still much for Lloyd George to do to make his achievement stick. Cave, as the minister responsible for the metropolitan police, offered to resign, but Lloyd George was in no mood for reconstructing the government at such a moment and would not let him go. Yet it was necessary for a head to roll, and the Prime Minister decided that it had to be Henry's. The commissioner had given good service according to his lights, but had stayed too long and lost control of his force. He was retired with the immediate award of a baronetcy, and Cave had the unpleasant task of communicating the decision to him. The Home Secretary was also authorized to make a statement to the press clarifying the position about recognition of the police union:

The prime minister said to the deputation of policemen who saw him that he could not in wartime sanction recognition . . . He pointed out that the trouble in Russia had to a great extent arisen from the existence of a union or a committee among the soldiers. He thought the police were a semi-military force, and . . . to a great extent the same conditions applied to them . . . [He] added that he thought there should be machinery under which the police force could bring before the police authorities any grievances which they had, as to their conditions of service. Subject to this, they should have no kind of power to interfere with the discipline of the force . . . Of course, that is quite a different thing from a union in the ordinary sense.

Asked by a reporter if the Prime Minister had not, in effect, recognized the union by receiving all its officers, Cave replied:

The prime minister said he would receive the men as policemen. He could not receive them as the executive of the union . . . Mr. Duncan was present to introduce them as a Member of Parliament.

The potentially awkward question of Carmichael's status at the meeting was not raised.[20]

It was essential for Lloyd George to find the right man to replace Henry, and his choice fell upon the Adjutant-General to the forces, Sir Nevil Macready. The selection might be risky, but he sensed that no merely competent, safe man would be equal to the challenge of the post. Someone

---

20. Cave resented the criticism of the Home Office that then followed the strike and told Crawford that his treatment had been 'damnable' (Crawford diary, 12 September 1918).

combining up-to-date practical ability with outstanding qualities of leadership was needed, and such qualities could never be free from risk.

Macready's background was certainly not that of the average army officer. His father was the famous actor-manager William Charles Macready, who married for the second time (at the age of sixty-seven) a granddaughter of the portrait painter Sir William Beechey. Nevil, the only child of this marriage, was himself a talented singer and amateur actor, who could probably have done as well on the stage as in the army. As it was, his thespian genes were of some value to him in the career that he did choose. Along with his soldierly attributes he was a man of wit and eloquence, who had the capacity to sway an audience and to reinforce his authority with calculated bluff. He had experience of military intervention in support of the civil power at Tonypandy in November 1910 – when he commanded a force sent to help the police to stop looting and window-breaking in the town, during a mining dispute in the Rhondda valley[21] – and during the past twenty-four hours he had been working with Smuts and the Home Office in the deployment of troops to guard public buildings. He was already well known to Lloyd George, having been Adjutant-General since 1916. As such he was a member of the War Office establishment with which the Prime Minister often clashed. All the same, Lloyd George had observed the General's personal strengths, and during the early afternoon of the 31st he asked Milner to telephone him at the War Office with the request that he assume the commissionership. Macready refused outright, and at 5 p.m. Lloyd George summoned him to Downing Street, where it took almost twice as long to persuade him to accept as it had taken to settle with the policemen. In Macready's own words:

In the Cabinet room were the Prime Minister, Lord Milner, Sir G. Cave . . . and a few more Cabinet Ministers. I took a chair opposite Mr. Lloyd George and then the fun began. For close on two hours I resisted the pressure . . . I suggested other men, younger and equally fit for the post . . . to which the Prime Minister replied that it was necessary to have someone in whom the public would have confidence. The obvious retort on my part was that . . . the police, having digested all the nonsense that had appeared in the Press [not least about Tonypandy], would at once jump to the conclusion that I had been selected in order to dragoon them into submission. At last the Prime Minister expressed the opinion that it was of national importance that I should take the post. I asked him if he really meant that, and had not said it as

21. The operation was conducted by the then Home Secretary, Churchill, and it came to be believed that civilians were killed by the troops – a myth which stuck to Churchill and, to a lesser extent, Macready.

an extra bit of gratifying whitewash. He said he did, on which of course I had nothing further to say, except that I would do my best to see the business through. The assent of the King was obtained through the telephone, and I left Downing Street in a very sad frame of mind about 7 p.m.[22]

Macready took over from Henry on 3 September and, though he held the post of commissioner for only a year and a half (before moving to an even more difficult assignment in Ireland), his impact upon the metropolitan force, and policing nationally, was remarkable. He introduced women police and improved relations with the press, as part of a general programme of modernization. While firmly refusing to recognize the union, he set up machinery for representing the men at all levels and enabling valid grievances to be promptly met. The union continued to organize, but its leaders were no match for Macready. In June 1919 he addressed a meeting of 3,000 police at Queen's Hall, and won overwhelming support for his methods. When, nevertheless, the union called a nation-wide strike in August, it was a complete failure, only 5 per cent of the police answering the call. They were then dismissed and there was no further trouble.

If Lloyd George had not acted as swiftly as he did, or with such a sure touch, the metropolitan police strike of August 1918 might have escalated out of control, with incalculable consequences. The rapid growth of the union, and its ever-closer links with trade union militants like Carmichael, posed a real danger to the state; and there was also a potential threat to discipline in the armed forces. The Prime Minister's deal with the strike leaders, mixing substantial concessions with firmness disguised in a necessarily equivocal formula, averted grave disaster, and his appointment of Macready proved to be a master-stroke.

Curiously, he makes no reference at all in his war memoirs to an episode in which his part was so decisive and providential. At the time he could hardly believe that such a crisis had been allowed to develop. When Riddell congratulated him on settling the strike, he said: 'The whole thing has been disgracefully mismanaged. The terms granted by me had been agreed upon for some time past, but the men had never been told.' This was essentially fair comment. If, as Riddell himself recalls, the occupants of Downing Street felt that they were 'face to face with a revolution', it may have been a moment that Lloyd George preferred to forget in later years.[23]

*

22. C. F. N. Macready, *Annals of an Active Life* (2 vols., 1924), vol. i, pp. 302–3.
23. *RWD*, August 1918.

Clemenceau's dissatisfaction with the number of divisions in the BEF was expressed again in a long message to Lloyd George which reached him at Criccieth. Since the British population of military age was 'very much greater' than the French and 'less tried by war losses', it seemed to Clemenceau that the United Kingdom should be able to maintain fifty divisions on the Continent without prejudice to its maritime effort or other 'very useful contributions towards general requirements of the Entente'. But the motive for his appeal seemed to have changed from earlier in the year, when the paramount question was how to hold the Germans. Now he was looking to the future and the need for the European Allies to avoid undue dependence on the United States. 'No one more than I', he said, 'appreciates the value of American assistance. But our old Europe, which engaged in war without counting on that help, cannot consider "passing the hand" to its trans-Atlantic Allies for completion of the military task which will found a new Europe.'

Lloyd George replied the day he settled the police strike. (He worked on war business before the union leaders arrived at noon.) Noting that Clemenceau was asking for fifty British divisions on the Continent in addition to the ten from the Dominions, he insisted that this was quite out of the question. Agreeing, by implication, with Clemenceau's view that the European Allies should be foremost in the defeat of Germany, he used it to justify the existing balance of effort:

The *reserves* [my italics] of the Allied army are in America. If we wait for the United States to manufacture the equipment, the guns and the munitions [needed by the American forces], and the shipping in which they are to be transported, the British and French Armies will be worn down before the American Army can reach Europe in sufficient numbers to enable the Allies to take the offensive in decisive strength.

In any case, he and his fellow prime ministers had been making 'a careful examination of the manpower resources of the British Empire' and had 'reluctantly come to the conclusion' that if the Empire were to 'prosecute the war with the utmost vigour' it could not 'call up anything like the same number of recruits in 1919 as . . . in 1918'.

He was fully conscious of the 'sufferings' of the French people, 'owing to their geographical position', and told Clemenceau (truthfully) that he often reminded audiences at home that British sufferings had 'not been nearly so great'. But it was obvious that France, compared with Britain, was 'an agricultural rather than a maritime and manufacturing country'. Moreover, a large part of her industrialized territory was occupied by the enemy. These facts had their own logic in determining war priorities. He only wished it were possible 'to equalise the sacrifice' between their two countries. But 'unfortunately' it was not possible.[24]

Though unpersuaded, Clemenceau had no choice but to accept Lloyd George's decision, conveyed on behalf of his Dominion colleagues as well as himself. But the French premier must have been uncomfortably aware that more was involved than a disagreement on *war* priorities. There was also, he must have felt, a growing divergence between France's interests and those of the British Empire, which was bound to have a serious bearing on the priorities of peace.

He was more successful on another issue, of lesser though more immediate import. On 4 September he sent General Louis Guillaumat, military governor of Paris, to talk to Lloyd George about launching an offensive against the Bulgarians at an early date. Guillaumat had been the Allied commander after Sarrail at Salonica, where he had recently been replaced by Franchet d'Esperey. He remained strongly committed to the idea of a Balkan offensive, which had been authorized in principle by the SWC at the beginning of August. Three days after the meeting at Versailles Clemenceau had sent Lloyd George Franchet d'Esperey's plan of campaign,[25] and now he was eager to obtain the Prime Minister's assent to its implementation in the near future. Clemenceau's advocacy, reinforced by Guillaumat's, proved effective. Despite opposition from the CIGS Lloyd George agreed to the proposal, with consequences that will be described in the next chapter.

On 11 September Lloyd George travelled to Manchester, accompanied by Margaret and their daughters, Olwen and Megan. The plan was that he would spend several days of varied activity in the north, after a speech in Manchester which would set the tone for a possible autumn election. Fate, however, ordained that his stay would be much longer than intended, entirely in Manchester and largely inactive.

On arrival the Lloyd Georges were met by the Lord Mayor, Sir Alexander Porter, whose guests they were to be in the palatial neo-Gothic Town Hall. They drove there in an open carriage through cheering crowds. At the Town Hall Lloyd George received addresses of welcome from leaders of the local Syrian, Armenian and Jewish communities, to each of which he made a suitable reply. The following morning he drove, again through densely crowded streets, to the Hippodrome, where he was to receive the freedom

24. Clemenceau to DLG, message sent through British embassy in Paris 17 August 1918, received by Lloyd George next day; DLG to Clemenceau, 31 August 1918.
25. Clemenceau to DLG, 6 August 1918, marked '*rigoureusement* secret'.

of his native city in the presence of 3,000 people, including many local MPs and mayors, and other representative men and women. He responded with an eagerly awaited speech lasting an hour and a half, which began with a reference to his own special connection with the city, and acknowledgement of its world-wide renown:

It is over half a century ago that I became a citizen of Manchester. I subsequently lost that privilege, through circumstances over which I had no control,[26] but I am deeply grateful – I am proud – that the lord mayor and corporation of Manchester, in the name of the citizens of Manchester, have restored to me my lost citizenship in no mean city, a city famed through the world for its endeavours . . . in commerce, in industry, in politics, in art . . . Manchester put forward new ideas in the past, and I know she will show the same courage in the future.

He spoke then of the progress of the war. The news was 'distinctly good', and he meant 'really good, not merely good in appearance'. He was at pains to emphasize his own share in the favourable turn of events, with a sly dig at his opponents. When the Germans attacked in March, the BEF had 'considerable reserves':

The Germans did not know it. And I have . . . expressed my gratitude to the newspapers which criticised the government on the ground that we had no reserves for so skilfully misleading the enemy. We . . . took very good care not to contradict them. As a matter of fact we have poured in hundreds of thousands of very fine troops since March 21, and the Germans never expected them in the least. They know now that they are there. (Cheers.)

Recent Allied victories were due above all, he suggested, to unity of command. 'It is not that one general is better than another, but that one general is better than two. (Laughter.)' He heaped praise on Foch, and took credit for 'the troublous part' he himself took in securing the appointment of a supreme commander. He did not mention the name of Haig.

'Nothing but heart failure', he said, could now prevent the Allies from winning the war, though he could not predict when final victory would come. Meanwhile he was concerned that when it came it should not be

26. When Lloyd George was born (on 17 January 1863) his father was holding a temporary headmastership in Manchester and living in a small (two-up, two-down) house, 5 New York Place, Chorlton-upon-Medlock. The house no longer exists, but before its demolition it was painted by L. S. Lowry. A plaque recording Lloyd George's birth now adorns the wall of a nearby council house.

wasted, and that the uniquely destructive war they had been living through should be the last in human history. He warned against illusions:

> I want to say to those who have the same horror of war that I have, who would like to see any rational means of bringing this madness to an end, do not . . . be misled into the belief that the establishment of a League of Nations without power will in itself secure the world against that catastrophe . . . I am for a League of Nations. In fact, the League of Nations has begun. The British empire is a League of Nations. The Allied nations who are fighting the battle of international right are all a League of Nations.

But, he indicated, any League of Nations would be a mockery without the means to combat 'brute force'.

A Germany 'freed from military domination' should be welcome to join, and the only sure foundation of security in the future would be a just peace: 'It must be a peace that will lend itself to the common sense and conscience of the nation as a whole. It must not be dictated by extreme men on either side . . . we must not arm Germany with a real wrong.' This was a far cry from the outburst that had somewhat shocked Hankey at Criccieth, but more in accordance with the views on Germany that Lloyd George had often expressed. (Unfortunately the issue was to prove one of supreme complexity, in which differing perceptions of justice were impossible to reconcile.) He turned to the lessons of the war for British society, and singled out the health of the people, the theme of his recent discussions with Addison, Dawson and others in Wales. Britain had used its human material 'prodigally, foolishly, cruelly', as the war had revealed:

> I asked the Minister of National Service how many more we could have put into the fighting ranks if the health of the country had been properly looked after. I staggered at the reply. It was a considered reply, and it was 'At least one million'[27] . . . And the vigour and strength of the workers of this country have been unsatisfactory even in pursuits where all conditions are favourable to the development of a fine physique. The results in agriculture have been almost as disappointing as in any other industry . . . I solemnly warn my fellow-countrymen that you cannot maintain an A1 Empire with a C3 population. (Cheers.)

---

27. By coincidence, one million was mentioned by Clemenceau to Lloyd George in their recent correspondence as the very figure by which recruitment for service at the front could be increased without prejudice to other necessary war work. Lloyd George did not choose to reply that one million Britons were physically unfit to fight.

Health was 'the secret of national efficiency and national recuperation'. The whole question had to be given the highest priority, and one particularly urgent aspect of it was housing.[28] While touching on other spheres of social reform, he mentioned 'Mr. Fisher's great bill' and said that an educated man was 'a better worker, a more formidable warrior and a better citizen'.

Moving towards a typical peroration he said he had found in his conversations with people 'of all ranks' since the war 'one sentiment among them all' – that the things that were tolerated before the war could be tolerated no longer:

There has been a community of sacrifice. The national conscience has been stirred in a way which is unparalleled in the history of this country, and the nation when the war is over will expect [us to] put right the wrongs, inequalities and stupidities from which millions have suffered and the community has suffered.

Though the word 'election' never passed his lips, he gave a clear hint that his appeal to the country would be as a coalition leader. He referred to 'sheds where the various party machines have rusted', implying that they should be left to rust away. Then he ended with a passage beginning 'In my Welsh home we have an infallible method of ascertaining when a storm is coming', which led somehow to a word-picture of 'settled weather for the great harvest'.[29]

Fisher, who was on the platform for the speech, recorded that Lloyd George was 'long' and 'not in his best form'.[30] Reading the speech now, many would be inclined to agree. But at the time it seems to have made a powerful impact. After delivering it, he attended a civic lunch at the Midland Hotel, where he made a shorter speech, praising the exploits of the Manchester regiment and other Lancashire units. During the afternoon he attended a gathering of the local Welsh community, to whom he spoke in Welsh. He would no doubt have felt obliged to make yet another speech in the evening, at a dinner at the Reform Club. But he felt too ill to go and took to his bed in the Town Hall. His illness was diagnosed as influenza, which must have been coming over him throughout the day.

For the next nine days the Town Hall of Manchester was his hospital. A programme planned to follow the Manchester speech, in which he would

28. The Boer War had already drawn attention to the unhealthy state of the British working class, and had given rise to a cult of national efficiency transcending party. The First World War produced further shocking evidence, enabling Lloyd George to preach the need for more extensive social reform, building upon his pre-war welfare legislation.
29. Speech reported in *The Times*, 13 September 1918.   30. Fisher diary, 12 September 1918.

have received other freedoms (for instance, of Salford and Blackpool) and made more speeches, had to be cancelled. He was under the professional care of the eminent Manchester ENT specialist, Sir William Milligan. Margaret Lloyd George stayed on, as did Olwen and Megan, though they both became ill themselves with 'colds'. Bulletins issued to the press were brief and made no suggestion that the Prime Minister was in any danger, no doubt because the truth would have been alarming to the British public and encouraging to the enemy. But Hankey (whom Lloyd George had sent on leave on 5 September) noted afterwards that he had been 'very seriously ill' and that his valet, Newnham, had said it was 'touch and go'.[31]

Lloyd George's bedroom in the Town Hall was at the front of the building, and he afterwards told Riddell that he could see from it the statue of John Bright 'dripping with constant rain'. When his fever subsided and he was allowed to get out of bed, he was visited by C. P. Scott and congratulated a private from the Manchester regiment who came to the Town Hall to be presented with the Military Medal.

On 21 September he returned to London, but still wearing a respirator and accompanied by Milligan as well as by Megan, Sutherland and the chief whip, Guest. Margaret and Olwen left for Criccieth. On arrival at Euston Lloyd George was met by J. T. Davies and driven to Downing Street. But he did not linger there or preside over any meeting of the War Cabinet. He went straight to Danny Park for a working convalescence, and from there wrote to Margaret a few days later: 'I am crawling upward but have not yet recovered strength. Unfortunately – or fortunately – things are moving so rapidly I cannot keep off affairs of State. Someone here every day.' Even at the end of the month he cancelled public meetings for a few more days 'under medical advice', and when on 4 October he travelled to France Milligan went with him. Early that morning he wrote from his bed to Margaret:

I am off by the 8 train from Charing X. Sir William Milligan insists on accompanying me. My temperature is still very low & my pulse too feeble . . .

I had my first Cabinet yesterday & it tired me so that I am not yet fit for much work. It is a pity that the Paris journey could not be put off until next week . . . I propose staying at Versailles . . . more reposeful than a Paris hotel.[32]

31. Hankey diary, 22 September 1918; Hankey to Lady Hankey, same date. Lloyd George's illness had the serendipitous effect of prolonging the overworked War Cabinet secretary's leave.
32. Reports in *The Times*; *RWD*, 21 September 1918; Scott diary, 18 September 1918; DLG to MLG, 27 September and 4 October 1918 (the first letter, from Danny, completed by Megan). Margaret seems to have caught the flu but did not tell him, because on 3 October he wrote that

Lloyd George combined enormous vitality with a strong streak of hypochondria, for which allowance must always be made. He hated illness, in himself and others, and was never one to make light of it. All the same, the evidence leaves little room for doubt that his medical experience in the latter half of September 1918 was one of the worst of his life. He seems to have been very acutely, perhaps critically, ill at a time of mounting crisis in the world, when he needed to be in full vigour to tackle a situation that took him by surprise.

---

he was distressed to read of her illness in the paper. Perhaps she did write and the letter did not reach him.

Milligan was a good Liberal as well as a good doctor. In 1922 he stood unsuccessfully for Parliament.

32

Decisive Success in the West

Decisive success in the West – Sideshows come good –
At Danny Park

While Lloyd George was lying, feverish and frustrated, in the Town Hall at Manchester, and during the period of shaky convalescence that followed, enormous events were unfolding on the battlefields which forced him to revise his assumptions about the war's likely duration, and which brought him, much sooner than expected, to grips with the daunting political problems of its imminent conclusion and aftermath. When he left for Criccieth in mid-August he knew from the victory of Amiens that the initiative in the West had passed to the Allies, and that, to judge from the toll of prisoners alone, the Germans must be seriously demoralized. But the British and French forces had recovered from similar disasters earlier in the year, and he still did not believe that the mighty German army could be comprehensively defeated before 1919. He was as concerned as ever to husband British strength in the West until the Americans were ready to play their full part there, and as eager as ever to exploit opportunities in other theatres which would weaken Germany, at relatively low cost, while also promoting British Imperial interests.

The course of events on the Western front was, however, largely out of his hands. Even the previous autumn Haig had got his way, and now he was in a much stronger position, partly for the ironical reason that the unity of command for which Lloyd George rightly claimed credit was working in his favour. He and Foch were in basic agreement about strategy, and if they disagreed on any particular issue Haig had shown that he was likely to emerge the winner. He was, in reality, free to make and carry out his own plans, though the existence of a generalissimo gave the impression that he was acting under orders. Any criticism of the strategic use of the BEF had to be directed at Foch rather than at him. Fortunately he had learnt important lessons since the year before, and the failure of Ludendorff's offensive, together with the gathering strength of the Americans (not to mention flu and the effects of the blockade), had at last palpably reduced the German army's will to resist. If in 1917 Haig's assessment of this factor had been wrong when Lloyd George's was right, a year later it was the other way round.

In the final decisive year of the war the BEF made the strongest showing on the Allied side, though it faced the largest number of German divisions.[1] During the five weeks following the Amiens victory three of Haig's armies (the First under Horne, the Third under Byng and the Fourth under Rawlinson) advanced an average of fourteen miles, over terrain ravaged in previous fighting, until they reached the edge of the Hindenburg defences, begun when the Germans made their tactical withdrawal in the spring of 1917 and since greatly elaborated. In the process Albert, Bapaume and Peronne were among the places retaken, the last named after the capture by a small force of Australians of the Mont Saint-Quentin, one of the war's outstanding exploits. Casualties in the advance were heavy on both sides, but the German figure, anyway substantially larger than the British, included 46,000 prisoners.

Meanwhile, in mid-September Pershing had conducted the first big all-American operation, when he eliminated the Saint-Mihiel salient south of Verdun. It had always been his wish that the independent American army should operate on the extreme right of the Allied line, with its own hospitals, training areas and communications to the French Atlantic ports. It also suited him to be as far removed as possible from the British. Yet his freedom of action was, in practice, severely limited, because he depended upon the French and British for tanks, guns and planes. He had intended his Saint-Mihiel attack to be far more ambitious than Foch eventually allowed it to be. In Pershing's original conception, his army would not only reduce the salient, but would then break through the German line beyond it, known as the *Michel Stellung*, and advance towards Metz. In so doing it would pose an immediate threat to the iron and coal regions of Briey and the Saar, and with luck even turn the whole German position from the South, forcing abandonment of the Hindenburg line.

Pershing's grand design ceased to appeal to Foch once he was convinced that the war could be ended in 1918 by a pincer movement against the bulk of the German army in the centre of the front. Haig was the man who convinced him, proposing that the BEF should make an assault on the Hindenburg defences, on condition that there would be a simultaneous Franco-American offensive in the Meuse–Argonne area. Foch's strategy of 'tout le monde à la bataille' would be given a convergent character, instead of taking the form of opportunistic pressure all along the line, in the hope that somewhere or other the Germans might crack. After a furious confrontation with the generalissimo, Pershing deferred to him to the extent

---

1. This did not, however, mean that it was outnumbered, because the German divisions were so far below strength.

of agreeing to stop the Saint-Mihiel attack when the salient was eliminated, and then to partake in a Franco-American attack north-westwards towards Sedan and Mezières. But he insisted on doing so in the form of an all-American force, the First US Army, consisting partly of troops transferred from Saint-Mihiel and partly of units without, as yet, any battle experience.

Within the limits imposed by Foch the Saint-Mihiel operation was an outstanding success. It was independent in the sense that it was carried out largely by American troops, and that the French divisions assigned to support it were placed under Pershing's command. But he was entirely dependent upon the Allies for the 3,000 guns whose four-hour bombardment preceded the attack; also for the 1,400 planes and 300 tanks that were put at his disposal.[2] The guns opened fire at 1 a.m. on 12 September, and by the end of the following day Pershing's men had reached the *Michel Stellung*, where to their frustration they were compelled to stop. They had taken 16,000 prisoners and 450 guns, and had liberated 200 square miles of French territory. Their own casualties amounted to 8,000.

Foch's plan then required Pershing to switch in no more than a fortnight from Saint-Mihiel to the Meuse–Argonne area sixty miles away. He chose to attack in the Argonne forest, to the right of the French Fourth Army, which proved to be a bad choice. It was hard enough to re-form his First Army on a new front in such a short time, but he compounded his difficulties by giving his units over-ambitious objectives, and by failing to anticipate that the Germans would be able to organize effective defence in depth in the forest. Altogether, the Franco-American offensive failed in its purpose of assisting and complementing Haig's assault on the Hindenburg line further north. It drew no German reserves from Haig's front, and, despite being opposed by fewer than half as many enemy divisions, achieved no comparable success.[3] Indeed, it made slow and painful progress, and in the end the breaching of the Hindenburg line owed virtually nothing to the convergent operation devised by Foch under Haig's influence.

The question has to be asked: was Pershing's aborted plan for exploiting

2. Pershing argued that this dependence upon the Allies for heavy arms was due solely to the Allies' own request for concentration upon the shipment of American infantry and machine-guns during the spring crisis. But in fact it was due quite as much to 'breakdowns in American industrial mobilisation' (David R. Woodward, *Trial by Friendship: Anglo-American Relations, 1917–1918* (1993), p. 201).

3. The Germans had 57 divisions against Haig's 42, whereas in the Meuse–Argonne only 20 German divisions faced 31 French and 15 American. In view of the reduced strength of German divisions Haig had numerical superiority, but Pershing and Gouraud (Fourth Army) had a superiority of six to one, granted the size of American divisions.

success at Saint-Mihiel in truth the better option? Might his army have been able to break through eastwards, perhaps capturing Metz and cutting the lateral railway from there to Thionville and Longuyon? If so, he would surely have threatened the enemy's whole position in the West more acutely than the Meuse–Argonne offensive ever did, and thus – together with Haig's breach of the Hindenburg line, soon to be described – possibly have contributed to a still earlier ending of the war. Opinions on the issue are divided. One of Pershing's own corps commanders is on record as a sceptic: 'The possibility of taking Metz and the rest of it, had the battle been fought on the original plan, existed . . . only on the supposition that our army was a well-oiled, fully coordinated machine, which it was not as yet.'[4] On the other hand, the German army group commander in the area, General Max von Gallwitz, said later that 'a successful attack launched against the *Michel Stellung* would have been more important than the successes gained along the Meuse and in the Argonne', and that 'an American advance to Longuyon would have been a blow which [his defensive front] could not have borne'.[5] His verdict might be regarded as decisive, but only on the assumption that American logistics would have been equal to the challenge.

The Germans were taken by surprise at Saint-Mihiel, and were already under orders to withdraw from the salient when the Americans attacked. The *Michel Stellung* was reached with remarkable speed, while the enemy was still making desperate efforts to improve its strength. Momentum and morale both favoured the Americans, and it seems likely that, if they had immediately pursued their attack, they would have broken through. As for the problems of transport, supply and staff work that would then have arisen, they could hardly have been as bad as those they had to face in switching from Saint-Mihiel to the Argonne. On the whole the case for Pershing's plan appears stronger than for the Haig–Foch alternative to which he was obliged to conform.

Incidentally, two names that were to become illustrious in the next war first figure at this time. Colonel George C. Patton was commanding the tanks at Saint-Mihiel, and it is tempting to think that he might have anticipated his later feats of armoured mobility had the Americans been free to operate beyond the *Michel Stellung* (though in fact even he could not have hoped to move a great distance with the tanks of 1918, which tended to break down at an early stage). The other name that stands out is that of Captain George

---

4. Woodward, *Trial by Friendship*, p. 202 (quoting General Hunter Liggett, *A. E. F.: Ten Years Ago in France*).
5. Basil Liddell Hart, *Foch, the Man of Orleans* (1931), p. 362.

C. Marshall, whose talents as a staff officer were tested, and not found wanting, in organizing the hasty transfer of troops and vehicles from Saint-Mihiel to the Argonne. The process was bound to be rather chaotic, but without him it would not have occurred at all.[6]

The American operation in the Argonne began on 26 September, and the following day Haig launched his attack on the Hindenburg line, the prospect of which had caused understandable misgivings in London. On 29 August he had received a 'personal' telegram from the CIGS: 'Just a word of caution in regard to incurring heavy losses in attacks on Hindenburg Line as opposed to losses when driving the enemy back to that line. I do not mean to say that you have incurred such losses, but I know the War Cabinet would become anxious if we received heavy punishment in attacking the Hindenburg Line, without success.' On this Haig comments in his diary:

It is impossible for a CIGS to send a telegram of this nature to a C. in C. . . . as a 'personal' one. The Cabinet are ready to meddle and interfere in my plans in an underhand way, but do not dare openly to say that they mean to take the responsibility for any failure though ready to take credit for every success! The object of this telegram is, no doubt, to save the Prime Minister in case of any failure. So I read it to mean that I can attack the Hindenburg Line if I think it right to do so. The CIGS and the War Cabinet already know that my arrangements are being made to that end. If any attack is successful, I will remain on as C. in C. If we fail, or our losses are excessive, I can hope for no mercy![7]

Lloyd George, in his memoirs, denies any knowledge of Wilson's telegram, and emphasizes his public tributes at the time to Haig's victory at Amiens. He protests too much. Whether or not the telegram was sent at his instigation, it certainly expressed his sentiments. Though he believed that the Germans had to be properly defeated in the West, he was also desperately concerned to limit the cost in British lives. His idea was that in the final stages of a war which he still did not expect to end in 1918 the Americans should do most of the fighting and make the largest sacrifice. Wilson may have sent the warning telegram on his own initiative, but if so he sent it in the knowledge that it faithfully reflected the War Cabinet's anxiety. He may also have

6. Marshall was already recognized in the AEF as one of the very few men who were prepared to stand up to Pershing.

The American First Army, incorporating new units as well as troops from Saint-Mihiel, fought in the Argonne. The troops left to hold the Saint-Mihiel salient, supplemented by others, became in mid-October the Second Army. Pershing assumed overall command of both.

7. Haig diary, 29 August 1918.

worded it in such a way as to suggest that his own sympathies were with the Field-Marshal. To that extent Lloyd George may have been justified in reading into it a desire on Wilson's part 'to ingratiate himself with the commander-in-chief, who distrusted him through and through'. But the retrospective attempt by Lloyd George to dissociate himself altogether from the view of the forthcoming operation conveyed in the telegram does not carry conviction.[8] In fairness one should add that Haig's misjudgements in the past, especially in the quite recent past – the latter part of 1917 – made it only natural that the Prime Minister and his colleagues should feel uneasiness about a plan to attack the Germans at their strongest point. And they were right to expect very heavy casualties. Milner spent ten days in France shortly before the attack, and on his return told the CIGS that Haig was 'ridiculously optimistic', though he admitted that other generals shared their commander's optimism. Milner himself feared that Haig was about to 'embark on another Passchendaele'.[9]

Events were very soon to prove him wrong. On 27 September Haig's First and Third Armies (Horne and Byng) attacked towards Cambrai, without tanks but with powerful artillery support. In this operation the Canadians managed to get across the Canal du Nord, forming a breach through which others could pass. By the end of the following day the British had advanced six miles on a twelve-mile front, beyond the furthest point reached the previous November, though the Germans were still holding out in Cambrai itself. On 29 September Rawlinson's Fourth Army struck against the toughest part of the Hindenburg line, mainly consisting of a stretch of the Saint-Quentin canal heavily fortified and with steep banks. This attack was preceded by a tremendous bombardment in which mustard gas was used for the first time. One hundred and eighty tanks were also available in support of the infantry. The canal was crossed and the German line penetrated to a depth of three and a half miles, but not by Monash's élite Australians or the two American divisions fighting under Rawlinson's command.[10] The heroes of the hour

8. WM, pp. 3403–4.
9. Wilson diary, 23 September 1918. Milner doubted the possibility of a comprehensive defeat of the German army in the West, and was in any case more concerned about Britain's Imperial interests than about changes to the map of Europe. Lloyd George, while sharing Milner's suspicion of Haig, and his Imperial concerns, did believe in total victory and was committed to war aims that had far-reaching implications for Europe's future. This difference of outlook on vital aspects of strategy and policy no doubt contributed to the Prime Minister's relative loss of confidence in Milner during the latter part of 1918.
10. After the Amiens offensive, in which only one American regiment took an active part, Pershing tried to reclaim all the five US divisions training in the BEF's sector. But in response to Haig's protests only three were moved, two remaining for the Hindenburg line operation.

were troops of an unglamorous British unit, the 46th (North Midland) division, which had been living under the shadow of supposed failure on the first day of the Somme in 1916. These men now carried out one of the most remarkable exploits of the war, overrunning German trenches on the near side of the waterway before swimming across it and storming the German defences on the far side. They were helped by early morning fog and an artillery barrage sustained until the last moment. They also had life-belts, collapsible boats, scaling ladders and other special equipment. But nothing can detract from the splendour of their achievement.

Within a fortnight little was left of the Hindenburg defences. By 5 October the Fourth Army alone had taken 15,000 prisoners. Four days later Cambrai fell. Haig's army had reached open country, and the Germans had no good defensive line to fall back on short of the Meuse.

While this triumphant breakthrough was being achieved in the centre of the front, offensive operations were proceeding all the way northward to the Channel, involving the Belgian army and the BEF's Second and Fifth Armies (Plumer and Birdwood). By the end of September two symbolic landmarks lost in the spring had changed hands for the last time, when Messines ridge was recaptured by Plumer and Passchendaele ridge fell to the Belgians. Soon the Germans had abandoned the whole of the Belgian coast and much of French Flanders. Lille was liberated and the River Lys was crossed.

In early September Churchill discussed with Lloyd George the BEF's newfound ability to win and gave four causes for it, listing them in what, apparently, he considered their order of importance: '(1) tanks, (2) deterioration of German Army, (3) valour of British Army, and (4) fighting on a wide battle-line.' Lloyd George argued that the change was due above all to unity of command and Foch's strategy.[11] It was perhaps as predictable for him to say this as it was for Churchill to give pride of place to tanks. Both men were favouring their own creations, or at any rate causes with which they were most notably associated. But what should we think of Churchill's list and Lloyd George's counter-claim? There can hardly be any argument about items 2 and 3 in the list. Most people would argue that the BEF's stamina should rate first, along with the German army's demoralization, to which it contributed. Unity of command was vital psychologically in the spring crisis of 1918, but Foch's strategy was of less importance, and, as we have seen, was besides at least as much Haig's as his own. On the technical side the tank was certainly a significant innovation, and the Germans

11. *RWD*, entry covering 4, 5 and 6 September 1918.

suffered from not having it. All the same, it counted for much less in the First World War than in the Second. It was slower-moving and far more subject to breakdown. (Of the tanks used in Rawlinson's attack on the Hindenburg line more than half were soon out of action.) A far more telling technical factor in the BEF was, by 1918, the artillery. British gunnery was so advanced and sophisticated that the Amiens offensive opened, 'despite poor visibility, with British shells falling with deadly precision upon the enemy's carefully concealed artillery pieces'.

Yet the true explanation of British technical superiority in the famous Hundred Days of 1918 was that all arms were well co-ordinated. 'Infantry, artillery, machine-guns, tanks, aircraft and wireless telegraphy all functioned as parts of a single unit. As a result of meticulous planning, each component in the offensive was integrated with, and provided maximum support for, every other component. [This] was the great technical achievement of these climactic battles.'[12] Human and material factors at last came together to form a war-winning combination. Without it, 'fighting on a wide battle-line' would have been of little more use than fighting in limited sectors.

Lloyd George received good news of the war during his period of sickness and isolation in Manchester Town Hall. The day of his speech in the city and his subsequent collapse was also the day of the American attack at Saint-Mihiel, of which he heard while his fever was at its height. But the best news came shortly afterwards, and not from the Western front. In mid-September the Salonica bridgehead finally justified its existence, becoming the scene of a swift and decisive Allied attack. And within a few days Allenby launched his long-delayed offensive to knock Turkey out of the war.

After Lloyd George had given his blessing to Franchet d'Esperey's Salonica plan early in the month, 'Desperate Frankie' (as the British nicknamed him) did not waste any time. He threw his army into action against the Bulgarians on 14 September. It was a remarkably variegated force, in which the French and British elements were combined with Greeks, Serbs and other southern Slavs, a Yugoslav division providing a foretaste of the Balkan future. Morale among the Bulgarians was low. Their country had been brought into the war on the Central Powers' side in 1915, and had helped them to overrun Serbia. The Bulgarian King Ferdinand, who was in any case German by birth and sympathy, calculated that the Allies would lose the war and that

12. Trevor Wilson, *The Myriad Faces of War: Britain and the Great War, 1914–1918* (1986), p. 586.

Bulgaria had a better chance, by opposing them, of regaining territory lost in the second Balkan war. In September 1917, when Roumania unwisely declared war on Austria-Hungary, and Germany countered by declaring war on Roumania, Bulgaria joined in and contributed to Roumania's defeat. At that time the Allied army at Salonica was too weak and uncoordinated to affect the issue. But a year later everything had changed. The Central Powers were losing, Allied morale was rising, and Ferdinand's subjects could see that he had miscalculated. At Salonica, the Greeks and southern Slavs, in particular, were fired with ambition and ready for action.

Franchet d'Esperey was an imaginative strategist, with the advantage of knowing the terrain of his new command well from travels in the area before the war. He decided to deliver his main attack on the left of his front, where it would be least expected because a barrier of mountains there favoured defence. He counted on surprise to enable him to storm the mountain positions, and then to advance rapidly through the valleys on the other side, so achieving a decisive breach in the Bulgarian front. This attack on the left would be entrusted to French and Serb units, while on the right the bulk of the Bulgarian army would remain facing the British and Greeks.

The offensive began on 14 September with a heavy bombardment of the mountain defences on the left. Despite the physical difficulties, surprise was achieved. As by the Germans before Caporetto, the guns were moved forward unobserved. After the bombardment the infantry (including French Senegalese troops) attacked with great determination and in two days dislodged the enemy from the peaks, using weapons ranging from bayonets to flame-throwers. As the Bulgarians retreated into the valleys, Franchet d'Esperey ordered an attack by the British and Greeks, to prevent any reinforcement of the now-collapsing left, and this was launched on 18 September.

The British commander, General George Milne, had been on the Salonica front since 1916. An Aberdonian, and a gunner, he had first made his mark at Omdurman, where he impressed Kitchener who had thereafter advanced his career. But he was also admired by those who served under him. At Salonica he was subordinate to the French commander, and had got on particularly well with Guillaumat. His relations with Franchet d'Esperey were at first less easy, but warmed over time into friendship as well as mutual respect. The British attack ordered by the Frenchman succeeded in its purpose of preventing any movement of Bulgarian reserves to the left. But at the start it was tactically unrewarding and very costly, one battalion losing over 70 per cent of its numbers. The Greeks also had a hard time. Yet while the infantry struggled, British aircraft were most effective on every part of the front, harrying the Bulgarians wherever they were in retreat.

Their retreat was soon general. All the positions around Lake Doiran, where the British and Greeks had been fighting, were abandoned, and on 25 September British troops entered Bulgaria. Four days later Skopje fell to the French, and the following day hostilities ceased. Ferdinand had told his troops to die rather than retreat, but they ignored him. The Allies were able to impose their own terms: evacuation of all Greek and Serbian territory, virtual demobilization of the Bulgarian army, removal of German and Austrian troops from Bulgaria, and the Allies' right to use railways and occupy key points in the country.

Thus was the first 'prop' in Germany's power structure removed. But it fell chiefly because Germany was no longer capable of propping up the so-called props. What happened was, in reality, more a consequence than a cause of German weakness. In the past there would have been German divisions available to help Bulgaria repel an Allied offensive, but in September 1918 the most that could be spared was a brigade from the Crimea which could not arrive in time to be of any use. The Austrians, themselves in increasingly desperate straits, could offer nothing.

The victorious campaign which ended the Allied commitment at Salonica was therefore of psychological rather than material significance. Originally, in 1915, Lloyd George had intended the bridgehead to provide support for a Balkan alliance against the Central Powers. But the opportunity for creating this was missed, and he may have been somewhat over-sanguine about it in any case. Since then Salonica had been an expensive luxury, but it was far less of a drain on Allied resources than the Italian campaign in the Second World War, the strategic value of which was always equally questionable.

While the Balkan campaign was in progress, and Lloyd George was still at Manchester, Allenby made his dramatic move in Palestine. By a combination of good generalship and good luck he achieved what Liddell Hart describes as 'one of the most quickly decisive campaigns ... in history'.[13] Luck favoured him, first of all, in the strategy decided on by the Turkish government, in which Enver Pasha was the War Minister. After the collapse of Russia, instead of taking advantage of the removal of pressure from Turkey's eastern frontier to switch forces to the south, with a view to recapturing all the ground lost in Mesopotamia and Palestine, Enver and his colleagues chose to mount an offensive towards Baku, with the longer-

13. Basil Liddell Hart, *History of the First World War* (1970), p. 432.

term aim of raising a *jihad* among the Muslims of central Asia and northern India. The Turkish position in Palestine was not reinforced, while Allenby was able to rebuild the strength of his army depleted during the spring crisis on the Western front. In the autumn the Turks had three nominal armies in the Levant but they numbered in all only 26,000 infantry and 3,000 cavalry, with 340 guns. Allenby, on the other hand, had 57,000 infantry, 12,000 cavalry and 540 guns. He also had overwhelming superiority in the air, and the substantial asset of his Arab allies. Nevertheless, he was rightly far from complacent about his prospects, knowing that the Turks were capable of dogged resistance and that the ground would in many ways help them, if they could establish themselves as at Gallipoli. Their German commander was, indeed, now the very man who had led them on those famous heights, Liman von Sanders having taken Falkenhayn's place; and the Turkish hero of Gallipoli, Mustafa Kemal, was now commanding an army on the Palestine front (being prepared to work with Liman as he had not been with Falkenhayn).

To win, Allenby had to break the Turks' morale, and he knew that the first necessity was surprise. His plan was to attack on the extreme left of his line, along the coast, but he went to enormous lengths to convince the enemy that he would be attacking in the centre or on the right. His tricks included laying out dummy camps, with 15,000 dummy horses. A Jerusalem hotel was commandeered as a bogus headquarters, and troops were marched eastwards by day, only to be driven back at night in lorries to their camps near the coast. Above all, Allenby used his control of the air to deny the enemy any scope for air reconnaissance, and he tried to enforce the strictest field security among all ranks of his army.

There was, however, a dangerous moment when an Indian deserter revealed Allenby's plan of attack the day before it was due to be launched. Fortunately Liman thought the information was a plant, and his view seemed to be corroborated when flying columns of Arabs attacked Turkish communications east and west of the Jordan. He would have had little time to change his dispositions even if he had believed the deserter's story (as Kemal, among others, did), but he continued to expect Allenby's main blow to be delivered further east. When, therefore, the British attacked along the coastal plain at dawn on 18 September, after an artillery bombardment lasting only a quarter of an hour, surprise was achieved and the Turkish defences were swiftly overwhelmed. By late afternoon British infantry had advanced fourteen miles and were preparing to turn inland, while the cavalry swept past them to cut enemy communications to the rear. The rapid advance of the cavalry was accompanied by relentless air attacks on the retreating enemy by RAF, Australian and New Zealand planes. Enemy airfields, telegraph offices and telephone exchanges also were put out of action. Near Megiddo (the Armageddon of the Book of Revelation) the Turks were ordered to make a stand, but their positions there were abandoned with only a few shots fired. On 20 September Liman's headquarters at Nazareth was taken, he himself narrowly escaping in his pyjamas. That day Allenby's army advanced forty miles.

The following day Haifa and Acre fell, while to the east Turkish troops in flight towards the Jordan either (if they were lucky) surrendered in thousands or were pulverized from the air. On 25 September Australian and New Zealand cavalry crossed the Jordan and entered Amman. Two days later more of Allenby's mounted troops crossed the Golan Heights into Syria, and on 1 October the advance guard of the Australian Light Horse entered Damascus. By the end of the month the whole of Syria was occupied and an armistice was signed with Turkey on the island of Mudros. In five weeks Allenby's army had advanced 300 miles and taken 75,000 prisoners, while incurring itself only 6,000 casualties in battle. (There were, however, many more casualties from disease, especially malaria and the Spanish flu. Mortality among the Australians was four times as great from these diseases as from enemy action.)

Allenby's remarkable victory was too late to contribute much to the defeat of Germany, which was already being determined on the Western front. But Lloyd George had some reason to believe that it could have occurred earlier, at a time when the Ottoman Empire's elimination from the war might have been a serious blow to the principal enemy:

Had we reinforced our Egyptian Army in 1916 with a few of the men we were wasting on the Somme, at a time when the Allies outnumbered the Germans on the Western Front by more than 50 per cent., we might have broken the Turkish power in time to save Roumania, equip Russia, and end the War two years before it finally dragged to its tragic close. In a Turkish campaign our sea communications gave us a decisive advantage over the Central Powers. The railway accommodation was so limited and so broken that Germany could not have reinforced the Turks, however desperate their plight might be. The military advisers who scorned the Palestine campaign as a futile and wasteful 'sideshow' have a heavy reckoning to settle.[14]

It is hard to share the absolute confidence of Lloyd George's retrospective judgement, which contains, as to detail, many highly debatable assumptions.

14. *WM*, p. 3226.

All the same, he was surely right to claim that his persistent advocacy of a forward strategy against the Turks was substantially vindicated.

While Lloyd George was ill at Manchester, Frances Stevenson also was an invalid. For six weeks she had been suffering from inflammation of the kidneys, and during this time Riddell had dutifully accommodated her at Danny Park under the care of two nurses.[15] When Lloyd George was there he visited her in her sickroom and also wrote her letters which suggest the rediscovery of pristine passion. For instance:

My sweet loving fond thrilling little worry – the dearest thing I have struck in life after meandering through its marshes plains mountains for over half a century. It was worth such a long strenuous & weary walk to come across you in the end. And now I mean to take you along with me – for ever . . . Oh I am full of things wild but true to tell you sweetheart & I'll tell them on your lips – soon.

And, in a slightly less exalted style:

This is to warn you at the earliest possible moment that I have once more fallen desperately in love with an absolutely new girl. She is the darlingest girl I ever met. I saw her for the first time yesterday afternoon lying (in the most seductive attitude) on a sofa. She had the dearest face I ever saw – the most alluring smile – her neck was simply provoking. Altogether I am clean gone. I hope one day to make her love me as much as if I were a grilled kidney swimming in fat. [A curious image, and hardly tactful in view of the nature of her complaint.][16]

At Criccieth in August Lloyd George must have been worried about her health and asked Addison to check up on her in his capacity as a doctor, because Addison later wrote to him reassuringly at Manchester:

15. Ruth Longford, *Frances, Countess Lloyd George: More than a Mistress* (1996), p. 523.
16. DLG to FLS, no precise dates, but attributed to August/September 1918. Since all the letters are written from Danny Park, A. J. P. Taylor considers that Frances was 'clearly back at her London flat' during at least part of the time she was ill (*My Darling Pussy: The Letters of Lloyd George and Frances Stevenson, 1913–41*, ed. Taylor (1975), p. 22). But it seems more likely that the letters were written while they were both at Danny. In one Lloyd George writes: 'Last night I got it into my silly head that you had a bad cold & it kept me waking from fitful sleep . . . I strolled in the night twice outside your door to find out whether all was quiet. I was so thankful to hear your voice . . . when I called out.' Ruth Longford (Frances's granddaughter) is definite that she was at Danny throughout her illness. Riddell is no help; his diary does not mention Frances until after the war.

As I suggested to you might be the case, Miss Stevenson's illness arose from a kidney affection ... I got in touch with the Doctor who had a good consultant down and ... it was quite clear that peritonitis was not in question. As you will have heard no doubt, she is making good progress and I hope that it is now only a matter of time to get her well again ...[17]

At the end of the month she and Lloyd George were convalescing together at Danny. Philip Kerr wrote to Nancy Astor, with suitable obeisances to Christian Science:

The P.M. is much better, & there have been many comings and goings of pundits ... But it's generally thought that he should stay here for a few more days, & so long as one believes in the laws of m.m. [materialist medicine?] it's best to obey them ... Miss Stevenson has been quite bad & is in bed, but gets up for a bit each day & will shortly be quite fit again.[18]

Before leaving for France in the first week of October, Lloyd George sent a 'Memo from D[avid] to P[ussy].'

This is not a love-letter – it is a purely business communication or rather a minute from a Chief to his Secretary. Instructions how to behave on my departure for & during my absence on the Continent.

1. Look today as if you rather liked my going – cheerful jolly, otherwise we shall both be miserable (pure selfish thought for himself as usual says Pussy).
2. After I have left & the whole time I am away you must not get depressed or miserable. Act as if you were right down glad to get rid of an old bore who is always hanging about your room when he is not wanted.
3. Get rid of the cold as soon as you can.
4. Don't be in too great a hurry to get well. It leads to fretting and impatience & overpersuading nurses & doctors to let you do things you ought not to – and ultimate disappointment. Climb back to strength slowly.
5. Seek nor desire any substitute for me (vide First Commandment for paraphrase of this).
6. Never forget that there is a fond old man who will not be too full of affairs for a single moment of his journey to find room – & the best room in his heart for you.

Whatever luggage I leave behind Pussy will be with me for the little witch has

17. Addison to DLG, 16 September 1918. Addison must surely have been aware of the relationship.   18. Philip Kerr to Nancy Astor, 28 September 1918.

done her own packing long long ago & she never leaves the valise whatever is taken out or put in.

Every morning I shall be eagerly awaiting news from Danny – yes & every evening and how happy I shall be to know you are getting on my darling cariad.[19]

Frances would have been justified in regarding injunctions 1, 2 and 5 in the memo as purely selfish in motivation. It must have been awkward for Lloyd George to have their affair, normally conducted in the privacy of her flat or his retreat at Walton Heath, potentially brought to the notice of distinguished visitors to Danny who as yet had no knowledge of it. He was therefore asking her to feign total indifference to his departure, even pleasure that the 'old bore' was away. At the same time he was reasserting his demand to be the only man in her life, daring to invoke the First Commandment. Despite the semi-jocular tone, she must have known that he was serious in not wanting her presence at Danny to involve him in needless embarrassment. The evidence of loving concern in other parts of the memo cannot have disguised its essential message.

All the same it is clear that his attachment to Frances, self-centred though it always was, became more ardent again after the spring crisis on the Western front, during which he had turned instinctively to Margaret. Relieved of acute anxiety about the progress of the war, and returning to health after his Manchester collapse, he was in a mood for the enchantments of his second love, whose own illness may, moreover, have enhanced his awareness of what she meant to him. But, whatever he might say to Frances, Margaret never ceased to be vital to him, as his wife and the mother of his children, and as the first woman he had really loved. She was on the level with him in a sense that Frances never was, not least because of their shared Welsh background. He needed both women, and it was lucky for him that the newspaper codes of the time enabled him to lead the life of a quasi-bigamist. In his feelings for Frances there was still plenty of passion, but it has to be stressed that the supreme passion of his life was politics, a fact of which his memo to her was a sharp reminder.

Another person very close to Lloyd George, and politically indispensable to him – Bonar Law – also showed at Danny that he was in a bad way, confessing to Riddell 'with the tears coursing down his cheeks':

It is useless to conceal that I am nearly at the end of my tether. I do my work from day to day because I have certain powers of endurance, but they are growing less

19. 5 October 1918.

and less ... If it were not so I should not give way like this. Ever since the death of my sons I have gradually been growing worse and worse.

When Riddell reported this sad outburst to the Prime Minister, Lloyd George replied: 'I don't know what to do with him. He has no outside interests and he won't go for a holiday. He does not even care for golf or bridge. He just reads and works and smokes all day. I feel very sorry for poor old Bonar.'[20] And his sympathy had not been confined to words, since he had arranged for Law's younger daughter, Kitty, to spend some time at Criccieth in September.[21]

Lloyd George seems to have found Danny Park a congenial place to conduct business, away from but within easy reach of London. The fact that it was a rather grand period house – described by Pevsner as 'a typical, stately Early Georgian job'[22] – evidently did not put him off it, though he normally disliked the atmosphere of such places. Riddell took it for him in July, and he spent two weekends there that month, two more in August before he went to Criccieth, and a week in early September after settlement of the police strike. He would have spent more of September there than he did but for being so disagreeably detained at Manchester. As it was, he went to Danny for ten days later in the month (as we have seen, before his trip to France in early October), and he was there again for a final weekend in mid-October after his return.

Apart from all the interviews and conferences, involving a shifting cast of leading figures, Lloyd George found time at Danny for exercise – he enjoyed climbing Wolstenbury Hill under which the house is built – and for reading and conversation unrelated to the war, of which Riddell gives us fascinating glimpses. One day he discusses Bright's speeches, and gets a volume of them

20. *R WD*, 27 and 28 September 1918.
21. 'Little Kitty Bonar Law very happy at the prospect of going to Criccieth' (DLG to MLG, 31 August 1918).
   Law and his wife (who died in 1909) had six children, four boys and two girls. Of the two sons who survived the war the younger, Richard, went into politics, in which he achieved modest success. Unlike his father, he ended his life a peer (Lord Coleraine). The elder daughter, Isabel, acted as hostess to her father until she married General Sir Frederick Sykes (Chief of Air Staff between Trenchard's first and second terms, and later Governor of Bombay). Kitty (Catherine) Law was born in 1905, and so was three years younger than Megan Lloyd George.
22. The house dates originally from the late sixteenth century, but another front was added in 1728, when changes were also made to the earlier building. As it stands it is E-shaped, built of red brick, with a 'very monumental' east front rising to three storeys. Inside the eighteenth-century staircase swings round 'elegantly' (Ian Nairn and Nikolaus Pevsner, *Sussex* (1965), pp. 517–18).

from the library in the house, from which he reads extracts to illustrate his points. He notes Bright's intimate introductory touches, referring to individuals he has just met or heard from, which are 'most valuable in enabling a speaker to get on intimate terms with his audience'. But Lloyd George also admires his noble flights, such as the peroration to his speech on the American Civil War. When Riddell suggests that the style of such passages might be rather too grandiloquent for contemporary taste, Lloyd George disagrees: 'I think it would have a great reception. He was discussing a great issue. The language was worthy of the occasion. The public like a high tone when a great moral issue is involved.'

Emphasizing that a 'clear style' is always an asset, Lloyd George turns to the letters of 'a very different man', Byron, from which he also reads extracts. This book is his own, and Riddell, noticing that he has made marks in it, asks when the marks were made. 'Years ago,' Lloyd George replies, 'when I first read it,' and he is pleased to see that he still most admires the passages that he marked about thirty years previously.[23]

On another occasion they talk about Lytton Strachey. Riddell has given the Prime Minister a copy of Strachey's book on French literature, with which he is delighted. He 'considers the author one of the best modern writers'.[24] When discussing Foch one day, he says: 'I often think of Cicero's oration when it was proposed to send Pompey on a campaign. Cicero gave various reasons why Pompey would be a good commander, and concluded "and lastly he is favoured by the gods". Some men are lucky and some unlucky. Foch, in addition to his other great qualities, is a lucky man.'[25]

Despite what is often alleged, Lloyd George was a literary as well as a political animal. Though not so regular a reader as Asquith, for instance, he had read widely in history and the English classics as a child and remembered what he had read. And the habit of reading stayed with him. He needed books for both solace and stimulus.

At Danny, Riddell marvels, as always, at his vitality. Before an expedition to Beachy Head for a picnic tea he is described as giving 'much consideration' to every detail of the picnic, 'how the tea was to be made, what sort of kettle we should take with us, etc.'[26] One evening, after he has gone to bed, Balfour and Law discuss his character. Balfour says 'the PM is certainly a very attractive creature', and Law remarks: 'When he is keen on

23. *RWD*, 29 July 1918.
24. *RWD*, 31 August 1918 (the evening Lloyd George drove to Danny after settling the police strike).
25. *RWD*, 7 September 1918. 26. *RWD*, 31 August 1918.

anything, he sweeps you along with him and imagines you are in agreement with him when probably you are not!' Balfour's final comment is: 'When he is wrong, he is usually wrong in a more interesting way than other people.'[27]

27. *RWD*, 27 September 1918.

33

Newspaper Coup

Throughout his career Lloyd George took the press very seriously. As a democratic politician whose power derived from Wales, nonconformity and the people at large, rather than from hereditary wealth and status or from big business, he was ever conscious that the press and those who controlled it had unique resources for interpreting and influencing public opinion. As prime minister he had even more reason to cultivate press support and, where possible, to avert press hostility, since he lacked the normal advantage of a majority in parliament based on a party led by himself. It was therefore highly satisfactory for him to obtain, on 1 October, control of a national daily, especially in view of the probable imminence of a general election.

The paper in question was the *Daily Chronicle*, established in 1876 by Edward Lloyd and currently owned by his son Frank.[1] The *Chronicle* was a Liberal organ, but during the Boer War it differed from Lloyd George in taking the pro-war stance. But in 1902 Robert Donald, an independent-minded Scot, was appointed editor, and three years later the Liberals were back in power, with Lloyd George in high office. Under Donald the paper gave solid support to the Liberal government, and not least to Lloyd George's policies of radical reform. The two men were on friendly personal terms, often playing golf together. Their good relations were maintained in the war, until a breach was caused when Donald supported Robertson in February 1918; and this offence was compounded in May, when he made Maurice the *Chronicle*'s military correspondent. In September Lloyd George was particularly riled when, after his Manchester speech, he was attacked by the paper's lobby correspondent, Harry Jones, for praising Foch without mentioning Haig, 'evidence of a small mind that petulantly refuses to

---

1. Edward Lloyd had created the enormously successful *Lloyd's Weekly London Newspaper*. When he acquired the *Chronicle*, an obscure local paper, for £30,000, he immediately spent £150,000 to put it on the map.

acknowledge the services of a great soldier'.[2] Now the Prime Minister was determined to gain control of the *Chronicle*, not only to keep it out of the hands of the rival Liberal faction, but also to remove an editorial team which was becoming increasingly vexatious.

Throughout 1917 Frank Lloyd had been willing to sell, and Lloyd George had hoped that his friend Lord Leverhulme would buy the paper on his behalf. Negotiations were conducted at that time with Donald's knowledge and involving no threat to his editorship. But they came to nothing, because the price demanded by Lloyd (£900,000 for the ordinary shares alone) was more than Leverhulme was prepared to pay. Beaverbrook was also active behind the scenes, but Lloyd George became uneasy about cooperating with him in such an enterprise. Apart from anything else it was awkward that he was a Conservative, however maverick. Eventually Lloyd George and Guest raised the money to pay Lloyd from their own Coalition Liberal resources, supplemented by contributions from a few new subscribers. One of these was the shipowner Andrew Weir (no relation of William Weir, the air minister), who was to succeed Churchill as minister of munitions in 1919, becoming Lord Inverforth.[3] Lloyd received a total of £1,600,000 for the *Chronicle*, evidence that Lloyd George's party chest, otherwise known as the Lloyd George Fund, was already very substantial.

The new set-up ensured that the paper would in all respects be subject to Lloyd George's control. A holding company was created, of which the prime minister's old ally and crony, Sir Henry Dalziel, became chairman. He was to act as 'in effect [Lloyd George's] agent'. Donald was kept in utter ignorance of the negotiation, but when the deal was done he was almost immediately removed from the editorship. He was succeeded by the news editor, E. A. Perris, on the understanding that the paper's political line would be set by Dalziel, in other words by Lloyd George. Maurice and Jones also left, to be taken on by the *Daily News*. But one important figure broke with Donald and stayed on under the new regime. He was the scholarly radical R. C. K. Ensor, who remained as chief leader-writer and so gave helpful moral endorsement to Lloyd George's coup. When the irrepressible Pringle alleged in Parliament that their coup indicated a tendency towards 'monopolistic control of the Press', Dalziel himself replied to him in the Commons,

2. *Daily Chronicle*, 13 September 1918. Lloyd George was always edgy about Haig.

3. Weir was a distinguished man, who would have deserved office and honour in any case. The same could not be said of another contributor, James White, a Lancashire company promoter who committed suicide in 1927 without ever receiving the knighthood which, apparently, he had been promised by Guest.

disingenuously repudiating the charge that the deal had anything to do with Lloyd George's political requirements.[4]

More should now be said about Beaverbrook's part in the affair. If his plans had been realized the complaint about a tendency to monopoly would have been rather less frivolous. His idea was to buy not only the *Chronicle* from Lloyd, but also the *Sunday Times* from the Berry brothers, William and Gomer (the future Lords Camrose and Kemsley). The resulting combination of daily and Sunday papers would still not have been strictly monopolistic, since plenty of rivals would have remained in both fields; but it would have been more nearly so than the mere acquisition of the *Chronicle*. Beaverbrook's interest in journalism was growing. Had he secured the *Chronicle* he would probably have merged it with his own *Daily Express*, for which, later in the year, he launched a weekend partner, the *Sunday Express*. His attempt to buy the *Sunday Times* was sabotaged by Guest, who told the Berry brothers (then Coalition Liberal supporters, though natural Conservatives and soon to gravitate that way) that they must not sell the paper to a Tory. The combination sought by Beaverbrook might or might not have been a reliable buttress to Lloyd George. Guest was extremely doubtful, and communicated his doubts to the Prime Minister. Beaverbrook was then excluded from the *Chronicle* negotiations. Doubts about him were surely justified. At any rate, his friend and biographer A. J. P. Taylor thinks so: 'Guest may well have recalled how [he] had gone into the *Daily Express* as agent for the Unionist Party and then carried it off for himself . . . he ran propaganda according to his own ideas, not at the direction of others. The Lloyd George group had some excuse for keeping him out.'[5]

At the time, Beaverbrook was trying to run propaganda for the country, as a member of the government. Since February he had been Minister of Information, as already briefly recorded.[6] He had been doing the same job for Canada (though without ministerial status) since the early months of the war, and was now asked to deploy his extraordinary talents as a publicist on behalf of his country of adoption. But his scope for action was limited.

---

4. Stephen Koss, *The Rise and Fall of the Political Press in Britain* (2 vols., 1981–4), vol. 2, pp. 334–7. Hansard, fifth ser., vol. cxviii, cols. 78–94. Dalziel was elected to Parliament soon after Lloyd George and was one of two friends and fellow MPs (the other being Herbert Lewis) who in 1896 accompanied him on a trip to Argentina in connection with a doomed Patagonian gold-mining project. (See Grigg, *The Young Lloyd George*, chap. 7). As a politician he concentrated upon journalism and the newspaper ownership, achieving great success with the *Sunday Reynolds News* and its adjuncts, and in 1917 gaining control of the *Pall Mall Gazette*. He held his Commons seat (Kirkaldy) until 1921, when he went to the House of Lords.

5. A. J. P. Taylor, *Beaverbrook*, p. 216.

6. See p. 388 above.

With his own agreement and active help, propaganda in enemy countries was entrusted to another man, Northcliffe. Northcliffe had no intention of compromising his freedom to comment and criticize by becoming a minister, but Beaverbrook devised a formula under which he would run his department on a quasi-independent basis, with direct access to the Prime Minister.

Beaverbrook, who was always touchy about his status, also insisted that he be given ministerial rank. To facilitate this, he was also offered the Chancellorship of the Duchy of Lancaster. When the King (who did not like him or, equally important, the idea of a Presbyterian in charge of Church of England appointments) resisted, Lloyd George told Stamfordham firmly that Beaverbrook was essential for the war effort. Beaverbrook's appointment was also attacked in Parliament where Austen Chamberlain led the accusations that the government had allowed himself to fall too much under the influence of newspaper magnates.

Although he briefly considered resigning – a threat he frequently used – Beaverbrook took up his duties with the same energy and enthusiasm he had shown for the Canadian propaganda effort. He set up an Overseas Press Centre and arranged special tours and interviews for foreign correspondents. Like Lloyd George himself, he went outside the civil service for expertise. He brought in a firm of chartered accountants to get the finances of his new ministry on a more businesslike footing and he appointed a number of his business acquaintances to posts. John Buchan stayed on as Director of Intelligence and Arnold Bennett became the resident expert on France while Hugh Walpole took on Russia. Lord Castlerose, a new friend who had been invalided out of the Irish Guards, shepherded influential Americans to France. Northcliffe stayed on as head of propaganda in enemy countries with a virtually independent office.

As Beaverbrook's plans grew increasingly ambitious, he ran up against entrenched interests. When he proposed that his ministry control the distribution of newsprint, the Board of Trade objected strongly. When he tried to set up his own intelligence network and demanded complete access to all political intelligence being produced by the War Office, the Admiralty and the Foreign Office, he was repeatedly frustrated. Lloyd George, who had felt that it was safer to have Beaverbrook in the government than outside, stood by his appointment but was not prepared to waste precious political capital and energy on fighting his battles for him.

Lloyd George liked Beaverbrook and was amused by him but he never trusted him completely. 'Max likes to strike down the tall poppies,' he told Frances Stevenson. By the summer of 1918, he was also tired of Beaverbrook's repeated demands and complaints. In the middle of June, for example, at a time when the Allies were battling back against the massive German attack, Beaverbrook sent a huge memorandum to the Prime Minister, full of detail about the ways in which other government departments had interfered with his work.

Beaverbrook's other role, as newspaper proprietor, also caused difficulties. When the Ministry of Information proposed establishing an imperial news service with imperial radio stations, Beaverbrook's enemies raised the alarm. Was this simply a way for the unscrupulous press lord to gain control over a new medium? Questions were raised about where the *Daily Express* was getting its information. In April, it caused a certain amount of embarrassment to the government by leaking the news of Derby's relegation to the Paris embassy. In a long letter to Lloyd George, Beaverbrook denied that he had had anything to do with the leak. He was, he insisted in an excuse which cannot have persuaded Lloyd George, merely the principal shareholder of the paper. Later that summer, when the *Daily Express*, in a leader, suggested that it would not support Lloyd George in the next election unless he supported tariff reform and imperial preference, Lloyd George was furious: 'That is Max. Having regard to the risks I ran for him and the way I stood up for him when he was attacked by his own party I regard this as a mean piece of treachery.' In October, Beaverbrook, whose health was giving way, resigned.

Afterword

by Margaret MacMillan

In some of the last passages he wrote before he so sadly died, John Grigg showed a weakened Germany, its forces being pushed out of Belgium and northern France, its allies dropping away one by one. It was clearly his intention to conclude this fourth volume of his magisterial life of Lloyd George with the final collapse of Germany and the end of the fighting on 11 November 1918. The last month of the war was a blur of events, as first Bulgaria then Turkey and finally Germany and Austria-Hungary requested ceasefires. These requests produced often tense negotiations among the Allies over the armistice which gave warning of the difficulties to come over the peace. In the meantime, of course, the fighting went on.

Lloyd George, like the other Allied war leaders, showed signs of strain in those crucial weeks. Hankey, who saw Lloyd George day in, day out, found him capricious and, on occasion, unwontedly petty. Perhaps Lloyd George had not yet fully recovered from his illness at Manchester. And he was living at a frenetic pace. In the last five weeks of the war, he had to go to Paris twice for high-level meetings. The pressures on him were enormous. At home, the police strike was a shocking indication of the depth of labour unrest; his Cabinet colleagues were restive with what they saw as his increasingly peremptory style; and his enemies, Asquith foremost among them, waited in anticipation of a fatal mistake.

The war was going well but for much of October it appeared to be far from over. Although the Allies thought from time to time about their peace aims, none had bothered to draw up armistice terms. Even as late as the third week of October, expert opinion held that Germany still had the capacity to fight on into the spring of 1919. As Henry Wilson wrote to Cavan: 'The Boche army is *not* beaten. It has been roughly handled and is sore and tired, but it is still well able to extricate itself from awkward angles and corners and to fall back in continuous and unbroken line to the Lys, to the Schedlt, to the Meuse – in short to wherever it *must* fall back.'[1]

1. Wilson to Cavan, 19 October 1918, *The Military Correspondence of Field-Marshal Sir Henry Wilson*, ed. Keith Jeffrey (1985), p. 56.

An armistice with Germany was tempting but it carried considerable risk. If its terms were not carefully worked out and close to those which the Allies hoped to gain in a final peace settlement, too early a ceasefire might damage their ability to bend Germany to their will. Allied leaders by now had very real concerns about the capacity of their forces to fight on. Once they had stopped it would be difficult, if not impossible, to get them moving again. True, the Americans were arriving in increasing numbers, but there were considerable doubts, if not about their fighting ability then about the quality of their officers and their logistics.

The very prospect of peace at last, so tantalizingly raised by the collapse of Germany's allies, had unsettled public opinion. Would the Allied publics continue to support the war effort? The demands of Bulgaria, then Turkey, and finally Austria-Hungary and Germany for armistice discussions and Woodrow Wilson's replies were published in the press on both sides. This was creating an 'irresistible peace atmosphere', Smuts warned his colleagues in the War Cabinet. 'Unless we feel certain that the war is really over, and that nothing now remains but for the diplomats to discuss and sign the peace treaties, this correspondence may really produce a disastrous handicap to us in renewing the campaign next year.'[2]

Smuts, like a number of the Allied leaders including Lloyd George himself, was also disturbed by Wilson's calm assumption that he had the right to arrange ceasefires even when, as in the case of Bulgaria and Turkey, the United States was not a belligerent. Wilson's own position was clear: Bulgaria had asked him for help in arranging a ceasefire with its enemies and he was prepared to do so in a helpful spirit. He was only interested, he told Wiseman on 27 September, in peace. Clemenceau threatened to tell the United States to stay out of what did not concern it. When the War Cabinet met on 3 October, there was qualified support. He felt considerable sympathy with Clemenceau, Lloyd George said, but he agreed that it would not do to alienate the United States at this stage. It was a pity though, he added, that Wilson had not sent a proper representative to Europe who could take part in decisions. As it was, the United States tended to make objections in an unhelpful manner.

It was unfortunate that British representation in Washington was almost equally unsatisfactory. Reading was back in London for consultations (he was never to return to his post). That left only a chargé in Washington in addition to Wiseman, who was more and more seeing issues from an American perspective. To geographic distance was added another sort.

2. HLRO. Lloyd George Papers. F160/1/15. 'Notes on a General Armistice', 23 October 1918.

Wilson came, Lloyd George later wrote in his memoirs of the Peace Conference, not quite from a different world but certainly from a different hemi-
sphere. 'Whilst we were dealing every day with ghastly realities on land and
sea, some of them visible to our own eyes and audible to our ears, he was
soaring in clouds of serene rhetoric.'[3] But the rhetoric, with its promise of a
fair and just peace, self-determination for captive nations, and, above all, a
new world order which would make war obsolete, was enormously appealing to the war-weary populations of Europe.

In the end Wilson's offer of mediation was not taken up as Bulgaria
collapsed quicker than expected. With Bulgaria out of the war, the way was
now open for Allied forces to strike southwards against Constantinople and
Turkey and north into Roumania, with its oil which was so crucial to the
Central Powers, and then, perhaps, into Austria-Hungary itself. With any
luck the long-postponed Italian offensive might also start.

This was not lost on Germany's military leaders, Ludendorff and Hindenburg. The Allied attacks along the length of the Western front which started
on 26 September were the final straw. On 28 September, Ludendorff
cracked; he raged around in his office, blaming everyone for Germany's
defeats – the Kaiser, the politicians, the German people – except of course
himself and his military. Germany must ask for an immediate ceasefire
before the situation became even worse. Hindenburg, who had reached the
same conclusion, agreed. The following day, they told an astonished Kaiser
and his Chancellor, the conservative Count Georg von Hertling, that the
government must ask for an immediate armistice. Moreover, it must make
itself more democratic by inviting the participation of Germany's leading
political parties. Having rigorously excluded Germany's civilian leaders
from the waging of the war, Ludendorff and Hindenburg wanted to make
them responsible for its loss. The Chancellor, Hertling, resigned in protest
and Prince Max of Baden, a known moderate, took his place.

On the evening of 3 October, the new German government dispatched a
telegram to President Wilson, requesting an armistice and asking Wilson to
invite the belligerents to send delegates to peace negotiations which would
be based on the Fourteen Points. Austria-Hungary, by now in desperate
straits, sent a similar note. The unexpected demand stunned the Allies as
much as it did the German population, which had been kept in the dark
about Germany's rapidly deteriorating situation.

With these two notes, a very public series of negotiations began. The *New
York Times* published the German note on 7 October and newspapers

---

3. Lloyd George, *The Truth about the Peace Treaties* (1938), vol. i, p. 222.

around the world followed suit. This of course put added pressure on the Allied leaders to make a quick armistice, something the Germans no doubt intended. Wilson himself was delighted by the Central Powers' move. He told the British chargé in Washington with a smile that he was not sure how he would respond; the position was tricky because the enemy appeared to be accepting his terms.

When what later came to be called the First German Note was sent, Lloyd George was in Paris for a series of meetings to discuss the next stage of the war, as well as the implications of Bulgaria's defeat, in particular for the campaign against Turkey. In the Cabinet before he left London, he had talked optimistically of making peace with Turkey right away, before any general peace conference. That would have the advantage of keeping the United States, and France, out of any settlement. (On the other hand, he occasionally contemplated asking the United States to take on responsibility for Armenia, much of which lay within Turkey, or for Palestine.) A quick peace might also limit French involvement since the majority of the forces fighting the Turks were from the British Empire. He had long since come to regret the secret Sykes–Picot Agreement which divided up the Ottoman Empire among the Allies. He had no wish to see the Italians laying claim to large parts of Asia Minor and, more importantly, he did not intend that France should get a large part of Syria and the Turkish province of Mosul as well. The French, he charged, were being greedy.

On 5 October Lloyd George had a private meeting with Clemenceau and Orlando, the Italian Prime Minister. Henry Wilson, who was summoned to give advice, found the three sitting round a small-scale atlas trying to plan Allied strategy. The British and the French disagreed strongly, the French arguing for a protracted campaign in the Balkans and the gradual isolation of Turkey, while the British wanted an all-out attack on Constantinople by British forces under General Milne, which would be detached from d'Esperey's command and placed under that of Allenby, who would simultaneously strike north from Syria. Franchet would remain in command only of operations in the northern part of the Balkans. The final campaign against Turkey would therefore be almost exclusively British. Clemenceau was outraged. (Foch further annoyed him by agreeing with Lloyd George.) The proposal amounted, he told Derby, now British Ambassador to France, to a veritable repudiation of the Anglo-French alliance.

To further complicate matters, Arthur Frazier, the American observer on the Supreme War Council, plaintively asked Hankey why Turkey and Bulgaria were being discussed in private meetings instead of those of the Council. 'We could hardly tell him point blank,' Hankey wrote in his diary, 'that we were holding conferences instead of the SWC because President Wilson would not declare war on Turkey and Bulgaria.'[4] Hankey gave, he said, a hint of the Allied feeling that they had no obligation to consult Wilson in the circumstances either on the war on those two countries or the peace.

Henry Wilson stirred up further wrangling between the British and the French when he prematurely sent a telegram to Allenby on 5 October to alert him to the proposed changes. The French not only protested vigorously but also countered on 7 October with a scheme of Franchet's under which Milne would now move north up the Danube and a French general would command the attack on Turkey. Franchet also started to divide Milne's army into two parts. Lloyd George in turn refused to agree. After a stormy meeting of the Allied prime ministers and the advisers, a compromise of sorts was cobbled together. Milne's army was left where it was, under Franchet's command, but a British general – unspecified – would command the attack on Constantinople, and his troops, while mainly British, would now include French, Italians, Greeks and Serbians. By that point, it looked increasingly unlikely that an attack would ever be necessary. News reached Paris on 6 October that the Turkish government had sent emissaries to Mitylene to ask for an armistice. In fact, the approach was not an official one and the war against Turkey was to drag on for some weeks more.

Lloyd George felt that the wranglings had done little damage. To Derby, he said: 'What I like is having a thing out. I do not bear any grudge afterwards.' The French and the Italians were different, Derby told him. 'They do not understand having a thing out when every sort of insulting thing is said on both sides and they do bear resentment.'[5] Lloyd George also found it extraordinary that, when Orlando was furious with Clemenceau, he never showed it. 'These Latins are very odd people,' he told Hankey.[6] The disputes were to flare up again later in the month when the Turkish armistice was actually negotiated.

As the Allied leaders discussed Turkey, they waited anxiously for Woodrow Wilson's reply to the German Note. Their fear was that the Germans had somehow persuaded Wilson that they were sincere in asking for a peace based on the Fourteen Points and that the American President would unilaterally agree to an armistice. This would put the European Allies in a very tricky position. They did not want Wilson to speak for them, especially

4. Stephen Roskill, *Hankey: Man of Secrets* (3 vols., 1970–74), vol. i, p. 608.
5. *Paris 1918: The War Diary of the British Ambassador, the 17th Earl of Derby*, ed. David Dutton (2001), p. 246.   6. Roskill, *Hankey*, vol. i, p. 608.

when he did not consult them. And they had very real concerns that a peace based on the Fourteen Points would not give them what they felt they were entitled to – Germany's colonies, for example, or war damages.

While they waited, the European leaders considered the military terms they wanted should Germany agree to an armistice. On 6 October, they decided to ask that Germany evacuate all the occupied territories in the West and that furthermore it withdraw its forces from Alsace-Lorraine and the Rhineland, that part of Germany west of the Rhine river. In the East, Germany and Austria-Hungary were to pull back along the Italian front, in the Balkans, along the Russian front and in the Caucasus. This would have given the Allies control of much of that which both France and Italy hoped to gain after the war. When the military advisers looked at the terms the following day, they added further provisions which effectively disarmed Germany. Lloyd George surprisingly found these too severe.

His attitude to Germany was a curious mixture at this point. Emotionally he hated, if not Germans, then German militarism. He was, he told his Cabinet colleagues, attracted by the school of thought that said: 'We ought to go on until Germany is smashed; that we ought to force our way on to German soil, and put Germany at our mercy; that we should actually dictate terms on German soil, very possibly such terms as we would not accept; but that the enemy should be shown that war cannot be made with impunity.'[7] On the other hand, he recognized that the time had probably come to stop the war. Was it worth driving Germany into a corner and forcing it to fight on?

The discussion of the military terms had an unfortunate impact on Washington where it was President Wilson's turn to complain that he had not been consulted. The terms appeared as further proof of what the Americans had always feared: that the Europeans did not really support the Wilsonian programme. When Wilson had made a rousing speech in New York on 27 September calling on the world's leaders to accept his vision for a new world order, run on new principles, the Europeans had responded politely but noncommittally. American suspicions of Europe, always near the surface, were particularly acute as the war wound down. Rumours reached Washington of secret deals, for example over the Turkish peace.

Fortunately wiser heads on both sides of the Atlantic realized that it would be disastrous for the coalition to fall to pieces before the successful conclusion of the war. Wilson was mollified when the Allies assured him that there had been no intention to exclude him. For his part, Wilson assured them that he was absolutely determined on a clear victory over Germany.

7. HLRO. Bonar Law Papers. Box 70. War Cab., 491B, 26 October 1918.

Colonel House, who enjoyed stirring up Wilson to think the worst of the Europeans, helped to calm him down.

On 9 October Wilson's reply to Germany reached Paris. (Much to the annoyance of some of the British it appeared in the press at virtually the same time.) Although the Europeans had not been consulted, they found it better than they expected. Wilson was under considerable pressure in the United States to be tough with Germany and he had moved away from his original impulse to send a moderate response. His Note asked the Germans whether they fully accepted his Fourteen Points but it also said firmly that as long as German forces remained on foreign soil, Wilson could not recommend that the Allies negotiate.

Lloyd George's first reaction nevertheless was one of anger, partly because Wilson had not consulted his Allies and partly because he did not mention evacuating Alsace-Lorraine. He had another, more serious, concern, which was that one of the Fourteen Points could not be accepted by Britain under any circumstances. Point Two talked about 'Absolute freedom of navigation upon the seas, outside territorial waters, alike in peace and in war . . .' What was called the Freedom of the Seas issue for short was one that cut at the heart of British naval power. If the British navy could not use its traditional weapon of blockade in war, then Britain lost its most potent weapon against its enemies. 'Wilson is adopting a dangerous line,' Lloyd George told Riddell. 'He wants to pose as the great arbiter of the war. His Fourteen Points are very dangerous. He speaks of freedom of the seas. That would involve the abolition of the right of search and seizure, and the blockade. We shall not agree to that; such a change would not suit the country.'[8] (In their darker moods, the British suspected the French of having done a secret deal with the Americans to go along with the Freedom of the Seas in return for American support for French designs on the Rhineland.)

For all their annoyance with Wilson, the Europeans confined themselves to sending two cables: the first, which praised his noble sentiments, asked that the military experts be allowed to advise on the armistice terms, and the second that he send a proper representative with sufficient powers to participate fully in the discussions and in the decisions. Wilson decided on House, the man he trusted most in the world. Quiet, self-effacing, delighting in the exercise of power from behind the scenes, House shared Wilson's ideals and goals completely. Although he never let Wilson know it, House felt that he was the better equipped to realize them. Like Wilson, House tended to see European duplicity and greed everywhere. He was also con-

8. *RWD*, pp. 366–7.

vinced that the European Allies were becoming more conservative and imperialistic as the war neared its end. Among the European leaders, he got on best with Clemenceau. Lloyd George he saw as an amoral politician who lacked any guiding principle beyond staying in power. As House saw Wilson for the last time before he sailed, Wilson told him, 'I have not given you any instructions because I feel you will know what to do.'[9]

By 11 October, Lloyd George was back in London, reporting on the Paris meetings to a joint meeting of the Imperial War Cabinet and War Cabinet. The next day he went off to Danny Park for the weekend with Reading and Riddell. At dinner the conversation turned to President Wilson. Lloyd George wondered what their first meeting would be like. Reading said that Clemenceau predicted there would be only a few feathers left. Lloyd George laughed but added that Wilson had placed the Allies in a difficult situation through his correspondence with Germany. 'I am not quite sure that it would not be a good thing for Clemenceau or me to make a speech indicating the position in an inoffensive way. The American public would soon understand and would speedily make it clear to Wilson that they must act in accord with the French and the British who have borne the heat of the day.'[10]

That night, after he had gone off to bed, the text of the Second German Note arrived. The Germans declared that they accepted the Fourteen Points without reservation and asked whether the European Allies accepted them as well. They would be happy to evacuate Allied territory and suggested that a joint commission supervise the withdrawal. They made no mention of handing over war equipment or withdrawing their troops from their own territory. Philip Kerr took it up to Lloyd George and came back to report: 'There is awful trouble upstairs, I can tell you! He thinks the Allies are now in a horrible mess. Wilson has promised them an armistice.'[11] Lloyd George assumed that the Germans were to get a ceasefire while they were still on occupied territory.

It was fortunate, at least from his point of view, that the German military, with the appalling timing that had characterized so many of their actions during the war, had decided to continue attacks on shipping warfare. Two days previously, German submarines had sunk a passenger steamer, the *Hiramo Maru*, as well as the Irish mail boat, the *Leinster*. 'There was a howl of indignation,' Lloyd George later wrote in his memoirs, 'which drowned

9. Edward Mandell House, *The Intimate Papers of Colonel House Arranged as a Narrative by Charles Seymour* (1926–8), pp. 4 and 88.
10. H. Montgomery Hyde, *Lord Reading* (1967), p. 296.   11. *RWD*, p. 370.

out the welcome that might otherwise have been given to the German Peace Note.'[12]

On Sunday morning, Lloyd George went for a brisk walk with Reading and Riddell, complaining vociferously about Wilson's propensity to ignore his allies. 'Wilson has put us in the cart and he will have to get us out.' What did the Fourteen Points mean? 'They are very nebulous.'[13] Balfour, Bonar Law, Milner, Churchill and Henry Wilson joined the party for lunch and Wemyss and Hankey arrived in the afternoon. The main topic for discussion was Wilson's latest Note to the Germans but the group went much further, discussing the armistice terms and those of the peace to follow. Later on, when Curzon and others including the Dominion leaders complained that they had been excluded, Reading gave the excuse that it was too difficult to get hold of everyone on a Sunday. In fact, Lloyd George had precisely whom he wanted.

There was general annoyance with President Wilson and what was seen as his hijacking of the armistice negotiations. Lloyd George opened the discussion by saying that it must be made clear to the public that Wilson alone was responsible for the negotiations so far and reiterated that Britain could not accept Wilson's Point Two about the Freedom of the Seas. On Germany, he was for stiff armistice terms; the Germans were near the end of their tether and it would be a mistake to allow them time to recover. In fact, he was prepared to go further, to carry the war on to German soil. The German public had not yet had a real taste of what defeat meant. Historical comparisons were not always useful, but look at the Second Punic War. 'The Romans might have made peace by insisting on Carthage clearing out of Italy and Spain. The Romans, however, said that this was not enough, that they must actually invade Carthaginian territory and achieve victory on Carthaginian soil. History had shown that they were right.' Balfour remarked that he hoped Lloyd George would not use the analogy in public. Law argued that disarming German troops was the same as a complete defeat. Balfour added that the loss of territory – Alsace-Lorraine, which Germany had vowed never to give up, and German Poland with its iron and steel – would be felt by the Germans as much as actual fighting on German soil. Unable to carry his colleagues with him, Lloyd George accepted that they should make an armistice on favourable terms as soon as possible. He had a warning though: 'if peace were made now in twenty years' time the Germans would say what Carthage had said about the First Punic War, namely that they had made this mistake and that mistake, and that by better

---

12. *WM*, p. 3288.   13. *RWD*, p. 371.

preparation and organisation they would be able to bring about victory next time'.[14]

The discussion then turned to the armistice itself. As Lloyd George pointed out, the moment an armistice was concluded the Allies lost their momentum and much of the upper hand they held over Germany. It was very important, therefore, to ensure that the terms left Germany unable to recover and renew the fighting. Henry Wilson argued, successfully, that the Germans must be disarmed before they marched back to Germany and Wemyss put in a demand for complete naval disarmament. Lloyd George agreed reluctantly. According to Riddell, he preferred Foch's earlier proposal to allow the German troops to withdraw behind the Rhine in good order, with the Allies holding the key bridgeheads for safety, on the grounds that Germany was more likely to accept.

The discussion came round to Wilson's Fourteen Points, particularly the Freedom of the Seas. In Wemyss's opinion it was clearly directed against the British navy. 'If it were adopted we should lose enormously in prestige and enormously in power.' They would no longer be able to use the blockade. 'This was very important,' said Lloyd George, 'since the blockade had been the primary factor in defeating Austria, and a very important one in defeating Germany.' There was general scepticism about the League using its collective authority as a substitute.

Lloyd George wondered whether the British should agree to discuss the peace on the basis of the Fourteen Points, as Germany had asked. The Germans were already putting their own construction on them. Was there an assumption that Britain had also agreed to Wilson's terms? That, everyone agreed, was dangerous. Churchill was optimistic: 'if the Freedom of the Seas was whittled down to our interpretation and the remainder of the Fourteen Points were screwed up to the interpretation we wished to put upon them, the situation would be all right.' Balfour wondered whether the British knew what their interpretation was. Out of a long and confused discussion, two main points emerged: that Freedom of the Seas was unacceptable and there must be some provision for reparation for war damage inflicted by Germany. In the end, though, for all the huffing and puffing against Wilson, discretion won out. It was decided simply to send him a telegram asking him to make it clear in his reply to Germany that he did not intend that Germany should get an armistice simply by promising to withdraw from occupied territory.[15]

While the world waited for Wilson's reply to the German Note of

14. Draft notes of a conference held at Danny Park, Sussex, on Sunday 13 October 1918 at 2.30 p.m. Public Record Office, CAB24/66. 15. Ibid.

12 October, the Allies continued to press ahead. Pershing's Americans finally cleared the Germans out of the Argonne forest on the south of the Western front and the British, the French and the Belgians attacked in the north. On 13 October, French forces retook Laon. In the Balkans, Serb and Allied forces pushed northwards. In the Middle East, Allenby's forces headed north through Syria towards Turkey proper. Although Ludendorff, now recovered from his earlier panic, talked wildly about a spring offensive, it was clear that Germany was nearly finished. Its remaining allies, Austria-Hungary and Turkey, were dropping away.

At home, the British government remained preoccupied with the Irish question and with industrial unrest. The War Cabinet talked about the impact of the end of the war on the home front, about the problems, for example, around demobilization. (It also took time to deal with a serious shortage of beer.) Lloyd George was thinking about his own political future, trying to decide when to have the long-overdue general election and how he should fight it. Would he return to the Liberal Party as its leader, an unappetizing prospect as long as Asquith and his other enemies remained powerful? Or might he take advantage of the flux in British politics and form his own new party? He was already well on the way to putting together a substantial war chest under his own control. Or would he keep the wartime Coalition alive and continue to govern as the Liberal leader of a largely Conservative group? He was to opt for the last alternative.

The war and the big strategic issues continued to take up much of the Cabinet's attention. What should Britain do in the Caucasus? In Siberia? In Russia as a whole? The discussion increasingly turned to what would happen after the war. Britain, or its dominions, must get Germany's colonies. The French must somehow be kept out of the Middle East, whatever the Sykes–Picot Agreement had promised.

On 15 October, Wilson's reply to the Second German Note arrived in London. It was significantly tougher than his earlier ones. Wilson was shocked by the sinking of the *Leinster* but he was also affected by the hardening of his own public opinion towards Germany. He may also have heeded his European Allies who insisted that German evacuation of the occupied territory was not sufficient to give them an advantage over Germany. He now stated that the armistice terms were to be left to the Allied military advisers who must ensure Allied supremacy. Germany must stop its submarine warfare, and, in a demand which was to reverberate in Germany, the 'arbitrary power' that had governed it must be removed. The British government greeted this with a certain amount of derision. Everyone was sarcastic, Hankey noted, about the change from excessive leniency to severity.

A few days later, on 19 October, Haig came over from France to discuss the armistice terms in a special secret meeting with Lloyd George, Law, Milner, Balfour and Henry Wilson. Haig argued that Germany was not yet desperate to accept complete disarmament and withdrawal of its forces east of the Rhine. He was also dubious about the ability of the Allied forces to carry on to victory. He was therefore for sending Germany back to its frontiers of 1870, before it had Alsace and Lorraine. Although Henry Wilson was for harsher terms, including the occupation of German soil, Lloyd George was persuaded by Haig's gloomy analysis.

Part way through the meeting, Wemyss arrived to present the Admiralty's view. The naval authorities were ambivalent about the prospect of peace. On the one hand, they did not want another year of war. Apart from anything else, worsening morale among their sailors was causing real concern. On the other hand, the navy had not played its traditional role. There had been no glorious victories at sea. If an armistice were to come, therefore, they wanted it to achieve what they had failed to do: the destruction of the German fleet. Wemyss asked for the surrender of two-thirds of the surface ships, including the most modern ones, and the whole of the submarine fleet. Lloyd George thought the terms far too stiff. They amounted to a complete surrender and ran the danger of stirring the Germans up to resistance.

What none of them knew, and there was no way they could have known, was how rapidly Germany's will to fight on was vanishing. Although Ludendorff and Hindenburg talked about fresh attacks, they were living in a fantasy. The German War Minister reported that if the oil supply from Roumania was cut off, which was about to happen, the army could last for only six weeks. From Belgium, where the Allies had now seized virtually the whole of the coast, the Commander-in-Chief of the German forces said that his men could not fight beyond the end of the year. Crown Prince Rupprecht of Bavaria wrote to Prince Max to say that his troops were at the end of their tether, short of everything from horses to officers. At the same time the beleaguered Chancellor was getting alarming reports about the state of public opinion in Germany.

After a terrific struggle with his military leaders, Prince Max sent off a reply to Woodrow Wilson. The Third German Note, which was broadcast on 20 October, threw Germany on Wilson's mercy. It trusted, it said, that he would not approve any demand which would damage the honour of the German people or the hopes of making a just peace. The Germans also undertook to stop submarine attacks on passenger ships. Wilson was generally pleased with its tone. He did not think that it was necessary to wait for an armistice until German troops were back across the Rhine. He was concerned to stop the fighting before his own public opinion grew any more vindictive towards Germany. His European Allies were asking for more than they were entitled to and if they did not agree, he told his Cabinet, he would force them to accept an armistice. (How this was to be done, he did not spell out.) As for Germany, the United States and the European Allies would remain strong enough to force it to abandon its old militaristic ways and build a new order based on the Fourteen Points. It is perhaps fortunate that the Europeans were not aware of this exchange.

In London, the War Cabinet was in session, discussing the news that the Turks had sent an official request for an armistice, when news of the Third German Note arrived. Again there was irritation with Wilson for carrying on the negotiations as well as a grudging admiration for the skill the Germans had shown in not mentioning the withdrawal of their forces from Alsace-Lorraine. After a rambling discussion, the Cabinet decided to ask Wilson not to reply without consulting his Allies.

In fact there was no time for consultation because Wilson drafted his reply rapidly and sent it on 23 October. His final Note to Germany said that he was laying the correspondence and the request for an armistice before the European Allies. He did not specify the military terms but simply said that they must be sufficient to ensure that the Allies remained in a position to safeguard and enforce the peace, which would, of course, be made on the basis of the Fourteen Points. He also hinted strongly that it was about time Germany got rid of the Hohenzollerns and became truly democratic. When the War Cabinet saw the Note the following day, they approved. 'The diplomatic wrangle was now over,' said Lloyd George, 'and the President had made it clear that the terms of the armistice would be such as to prevent the resumption of hostilities by the Germans.'[16]

In Germany, Ludendorff and Hindenburg decided that the armistice conditions were unacceptable. They sent a telegram to all their senior army commanders ordering a fight to the finish. On 25 October, Prince Max demanded that the Kaiser dismiss them. In one of the last and most constructive acts of his reign, Wilhelm, who up to this point had stood by his High Command, forced Ludendorff's resignation. Hindenburg remained, reduced by now to a mere figurehead. On 28 October, the German government informed Wilson that it was waiting for the Allied armistice terms.

By that point, House had arrived in Paris to take part in the Supreme War Council. Lloyd George arrived on the 28th in a cheerful mood: Aleppo had fallen to Allenby's forces; Ludendorff had finally gone; and Austria was

16. HLRO. Lloyd George Papers. F105, vol. ii. War Cab., 490, 24 October 1918.

about to ask for an armistice. Lloyd George's instructions from the War Cabinet were to get an armistice with Germany as soon as possible. He was also to deal with the Freedom of the Seas issue. On 29 October, he had a private lunch with House, who reported to Wilson that Lloyd George was feeling the pressure from the British press for harsh armistice terms. Lloyd George claimed that he was resisting this. (House was confident that the British had no idea what was in his reports back to Washington; in fact the British broke his codes easily.)

Lloyd George remained in Paris for a week, one of the most crucial ones in the war. In their meetings, both the formal ones of the Supreme War Council and the less formal ones, the Europeans and the Americans not only wound up the war but they also started to shape the peace. Much of the time was occupied with drawing up the armistices with Turkey, Austria-Hungary and Germany, but much was also taken up with debates, sometimes quite difficult ones, among themselves.

The Turkish armistice caused particular friction between the British and the French. The Italians, who also had a stake in the fate of the Turkish territories, watched with a certain amount of annoyance from the sidelines. On 20 October, General Townshend, the man responsible for the British disaster in Mesopotamia earlier in the war and who had been living in considerable comfort under house arrest in Constantinople, had appeared at Mitylene with an official Turkish request for an armistice. The terms amounted to a capitulation.

Lloyd George had managed to get a British admiral, Calthorpe, as Commander-in-Chief for Allied forces for the final attack on Constantinople. He now intended to use him to negotiate an armistice with the Turks on the island of Mudros. Calthorpe was instructed to move quickly and to protect British interests. Although the Allies had agreed on twenty-four separate points to be included in an armistice, Calthorpe was told to concentrate only on such issues as the opening of the Straits, the occupation of the Constantinople and Dardanelles forts by the British, and the surrender of the Turkish navy. The French, for their part, had no intention of being cut out and protested strongly against the British action. Lloyd George somewhat disingenuously claimed in his *War Memoirs* that the Turks preferred to negotiate with the British and had approached Calthorpe directly. When the French admiral on Mudros tried to join in the discussions, Calthorpe, on instructions from London, refused to allow him to take part.

Back in Paris, on 30 October, there was a scene in the Supreme War Council. Clemenceau complained vociferously. He did not want, he said, to indulge in recriminations, but the British should recognize French sensitivities. The overall naval command in the Mediterranean was French; a French admiral should be allowed to sign the armistice agreement with Turkey. Sonnino added that an Italian admiral should sign as well. Lloyd George responded by pointing out that the armistice with Bulgaria had been negotiated by Franchet d'Esperey alone, and then he turned to the British military campaign in the Middle East. 'The British had captured three or four Turkish armies and had incurred hundreds of thousands of casualties in the war with Turkey. The other Governments had only put a few nigger policemen to see that we did not steal the Holy Sepulchre. When, however, it came to signing an armistice all this fuss was made.'[17] The French and the Italians backed down and Calthorpe signed the armistice on his own, but the episode left Clemenceau angry and even more suspicious of Lloyd George's intentions in the Middle East than before. On 31 October, when he received confirmation of the armistice, Lloyd George sent a message to the House of Commons which stressed that only a British admiral had signed. That evening he went out to celebrate with dinner at the Meurice and an evening at a musical comedy. 'It would be less intolerable,' said Bonar Law, 'if only they wouldn't sing.'[18]

Austria-Hungary's armistice drew less attention from the British leaders. After all, Britain had few direct interests in its territory and had not played a significant role in its defeat. The Austrian government had asked Wilson on 7 October to help it secure an armistice based on the Fourteen Points. Preoccupied with the German terms, Wilson had been slow to reply. His answer, when it came on 20 October, offered little help to the beleaguered monarchy. He had changed his mind, he said, on Point Ten of the Fourteen Points, which had called for autonomous development of the nationalities within Austria-Hungary: they must now be allowed to control their own destinies. The nationalities needed little encouragement. As the Italians finally launched their great attack, the Czechs and the Yugoslavs declared their independence. On 31 October, the leader of the Independence Party became Prime Minister of Hungary.

The Austrian government pleaded for an armistice on 29 October, saying that it accepted all of Wilson's Points. In Paris, the Supreme War Council met the following day to consider the terms to be offered. Lloyd George argued that it would help to settle the armistice quickly as a way of showing Germany what the Allies intended to do to it. He recommended that Austria

---

17. HLRO. Lloyd George Papers. F120–21. I.C.-84 Notes of a Conversation in M. Pichon's Room at the Quai D'Orsay on Wednesday 30 October 1918 at 3 p.m.
18. Roskill, *Hankey*, vol. i, p. 625.

be made to demobilize its forces and allow Allied forces to move freely through its territory. The greater part of its navy must be handed over. (Clemenceau exclaimed, 'They have left the breeches of the Emperor and not much else!'[19]) Austria must also evacuate all occupied territories as well as those promised to Italy in the Treaty of London.

The discussion on the terms brought a clash between Italy and Serbia, who objected to Italy's occupying what were Slav territories in Austria-Hungary. When the Italians proposed to continue the blockade of Austria-Hungary, the Serbians again objected. Many of the merchant ships in the Adriatic belonged to South Slavs, who, while technically subjects of the old empire, had always supported the Allies. Surely they could be allowed to go about their business? In the Adriatic, the clash turned bloody. As one of his last acts, the Austrian Emperor had handed over the bulk of his navy at Pula in the Istrian peninsula to a self-appointed council of his South Slav subjects at Zagreb. On the night of 31 October an Italian torpedo boat slipped into the harbour and sank a dreadnought, *Viribus Unitis*, drowning several hundred largely South Slav sailors.

The Supreme War Council instructed the Chief of the Italian General Staff, General Armando Diaz, to negotiate with the Austrian envoys, who were by now extremely anxious to get a reply. On 3 November, as the Supreme War Council discussed the terms to be offered to Germany, Orlando got a telegram to say that the Austrian armistice had been signed at the Villa Giusta near Padua. (A separate one had to be signed in Belgrade on 13 November with Hungarian representatives.) The room erupted with rejoicing. Lloyd George alone was subdued. As a Celt, he told Hankey, he could not help feeling superstitious about so much success.

That left Germany: but before the Allies and the Americans could settle the German armistice terms, they had to sort out their differences over the Fourteen Points. While the French feared that the Points ruled out reparations and the Italians worried about their frontiers, the main attack came from the British. On 29 October, Lloyd George asked House whether the Germans were counting on making peace on the basis of the Fourteen Points. When House said undoubtedly, both Lloyd George and Clemenceau pointed out that they had never been consulted. Lloyd George must speak out now, he said, or the British government would find itself committed to those terms. He was prepared to state clearly which ones he could not accept. Pichon, the French Foreign Minister, read out the Points one by one. When he came to the second, on the Freedom of the Seas, Lloyd George

19. WM, p. 3316.

said sharply that he could not accept this under any conditions. If the League of Nations was formed and was successful, then Britain might discuss handing over responsibility for blockades to it. House, Hankey reported, looked very sick. The Colonel tried threats. If the Europeans did not accept the Fourteen Points then Wilson would have to tell Germany and Austria so. The negotiations up to this point would have been fruitless and the United States might well have to make a separate peace. 'We shall be very sorry,' said Lloyd George, 'but we shall fight on.'[20] Clemenceau, so Lloyd George told Riddell later, slapped his chest and said, 'Yes, and we shall fight with you!'[21] House cabled Wilson to advise him of the situation and to suggest that he open a debate in Congress on whether the United States should make peace separately or go on fighting with such ungrateful Allies. He also advised Wilson to start reducing American loans and shipments of troops and supplies. For his part, Wilson contemplated threatening to open a naval race with Great Britain, and, in what was a favourite threat, to appeal to public opinion both in the United States and in Europe. Lloyd George, who may well have been reading the decoded cables of the exchange, later wrote in his memoirs, 'I need hardly say this unloaded blunderbuss did not intimidate either Clemenceau or the British leaders.'[22]

The statesmen, perhaps recognizing that they had reached a dangerous impasse, agreed to adjourn and think over their amendments to the Fourteen Points. The next morning, House, Clemenceau and Lloyd George held a private meeting. Lloyd George produced written reservations to the Fourteen Points. (In diplomatic practice, nations could register reservations or interpretations of documents, even of treaties, which stood as long as the other parties agreed.) He concentrated on two, the Freedom of the Seas and reparations. The former, he had written, was open to various interpretations, some of which Britain could not accept. On the second, the President had said that occupied territories must be restored; the Allies assumed that this implied that Germany would make compensation for all damage done to Allied property and civilians by German forces. House hesitated; even if he were prepared to accept their reservations, Wilson was not. From Washington, over the next few days, the President sent repeated instructions to stand firm. On 3 November, Lloyd George proposed a face-saving compromise: that they postpone their discussion of Freedom of the Seas for the coming peace conference. House persuaded Wilson that this was a good solution. 'I felt confident,' Lloyd George wrote in his memoirs, 'that nothing more

20. Roskill, *Hankey*, vol. i, p. 623.   21. *RWD*, p. 380.
22. Lloyd George, *The Truth about the Peace Treaties*, vol. i, p. 75.

would be heard of the subject.'[23] House also acquiesced in the reservation on reparations.

When Sonnino, speaking for the Italians, tried to enter a reservation to Wilson's Ninth Point, which talked about the readjustment of Italy's boundaries along lines of nationality, to include strategic necessity (which would have opened the door to Italy's taking German and Slav areas), Lloyd George was uncooperative. They were only talking about the Fourteen Points where they applied to Germany, he argued rather unfairly. They could deal with Italy's reservations at a later time. Since that time never came, the Italians logged yet another grievance in the list they were accumulating against their allies.

After the dispute over the meaning of the Fourteen Points, the military and naval terms were relatively easy. Foch, speaking for the military advisers, insisted on Germany withdrawing its forces from Belgium, Luxembourg, Alsace-Lorraine and from its own territory west of the Rhine as well as a strip about thirty kilometres deep to the east of the river. Allied forces would hold the bridgeheads. Germany was also required to stop its systematic destruction of Allied property as it retreated. Furthermore, it was to hand over virtually all its weapons as well as huge numbers of locomotives, railway cars and lorries. It was also to return the cash and securities looted from Belgium. Lloyd George still found the evacuation terms too severe but gave way when Clemenceau and House presented a united front. Foch initially had not mentioned the Eastern front but, at the insistence of his political superiors, he drew up a provision that Germany should pull its troops back from all territory outside its 1914 borders.

On the naval terms, the British asked for the surrender of roughly two-thirds of the German surface fleet and all of the submarine fleet. This demand was opposed by the French, who were afraid that it would stiffen German resistance. Lloyd George suggested a possible compromise: that the German battleships be interned in neutral ports under Allied supervision instead of being surrendered. Over the strenuous objections of the British naval authorities, the Supreme War Council finally decided on 4 November to intern all the surface ships in neutral ports if these could be found, and in Allied ones if not. (That last proviso opened the door for the eventual sending of much of the German fleet to Scapa Flow.)

Lloyd George met House and Clemenceau for the last time on the morning of 4 November. The three decided that Wilson should send one last Note to the German government telling it to send emissaries under a white flag

23. Lloyd George, *The Truth about the Peace Treaties*, vol. i, p. 85.

AFTERWORD

to Foch to ask for an armistice. The work of the armistice terms done, Lloyd George decided to leave at once for London. 'Very peaceful now that Lloyd George has gone home,' wrote Henry Wilson in his diary.[24]

The trip back across the Channel was not as peaceful. Lloyd George's destroyer was caught in rough seas and the party, including a seasick Hankey, had to be taken off by boat at Dover late that night. Lloyd George remained in good spirits. 'We have detached Germany's allies one by one,' he told Riddell the next day, 'and now she is alone, and we have sent her some hot pepper in the shape of our armistice terms.'[25] The Prime Minister went straight on to London where he reported to the Cabinet on the Paris meetings. When Hughes of Australia complained about the Fourteen Points, Lloyd George was reassuring: he had been through them carefully and, apart from Freedom of the Seas and reparations, where Britain had now registered its viewpoints, there was nothing to trouble them. He briefly discussed future war plans if Germany should refuse to ask for an armistice, which included an attack through southern Germany and possibly aerial bombing of Berlin. Foch had assured him that there would be victory by Christmas. That afternoon, he read the Austrian armistice terms to the House of Commons. On 5 November he had seen the King and informed him that he would be asking for a dissolution in the near future.

In fact, although few on the Allied side realized it yet, Germany was no longer capable of organized resistance. On the battle fronts, the authorities were hastily consolidating their divisions in a desperate attempt to eke out their dwindling manpower. Infantry battalions were down to about half their usual size. Desertions mounted rapidly. In Germany, what looked like revolution was breaking out. At Kiel on 3 November the sailors of the Grand Fleet had mutinied, rather than make one last 'death-ride' out against the British, and the town was now under their control. The mutiny spread rapidly across the ports of north Germany. In their barracks, soldiers started to form their own councils, ignoring their officers. In Berlin, revolutionary socialists led huge demonstrations against the government. By 8 November, most of the major cities were flying the red flag. In Bavaria, a Council of Workers and Soldiers had taken over. Even the moderate socialists, who were part of the German government, now demanded the Kaiser's abdication. Tucked away safely in Spa, Wilhelm adamantly refused to consider it. By 9 November, he no longer had a choice. His government made the announcement for him. An exhausted Prince Max resigned as Chancellor and a socialist, Friedrich Ebert, took over.

24. Wilson diary, vol. ii, p. 148.   25. *RWD*, p. 378.

While Germany fell apart, the armistice negotiations moved rapidly ahead. On the evening of 7 November, the German emissaries made their way along a track that had been cleared through the front lines towards La Capelle. The first automobile bore a white flag (actually a large towel), and, in a reminder of an earlier age, a trumpeter stood on its running board repeatedly sounding a four-note refrain. Under French escort, the Germans made their way by moonlight from La Capelle to a train which took them to a siding in the Forest of Compiègne early on the morning of 8 November. Foch waited in his railway car. Wemyss, who was there to deal with naval matters, remembered a melancholy atmosphere, with the leaves gently falling. When the Germans asked to hear the Allied terms, Foch said he had no proposals to make. In confusion, the Germans asked again and again until they understood that Foch wanted them to request an armistice.

As a French general read out the terms, the Germans listened in consternation. One officer had tears running down his face. The Germans begged for an immediate ceasefire, pointing to the dangers of Bolshevism taking over Germany if the war went on. Foch refused. The Germans had seventy-two hours to sign. The Germans attempted to modify the terms. 'We cannot surrender all our weapons,' said one, 'or we will have nothing to use against the Bolsheviks.' Foch remained adamant, conceding only some minor changes: he lowered the numbers of machine guns and trucks to be surrendered and he extended the length of time allowed for the evacuation of German troops. On the Eastern front, though, he made a significant concession, which reflected his and other Allied leaders' fears of Bolshevism: German troops would remain on Russian soil until the Allies decided the time had come for them to withdraw. At 5.10 a.m. on the morning of 11 November, the Germans signed. Foch's railway carriage was later put in a museum. In 1940, German army engineers broke open the carriage and France signed its capitulation. The carriage was later destroyed but the French have made a replica.

Although Foch kept the Allies fully briefed, they watched with a certain amount of anxiety. It was not clear up to the last moment whether the Germans would sign or whether in fact they represented a government at all. On 9 November, Clemenceau sent a telegram to Lloyd George warning him that he may have to come to Paris immediately. The following day Lloyd George told his Cabinet that, although Foch seemed inclined to go on fighting, he himself was reluctant to send troops into Germany where they might catch the 'cholera' of revolution. The Cabinet agreed that they would rather have an armistice.

Lloyd George does not appear to have been seriously concerned about the armistice. On 9 November he made a stirring speech at the Lord Mayor's banquet. 'A terrible tragedy nearly took place this evening,' he told Riddell. 'Look at my uniform. I have outgrown it. I have not had it on for nearly five years.' The collar had been much too tight. 'But there was a greater danger down below. The breeches nearly gave way! What a catastrophe that would have been!'[26]

By 10 November, with the new socialist government in place in Berlin, there seemed little doubt that Germany would sign. Lloyd George went off to Walton Heath for the day with Margaret, Megan and Riddell. At 6 a.m. the next day he was wakened by a phone call from Wemyss with the good news that the armistice had just been signed. At 9.30 a.m. he met the Cabinet. It was decided to tell the home military authorities to pull out all the stops to celebrate. They were to fire guns, blow bugles, set their bands marching and church bells ringing. Lloyd George sounded a warning; they must not treat the defeated too harshly. 'It behooved us now to behave as a great nation and to do nothing which might arouse and harbour a spirit of revenge later. The future peace of the world would depend more on the way in which we behaved after victory than upon victory itself.'[27]

Shortly before 11 a.m. Harold Nicolson looked out the window of the Foreign Office to see a crowd gathering outside 10 Downing Street. Suddenly Lloyd George appeared on the doorstep and shouted out, 'At eleven o'clock this morning the war will be over!'[28] Smiling, he went back inside as the crowd filled Downing Street and overflowed into Horse Guards Parade. Lloyd George appeared in his back garden with two secretaries, looking nervous and enthusiastic. He stepped out into the Parade and the crowd surged around, patting him on the back. Lloyd George retreated to his garden, laughing.

As the news spread like wildfire through London, people poured out into the streets in spontaneous celebrations. Bonar Law, Smuts, Balfour and Milner struggled through the throngs to give Lloyd George their congratulations. Churchill's car, with a very pregnant Clementine inside, was surrounded by cheering crowds. From Kensington, Chaim Weizmann, leader of the World Zionist Organization, set out for a long-arranged lunch with Lloyd George. At 1.30 p.m. he finally made it to Downing Street where a policeman told him that a great many people were claiming to have appointments with the Prime Minister that day. Once inside, Weizmann

26. *RWD*, pp. 378–9.
27. HLRO. Bonar Law Papers. Box 70. War Cab., 500B, 11 November 1918.
28. Harold Nicolson, *Peacemaking 1919* (1964), p. 9.

found Lloyd George reading the Psalms, near to tears. This was not, as some cynics later suggested, carefully staged. Although he was not a believer, Lloyd George often drew on the Bible for inspiration and for comfort. 'I am feeling', he had said to Riddell the previous day, 'like a man who has been in a big thing that is over. He is at a loose end; he does not know what to do. I feel like that. I have had a terrible time during the past four and a half years.'[29]

After a rushed lunch, Lloyd George left to make a statement to the House of Commons. Weizmann watched as a crowd seized him and carried him off on their shoulders. In the House, Lloyd George read out the armistice conditions and concluded: 'Thus at eleven o'clock this morning came to an end the cruellest and most terrible war that has ever scourged mankind. I hope we may say that thus, this fateful morning, came to an end all wars.'[30] He then moved an adjournment and the members walked across to St Margaret's Church for a service of thanksgiving. That evening, as London went mad, Lloyd George dined at Downing Street with Churchill, F. E. Smith and Henry Wilson. The talk was mainly about the coming general election but it inevitably turned to the war that had just ended. Lloyd George wanted to shoot the Kaiser; Churchill disagreed. The party agreed, however, that the German people had many great qualities and that Europe could not be rebuilt without them.

Lloyd George was shortly to be christened 'The Man Who Won the War', and there was much truth in the description. On November 11, he could look back with pride on his prime ministership. He had carried Britain and the Empire through a political crisis which had threatened to cripple the government and the war effort. He had done much to mobilize both people and resources for the war. He had worked successfully with his allies. He had won on the principle of unity of command. He also had much to preoccupy him that night: an election in the near future where both his own record and the mood of the British electorate would be tested; the huge tasks of demobilizing the armed forces and restoring and rebuilding a society and an economy which had been badly strained by the war; and, above all, the making of a lasting peace.

29. *RWD*, p. 380.   30. *WM*, pp. 3329–30.

Index

468, 506–7, 589, 591; progress
during 1918 597; Robertson and
490; strategic use of 596; transfers of
troops to 516, 546; and US troops
527, 529; Henry Wilson and 286
British Legion 503
British Medical Association 113
British Museum, London 483
British War Mission 126n, 128
British Weekly 256, 339n
Broodseinde ridge 259–60
Brownlie, R. 112
Bruce, W. N. 570
Bruges 514
Brunel, Isambard Kingdom 138
Brusilov, Alexei 90, 203
Bryan, William Jennings 126n, 307
Bryce, James, 1st Viscount 76,
105n
Brynawelon 578
Buchan, John 36n, 617
Buchanan, Sir George 199–200,
432
Bucharest, treaty of 436
Buckmaster, Lord 379–80
Budget League 577
Bukharin, Nikolai 430, 434
Bukovina 203
Bulgaria; as ally of Austria 6–7, 89;
armistice 619, 620, 633; attack on
151, 603–5; collapse of 621; defeat
of 622–3; and Germany 93; war
never declared on 72; Woodrow
Wilson on 335
Bullecourt 541
Bunbury, Henry 46n
Burdett-Coutts, Angela , Baroness 142n
Burge, Dr, Bishop of Southwark 363
Burke, Edmund 103n
Burke's Peerage 144
Burnham, Harry Lawson, 1st Viscount
139, 226n, 329, 571
Burns, Robert 518–19
Burton, Henry 539
Butler, Geoffrey 126

Byng, Sir Julian 313–14, 440–41, 442,
444–5, 559, 597, 601
Byron, George Gordon, Lord 612
Byron, Lady 143
Bystander 219

Cabot Lodge, Henry 70
Cadorna, General Luigi 27, 28, 35, 92,
162, 225–6, 227, 269–71, 273, 274,
285, 325, 406
Caernarfon Cottage Hospital 219
Caillaux, Joseph 162, 289, 392–3
Caird, Andrew 124
Cairo 150
Calais 460; conference 41–4, 83, 93,
97, 155, 160, 172, 221
Calthorpe, Admiral Sir Arthur Gough
632–3
Cambon, Jules 90n
Cambon, Paul 36, 90n
Cambrai 601–2; battle of 313–18, 323,
332, 423, 439, 440, 443, 445, 450,
558
Campbell-Bannerman, Sir Henry 26,
134, 145, 195
Camrose, William Berry, Lord (earlier
Sir William Berry) 141n, 616
Canada 61, 63, 126, 128, 538–9, 540,
543, 576
Canadian Army Corps 552, 557
Canadian troops 558
Canal du Nord 601
Canrobert, Marshal François 22
Cantigny 530
Capello, General Luigi 269–71
Caporetto (Karfreit) 270, 271, 283,
284, 287–8, 322, 443, 604
Carey Evans, Margaret (LG's
granddaughter, later Barrett) 147,
424–5
Carey Evans, Captain Thomas 146–8
Carlsbad 294
Carmichael, James 585, 588
Caroline islands 563
Carr, Lascelles 217